Lecture Notes in Computer Science

Lecture Notes in Artificial Intelligence   **15450**

Founding Editor

Jörg Siekmann

Series Editors

Randy Goebel, *University of Alberta, Edmonton, Canada*
Wolfgang Wahlster, *DFKI, Berlin, Germany*
Zhi-Hua Zhou, *Nanjing University, Nanjing, China*

The series Lecture Notes in Artificial Intelligence (LNAI) was established in 1988 as a topical subseries of LNCS devoted to artificial intelligence.

The series publishes state-of-the-art research results at a high level. As with the LNCS mother series, the mission of the series is to serve the international R & D community by providing an invaluable service, mainly focused on the publication of conference and workshop proceedings and postproceedings.

Alessandro Artale · Gabriella Cortellessa ·
Marco Montali
Editors

AIxIA 2024 – Advances in Artificial Intelligence

XXIIIrd International Conference
of the Italian Association for Artificial Intelligence, AIxIA 2024
Bolzano, Italy, November 25–28, 2024
Proceedings

 Springer

Editors
Alessandro Artale (iD)
Free University of Bozen-Bolzano
Bolzano, Italy

Gabriella Cortellessa (iD)
Consiglio Nazionale delle Ricerche
Rome, Italy

Marco Montali (iD)
Free University of Bozen-Bolzano
Bolzano, Italy

ISSN 0302-9743   ISSN 1611-3349 (electronic)
Lecture Notes in Artificial Intelligence
ISBN 978-3-031-80606-3   ISBN 978-3-031-80607-0 (eBook)
https://doi.org/10.1007/978-3-031-80607-0

LNCS Sublibrary: SL7 – Artificial Intelligence

This Springer imprint is published by the registered company Springer Nature Switzerland AG
The registered company address is: Gewerbestrasse 11, 6330 Cham, Switzerland

If disposing of this product, please recycle the paper.

Preface

This volume contains the proceedings of the 23nd International Conference of the Italian Association for Artificial Intelligence (AIxIA 2024), the primary scientific event of the Associazione Italiana per l'Intelligenza Artificiale (AIxIA). AIxIA is a non-profit organization, dedicated to promoting the advancement of Artificial Intelligence (AI) within academic, social, and production contexts. The association established the series of international conferences in 1991, initially organizing an event every two years, and then maintaining an annual schedule from 2015 onwards. Over the years, the conference has visited many cities throughout the national territory, as reported in the LNCS proceedings of the various editions (https://link.springer.com/conference/aiia).

AIxIA 2024 was held in Bolzano, Italy, during November 25–28, hosted by the Free University of Bozen-Bolzano. The conference received 41 submissions for the regular research papers track. Each paper was peer reviewed by at least three members of the Program Committee, and finally 24 papers were accepted for publication in these proceedings and presented at the conference. Besides regular papers, the conference also received the submission of 21 discussion papers, i.e., position papers or extended abstracts of articles recently published in premier international conferences and journals related to AI. After a dedicated review process, 15 discussion papers were accepted for presentation at the conference.

AIxIA 2024 featured three renowned keynote speakers: "*Representation learning for acting and planning*" by Hector Geffner (RWTH Aachen University); "*Against the clock: lessons learned by applying temporal planning in practice*" by Andrea Micheli (Fondazione Bruno Kessler, Trento); and "*The language factor*" by Malvina Nissin (University of Groningen). The conference agenda also included two tutorials: "*Designing Virtual Knowledge Graphs*" by Davide Lanti and Diego Calvanese (Free University of Bozen-Bolzano) and "*Learning and Reasoning in Neuro-Symbolic Systems*" by Luciano Serafini (Fondazione Bruno Kessler, Trento).

Besides the main track, AIxIA 2024 encompassed a wide range of theoretical and applied AI aspects, with 22 co-located workshops dedicated to specific topics, bringing together AI communities with related interests. In addition, the following collateral events were organized: a Doctoral Consortium, award events, and a public panel focused on the impact of generative AI and Large Language Models.

We express our gratitude to the various institutions and sponsors who supported AIxIA 2024, the AIxIA Executive Board for its steadfast assistance, and the Free University of Bozen-Bolzano for granting us the opportunity to host the conference in its facilities. We also want to thank all authors for submitting high-quality research papers, and the members of the Program Committee and the additional reviewers for their efforts to produce fair and thorough evaluations of the submitted papers. Our heartfelt thanks also go to the Workshop and Tutorial chairs, Antonella Guzzo (University of Calabria) and Oliver Kutz (Free University of Bozen-Bolzano), and the Doctoral Consortium chairs, Davide Bacciu (University of Pisa) and Ivan Donadello (Free University of Bozen-Bolzano), for their invaluable contributions in shaping an exciting program for AIxIA 2024. We would also like to thank the Proceedings Chair, Sergio Tessaris (Free University of Bozen-Bolzano), for his assistance in gathering the papers and organizing the final version of this volume. Finally, we would like to express our gratitude to all those who, in various capacities, contributed to the success of AIxIA 2024.

October 2024

Gabriella Cortellessa
Alessandro Artale
Marco Montali

Organization

General Chair

Marco Montali   Free University of Bozen-Bolzano, Italy

Program Committee Chairs

Gabriella Cortellessa   Consiglio Nazionale delle Ricerche, Rome, Italy
Alessandro Artale   Free University of Bozen-Bolzano, Italy

Workshop Chairs

Antonella Guzzo   University of Calabria, Italy
Oliver Kutz   Free University of Bozen-Bolzano, Italy

Doctoral Consortium Chairs

Davide Bacciu   University of Pisa, Italy
Ivan Donadello   Free University of Bozen-Bolzano, Italy

Sponsorship Chairs

Alessandro Mosca   Smart Data Factory, FUB, Italy
Floriano Zini   Smart Data Factory, FUB, Italy

Social Chairs

Tiziano Dalmonte   Free University of Bozen-Bolzano, Italy
Floriano Zini   Free University of Bozen-Bolzano, Italy
Ognjen Savkovic   Free University of Bozen-Bolzano, Italy

Proceedings Chair

Sergio Tessaris   Free University of Bozen-Bolzano, Italy

Web Chairs

Nicola Gigante   Free University of Bozen-Bolzano, Italy
Alessandro Burigana   Free University of Bozen-Bolzano, Italy

Travel Grant Chairs

Valentina Poggioni   Università degli Studi di Perugia, Italy
Riccardo Rasconi   Consiglio Nazionale delle Ricerche, Rome, Italy
Christian Tamantini   Consiglio Nazionale delle Ricerche, Rome, Italy

Program Committee

Marco Baioletti   Università degli Studi di Perugia, Italy
Matteo Baldoni   Università di Torino, Italy
Adriano Barra   Università del Salento, Italy
Roberto Basili   University of Roma Tor Vergata, Italy
Gloria Beraldo   ISTC-CNR & University of Padua, Italy
Stefano Berretti   University of Firenze, Italy
Andrea Burattin   Technical University of Denmark, Denmark
Francesco Calimeri   University of Calabria, Italy
Alberto Casagrande   Università degli Studi di Udine, Italy
Antonio Chella   Università di Palermo, Italy
Alessandro Cimatti   Fondazione Bruno Kessler, Italy
Luca Console   Università di Torino, Italy
Flavio S. Correa Da Silva   University of São Paulo, Brazil
Stefania Costantini   Università dell'Aquila, Italy
Dario Della Monica   Università degli Studi di Udine, Italy
Francesco M. Donini   Università della Tuscia, Italy
Johannes K. Fichte   Linköping University, Sweden
Alberto Finzi   Università di Napoli "Federico II", Italy
Fabio Fioravanti   University of Chieti-Pescara, Italy
Andrea Formisano   Università di Udine, Italy
Marco Gavanelli   University of Ferrara, Italy
Nicola Gigante   Free University of Bozen-Bolzano, Italy

Laura Giordano	Università del Piemonte Orientale, Italy
Davide Lanti	Free University of Bozen-Bolzano, Italy
Maurizio Lenzerini	Sapienza University of Rome, Italy
Francesca Alessandra Lisi	Università degli Studi di Bari "Aldo Moro", Italy
Marin Lujak	University Rey Juan Carlos, Spain
Bernardo Magnini	FBK-irst, Italy
Marina Mongiello	Politecnico di Bari, Italy
Angelo Montanari	University of Udine, Italy
Alessandro Mosca	Institute for Cognitive Sciences and Technologies (ISTC-CNR), Italy
Angelo Oddi	ISTC-CNR, Italian National Research Council, Italy
Andrea Orlandini	CNR, Italy
Luigi Portinale	Università del Piemonte Orientale "A. Avogadro", Italy
Alessandra Raffaetá	Università Ca' Foscari Venezia, Italy
Riccardo Rasconi	ISTC-CNR, Italy
Andrea Roli	University of Bologna, Italy
Marco Roveri	University of Trento, Italy
Salvatore Ruggieri	Università di Pisa, Italy
Giuseppe Sansonetti	Roma Tre University, Italy
Domenico Fabio Savo	University of Bergamo, Italy
Enrico Scala	Università di Brescia, Italy
Francesco Scarcello	University of Calabria, Italy
Alessandro Sperduti	Università di Padova, Italy
Christian Tamantini	Institute of Cognitive Sciences and Technologies, CNR, Italy

Additional Reviewers

Baiardi, Fabrizio	Mauro, Noemi
Bonassi, Luigi	Poe, Robert
Brunello, Andrea	Setzu, Mattia
Dal Palù, Alessandro	Sterlicchio, Gioacchino
Hromei, Claudiu Daniel	Theseider Dupre, Daniele
Irwin, Christopher	Tortora, Matteo
Longo, Davide Mario	

Contents

Against the Clock: Lessons Learned by Applying Temporal Planning in Practice

Andrea Micheli$^{(\boxtimes)}$ [iD]

Fondazione Bruno Kessler, Trento, Italy
amicheli@fbk.eu

Abstract. Automated Planning is a foundational area of AI research, focusing on the automated synthesis of courses of actions to achieve a desired goal within a formally-modeled system. When dealing with time and temporal constraints, this problem is known as Temporal Planning. In this paper, we will present our research on the application of temporal planning to real-world scenarios, and highlight the open research directions in this field. Starting from a series of projects in different application domains – including robotics, manufacturing, and logistics – we will explore key challenges encountered, the (sometimes hard) lessons learned, and the techniques, tools, and methodologies that have emerged from these efforts. Additionally, we will introduce and discuss preliminary results on applying Reinforcement Learning techniques to tailor temporal planners to specific application contexts.

Keywords: Automated Temporal Planning · Planning and Scheduling · Applications of Planning

1 Introduction

Automated planning is a historical research area in Artificial Intelligence focusing on the synthesis of "plans" to achieve specified goals in formally modeled systems [10]. Several concrete problems have been defined by requiring certain formulations of plans or by limiting the system models to some expressiveness class. As a motivating example, consider a fleet of robots that can move among a set of locations and perform logistic operations (such as picking objects, transporting and depositing cargo); further suppose that each operation has known duration and that some operations might consume resources (such as the robot batteries). Temporal planning formalisms are designed to faithfully model a situation like this[1] and allow the automated synthesis of courses of actions to achieve a desired objective, possibly within a specified deadline.

This paper summarizes the contents of the homonymous AIxIA 2024 invited talk.

[1] Disregarding, for the sake of computational efficiency, uncertainties in the robot and environment behaviors.

A. Artale et al. (Eds.): AIxIA 2024, LNAI 15450, pp. 1–11, 2025.
https://doi.org/10.1007/978-3-031-80607-0_1

This paper surveys the approaches to Temporal Planning developed in recent years in the Planning, Scheduling and Optimization unit (PSO) that I lead at Fondazione Bruno Kessler[2]. We have in fact participated in a number of research and technology transfer projects concerning planning and scheduling: we will here discuss the methodology developed in the most significant ones, focusing on the practical challenges that generated research ideas, and introducing the reusable assets we implemented to address them.

We will first present the iLAADR project, aiming at automating the intra-logistics operations in a factory, which served as a real-world use-case for the advanced modeling features of the ANML language. These features are rarely supported by off-the-shelf automated planners and motivated a line of theoretical and practical research to offer them effectively. Then, we will summarize our collaboration in the area of underwater robotics, where the planner is tasked to decide and schedule the operations needed to perform a surveillance mission and to safely overcome problematic situations. In this context, the optimization of resources is of paramount importance: we tackled the open problem of Optimal Temporal Planning with an approach grounded in Optimization Modulo Theory (OMT) [21]. Third, we motivate and report on the technological effort to bring a convenient and reusable platform for the modeling, manipulation and solving of automated planning problems. We built and validated such a platform in the context of the AIPlan4EU project; other project partners, us, and also third parties are currently re-using this open-source infrastructure for new projects and research. Finally, we discuss the extremely challenging MAIS project, aimed at the automated control of electroplating production factories, which inspired an ambitious line of research focused on the combination of Reinforcement Learning and Automated Planning for the synthesis of specialized planners.

Structure of the Paper. This paper is structured as follows. We first report some minimal background notions needed to set the stage of the paper; then, we discuss the four mentioned projects with the technical results that emerged and lessons learned in four separate sections. Finally, we draw our conclusions in Sect. 7.

2   Background

Before delving into the projects and the research ideas, we provide a brief overview of the area of temporal planning, relevant to explain the contributions reported in this paper.

Temporal planning is a vast area of Artificial Intelligence and over the years a number of models and techniques have been proposed within it. At the core of the problem lays the interplay between deciding which actions/activities need to be performed to reach a desired goal (the planning part) and choosing an appropriate timing (or a set of possible timings) for such activities (the scheduling part). The combination of planning and scheduling is what makes the problem

---

[2] https://pso.fbk.eu.

hard and challenging. Being at the border of planning and scheduling implies that often a problem could be addressed both by temporal planning and scheduling techniques: for example, if the number of possible activities to choose from could be bound, a problem might be equivalently framed as a scheduling problem with optional activities or as a temporal planning problem. The best approach is not always clear and strongly depends on the problem size and the kind and number of constraints.

In the area of temporal planning, two major formalisms emerged: action-based planning [2,3,27] and timeline-based planning [1,9,26]. In extreme simplification, action-based approaches and languages augment classical planning formalisms with time and temporal constraints, while timeline-based planning consists in augmenting scheduling techniques to constrain the possible instantiations of activities and their constraints.

In our work, we focused on action-based planning. In this area, two major languages have been proposed, namely PDDL 2.1 [6] and ANML [22]. PDDL 2.1 is by far the most common language for temporal planners: it extends the well-known PDDL language by allowing "durative-actions", i.e. actions that correspond to an interval of time and can have conditions and effects either at the beginning or at the ending, plus an invariant (overall) condition. In addition to temporal constraints, PDDL 2.1 also supports continuous change, but for the sake of this paper we limit ourselves to the temporal and numeric fragment (generally called PDDL 2.1 Level 3). As shown by Cushing et al., PDDL 2.1 is a temporally-expressive language, meaning it can express problems in which all valid plans require actions to run concurrently [4]. Despite its widespread adoption and its theoretical expressiveness, PDDL 2.1 is not always easy to use in practical settings and requires several compilation constructions to express interesting behaviors such as Intermediate Conditions and Effects (ICE) [8,23]. The Action Notation Modeling Language (ANML) is an alternative action-based language proposed by NASA, designed to be more user-friendly by providing higher-level constructs such as a richer type system, ICE, structured types, richer temporal constraints and hierarchical structures. In the following, we will motivate how we chose to use ANML over PDDL 2.1 for several projects and how we formally studied the complexity of some of the features offered by either languages. For the sake of completeness, other action-based languages exists: PDDL+ [7] is an evolution of PDDL 2.1 that retains the durative-action concept, but focuses on continuous and exogenous processes and events; NDL [20] is another temporally-expressive language with an explicit notion of resources and where actions are not intervals, but rather events with conditions and effects scheduled in the future.

3   iLAADR: Temporal Planning Expressiveness

The first project experience we report on is iLAADR[3], a project funded by the European Institute of Technology aiming at the automation of intra-logistic

---

[3] https://robotik.dfki-bremen.de/en/research/projects/ilaadr.

operations using robots. The use-case of the project, provided by a leading automotive manufacturer, is centered on "kitting" operations: a robot equipped with a robotic arm is tasked to pick a set of pieces from a small warehouse (Fig. 1a) and to bring it to a second automated guided vehicle serving the production line (Fig. 1b) just in time for a human operator to get the kit for the specific car being manufactured in that moment. Consider the following example: the car currently being assembled in the production line is red, whereas the next one is green. This means that the operator needs to receive a "red kit" in time for completing the red car assembly and before receiving the "green kit". In this project, we were in charge of the automated planning operations, consisting in the synthesis of plans for each of the robots involved in the scenario.

We focused on the faithful modeling of the system constraints and developed an automated procedure to construct planning problems from the factory Warehouse Management System (WMS) and Manufacturing Execution System (MES). The key challenges we encountered concerned the complexity and maintainability of the models, and the scalability of tools on such models.

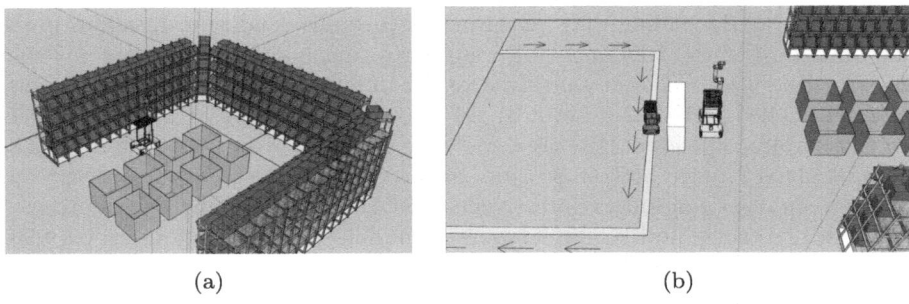

(a)   (b)

Fig. 1. 3D renderings of the iLAADR scenario. (a) the robot navigates the warehouse to pick the components of a kit. (b) the kit is exchanged between two robots.

We tried to modeled the problem in different languages, and we soon realized that the "queue of orders" is not easy (although possible) to model in PDDL 2.1: to order objectives in time, one needs to use "Timed Initial Literals" [5] (which are not part of PDDL 2.1, but are supported by several planners) and monitor fluents to record what has been achieved so far. Modeling the scenario with ANML is much easier: one can use object fluents and structured types to represent the sequence of orders[4] and ANML natively supports both absolute timing constraints for timed goals as well as Intermediate Conditions and Effects (ICE) to express constraints happening during the execution of the activities. Maintaining a high-level representation, close to the problem domain, allows

---

[4] In particular, we could define a list of n orders as a fluent with a numeric parameter in the domain $\{1, \ldots, n\}$ and type *Order*. This essentially represents an array of variables that can then be filled by actions in a very natural way.

the creation of domain-specific heuristics (in the project, we constructed a simple domain-dependent goal-counting heuristic that was extremely effective in practice): these can be embedded in the final planner together with standard heuristics in a portfolio approach.

The use of the ANML language in this project motivated a line of research that is both practical and theoretical. We developed a planner, called TAMER[5], for solving planning problems modeled in ANML and we focused on the problem of how to embed ICE as a native feature of our planner; we extended the decoupled approach used by the POPF [2] and other planners to support these features. The resulting planner is shown [27] to be much more efficient than state-of-the-art competitors on problems having ICE with respect to different ways this feature can be compiled into PDDL 2.1 [8,23].

In a theoretical line of papers, we set ourselves to understand the computational complexity of temporal planning when time is interpreted over a dense domain (as prescribed by the ANML semantics). Interestingly, we discovered that temporal planning is not harder than classical planning (PSPACE-complete) if we forbid self-overlapping of ground actions: this means that two instances of the same action with the same parameters are not allowed to overlap in time, although the same action can be repeated multiple times, as needed. Instead (and surprisingly), if a separation of a known time quantum (generally referred to as ϵ) is enforced between interfering events (e.g., between an effect setting a fluent to true and a condition requiring the fluent to be true) the temporal planning problem is shown to be EXPSPACE-complete. When no ϵ-separation is assumed and actions can self-overlap, the problem becomes undecidable [11]. These results gave a clear theoretical view on the role of self-overlapping and ϵ-separation in the realm of temporal planning inspiring new planners such as CTP, the first decision procedure for temporal planning in dense time without action self-overlapping [19]. Finally, we also proved that advanced temporal planning features, such as conditional effects and ICE do not impact these core results [12].

4   HyDrone: Optimal Temporal Planning

A second technology-transfer project, named HyDrone[6], concerned the use of automated planning for the synthesis of mission plans and recovery procedures for an underwater surveillance drone. The characteristics of the drone have been presented in [24], as well as the general architecture of the automated decision system we designed and implemented. Focusing on the computational challenges of the project, we needed a system capable of optimizing resources in addition to finding valid plans. In the project, we had three major quantities to consider and optimize: the total mission time (i.e., the makespan of the plan), the data being produced (as the system has limited data storing capacity) and, naturally, the battery level to allow for safer and more efficient operation of the robot. In this

---

[5] https://tamer.fbk.eu.
[6] https://pso.fbk.eu/articles/hydrone.

respect, we started exploring the area of optimal temporal planning, consisting in finding a valid plan that is optimal with respect to a specified cost function. The problem itself is extremely hard, with very few approaches in the literature either aimed at minimizing the plan makespan or limited to specific problem formulations.

We took inspiration from this challenge to tackle the optimal temporal planning problem in a principled way. We started from the work by Leofante et al. for optimal numeric planning via Optimization Modulo Theory (OMT) [13], and we generalized it to the case of temporal planning. The basic idea behind the approach is to use a bounded encoding into OMT that can capture in a single formula both the concrete plans of the system within the bound (in terms of number of steps) as well as an abstraction of plans that are longer (and might not exist); if the OMT solver returns a concrete plan while optimizing the objective function, we can prove that such a plan is globally optimal, because no other plan, however long, can have a better objective value [17].

Our generalization to temporal planning is far from trivial, because temporal planning (unlike classical and numeric planning) requires to tackle "future commitments": if an action is started, but not yet completed, one must take care of the consequences of the inevitable termination of such action. In this line of research, we also devised specialized encodings for the optimization of the makespan and we fully support the linear combination of makespan and action cost objectives in our planner [18].

5   AIPlan4EU: Making Planning Easier to Use

Among the major hindrances for practitioners wanting to explore the use of automated planning (and temporal planning in particular), we note the steep learning curve needed to gain familiarity with the modeling principles, the heterogeneity of input languages and dialects, and the diverse technical characteristics of available tools. Moreover, real-world applications require the use of planning as a component integrated in a wider ICT solution, not as a standalone software as it is the case for most planning tools. In the AIPlan4EU project[7], we worked to mitigate these issues by providing a convenient programmatic interface to model, manipulate and ultimately solve planning problems of various kind.

In practice, we developed a Python library, called Unified Planning (UP)[8], for representing, manipulating and solving classical, numerical, temporal, hierarchical and other kinds of planning problems. A user can either model a problem directly using the provided Python API, or by employing one of the provided parsers (PDDL 2.1 and ANML). Since UP is library, it is easy to use data sources (e.g. the WMS of a plant or the sensors of a robot) to dynamically construct the planning problems. UP also allows the manipulation of the problem, for example by compiling away some modeling features such as disjunctive preconditions, or

---

[7] https://aiplan4eu-project.eu.
[8] https://github.com/aiplan4eu/unified-planning.

performing the grounding of the problem. Moreover, the library offers a plug-in system for interfacing external planning engines that can be used to further manipulate or solve a planning problem. Finally, the solution plans are exposed as Python objects for easy inspection and use of produced results.

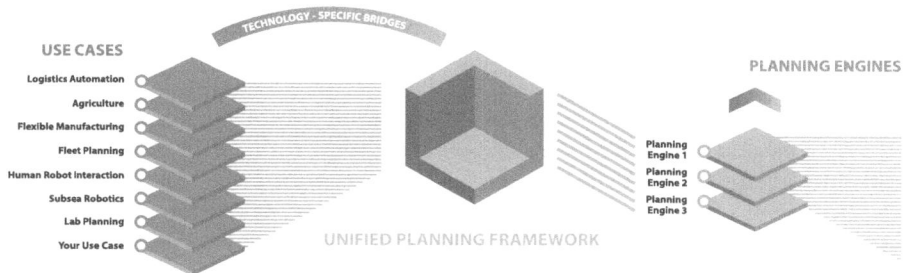

Fig. 2. Overview of the The Unified Planning framework.

In the project, we demonstrated the technology on a wide variety of use-cases and scenarios; in addition, project partners and third parties developed specialized libraries and tools for some application domains. We call such integrations "Technology-Specific Bridges" (TSB): they allow the easy re-use of the library in a certain ICT environment. To mention some examples, the Embedded Systems Bridge[9] permits the use of UP in a framework-independent robotic setting, while UP4ROS2[10] focuses on the Robotic Operating System integration. Figure 2 depicts the general, high-level architecture of the project solution.

In addition to simplifying technology transfer, this technical effort enables the exploration of advanced features, such as procedural modeling of effects or custom heuristics. The former consists of specifying the effects of an action as a Python function that can be executed but not inspected, whereas the latter allows to programmatically describe a domain-specific heuristic within the framework. Moreover, the library offers support for the simulation and validation of planning problems, which are essential ingredients for approaches combining planning with other technologies such as Reinforcement Learning. In fact, the library is currently being used as the basis for new research: we recently extended it to model Task and Motion Planning (TAMP) problems, exploiting the manipulation capabilities of the library to automate the refinements in a Benders decomposition schema [25].

6   MAIS: Specialization of Temporal Planners

The final project we report in this survey is called Mechanical Automation Integration System (MAIS). The context of the project is the automation of electro-

---

[9] https://github.com/aiplan4eu/embedded-systems-bridge.
[10] https://github.com/aiplan4eu/UP4ROS2.

plating plants, where hoists are used to move the products being treated along a predefined sequence of chemical (and electro-chemical) baths. The goal of the project was to develop a planning solution capable of automating the decisions of when and where each hoist should move the products around to achieve the maximal throughput of the plant. We approached the problem in different ways and with diverse technologies, but no planner nor scheduler was capable of getting close to the real-world scale of the problem we faced. In the scheduling literature, a simplified version of the problem is called Hoist Scheduling Problem (HSP) and is shown to be strongly NP-hard even with very strong assumptions [14].

The complexity of the problem lies in the interaction of planning decisions (i.e., where to send the hoist and which operation to perform) with the scheduling constraints emerging from the very precise timings each piece can stay in each bath. Practically, in driving the hoists to bring many pieces into production, we are creating a lot of deadlines for taking the pieces out of the respective bath and such deadlines quickly become unachievable due to the finite speed of the hoist. A search-based approach discovers these constraints by extensive search, but fails to effectively back-jump to the root-cause of a problem. Instead, a scheduling-based approach quickly explodes due to the very high number of hoists movements involved in the problem. Moreover, it is very hard to model the spatial constraints emerging from the relative positioning of the hoists in scheduling.

The solution we settled on was developing a domain-specific planner embedding lots of domain knowledge into the search, together with a strategy to combine solutions for parts of the plant into a global one. To cope with the deadlines emerging from the electroplating process, we devised a method to impose long-term constraints in a heuristic-search approach.

Our solution was adequate for the MAIS project, but we are unsatisfied with the generality of the approach; yet, this project was very instrumental in terms of lessons learned. First, we realized that the constraints expressible in either PDDL 2.1 or ANML are too "local" for some problems, whereas scheduling often requires expressing global constraints. As a first step to address these limitations we developed the TPACK planner [15], which can express temporal constraints as a quantified logic over time points, allowing the user to express complex global constraints such as the electroplating "recipes" of the MAIS project.

The second, and perhaps more radical, research idea stemmed from this project consists in tackling the problem of automatically specializing a planner for a certain domain: in fact, during the MAIS project we had to manually adapt our planner to the characteristics of the domain and we embedded in the planner heuristic the knowledge gathered from domain experts. We started working on this idea using Reinforcement Learning (RL) methods to synthesize domain-specific heuristics from a simulator of the distribution of planning problems of interest. Importantly, and differently from other approaches in the state of the art, we do not assume that a set of example plans is given. Instead, we take as input a set of planning problems that is intended to be a representative sample of the problem expected at run-time, and we use RL to devise a general policy

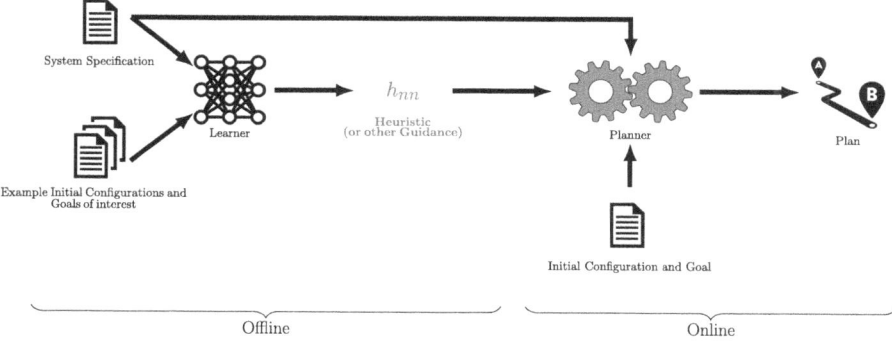

Fig. 3. Overview of the general learning schema for the specialization of temporal planning by synthesizing heuristic guidance. The offline phase is devoted to the synthesis of a guidance artifact, which is the used online by the planner to solve planning problems.

for such a distribution. Then, instead of using the policy directly, we convert it into a planning heuristic to balance the exploitation of learned information and systematic search, thus retaining the formal guarantees of a temporal planner. The general schema of this solution is depicted in Fig. 3, and our initial solution beats our purely-symbolic planner on some domains [16]. This idea has been proposed and articulated in my own ERC project, called STEP-RL[11] (Specializing TEmporal Planning using Reinforcement Learning), which will focus on exploring, in a principled and well-founded way, the combination of temporal planning and reinforcement learning.

7   Conclusions

In this paper, we surveyed a series of works inspired by challenges emerged in a variety of technology-transfer projects centered on the theme of temporal planning we have been involved in. Considering both theoretical and practical aspects, we worked to extend the applicability of temporal planning also to make it more usable by practitioners.

Our quest is still far from over, as many challenges still need more research to be addressed; because of this, we are currently working along different lines. First of all, we are expanding our approach using RL in combination with planning along two major directions. The first concerns the learning of a residual of a planning heuristic, instead of learning a heuristic from scratch: the idea is to simplify the learning effort and exploit the volume of work in domain-independent planning. The second direction aims at learning macro-actions for temporal planning, which are "shortcuts" in the search space of a planner, from RL explorations.

---

[11] https://pso.fbk.eu/articles/step-rl.

Furthermore, we are exploiting the UP library to advance our Task and Motion Planner to support time and temporal constraints. Finally, we are exploring the use of simulated entities as a mean to incorporate learned knowledge into a digital-twin model for space applications.

Acknowledgments. This work has been partially supported by the STEP-RL project funded by the European Research Council under GA n. 101115870.

I am very grateful to all my co-authors over the years in this line of research. In particular, Alessandro Cimatti, Nicola Gigante, Marco Roveri, Enrico Scala, and Alessandro Valentini hugely contributed with discussions, insights and technical effort.

References

1. Cesta, A., Cortellessa, G., Fratini, S., Oddi, A., Rasconi, R.: The APSI framework: a planning and scheduling software development environment. In: Working Notes of the ICAPS-09 Application Showcase Program. Thessaloniki, Greece (2009)
2. Coles, A.J., Coles, A., Fox, M., Long, D.: Forward-chaining partial-order planning. In: ICAPS 2010 (2010)
3. Coles, A., Fox, M., Long, D., Smith, A.: Planning with problems requiring temporal coordination. In: AAAI (2008)
4. Cushing, W., Kambhampati, S., Mausam, Weld, D.S.: When is temporal planning really temporal? In: IJCAI 2007 (2007)
5. Edelkamp, S., Hoffmann, J.: PDDL2.2: The language for the classical part of the 4th international planning competition, Technical report, Technical Report 195, University of Freiburg (2004)
6. Fox, M., Long, D.: PDDL2.1: an extension to PDDL for expressing temporal planning domains. J. Artif. Intell. Res. (2003)
7. Fox, M., Long, D.: Modelling mixed discrete-continuous domains for planning. J. Artif. Intell. Res. (2006)
8. Fox, M., Long, D., Halsey, K.: An investigation into the expressive power of PDDL2.1. In: ECAI 2004 (2004)
9. Frank, J., Jónsson, A.: Constraint-based attribute and interval planning. Constraints (2003)
10. Ghallab, M., Nau, D.S., Traverso, P.: Automated Planning - Theory and Practice. Elsevier (2004)
11. Gigante, N., Micheli, A., Montanari, A., Scala, E.: Decidability and complexity of action-based temporal planning over dense time. Artif. Intell. **307**, 103686 (2022). https://doi.org/10.1016/j.artint.2022.103686
12. Gigante, N., Micheli, A., Scala, E.: On the expressive power of intermediate and conditional effects in temporal planning. In: Kern-Isberner, G., Lakemeyer, G., Meyer, T. (eds.) Proceedings of the 19th International Conference on Principles of Knowledge Representation and Reasoning, KR 2022, Haifa, Israel, July 31 - August 5, 2022 (2022). https://proceedings.kr.org/2022/18/
13. Leofante, F., Giunchiglia, E., Ábrahám, E., Tacchella, A.: Optimal planning modulo theories. In: Bessiere, C. (ed.) Proceedings of the Twenty-Ninth International Joint Conference on Artificial Intelligence, IJCAI 2020, pp. 4128–4134 (2020). https://doi.org/10.24963/IJCAI.2020/571
14. Manier, M.A., Bloch, C.: A classification for hoist scheduling problems. Int. J. Flex. Manuf. Syst. **15**, 37–55 (2003)

15. Micheli, A., Scala, E.: Temporal planning with temporal metric trajectory constraints. In: AAAI 2019, pp. 7675–7682 (2019)
16. Micheli, A., Valentini, A.: Synthesis of search heuristics for temporal planning via reinforcement learning. In: Thirty-Fifth AAAI Conference on Artificial Intelligence, AAAI 2021, Thirty-Third Conference on Innovative Applications of Artificial Intelligence, IAAI 2021, The Eleventh Symposium on Educational Advances in Artificial Intelligence, EAAI 2021, Virtual Event, February 2-9, 2021, pp. 11895–11902. AAAI Press (2021). https://doi.org/10.1609/AAAI.V35I13.17413
17. Panjkovic, S., Micheli, A.: Expressive optimal temporal planning via optimization modulo theory. In: Williams, B., Chen, Y., Neville, J. (eds.) Thirty-Seventh AAAI Conference on Artificial Intelligence, AAAI 2023, Thirty-Fifth Conference on Innovative Applications of Artificial Intelligence, IAAI 2023, Thirteenth Symposium on Educational Advances in Artificial Intelligence, EAAI 2023, Washington, DC, USA, February 7-14, 2023, pp. 12095–12102. AAAI Press (2023). https://doi.org/10.1609/AAAI.V37I10.26426
18. Panjkovic, S., Micheli, A.: Abstract action scheduling for optimal temporal planning via OMT. In: Wooldridge, M.J., Dy, J.G., Natarajan, S. (eds.) Thirty-Eighth AAAI Conference on Artificial Intelligence, AAAI 2024, Thirty-Sixth Conference on Innovative Applications of Artificial Intelligence, IAAI 2024, Fourteenth Symposium on Educational Advances in Artificial Intelligence, EAAI 2014, February 20-27, 2024, Vancouver, Canada. pp. 20222–20229. AAAI Press (2024). https://doi.org/10.1609/AAAI.V38I18.30002
19. Panjkovic, S., Micheli, A., Cimatti, A.: Deciding unsolvability in temporal planning under action non-self-overlapping. In: Thirty-Sixth AAAI Conference on Artificial Intelligence, AAAI 2022, Thirty-Fourth Conference on Innovative Applications of Artificial Intelligence, IAAI 2022, The Twelveth Symposium on Educational Advances in Artificial Intelligence, EAAI 2022 Virtual Event, February 22 - March 1, 2022, pp. 9886–9893. AAAI Press (2022). https://doi.org/10.1609/AAAI.V36I9.21225
20. Rintanen, J.: Discretization of temporal models with application to planning with SMT. In: Bonet, B., Koenig, S. (eds.) Proceedings of the Twenty-Ninth AAAI Conference on Artificial Intelligence, January 25-30, 2015, Austin, Texas USA, pp. 3349–3355. AAAI Press (2015). https://doi.org/10.1609/AAAI.V29I1.9644
21. Sebastiani, R., Tomasi, S.: Optimization modulo theories with linear rational costs. ACM Trans. Comput. Log. **16**(2), 12:1–12:43 (2015). https://doi.org/10.1145/2699915
22. Smith, D., Frank, J., Cushing, W.: The ANML language. In: KEPS 2008 (2008)
23. Smith, D.E.: The case for durative actions: a commentary on PDDL2.1. J. Artif. Intell. Res. (2003)
24. Tosello, E., et al.: Opportunistic (re)planning for long-term deep-ocean inspection: an autonomous underwater architecture. IEEE Rob. Autom. Mag. **31**(1), 72–83 (2024). https://doi.org/10.1109/MRA.2024.3352810
25. Tosello, E., Valentini, A., Micheli, A.: A meta-engine framework for interleaved task and motion planning using topological refinements. In: Proceeding of the European Conference in AI (to appear) (2024)
26. Umbrico, A., Cesta, A., Mayer, M.C., Orlandini, A.: Integrating resource management and timeline-based planning. In: ICAPS (2018)
27. Valentini, A., Micheli, A., Cimatti, A.: Temporal planning with intermediate conditions and effects. In: AAAI 2020 (2020)

A Novel Approach for Leveraging Agent-Based Experts on Large Language Models to Enable Data Sharing Among Heterogeneous IoT Devices in Agriculture

Nur Arifin Akbar[(✉)] ⓘ, Biagio Lenzitti[(✉)] ⓘ, and Domenico Tegolo[(✉)] ⓘ

Dipartimento Matematica e Informatica, Universitá degli Studi di Palermo, 90123 Palermo, Italy
{nurarifin.akbar,biagio.Lenzitti,domenico.tegolo}@unipa.it

Abstract. The rapid adoption of Internet of Things (IoT) devices in agriculture has led to the generation of diverse data types, creating challenges in data sharing and integration across heterogeneous platforms. This paper presents a novel approach to facilitate data sharing among heterogeneous IoT devices in agriculture using agent-based experts built on large language models (LLMs).

Background: Traditional methods of data sharing in agriculture face limitations due to the lack of standardization and interoperability among IoT devices. Previous approaches, such as model fine-tuning and prompt engineering, have shown promise but struggle with open-ended agricultural queries and context comprehension.

The proposed Agent-based Data Sharing (ADS) framework combines semantic web technologies with agent-based design and LLMs to enable seamless information exchange, decentralized data sharing, and knowledge transfer through intelligent expert agents. This approach leverages the strengths of LLMs in understanding text and their extensive training data while addressing the challenges of data interoperability and context-aware decision-making in agriculture.

Using synthetic agricultural data, we evaluated the framework's performance in disease diagnosis and precision farming recommendations. The results demonstrate significant improvements in data integration, interoperability, and decision-making efficiency. With extensive data sharing, mean performance scores increased by 16% for disease diagnosis and 25% for precision farming compared to baseline scenarios.

The framework's ability to manage diverse devices and handle natural language queries through agent-based experts highlights its potential for real-world agricultural applications. This approach could support the advancement of smart farming through IoT applications and pave the way for improved efficiency in sustainable agriculture. However, challenges such as data privacy, standardization, and incentive structures need to be addressed in future research.

Keywords: large language models · agriculture · expert agents · data sharing · heterogeneous devices · agent-based systems

A. Artale et al. (Eds.): AIxIA 2024, LNAI 15450, pp. 12–22, 2025.
https://doi.org/10.1007/978-3-031-80607-0_2

1 Introduction

The advancement of technology, specifically the incorporation of IoT devices within agriculture, has made it possible to collect a considerable volume of heterogeneous data. However, the standardization and interoperability issues of these devices prevent us from meeting the main goal of data sharing and exchange. Large language models can help fill the gaps because they have the ability to understand and process natural language.

In this capacity, LLMs can be very effective for LLM-based agricultural applications, tapping into their ability to read beyond the text and answer questions accurately. However, for some specific applications, such as crop yield prediction or disease recognition in crops, their value is proportional to the number of examples that can be collected and how deeply the matrix understands the specifics of the problem at hand. Implementing LLMs to answer open-ended agricultural questions depends on how rich the examples provided are and how well the models understand the situation at hand.

Model fine-tuning is one of the most common ways to adapt LLM for agricultural problem solving [7]. However, existing methodology, such as prompt engineering and in-context learning, have been recently developed and applied in some cases [1, 14]. These techniques strive to increase the performance of LLM while addressing concerns such as data security and bias reduction issues [22]. Prompt engineering generates requests or directions to shape the output of LLM, thereby increasing the likelihood of accurate output in various tasks [6].

Nevertheless, these approaches tend to have many areas for improvement in responding to unstructured agricultural questions or issues and evaluating context comprehension. Giving more problem descriptions may also help block the agent's comprehension, and due to the limited variety of external agricultural knowledge bases available, there may also be limitations in the range of consultable resources.

This paper will present a new approach to agriculture data sharing by proposing an agent-based data sharing (A.D.S.) framework, which uses agents for data sharing between heterogeneous IoT devices based on generative AI on a large language model. Our primary contributions to this paper are as follows:

a. *Introducing the ADS Framework:* The combination of agent-based systems and LLM enables decentralized information and knowledge transfer among agricultural IoT devices.
b. *Improving Data Interoperability:* Using the strengths of LLM and agent-based systems to overcome data interoperability issues and contextually driven agricultural decision-making processes.
c. *Experimental Validation:* We illustrate the A.I. through experiments on agronomically sworn synthetic data, and show how the problem diagnosis or precision farming recommendations improve when agents share the data in the ADS. Paradigm.

2   Related Works

2.1   In-Context Learning for Agricultural Applications: Capabilities and Limitations

In-context learning in agriculture has the potential to improve its energy efficiency, resource allocation, and promote environmentally friendly attitudes through smart agricultural activities. Context learning can interact with various channels such as IoT sensors or intelligent monitoring systems, thereby enhancing data collection, reasoning, and decision-making for farmers. This may result in better production yields, less wastage of resources, and positive stewardship of the environment [23].

There are constraints on the use of in-context learning in the field, particularly in its application to agriculture. One major limitation is the issue of data standards, and interoperability is another. Agricultural databases are heterogeneous in terms of data format, quality, and availability. In order to maintain the quality and credibility of the learning setups, combining and using these dataset for agricultural decision-making requires significant effort in data processing and standardization procedures [23].

2.2   Retrieval-Augmented Generation: Enhancing LLMs with External Agricultural Knowledge

The retrieval-augmented method generation is a new and hopeful technique to improve Large Language Models (LLMs). In this method, external knowledge from agriculture can be added to the input through attention blending or output interpolation[15]. This way, LLMs can give accountability for information and create more precise and suitable for farming purposes [24].

Different approaches have been applied to retrieval-augmented generation in the field of agriculture, such as:

a. *BM25 Algorithm:* Used to select the most similar farming details to a query by considering term frequency and document length [13].
b. *Sentence-BERT (SBERT):* A sentence-level embedding model used for effective example retrieval using contrastive learning [11].
c. *Dense Retrieval Models:* Utilizing feedback-driven dense retrievers for farming-related tasks, significantly impacting practical learning in context [11].

3   Agent-Based Data Sharing Framework

3.1   A Conceptual Overview of the ADS Framework

The ADS framework models the system with autonomous agents that represent the diverse players in agriculture, such as a farmer, researcher, or policymaker, using an agent-based architecture. There's a clear division of task, including goals, knowledge, and faculties, allowing them to cooperate in a distributed manner [2]. Within this framework, the decentralized data pool acts as a distributed database where agents can store and access shared data without a central point of control. Such a structure guarantees the control of the data with the individual agents, yielding independence and privacy in data use. Each agent makes an autonomous decision on what information to disclose to protect their own databases [Fig. 1].

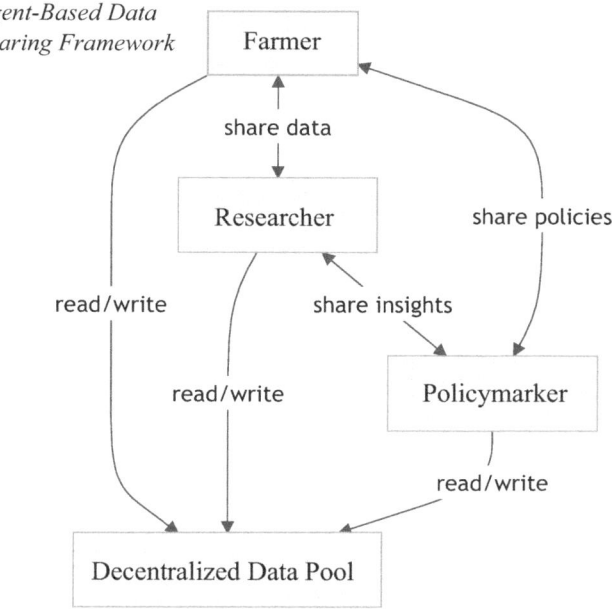

Agent-Based Data Sharing Framework

Fig. 1. Interconnected Agricultural System with three agents - Farmer, Researcher, and Policymaker - sharing data and insights, all linked to a Decentralized Data Pool for data storage and access.

3.2   Data Retrieval and Storage

Each agent in the framework is responsible for creating and maintaining its own dataset containing information such as crop yields, soil content, weather, or market price. This innovative method of producing and storing agriculture information captures and adds more localized agricultural data to the existing sets of data. When an agent tackles a wide-ranging agricultural problem, it initiates a complex process of product retrieval to identify the most pertinent instance, knowledge, or concept from a vast pool of resources (Fig. 2). This includes techniques like semantic space matching and context ranking, which aim to fit the query to the extent of available information. Such algorithms accomplish the task by reasoning about the asker's goals and objectives, the questions' reasons and context, and the agent's area of knowledge, thereby selecting and rendering the most attractive facts from the knowledge base. This, in turn, improves the agent's performance in context retrieval, aiding in additional decision-making aimed at improving agricultural practices.

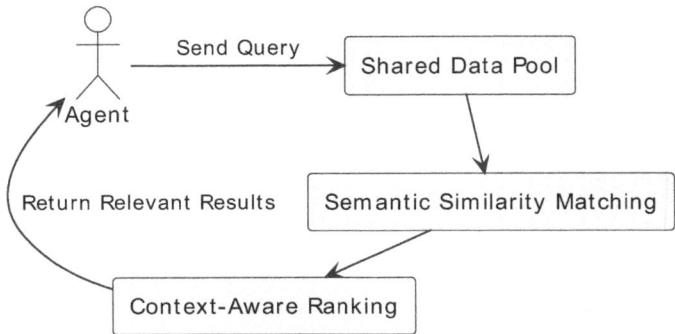

Fig. 2. Agent interacting with a Shared Data Pool, The Shared Data Pool processes this question through a two-step retrieval process involving Semantic Similarity Matching and Ranking Algorithms with Context.

4   Experiment

4.1   Dataset Description

For testing the proposed ADS framework, we utilized DataDreamer, an open-source Python library [3], to generate synthetic datasets simulating real-world agricultural scenarios using the Phi-3 foundational model [17]. The details of these datasets are summarized in Table 1.

4.2   Experiment Setup

In our experiment, we approached two main areas of application: disease detection and agronomic precision recommendations. For the disease detection area, we created agents well-skilled in diagnosing plant diseases through the incorporation of LLM-symptom analysis, climate, and plant metadata. In the area of providing precision farming recommendations, agents rendered advisory services by analysing data sourced from soil sensors, weather stations, and management activities in particular regions.

We created an instruction set to operationalize the agents, tailored to each agent's domain of knowledge. They used the OpenAI Compatible API [14] with the Llama 3 8B model. Furthermore, the agents used a code interpreter tool in real-time data analysis and computation, allowing them to analyse a large amount of data.

In order to check the data distribution effect on the agents' work, we implemented three different variants of data sharing:

a. Baseline (No Sharing): The agents worked separately with no data exchange.
b. Limited Sharing (Partial): The agents engaged in modest data sharing with one another in such matters as soil or weather data.
c. Extensive Sharing (All): The agents exchanged all available data and resources internally, without any restrictions on external sources.

Table 1. Dataset Description

Component	Sample Number	Features	Target Variable	Data Split
Crop Yield Prediction	10,000	Historical yield data, weather conditions (temperature, precipitation, humidity), soil characteristics, management practices (irrigation, fertilization, pest control)	Crop yield (tons per hectare)	Training: 70%, Validation: 15%, Testing 15%
Plant Disease Diagnosis	5,000	Visual symptoms (leaf discoloration, lesions, wilting), environmental conditions (temperature, humidity), plant metadata (species, growth stage)	Disease class (10 distinct classes)	Training: 60%, Validation: 20%, Testing: 20%

In each of the data sharing scenarios, we posed a combination of 50 open-ended agronomy-related questions to the agents, simply focusing on disease diagnosis and precision agriculture, among other aspects. It allowed us to evaluate the impact of changes to levels of data sharing on the agents' response quality, completeness, and context relevance [Fig. 3].

4.3   Evaluation Methodology

To evaluate the effectiveness of data sharing among the agents, we developed a scoring formula that assesses their responses based on five key criteria: relevance (s_r), accuracy (s_a), completeness (s_c), clarity (s_l), and originality (s_o). Each criterion was assigned a score ranging from 0 to 1. The overall response score was calculated using the formula.

$$\text{Score} = \frac{w_r s_r + w_a s_a + w_c s_c + w_l s_l + w_o s_o}{\sum_{i \in \{r,a,c,lo\}} w_i} \quad (1)$$

where w_i are the weights assigned to each criterion.

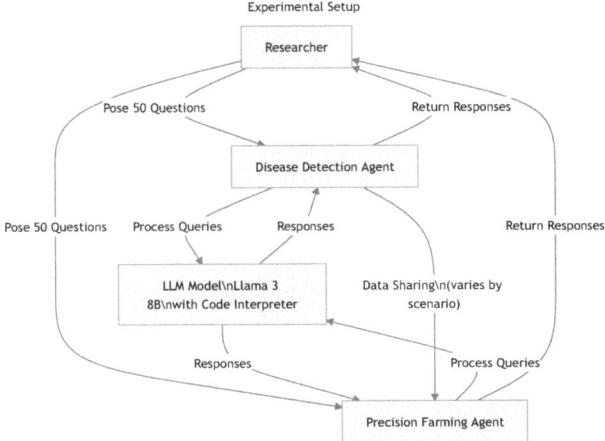

Fig. 3. The diagram experimental setup involves two specialized agents: one for disease detection and another for precision farming recommendations. The agents interact with the Llama 3 8B model via the OpenAI Compatible API, utilizing a code interpreter tool for real-time data analysis.

For simplicity and to assign equal importance to all evaluation criteria, we set all weights to 1.

$$(w_r = w_a = w_c = w_l = w_o = 1) \qquad (2)$$

The denominator ensures that the resultant score is not greater than 1. We define the criteria as follows: relevance measures the response's ability to address the question; accuracy evaluates the truthfulness of the provided information; completeness gauges the extent of the answer to the question; clarity scrutinizes the answer and its presentation; and originality gauges the creativity and perception inherent in the response. We used this linear sum formula to add up the scores for each criterion and get the overall score.

4.4 Results

When comparing all three scenarios, the evaluation indicated very positive changes in agent performance as a function of the level of data sharing. The average performance measures of each domain with respect to the data sharing scenarios have been given in Table 2.

Table 2. Mean Performance Scores Across Data Sharing Scenarios.

Domain	Baseline	Limited Sharing	Extensive Sharing
Disease Diagnosis	0.7474	0.8190	0.9137
Precision Farming	0.5933	0.7208	0.8447

To illustrate the impact of data sharing on the quality of agent responses, we present a comparative analysis based on the agents' answers to the following question:

"What is the optimal soil pH for growing tomatoes?"

The agents' responses and corresponding scores under each data sharing scenario are summarized in Table 4, while the details shown in Table 3.

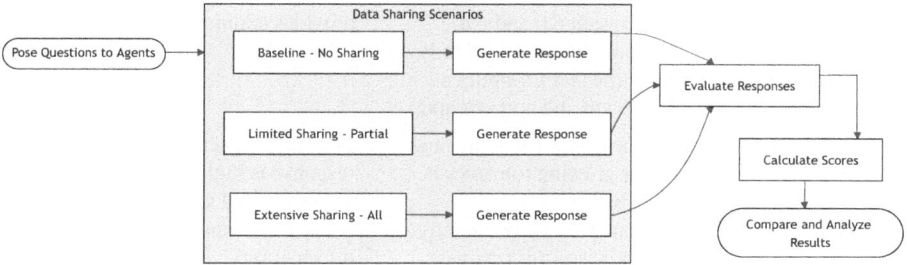

Fig. 4. Evaluation Process of Agent Responses

In the baseline scenario, agents operate independently without exchanging data. Partial sharing allows limited data exchange, such as weather or soil information, while keeping proprietary practices private. Full sharing involves complete pooling of all data and resources among agents. These scenarios represent a spectrum from isolated operation to full collaboration, enabling assessment of data sharing's impact on agricultural decision-making and overall system performance.

The results of the performance evaluation showed significant improvements in agent performance when extensive data sharing was employed [Fig. 4]. As a result, the mean performance metrics for each domain under different sharing scenarios were as follows.

Table 3. Scoring of Shared Data (Evaluated by Agent)

Sharing Scenario	Relevance	Accuracy	Completeness	Clarity	Originality
Baseline (No Sharing)	0.65	0.70	0.60	0.68	0.62
Limited Sharing	0.78	0.80	0.75	0.77	0.73
Extensive Sharing	0.90	0.92	0.88	0.91	0.89

In the disease diagnosis domain, mean performance scores increased approximately by 22% from the mean of 0.7474 to that of 0.9137. In precision farming, scores increased approximately 42% to 0.8447 from 0.5933. These huge gains show that the agents have a better capacity to deliver accurate, complete, and contextualized responses when presented with a larger amount of data.

Table 4. Agents' Responses and Scores Across Data Sharing Scenarios

Sharing Scenario	Response	Explanation	Score
Baseline (No Sharing)	The optimal soil pH for growing tomatoes is between 6.0 and 6.8	The LLM-generated response is mostly accurate but lacks some specificity	0.7
Limited Sharing (Partial)	The optimal soil pH range for growing tomatoes is between 6.0 and 6.8. Tomatoes prefer slightly acidic soil for optimal growth and nutrient uptake	The LLM-generated response is accurate and provides additional relevant information	0.85
Extensive Sharing (All)	The optimal soil pH range for growing tomatoes is between 6.0 and 6.8. Tomatoes prefer slightly acidic soil for optimal growth and nutrient uptake. Soil pH affects the availability of essential nutrients, and maintaining the proper pH range ensures the best possible growth, yield, and fruit quality	The LLM-generated response is highly accurate complete, and provides detailed relevant information	0.95

5 Conclusion

The experimental results show that there is a greater improvement in response quality when agents share more information in both the disease diagnosis and precision farming areas. These details hold greater significance in agricultural decision-making, as even the smallest details significantly influence the process and outcome of the decisions.

Acknowledgments. This project has received funding from the European Union's Horizon 2021 research and innovation program under the Marie Skłodowska-Curie grant agreement No 101073381.

References

1. Luo, M., Xu, X., Liu, Y., Pasupat, P., Kazemi, M.: In-context Learning with Retrieved Demonstrations for Language Models: A Survey, https://arxiv.org/abs/2401.11624 (2024). https://doi.org/10.48550/ARXIV.2401.11624
2. Ault, A., Palacios, S., Evans, J.: Agriculture data sharing: conceptual tools in the technical toolbox and implementation in the open Ag data alliance framework. Agron. J. **114**(5), 2681–2692 (2022). https://doi.org/10.1002/agj2.21007
3. Patel, A., Raffel, C., Callison-Burch, C.: DataDreamer: A Tool for Synthetic Data Generation and Reproducible LLM Workflows, https://arxiv.org/abs/2402.10379 (2024). https://doi.org/10.48550/ARXIV.2402.10379
4. Condran, S., Bewong, M., Islam, Z., Maphosa, L., Zheng, L.: Machine learning in precision agriculture: a survey on trends, applications, and evaluations over two decades. IEEE Access **10**, 73786–73803 (2022). https://doi.org/10.1109/ACCESS.2022.3188649
5. Cooper, N.: Harnessing large language models for coding, teaching, and inclusion to empower research in ecology and evolution. Methods Ecol. Evol. (2024). https://doi.org/10.1111/2041-210X.14325
6. Dwivedi, S.: Breaking the bias: gender fairness in LLMs using prompt engineering and in-context learning. Rupkatha J. Interdisc. Stud. Humanit. **15**(4) (2023). https://doi.org/10.21659/rupkatha.v15n4.10
7. Zheng, H., et al.: Learn From Model Beyond Fine-Tuning: A Survey, https://arxiv.org/abs/2310.08184 (2023). https://doi.org/10.48550/ARXIV.2310.08184
8. Griend, R.: Artificial intelligence and scholarly publication in foot & ankle international and foot & ankle orthopaedics. Foot Ankle Int. **45**(3), 207 (2024). https://doi.org/10.1177/10711007241232288
9. Haileslassie, A., Mekuria, W., Schmitter, P., Uhlenbrook, S., Ludi, E.: Review of lessons learned in changing agricultural landscapes in Ethiopia: what worked well and what did not work so well? (2020). https://doi.org/10.20944/preprints202010.0124.v1
10. Hou, J.: Assessing large language models in mechanical engineering education: a study on mechanics-focused conceptual understanding (2024). https://doi.org/10.31219/osf.io/d3nc6
11. Reimers, N., Gurevych, I.: Sentence-BERT: Sentence Embeddings using Siamese BERT-Networks. https://arxiv.org/abs/1908.10084 (2019). https://doi.org/10.48550/ARXIV.1908.10084
12. Li, W.: Segment, anything model, can not segment anything: assessing AI foundation model's generalizability in permafrost mapping. Remote Sens. **16**(5), 797 (2024). https://doi.org/10.3390/rs16050797
13. Sawarkar, K., Mangal, A., Solanki, S.R.: Blended RAG: Improving RAG (Retriever-Augmented Generation) Accuracy with Semantic Search and Hybrid Query-Based Retrievers, https://arxiv.org/abs/2404.07220. (2024). https://doi.org/10.48550/ARXIV.2404.07220
14. Allen, M., Pearn, K., Monks, T.: Developing an OpenAI Gym-compatible framework and simulation environment for testing Deep Reinforcement Learning agents solving the Ambulance Location Problem, https://arxiv.org/abs/2101.04434. (2021). https://doi.org/10.48550/ARXIV.2101.04434
15. Radeva, I.: Web application for retrieval-augmented generation: implementation and testing. Electronics **13**(7), 1361 (2024). https://doi.org/10.3390/electronics13071361
16. Raiaan, M.: A review on large language models: architectures, applications, taxonomies, open issues, and challenges (2023). https://doi.org/10.36227/techrxiv.24171183.v1
17. Abdin, M., et al.: Phi-3 Technical Report: A Highly Capable Language Model Locally on Your Phone, arXiv:2404.14219. (2024)

18. Shutske, J.: Editorial: harnessing the power of large language models in agricultural safety & health. J. Agric. Saf. Health **29**(4), 205–224 (2023). https://doi.org/10.13031/jash.15841
19. Sivarajkumar, S.: An empirical evaluation of prompting strategies for large language models in zero-shot clinical natural language processing: algorithm development and validation study. JMIR Med. Inform. **12**, e55318 (2024). https://doi.org/10.2196/55318
20. Stoyanov, S.: Using LLMs in cyber-physical systems for agriculture - ZEMELA (2023). https://doi.org/10.1109/BDKCSE59280.2023.10339738
21. Ubah, C.: Evaluation of AI models to update cybersecurity curriculum. J. Colloquium Inf. Syst. Secur. Educ. **11**(1), 8 (2024). https://doi.org/10.53735/cisse.v11i1.183
22. Woo, B.: Transforming nursing with large language models: from concept to practice. Eur. J. Cardiovasc. Nurs. (2024). https://doi.org/10.1093/eurjcn/zvad120
23. Qamar, T., Bawany, N.Z.: Understanding the black-box: towards interpretable and reliable deep learning models. https://doi.org/10.7717/peerj-cs.1629. (2023)
24. Lewis, P., et al.: Retrieval-Augmented Generation for Knowledge-Intensive NLP Tasks, https://arxiv.org/abs/2005.11401. (2020). https://doi.org/10.48550/ARXIV.2005.11401

An Extensive Empirical Analysis of Macro-actions for Numeric Planning

Diaeddin Alarnaouti$^{(\boxtimes)}$, Francesco Percassi⦿, and Mauro Vallati⦿

University of Huddersfield, Huddersfield, UK
diaeddin.alarnaouti@hud.ac.uk

Abstract. Automated Planning is a pivotal field of artificial intelligence, focusing on intelligent agents' ability to generate action sequences leading from an initial state to a desired goal condition. A well-known technique to improve planning performance is based on macro-actions, which can reduce search depth by merging multiple primitive actions together, generating "shortcuts" in the search space. Macros have been studied extensively in classical planning, but rarely in more expressive formalisms.

In this study, we investigate macro-actions in numeric planning, formalising the macro generation process and exploring a semi-automated methodology for selecting candidate primitive actions to be combined into macro-actions. Our extensive experimental analysis demonstrates the potential benefits of macros for numeric planning engines, providing useful insights into their effectiveness for efficient plan generation.

Keywords: Automated Planning · Macro Actions · Numeric Planning

1 Introduction

Automated Planning is a prominent field of artificial intelligence, that focuses on the capability of intelligent agents to generate sequences of actions whose application, starting from a given initial state, would lead to a state where a given goal condition is satisfied [15].

In domain-independent planning, the separation between planning knowledge and reasoning supports the use of reformulation approaches [23]. These techniques involve automatically re-formulating, re-representing, or adjusting the planning knowledge [21,25,26,30] to enhance the efficiency of planning engines or to allow the use of different classes of solving approaches. In literature, there is a substantial body of work on reformulation techniques, primarily focused on the classical planning paradigm [1]. Among other reformulation techniques, macro-actions are a well-studied approach, that aims to reduce the search depth by merging actions together, to provide shortcuts in the search space [2,6,8,9,22]. Scala [27] proposed the most relevant work on macro actions in numeric planning. Still, the work focuses on macros for repairing plans, rather than macros that can boost the plan generation process. Given the positive performance impact

A. Artale et al. (Eds.): AIxIA 2024, LNAI 15450, pp. 23–36, 2025.
https://doi.org/10.1007/978-3-031-80607-0_3

that macro techniques allow to achieve in classical planning, a promising avenue for research is using macros in more expressive planning formalisms.

Given the recent renewed interest in numeric planning, both from a practical and theoretical point of view [5,7,16,17,19,24,28,29], in this study, we investigate macro-actions in the context of numeric planning. We formalise the macro process generation in numeric planning, and introduce a semi-automated methodology for selecting candidate primitive actions to be combined into macro-actions. We introduce a categorisation of macros for numeric planning by accounting for syntactical aspects, which can help shed some light on performance and the expected impact of macros. Finally, we run an extensive empirical evaluation of macros in numeric planning to assess their impact on plan generation performance.

2   Background

Traditionally, numeric planning tasks are described by means of PDDL2.1 [11]. A *numeric planning task* is a pair $\Pi = \langle \mathcal{D}, \mathcal{P} \rangle$ where $\mathcal{D}$ is a *planning domain model* and $\mathcal{P}$ is a *planning problem*. $\mathcal{D}$ is a tuple $\langle F, X, A \rangle$ where F and X are sets of Boolean and numeric functions returning values in $\mathbb{B} = \{\bot, \top\}$ and $\mathbb{Q}$, respectively, and A is a set of lifted actions. Elements from $F \cup X$ are referred to as lifted functions. $\mathcal{P}$ is a tuple $\langle O, I, G \rangle$ where O is a set of objects, I is the initial state, and G is the goal description. A function $p \in F \cup X$ has arity k, and every occurrence of p in Π features k arguments $\{v_1, \ldots, v_k\}$, written as $p(v_1, \ldots, v_k)$. Numeric functions can be combined to obtain mathematical expressions defined as $\varphi := \varphi + \varphi \mid \varphi * \varphi \mid x \mid q$, where $x \in X$ and $q \in \mathbb{Q}$.

Let F^O (X^O) be the sets of all Boolean (numeric) variables formed from the functions F (X) by substituting objects O in the functions' arguments. Elements from $F^O \cup X^O$ are referred to as grounded variables. A state s is a complete assignment over the variables $F^O \cup X^O$, mapping elements from F^O to $\mathbb{B}$ and from X^O to $\mathbb{Q}$. The initial state I is then a complete assignment over $F^O \cup X^O$. The goal G is a partial assignment over $F^O \cup X^O$.

A lifted action a is a tuple $\langle \mathrm{par}(a), \mathrm{name}(a), \mathrm{pre}(a), \mathrm{eff}(a) \rangle$, where $\mathrm{par}(a)$ is the set of arguments of a, $\mathrm{name}(a)$ is the unique identifier of the action, $\mathrm{pre}(a)$ (preconditions of a) is a set of conditions, $\mathrm{eff}(a)$ (effects of a) is a set of effects. $\mathrm{pre}(a)$ is partitioned in numeric and Boolean conditions, i.e., $\mathrm{pre}(a) = \mathrm{pre}_{\mathsf{num}}(a) \cup \mathrm{pre}_{\mathsf{prop}}(a)$. A numeric condition in $\mathrm{pre}_{\mathsf{num}}(a)$ has the form $\langle \varphi \bowtie 0 \rangle$, where φ is a mathematical expression defined over X and $\mathbb{Q}$ and $\bowtie \in \{<, \leq, =, \geq, >\}$. A Boolean condition in $\mathrm{pre}_{\mathsf{prop}}(a)$ has the form p or $\neg p$ where $p \in F$. Similarly, the effects are partitioned into numeric and Boolean effects, i.e., $\mathrm{eff}(a) = \mathrm{eff}_{\mathsf{num}}(a) \cup \mathrm{eff}_{\mathsf{prop}}(a)$. A numeric effect in $\mathrm{eff}_{\mathsf{num}}(a)$ has the form $\langle x := \varphi \rangle$ where $x \in X$ and φ is a mathematical expression defined over X and $\mathbb{Q}$. A Boolean condition in $\mathrm{pre}_{\mathsf{prop}}(a)$ has the form p or $\neg p$ where $p \in F$. To differentiate between positive and negative effects, we use $\mathrm{eff}_{\mathsf{prop}}^{+}(a)$ and $\mathrm{eff}_{\mathsf{prop}}^{-}(a)$, respectively.

Let A^O be the set of all grounded actions formed from the lifted actions A by substituting objects O for the parameter symbols in their preconditions and effects. This process produces *grounded actions* $\langle \text{pre}(a), \text{eff}(a) \rangle$ without arguments, where $\text{pre}(a)$ and $\text{eff}(a)$ are defined over variables $F^O \cup X^O$. All definitions of lifted conditions, effects, and mathematical expressions defined over $F \cup X$ can be syntactically redefined for grounded variables.

Let s be a state, v a variable in $F^O \cup X^O$ and φ a mathematical expression defined over X^O and $\mathbb{Q}$, we denote with $s[v]$ the value assumed by v in s, and with $s[\varphi]$ the evaluation of φ in s. A numeric condition $c = \langle \varphi \bowtie 0 \rangle$ is satisfied by a state s, denoted $s \models c$, if and only if $s[\varphi] \bowtie 0$ holds. Similarly, the Boolean condition v ($\neg v$) is satisfied if and only if $s[v] = \top$ ($s[v] = \bot$). A state s satisfies a set of conditions C, denoted $s \models C$ if and only if $\bigwedge_{c \in C} s \models c$. Applying a grounded action a in a state s yields a new state $s' = \gamma(s, a)$ where:

$$
s[v] = \begin{cases}
\top & \text{if } v \in \text{eff}(a), v \in F^O \\
\bot & \text{if } \neg v \in \text{eff}(a), v \in F^O \\
s[\varphi] & \text{if } \langle v := \varphi \rangle \in \text{eff}(a), v \in X^O \\
s[v] & \text{otherwise (frame axiom)}
\end{cases}
$$

An action is applicable in a state s if $s \models \text{pre}(a)$, there are no conflicting effects, i.e., more than one effect affecting the same variable differently, and the result of each numeric effect $s[\varphi]$ is well-defined. A plan π for Π is a sequence of grounded actions, i.e., $\langle a_1, \ldots, a_n \rangle$. A plan π is valid for Π if each action is iteratively applicable starting from I and the resulting state achieves G.

2.1   Example

To illustrate the concepts presented in the background, we will refer to a well-known domain, namely SETTLERS [20]. We will focus on two actions that will be used to demonstrate the generation of macro-actions.

Let $O = \{p_1, p_2\}$ be a set of objects representing two places. We consider a single Boolean function, parameterised by p, that indicates whether a coal stack is present at place p, i.e., $F = \{has\text{-}coal\text{-}stack(p)\}$. Additionally, we use numeric functions to track the available timber or coal at each location, as well as the overall pollution emitted or labour consumed, i.e., $X = \{timb(p), coal(p), poll, lab\}$.

We consider two lifted actions a_1 and a_2 to build a coal stack or to burn the coal, respectively. Both actions are parametrised in p, i.e., $par(a_1) = par(a_2) = \{p\}$ and $name(a_1) = build\text{-}coal\text{-}stack$ and $name(a_2) = burn\text{-}coal$. The preconditions and effects of these actions are defined as:

$\text{pre}(a_1) = \{\langle timb(p) \geq 1 \rangle\}$

$\text{eff}(a_1) = \{has\text{-}coal\text{-}stack(p), \langle lab := lab + 2 \rangle, \langle timb(p) := timb(p) - 1 \rangle\}$

$\text{pre}(a_2) = \{has\text{-}coal\text{-}stack(p), \langle timb(p) \geq 1 \rangle\}$

$\text{eff}(a_2) = \{\langle timb(p) := timb(p) - 1 \rangle, \langle coal(p) := coal(p) + 1 \rangle, \langle poll := poll + 1 \rangle\}$.

The grounded variables instantiated through the objects $O = \{p_1, p_2\}$ are $F^O = \{has\text{-}coal\text{-}stack(p1), has\text{-}coal\text{-}stack(p2)\}$ and $X^O = \{timb(p1), timb(p2), coal(p1), coal(p2), poll, lab\}$. To illustrate the grounding process for the lifted actions, we consider action a_1 grounded using place p_1. The resulting grounded action is $a_1^{p_1}$, where $\text{pre}(a_1^{p_1}) = \{\langle timb(p_1) \geq 1 \rangle\}$ and $\text{eff}(a_1^{p_1}) = \{has\text{-}coal\text{-}stack(p_1), \langle lab := lab + 1 \rangle, \langle timb(p_1) := timb(p_1) - 1 \rangle\}$.

3   Generating Macro-actions

This section describes how a pair of candidate lifted actions can be combined to obtain an equivalent macro-action. We refer to the input actions as candidates because two actions may not be combinable, for instance, if the first action consumes a resource violating a precondition of the second one.

The generation of macro-actions in the numeric context must consider the Boolean and numeric components. For the Boolean component, a standard approach from classical planning is used. On the other hand, the numeric component is handled by adopting a technique from the work of Scala [27].

Algorithm 1 outlines the overall methodology. This algorithm takes two candidate actions, namely a_i and a_j, along with an identifier id that ensures the generation of uniquely named macro-actions. The resulting macro-action, denoted as $a_{i,j}$ is obtained by separately combining the propositional and numeric preconditions, as well as effects.

The parameters of $a_{i,j}$ are obtained by merging the parameters of the candidate actions, while the name is obtained by simply chaining the names of a_i and a_j and the unique identifier id. The propositional precondition of $a_{i,j}$ is obtained by merging the preconditions of a_i and a_j, from which the additive effects of a_i are removed. Specifically, these are removed because they may not hold before applying a_i.

The merging of numeric preconditions is accomplished using the procedure MERGENUMPRECS($\cdot$), the pseudocode of which is outlined in Algorithm 2. Specifically, the numeric preconditions of $a_{i,j}$ are constructed by directly including all the preconditions of a_i in their original form. In contrast, the preconditions of a_j must be manipulated to account for the effects of a_i. Specifically, the algorithm iterates over all the numeric conditions $\langle \varphi \bowtie 0 \rangle \in \text{pre}(a_j)$, and adds the regressed condition $\langle S(\varphi, \text{eff}(a_i)) \bowtie 0 \rangle$ to $\text{pre}(a_{i,j})$. Here, S is a function that substitutes each numeric function x appearing in φ with the right-hand side expression of the numeric effect involving x in $\text{eff}(a_j)$. If there is no interaction between $\text{eff}(a_i)$ and φ the substitution function returns φ untouched.

Similarly, for the effects, it is necessary to assemble the Boolean and numeric effects of the two actions. For the former, the positive (negative) effects of $a_{i,j}$ are obtained by merging the positive (negative) effects of the two actions, from which the negative (positive) effects of a_j are subtracted. The numeric effects of $a_{i,j}$ are obtained using the procedure MERGENUMEFFS($\cdot$), the pseudocode of which is provided in Algorithm 3. Intuitively, the effects of $a_{i,j}$ are obtained (i) by adding all the effects of a_j and projecting forward the effects of a_i. (ii) All

---

Algorithm 1. Generation of a numeric macro-action.

Input: A pair of actions a_i, a_j and a unique identifier id.
Output: A macro-action $a_{i,j}$.

1: **procedure** GENERATEMACRO(a_i, a_j, id)
2:     $\text{par}(a_{i,j}) \leftarrow \text{par}(a_i) \cup \text{par}(a_j)$
3:     $\text{name}(a_{i,j}) \leftarrow \text{name}(a_i) + \text{``}+\text{''} + \text{name}(a_j) + \text{``\_''} + id$
4:     $\text{pre}_{\text{prop}}(a_{i,j}) \leftarrow (\text{pre}_{\text{prop}}(a_i) \cup \text{pre}_{\text{prop}}(a_j)) \setminus \text{eff}^+_{\text{prop}}(a_i)$
5:     $\text{pre}_{\text{num}}(a_{i,j}) \leftarrow \text{MERGENUMPRECS}(\text{pre}_{\text{num}}(a_i), \text{pre}_{\text{num}}(a_j))$
6:     $\text{pre}(a_{i,j}) \leftarrow \text{pre}_{\text{num}}(a_{i,j}) \cup \text{pre}_{\text{prop}}(a_{i,j})$ ▷ $a_{i,j}$ preconditions
7:     $\text{eff}^-_{\text{prop}}(a_{i,j}) \leftarrow (\text{eff}^-_{\text{prop}}(a_i) \cup \text{eff}^-_{\text{prop}}(a_j)) \setminus (\text{eff}^+_{\text{prop}}(a_j))$
8:     $\text{eff}^+_{\text{prop}}(a_{i,j}) \leftarrow (\text{eff}^+_{\text{prop}}(a_i) \cup \text{eff}^+_{\text{prop}}(a_j)) \setminus (\text{eff}^-_{\text{prop}}(a_j))$
9:     $\text{eff}_{\text{prop}}(a_{i,j}) \leftarrow \text{pre}^+_{\text{prop}}(a_{i,j}) \cup \text{pre}^-_{\text{prop}}(a_{i,j})$
10:    $\text{eff}_{\text{num}}(a_{i,j}) \leftarrow \text{MERGNUMEFFS}(\text{eff}_{\text{num}}(a_i), \text{eff}_{\text{num}}(a_j))$
11:    $\text{eff}(a_{i,j}) \leftarrow \text{eff}_{\text{num}}(a_{i,j}) \cup \text{eff}_{\text{prop}}(a_{i,j})$ ▷ $a_{i,j}$ effects
12:    $a_{i,j} \leftarrow \langle \text{par}(a_{i,j}), \text{name}(a_{i,j}), \text{pre}(a_{i,j}), \text{eff}(a_{i,j}) \rangle$
13:    **return** $a_{i,j}$
14: **end procedure**

---

effects of a_i that do not interfere with the effects of a_j, and therefore have not been projected forward through a_j, must be added to the effects of $a_{i,j}$.

Point (i) is handled by the first *for* loop. Each effect $\langle x := \varphi \rangle \in \text{eff}_{\text{num}}(a_j)$ is added to the effects of $a_{i,j}$ by projecting the effects of a_i using the substitution function $\mathcal{S}$. If a_i does not interfere, the function returns φ unchanged.

Algorithm 2. Merging of numeric preconditions.

Input: A pair of numeric preconditions $\text{pre}_{\text{num}}(a_i)$ and $\text{pre}_{\text{num}}(a_j)$.
Output: A numeric precondition $\text{pre}_{\text{num}}(a_{i,j})$.

1: **procedure** MERGENUMPRECS($\text{pre}_{\text{num}}(a_i), \text{pre}_{\text{num}}(a_j)$)
2:     $\text{pre}_{\text{num}}(a_{i,j}) = \text{pre}_{\text{num}}(a_i)$
3:     **for** $\langle \varphi \bowtie 0 \rangle \in \text{pre}_{\text{num}}(a_j)$ **do**
4:         $\text{pre}_{\text{num}}(a_{i,j}) = \text{pre}_{\text{num}}(a_{i,j}) \cup \{ \langle \mathcal{S}(\varphi, \text{eff}(a_i)) \bowtie 0 \rangle \}$
5:     **end for**
6:     **return** $\text{pre}_{\text{num}}(a_{i,j})$
7: **end procedure**

---

4   Selecting Candidates

This section outlines the methodology for selecting candidates for macro-actions in numeric planning, based on the algorithm described in the previous section.

The efficient generation of macro-actions is well-known to be extremely challenging, due to the potentially large number of possible combinations of actions.

Generating macro-actions efficiently is well-known to be extremely challenging, due to the potentially large number of possible combinations of actions to

---

Algorithm 3. A pair of set of numeric conditions $\text{eff}_{\text{num}}(a_i)$ and $\text{eff}_{\text{num}}(a_j)$.

Input: a_i and a_j actions.
Output: A macro-action $a_{i,j}$

1: **procedure** MERGENUMEFFS($\text{eff}_{\text{num}}(a_i)$, $\text{eff}_{\text{num}}(a_j)$)
2:     $\text{eff}_{\text{num}}(a_{i,j}) \leftarrow \emptyset$
3:     **for** $\langle x := \varphi \rangle \in \text{eff}_{\text{num}}(a_j)$ **do**
4:         $\text{eff}_{\text{num}}(a_{i,j}) \leftarrow \text{eff}_{\text{num}}(a_{i,j}) \cup \{\langle x := \mathcal{S}(\varphi, \text{eff}_{\text{num}}(a_i)) \rangle\}$
5:     **end for**
6:     **for** $\langle x := \varphi \rangle \in \text{eff}_{\text{num}}(a_i)$ s.t. φ does not interfere with $\text{eff}_{\text{num}}(a_j)$ **do**
7:         $\text{eff}_{\text{num}}(a_{i,j}) \leftarrow \text{eff}_{\text{num}}(a_{i,j}) \cup \{\langle x := \varphi \rangle\}$
8:     **end for**
9:     **return** $\text{eff}_{\text{num}}(a_{i,j})$
10: **end procedure**

---

be considered. For instance, when considering only pairs of actions to combine, the number of candidates grows quadratically with respect to the number of actions. For this reason, in this work, we initially explored possible macros for each domain by partially adopting an approach used in classical planning [9,10]. This approach generates macro-actions by analysing several plans and extracting pairs or groups of actions that are promising candidates for combination. Specifically, to select actions for creating effective macro-actions, we applied the following conditions:

- Actions were identified to often occur sequentially in generated plans across various problem instances, using different planning engines. This suggests that these actions are likely needed to be used in sequence to achieve common goals in the considered domain.
- There should be no conflicts between the preconditions and effects of candidate actions. In particular, the effects of the first action should not delete preconditions of the following.

After selecting the candidate actions for each domain, the input for the Algorithm 1 is ready.

The increased expressiveness of PDDL2.1 when compared to classical planning allows for a classification of generated macros based on a syntactic criterion. We did this to investigate whether different kinds of macro-actions might have varying experimental impacts. Specifically, we consider the following types:

- *same numeric fluent* (shortened as SNF): this category includes all macro-actions obtained by combining two primitive actions that share at least one numeric fluent in their preconditions or effects;
- *different numeric fluent* (shortened as DNF): this category includes all macro-actions in which the two primitives involve at least one numeric variable, and these variables do not overlap;
- *propositional* (shortened as PROP): this category includes all macro-actions in which at least one of the two primitives has no numeric component.

It is worth to remind that the most intuitive class to consider is SNF, as it represents macro-actions formed by combining actions that share at least one numeric variable and are therefore believed to be useful in a numeric setting.

For our investigation, we consider well-known numeric domains: DEPOTS, ROVERS, SETTLERS, TPP, and ZENOTRAVEL. These domains are taken from different editions of the International Planning Competition (IPC). Specifically, DEPOTS is from the second IPC [3]; ROVERS, SETTLERS, and ZENOTRAVEL are from the third IPC [20]; and TPP is from the fifth IPC [14]. In the following, we provide a brief description of each domain, followed by a description of the macro-actions that were derived from the original formulation, classifying them by type.

DEPOTS. The domain focuses on actions involving loading and unloading trucks using hoists fixed at specific locations. The loads are crates, which can be stacked and unstacked onto pallets available at these locations. Trucks hold crates flexibly, allowing crates to be rearranged as needed. The trucks can be moved between locations, to deliver packages to specific depots. The numeric version includes weight attributes for crates and weight capacities for trucks, with fuel consumption needing to be minimised during travel and crate handling.

The actions in many plans often follow a similar pattern, with `lift` and `load` complementing each other, as well as `unload` and `drop`. Driving the truck to the required locations can occur before or after these actions. The macro-action `lift+load` is classified as DNF because the first action involves the `fuel-cost` variable, while the second action involves the `current_load` variable. The macro-action `unload+drop` is classified as PROP because `drop` is a pure propositional action. Additionally, we consider a macro-action obtained by sequencing three actions, i.e., `lift`, `load`, and `drive`. This macro-action is classified as SNF as `lift` and `drive` share the `fuel-cost` variable.

ROVERS. Inspired by planetary rover problems, this domain involves navigating a planet's surface, collecting samples, and communicating findings to a lander. Some rovers can only traverse specific terrains, and data transmission requires direct visibility between waypoints and the lander. The numeric component of the domain introduces energy consumption for rover activities and allows recharging only in sunlight, emphasising efficient energy management.

According to our methodology, firstly, we combined the actions `calibrate` and `take_image`. We observed that whenever `calibrate` is used in any generated plan, the action `take_image` always follows for the same objects because the camera must be calibrated before use. This macro-action is classified as SNF because the `calibrate` action involves `energy` both in its preconditions and effects, and the same applies to the `take_image` action.

Secondly, we combined the actions `sample_soil` and `sample_rock` with `drop`. In both instances, the `sample` action should be followed by the `drop` action to ensure that the rover's storage is empty and available for other operations. These macros are classified as PROP since `drop` is a propositional action.

SETTLERS. Due to the numerous actions available in this domain, it is particularly well-suited for exploring macro-actions. The analysis of the plans generated for settlers resulted in 16 macro-actions, covering the SNF and DNF classes, each with the same number of actions (see Table 1 for details).

TPP. The Traveling Purchaser Problem (TPP) is an extension of the Traveling Salesman Problem. It involves selecting markets to buy a set of products, minimising both travel and purchase costs. Each market offers products at different prices and limited quantities. The numeric version features three operators, two of them, buy-all and buy-allneeded, handle purchasing actions. The buy-all operator buys all available goods of a specific type at a market, while the buy-allneeded operator buys only the remaining amount needed to meet the purchase goals. In this model, all markets are interconnected and linked to depots. There is one depot and one truck available for transportation.

In most generated plans, the action drive consistently precedes the actions buy-all and buy-allneeded. The two resulting macro-actions are thus classified as SNF since they involve distinct numeric variables. Specifically, both actions involve the total-cost variable, but even other variables.

ZenoTravel. This domain revolves around transportation, utilising planes to carry passengers through two modes: fast movement, called zoom, and slow movement, called fly. In the numeric formulation, aircraft fuel consumption varies based on the mode of travel. Each plane is characterised by its unique fuel consumption rate and passenger capacity.

Analysing a multitude of plans, we have observed that the board action is typically followed by either fly or zoom. This makes sense since passengers are boarded to be transported. Similarly, the fly and zoom actions are always followed by debark. All of these macro-actions involve different numeric variables and are therefore classified as DNF.

Table 1. Summary of all the macro-actions generated in the domains.

Domain	Macro Class		
	SNF	DNF	PROP
DEPOTS	lift+load+drive	lift+load	unload+drop
ROVERS	calibrate+take_image	*na*	sample_soil+drop, sample_rock+drop
SETTLERS	load+move-cart, move+cart-load, move+cart-unload, b-cabin+fell-timber, b-quarry+break-stone, b-coalstack+burn-coal, b-sawmill+saw-wood, b-docks+b-wharf	load+move-train, load+move-ship, move+train-load, move+ship-load, move+ship-unload, b-mine+mine-ore, b-ironworks+make-iron, b-docks+b-wharf	*na*
TPP	drive+buy-all, drive+buy-allneeded	*na*	*na*
ZENOTRAVEL	*na*	board+fly, board+zoom fly+debark, zoom+debark	*na*

4.1 Example

In this example, we analyse the generation of an SNF macro-action by referring to the SETTLERS example using Algorithm 1. We combine the actions a_1 (build-coal-stack) and a_2 (burn-coal).

The two involved actions share the same parameter p representing a place, then $par(a_{1,2}) = \{p\}$. Given a unique identifier $id =$ "1", we combine the names of a_1 and a_2 obtaining $name(a_{1,2}) = build\text{-}coal\text{-}stack+burn\text{-}coal\_1$.

As for the Boolean preconditions, note that the only Boolean condition of a_2 is $has\text{-}coal\text{-}stack(p) \in pre_{prop}(a_2)$. However, $has\text{-}coal\text{-}stack(p) \in eff^+_{prop}(a_1)$. Then, by Line 4 of Algorithm 1, we obtain $pre(a_{i,j}) = (pre_{prop}(a_1) \cup pre_{prop}(a_2)) \setminus eff^+_{prop}(a_1) = (\emptyset \cup \{has\text{-}coal\text{-}stack(p)\}) \setminus \{has\text{-}coal\text{-}stack(p)\}\} = \emptyset$.

As for the numeric preconditions, note that there is an interaction between the effect $e = \langle timb(p) := timb(p) - 1\rangle \in eff_{num}(a_1)$ and the condition $c = \langle timb(p) \geq 1\rangle \in pre_{num}(a_2)$. Therefore the formula involved in the condition c, i.e., $timb(p) - 1$, must be regressed considering the effect e. By applying the substitution function as Line 4 from Algorithm 2, i.e., $\mathcal{S}(timb(p) - 1, \{timb(p) := timb(p) - 1, \ldots\}) = timb(p) - 2$, we obtain the numeric condition $\langle timb'p) \geq 2\rangle$ to be added to $pre_{num}(a_{i,j})$. This condition reflects that a_2 requires one unit of fuel and, since a_1 consumes one unit, their sequential execution requires at least two units of fuel.

As for the Boolean effects, the only effect to be added to the effects of $a_{i,j}$ is $has\text{-}coal\text{-}stack(p) \in eff_{prop}(a_1)$ as it is not negated by a_2. By applying Line 8 of Algorithm 2, we obtain $eff^+_{prop}(a_{i,j}) = (eff^+_{prop}(a_1) \cup eff^+_{prop}(a_2)) \setminus eff^-_{prop}(a_2) = (\{has\text{-}coal\text{-}stack(p)\} \cup \emptyset) \setminus \emptyset = \{has\text{-}coal\text{-}stack(p)\}$. Since there are no negated effects we have that $eff^-_{prop}(a_{1,2}) = \emptyset$ and then $eff_{prop}(a_{1,2}) = \{has\text{-}coal\text{-}stack(p)\}$.

As for the numeric effects, note that the only effects to be combined are those concerning the available timber. In contrast, all others can be merged without further manipulations as no interactions exist among them. Specifically, the right-hand-side effect $\langle timb(p) := timb(p) - 1\rangle \in eff_{num}(a_2)$ must undergo the substitution function to take into account the effect of a_1 affecting $timb(p)$. Then, by applying Line 4 of Algorithm 3, i.e., $\mathcal{S}(timb(p) - 1, eff_{num}(a_1)) = \mathcal{S}(timb(p) - 1, \{timb(p) := timb(p) - 1\}) = timb(p) - 2$, we obtain a new composite effect $\langle timb(p) := timb(p) - 2\rangle$ to be added to the effect of $a_{1,2}$. This effect reflects the fact that, since both actions consume one unit of fuel, their sequential execution results in the consumption of two units of fuel. Assembling all the elements obtained, the action $a_{1,2}$ has the following preconditions and effects:

$$pre(a_{1,2}) = \{\langle timb(p) \geq 2\rangle\}$$
$$eff(a_{1,2}) = \{has\text{-}coal\text{-}stack(p), \langle lab := lab + 2\rangle, \langle timb(p) := timb - 2\rangle.$$
$$\langle coal(p) := coal(p) + 1\rangle, \langle poll := poll + 1\rangle\}$$

5 Experimental Analysis

The experimental analysis aims to empirically assess the effectiveness of the macros in the context of numeric planning. We evaluated the impact of using different types of reformulations-SNF, DNF, and PROP-compared to the original version of the models, across four well-established numeric planners. We also considered a fourth formulation, called ALL, in which we combined all macros of different types. Regarding the numeric planning systems, to explore a variety of methodologies, the following planners have been considered: ENHSP [27], LPG [12,13], METRIC-FF [18], and OPTIC [4]. All experiments run on an Intel Core i9-10885H CPUs with 2.40GHz with a cutoff time of 900 s, and 8GB of RAM.

Table 2 provides an overview of the results in terms of coverage, i.e., the number of problems solved, and IPC-Score calculated for the runtime, denoted as IPC-Score(T). The IPC-Score for the runtime is calculated according to the metric commonly used in the International Planning Competitions [29]. Specifically, given a planning problem p in the test suite solved in t seconds, the IPC-Score(T) of p is assigned to 1 if $t \leq 1$, $1 - \log(t)/\log(900)$ otherwise.

As a first interesting result, it is easy to note that the effectiveness of macros in improving planning performance varies widely. This is influenced by several factors, including the type of macro employed, the characteristics of the domain, and the planning system. For example, in the case of DEPOTS, applying reformulation techniques consistently proves beneficial for ENHSP. When all macros are utilised together in this domain, there is a notable increase in coverage, with six additional instances being solved. Conversely, in the ZENOTRAVEL domain, the impact of macros is less favourable. Here, we observe a decrease in coverage for both ENHSP and LPG. This indicates that these macros in ZENO-TRAVEL might introduce additional complexities to the problem, in the form of increased breadth, that outweigh their potential benefits. However, for other systems within this domain, the coverage is unaffected.

In all other examined benchmark domains, the influence of macros on coverage is minimal, with only minimal fluctuations observed. These oscillations are both positive and negative, indicating that the impact of macros is not uniformly beneficial or detrimental but varies depending on the specific circumstances, as observed in previous work on macros.

To clarify the mixed results, we measured the frequency with which macros provided faster solutions compared to the original formulation. Figure 1 illustrates, for each planner, the proportion of instances where a specific type of macro allows a planner to solve a problem instance faster. It is clear that ENHSP benefited the most from macros, especially with SNF, PROP, and ALL macros. Other planners saw more modest, but still significant, improvements, with up to 20% of instances being solved faster. Additionally, Fig. 2 shows, for each planner, the proportion of instances where any macro enabled a faster solution than the original formulation, with results broken down by domain.

Overall, the performed analysis indicates that some planners are more prone than others to exploit the potential benefits of macros in numeric planning problems. However, for all considered planners macros have been beneficial for solving at least a few instances from the benchmarks. Turning our attention to the domains, ZENOTRAVEL is not suitable for using macros, while most of the others show significant benefits.

Table 2. Results about the macro reformulation versus the original formulation (ORIGINAL) in terms of coverage and IPC-Score(T). *na* denotes the absence of macros of the considered type.

		Coverage					IPC-Score(T)				
		ORIGINAL	SNF	DNF	PROP	ALL	ORIGINAL	SNF	DNF	PROP	ALL
Depots	ENHSP	8	11	11	10	14	5.0	4.6	4.9	4.5	5.2
	LPG	20	20	20	20	20	18.8	15.5	18.2	17.3	12.8
	METRIC-FF	0	0	0	0	0	0	0	0	0	0
	OPTIC	0	0	0	0	0	0	0	0	0	0
	Σ	28	31	31	30	34	23.8	20.1	23.0	21.8	18.1
		ORIGINAL	SNF	DNF	PROP	ALL	ORIGINAL	SNF	DNF	PROP	ALL
Rovers	ENHSP	0	0	*na*	0	0	0	0	*na*	0	0
	LPG	19	19	*na*	19	20	17.0	17.7	*na*	17.5	17.7
	METRIC-FF	0	0	*na*	0	0	0	0	*na*	0	0
	OPTIC	0	0	*na*	0	0	0	0	*na*	0	0
	Σ	19	19	*na*	19	20	17.0	17.7	*na*	17.5	17.7
		ORIGINAL	SNF	DNF	PROP	ALL	ORIGINAL	SNF	DNF	PROP	ALL
Settlers	ENHSP	0	0	0	*na*	0	0	0	0	*na*	0
	LPG	0	0	0	*na*	0	0	0	0	*na*	0
	METRIC-FF	7	4	8	*na*	5	4.5	3.3	4.5	*na*	2.8
	OPTIC	4	3	1	*na*	1	1.9	2.2	0.5	*na*	0.5
	Σ	11	7	9	*na*	6	6.4	5.6	5.0	*na*	3.3
		ORIGINAL	SNF	DNF	PROP	ALL	ORIGINAL	SNF	DNF	PROP	ALL
TPP	ENHSP	9	9	*na*	*na*	9	7.2	7.2	*na*	*na*	7.2
	LPG	20	19	*na*	*na*	19	20.0	13.0	*na*	*na*	13.0
	METRIC-FF	0	0	*na*	*na*	0	0	0	*na*	*na*	0
	OPTIC	20	20	*na*	*na*	20	15.0	13.7	*na*	*na*	13.7
	Σ	49	48	*na*	*na*	48	42.2	33.9	*na*	*na*	33.9
		ORIGINAL	SNF	DNF	PROP	ALL	ORIGINAL	SNF	DNF	PROP	ALL
ZenoTravel	ENHSP	19	*na*	17	*na*	17	17.1	*na*	13.5	*na*	13.5
	LPG	20	*na*	15	*na*	15	19.7	*na*	14.5	*na*	14.5
	METRIC-FF	20	*na*	20	*na*	20	19.8	*na*	16.8	*na*	16.8
	OPTIC	17	*na*	17	*na*	17	16.0	*na*	14.3	*na*	14.3
	Σ	76	*na*	69	*na*	69	72.6	*na*	59.2	*na*	59.2

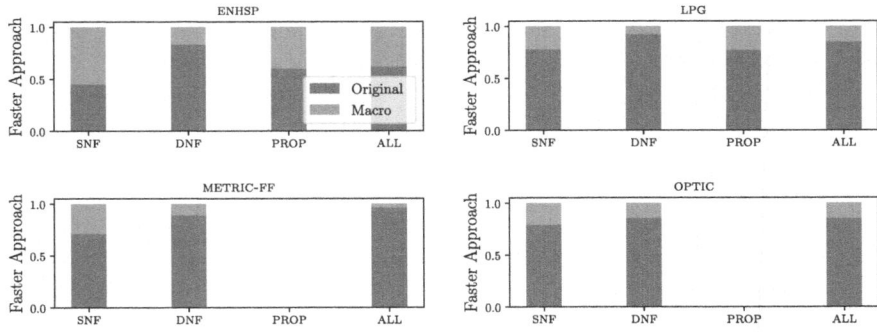

Fig. 1. Percentage of problems solved faster by a given planner when using the original domain model (blue) or the corresponding macro set (orange). Results are cumulative across all considered benchmarks. (Color figure online)

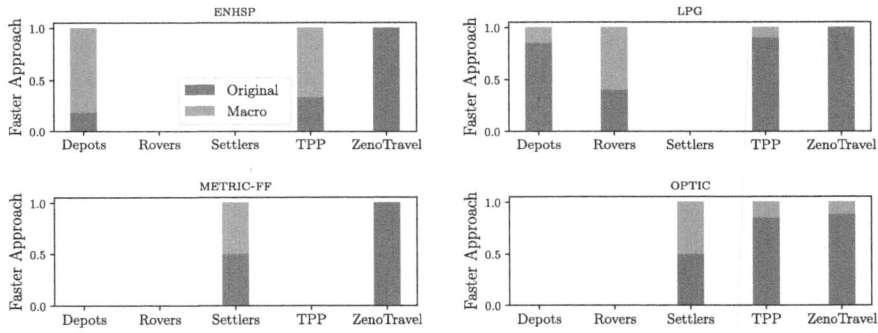

Fig. 2. Percentage of problems solved faster by a given planner when using the original domain model (blue) or any corresponding macro set (orange) on each considered benchmark domain. (Color figure online)

6   Conclusions

In this study, we conducted an extensive investigation into the use of macro-actions in numeric planning. We formalised the macro generation process and explored a semi-automated methodology for selecting candidate primitive actions to be combined into macro-actions. Our experimental analysis demonstrates both the potential benefits and drawbacks of using macros in numeric planning engines. The results highlight that planners can respond very differently to domain models enhanced with macro-actions, and that some domain models may not be suitable for reformulation.

Future work will focus on identifying techniques for filtering and selecting macros that are tailored to the needs of the planning system, to characterise domain models suitable for macros reformulation, and explore the possibility to generate macros by combining more primitive actions together.

References

1. Alarnaouti, D., Baryannis, G., Vallati, M.: Reformulation techniques for automated planning: a systematic review. Knowl. Eng. Rev. **38**, e9 (2023)
2. Asai, M., Fukunaga, A.: Solving large-scale planning problems by decomposition and macro generation. In: ICAPS, pp. 16–24 (2015)
3. Bacchus, F.: The AIPS '00 planning competition. AI Mag. **22**(3), 47–56 (2001)
4. Benton, J., Coles, A., Coles, A.: Temporal planning with preferences and time-dependent continuous costs. In: ICAPS, vol. 22, pp. 2–10 (2012)
5. Bonassi, L., Gerevini, A.E., Scala, E.: Dealing with numeric and metric time constraints in PDDL3 via compilation to numeric planning. In: AAAI, pp. 20036–20043 (2024)
6. Botea, A., Enzenberger, M., Müller, M., Schaeffer, J.: Macro-FF: improving AI planning with automatically learned macro-operators. J. Artif. Intell. Res. **24**, 581–621 (2005)
7. Cardellini, M., Giunchiglia, E., Maratea, M.: Symbolic numeric planning with patterns. In: AAAI, vol. 38, pp. 20070–20077 (2024)
8. Castellanos-Paez, S., Pellier, D., Fiorino, H., Pesty, S.: Mining useful macro-actions in planning. In: AIPR, pp. 1–6. IEEE (2016)
9. Chrpa, L.: Generation of macro-operators via investigation of action dependencies in plans. Knowl. Eng. Rev. **25**(3), 281–297 (2010)
10. Chrpa, L., Barták, R.: Towards getting domain knowledge: plans analysis through investigation of actions dependencies. In: FLAIRS, pp. 531–536 (2008)
11. Fox, M., Long, D.: PDDL2.1: an extension to PDDL for expressing temporal planning domains. J. Artif. Intell. Res. **20**, 61–124 (2003)
12. Gerevini, A., Saetti, A., Serina, I.: Planning through stochastic local search and temporal action graphs in LPG. J. Artif. Intell. Res. **20**, 239–290 (2003)
13. Gerevini, A., Saetti, A., Serina, I.: An approach to efficient planning with numerical fluents and multi-criteria plan quality. Artif. Intell. **172**(8–9), 899–944 (2008)
14. Gerevini, A.E., Haslum, P., Long, D., Saetti, A., Dimopoulos, Y.: Deterministic planning in the fifth international planning competition: PDDL3 and experimental evaluation of the planners. Artif. Intell. **173**(5–6), 619–668 (2009)
15. Ghallab, M., Nau, D., Traverso, P.: Automated Planning: Theory and Practice. Elsevier (2004)
16. Gigante, N., Scala, E.: On the Compilability of Bounded Numeric Planning. In: IJCAI, pp. 5341–5349 (2023)
17. Helal, H., Lakemeyer, G.: An analysis of the decidability and complexity of numeric additive planning. In: ICAPS, pp. 267–275. AAAI Press (2024)
18. Hoffmann, J.: The Metric-FF planning system: translating ignoring delete lists to numeric state variables. J. Artif. Intell. Res. **20**, 291–341 (2003)
19. Kouaiti, A.E., Percassi, F., Saetti, A., McCluskey, T.L., Vallati, M.: PDDL+ models for deployable yet effective traffic signal optimisation. In: ICAPS, pp. 168–177. AAAI Press (2024)
20. Long, D., Fox, M.: The 3rd international planning competition: results and analysis. J. Artif. Intell. Res. **20**, 1–59 (2003)

21. Long, D., Fox, M., Hamdi, M.: Reformulation in planning. In: Koenig, S., Holte, R.C. (eds.) SARA, vol. 2371, pp. 18–32 (2002)
22. McCluskey, T.L.: Combining weak learning heuristics in general problem solvers. In: IJCAI, pp. 331–333 (1987)
23. McCluskey, T.L., Vaquero, T.S., Vallati, M.: Engineering knowledge for automated planning: towards a notion of quality. In: Proceedings of the Knowledge Capture Conference, K-CAP, pp. 14:1–14:8 (2017)
24. Percassi, F., Scala, E., Vallati, M.: A practical approach to discretised PDDL+ problems by translation to numeric planning. J. Artif. Intell. Res. **76**, 115–162 (2023)
25. Riddle, P.J., Barley, M., Franco, S.: Problem reformulation as meta-level search. In: Proceedings of the Conference on Advances in Cognitive Systems, pp. 199–216 (2013)
26. Riddle, P.J., Holte, R.C., Barley, M.W.: Does representation matter in the planning competition? In: Proceedings of the Ninth Symposium on Abstraction, Reformulation, and Approximation, SARA (2011)
27. Scala, E.: Plan repair for resource constrained tasks via numeric macro actions. In: ICAPS, vol. 24, pp. 280–288 (2014)
28. Shleyfman, A., Kuroiwa, R., Beck, J.C.: Symmetry detection and breaking in linear cost-optimal numeric planning. In: ICAPS, pp. 393–401. AAAI Press (2023)
29. Taitler, A., et al.: The 2023 international planning competition. AI Mag., pp. 1–17 (2023)
30. Vallati, M., Chrpa, L., McCluskey, T.L., Hutter, F.: On the importance of domain model configuration for automated planning engines. J. Autom. Reason. **65**(6), 727–773 (2021)

Feature Selection on Contextual Embedding Pushing the Sparseness

Stefano Bistarelli[1(✉)] 🆔 and Marco Cuccarini[1,2] 🆔

[1] University of Perugia, Perugia, Italy
stefano.bistarelli@unipg.it
[2] University of Naples Federico II, Naples , Italy
marco.cuccarini@unina.it

Abstract. The question-answering task is a classical problem of natural language processing and is largely applied to a plethora of possible situations. There are different domains of application; one of these is providing an answer considering a text or a document, expecting to retrieve the user with the required information.

For doing that, the state-of-the art approach is to represent each sentence of the document with a contextual embedding and select the closer sentence in terms of space (and consequential meaning) with respect to the question of the user. Indeed, the position of the sentences in the space can deeply influence the model and affect the correctness of the answer, and a crowded space will cause problems for the selection of the best answer. On the other side, a well-spaced space will provide better results. Starting from this idea, we will use weighted feature selection with the objective of obtaining more space among the points representing the document and consequently improving the performance.

Keywords: Contextual Embedding · BERT · Features Selection · Density

1 Introduction

The Large Language Models (LLMs) advent of the last few years has totally revolutionised the field of Natural Language Processing (NLP). In fact, models that exploit a large amount of pre-training are capable of deeply understanding the language and producing very meaningful word and sentence embeddings. The sentence or word embedding has the goal of producing a vector that can encode semantic characteristics of texts. If two sentences are semantically similar, the model will produce two vectors that are close according to the similarity function (Euclidean distance, cosine similarity, dot product, etc.). If the two sentences are different, it will append the contrary. It is called context embedding because the encoding process also considers the context of each word and not only their meaning. As an example of contextual embedding, we will use the one produced by Siamese BERT, a BERT-based model that is composed of two BERT models that share the same error function.

A. Artale et al. (Eds.): AIxIA 2024, LNAI 15450, pp. 37–49, 2025.
https://doi.org/10.1007/978-3-031-80607-0_4

The capability of encoding is a characteristic of the BERT-based models that, unfortunately, require fine tuning. For fine-tuning, it is necessary to arrange an important amount of data and computational power. Besides, it causes the specialisation of the model and, consequently, the loss of generalisation. The characteristic of the embedding is the large dimensionality of the vector produced, and we can assume that each of these dimensions represents one, more, or part of some linguistic rules. Not all linguistic concepts are helpful for all kinds of tasks, and someone in certain situations can also represent noise and deteriorate the performance of the model.

Our idea is to consider only the meaningful elements of the embedding for a certain task and discard all the information that is not helpful for the problem that we want to solve. For this, we will use a form of feature selection (FS). FS is usually used to solve problems with large dimensions of data in the context of machine learning. It helps to increase performance, reduce computational expenditure, and avoid overfitting. The FS is also useful in instance-base algorithms [1] (or lazy learning algorithms), where samples are classified according to the similarity of other samples, exploiting some similarity function. The most classical case is k-Nearest Neighbours (k-NN) [6].

There are different possibilities for the FS; the most common classification is supervised or not supervised. In our implementation, we want to keep the solution general and applicable to other contexts. For this reason, we chose an approach that is not supervised. At the same time, it is also reasonable to assume that well-spaced points (that represent the sentences) may reduce the risk of error. If the question is present in a crowded space, it is more probable that the model will equivocally predict the answer. For this reason, the goal of the featured selection that we are going to apply is to space out the points representing the possible answers and, consequentially, improve the performance.

So in this work, we try to push the sparsity of the representations to create the most efficient configuration for the identification of the right query and avoiding the use of training data, the computational expense, and the time required for fine-tuning.

In fact, the fine-tuning of a BERT-based [8] model in a problem of text classification can be seen as a procedure that pushes the representation of the text of one class away from the representation of the text of another class. This is done for better separation and to reduce cases of misclassification by focussing on the features (or dimensions) of the vector embedding that highlight the differences between the samples of different classes.

The paper is structured as follows: in Sect. 2, we introduce all the context necessary for the understanding of the paper. In Sect. 3 we present the task that we want to solve and the dataset that we will use. For Sect. 4, we show techniques chosen for: text division, text embedding, and evaluating functions. Section 5 is related to the choice of the method of FS and how we apply it to the work. In Sect. 6 we comment on all the results in terms of sparsity and right answer. In Sect. 7 we introduce all the related works, and in Sect. 8 we take the conclusions and propose some possible feature works.

2 Background

In this section, we introduce all the concepts necessary to understand the paper, starting with a definition of contextual embedding, showing the state-of-the art methodology for question answering on the close domains system, and the methods used on instance-based problems for feature selection.

2.1 Contextual Embedding Methods

There are many ways to produce contextual embeddings; the most commonly used are BERT-based models. An example that works very well in cases where it is necessary to use the semantic similarity is Siamese-BERT (SBERT) [14]. SBERT is a model based on BERT (Bidirectional Encoder Representation for Transformers) specifically designed to quantify the similarity between two sentences. The structure of SBERT is represented by two BERT models that share the same objective function. This can be a continuous value in the case of sentence similarity or a class for classification. In the training process, they share the backpropagation error, with one model being influenced by the other's error. In particular, we will consider two pre-train models:

- "multi-qa-mpnet-base-dot-v1" [13]: this model is trained to recognise the similarity between an answer and a question; it returns the best performance on the task of semantic search. It has been trained on 215 million samples (questions and answers). The model accepts a maximum sequence length of 512 tokens and returns a vector of size 768. The similarity metric used is the dot product.
- "all-mpnet-base-v2" [12]: this model is trained for the general task of semantic similarity and has the best results on sentence embedding. It accepts a maximum sequence of 384 tokens and returns a vector of 768 elements. In this model, it is possible to use all the evaluation metrics: cosine similarity, dot product, and Euclidean distance.

2.2 Overview of Question Answering in Close Domain

There are a lot of solutions to the problem of question answering in close domains [2], where the goal is to provide the information contained inside a document requested by the user. There are different variations, but fundamentally, the possible approaches are the following four techniques:

- Sentence Splitting: the first step is to divide the document into different chunks of text; this text can be a simple sentence or an entire paragraph, with or without overlap or other characteristics. The choice of solution for this part is fundamental and will influence the future performance of the models.

- Sentence representation: the second step is to find a way to measure the semantic similarity between them. The solution most commonly adopted is usually embedding. The goal of the embedding is to create a vector that can represent a sentence and the relationship between different sentences. If two sentences are similar, the two encoded vectors will be similar according to the evaluation functions.
- Evaluation of similarity: for the selection of the answer, it is necessary to use some measure of similarity between a sentence in the document and the query.
- Evaluation of the performance: it is possible to use a method similar to the ones cited in the previous step, or it is also possible to human-check or use methods that evaluate how many words the two sentences share.

2.3   Instance-Based Learning

The core problem that we plan to solve can also be defined as instance-based learning, or lazy learning. The standard approach to machine learning involves splitting the work into two principal phases: we train the model on portions of data, and after that, these data are tested on a smaller dataset. In instance-based learning, these two phases are not always well defined. This type of learning method is based on the idea that samples that are similar need to be classified in the same way.

2.4   The Nearest Neighbor Classifier

The most classical example of an instance-based algorithm is the k-Nearest Neighbor (k-NN), a non-parametric algorithm based on the proximity of the samples. In k-NN, each example is classified based on the vote of the k most near examples present in the space. This algorithm can be used for classification or regression problems. It is sensible to noise and to high-dimensional data; the normalisation of the features can fix those limitations.

If an abnormal value is present for one of the features (very influential for the classification), it will be biassed by the other values. More irrelevant features are added to the data, the less influence will be exerted on the relevant features. To correct this tendency, it can be helpful to use normalisation approaches or, in the most critical cases, remove irrelevant features.

Attribute-Weighted K-Nearest Neighbor Methods One of the most important techniques for improving k-NN algorithm performance is the selection of features. As mentioned before, one of the major limitations of the k-NN classifier is having samples with high dimensions because this can add a lot of noise. Some cases exist where a feature provides a lot of information and another feature is irrelevant (see Fig. 1). In this case, the X will be selected, while the Y will be rejected. The illustrated case is an ideal situation (see Fig. 1a); in the real-world scenario, there is no clear division between useful and not-useful information (see Fig. 1b). Natural noise or the correlation between the features that makes it necessary to use some weights for defining their importance.

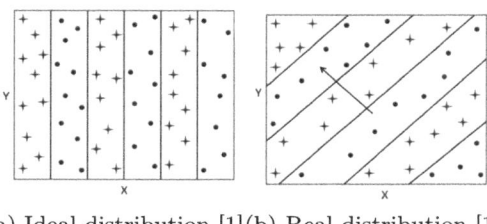

(a) Ideal distribution [1](b) Real distribution [1]

Fig. 1. Comparison of the ideal distribution of the features (a) and a real distribution (b)

2.5   Evaluation Metric

As previously mentioned, the evaluation function has a strong influence on the results of the classification as it represents prior knowledge.

Dot-Product. The projection of one vector onto another is known as the dot product. This calculation considers the angle and the magnitude of the two vectors, making it more advantageous than cosine similarity, which only considers the angle. One drawback is that the outcome is not normalized. In order to increase similarity, it is necessary to maximise the value. The formal definition is:

$$dot\_prod(a, b) = \mathbf{a} \cdot \mathbf{b} = \sum_{i=1}^{n} a_i \cdot b_i = |\mathbf{a}|\,|\mathbf{b}| \cos(\theta) \tag{1}$$

The product between —a— and —b— is always positive. The negativity is given by the cosine of the angle. If it is between 0 and 90°C, then the result will be positive; otherwise, it will be negative.

3   Datasets and Task

Our aim is to develop a system capable of providing users with the required information in response to their questions, using information that is already available. The system's core functionality is to identify and extract relevant text segments with the goal of answering user information queries accurately. This case study focusses on documents and policy structures within the tourism industry and hotels.

The dataset used for this implementation is the same as in the previous paper [4], where we approached the task and started to analyse the correlation between the sparsity of the sentence's point and performance. This dataset is composed of 820 questions pertaining to 41 different policies or rules sourced from the internet. These documents vary in structure and length and originate from various parts of the world.

In addition, generative models are also used to answer the questions, allowing comparison with other approaches, typically based on state-of-the-art methods. The nature of the questions varies significantly: some can be answered with a simple yes or no, while others require more detailed information. In more complex cases, it is necessary to contextualise the information provided to ensure a complete answer.

4   Text Division and Text Embedding

The text splitting is a fundamental choice that deeply influences the performance of the model. In some cases, the sentence division can be used. At each dot present, the text is divided, and that would represent an answer. This approach has the pros of being very careful in choosing the sentence and avoiding possible confusion. The problem is that dividing two answers of the same period can mean removing the context for one of the two, resulting in an answer that is often incomplete or without meaning.

A better solution can be the division by periods. A period contains more sentences interconnected by reciprocal references and would always help to contextualise the right answer. The critical issue is that the relevant part of the text that provides the correct answer is covered by all the information from the other sentences present.

For the embedding part, we simply applied the two S-BERT models: "multi-qa-mpnet-base-dot-v1" ($MODEL_Q$) and "all-mpnet-base-v2" ($MODEL_G$), as described in Sect. 2. With each of the two models, we produce two different embedding vectors, one for the question and one for the answers, and we save them into a file. For each of the two types of embedding, we have to evaluate the similarity between the question and all the possible answers for each document. For both models, we used the dot product.

Performance is impacted by the way the points are distributed. Zones with a large presence of points can negatively influence the performance (see Fig. 2a) by having a larger pool of possible answers. In case the points that indicate the query have just one obvious choice, we probably achieve better results when the points are distributed equally (see Fig. 2b). While the second scenario is ideal, the main objective should be to tend to that solution.

The correctness of the answers is verified using a human-check. For each question, different possible answers can be considered correct. The results are expressed using accuracy (correct answers/all the answers). We try to explore other methods for performance evaluation, but they cannot be helpful in this situation. The F1 score, precision, or recall makes sense when the task involves the use of classes. For question answering, models that measure semantic similarity are usually used, but these would be the same methods used for the selection of the best answer.

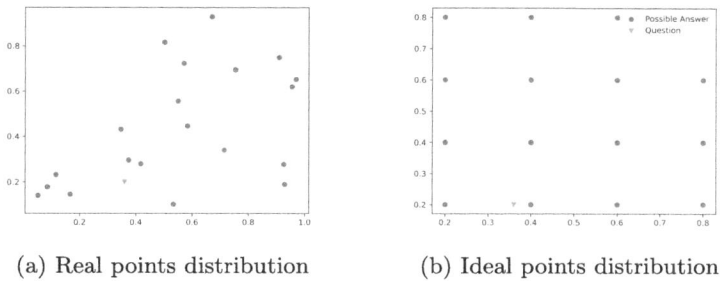

(a) Real points distribution   (b) Ideal points distribution

Fig. 2. Comparison of the real distribution of the points (a) and an ideal distribution (b)

The results showed (see Fig. 1) that the specific model $MODEL_Q$ has better performance compared to $MODEL_G$. This approach offers good results; we have tested the answers provided by the $MODEL_Q$ and the $MODEL_G$. Compared to the one already tested in the state of the art, the model trained on a specific question answer performs slightly better than the model trained on the generic task of semantic similarity. The results are impressive in the case of $MODEL_Q$ reaching a value of 0.860 and in the case of $MODEL_G$ reaching a value of 0.830, considering that we don't apply any type of fine-tuning and that the goal of the system is to remain general and be applied to each context in which some document is presented.

5   Instance-Based Feature Selection

The FS in the state-of-the-art is usually applied to the problem of classification or to instance-based methods. From what we know, this has never been applied in the case of contextual embedding. The FS methods have the goal of maximising the performance on the classification problem; in this case, it will be a little different. The objective is to increase the sparsity of the points that encode the semantic meaning of the sentences. This, according to our assumption, will make it more difficult for the question to confuse the right answer.

The most similar case of our problem is the k-NN, which is a problem of instance-based learning. The k-NN uses a distance function to evaluate the similarity of some points represented in a space and, based on this similarity, classifies each point. The way that we use the S-BERT model (without fine-tuning) can be defined as an instance-based algorithm, exploiting already pre-trained concepts that encode linguistic properties with the goal of creating a contextual embedding that can correctly represent the semantic relation present between some sentences. In the test phase, we simply select the most similar sentence with respect to the question present in the space using some distance function.

The innovation in this work is the use of weighted feature selection with the embedding methods. In that way, we try to artificially imitate the behaviour of the fine-tuning process in a faster and more adaptable way.

If we interpret each dimension as an embedding representation of a property of the text, we cannot simply assume that all these properties are helpful. In an ideal world, we have a space where for each dimension there is a precise rule, but this isn't an ideal case, so we can't simply remove or keep a feature. It is essential to find a way to weigh their importance.

5.1   Similarity Function and Weight of the Features

To apply the FS, the most straightforward solution is to modify the similarity function. The similarity function measures the similarity between two vectors; in the case of the dot product, we multiply each dimension and sum the results. The more similar two texts are, the higher the result of the dot product will be. For this reason, a weight function will be applied that increases the influence of the relevant features and decreases the influence of the irrelevant one.

$$\bar{X} = (x_1 \ldots x_d) \text{ and } \bar{Y} = (y_1 \ldots y_d) \text{ and } \bar{W} = (w_1 \ldots w_d)$$

$$WeightedDotProduct(\bar{X}, \bar{Y}, \bar{W}) = \sum_{i=1}^{d} w_i \cdot (x_i \cdot y_i) \tag{2}$$

Once the formula for the calculation of the similarity is defined, it remains to define the weight function. To keep this work general, we cannot consider the question but only the sentences of the document. A method usually used in the state of the art for identifying the most relevant features without supervision is the variance. If a feature has a higher variance, it is more probable that the feature will contain discriminant information. It is also fast to calculate and perfect for this situation.

To obtain the weight from the variance, it is sufficient to normalise the value, dividing by the greatest value of the variance and obtaining and returning a value that is between 0 and 1. In our case, we can consider two types of feature variance:

- Local variance: in the case of local variance, we consider the variance of the features for each document, recognising that each document has its own unique characteristics.
- Global variance: in this case, we consider one global variance for all the documents with a more generalised assumption.

6   Comparison Between Methods with and Without Feature Selection

To verify the effectiveness of this method, we decided to test it in the same way we did for the method in Sect. 4, changing only the similarity function that uses the information provided by the variance. After that, we will analyse the results in terms of performance and sparsity of points.

6.1   Performance

The results obtained are very promising (see Table 1), considering the unsupervised approach. We have seen an increase in performance for both models. In the case of $MODEL_Q$ Global FS, the results are near 1%. In the case of the local FS, the increase is more contained but still present. The same applies to $MODEL_G$.

We can notice that the FS method tends to change the most uncertain answer, changing the prediction in case an answer is misclassified. Sometimes it predicts the right answer (which increases performance), while a lot of others predict another wrong answer. In any case, this opens up a lot of new possibilities, giving us the possibility to also use the FS as a technique for identifying the most uncertain answers. This can be exploited to try to reformulate the question to clarify the most ambiguous request of the user.

The major pros of this method based on FS are principally two:

– **Generality**: it does not require any specific training or data and can be applied to all possible topics. It is possible to define a pipeline that automatically extracts the variance from the data and uses it for the FS. This method can also be applied to every case that involves the use of embedding (text classification, similarity quantification, etc.).
– **Speed**: this method is very rapid; the evaluation of the variance requires a few moments, and it is so much more efficient than any other method of fine-tuning; and it can also be applied in addition to it.

Table 1. Accuracy with and without FS.

Example	Acc	Example	Acc
$Model_Q$ (**Baseline method**)	0.860	$Model_G$ (**Baseline method**)	0.830
$Model_Q$ + **FS with Loc Var**	0.864	$Model_G$ + **FS with Loc Var**	**0.833**
$Model_Q$ + **FS with Glob Var**	**0.869**	$Model_G$ + **FS with Glob Var**	0.836

6.2   Sparsity of the Points

The previous performance gives us the idea of how well the model performs generally, but if we want to analyse the effect of the FS in terms of sparsity, we have to see its effect on a single document. If our assumption is confirmed, a question that passes from being labelled as wrong to being labelled as correct will also change the distribution of its neighbor points. This can prove the correlation between good performance and the sparsity of features. For this reason, it is not helpful to analyse all the space occupied by the sentence's document because the questions are not distributed in all the space. If there is a poorly spaced zone and there is no question around it, this will not affect the performance. So the analysis will only consider the density around the points that represent the questions. For the visualisation of the plot, we use Principal Component Analysis (PCA) [11]. The PCA allows us to preserve the dependencies that exist between points in n dimensions and transpose them to a set of points in two dimensions. This is very helpful for visualisation, or also for feature selection (FS).

It is clear how there is a change in the point distribution according to the type of FS applied (see Fig. 3). We take as an example a document that misclassifies two questions in case no FS is applied (see Fig. 3a and Fig. 3d), misclassifies one question when Local FS is used (see Fig. 3c and Fig. 3f), and classifies all questions correctly in the case of Global Feature Selection (see Fig. 3b and Fig. 3e).

For question Q1, which is classified correctly only by the Global FS (correct predict), there are fewer points around the neighbor, and those points have more space between each other, whereas in the case of the Local and No FS (wrong predict), there are more points, and these points are also more crowded. Meanwhile, for question Q2, both methods that use feature selection correctly predict the answer. They tend to have a larger number of points around the neighbor compared to the method that doesn't use feature selection, but those points are well spaced and present in a more uniform way in all the space around the question point. Meanwhile, in the case where the FS is not applied, there are fewer points, but these points are concentrated in the upper part of the neighborhood.

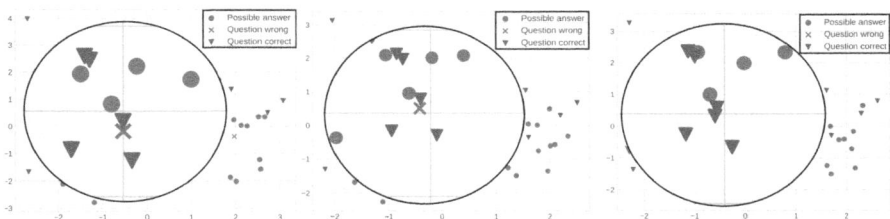

(a) Normal embedding Q1 (b) Local FS embedding Q1 (c) Global FS embedding Q1

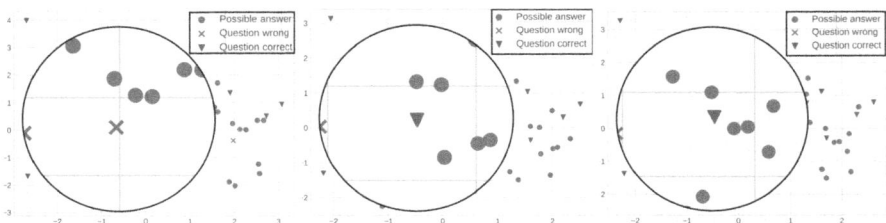

(d) Normal embedding Q2 (e) Local FS embedding Q2 (f) Global FS embedding Q2

Fig. 3. 2D representation of the embedding in the case of performance-increased

We can notice that the questions in general aren't influenced by the FS in terms of space position. This can be explained by the fact that in the variance evaluation, the question was never taken into consideration. In any case, this is a positive phenomenon, seeing that our goal is to push only the sparsity of the sentences. It is also important to consider that in this case we are using the dot product as a distance function, which means that we don't have to consider only the distance between the two functions but also the angle of the two vectors.

7   Related Work

The focus of this work is to define an FS on contextual embeddings produced by a BERT-based model, with the objective of extracting the relevant information for a certain task, and trying to move some steps on the path towards understanding the mechanism of encoded-based models. In the majority of cases, this kind of work focusses on the architecture of the transformers [15] and tries to extract and interpret information provided by the neurons or attention mechanisms [3].

One example is the work of Dai et al. [7], where they identify some neurons that express certain knowledge and tend to be activated by some prompts that express the same knowledge. So, taking a BERT model without any kind of fine-tuning, they noticed that some neurons tend to be involved when the prompt expresses a certain type of concept.

Another case where BERT-based models are investigated for extracting knowledge is the case of Kevin Clark et al. [5], where they focus on analysing the attention mechanism. The study of attention mechanisms has pros that permit an easy interpretation of the values because they give the weight that each word has on the process of computing the next word representation, and they discover how the attention mechanism tends to follow defined patterns and linguistic rules.

There are different feature selection methods that involve the use of the BERT model; they are mainly focused on the selection of the relevant part of the text to provide as input. An example is the work of Wang et al. [16], where, with the goal of reducing the length of the text (BERT has a maximum length of 512 subtokens), they select 4 different FS methods that help to keep only the key concept. This is done to reduce the computational power required for fine-tuning the model.

Another example where the FS is applied to text classification is the work of Hong et al. [10], where they focus on selecting discriminative-keywords from the text using long short-term memory(LSTM) [9] for extracting in an unsupervised way deep features from a bag-of-word vector.

From what we know, there isn't an approach that weights the contextual vector produced by a BERT-based model.

8   Conclusions and Future Work

The outcomes demonstrate how successful FS may be in sparsifying the points that represent the sentences and improving performance. This method can be quite useful in many situations, offering a quick and automated solution to enhance performance regardless of the sample labels. This work opens up opportunities for more research. To determine the significance of each contextual embedding feature, one could opt for a more sophisticated approach that makes use of additional unsupervised techniques (PCA, autoencoders, information gain, etc.). It can also be considered to apply selection in every case where text similarity is applied (text classification, QA, Natural Language Inference, etc.).

It can be very interesting to see what features are involved for each task and domain; this can help explain the embedding process. Each feature can represent a precise characteristic and push a clear division of this characteristic; this can greatly assist the process of understanding natural language processing. It would be interesting to try to compare fine-tuning and FS to check if the points that encode the sentences tend to sparse their positions in a similar way and propose a solution that avoids data and computational power consumption. In addition, we could take into account a function that quantifies the density of the surrounding space of a point, abandoning merely visual assessment with the objective of proposing a function that can maximise the sparsity and, consequently, improve performance.

Acknowledgments. The authors are member of the INdAM Research group GNCS and of Consorzio CINI. This work has been partially supported by: GNCS-INdAM, CUP_E53C23001670001; MUR project PRIN 2022 EPICA (CUP H53D23003660006), funded by the European Union - Next Generation EU; MUR PNRR project SERICS (PE00000014), funded by the European Union - Next Generation EU; EU MUR PNRR project VITALITY (J97G22000170005), funded by the European Union - Next Generation EU; University of Perugia - Fondo Ricerca di Ateneo (2020, 2022) - Projects BLOCKCHAIN4FOODCHAIN, FICO, RATIONALISTS, "Civil Safety and Security for Society"; Piano di Sviluppo e Coesione del Ministero della Salute 2014–2020 - Project I83C22001350001 LIFE: "the itaLian system Wide Frailty nEtwork" (Linea di azione 2.1 "Creazione di una rete nazionale per le malattie ad alto impatto" - Traiettoria 2 "E-Health, diagnostica avanzata, medical devices e mini invasività").

References

1. Aggarwal, C.C.: Instance-based learning: a survey. In: Aggarwal, C.C. (ed.) Data Classification: Algorithms and Applications, pp. 157–186. CRC Press (2014). https://doi.org/10.1201/B17320-7
2. Badugu, S., Manivannan, R.: A study on different closed domain question answering approaches. Int. J. Speech Technol. **23**(2), 315–325 (2020). https://doi.org/10.1007/S10772-020-09692-0
3. Bahdanau, D., Cho, K., Bengio, Y.: Neural machine translation by jointly learning to align and translate. In: Bengio, Y., LeCun, Y. (eds.) 3rd International Conference on Learning Representations, ICLR 2015, San Diego, CA, USA, May 7-9, 2015, Conference Track Proceedings (2015). http://arxiv.org/abs/1409.0473
4. Bistarelli, S., Cuccarini, M.: BERT-based questions answering on close domains: preliminary report. In: Angelis, E.D., Proietti, M. (eds.) Proceedings of the 39th Italian Conference on Computational Logic, Rome, Italy, June 26-28, 2024. CEUR Workshop Proceedings, vol. 3733. CEUR-WS.org (2024). https://ceur-ws.org/Vol-3733/short4.pdf

5. Clark, K., Khandelwal, U., Levy, O., Manning, C.D.: What does BERT look at? An analysis of BERT's attention. In: Linzen, T., Chrupala, G., Belinkov, Y., Hupkes, D. (eds.) Proceedings of the 2019 ACL Workshop BlackboxNLP: Analyzing and Interpreting Neural Networks for NLP, BlackboxNLP@ACL 2019, Florence, Italy, August 1, 2019, pp. 276–286. Association for Computational Linguistics (2019). https://doi.org/10.18653/V1/W19-4828

6. Cover, T.M., Hart, P.E.: Nearest neighbor pattern classification. IEEE Trans. Inf. Theory **13**(1), 21–27 (1967). https://doi.org/10.1109/TIT.1967.1053964

7. Dai, D., Dong, L., Hao, Y., Sui, Z., Chang, B., Wei, F.: Knowledge neurons in pre-trained transformers. In: Muresan, S., Nakov, P., Villavicencio, A. (eds.) Proceedings of the 60th Annual Meeting of the Association for Computational Linguistics, vol. 1, Long Papers, ACL 2022, Dublin, Ireland, May 22-27, 2022, pp. 8493–8502. Association for Computational Linguistics (2022). https://doi.org/10.18653/V1/2022.ACL-LONG.581

8. Devlin, J., Chang, M., Lee, K., Toutanova, K.: BERT: pre-training of deep bidirectional transformers for language understanding. In: Burstein, J., Doran, C., Solorio, T. (eds.) Proceedings of the 2019 Conference of the North American Chapter of the Association for Computational Linguistics: Human Language Technologies, NAACL-HLT 2019, Minneapolis, MN, USA, June 2-7, 2019, vol. 1, Long and Short Papers, pp. 4171–4186. Association for Computational Linguistics (2019). https://doi.org/10.18653/V1/N19-1423

9. Hochreiter, S., Schmidhuber, J.: Long short-term memory. Neural Comput. **9**(8), 1735–1780 (1997). https://doi.org/10.1162/NECO.1997.9.8.1735

10. Hong, M., Wang, H.: Feature selection based on long short term memory for text classification. Multim. Tools Appl. **83**(15), 44333–44378 (2024). https://doi.org/10.1007/S11042-023-16990-7

11. Lee, R.C.T., Chin, Y.H., Chang, S.C.: Application of principal component analysis to multikey searching. IEEE Trans. Softw. Eng. **2**(3), 185–193 (1976). https://doi.org/10.1109/TSE.1976.225946

12. Reimers, N.: all-MPNet-base-v2. https://huggingface.co/sentence-transformers/all-mpnet-base-v2. Accessed 30 Sep 2010

13. Reimers, N.: multi-qa-mpnet-base-dot-v1. https://huggingface.co/sentence-transformers/multi-qa-mpnet-base-dot-v1. Accessed 30 Sep 2010

14. Reimers, N., Gurevych, I.: Sentence-BERT: sentence embeddings using Siamese BERT-networks. In: Inui, K., Jiang, J., Ng, V., Wan, X. (eds.) Proceedings of the 2019 Conference on Empirical Methods in Natural Language Processing and the 9th International Joint Conference on Natural Language Processing, EMNLP-IJCNLP 2019, Hong Kong, China, November 3-7, 2019, pp. 3980–3990. Association for Computational Linguistics (2019). https://doi.org/10.18653/V1/D19-1410

15. Vaswani, A., et al.: Attention is all you need. In: Guyon, I., et al. (eds.) Advances in Neural Information Processing Systems 30: Annual Conference on Neural Information Processing Systems 2017, December 4-9, 2017, Long Beach, CA, USA, pp. 5998–6008 (2017). https://proceedings.neurips.cc/paper/2017/hash/3f5ee243547dee91fbd053c1c4a845aa-Abstract.html

16. Wang, K., Huang, J., Liu, Y., Cao, B., Fan, J.: Combining feature selection methods with BERT: an in-depth experimental study of long text classification. In: Gao, H., Wang, X., Iqbal, M., Yin, Y., Yin, J., Gu, N. (eds.) Collaborative Computing: Networking, Applications and Worksharing - 16th EAI International Conference, CollaborateCom 2020, Shanghai, China, October 16-18, 2020, Proceedings, Part I. LNCS, Social Informatics and Telecommunications Engineering, vol. 349, pp. 567–582. Springer (2020). https://doi.org/10.1007/978-3-030-67537-0_34

Neuro-Symbolic Integration for Open Set Recognition in Network Intrusion Detection

Alice Bizzarri[1(✉)], Chung-En Yu[2], Brian Jalaian[2,3], Fabrizio Riguzzi[1],
and Nathaniel D. Bastian[4]

[1] University of Ferrara, Ferrara, Italy
{alice.bizzarri,fabrizio.riguzzi}@unife.it
[2] University of West Florida, Pensacola, FL, USA
cy31@students.uwf.edu, bjalaian@uwf.edu.org, bjalaian@ihmc.org
[3] Institute for Human and Machine Cognition, Pensacola, FL, USA
[4] United States Military Academy, West Point, NY, USA
nathaniel.bastian@westpoint.edu

Abstract. Open Set Recognition (OSR) addresses the challenge of classifying inputs into known and unknown categories, a crucial task where labeling is often prohibitively expensive or incomplete. This is particularly vital in applications like Network Intrusion Detection Systems (NIDS), where OSR is used to identify novel, previously unknown attacks. We propose a neuro-symbolic integration approach that combines deep learning and symbolic methods, enhancing deep embedding for clustering with custom loss functions and leveraging XGBoost's decision tree algorithms. Our methodology not only robustly addresses the identification of previously unknown attacks in NIDS but also effectively manages scenarios involving covariance shift. We demonstrate the efficacy of our approach through extensive experimentation, achieving an AUROC of 0.99 in both contexts. This paper presents a significant step forward in OSR for network intrusion detection by integrating deep and symbolic learning to handle unforeseen challenges in dynamic environments.

Keywords: Neuro-symbolic Integration · Deep Embedding for Clustering · XGBoost · Open Set Recognition · Network Intrusion Detection

1 Introduction

Machine learning systems are commonly trained under the closed-world assumption, where it is presumed that every test class corresponds to a training class [13,16,23]. There has been a concerted effort to augment the ability of these systems to recognize and disregard unknown inputs. This effort has been particularly pronounced in the domains of anomaly detection, out-of-distribution

(OOD) detection, and open set recognition (OSR). Traditionally, the focus was more on anomaly detection, but recent shifts have prioritized OOD detection and OSR. The fundamental differences between OOD detection and OSR are twofold: firstly, OOD detection involves a greater semantic gap between data considered outside and within the distribution. Conversely, OSR deals with classifying subsets of data as either within or outside the distribution in the same dataset. Secondly, unlike OOD detection which primarily differentiates between external and internal samples, OSR also assesses classification efficacy on known classes within a closed-world setup [30]. As delineated in [28], a distinction is made between semantic shift and covariate shift. Semantic shift pertains to OOD samples emanating from different classes, whereas covariate shift relates to samples originating from varying domains.

A pertinent example of an OSR challenge is the detection of previously unknown attacks facing by Network Intrusion Detection Systems (NIDS). Our proposed solution, TEX-DEC, integrates Deep Embedding for Clustering (DEC) [27] with XGBoost [7] to address this. DEC extracts pertinent features and clusters them to form a condensed latent space, while XGBoost is utilized to identify novel samples within this space. Notably, our approach employs a neuro-symbolic methodology, merging neural network-based deep learning with symbolic techniques that process data representations symbolically. This fusion enhances the system's adaptability and robustness, enabling it to tackle the diverse and complex challenges presented by OSR effectively. We implemented TEX-DEC in identifying previously unknown attacks in NIDS and in recognizing handwritten images, achieving an impressive AUROC of 0.99 in both applications.

The remainder of this paper is structured as follows: Sect. 2 reviews relevant literature and prior work concerning OSR and NIDS. Section 3 elucidates key concepts crucial for a comprehensive understanding of our methodology. The details of our proposed approach are elaborated in Sect. 4. Section 5 describes the experimental setup, datasets used, and the results obtained. An ablation study examining our custom loss function is discussed in Sect. 6. Finally, Sect. 7 provides our concluding thoughts and findings.

2   Related Work

Recent advancements in machine learning have significantly enriched the research landscape of OSR. OSR methodologies, pivotal in scenarios with an open-ended or evolving set of possible classes, are generally bifurcated into discriminative and generative approaches [9]. Discriminative models, such as those discussed by Scheirer et al. [25], Hassen and Chan [11], and Bendale et al. [4], utilize probability- or learning-based techniques to distinguish known from unknown classes. Conversely, generative models, exemplified by the works of Neal et al. [22] and Ge et al. [8], deploy generative techniques to identify OSR samples.

Scheirer et al. [25] introduced the Compact Abating Probability (CAP) model, which reduces the probability of class membership as samples diverge from training data towards open space, demonstrating successful application in OSR scenarios. Bendale et al. [4] expanded upon this with OpenMax, incorporating Extreme Value Theory (EVT) to build a CAP model for each class, enhancing robustness by rejecting unknown inputs via thresholding. Although not primarily focused on adversarial inputs, OpenMax exhibits superior resilience compared to traditional softmax models.

Hassen and Chan [11] explored intermediate representations to create a spatial distinction where samples from the same class are clustered together while distinctly separating different classes, enabling the identification of unknown examples through Euclidean distance and predefined thresholds. Neal et al. [22] employed generative adversarial networks to create examples mimicking the training set yet belonging to no known category, training OSR models with these synthetic samples. Ge et al. [8] introduced Generative OpenMax (G-OpenMax), extending OpenMax capabilities to better detect unknown samples.

In our work, we adopt a methodology resonating with the approach of Hassen and Chan [11], enhancing it with a clustered latent space and XGBoost to augment both performance and robustness. Notably, the use of XGBoost obviates the need for threshold-based classification of unknown examples.

The NIDS domain, predominantly using known datasets for attack classification [2,3,15], faces challenges in detecting previously unknown attacks. Traditional anomaly-based methods, which rely on deviations from normative behavior and typically require network flow data, necessitate additional information [1,14,24,29]. Addressing these challenges, we propose a novel DEC and XGBoost approach for packet-level detection of previously unknown attacks, comparing its efficacy against existing packet-based and flow-based systems [19,29].

3   Background

In this section, we provide an overview of key concepts that are needed to understanding our proposed approach. Specifically, we introduce DEC and XGBoost.

3.1   Deep Embedding for Clustering

Cluster analysis holds a crucial role in machine learning and data mining. Deep clustering refers to a set of techniques that combine deep learning with traditional clustering algorithms. Unlike conventional clustering methods, that rely on handcrafted features or distance metrics, deep clustering leverages the representation learning capabilities of DNNs to automatically learn feature representations directly from raw data. Deep clustering takes the feature extraction prowess of deep neural networks to autonomously acquire richer and more representative data representations. This methodology handles high-dimensional and intricate datasets, making it especially suited for scenarios where the inherent structure of the data is not known. By employing gradient-based optimization methods, DNNs can be trained to enhance cluster homogeneity while simultaneously maximizing inter-cluster heterogeneity. The outcome is a resilient and adaptable clustering approach effective on different datasets sourced from various origins and domains.

This study builds upon DEC [27], which employs DNNs to simultaneously learn feature representations and cluster assignments. This is achieved by mapping the data space to a low-dimensional feature space and iteratively optimizing a clustering objective. DEC comprises encoders responsible for acquiring a latent representation, coupled with a cluster layer. This cluster layer generates a *soft assignment q* for each sample, reflecting the likelihood of its membership in each cluster. Loss is defined as the Kullback-Leibler (KL) divergence between the *soft assignment q* and a target distribution *p*. DEC initially pre-trains the encoder part of the network using the autoencoder (AE) framework. The purpose is to initialize the weights and significantly reduce the effort required to achieve the clustering objective. A *Cluster layer* is appended to the end of the encoder to generate the *soft assignments*. The *Cluster layer* incorporates centroids as a parameter and uses the output of encoder, z, as an input, subsequently calculating the *soft assignment* in the manner described in Eq. 1.

As mentioned above, DEC training is done in several phases, first an AE is pretrained to initialize the parameters. Alternatively, DEC can be trained from scratch, but this requires more effort in terms of training epochs. The AE learns a latent representation that naturally facilitates identifying clustering representations with DEC. The feature space of AE is used as the starting point for training DEC. The algorithm *k-means* is applied to initialize the centroids. After using the AE encoder as the basis for DEC, a clustering layer was added. Both centroids and parameters of encoder, Θ, are now trainable parameters, and Stochastic Gradient Descent (SGD) can be used to learn the feature space and its clustering representation. In [27], the authors used a KL divergence to train the neural network.

In the first step, a *soft assignment* between the embedded points and cluster centroids is computed using Student's t-distribution [18] as a kernel to measure the similarity between the embedded point z_i and the centroid μ_j; in this way we can get the probability q_{ij} that sample i is assigned to cluster j (*soft assignment*).

$$q_{ij} = \frac{\left(1 + \|z_i - \mu_j\|^2 / \alpha\right)^{-\frac{\alpha+1}{2}}}{\sum_{j'} \left(1 + \|z_i - \mu_{j'}\|^2 / \alpha\right)^{-\frac{\alpha+1}{2}}} \tag{1}$$

where α is the number of degrees of freedom of the Student's t-distribution, we let $\alpha = 1$ for all experiments in accordance with [27].

The second step involves updating both cluster centroids and deep mapping f_Θ parameters by learning from the current high confidence assignments using an auxiliary target distribution. In other words, the loss is obtained by a KL divergence between q and p, where p is a target distribution defined as follows:

$$p_{ij} = \frac{q_{ij}^2 / f_j}{\sum_{j'} q_{ij'}^2 / f_{j'}} \tag{2}$$

Here $f_j = \sum_i q_{ij}$ is the soft cluster frequency. For more details about target and *soft assignment* please refer to [27]. So, we can use KL divergence as the loss to train the network.

$$\mathcal{L}_{kld} = \text{KL}(P\|Q) = \sum_i \sum_j p_{ij} \log \frac{p_{ij}}{q_{ij}} \tag{3}$$

3.2   Extreme Gradient Boosting

XGBoost [7] is a ensemble learning algorithm. Based on the gradient boosting framework, XGBoost constructs a sequence of decision trees, with each subsequent tree aiming to correct the errors made by the previous ones. By iteratively refining the predictions of weak learners, XGBoost effectively captures complex relationships between input features and target variables, leading to high predictive performance and robust generalization capabilities. XGBoost uses classification and regression trees (CART) as weak learners. Trees try to complement each other. Mathematically, we can write our model in the form:

$$\hat{y}_i = \sum_{k=1}^{K} f_k(x_i), f_k \in \mathcal{F} \tag{4}$$

where K is the number of trees, f_k is a function in space $\mathcal{F}$, and $\mathcal{F}$ is the set of all possible CARTs.

The objective function to be optimized is given by the sum of the losses $l(y_i, \hat{y}_i)$ for all examples plus the sum of the tree complexities $\omega(f_k)$. The latter is used as a regularization term computed on the basis of the number of leaves and the scores assigned to the leaves. More details can be found in [7].

We used *XGBClassifier* with optimization for logistic regression, designed to handle binary classification tasks. XGBClassifier optimizes the logistic regression-specific loss function and uses the logistic activation function to produce predicted probabilities. In addition, XGBoost is known for its ability to efficiently handle problems with large data sets and high data sizes due to its highly efficient implementation and ability to take advantage of computational parallelization.

In conclusion, XGBoost is a powerful machine learning algorithm that combines gradient boosting with decision trees to obtain accurate and generalizable predictive models. With built-in regularization techniques such as tree pruning and column sampling, the model is able to avoid overfitting to training data, ensuring good generalization to new instances.

3.3   Contrastive Learning

Contrastive learning [10] is a self-supervised learning technique that aims at learning useful representations by maximizing the agreement between similar samples and minimizing the agreement between dissimilar ones. By encouraging similar samples to be closer together and dissimilar samples to be farther apart in the learned representation space, contrastive learning enables the discovery of semantically meaningful features that capture underlying patterns in the data. This makes contrastive learning particularly well-suited for tasks such as representation learning, feature extraction, and unsupervised feature learning.

4   Proposed Method

Let D be a dataset comprising pairs (x, y), where $x \in X$ and $y \in C$. Here, X represents the input space and C represents the label set. D is divided into a training set, D_{tr}, and a test set, D_{test}. Additionally, we define two subsets of C: C_k, containing the known classes, and C_u, containing the unknown classes. The objective is to construct a function $f : X \to \{known, novelty\}$ that assigns each input x to one of two categories: $known$ if $y \in C_k$, and $novelty$ if $y \in C_u$.

We propose Tree EXtreme Gradient Boosting with Deep Embedding for Clustering (**TEX-DEC**) exploits DEC and XGBoost, as shown in Fig. 1.

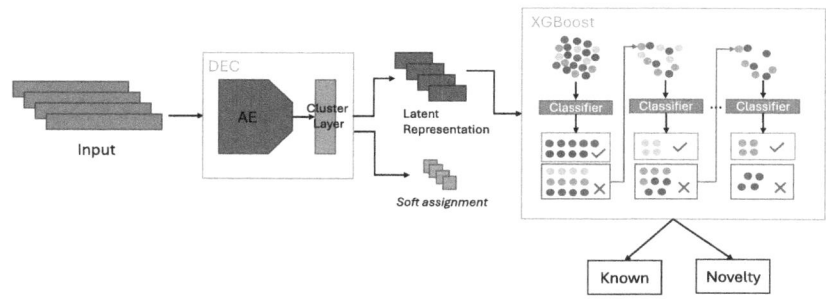

Fig. 1. DEC first extracts the latent representation and performs soft assignment. XGboost then uses the latent representation to detect Known and Novel sample.

We segmented the dataset D into three categories: *Known, Novelty 1*, and *Novelty 2*, as illustrated in Fig. 2. We denote by *Novelty 1* and *Novelty 2* respectively the examples of novelty classes used for training the XGBoost model and the examples of novelty classes reserved exclusively for the testing phase. The *Known* subset is divided into three parts: one for training DEC, the second, along with *Novelty 1*, for training XGBoost, and the last, along with *Novelty 2*, for test TEX-DEC. One *Novelty 2* class is used at a time, allowing for the training of a separate XGBoost model for each class using a one-vs-all approach. For instance, if we have classes *A, B,* and *C* as novelty, we train three separate XGBoost models, one for each class. Each model uses only one class as *Novelty 2*. For example, if the test class *Novelty 2* is *A*, the remaining classes (*B* and *C*) are treated as *Novelty 1*.

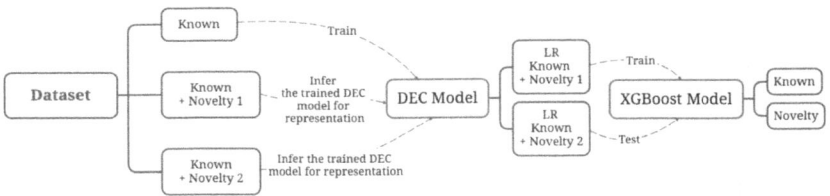

Fig. 2. The dataset is divided into three subsets: *Known, Novelty 1* and *Novelty 2*. The known subset is used to train DEC. A latent representation (LR) is obtained from each of the three subsets (note: DEC parameters are not changed at this stage). These LRs are then used to train (*Known* and *Novelty 1*) and test (*Known* and *Novelty 2*) an XGBoost classifier for sample classification.

4.1 Deep Embedding for Clustering

We leverage contrastive learning to enhance the distinctiveness of clusters obtained through DEC. By harnessing the complementary strengths of contrastive learning and traditional clustering techniques, we seek to achieve more effective data representation and clustering performance in our proposed approach. Our contribution is the addition of a contrastive loss and classification loss to the KL divergence used in DEC. This aids the second part of the architecture in distinguishing between novel and known samples. Below, we describe the loss components used for training.

- *KL Divergence:* as DEC, see Sect. 3.1, Eqs. 1, 2 and 3.
- *Contrastive Loss:* We calculate the average $C_{distance}$ of the Euclidean distance between each pair of centroid as follows:

$$C_{distance} = \frac{\sum_{i,j} \|\mu_i - \mu_j\|_2}{k(k-1)} \qquad (5)$$

where k is the number of clusters. This loss measures the mean Euclidean distance between cluster centroids, rather than focusing on individual sample pairs as in traditional contrastive losses [10]. To our knowledge, this specific formulation is novel. The contrastive loss we use is then:

$$\mathcal{L}_{contrastive} = \frac{1}{C_{distance}} = \frac{k(k-1)}{\sum_{i,j} \|\mu_i - \mu_j\|_2} \qquad (6)$$

The aim of this loss is to increase the distance between the centroids.

- *Classification Loss:* Since the clusters should accurately represent the actual classes of known samples. We used the Cross Entropy loss (L_{CE}), define as follow:

$$L_{CE} = -\frac{1}{N} \sum_{i=1}^{i=N} y_i \cdot \log(\widehat{y}_i) \qquad (7)$$

where $\widehat{y}_i$ and y_i are the predicted and real labels, respectively.

The final loss is then:

$$\mathcal{L} = \alpha \cdot \mathcal{L}_{kld} + \beta \cdot \mathcal{L}_{contrastive} + \omega \cdot L_{CE} \tag{8}$$

The ablation study in Sect. 6 shows that each of the three terms is essential for the performance of the system. α, β and ω are used as weights during ablation study to analyze the impact of each loss component.

4.2 XGBoost

After DEC creates a smaller latent representation of the input, XGBoost is used to distinguish between known and novel instances, exploiting both known instances and a small subset of novel examples for training. Notably, our dataset is partitioned into three distinct sets: the first for training DEC exclusively with known instances, the second for training XGBoost with a mix of known and novel examples, and the third for testing, which is composed in a balanced way of novel and known instances. Importantly, the novelty classes employed in XGBoost training differ from those considered as novel in the final test set, ensuring a consistent assessment of novelty detection performance.

5 Experiments

In this section, we present the results of our experiments conducted with TEX-DEC using data described in Sect. 5.1. The outcomes of these experiments are detailed in Sect. 5.2.

5.1 Datasets

The system is applied to the task of OSR in network intrusion detection using the CIC-IDS2017 dataset [26]. As the field of NIDS is continually evolving, with the detection of new types of attacks being crucial, as mentioned above, we segmented the dataset into three categories: *Known*, *Novelty 1*, and *Novelty 2*. We also test TEX-DEC using the classical MNIST dataset [5].

NIDS Datasets. In domain of NIDS, we used the CIC-IDS2017 and UNSW-NB15 datasets. The CIC-IDS2017 dataset, created by the Canadian Institute for Cybersecurity in 2017, contains packet-based data in packet capture (PCAP) format and flow-based data in CSV format. Both types of data were captured during simulated network traffic in packet-based and bidirectional flow-based formats, including the latest attacks and benign traffic. For our study, we used only packet-based data. The dataset collects simulated traffic information for an acquisition period of five days. The packet-based information in CIC-IDS2017 is unlabeled, making it necessary to use the Payload-Byte tool [6] for the extraction and labeling of network traffic packet capture files using the metadata provided in the dataset. The tool uses the features described in PCAPs to match packets with flow-based labeled data instances. Due to the variability in packet size, Payload-Byte uses a maximum payload length of 1500 bytes, with each byte converted into an 8-bit integer feature. Upon data labeling, any duplicate instances and those devoid of payload data are eliminated. The dataset contains 14 different types of attack and 1 benign class. The dataset was split as shown in Table 1. Three attacks were chosen as novel as in [19], where the authors considered each type of attack in turn as previously unknown, and identified these three attacks as those that showed the greatest performance degradation in terms of detection. Therefore, we also chose to use the same attacks as novelties.

Table 1. The dataset split into *Known, Novelty 1 & 2*

Class	# sample	Subset
Benign	3.328.591	Known
DoS Hulk	2.219.061	Known
DoS Slowhttptest	9.778	Known
Heartbleed	41.283	Known
Brute Force (Web Attack)	28.920	Known
Sql Injection (Web Attack)	45	Known
XSS (Web Attack)	6.767	Known
Bot	5.143	Known
PortScan	946	Known
DoS GoldenEye	34.293	Novelty 1
DoS slowloris	20.877	Novelty 1
DDoS	618.544	Novelty 1
SSH-Patator	181.147	Novelty 1 or 2
FTP-Patator	110.636	Novelty 1 or 2
Infiltration	41.725	Novelty 1 or 2

The UNSW-NB15 dataset [21] is a NIDS dataset developed to identify normal and attack network traffic. The raw network packets were generated by the Australian Centre for Information Security (ACCS) [20]. This dataset was preprocessed in the same manner as the previous one. The Payload-Byte tool [6] was applied to it. This dataset is used as a covariate to test the robustness of our approach, even with datasets from different network configurations. The UNSW dataset is used only during the testing phase and is labeled as *Novelty 2*.

MNIST Dataset. In our experimental evaluation, we also used the MNIST dataset [5], a well-established benchmark comprising simple handwritten digits. MNIST comprises ten classes representing numbers from 0 to 9. We partitioned this dataset into three subsets: *known, Novelty 1*, and *Novelty 2*: digits 0 through 4 were designated as *known*, while digits 5 through 9 were categorized as both

Novelty 1 and *Novelty 2*. During the testing phase, we employed a one-vs-all strategy, wherein a single *Novelty 2* class was utilized at a time, enabling the training of individual XGBoost models for each class.

5.2   Results

As previously mentioned, we tested our approach on different datasets. DEC was trained using different loss configurations, as discussed in Sect. 6. Additionally, we conducted a grid search on the hyper-parameters of XGBoost, including the number of components and maximum depth, to achieve optimal results. We evaluated the models using the Area Under the Receiver Operating Characteristic Curve (AUROC) because it proves effective in measuring the performance of a binary classification model under various scenarios. AUROC provides a comprehensive assessment of the model's ability to discriminate between positive and negative classes, considering both sensitivity and specificity.

For the CIC-IDS2017 dataset, we compared our results with those of [19, 29]. Specifically, we compared the AUROC for the *Novelty 2* classes. Additionally, we compared the AUROC for the UNSW-NB15 dataset with [19]. In this case, we did not encounter a semantic shift, but rather a covariate shift. Essentially, we had the same classes but from different datasets and thus different distributions. The results, reported in Table 2, show a significant improvement in the performance of our method compared to previous approaches. For instance, in detecting the previously unknown Infiltration attack, we achieved an AUROC of 0.9843, surpassing the performance of existing methods. Similarly, our method exhibited an AUROC score of 0.9939 for the previously unknown SSH-Patator attack, slightly outperforming [19] (0.9921) and significantly surpassing [29] (0.6787). In the case of the previously unknown FTP-Patator attack, although our AUROC of 0.9950 is slightly lower than [19] (0.9957), it notably outperforms [29] (0.7955). Moreover, when assessing the UNSW-NB15 dataset, which was generated from an entirely different distribution than CIC-IDS2017, our AUROC of 0.9939 surpassed the result reported by [19] (0.9583). This fact underscores the robustness and generalizability of our methodology for detecting novelty across different datasets. While the first three attacks are novel within the same dataset, our method demonstrates high adaptability and detection capability even on a completely different dataset like UNSW-NB15. This generalization ability instills confidence in the validity and utility of our approach across a variety of real-world scenarios.

For the MNIST dataset, during the training phase samples labeled as known were used to train the DEC model, with the aim of establishing a robust representation of these digits. Separate XGBoost models were trained for each number within the Novelty interval (5, 6, 7, 8, 9) using a one-vs-all classification strategy. This training process allowed the development of specialized classifiers to distinguish each novelty class from the normal class. The performance was compared with AAE-II [12] and Isolation Forest [17], the latter two obtaining an AUROC of 0.619, and 0.841, respectively. TEX-DEC achieved 0.935, which significantly

Table 2. The AUROC results of the methods for specified previously unknown attacks

	AUROC		
Novelty Type	Matejek et al. [19]	Zavrak et al. [29]	TEX-DEC
FTP-Patator	**0.9957**	0.7955	0.9950
Infiltration	0.9742	0.8965	**0.9843**
SSH-Patator	0.9921	0.6787	**0.9939**
UNSW-NB15	0.9583	-	**0.9939**

exceeded the results obtained in [12]. These results indicate the effectiveness of our approach in detecting novel samples in the MNIST dataset.

6   Ablation Study

As mentioned previously, our work relies on a loss function with three components: KL divergence (L_{kld}), contrastive loss ($L_{contrastive}$), and classification loss (L_{CE}). In this section, we investigate various configurations of this loss to achieve the best results. To conduct this study, we partitioned the dataset consistently and trained only one autoencoder for all configurations, ensuring a common starting point for comparison. The loss function is described in Eq. 8. We set the weights α, β, and ω by considering all possible combinations of 0 and 1 to *turn off* individual loss components.

The results are presented in Table 3. Each cell in the table reports the AUROC value for the specific configuration, along with the difference compared to the optimal configuration (highlighted in bold).

Table 3. The table displays the AUROC for the different test *Novelty 2*: SSH-Patator, Infiltration, FTP-Patator, and UNSW-NB15.

α	β	ω	SSH-Patator	Infiltration	FTP-Patator	UNSW-NB15	Average
1	1	1	99.50	98.43	99.39	**99.39**	**99.28**
1	0	0	99.66	84.54	99.03	98.88	95.53
0	1	0	99.41	98.29	99.52	99.28	99.13
0	0	1	99.57	**98.61**	**99.56**	99.35	99.27
1	1	0	**99.69**	84.52	99.03	98.85	95.52
1	0	1	99.68	84.40	99.05	98.88	95.51
0	1	1	99.51	98.38	99.36	**99.39**	99.16

The results, summarized in Table 3, show discernible trends among different configurations. In particular, configurations in which all loss components are turned on ($\alpha = \beta = \omega = 1$) consistently produce AUROC values close to optimal levels, underscoring the synergistic contribution of each component to overall model performance levels. In contrast, configurations with the KL divergence component active and one or more components at 0 ($\alpha = 1$ *and* $\beta = \omega = 1$ *or* 0) show lower performance, particularly in the case of *Infiltration*, emphasizing the indispensable role of each component in facilitating effective novelty detection.

Intermediate configurations, in which specific loss components are selectively activated, reveal nuances about their respective contributions. They show how the use of classification and contrastive loss lead to improved novelty detection. Systematic exploration of loss function configurations provides valuable insights into the interaction between individual components and their collective impact on novelty detection performance. Such insights are critical in guiding the refinement and optimization of novelty detection systems, thereby advancing the state of the art in novelty detection research.

7 Conclusion

This research was primarily aimed at enhancing the robustness of machine learning by NIDS by improving the detection capabilities for previously unknown attacks, a critical aspect of modern network security. As we navigate through an era of rapidly advancing technological threats, the ability to identify novel, complex attacks becomes imperative. The system presented in this paper, which synergistically combines a neural component (DEC) with a symbolic component (XGBoost), leverages the strengths of neural networks in feature extraction from extensive data sets along with the robust decision-making capabilities of decision tree ensembles. This neuro-symbolic artificial intelligence approach not only enhances the robustness and adaptability of NIDS but also contributes significantly to the domain by improving the system's ability to recognize and react to new threats dynamically. Moreover, the integration of these technologies offers improved explainability and the ability to discern complex relationships within the input data, setting a foundation for addressing more intricate challenges in network security. The effectiveness and innovative aspects of this approach are underscored by its application to both previously unknown attack detection in NIDS and scenario involving handwriting recognition, achieving a high AUROC of 0.99 in both domains. This underscores the versatility and potential of our approach to generalize across different types of data and applications, paving the way for broader implementations in cybersecurity and beyond.

Acknowledgments. This work was supported in part by the Italian Ministry of University and Research through PNRR - M4C2 - Investimento 1.3 (Decreto Direttoriale MUR n. 341 del 15/03/2022), Partenariato Esteso PE00000013 - "FAIR - Future Artificial Intelligence Research" - Spoke 8 "Pervasive AI", funded by the European Union under the NextGeneration EU programme"; and by the U.S. Military Academy (USMA) under Cooperative Agreement No. W911NF-23-2-0108, the U.S. Army Combat Capabilities Development Command Army Research Laboratory under Support Agreement No. USMA 21050, and the Defense Advanced Research Projects Agency under Support Agreement No. USMA 23004. The views and conclusions expressed in this paper are those of the authors and do not reflect the official policy or position of the U.S. Military Academy, U.S. Army, U.S. Department of Defense, or U.S. Government.

References

1. Abdalgawad, N., Sajun, A., Kaddoura, Y., Zualkernan, I.A., Aloul, F.: Generative deep learning to detect cyberattacks for the IoT-23 dataset. IEEE Access **10**, 6430–6441 (2021)
2. Andresini, G., Appice, A., Di Mauro, N., Loglisci, C., Malerba, D.: Multi-channel deep feature learning for intrusion detection. IEEE Access **8**, 53346–53359 (2020)
3. Asam, M., Khan, S.H., Akbar, A., Bibi, S., Jamal, T., Khan, A., Ghafoor, U., Bhutta, M.R.: IoT malware detection architecture using a novel channel boosted and squeezed CNN. Sci. Rep. **12**(1), 15498 (2022)
4. Bendale, A., Boult, T.E.: Towards open set deep networks. In: Proceedings of the IEEE Conference on Computer Vision and Pattern Recognition, pp. 1563–1572 (2016)
5. Deng, L.: The MNIST database of handwritten digit images for machine learning research. IEEE Sig. Process. Mag. **29**(6), 141–142 (2012)
6. Farrukh, Y.A., Khan, I., Wali, S., Bierbrauer, D., Pavlik, J.A., Bastian, N.D.: Payload-byte: a tool for extracting and labeling packet capture files of modern network intrusion detection datasets. In: 2022 IEEE/ACM International Conference on Big Data Computing, Applications and Technologies (BDCAT), pp. 58–67. IEEE (2022)
7. Friedman, J.H.: Greedy function approximation: a gradient boosting machine. Ann. Stat., 1189–1232 (2001)
8. Ge, Z., Demyanov, S., Chen, Z., Garnavi, R.: Generative OpenMax for multi-class open set classification. arXiv preprint arXiv:1707.07418 (2017)
9. Geng, C., Huang, S.J., Chen, S.: Recent advances in open set recognition: a survey. IEEE Trans. Pattern Anal. Mach. Intell. **43**(10), 3614–3631 (2020)
10. Hadsell, R., Chopra, S., LeCun, Y.: Dimensionality reduction by learning an invariant mapping. In: 2006 IEEE Computer Society Conference on Computer Vision and Pattern Recognition (CVPR'06), vol. 2, pp. 1735–1742. IEEE (2006) vol. 2, pp. 1735–1742. IEEE (2006)
11. Hassen, M., Chan, P.K.: Learning a neural-network-based representation for open set recognition. In: Proceedings of the 2020 SIAM International Conference on Data Mining, pp. 154–162. SIAM (2020)
12. Hassen, M., Chan, P.K.: Unsupervised open set recognition using adversarial autoencoders. In: 2020 19th IEEE International Conference on Machine Learning and Applications (ICMLA), pp. 360–365. IEEE (2020)
13. He, K., Zhang, X., Ren, S., Sun, J.: Delving deep into rectifiers: surpassing human-level performance on ImageNet classification. In: Proceedings of the IEEE International Conference on Computer Vision, pp. 1026–1034 (2015)
14. Hwang, R.H., Peng, M.C., Huang, C.W., Lin, P.C., Nguyen, V.L.: An unsupervised deep learning model for early network traffic anomaly detection. IEEE Access **8**, 30387–30399 (2020)
15. Khan, A.S., Ahmad, Z., Abdullah, J., Ahmad, F.: A spectrogram image-based network anomaly detection system using deep convolutional neural network. IEEE Access **9**, 87079–87093 (2021)

16. Krizhevsky, A., Sutskever, I., Hinton, G.E.: ImageNet classification with deep convolutional neural networks. Adv. Neural Inf. Process. Syst. **25** (2012)
17. Liu, F.T., Ting, K.M., Zhou, Z.H.: Isolation forest. In: 2008 Eighth IEEE International Conference on Data Mining, pp. 413–422. IEEE (2008)
18. Van der Maaten, L., Hinton, G.: Visualizing data using t-SNE. J. Mach. Learn. Res. **9**(11) (2008)
19. Matejek, B., Gehani, A., Bastian, N.D., Clouse, D., Kline, B., Jha, S.: Safeguarding network intrusion detection models from zero-day attacks and concept drift (2017)
20. Moustafa, N.: Designing an online and reliable statistical anomaly detection framework for dealing with large high-speed network traffic, Ph.D. thesis, UNSW Sydney (2017)
21. Moustafa, N., Slay, J.: The evaluation of network anomaly detection systems: statistical analysis of the UNSW-NB15 data set and the comparison with the KDD99 data set. Inf. Secur. J. Glob. Perspect. **25**(1–3), 18–31 (2016)
22. Neal, L., Olson, M., Fern, X., Wong, W.K., Li, F.: Open set learning with counterfactual images. In: Proceedings of the European Conference on Computer Vision (ECCV), pp. 613–628 (2018)
23. Parmar, J., Chouhan, S., Raychoudhury, V., Rathore, S.: Open-world machine learning: applications, challenges, and opportunities. ACM Comput. Surv. **55**(10), 1–37 (2023)
24. Sabeel, U., Heydari, S.S., Elgazzar, K., El-Khatib, K.: Building an intrusion detection system to detect atypical cyberattack flows. IEEE Access **9**, 94352–94370 (2021)
25. Scheirer, W.J., Jain, L.P., Boult, T.E.: Probability models for open set recognition. IEEE Trans. Pattern Anal. Mach. Intell. **36**(11), 2317–2324 (2014)
26. Sharafaldin, I., Lashkari, A.H., Ghorbani, A.A.: Toward generating a new intrusion detection dataset and intrusion traffic characterization. ICISSP **1**, 108–116 (2018)
27. Xie, J., Girshick, R., Farhadi, A.: Unsupervised deep embedding for clustering analysis. In: International Conference on Machine Learning, pp. 478–487. PMLR (2016)
28. Yang, J., Zhou, K., Li, Y., Liu, Z.: Generalized out-of-distribution detection: a survey. arXiv preprint arXiv:2110.11334 (2021)
29. Zavrak, S., Iskefiyeli, M.: Anomaly-based intrusion detection from network flow features using variational autoencoder. IEEE Access **8**, 108346–108358 (2020)
30. Zhu, F., Ma, S., Cheng, Z., Zhang, X.Y., Zhang, Z., Liu, C.L.: Open-world machine learning: a review and new outlooks. arXiv preprint arXiv:2403.01759 (2024)

MM-IGLU-IT: Multi-modal Interactive Grounded Language Understanding in Italian

Federico Borazio$^{(\boxtimes)}$, Claudiu Daniel Hromei$^{(\boxtimes)}$, Elisa Passone ,
Danilo Croce$^{(\boxtimes)}$, and Roberto Basili

Department of Enterprise Engineering, University of Rome Tor Vergata, Via del
Politecnico, 1, Tor Vergata, Italy
{borazio,hromei,passone}@ing.uniroma2.it, {croce,basili}@info.uniroma2.it

Abstract. This paper explores Interactive Grounded Language Understanding (IGLU) within Human-Robot Interaction (HRI). Here, a robot interprets user commands related to its environment, determining if a specific command can be executed. When ambiguities or incomplete data arise, the robot asks relevant clarification questions. Current models, trained on English datasets, leverage multi-modal and end-to-end capabilities by fine-tuning architectures like LLaVA. These models combine a Visual Encoder, processing images of the environment, with Large Language Models (LLMs) encoding user requests, enabling agents to discern command executability and seek clarifications when necessary. While many LLMs are inherently multi-lingual, fine-tuning them on English-only datasets limits their application in other languages, such as Italian. To address this, we developed MM-IGLU-IT, a dataset for Multi-Modal Interactive Grounded Language Understanding in Italian. This dataset was created by automatically translating existing large-scale datasets and manually validating them for accuracy, resulting in over 6,800 command examples. Training a model like LLaVA, fine-tuned over a multi-lingual base model such as LLaMA2, allowed us to achieve comparable performance in both English and Italian. This resource is released on a dedicated GitHub page at https://github.com/crux82/MM-IGLU-IT and we hope it will advance multi-modal models in the Italian language, providing a valuable resource for ongoing research.

Keywords: Human-Robot Interaction · Interactive Grounded Language Understanding · Large Language Models · Multi-Modality

1 Introduction

In recent years, significant progress has been made in developing models for text comprehension and interpretation. These models can answer questions, generate narratives, and interpret natural language and images [14,23,35,39]. Additionally, there is a growing interest in models focused on interpreting commands, evidenced by the proliferation of Large Language Models (LLMs) like ChatGPT.

A. Artale et al. (Eds.): AIxIA 2024, LNAI 15450, pp. 64–78, 2025.
https://doi.org/10.1007/978-3-031-80607-0_6

In robotics, while models excel at understanding human instructions, interpreting commands in real-world scenarios adds complexity. For instance, commands may be ambiguous, requiring clarification to ensure correct actions. The Interactive Grounded Language Understanding (IGLU) [13] task at NeurIPS 2022 showcased advances in natural language command interpretation. Here, "Understanding" involves interpreting a user's command, checking its feasibility, and generating an appropriate response. In this task, a human "Architect" gives commands to a robotic "Builder" in a Minecraft-like environment, such as *"Place 3 green blocks vertically above the red block"*. The robot must determine if the commands are executable or need clarification. To address the challenges of command interpretation in Human-Robot Interaction (HRI), two primary strategies have emerged: *(i)* utilizing a Knowledge Base (KB) to store comprehensive entity information and integrate this knowledge into models; *(ii)* leveraging images to capture intricate details of nearby objects, including their spatial relationships, shapes, and colors, to develop end-to-end systems capable of accurately understanding and responding to user queries. These two strategies can be used independently or combined within a more complex system. Inspired by the latter method, the MM-IGLU [11] resource expands the original IGLU resource by incorporating images that depict block arrangements with their respective colors, paired with textual commands and expected responses from the robot, which include phrases like *"Yes, I can execute this command"* or *"Do you want me to move the red block positioned on the right or left?"*. This enhancement enables the adoption of multi-modal approaches that merge visual perception encoding, obtained through advanced computer vision techniques, with text encoding. Notable examples of this class include ChatGPT4 [26], Flamingo [1], LLaVA [20], CogAgent [9] and Idefics [17].

However, MM-IGLU is exclusively for English language data, allowing for the training and evaluation of multi-modal LLMs only in English. To enable multi-modal LLMs to work with the Italian language, we created MM-IGLU-IT by translating and, most importantly, manually validating the available English data from MM-IGLU into Italian, resulting in more than 6,800 examples of commands. By training a multi-modal LLM, such as LLaVA, fine-tuned over a multi-lingual base model like LLaMA2 with the Italian data, we achieved comparable performance in both English and Italian. We hope this dataset will support the advancement of multi-modal models for the Italian language, providing a valuable resource for ongoing research in this domain.

In the rest of the paper, Sect. 2 describes the related work, Sect. 3 describes the resources and architectural frameworks used, Sect. 4 presents and discusses the experimental evaluation while Sect. 5 derives the conclusion.

2   Related Works

The generation of clarifying questions for human-robot interaction dates back to Winograd's foundational research [38]. Since then, many approaches have been developed, from human-made templates, such as cloze-type [8], rule-based

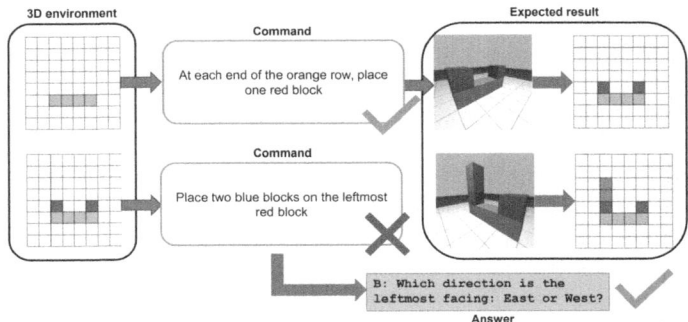

Fig. 1. Taken from the IGLU challenge description. *Top*: The architect's command was clear and no questions were needed, thus the Builder can execute it. *Bottom*: The word *'leftmost'* in the Command is ambiguous, so the Builder asks a clarifying question.

[24, 34], to semi-automatic questions [19, 33]. The most recent research has introduced Transformer-based techniques. This attention-based architecture, presented by [37], is an encoder-decoder architecture that has led to different model families. The encoder component, which may correspond to models like BERT [6], RoBERTa [21], and DeBERTa [7], encodes input sequences by using self-attention. In contrast, decoders, such as GPT [30], GPT-3 [4], and LLaMA [36], generate output sequences auto-regressively. LLaMA is a massive model with various applications to linguistic tasks, as shown in [10]. Examples of encoder-decoder models include T5 [31] and BART [18], which excel in tasks like translation, summarization, and question-answering. More recent research on generating clarifying questions has introduced transformer-based techniques. In [16], BERT is trained on an inverted SQuAD dataset [32], generating questions from provided text and answers. A different approach is expressed in [22] where GPT-2, used for the same dataset excluding answers, generates questions based purely on the context.

Despite these advancements, existing architectures focus on generating questions about a text but do not attempt to interact directly with the user to gather additional information in a specific environment. This limitation hinders the development of truly interactive systems that can dynamically engage with users. In the context of HRI, the successful interaction between the human and the robot is crucial. Effective collaboration requires clear roles and an understanding of each participant's position in the space [28]. For instance, [15] explores simulations of human behaviors where a robotic leader provides natural language commands, and the evaluation focuses on human task execution. However, this setup lacks full interactivity, as the human follower cannot ask questions but must follow the given instructions. Conversely, [25] investigates a dynamic interaction between a human and a robot capable of identifying when provided information is inadequate, a feature extended in [11].

The Interactive Grounded Language Understanding (IGLU) challenge, presented in [13], promotes research in Human-Robot Interaction, emphasizing collaboration via natural language. The challenge involves generating interactive agents that execute tasks using grounded language instructions in teamwork settings. Within IGLU, the "Architect" (Human Agent) instructs the "Builder" (AI Agent) on arranging colored blocks in a voxel environment. The Builder can seek clarifications if instructions are ambiguous, posing questions, as shown in Fig. 1. In this context, interactions are single-turn: the Architect instructs, and the Builder acts or asks for clarity. More details about data gathering can be found in [2,3,12,13]. However, the IGLU dataset lacks real-world images or natural language descriptions, and examples aren't categorized by command objectives, limiting the possibility of investigating multi-modal models. The work described in [11] aims to generate fully interactive systems based on Language Models, addressing these gaps by introducing multi-modal data and natural language descriptions. They integrate visual information, such as images of the environment, to explore unified visual and language systems. The paper tackles the task of Grounded Question Generation via a multi-modal approach integrating a Language Model based on LLaMA [36] with a Vision Model based on CLIP [29], merging both visual and textual data.

Although many models, including [36], are inherently multi-lingual, fine-tuning on English-only datasets limits their applicability to other languages. This work investigates the positive impact of creating an Italian dataset to enable effective evaluation and fine-tuning of multi-modal models in Italian. By developing MM-IGLU-IT, we aim to extend these models' capabilities to operate in Italian, thus broadening their applicability in human-robot interaction.

3   MM-IGLU-IT: An Italian Multi-modal Dataset for Grounded Language Understanding

The original IGLU dataset primarily provided data that are numerical-only (such as the positions of the blocks and the numerical identifier of the color), which limited its direct applicability to multi-modal neural approaches that integrate vision and language, usually based on images of the environment. MM-IGLU [11] overcomes these limitations by incorporating images showing block configurations and natural language descriptions of the environment. As illustrated in Fig. 2, an instruction like *"Break the green blocks"* cannot be executed if there are no green blocks in the environment, prompting the agent to seek clarification from the architect. The visual representation provided by these images enables the application of advanced computer vision techniques. Furthermore, MM-IGLU includes detailed textual descriptions of the blocks, such as *"There are no blue blocks, no yellow blocks, no green blocks, no orange blocks, eight purple blocks, four of which are on the ground, six red blocks, one of which is on the ground"*. They are made by converting the three-dimensional block coordinates into detailed narratives that enumerate the number of blocks, classify them by color, and specify their positions, enhancing the model's ability to interpret and respond to commands accurately. These linguistic descriptions allow the use of Large Language Models (LLMs) even in the absence of visual inputs, enhancing the dataset's versatility.

While multi-modal models like LLaVA can leverage LLMs agnostically, whether language-specific or multi-lingual, MM-IGLU's exclusive use of English data restricts the training and evaluation of models in other languages, such as Italian. To overcome this limitation, we developed MM-IGLU-IT by translating the English data from MM-IGLU into Italian and performing manual validation. This enabled the creation and assessment of multi-modal models in the Italian language. Inspired by the approach of [5], which translated the Visual Question Answering dataset into Italian, we utilized DeepL for the initial translation[1]. However, unlike [5], which validated only the test set, our process involved manual validation of the entire dataset-including training, validation, and test sets-by two annotators. This comprehensive validation ensured the integrity of the data, reducing the exposure of models to synthetic data and enhancing the overall quality of the training process.

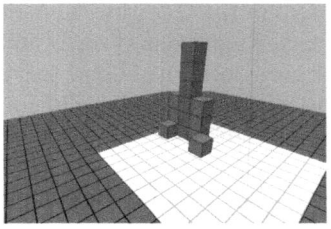

Fig. 2. An example of visual rendering of the environment, where the Instruction given by the Human is *"Break the green blocks"* and the expected answer is *"There are no green blocks, which blocks should I break?"*. (Color figure online)

Before completing validation, we evaluated the translation quality using the well-known BLEU scores [27] on the test set for both user commands and clarification questions. The BLEU-n scores for the commands are, in increasing lengths n of the target n-grams: 0.88, 0.83, 0.78 and 0.73, for $n=1,2,3,4$ respectively. For the questions, the corresponding scores are 0.95, 0.92, 0.48, and 0.39. High BLEU-1 scores suggest good overall translation quality, but the decline in scores with higher n-grams highlighted the need for further corrections. This prompted a manual validation of all translations to ensure accuracy. Consequently, MM-IGLU-IT encompasses over 6,800 examples, as detailed in Table 1. Each example includes an image depicting the arrangement and colors of blocks in the environment, accompanied by a command. If the command is not executable given the configuration, an expected clarification statement from the robot is included. Similar to IGLU and MM-IGLU, 13% of the examples require clarification. Furthermore, each Italian example is aligned with the original image and the corresponding command in English, supporting future cross-lingual research.

The main sources of error that were corrected include incorrect verb conjugations (e.g., *"Rimuovete"* → *"Rimuovi"*), rephrasing expressions (e.g., *"Vista a Nord"* → *"Guardando a Nord"*), and fixing mistranslations (e.g., *"Towel"*

---

[1] Source accessed in March 2024 at https://www.deepl.com/it/translator.

Table 1. Statistics of the datasets for total examples (#Exs), clear commands (#Clear), ambiguous commands (#Amb), and average word length for commands (C) and questions (Q).

Section	Instructions			Avg Len	
	#Exs	#Clear	#Amb	C	Q
Train	5,530	4,813	717	17.35	11.35
Val	615	531	84	16.39	10.79
Test	683	593	90	17.34	10.67

→ "*Asciugamano*" instead of "*Torre*", i.e. "*Tower*"). For example, the English word "*block*" was often mistranslated as "*isolato*" (i.e. *city block*) instead of "*blocco*". Only about 1% of the commands were nonsensical, such as "*Facing north and green purple blocks will be destroyed*" which was translated to "*Rivolto a nord e blocchi verdi viola saranno distrutti*" despite not being actionable. We maintained ambiguous commands to highlight cases needing clarification questions and test the robustness of the neural models. For instance, "*Istruzione non chiara, cosa vuoi che faccia?*" translated from "*The command is not clear, what do you want me to do?*". It is interesting to note that verbs like *to destroy* were translated to Italian verbs *distruggere, cancellare*, or *rimuovere*, maintaining a broader linguistic variability than the original dataset. This variability can enhance an LLM's robustness by minimizing overfitting to specific verbs and actions. Similar to [11], for each command in the test set that exhibits ambiguity, we reassigned the same classification label of the original dataset specifying the type of information that the command lacks, prompting the need for a clarifying question. These categories include: BLOCK, indicating uncertainty about which block the command refers to, e.g., "*Which specific block do you mean?*", or COLOR, when clarification about the color of the block is required. We believe this categorization is very useful for understanding the need for additional information, but for more details, we refer to [11].

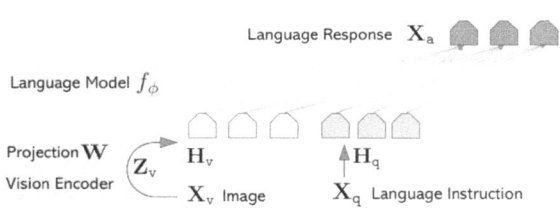

Fig. 3. The LLaVA network architecture, as presented in [20]

LLMs for Multi-modal IGLU. To address the above multi-modal task, we adopt the approach described in [11], utilizing the LLaVA framework [20]. This model integrates visual information from images of the environment using an image encoder like CLIP [29], with linguistic information using a Large Language Model (LLM) such as LLaMA2 Chat-13b [36]. The model processes commands and generates textual outputs, such as *"Posso eseguirlo."* (in English *"I can execute it"*) if the command is executable, or a clarification request is needed, otherwise.

In practice, LLaVA combines visual models with linguistic models using a single-layer neural network called the Projector to align the visual model's output representation with the language model's input representation. The architecture, illustrated in Fig. 3, shows X_v as the image and X_q as the input text. The Vision Encoder processes X_v to produce visual features Z_v, which are then projected by the Projection layer W to align with the language model's vector space, resulting in H_v. Simultaneously, the input text X_q is tokenized and embedded into the language model, producing H_q. These aligned visual and linguistic embeddings, H_v and H_q, are combined within the language model to generate a coherent language response X_a. This alignment is crucial for effective communication between the language and vision components of the model, enabling it to leverage both modalities effectively.

In this setup, the model is fine-tuned[2] by taking as input the tuple:

$$\langle \texttt{Introduction}, \texttt{Prompt}, \texttt{Image}, \texttt{Command} \rangle$$

The Introduction provides a contextual backdrop for the overarching task[3]:

In this virtual world reminiscent of Minecraft, you are a robotic entity equipped with the ability to move freely, and place or remove blocks within the environment. Imagine you are situated in the environment depicted in the image provided. Your task is to determine whether you can execute a given command based on the current configuration of the world. If you require additional information to carry out the command effectively, you should respond by asking relevant clarifying questions, such as inquiring about block colors, quantities, directions, or any other necessary details.

The IGLU tasks can be modeled into two modalities: classification and generation. In the classification modality, the agent determines whether a command can be executed and responds with either *"Yes"* or *"No"*. In the generation task, the agent generates a textual response to indicate whether the command can be executed and, if not, produces a clarification question. While these tasks only affect the Prompt, they could lead to two separate datasets. The Prompt element delineates the specific subtask at hand. For the classification task, it states:

Respond with 'Yes' if you can execute the command, or 'No' if additional information is required.

---

[2] Initially, this model was tested in a zero-shot manner but it resulted in unstable outcomes, often leading to hallucinated answers. While most sentences generated were sensible, they typically failed to show an understanding of the need to perform actions within the environment, often miscounting blocks.

[3] All the following texts are translated in Italian when used in the model.

For generation tasks, the prompt is:

Answer with 'I can execute it' if the command is executable, or pose a pertinent clarifying question if further details are needed.

The `Image` token serves as a placeholder that the vision encoder subsequently replaces with X_v. Meanwhile, the `Command` represents the robotic directive. Thus, X_q is the concatenation of `Instruction`, `Prompt` and `Command`.

The model's output X_a conforms to a *"Yes/No"* structure for classification, or it produces the direct question for generation tasks or, again, the affirmative response *"I can execute it"*. Inspired by the recent findings in [10,11], which demonstrated the effective fusion of data from multiple tasks to guide the prompting of an LLM, we have introduced the capability for multi-modal models to train a single LLaVA model by combining data from both the classification and generation task prompts. This multi-task learning approach shows great potential, as we expect, based on findings from [10], that the tasks will complement and enhance each other's performance. In particular, the generation task might see improvements as the model implicitly specializes in the classification task. From a practical standpoint, it simply requires merging the training datasets generated from both modalities and ad hoc instructions.

In [11], the language model was based on LLaMA2 Chat-13b[4] with 13 billion parameters. In this work, we use the same LLaMA2 Chat-13b, since it has been partially trained on Italian data from previous versions, demonstrating high performance in processing Italian texts [10]. This choice ensures better adaptability and effectiveness for tasks in Italian, leveraging the strengths of both visual and linguistic modalities in a multi-modal framework.

4   Experimental Evaluation

In this section, we evaluate the performance of the proposed architecture in generating contextually grounded clarifications, providing insights into its understanding of instructions and its ability to identify missing information that can be transformed into queries. We utilize the LLaMA2-chat model as a generative decoder for the robot's responses, leveraging its multi-lingual capabilities to investigate and compare performance when fine-tuned on tasks using English or Italian data. Our analysis focuses on three main areas: *Quality of Generated Answers*, which assesses both the model's decision to refrain from asking questions and the nature of the questions it generates; *In-Depth Error Analysis*, which examines the model's limitations and areas of difficulty; and *End-to-End Question-Answer Generation*, which explores the capability of a holistic system to produce valid responses. Given the multi-lingual nature of the LLaMA model, we test different language combinations between English and Italian. Specifically, we compare the multi-modal model introduced in [11] and trained on the English dataset (`LLaMA2Chat-13b-EN`) with the model trained using the

---

[4] https://huggingface.co/meta-llama/Llama-2-13b-chat-hf.

Italian dataset (`LLaMA2Chat-13b-IT`). This comparison allows us to assess the impact of language-specific training on model performance. As in [11], the linear projector, initially derived from LLaVA's release, was later completely re-tuned to achieve slight improvements in convergence. The hyper-parameters remain unchanged and are referenced in detail in that work.

Table 2. The Classification performance is divided into F1 of the positive class (the command is clear), F1 of the negative class (the command is ambiguous), and the Macro F1 of the two. The evaluation is divided into the Language of Training (Tr. Lan) and the Language of Testing (Test Lan).

Model name	Tr. Lan	Test Lan	F1 Pos	F1 Neg	M-F1
`LLaMA2Chat-13b-EN`	EN	EN	96.43%	67.16%	81.80%
`LLaMA2Chat-13b-EN`	EN	IT	70.07%	24.29%	47.18%
`LLaMA2Chat-13b-IT`	IT	IT	97.81%	66.67%	82.24%

Recognizing Ambiguous Commands. An interesting aspect of this evaluation is testing the multi-modal model introduced in [11], trained on the English dataset, on our Italian test set. This comparison helps us to understand whether translating the data into Italian and re-training the model is necessary or if the English-trained model, with the "emergent" capabilities of a multi-lingual LLM, is sufficient. First, we evaluate the system's ability to recognize ambiguous or problematic commands where clarifications are needed (without assessing the quality of these clarifications). We present results from various models applied to two tasks: *Classification* (determining whether to respond with "*Yes*" or "*No*") as shown in Table 2, and *Generation* (where the generated text is "*I can execute it*" or any clarification question) as shown in Table 3. Each model's language configuration, fine-tuned using the LLaVA framework, utilizes the same CLIP visual encoder, which remained "frozen" during the fine-tuning process. Being a binary classification task, we used Precision, Recall, and F1 metrics to evaluate the model's ability to say "*Yes*" or "*No*". The overall model performance is measured using Macro-F1 scores. Observing the results in Table 2, which includes model responses in the form of Yes/No, the `LLaMA2Chat-13b-EN` model reflects the results from [11] and is used as a reference. Its F1 Positive score is 96.43% when asserting its ability to recognize commands consistent with the environment. However, its performance decreases when ambiguous commands need clarifications, resulting in an overall Macro-F1 of 81.80%. This is plausible given the dataset's imbalance, with only 13% of cases expecting a "*No*". Leveraging the multi-lingual capabilities of the LLaMA2 model, we validated its behavior on Italian data without further tuning: performance dropped significantly (Macro-F1 of 47.18%), highlighting the difficulty in identifying ambiguous commands (F1 Neg is 24.29%). Nonetheless, this is an interesting result, as in 24.29% of cases, the system, likely inspired by some similarities between English and Italian terms like "*destroy*"/"*distruggere*" or "*blue*"/"*blu*" and the common vision model, manages to (rarely) respond correctly. Finally, a fairer evaluation was conducted by assessing the model trained on Italian-translated data, `LLaMA2Chat-13b-IT`, on the Italian test data: it is interesting to note that not only this model does achieve comparable quality to the English version in correctly identifying when a command is executable or ambiguous, but it shows also a slightly higher Macro-F1. Moreover, the model's quality in correctly identifying an ambiguous command in the Italian test more than doubled compared to its English counterpart (F1 Neg: 66.67% vs 24.29%). Finally, we evaluated the models in a generation setup where the task is to produce a complete phrase, either affirming the command or generating a clarification if the command is ambiguous. Table 3 presents the results for this task. The `LLaMA2Chat-13b-EN` model, trained and tested in English, shows an F1 Positive score of 93.95% and an F1 Negative score of 47.89%, resulting in a Macro-F1 of 70.92%. This model serves as our baseline. When the same model is applied to the Italian test set without any further tuning, its performance drops significantly, with an F1 Positive score of 70.01%, an F1 Negative score of 0.00%, and a Macro-F1 of 35.00%. This indicates that the model struggles significantly with ambiguous commands in Italian, often failing to generate appropriate clarifications and instead defaulting to incorrect responses. In contrast, the `LLaMA2Chat-13b-IT` model, fine-tuned on the Italian dataset, performs comparably to the English baseline on the Italian test set. It achieves an F1 Positive score of 93.62% and an F1 Negative score of 44.16%, resulting in a Macro-F1 of 68.89%. In general, a model trained solely on Yes/No responses appears more effective in recognizing this specific task, suggesting, as in [11], that an effective system should still use a multi-step approach: first, determine if the command is ambiguous, and second, generate the necessary clarification if the command is recognized as ambiguous. In summary, the results indicate that while the LLaMA2Chat-13b model trained in English can somewhat handle Italian data due to its multi-lingual capabilities, its performance is mostly divergent and it is significantly enhanced when specifically fine-tuned on the Italian dataset. This underscores the importance of localized training for achieving high performance in different languages, demonstrating the necessity and effectiveness of our MM-IGLU-IT dataset.

Table 3. The Generation performance is divided into F1 of the positive class (the command is clear), F1 of the negative class (the command is ambiguous), and the Macro F1 of the two.

Model name	Tr. Lan	Test Lan	F1 Pos	F1 Neg	M-F1
LLaMA2Chat-13b-EN	EN	EN	93.95%	47.89%	70.92%
LLaMA2Chat-13b-EN	EN	IT	70.01%	0.00%	35.00%
LLaMA2Chat-13b-IT	IT	IT	93.62%	44.16%	68.89%

Evaluating the Generated Clarifications. To evaluate the quality of the generated clarifications, we used the same approach as in [11]. Instead of mea-

Table 4. The categories of "missing" information in the command identified in this work. Each category is described by a question example. A Relaxed Accuracy is computed for each category on the test set.

Category	LLaMA2Chat-13b-IT	LLaMA2Chat-13b-EN
BLOCK	30.00%	60.00%
VERTICAL-HORIZONTAL	50.00%	70.00%
NUMBER	66.67%	55.56%
SQUARE	62.63%	65.79%
COLOR	33.34%	66.67%
DIRECTION	60.00%	80.00%
BLOCK MISSING	27.28%	54.55%
COMPLETE	97.63%	97.11%
OVERALL	92.34%	93.24%

suring the quality of generations in terms of exact accuracy or BLEU scores, we isolated 90 instances where requests were generated: we assessed them using the Relaxed Accuracy metric. This metric determines the percentage of cases where, despite deviations from the original, the generated questions effectively addressed the ambiguity. If the generated query resolved the ambiguity, it was deemed correct; otherwise, it was incorrect. Building on the categorizations introduced in the original MM-IGLU [11], we further analyzed the system's effectiveness in addressing specific missing information classes. In Table 4, Relaxed Accuracy values for LLaMA2Chat-13b-IT are reported along with those for the original English model (LLaMA2Chat-13b-EN), divided by the meta-categories of the questions introduced in the original paper [11]. The results indicate that in both cases, the system achieves a Relaxed Accuracy between 92.34% and 93.24%. These comparable results highlight the utility of MM-IGLU-IT, demonstrating that over 90% of the agent's requests help the hypothetical human user understand what information is missing.

Table 5. Scores for the Utility and Fluency metrics from 1 to 3, where both need to be maximized.

Score	Utility	Fluency
1	*Incorrect classification*	*Not Italian or random Italian words*
2	*The clarification suggests awareness of the task but misses some key aspects*	*Italian with grammatical errors*
3	*Perfect*	*Perfect*

To better understand the utility and naturalness of the generated clarification requests, we enlisted two (human) external annotators unfamiliar with the project's specifics. They received both system-generated and gold-standard examples requiring clarifications, without any indication of the source, shuffled in a random order. Each annotator rated the clarifications on two dimensions: *Utility* and *Fluency*. Utility was scored between 1 and 3 based on the guidelines in the second column of Table 5, capturing the effectiveness of the clarification. Fluency was scored between 1 and 3 based on the criteria in the third column of Table 5, assessing the quality of the Italian writing[5]. The results, presented in Table 6, show that the `LLaMA2chat-13b-IT` model achieved the highest Utility score of 2.79 (out of 3), reflecting its ability to generate relevant questions and address important missing information, albeit with occasional inaccuracies. In terms of Fluency scores, all models performed very well: 2.98 for the Gold Standard annotation and 2.99 for the `LLaMA2chat-13b-IT` model. The generated clarifications are straightforward enough to appear even more useful than those suggested by the original annotators. For example, for the command *"Distruggi 1 blocco e mettine altri 3 in fila"*[6], the expected output is simply *"Distruggere quale blocco?"*[7], while our `LLaMA2-chat-13b-IT` model produces a much more comprehensive question, addressing all crucial points (missing information): *"Quale specifico blocco devo distruggere e quale colore/posizione/direzione deve avere la fila di 3 blocchi?"*[8].

Table 6. Utility and Fluency results for the Gold Standard and the Multi-Modal model (LLaMA2chat-13b-IT).

Dataset	Language	Utility	Fluency
Gold standard	EN	2.16	2.91
`LLaMA2Chat-13b-EN`	EN	2.73	2.99
Gold standard	IT	2.69	2.98
`LLaMA2chat-13b-IT`	IT	2.79	2.99

5   Conclusions

In this paper, we addressed the complexities of Interactive Grounded Language Understanding (IGLU) within the scope of Human-Robot Interaction (HRI). Our investigation focused on the robot's ability to comprehend and execute user instructions, particularly in scenarios with ambiguities or incomplete information. Leveraging the existing MM-IGLU resource, which aims to bridge gaps

---

[5] The inter-annotator agreement was judged to be very good, with a Pearson correlation of 0.81 for Utility and 0.83 for Fluency.

[6] In English *"Destroy 1 block and build another 3 in a row"*.

[7] In English *"Destroy which one block?"*.

[8] In English *"Which specific block should I destroy, and what color/direction/position should the three-block row be?"*.

between user intent and robot understanding, we expanded its applicability to the Italian language. This involved translating and manually validating both commands and clarification questions to ensure accuracy. Our contribution lies in adapting the MM-IGLU resource to Italian and demonstrating that pre-training on English data alone is insufficient for optimal performance. The study showed that fine-tuning the model on Italian commands significantly enhances its effectiveness, underscoring the necessity of language-specific training for multi-modal models. Future research should explore the transition from controlled, synthetic environments to more dynamic and realistic settings. While current computer vision techniques provide robust tools, real-world scenarios pose unique challenges that need addressing. Additionally, evaluating large-scale Multi-Modal LLMs, such as GPT-4, in zero-shot learning scenarios could yield valuable insights.

Acknowledgements. Claudiu Daniel Hromei is a Ph.D. student enrolled in the National Ph.D. in Artificial Intelligence, XXXVII cycle, course on *Health and life sciences*, organized by the Università Campus Bio-Medico di Roma. We acknowledge financial support from the PNRR MUR project PE0000013-FAIR.

References

1. Alayrac, J.B., et al.: Flamingo: a visual language model for few-shot learning. arxiv preprint arXiv:2204.14198 (2022)
2. Aliannejadi, M., Kiseleva, J., Chuklin, A., Dalton, J., Burtsev, M.: Building and evaluating open-domain dialogue corpora with clarifying questions. In: Moens, M.F., Huang, X., Specia, L., Yih, S.W.t. (eds.) Proceedings of the 2021 Conference on Empirical Methods in Natural Language Processing, pp. 4473–4484. Association for Computational Linguistics, Online and Punta Cana, Dominican Republic (2021). https://doi.org/10.18653/v1/2021.emnlp-main.367
3. Aliannejadi, M., Zamani, H., Crestani, F., Croft, W.B.: Asking clarifying questions in open-domain information-seeking conversations. arXiv preprint arXiv:1907.06554 (2019)
4. Brown, T.B., et al.: Language models are few-shot learners. arXiv preprint arXiv:2005.14165 (2020)
5. Croce, D., Passaro, L.C., Lenci, A., Basili, R.: GQA-it: Italian question answering on image scene graphs. In: Fersini, E., Passarotti, M., Patti, V. (eds.) Proceedings of the Eighth Italian Conference on Computational Linguistics, CLiC-it 2021, Milan, Italy, January 26-28, 2022. CEUR Workshop Proceedings, vol. 3033. CEUR-WS.org (2021). http://ceur-ws.org/Vol-3033/paper42.pdf
6. Devlin, J., Chang, M., Lee, K., Toutanova, K.: BERT: pre-training of deep bidirectional transformers for language understanding. In: Burstein, J., Doran, C., Solorio, T. (eds.) Proceedings of the NAACL 2019, pp. 4171–4186 (2019)
7. He, P., Liu, X., Gao, J., Chen, W.: DeBERTa: decoding-enhanced BERT with disentangled attention. In: 9th International Conference on Learning Representations, ICLR 2021, Virtual Event, Austria, May 3-7, 2021 (2021)
8. Hermann, K.M., et al.: Teaching machines to read and comprehend. In: Cortes, C., Lawrence, N., Lee, D., Sugiyama, M., Garnett, R. (eds.) Advances in Neural Information Processing Systems, vol. 28. Curran Associates, Inc. (2015)

9. Hong, W., et al.: CogAgent: a visual language model for GUI agents. arXiv preprint arXiv:2312.08914 (2023)
10. Hromei, C.D., Croce, D., Basile, V., Basili, R.: ExtremITA at EVALITA 2023: multi-task sustainable scaling to large language models at its extreme. In: Proceedings of the Eighth Evaluation Campaign of Natural Language Processing and Speech Tools for Italian. Final Workshop (EVALITA 2023). CEUR.org, Parma, Italy (2023)
11. Hromei, C.D., Margiotta, D., Croce, D., Basili, R.: MM-IGLU: multi-modal interactive grounded language understanding. In: Calzolari, N., Kan, M.Y., Hoste, V., Lenci, A., Sakti, S., Xue, N. (eds.) Proceedings of the 2024 Joint International Conference on Computational Linguistics, Language Resources and Evaluation, LREC-COLING 2024, pp. 11440–11451. ELRA and ICCL, Torino, Italia (2024). https://aclanthology.org/2024.lrec-main.1000
12. Kiseleva, J., et al.: Interactive grounded language understanding in a collaborative environment: IGLU 2021. In: NeurIPS 2021 Competitions and Demonstrations Track, pp. 146–161. PMLR (2022)
13. Kiseleva, J., et al.: IGLU 2022: Interactive grounded language understanding in a collaborative environment at NeurIPS 2022 (2022)
14. Koh, J.Y., Salakhutdinov, R., Fried, D.: Grounding language models to images for multimodal inputs and outputs. In: Proceedings of the 40th International Conference on Machine Learning. ICML'23, JMLR.org (2023)
15. Kojima, N., Suhr, A., Artzi, Y.: Continual learning for grounded instruction generation by observing human following behavior. Trans. Assoc. Comput. Linguistics 9 (2021).https://doi.org/10.1162/tacl_a_00428
16. Kriangchaivech, K., Wangperawong, A.: Question generation by transformers. arXiv preprint arXiv:1909.05017 (2019)
17. Laurençon, H., et al.: Obelics: an open web-scale filtered dataset of interleaved image-text documents. arXiv preprint arXiv:2306.16527 (2023)
18. Lewis, M., et al.: BART: denoising sequence-to-sequence pre-training for natural language generation, translation, and comprehension. arXiv preprint arXiv:1910.13461 (2019)
19. Liu, D., Lin, C.: Sherlock: a semi-automatic quiz generation system using linked data. In: International Semantic Web Conference (Posters & Demos), pp. 9-12. Citeseer (2014)
20. Liu, H., Li, C., Wu, Q., Lee, Y.J.: Visual instruction tuning. In: Oh, A., Naumann, T., Globerson, A., Saenko, K., Hardt, M., Levine, S. (eds.) Advances in Neural Information Processing Systems, vol. 36, pp. 34892–34916. Curran Associates, Inc. (2023)
21. Liu, Y., et al.: RoBERTa: a robustly optimized BERT pretraining approach. arXiv preprint arXiv:1907.11692 (2019)
22. Lopez, L.E., Cruz, D.K., Cruz, J.C.B., Cheng, C.: Transformer-based end-to-end question generation. arXiv preprint arXiv:2005.01107 (2020)
23. Mirowski, P., Mathewson, K.W., Pittman, J., Evans, R.: Co-writing screenplays and theatre scripts with language models: an evaluation by industry professionals. arXiv preprint arXiv:2209.14958 (2022)
24. Mitkov, R., Ha, L.A.: Computer-aided generation of multiple-choice tests. In: Proceedings of the HLT-NAACL 03 Workshop on Building Educational Applications Using Natural Language Processing, pp. 17–22 (2003). https://aclanthology.org/W03-0203

25. Narayan-Chen, A., et al.: Towards problem solving agents that communicate and learn. In: Proceedings of the First Workshop on Language Grounding for Robotics. Association for Computational Linguistics, Vancouver, Canada (2017). https://doi.org/10.18653/v1/W17-2812
26. OpenAI: GPT-4 technical report (2023)
27. Papineni, K., Roukos, S., Ward, T., Zhu, W.J.: Bleu: a method for automatic evaluation of machine translation. In: Isabelle, P., Charniak, E., Lin, D. (eds.) Proceedings of the 40th Annual Meeting of the Association for Computational Linguistics, pp. 311–318. Association for Computational Linguistics, Philadelphia, Pennsylvania, USA (2002). https://doi.org/10.3115/1073083.1073135
28. Pustejovsky, J., Krishnaswamy, N.: Multimodal semantics for affordances and actions. In: Kurosu, M. (ed.) Human-Computer Interaction: Theoretical Approaches and Design Methods, pp. 137–160. Springer, Cham (2022)
29. Radford, A., et al.: Learning transferable visual models from natural language supervision. arXiv preprint arXiv:2103.00020 (2021)
30. Radford, A., Narasimhan, K., Salimans, T., Sutskever, I., et al.: Improving language understanding by generative pre-training (2018)
31. Raffel, C., et al.: Exploring the limits of transfer learning with a unified text-to-text transformer. J. Mach. Learn. Res. **21**, 140:1–140:67 (2020). http://jmlr.org/papers/v21/20-074.html
32. Rajpurkar, P., Zhang, J., Lopyrev, K., Liang, P.: SQuAD: 100,000+ questions for machine comprehension of text. In: Proceedings of the 2016 Conference on Empirical Methods in Natural Language Processing, pp. 2383–2392. Association for Computational Linguistics, Austin, Texas (2016).https://doi.org/10.18653/v1/D16-1264
33. Rey, G.A. et al.: Semi-automatic generation of quizzes and learning artifacts from linked data. In: Conference: Proceedings of the 2nd International Workshop on Learning and Education with the Web of Data (LiLe2012), co-located with the World Wide Web Conference (WWW2012) (2012)
34. Rus, V., Wyse, B., Piwek, P., Lintean, M., Stoyanchev, S., Moldovan, C.: The first question generation shared task evaluation challenge. In: Kelleher, J., Namee, B.M., Sluis, I.v.d. (eds.) Proceedings of the 6th International Natural Language Generation Conference. Association for Computational Linguistics (2010). https://aclanthology.org/W10-4234
35. Su, D., et al.: Generalizing question answering system with pre-trained language model fine-tuning. In: Proceedings of the 2nd Workshop on Machine Reading for Question Answering. Association for Computational Linguistics, Hong Kong, China (2019). https://doi.org/10.18653/v1/D19-5827
36. Touvron, H., et al.: Llama: open and efficient foundation language models. arXiv preprint arXiv:2302.13971 (2023)
37. Vaswani, A., et al.: Attention is all you need. In: Guyon, I., et al. (eds.) Advances in Neural Information Processing Systems, vol. 30. Curran Associates, Inc. (2017)
38. Winograd, T.: Procedures as a representation for data in a computer program for understanding natural language, Technical report, Massachusetts Inst of Tech Cambridge Project Mac (1971)
39. Zhu, D., Chen, J., Shen, X., Li, X., Elhoseiny, M.: MiniGPT-4: enhancing vision-language understanding with advanced large language models. arXiv preprint arXiv:2304.10592 (2023)

IDADA: A Blended Inductive-Deductive Approach for Data Augmentation

Pierangela Bruno$^{(\boxtimes)}$ (iD), Francesco Calimeri$^{(\boxtimes)}$ (iD), Francesca Filice$^{(\boxtimes)}$ (iD), Cinzia Marte$^{(\boxtimes)}$ (iD), and Simona Perri$^{(\boxtimes)}$ (iD)

Department of Mathematics and Computer Science, Via P. Bucci, Rende 87036, Italy
{pierangela.bruno,francesco.calimeri,cinzia.marte,simona.perri}@unical.it,
filicefrancesca.ff@gmail.com

Abstract. This work proposes a hybrid approach to Data Augmentation that blends inductive and deductive reasoning. In particular, the approach effectively utilizes a modest collection of labeled images while employing logic programs to declaratively define the structure of new images, allowing for flexible and dynamic image generation; the use of logic programming ensures adherence to both domain-specific constraints and given desiderata. The resulting structures are then used for guiding the generation of new realistic images based on a dedicated Deep-Learning process. The general approach can be particularly of use in biomedical and healthcare scenarios, where building extensive datasets of quality images is in general a hard prerequisite for many applications that is challenging to meet. The approach is specialized to two real-world case studies featuring laryngeal endoscopic and cataract images, respectively, and experiments conducted for assessing the method are discussed.

Keywords: Data Augmentation · Hybrid Approaches · Deep Learning · Deductive Reasoning · Inductive Reasoning

1 Introduction

In recent years, Deep Learning (DL) applications have gained significant attention for their impressive results in various fields such as image processing, pattern recognition, object recognition [27,32]. However, these methodologies depend on models that require training on proper background knowledge, which must be represented in datasets that are adequate in terms of size, quality, and various other factors. Obtaining a substantial amount of "good" training data can be challenging in certain domains; this is particularly common in biomedicine, due to factors such as accessibility, costs, manual annotation effort, data availability, and class imbalance. To address this challenge, data augmentation techniques have been extensively researched to enrich and enhance poor datasets. Generative models like Generative Adversarial Networks (GANs) have been proposed, in particular to create synthetic yet realistic images, showing significant potential. However, these approaches also suffer from drawbacks and limitations. For

A. Artale et al. (Eds.): AIxIA 2024, LNAI 15450, pp. 79–91, 2025.
https://doi.org/10.1007/978-3-031-80607-0_7

instance, their training can be unstable and slow [16]; moreover, guiding feature extraction and image generation typically relies on the composition and adaptation of the training dataset, making it challenging to leverage available knowledge and express preferences for data generation. Nonetheless, such knowledge can be valuable in avoiding the generation of erroneous images, reducing generation times, and enhancing overall result quality by ensuring reliable generation of images aligned with specific criteria.

In this work, we present IDADA, a framework blending inductive and deductive strategies for data augmentation. IDADA relies on Answer Set Programming (ASP), a purely declarative formalism rooted in logic programming and non-monotonic reasoning [4,17,18]. ASP offers explainability by design, suitability for complex Knowledge Representation and Reasoning (KRR) tasks, and benefits from available efficient implementations [22]; its use for data augmentation facilitates the expression of constraints arising from background knowledge and desired features, thus allowing for guiding the automatic generation of new data that comply with domain knowledge.

Currently, IDADA focuses on image data generation. Basically, starting from a set of real (or realistic) images, IDADA: (*i*) identifies (at a semantic level) a set of distinctive elements that are supposed to be present in the images to be created; (*ii*) produces a knowledge base by encoding in ASP needed domain knowledge along with constraints and desiderata about how the new images should appear, in terms of the identified elements; (*iii*) generates a number of image structures by placing instances of distinctive elements and arranging them according to the encoded knowledge base, thus obtaining new labeled images (that are, essentially, semantically segmented images); (*iv*) employs DL methods to "fill" the image areas, thus producing plausible synthetic images based on the labeled image structures already generated.

To the best of our knowledge, this work represents one of the pioneering attempts in using Answer Set Programming (ASP) for medical image generation and augmentation.

We experiment with IDADA for generating synthetic images in two biomedical scenarios: cataract images starting from the Cataract Dataset (CaDIS) [19] and laryngeal endoscopic images, starting from the Laryngeal Endoscopic Dataset [25]. The results are encouraging, and demonstrate the effectiveness of IDADA in enabling the generation of new images based on declaratively expressed criteria.

The remainder of the paper is structured as described next. In Sect. 2 we provide some background and discuss related works, before introducing IDADA, the herein proposed framework for data augmentation, in Sect. 3. In Sect. 4 we report on the result of the experimental campaign, and eventually present our conclusion and briefly discuss future perspectives in Sect. 5.

2   Related Work

Image data augmentation techniques have been widely studied in the literature and used in state-of-the-art solutions to reduce overfitting, increase generalizability, and overcome the lack of data or other limitations that could affect algorithm performance. Indeed, data augmentation: (i) results in general much less expensive than regular data collection with its label annotation; (ii) can be extremely accurate (it is generated from ground-truth data); (iii) is controllable, to some extent, in generating balanced data [23].

Typically, image data augmentation is performed relying on "classical" strategies or methods based on DL techniques. In the first case, geometric transformation (i.e., flipping, rotation, shearing, cropping, translation in the geometric transformation) and photometric shifting (i.e., color space shifting, image filtering, addition of noise) are applied to existing available images in order to enrich the collection [23]. However, these techniques present some disadvantages, including memory consumption, transformation costs, and additional training time. Also, some strategies, such as photometric shifting, can produce the eliminations of important color information or specific features in the image, thus not always guaranteeing the preservation of nature and meaning of the image labels [29]. Hence, DL-based methods have been increasingly employed. Indeed, DL methods, especially Generative Adversarial Networks (GAN)-based ones, represent a huge breakthrough in image generation, due to the ability to generate artificial images from an initial dataset and then make use of them to "predict" image features. GANs are composed of two networks: a *generator* network, that creates tentative fake images, and a *discriminator* network, that aims at identifying whether the generated images are indicative of real-world evidence or not [1]. Nevertheless, GANs are inherently unstable, and suffer from both the lack of meaningful measures to evaluate the quality of their result and limited sample generation capabilities when only a little representative of the population is available.

In the biomedical context, the availability of huge datasets is a major concern: it is indeed a difficult task, as it requires continuous efforts, especially in the long term. Recent advancements in deep learning have shown promising results in classifying pathologies and segmenting medical images [5,9,20,21]. However, these improvements necessitate a consistent and diverse dataset for effective training, highlighting the urgent issue of data scarcity and the need for effective solutions. Image data augmentation techniques address this limitation by generating additional medical images, which can be used to design and refine automated assessment methods for pathological conditions. By doing so, these techniques assist healthcare providers in identifying the most appropriate preventive interventions and therapeutic strategies without relying solely on large medical datasets [12].

Kossen et al. [24] used GANs to create synthetic brain data and corresponding labels, showing good performance in the arterial brain vessel segmentation task. Similarly, Toikkanen et al. [31] used GAN to improve the quality of the predictive model in localizing the hemorrhage from computerized tomography (CT) scans. Synthetic samples from generative models have been demonstrated to alleviate the in-balance and scarcity of labeled training issues. In the same context, Zhai et al. [33] proposed a novel asymmetric semi-supervised GAN (ASSGAN) to

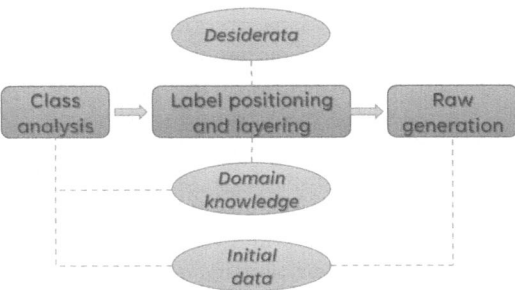

Fig. 1. IDADA Workflow: The process begins with analyzing the classes to identify dynamic and static classes based on the initial data. Next, it computes the label positioning for each dynamic class and generates a comprehensive label encompassing all classes, according to the desired criteria and domain knowledge. Finally, a photo-realistic raw image referencing the initial data is created.

generate reliable segmentation-predicted masks. The authors show that in the absence of labeled data, the network can make use of unlabeled data to improve segmentation performance.

ASP can be used to declaratively express quantitative and qualitative desiderata as well as content generation strategies, providing one with the possibility to easily increment, modify, and update new knowledge at will. Among the different applications, ASP has also been explored in the realm of scheduling, where it can optimize resource allocation and improve operational efficiency [13–15]. Moreover, ASP has been applied in the improvement of medical image segmentation and quality (e.g., [6,7]), although these efforts primarily focus on enhancing existing images rather than generating new ones. Other logic-based contributions have emerged in the related field of Content Generation, where, for example, ASP has been employed to produce game content with desirable properties [11,28,30]. To the best of our knowledge, IDADA, a work inspired by [8], represents one of the first logic-based approaches specifically designed for image data augmentation.

3   The IDADA Framework

In this section we introduce IDADA, a framework built upon an Inductive-Deductive Approach for Data Augmentation. We start by illustrating the general workflow; then, we discuss a more detailed application to a specific case study.

3.1   Workflow

The workflow of the proposed framework is illustrated in Fig. 1. At the first step, original images are analyzed in order to find all possible featured objects. Thus, a number of classes are identified collecting such objects, and are properly assigned with a label. Note that, depending on the specific scenario, this phase might require the availability of proper domain knowledge. Hence, two kinds of classes are defined, producing a grouping of all possible objects into two categories: *dynamic classes*, featuring objects that can significantly vary from image to image (e.g., size, position, shape, orientation, etc.); and *static classes*, which can be basically considered "fixed" due to their minimal variation across different images.

The second step focuses on dynamic classes, and consists of the generation of new eligible combinations (in terms of position or other spatial features) of objects of such classes. To achieve this, we rely on Answer Set Programming (ASP) to declaratively express how such combinations must be performed. In particular, ad hoc ASP programs produce proper label positioning in images, according to given requirements that can be related to both absolute location and relative positioning/layering of objects of dynamic classes within the image itself. The output is basically a set of (labeled) image structures. Notably, the declarative ASP-based approach allows us to easily integrate the domain knowledge and custom criteria to which all generated image structures and labels must comply.

The last step consists of the generation of new raw images corresponding to the previously created labels (i.e.: if semantically segmented, the raw images match the corresponding labels produced earlier); in particular, the final result is a set of images that: (*i*) differ from the original ones in terms of position of dynamic classes; (*ii*) comply with all the specified criteria (both domain knowledge and custom desiderata); (*iii*) are photo-realistic and can be used for augmenting the original dataset.

3.2   IDADA at Work

In the following we illustrate the application of the framework on a case study: the Cataract Dataset for Image Segmentation (CaDIS) [19].

Class Analysis. As introduced above, the first step requires to analyze the dataset with the aim of identifying the classes comprising all elements possibly featured in the images. In general, this would benefit from proper domain knowledge and potentially even interactions with domain experts, for correctly performing semantic segmentation. As for the CaDIS dataset, this information is already available, as each of the 4670 raw frames extracted from 25 videos of cataract surgery is paired with a semantic labelling annotated by experts (from this point onward, they will be referred to as "original labelling" for ease of reading). In particular, images comprise 36 classes: 29 surgical instrument classes, 4 anatomy classes, and 3 miscellaneous classes.

The analysis was completed by determining, for each class, whether it should be considered dynamic; the choice for each class is made based on prior knowledge and input from domain experts. In this case, we checked how classes change across images (in doing this, given that this is a medical domain, we relied both on the labeled images and the raw frames). Specifically, in the CaDIS dataset, the *pupil*, the *iris*, and the *surgical instruments* classes are considered as dynamic classes, while the classes *cornea*, *skin*, *surgical tape*, and *eye retractors* are considered as static ones.

Next, the actual input for the next step in the framework is prepared. In particular, each label corresponding to a dynamic class is extracted to generate a segmentation for that specific class (referred to as binary segmentation). All the binary segmentations of each dynamic class are collected together to create a representative dataset of the possible shapes assumed by that specific object, which will be layered with the other labels afterward to create a new label. Figure 2 shows an example of classification comprising the classes iris and pupil. Specifically, starting from the original label (Fig. 2 (a)), the static classes are selected and fixed as background (Fig. 2 (b)). In contrast, the dynamic ones, (i.e., iris and pupil) are split into single binary segmentation (Fig. 2 (c) and (d), respectively).

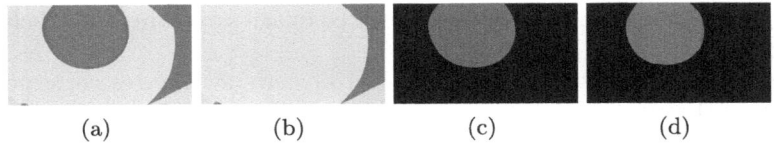

(a)	(b)	(c)	(d)

Fig. 2. Example of class analysis: (a) original label; (b) static classes considered as fixed background; (c) iris and (d) pupil, as dynamic classes, split in single binary segmentation.

Label Positioning and Layering. At the second step, we make use of an ad-hoc ASP program for managing combinations and layering of labels. The design of this stage can vary significantly, depending on the specific domain and the type of images one aims to generate, to the greatest extent. In this regard, the flexibility of ASP in Knowledge Representation and Reasoning is extremely beneficial.

In the following, we describe how we approach the problem in the chosen domain; we assume that the reader is familiar with the basic notions of the ASP language and refer to [10] for details.

As already mentioned, the main task in this phase consists in the design of proper ASP programs encoding the needed knowledge. For the case of images in the CaDIS dataset, we built an ASP program that takes as input labels of size 540×960 pixels, represented as matrices of the same size. Matrix elements are modeled by facts of the form cell(R, C, CLASS), where variables R, C, and CLASS are mapped to rows and columns of the matrix and the class associated to that cell, respectively. The output produces a new valid positioning of the objects in the image, represented by atoms of the form new_cell(R, C, CLASS), denoting the class CLASS that is contained in each cell (R,C). In order to effectively express viable choices for the new positions of objects, the idea is to identify a specific number of "pivot points", which can vary depending on the object.

These pivot points are then used to accurately reposition the object within the image. The repositioning approach takes into account the hierarchical relationships between classes, determining the sequence in which each class should appear based on prior knowledge or desiderata. This also dictates the order in which the final label is reassembled. In the case of discourse, i.e., cataract images, the process begins with the fixed background layer, followed by the addition of the iris layer, and finally the placement of the pupil layer on top. Each label corresponds to a layer that contributes to the final image. For the pupil and iris classes, we opted to identify 12 pivot points situated along the contour of both the pupil and iris classes, thus simplifying the modeling of their shapes and positions. More in detail, we first guess four main pivots, one for each cardinal point, by means of the following choice rules [10]:

```
{pivot(R,C,3,pupil) : max_col(C,pupil), cell(R,C,pupil)} = 1.
{pivot(R,C,6,pupil) : max_row(R,pupil), cell(R,C,pupil)} = 1.
{pivot(R,C,9,pupil) : min_col(C,pupil), cell(R,C,pupil)} = 1.
{pivot(R,C,12,pupil) : min_row(R,pupil), cell(R,C,pupil)} = 1.
```

where predicates `max_col(C,pupil)`, `max_row(R,pupil)`, `min_col(C,pupil)`, and `min_row(R,pupil)` represent the column C and the row R having the maximum (resp., minimum) index cell containing the class pupil. The remaining eight pivots are then identified as follows: we derive two additional pivots from each pair of adjacent main pivots $(3 - 6, 6 - 9, 9 - 12, 12 - 3)$ by first calculating the difference between the rows and columns of the considered pair; one of the two pivots corresponds to the cell lying on the contour of the pupil with a row equal to the midpoint between the rows of the two main pivots. Similarly, the remaining pivot is calculated using the same reasoning applied to the columns.

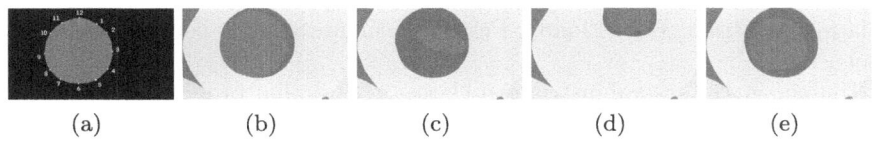

(a)   (b)   (c)   (d)   (e)

Fig. 3. Example of positioning and layering of iris and pupil classes: (a) identification of pivot points for the pupil, (b) incorrect layering of the pupil on top of the iris, (c) incorrect shape and proportion of the pupil relative to the iris, (d) incorrect proportion of the iris relative to the cornea, and (e) correct positioning and layering of the pupil and iris.

We point out that the identification of the pivot points is crucial for understanding, for instance, the object inclination, and thus for selecting (via choice rules) from the representative dataset the appropriate label for the construction of the new image. This process is essential for accurate image generation.

Next, we define the following constraints to ensure that the construction of the image follows the (medical) domain knowledge:

(c_1) :- pivot(R,C,_,pupil), not cell(R,C,iris).
(c_2) :- pivot(R,C,_,iris), not cell(R,C,cornea).
(c_3) :- centers_distance(D), D > 70.
(c_4) :- width(WP,pupil), width(WI,iris), height(HP,pupil),
        height(HI,iris), WP > HP*WI/HI + 80.
(c_5) :- width(WP,pupil), width(WI,iris), height(HP,pupil),
        height(HI,iris), WP < HP*WI/HI - 80.
(c_6) :- area(AI,iris), area(AC,cornea), R = AC/AI, R > 4.

Here, (c_1) ensures that the pupil lies on the iris. (c_2) forces all of the *iris* class pivots to lie on a cell of the *cornea* class. (c_3) forbids the generation of images where the pupil is not properly centered with respect to the iris. Specifically, the predicate centers_distance(D) stands for the distance D, expressed in pixel, between the pupil's and the iris' centers. We impose this distance not to exceed an empirically chosen threshold, which amounts to 70 pixel. (c_4) and (c_5) force the iris and the pupil to have similar shapes. The predicates width and height indicate, for both pupil and iris, the width and height, respectively; for ensuring that their dimensions are proportionate, we impose an empirical tolerance of ± 80 pixels. (c_6) ensures that the proportion between the iris and cornea is correctly observed. We use the predicate area to address the area of the iris and cornea; we then force that the cornea area is at most 4 times the iris area. Figure 3 illustrates the application of the approach to the iris and pupil classes. The ASP program generates the twelve pivot points for the pupil class (Fig. 3 (a)), ensuring (thanks to the modelled constraints) that the pupil's positioning over the iris aligns with domain knowledge. For instance, Fig. 3 (b) depicts a pupil incorrectly positioned on the iris, violating constraint (c_1). Figure 3 (c) shows a pupil with incorrect shape and proportion placed over the iris, violating constraints (c_4) and (c_5). Figure 3 (d) shows an iris with incorrect proportion relative to the cornea, violating constraint (c_6). Finally, Fig. 3 (e) demonstrates a correctly generated label.

To manage the several instrument classes with similar properties, we grouped 26 out of the 29 instrument classes into seven categories, and the remaining three classes into class *eye retractors*, which is identified as a fixed class and is already part of the background, whereas the remaining two classes *iris hooks* and *marker* required special pre-processing. Since multiple instances of the same instrument often appear in a single image, we defined a pre-processing used to increase the number of labels depicting the available instruments: in particular, we generated separate binary segmentation for each instance using Python and ASP scripts.

The modeling of surgical instruments follows the strategy described above, including identifying the pivot point(s) and choosing an appropriate binary segmentation to add to the image we are creating.

The interested reader can find all material at https://github.com/DeMaCS-UNICAL/Data-augmentation-via-ASP.

Raw Generation. At this step, the goal is to create realistic images that comply with the semantically-guided image structure generation. To this aim, in this case we use SPADE (Semantic Image Synthesis With Spatially-Adaptive Normalization) [26], a state-of-the-art paired-data technique, for generating proper textures for each image part. SPADE processes the input semantic layout (defining parts or objects and their spatial relationships) using convolution, normalization, and nonlinearity layers. In SPADE, the mask is projected onto an embedding space and convolved to produce modulation parameters, which are tensors with spatial dimensions. These tensors are multiplied and added to the normalized activation element-wise. We used the same configuration as the original authors [26], i.e., learning rates of 0.0001 for the generator, 0.0004 for the discriminator, and ADAM optimizer, and trained the network for 100 epochs.

4   Experimental Analysis

In order to assess the overall effectiveness of the IDADA approach to data augmentation, along with its versatility when dealing with different scenarios, we tested the presented framework over two very diverse real datasets. In particular, besides the already mentioned CaDIS dataset that features cataract images, we considered also the Laryngeal Endoscopic Images dataset [25]. Just like for the CaDIS dataset, also for this case all material is completely available at https://github.com/DeMaCS-UNICAL/Data-augmentation-via-ASP.

The Laryngeal Endoscopic Images dataset contains 536 manually segmented *in vivo* color images of the larynx, captured from videos recorded during two resection surgeries. The images include seven classes: *void, vocal folds, other tissue, glottal space, pathology, surgical tool,* and *intubation.* The dataset includes eight sequences from two patients, categorized into five different groups based on the features exhibited by the images. We divided the classes into two categories based on their relevance. In particular, we designated *vocal folds, glottal space,* and *other tissue* as static classes, as their shapes and appearances remain relatively consistent across different images. In contrast, we focused on the *pathology, intubation,* and *surgical tool* classes, chosen as dynamic classes.

In both the scenarios of test, IDADA proved to be a viable approach for agumenting the image datasets, granting coherence with background knowledge, compliance with custom desiderata and similarity of the final results. This is particularly encouraging, especially noting that the two case studies significantly differ to a large extent. For a qualitative evaluation of our approach, we showcase selected results in Fig. 4. The examples illustrate the effectiveness of our method in generating images that closely match the originals.

For the sake of reproducibility and transparency, all results of our experiments can be found at https://github.com/DeMaCS-UNICAL/Data-augmentation-via-ASP.

Furthermore, besides considerations about the viability of the approach and qualitative assessments, we also wanted to perform a more formal analysis. In particular, we wanted to quantitatively evaluate the similarity between the original images and the generated synthetic ones. To this aim, we used the Kernel Inception Distance (KID) [2]. KID is typically used for measuring the quality of

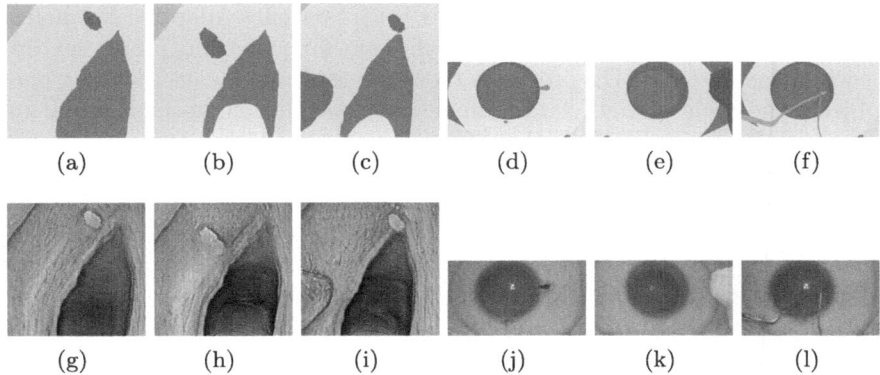

Fig. 4. Examples of laryngeal endoscopic images (a-g,b-h,c-i) and cataract images (d-j,e-k,f-l) obtained by IDADA. Labeled images and the corresponding raw ones are reported in the first and second row, respectively.

generative models [3] by comparing the distributions of generated and real images using the squared Maximum Mean Discrepancy (MMD) with a polynomial kernel. Lower KID scores indicate higher similarity and better quality of generated images. KID is advantageous for its unbiased nature and reliability, particularly with smaller sample sizes. On the CaDIS dataset, the resulting KID score is 0.10, indicating a very high level of similarity. This proves the quality of the results obtained by means of IDADA, due to both the semantically-guided label generation pervormed via ASP and SPADE's impressive capability to capture the nuanced characteristics of the original data, along with robustness and precision in generating high-fidelity images from labels. Similarly, on the vocal folds dataset, the KID score of 0.26 shows a commendable level of similarity between the generated and original images. While slightly higher than the CaDIS score, this still reflects a strong performance of SPADE, effectively capturing many important features of the original images; on the overall, results underscore its versatility and effectiveness across different datasets. The significant performance on CaDIS, combined with the solid results on vocal folds, suggests that the use of ASP for label generation combined with SPADE for finishing the raw images make IDADA a powerful and reliable tool for generating realistic images from original (potentially limited) datasets.

5   Conclusion and Perspectives

In this paper we presented IDADA, a framework aimed at enabling the declarative specification of data augmentation processes. In particular, we relied on Answer Set Programming (ASP) to guide the generation of realistic images within the biomedical domain. Our methodology involves collecting a dataset of labeled images and identifying the static and dynamic classes to work exclusively with those classes that show a significant change in the images; this allows for more efficient processing and enhances the relevance of the generated images. Using ASP reasoning tasks, we generate new labeled images by detailing the possible appearances of these elements and composing the output appropriately. The newly created semantically labeled images are used as input for proper DL-based methods, which then produce the final pseudo-realistic images.

We assessed the effectiveness of IDADA using images from two distinct datasets, featuring cataract and laryngeal endoscopic images, respectively, yielding promising results. The experiments show that declarative specifications can be seamlessly integrated into the image data augmentation process.

It is worth noting that ASP-encoded specifications allow us to incorporate both domain knowledge and desiderata, providing significant customization capabilities for generating new raw images. The approach eliminates the need for manually finding, collecting, and adapting data within a domain (e.g., surgical images with a specified number of instruments or particular organ positions). Furthermore, ASP grants robustness in handling knowledge updates, for instance allowing easy modifications of logic programs to change the number of elements in a given class or to adjust spatial relationships among elements (e.g., generating images with different numbers of instruments).

On a broader scale, incorporating ASP as the declarative formalism within the data augmentation process enables the collection and translation of declarative specifications (i.e., logic programs) into properly generated labeled images suitable for DL methods. With this respect, SPADE, in particular, has shown satisfactory results, producing realistic raw images that accurately correspond to their labeled counterparts.

Future work will focus on conducting experimental campaigns to evaluate the quality of the generated images in relation to specific tasks in the biomedical domain, and to assess the performance of our approach on additional datasets.

Acknowledgements. This work has been partially supported by: PNRR project FAIR - Future AI Research (PE00000013), Spoke 9 - Green-aware AI, under the NRRP MUR program funded by the "NextGenerationEU"; PNRR project Tech4You "Technologies for climate change adaptation and quality of life improvement", CUP H23C22000370006, under the NRRP MUR program funded by the "NextGenerationEU"; PON "Ricerca e Innovazione" 2014–2020, CUP: H25F21001230004. Francesco Calimeri is member of the Gruppo Nazionale Calcolo Scientifico-Istituto Nazionale di Alta Matematica (GNCS-INdAM).

References

1. Aggarwal, A., Mittal, M., Battineni, G.: Generative adversarial network: an overview of theory and applications. Int. J. Inf. Manag. Data Insights **1**(1), 100004 (2021)
2. Bińkowski, M., Sutherland, D.J., Arbel, M., Gretton, A.: Demystifying mmd gans. arXiv preprint arXiv:1801.01401 (2018)
3. Böhland, M., Bruch, R., Löffler, K., Reischl, M.: Unsupervised GAN epoch selection for biomedical data synthesis. In: Current Directions in Biomedical Engineering, vol. 9, pp. 467–470. De Gruyter (2023)

4. Brewka, G., Eiter, T., Truszczynski, M.: Answer set programming at a glance. Commun. ACM **54**(12), 92–103 (2011). https://doi.org/10.1145/2043174.2043195
5. Bruno, P., Calimeri, F., Kitanidis, A.S., De Momi, E.: Understanding automatic diagnosis and classification processes with data visualization. In: 2020 IEEE International Conference on Human-machine Systems (ICHMS), pp. 1–6. IEEE (2020)
6. Bruno, P., Calimeri, F., Marte, C.: DeduDeep: an extensible framework for combining deep learning and asp-based models. In: Logic Programming and Nonmonotonic Reasoning: 16th International Conference, LPNMR 2022, Genova, Italy, September 5–9, 2022, Proceedings, pp. 505–510. Springer (2022)
7. Bruno, P., Calimeri, F., Marte, C., Manna, M.: Combining deep learning and asp-based models for the semantic segmentation of medical images. In: Rules and Reasoning: 5th International Joint Conference, RuleML+ RR 2021, Leuven, Belgium, September 13–15, 2021, Proceedings 5, pp. 95–110. Springer (2021)
8. Bruno, P., Calimeri, F., Marte, C., Perri, S.: Data augmentation: a combined inductive-deductive approach featuring answer set programming. arXiv preprint arXiv:2310.14413 (2023)
9. Bruno, P., et al.: Assessing vascular complexity of PAOD patients by deep learning-based segmentation and fractal dimension. Neural Comput. Appl. **34**(24), 22015–22022 (2022)
10. Calimeri, F., et al.: Asp-core-2 input language format. Theory Pract. Log. Program. **20**(2), 294–309 (2020). https://doi.org/10.1017/S1471068419000450
11. Calimeri, F., Germano, S., Ianni, G., Pacenza, F., Pezzimenti, A., Tucci, A.: Answer set programming for declarative content specification: a scalable partitioning-based approach. In: Ghidini, C., Magnini, B., Passerini, A., Traverso, P. (eds.) AI*IA 2018 - Advances in Artificial Intelligence - XVIIth International Conference of the Italian Association for Artificial Intelligence, Trento, Italy, November 20-23, 2018, Proceedings. Lecture Notes in Computer Science, vol. 11298, pp. 225–237. Springer (2018). https://doi.org/10.1007/978-3-030-03840-3_17
12. Chen, Y., et al.: Generative adversarial networks in medical image augmentation: a review. Comput. Biol. Med. **144** 105382 (2022)
13. Dodaro, C., Galatà, G., Gebser, M., Maratea, M., Marte, C., Mochi, M., Scanu, M.: Operating room scheduling via answer set programming: improved encoding and test on real data. J. Logic Comput. exae041 (2024)
14. Dodaro, C., Galatà, G., Marte, C., Maratea, M., Mochi, M.: Nuclear medicine scheduling via answer set programming (2024)
15. Dodaro, C., Maratea, M.: Nurse scheduling via answer set programming. In: Logic Programming and Nonmonotonic Reasoning: 14th International Conference, LPNMR 2017, Espoo, Finland, July 3-6, 2017, Proceedings 14, pp. 301–307. Springer (2017)
16. Durgadevi, M., et al.: Generative adversarial network (GAN): a general review on different variants of GAN and applications. In: 2021 6th International Conference on Communication and Electronics Systems (ICCES), pp. 1–8. IEEE (2021)
17. Eiter, T., Ianni, G., Krennwallner, T.: Answer set programming: a primer. In: Tessaris, S., et al. (eds.) Reasoning Web. Semantic Technologies for Information Systems, 5th International Summer School 2009, Brixen-Bressanone, Italy, August 30 - September 4, 2009, Tutorial Lectures. Lecture Notes in Computer Science, vol. 5689, pp. 40–110. Springer (2009).https://doi.org/10.1007/978-3-642-03754-2_2
18. Gelfond, M., Lifschitz, V.: Classical negation in logic programs and disjunctive databases. N. Gener. Comput. **9**(3/4), 365–386 (1991). https://doi.org/10.1007/BF03037169

19. Grammatikopoulou, M., et al.: Cadis: cataract dataset for surgical RGB-image segmentation. Med. Image Anal. **71**, 102053 (2021)
20. Huang, Y., et al.: Segment anything model for medical images? Med. Image Anal. **92**, 103061 (2024)
21. Jiang, H., et al.: A review of deep learning-based multiple-lesion recognition from medical images: classification, detection and segmentation. Comput. Biol. Med. **157**, 106726 (2023)
22. Kaufmann, B., Leone, N., Perri, S., Schaub, T.: Grounding and solving in answer set programming. AI Mag. **37**(3), 25–32 (2016)
23. Khalifa, N.E., Loey, M., Mirjalili, S.: A comprehensive survey of recent trends in deep learning for digital images augmentation. Artif. Intell. Rev. **55**(3), 2351–2377 (2022)
24. Kossen, T., et al.: Synthesizing anonymized and labeled TOF-MRA patches for brain vessel segmentation using generative adversarial networks. Comput. Biol. Med. **131**, 104254 (2021)
25. Laves, M.H., Bicker, J., Kahrs, L.A., Ortmaier, T.: A dataset of laryngeal endoscopic images with comparative study on convolution neural network-based semantic segmentation. Int. J. Comput. Assist. Radiol. Surg. **14**(3), 483–492 (2019)
26. Park, T., Liu, M.Y., Wang, T.C., Zhu, J.Y.: Semantic image synthesis with spatially-adaptive normalization. In: Proceedings of the IEEE/CVF Conference on Computer Vision and Pattern Recognition, pp. 2337–2346 (2019)
27. Roß, T., Bruno, P., Reinke, A., Wiesenfarth, M., Koeppel, L., Full, P.M., Pekdemir, B., Godau, P., Trofimova, D., Isensee, F., et al.: Beyond rankings: learning (more) from algorithm validation. Med. Image Anal. **86**, 102765 (2023)
28. Shaker, N., Togelius, J., Nelson, M.J.: Procedural Content Generation in Games. Computational Synthesis and Creative Systems, Springer (2016). https://doi.org/10.1007/978-3-319-42716-4
29. Shorten, C., Khoshgoftaar, T.M.: A survey on image data augmentation for deep learning. J. big data **6**(1), 1–48 (2019)
30. Smith, A.M., Mateas, M.: Answer set programming for procedural content generation: a design space approach. IEEE Trans. Comput. Intell. AI Games **3**(3), 187–200 (2011). https://doi.org/10.1109/TCIAIG.2011.2158545
31. Toikkanen, M., Kwon, D., Lee, M.: ReSGAN: intracranial hemorrhage segmentation with residuals of synthetic brain CT scans. In: Medical Image Computing and Computer Assisted Intervention–MICCAI 2021: 24th International Conference, Strasbourg, France, September 27–October 1, 2021, Proceedings, Part I 24, pp. 400–409. Springer (2021)
32. Wu, H., Liu, Q., Liu, X.: A review on deep learning approaches to image classification and object segmentation. Comput. Mater. Continua **60**(2) (2019)
33. Zhai, D., Hu, B., Gong, X., Zou, H., Luo, J.: ASS-GAN: asymmetric semi-supervised GAN for breast ultrasound image segmentation. Neurocomputing **493**, 204–216 (2022)

HaWANet: Road Scene Understanding with Multi-modal Sensor Data Using Height-Width-Driven Attention Network

Soumick Chatterjee[1,2,3](✉)📖, Jiahua Xu[1,2,4]📖, Adarsh Kuzhipathalil[1,5], and Andreas Nürnberger[1,2]📖

[1] Faculty of Computer Science, Otto von Guericke University Magdeburg, Magdeburg, Germany
Jiahua.Xu@med.uni-tuebingen.de, adarsh.kuzhipathalil@xenomatix.com, andreas.nuernberger@ovgu.de
[2] Data and Knowledge Engineering Group, Otto von Guericke University Magdeburg, Magdeburg, Germany
[3] Genomics Research Centre, Human Technopole, Milan, Italy
soumick.chatterjee@ovgu.de,soumick.chatterjee@fht.org
[4] Hertie Institute for Clinical Brain Research, Tuebingen, Germany
[5] XenomatiX NV, Leuven, Belgium

Abstract. In recent years, the field of autonomous vehicles and driverless technology has seen remarkable advancements, driven by contributions from mainstream automotive manufacturers and open-source projects. This research aims to develop a pipeline for road scene understanding through semantic segmentation. The proposed pipeline utilises a multi-modal segmentation model, incorporating greyscale images and point cloud data from Xenolidar, specifically designed to capture the structural priors of highway road scenes. The fusion of input modalities and the design of an encoder-decoder architecture with a novel attention scheme called HaWANet is introduced, which focuses on the height and width contextual information to improve the accuracy of road segmentation, are the primary aspects explored for the proposed model. The output of the encoder is a two-dimensional point cloud, which effectively represents the road's planar nature, and is crucial for improving the accuracy of road segmentation, particularly in edge cases, addressing current challenges in autonomous driving research. This research, aimed at addressing the segmentation problem for multimodal sensor data, has presented significant performance improvement over single-modal approaches.

Keywords: Road Scene Understanding · Multimodal Segmentation · Deep Learning · Attention

---

J. Xu and A. Kuzhipathalil—equal contribution

A. Artale et al. (Eds.): AIxIA 2024, LNAI 15450, pp. 92–104, 2025.
https://doi.org/10.1007/978-3-031-80607-0_8

1   Introduction

Recent years have seen significant advances in the field of autonomous vehicles and driverless technology, with mainstream automotive manufacturers and open-source projects contributing high-quality research to solve autonomous driving problems. This progress can be attributed to the availability of open-source datasets and improvements in computational capabilities. This research aims to develop a pipeline for road scene understanding through semantic segmentation.

Despite significant improvements, fully autonomous driving remains a challenging goal due to its safety-critical nature. Current research focuses on addressing edge cases and improving system robustness. The choice of sensors in the perception stack is crucial in this context. LIDAR (Light Detection and Ranging) is widely used for long-range obstacle detection and is a key component of autonomous vehicle perception systems. It functions by emitting light pulses and measuring the time it takes for them to return after bouncing off objects, generating extensive data.

The challenge lies in extracting usable information from these data to perceive the vehicle's surroundings. Advances in LiDAR technology now provide high-quality 3D information. Combining 3D LiDAR data with the rich semantic information from camera images can enhance perception algorithms. Such data fusion strategies leverage the strengths of each sensor modality. For example, LiDAR performs well in low-light conditions, whereas cameras provide semantically rich data.

The efficient fusion of sensor modalities and the design of neural networks to solve various computer vision problems are crucial to the advancement of autonomous driving. This research explores data fusion between multimodal sensor data from a solid-state LiDAR with a proposed segmentation model. The aim is to contribute to improving robustness and accuracy, particularly in edge cases, by addressing current challenges in autonomous driving research.

1.1   Background

Perception systems form a crucial component of the autonomous driving stack. Over the past decade, these systems have significantly evolved, integrating high-accuracy sensor systems to process data about the vehicle's surroundings. Modern driverless cars use a sensor stack that includes cameras, LiDARs (light detection and range), radars (radio detection and range), and ultrasonic sensors. Real-time processing of data from these multimodal sensors presents a major challenge in autonomous driving. This research focuses on LiDARs, whose capabilities in low-light and nighttime conditions are invaluable, despite ongoing debates about their necessity in autonomous vehicles.

LiDARs in Automotive Perception Systems. LiDAR sensors have become a standard component in the perception stack for autonomous vehicles. Although there is a debate about their necessity, LiDARs provide efficient and accurate 3D perception with minimal post-processing. They offer precise 360-degree vision and faster depth sensing compared to other methods such as stereo vision. The requirements for LiDAR sensors in safety-critical applications such as autonomous vehicles include long range, real-time response, high spatial resolution, and tolerance to sunlight [8].

LiDAR technology works on the Time of Flight (ToF) principle, which measures the time between sending and receiving reflection of a light beam [1]. LiDARs generate point clouds by repeating these point measurements, and they are classified into two main types: Spinning LiDARs and Solid-state LiDARs.

Spinning LiDARs feature a rotating element that scans light around it and a receiver element that calculates the ToF to generate point clouds. These were the first 360-degree scanning devices used in the autonomous vehicle industry.

Solid-state LiDARs, a term from the semiconductor industry, use static scanners and receivers. Notable types include Microelectromechanical Systems (MEMS) based LiDARs, which use tiny mirrors to control the direction of the laser beam by adjusting the tilt angle with a stimulus voltage [15]. Another type is Vertical-Cavity Surface-Emitting Lasers (VCSEL) scanners, known for their precision and efficiency [2,16]. The LiDAR scanner used in this research employs VCSEL technology [17].

HANet: Attention for Semantic Segmentation. Incorporating the intrinsic nature of different scenes into computer vision tasks is an area with relatively little research. Specifically, for road scene understanding, many inherent presets can enhance algorithm design. Height-driven Attention Networks (HANet), proposed by Sungha Choi et al. [3], exemplifies this approach.

HANet capitalises on the structural priors of road scenes captured by front-mounted cameras in vehicles. This approach splits road scene images into three height-based regions and evaluates the class probability distribution in these regions compared to the whole image. The study found lower entropy in the height-based regions, confirming the potential to integrate these structural priors into semantic segmentation frameworks. HANet adds a height-driven attention mechanism to the segmentation framework, leveraging these spatial distributions to improve scene understanding.

Deep Data Fusion. When multimodal data is available, as in this research, a fusion strategy can be used to potentially improve the performance of the semantic segmentation problem. In general, data fusion can be categorised as: early fusion, late fusion, and hybrid fusion [19] - presented in Fig. 1

Early fusion combines different modalities before feeding them into feature extraction models. Camille Couprie et al. [5] introduced early fusion in 2013 for indoor scene segmentation by combining RGB and depth information using a Laplacian pyramid. Another notable method, FuseNet [6], fuses RGB and depth modalities at each feature extraction level within two encoder networks.

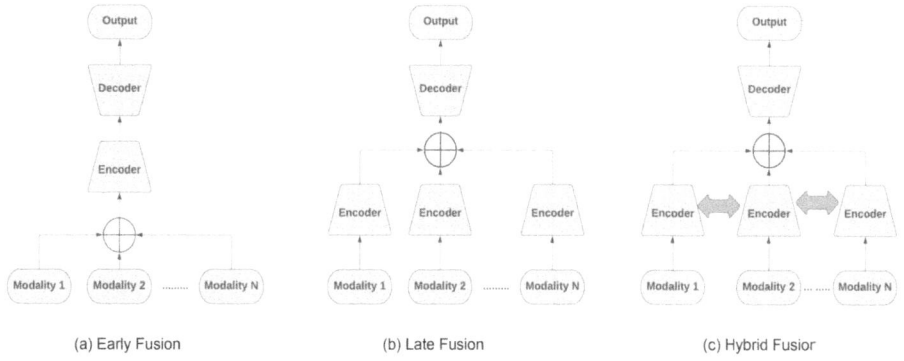

(a) Early Fusion   (b) Late Fusion   (c) Hybrid Fusion

Fig. 1. Deep Multimodal fusion strategies

Late fusion involves feeding each modality into separate encoder models and combining the extracted features at a later stage. Gupta et al. [4] employed late fusion in 2014 by extracting RGB and depth features with two encoders and combining them using an SVM classifier. Valada et al. [13] later summed features from different modalities and fed this joint representation into a series of convolution layers.

Hybrid Fusion combines early and late fusion techniques to enhance segmentation quality. Valada et al. [12] developed a Self-Supervised Model Adaptation (SSMA) module, which adapts semantically mature feature representations at different scales. The SSMA blocks successfully exploit modal-specific features and enhance discriminative factors in the feature map.

2   Methodology

2.1   Dataset

This research uses data from Xenolidar, consisting of two primary modalities: a 2D greyscale image and a 3D point cloud. The initial phase of this research involved data preparation and annotation, which is recognised as the most time-consuming and costly aspect of machine learning projects. This research utilised advanced deep learning methods to minimise the required time and effort

Data Collection. The data collection setup comprises Xenolidar housings developed by Xenomatix and an RGB camera that captures the same scene. Data from both sensors are time-stamped. The RGB camera is included to generate accurate predictions from existing model architectures trained on RGB images.

Generating Annotations. Initial attempts to generate rough segmentation masks involved inputting Xenolidar greyscale images into a pretrained segmentation network. Two methods were tested: stacking the greyscale image to create three channels and modifying the network for single-channel input. Both methods were unsuccessful due to the unique nature of Xenolidar images, leading to an alternative approach.

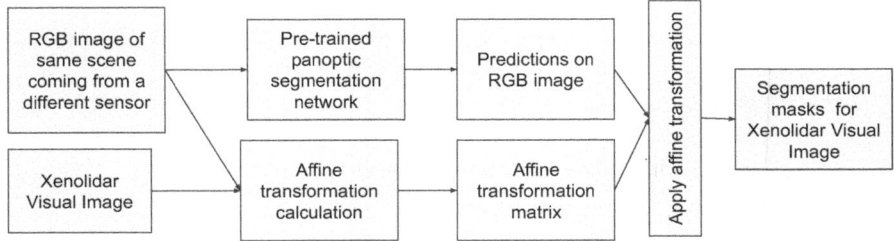

Fig. 2. Designed data preparation scheme where the affine transformation between RGB images and greyscale images from two different sensors is calculated first and then used to transfer segmentation masks

The data flow of the annotation scheme, illustrated in Fig. 2, starts with RGB images processed by the DeepLabV3 model, pretrained on the Cityscapes dataset. The semantic segmentation masks obtained for RGB images are transferred to the Xenolidar image space using affine transformations. For this, three corresponding points are selected from a sample RGB and greyscale Xenolidar image. Although manual selection is possible, automation using SIFT feature correspondence is preferred for accuracy. From the list of corresponding points, three distant points are chosen to calculate the affine transformation matrix, which is used to transform RGB images into the Xenolidar image space. This process is repeated multiple times to refine the transformation matrix.

The same affine transformation matrix is applied to convert segmentation masks of RGB images into masks for Xenolidar greyscale images, creating a rough set of segmentation masks. These masks are manually corrected using a modified Labelme tool [14], which accepts Xenolidar greyscale images and displays the corresponding RGB images and point-cloud overlays. Nine classes from the Cityscapes dataset were selected for annotation: car, truck, person, road, sidewalk, building, sky, vegetation, and bicycle + motorcycle.

The dataset, consisting of 12,000 frames (8,000 recorded in Belgium and 4,000 in Japan), required over four months of manual correction despite automation to achieve the desired quality.

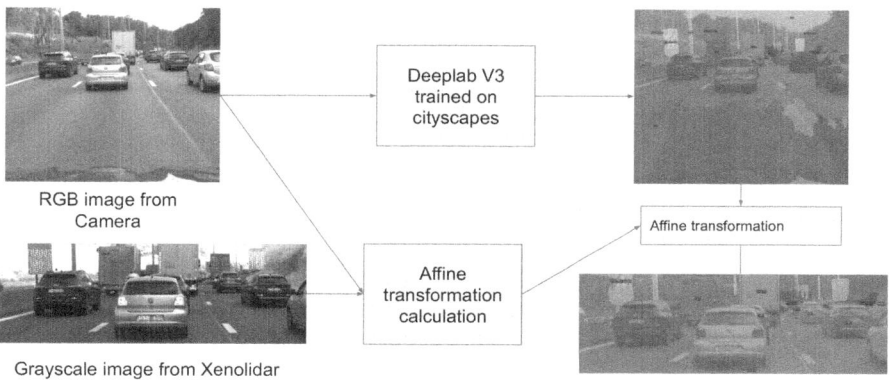

RGB image from Camera

Grayscale image from Xenolidar

Fig. 3. Sample result from the data annotation pipeline

2.2   Semantic Segmentation Network

A semantic segmentation model was developed during this research that processes multi-modal input, incorporating greyscale images and point cloud data from Xenolidar to generate semantic predictions. The primary aspects explored for the semantic segmentation model include the fusion of input modalities and the design of an encoder that efficiently extracts features from road scenes. The preprocessing and semiautomatic annotation methodology developed is detailed in the previous section. This section provides an in-depth description of the developed segmentation network.

The segmentation network architecture is inspired by UNet [9]. To accommodate multi-modal inputs, several modifications were necessary. Various encoder networks were experimented with in this research to determine the most effective models for this use case. The encoders selected for the experimentation were ResNet [7] and EfficientNet [11]. The methods for data fusion and feature extractor design are explained in detail in this section.

Fusion of 2D and 3D Modalities. The main aspect addressed is the fusion of the 2D image modality and the 3D point clouds. A late fusion strategy was adopted, where features are extracted from both greyscale images and point clouds from Xenolidar, and then fused in the feature extraction backbone.

Before fusion, the point clouds are converted into an intermediate 2D representation by creating a 2D depth image. This process involves creating an empty array of the same size as the greyscale image and filling it with the depth values from the point cloud. The position of each point in the 2D array is determined by the position of the reflected laser spots on the CMOS sensor, as calibrated by the manufacturer and encoded with the data. Each point in the point cloud includes 2D coordinates, facilitating the conversion to a 2D array. Figure xx shows the 2D depth image generated from the corresponding 3D point cloud. This 2D depth image is then used in the data fusion with the greyscale image.

The generated 2D depth image is fed into a small network with a few convolutional blocks. The resulting feature vector is concatenated with features from the greyscale images at a later stage in the main feature extraction backbone. The depth feature extractor consists of three convolutional layers followed by average pooling layers, converting a depth image of shape $1 \times 256 \times 768$ into $64 \times 64 \times 192$.

Proposed Height and Width Attention Block. To incorporate the intrinsic features of driving datasets, a custom attention block inspired by HANet [3] was designed and developed. HANet explores the class distribution in the vertical pixel scale, whereas this research proposes a height- and width-driven attention mechanism.

Since the dataset predominantly features highway scenes, a unique class distribution across width and height is present. Vertically, lower sections are expected to have more pixels labelled as roads, while upper sections contain more pixels labelled as sky. Horizontally, the road class is more likely to appear in the middle section, with buildings and vegetation more prominent on the left and right sections.

These observations motivated the design of an additional attention block, named Height- and Width-driven Attention Network (HaWANet). This block is integrated into the later stages of feature extraction and earlier stages of the decoder. HaWANet processes the feature map and, based on height and width-wise contextual information, identifies important features or classes within horizontal and vertical sections, combining this information with features from the main encoder.

The architecture of HaWANet is shown in Fig. 4. The input to this attention block is the feature map of the main segmentation network. HaWANet consists of two almost identical parts: the upper section processes height-wise information, while the lower section processes width-wise information. The height attention A_h is calculated in the upper section, and the width attention A_w in the lower section. Then both attention maps are multiplied by the main feature map.

The details of each subsection are as follows:

- **Height-wise pooling (a-h):** Average pooling is applied to the feature map in the width direction to generate a $C_l \times H_l \times 1$ matrix.
- **Downsampling (b-h):** The matrix is downsampled to size $C_l \times H_- \times 1$.
- **Attention map computation (c-h):** Three convolutional layers generate the attention map from the width-wise pooled and downsampled feature map.
- **Upsampling (d-h):** The attention map is upsampled to match the dimensions of the feature map.
- **Positional encoding (e-h):** A sinusoidal positional encoding, as used in HANet, is added to the feature map.
- **Width-wise pooling (a-w):** Average pooling is applied to the feature map in the height direction to generate a $C_l \times W_l \times 1$ matrix.
- **Downsampling (b-w):** The matrix is downsampled to size $C_l \times W_- \times 1$.

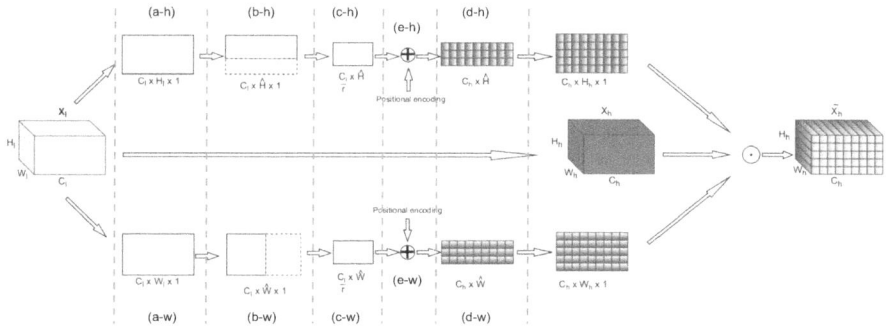

Fig. 4. Height and Width aware Attention Network (HaWANet Architecture)

- **Attention map computation (c-w):** Three convolutional layers generate the attention map from the height-wise pooled and downsampled feature map.
- **Upsampling (d-w):** The attention map is upsampled to match the dimensions of the feature map.
- **Positional encoding (e-w):** A sinusoidal positional encoding is added to the feature map.

HaWANet is an add-on module that can be inserted between different feature extraction blocks in the architecture. The entire encoder-decoder architecture that incorporates data fusion and HaWANet is explained in a subsequent section.

Encoder Decoder Segmentation Network. This research attempts to reuse the concept of UNet [9] to develop a segmentation model. For the encoder part, a ResNet-based feature extractor is used. Performance of multiple variants of ResNet [7] including ResNet-18, ResNet-50, ResNet-101, and EfficientNet [11] was tested. The main modifications made to the encoder part from the standard ResNet are the data fusion scheme and the custom attention block, HaWANet. The model architecture developed is depicted in Fig. 5.

Data fusion occurs in the third ResNet block, where features from the greyscale images and the depth image are concatenated. The concatenated feature matrix then progresses through the subsequent stages of feature extraction.

The HaWANet block is added in five positions of the model architecture, specifically in the later stages of feature extraction. This strategy is based on the understanding that the feature matrix is more concise in these stages and can be effectively utilised in the attention layers of HaWANet.

The model follows an encoder-decoder architecture. At intermediate stages, the feature matrix from the encoder section is concatenated with the corresponding sections of the decoder section, inspired by the UNet architecture. Finally, the decoder section outputs the segmentation masks for each class.

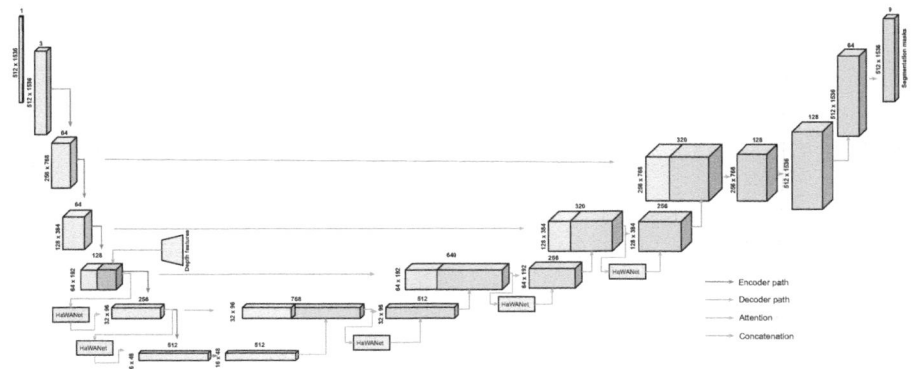

Fig. 5. Encoder - Decoder Network architecture incorporating data fusion and HaWANet attention module

The model was trained with approximately 12,000 greyscale images and corresponding depth images for 200 epochs. The loss functions used were a combination of cross-entropy loss and dice loss.

2.3   Model Training

Loss Functions. The proposed network architecture was trained using cross entropy [18] and dice loss [10] functions. Cross-entropy loss was implemented to measure the difference between the probability distributions of the predictions and the ground-truth, while the Dice loss was employed to evaluate the segmentation performance.

Data Augmentation. This research employed the following data augmentation steps andomly with random intensity to artificially increase the size of the dataset and improve the genaralisation capabilities of the model: rotation from -15 to 15 degrees, horizontal and vertical flip, translation of up to 50 pixels, random signal contrast, and random brightness.

2.4   Design of Experiments

Experiments were designed to study the influence of depth fusion with visual image modality and to test the HaWANet attention module proposed in this research. Multiple models with different backbones were developed to test their performance. Each model was trained with and without depth fusion and tested with the original HANet module and the proposed HaWANet. The backbones included ResNet-18, ResNet-50, ResNet-101, and EfficientNet. These combinations of backbones, data fusion, and attention modules were grouped and all models were trained.

Evaluated Configurations. Different configurations of the proposed architecture were evaluated in this research: baseline UNet, data fusion on UNet, depth fusion HANET block on UNet, HaWANET block on UNet, and finally, depth fusion and HaWANET block on UNet. For feature extraction, four different backbones were evaluated: ResNet18, ResNet50, ResNet101, and EfficientNet.

Evaluation Metrics. The ground-truths and the predictions were converted into a bitmap for each class in such a way that a pixel is assigned a value of 1 if it is assigned to that particular class and 0 if it is not, which were then used to calculate *TP, TN, FP* and *FN*. These were then used to computed the *Intersection over Union (IoU)* (also called the *Jaccard Index*).

3   Results

The segmentation model detailed in the previous section was modified with various feature extractors, attention mechanisms, and data fusion schemes, and tested extensively. This section presents the different configurations used to design multiple semantic segmentation models and the training setup. The results of each configuration are described, followed by an overview of the experiments and the final outcomes.

The different configurations were evaluated in terms of accuracy (usig IoU) and speed (using frames per second or FPS), and the scores are presented in Table 1. It was observed that HaWANet with data fusion resulted in the best performance among all configurations evaluated. Furthermore, it was noted that data fusion, through the introduction of the additional modality, improved the performance of HANet, HaWANet, and the baseline model. Table 2 presents the resultant class-wise scores achieved by the best performing model HaWANet with data fusion. Some visual explains of the segmentation results are presented in Figs. 6 and 7, for highways or outer road and urban scenes, respectively.

4   Discussion

The primary objective of this research was to develop a multi-modal scene understanding pipeline. The proposed semantic segmentation network utilises an encoder-decoder architecture with a height- and width-driven attention scheme, specifically designed to capture the structural priors of highway road scenes. This architecture integrates depth data from point clouds within the encoder to enhance segmentation accuracy.

The segmentation results presented here demonstrate the model's efficacy in highway scenes. The predicted masks for cars and trucks are highly accurate. However, the model occasionally misclassifies pixels on the sidewalk as road. The inclusion of point-cloud data, which effectively represents the road's planar nature, is crucial for improving the accuracy of road segmentation.

Table 1. Comparison of different configurations with different feature extraction backbones using IoU and FPS

	ResNet 18		ResNet 50		ResNet 101		EfficientNet	
	IoU	FPS	IoU	FPS	IoU	FPS	IoU	FPS
Baseline	0.55±0.04	4.7	0.61±0.07	4.3	0.62±0.04	3.7	0.59±0.05	4.2
Baseline with data fusion	0.57±0.05	4.1	0.63±0.08	3.5	0.64±0.03	3.0	0.61±0.04	3.9
With data fusion and HANet	0.66±0.04	3.8	0.71±0.03	2.9	0.72±0.05	2.5	0.68±0.06	3.7
With HaWANet (without data fusion)	0.65±0.04	3.4	0.70±0.03	2.7	0.71±0.05	2.2	0.70±0.06	3.5
With HaWANet (with data fusion)	0.67±0.04	3.2	0.75±0.03	2.1	**0.78±0.05**	1.9	0.72±0.06	2.9

Table 2. IoU results for individual classes for the best performed model

Class	IoU	Class	IoU	Class	IoU
Car	0.81	Person	0.70	Sidewalk	0.80
Truck	0.73	Sky	0.75	Building	0.79
Road	0.89	Vegetation	0.78	Bicycle + Motorcycle	0.75

In urban scenes, despite fewer training samples, the segmentation network performs reasonably well. However, the sidewalk class is sometimes misclassified, likely because the sidewalk and road are at the same level, making them appear similar in the point-cloud data. This misclassification suggests that further refinement is needed in distinguishing these classes.

The limitations of the LiDAR sensor, particularly its maximum range, affect the segmentation of distant objects. Objects far from the sensor lack point cloud data, while the sky often contains invalid data points (e.g., -1 or -9999). Interestingly, these negative values help to segment the sky class effectively, indicating that even seemingly invalid data can provide useful features for segmentation.

The *Person* class has the lowest IoU score among all classes. This poor performance is attributed to the limited number of training samples for this class, primarily because the dataset consists mostly of highway scenes where pedestrians are infrequent. This finding underscores the need for a more balanced dataset or additional data augmentation techniques to improve the segmentation of under-represented classes.

5   Conclusion and Future Work

This research, aimed at addressing the segmentation problem for multimodal sensor data, has presented significant performance improvement over single-modal approaches. The developed multi-modal segmentation network successfully integrates point cloud data to enhance the understanding of road scenes. The HaWANet attention mechanism effectively captures structural priors, leading to accurate segmentation in various scenarios. However, challenges remain in distinguishing closely related classes and in segmenting under-represented classes.

Fig. 6. Predictions of the semantic segmentation model from highways or outer road scenes.

Fig. 7. Predictions of the semantic segmentation model from urban scenes.

Future work would focus on expanding the dataset, refining the attention mechanism, and improving the integration of point-cloud data to address these challenges. Additionally, further development and optimisation of object detection models using Xenolidar data can extend the applicability of this research in real-world scenarios.

Acknowledgement. The authors would like to thank Dr Hung Nguyen-Duc, Senior Computer Vision Engineer at Xenomatix NV, Leuven, Belgium, for the support and guidance.

References

1. Chazette, P., Totems, J., Hespel, L., Bailly, J.S.: Principle and Physics of the LiDAR Measurement, pp. 201–247 (2016). https://doi.org/10.1016/B978-1-78548-102-4.50005-3
2. Chen, B.S., Foster, P., Warkentine, R.: Research and development of VCSEL-based optical sensors in industrial applications. In: Choquette, K.D., Lei, C. (eds.) Vertical-Cavity Surface-Emitting Lasers V. vol. 4286, pp. 210 – 218. International Society for Optics and Photonics, SPIE (2001). https://doi.org/10.1117/12.424806
3. Choi, S., Kim, J.T., Choo, J.: Cars can't fly up in the sky: improving urban-scene segmentation via height-driven attention networks. In: Proceedings of the

IEEE/CVF Conference On Computer Vision And Pattern Recognition, pp. 9373–9383 (2020)

4. Cortes, C., Vapnik, V.: Support-vector networks. Mach. Learn. **20**, 273–297 (1995). https://doi.org/10.1007/BF00994018

5. Couprie, C., Farabet, C., Najman, L., LeCun, Y.: Indoor semantic segmentation using depth information. arXiv preprint arXiv:1301.3572 (2013)

6. Hazirbas, C., Ma, L., Domokos, C., Cremers, D.: FuseNet: incorporating depth into semantic segmentation via fusion-based CNN architecture. In: Computer Vision–ACCV 2016: 13th Asian Conference on Computer Vision, Taipei, Taiwan, November 20-24, 2016, Revised Selected Papers, Part I 13, pp. 213–228. Springer (2017)

7. He, K., Zhang, X., Ren, S., Sun, J.: Deep residual learning for image recognition. In: Proceedings of the IEEE Conference on Computer Vision and Pattern Recognition, pp. 770–778 (2016)

8. Li, Y., Ibanez-Guzman, J.: Lidar for autonomous driving: the principles, challenges, and trends for automotive lidar and perception systems. IEEE Signal Process. Mag. **37**(4), 50–61 (2020). https://doi.org/10.1109/MSP.2020.2973615

9. Ronneberger, O., Fischer, P., Brox, T.: U-net: convolutional networks for biomedical image segmentation. In: Medical Image Computing and Computer-assisted Intervention–MICCAI 2015: 18th International Conference, Munich, Germany, October 5-9, 2015, proceedings, part III 18, pp. 234–241. Springer (2015)

10. Sudre, C.H., Li, W., Vercauteren, T., Ourselin, S., Jorge Cardoso, M.: Generalised dice overlap as a deep learning loss function for highly unbalanced segmentations. In: Deep Learning in Medical Image Analysis and Multimodal Learning for Clinical Decision Support: Third International Workshop, DLMIA 2017, and 7th International Workshop, ML-CDS 2017, Held in Conjunction with MICCAI 2017, Québec City, QC, Canada, September 14, Proceedings 3, pp. 240–248. Springer (2017)

11. Tan, M., Le, Q.: Efficientnet: rethinking model scaling for convolutional neural networks. In: International Conference on Machine Learning, pp. 6105–6114. PMLR (2019)

12. Valada, A., Mohan, R., Burgard, W.: Self-supervised model adaptation for multimodal semantic segmentation. Int. J. Comput. Vision **128**(5), 1239–1285 (2020)

13. Valada, A., Oliveira, G.L., Brox, T., Burgard, W.: Deep multispectral semantic scene understanding of forested environments using multimodal fusion. In: 2016 International Symposium on Experimental Robotics, pp. 465–477. Springer (2017)

14. Wada, K.: Labelme: Image Polygonal Annotation with Python.https://doi.org/10.5281/zenodo.5711226, https://github.com/wkentaro/labelme

15. Wang, D., Watkins, C., Xie, H.: MEMS mirrors for lIDAR: a review. Micromachines **11**(5), 456 (2020). https://doi.org/10.3390/mi11050456, https://www.mdpi.com/2072-666X/11/5/456

16. Warren, M., et al.: Low-divergence high-power VCSEL arrays for lidar application. pp. 14 (02 2018). https://doi.org/10.1117/12.2290937

17. XenomatiX: XenomatiX solidstate lidar scanner (2022). https://xenomatix.com/solid-state-lidar/ Accessed 19 April 2022

18. Yi-de, M., Qing, L., Zhi-bai, Q.: Automated image segmentation using improved PCNN model based on cross-entropy. In: Proceedings of 2004 International Symposium on Intelligent Multimedia, Video and Speech Processing, 2004, pp. 743–746 (2004). https://doi.org/10.1109/ISIMP.2004.1434171

19. Zhang, Y., Sidibé, D., Morel, O., Mériaudeau, F.: Deep multimodal fusion for semantic image segmentation: a survey. Image Vis. Comput. **105**, 104042 (2021). https://doi.org/10.1016/j.imavis.2020.104042

Hybrid Classification of European Legislation Using Sustainable Development Goals

Michele Corazza[✉], Franco M. T. Gatti, Salvatore Sapienza[✉],
and Monica Palmirani[✉]

University of Bologna, CIRSFID-ALMA AI, Bologna, Italy
{michele.corazza2,salvatore.sapienza,monica.palmirani}@unibo.it

Abstract. This study focuses on the automatic classification of European Union legislative documents according to the United Nations Sustainable Development Goals (SDGs) to monitor and improve government policies and legislation. This allows *ex-ante* checks during legal drafting to better align the new proposal with SDG policies and *ex-post* evaluation tools for monitoring the implementation and effectiveness of SDG strategies in the European legislation over time. The research aims to assess the alignment of legislative efforts with these global goals by utilizing an extensive corpus of regulations and directives from the Juncker (2014–2019) and von der Leyen Commission periods (2020–2024). The proposed Hybrid AI methodology employs an unsupervised deep learning approach, leveraging the structure of legislative documents formalized in the Akoma Ntoso XML standard. The research has two primary objectives: first, to examine a novel weighted approach where classifications of the initial articles guide the classification of subsequent articles using an unsupervised sentence embedding model. Second, to monitor document-level classifications over time, tracking legislative evolution and comparing policies under different European Commission presidencies. Initial findings, based on legal expert validation of the technical findings expressed to metrics, reveal that the first articles of legislative documents are crucial in determining the correct SDG classifications and that these classifications may evolve over time with normative modifications and new strategic policies.

Keywords: Hybrid AI · Unsupervised Classification · Temporal Tracking · LegalXML

1 Introduction

Deliberative institutions face an urgent need to detect and track policy implementation in legal acts, measure norm effectiveness, and evaluate societal impact. The Sustainable Development Goals (SDG) program serves as a crucial tool for monitoring global policies, while emerging AI applications in the legislative domain aim to find correspondences between laws and policies defined by deliberative bodies. In 2017, the European Commission's Joint Research Centre (JRC) initiated a policy mapping of Juncker Commission's actions (2014–2019), linking them to the 17 SDGs [6]. This process involved manual mapping and expert analysis of EU legislative documents, followed by automation using text mining and NLP techniques. A 2022 collaboration between the authors, European DG Informatics, and the European Publication Office resulted in a database of 21991 EU regulations and directives (2010–2019) converted to Akoma Ntoso XML format, and including consolidated versions. Further reviews, and the implementation of text mining and natural language processing techniques, led to an automatisation of the policy mapping process that was implemented starting from the documents of the Von Der Leyen Commission (2020–2024). For our scope we have considered only the manually annotated dataset (Juncker presidency) for creating a ground truth baseline.

However, this dataset classifies the European legislation at the document level. Crucially, legal practitioners - especially at the legislative level, like legal drafters - are interested in knowing precisely the article/portion of the text connected to SDGs in order to track policies and, in case of modifications, to detect improvements over time. Secondly, if the legislator intends to reinforce the SDGs indicators within the legal text, it is important to know exactly what provisions are not sufficient or "weak" in order to reinforce the strategy. Thirdly, legislative documents include modifications/derogations to other documents and the quoted text should be influential in the identification of the correct SDGs.

Some qualified parts of the legislative document express better the scope and the objective of the provision. For instance, the first articles usually describe the objective scope ("what" is regulated), the subjective scope ("who" is regulated) and definitions, which are crucial to contextualise the meaning of the norms. Finally, AI methods are usually applied at a document level. Given limitations in token-handling, legal documents are usually segmented in chunks, with no difference between parts (preamble, definition, articles, final provisions, etc.). This implies that the hierarchical structure of the legal document, which is crucial for the legal significance of the provisions is lost in the AI-friendly representation of the legal text. For these reasons, the main research questions are the following:

- **RQ1**: which parts (Recitals, definition, main body, etc.) of the legislative document are connected with the targets of the SDGs taxonomy? We intend to reach a better granularity of the classification, in order to provide an accurate instrument to the legislator, while maintaining the hierarchical legal significance of the document (e.g., chapters, articles, paragraphs)
- **RQ2**: what is the evolution of SDGs classification over time? We intend to exploit the evolution of the SDGs over time, monitoring the documents, including their consolidated versions, using the temporal metadata of Akoma Ntoso. The temporal spans are in ranges of 3 years (2015–2017, 2018–2020, 2021–2023, 2024) and 5 years (2015–2019, 2020–2024). (e.g., the SDGs 7 related to Affordable and Clean Energy has grown about 1% in the last 5 years monitoring the same documents because the legislator amended them).

We use Akoma Ntoso[1] because it is the official standard in EU institutions for modelling the legislative documents (AKN4EU[2]) and similarly is the standard for the documents in the UN (AKN4UN[3]).

2 Related Work

In the Natural Language Processing (NLP) field, the emergence of the transformer models [18] first and subsequently BERT [4] lead to a paradigm where a large model is pre-trained on a self-supervised task, allowing the model to be adapted to a multitude of tasks in a process called fine-tuning. In this context, some models have been fine-tuned from general purpose transformers for the legal domain. One such model is LEGAL-BERT [1], which was fine-tuned on both legislative documents from the EU, UK and US, as well as court documents from the European Court of Justice. In the same family there is another model called custom LEGAL-BERT [21], which was trained on a corpus of case low from the Harvard Law Library. Another dataset is called Pile-of-Law, and it was obtained from 35 different sources in English and used to train a model called PoL [9].

Beside pre-trained models, the application of NLP techniques to the legal domain has produced a multitude of tasks and models. Most of these approaches are related to the judiciary, with a multitude of different tasks such as the prediction of court rulings. In [20], in particular, a pre-trained model is fine-tuned to retrieve similar cases, predict the judgment, and answer legal question in Chinese. Another contribution [5] a transformer model is used to determine which articles have been violated in a given case, by using a global consistency graph which links charge (e.g., abuse) with article and term (e.g., 5 years). Similarly, a model and dataset have been proposed to predict and explain rulings of the Indian supreme court [11]. Beside these models, an evaluation campaign called the Competition on Legal Information Extraction/Entailment [8].

While most of the approaches described in this section are related to the judiciary, the application of NLP approaches to the legislative domain is less explored. However, there is a long standing tradition in the creation of machine-readable representation of legislative documents. In our research, we use the Akoma Ntoso [14,19] XML standard, which is used across a multitude of institutions around the world [3,7,12,13,15] and it creates a machine-readable representation that can encode legal definitions, the hierarchical structure of legal documents, temporal aspects (e.g., amendments, consolidation) and nonrmative references.

---

[1] http://docs.oasis-open.org/legaldocml/akn-core/v1.0/akn-core-v1.0-part1-vocabulary.html.

[2] https://op.europa.eu/it/web/eu-vocabularies/akn4eu.

[3] https://unsceb.org/unsif-akn4un, https://unsceb-hlcm.github.io/.

3   Document Collection

The ground truth baseline is composed by 2791 documents along with their associated SDGs, sourced from the JRC portal and derived from the manual policy mapping conducted by the JRC starting in 2017, covering documents produced during the Juncker Commission's mandate (2015–2019). Based on the mapping, each document was linked to at least one SDG, and many documents were connected to multiple SDG.

Our experiment was conducted on a document collection made starting from the 21991 regulations and directives (including consolidated versions) contained in the European legislation database EUR-LEX (2010–2021), converted in Akoma Ntoso format. From this dataset, we have filtered the documents matching the ground truth arriving at a set collection composed of 3846 items. It is important to notice that a consolidation is the version of an act comprising the original act and all the subsequent amendments and corrections to that act. For this reason, the analysis of the documents' evolution over time could reveal the trend of the EU Commission while implementing the SDGs.

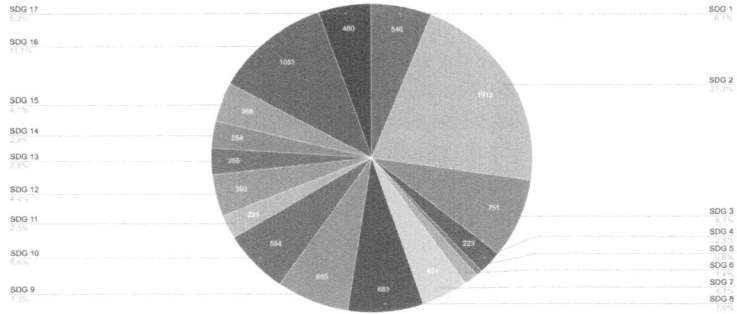

Fig. 1. Number of documents per each SDG in our document collection.

Figure 1 shows how many documents in our dataset are pertaining each SDG by the manual mapping. SDG number 2, which aims at "zero hunger" is the most frequently featured, appearing in 1,913 documents, while goal number 5, focused on "gender equality" is the least featured, appearing in only 5 documents.

Among the 169 targets specified in the 17 SDGs, 39 are absent from all 3846 documents in our dataset. Moreover, 71 targets are found in just 1 to 94 documents, and 31 appear between 103 and 283 times across the entire collection. The 28 most frequently featured targets (appearing between 301 and 1372 times) are depicted in Fig. 2. The top two targets (2.3 and 2.1), both pertaining to SDG number 2, are mentioned in 1372 and 1297 documents, respectively.

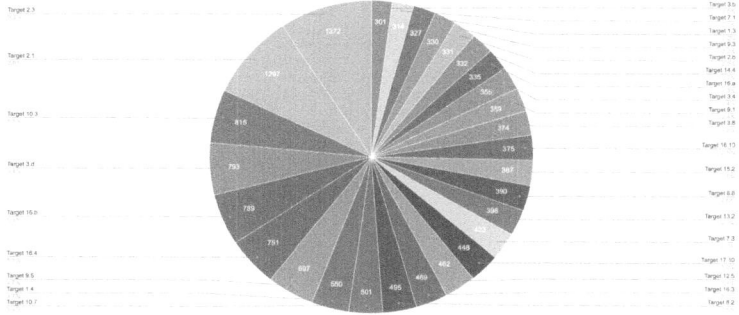

Fig. 2. The 27 most featured targets in our document collection.

4   Methods

In this article, our goal is to asses whether it is feasible to leverage an unsupervised approach in order to determine whether a document is related to one or more SDG targets. To achieve this goal, we use a sentence embedding approach based on Sentence-BERT and the SentenceTransformers library [16]. These models have been fine-tuned to produce vector representations for sentences which can be compared using cosine similarity or euclidean distance as metrics. This way, they can be used in an unsupervised way to assess the semantic similarity between two different portions of text.

In our experiments, we opted to use the "all-distilroberta-v1" model, due to the fact that it shows good performance on various datasets and that it still retains the maximum number of tokens from RoBERTa, namely 512. This model was fine-tuned from the DistillRoBERTa model [17], which in turn was distilled from RoBERTa [10]. This particular model was trained using a contrastive learning procedure, leveraging datasets annotated for semantic similarity. The model M is trained on matched pairs of sentences a, b such that a_i and b_i are semantically related according to the dataset. The two sets of sentences have the same cardinality $|a| = |b| = b_s$ which corresponds to the batch size. In order to proceed with the training, the first step is to obtain the vector representations of these two sets of sentences, normalized so that they have unit norm:

$$\bar{A} = \frac{M(a)}{|M(a)|} \quad \bar{B} = \frac{M(b)}{|M(b)|} \tag{1}$$

where we assume that each row of the matrices is divided by its own norm. By applying these formulas we obtain two matrices $\bar{A}, \bar{B}$ of size $b_s \times e_s$, where e_s represents the size of the outputs of the model (768 in the case of distillRoBERTa). In order to obtain the cosine similarity between the sentence embeddings in $\bar{A}, \bar{B}$ it is then possible to apply a simple matrix multiplication:

$$S = \bar{A}\bar{B}^T \tag{2}$$

Due to the fact that all vectors $a_i \in \bar{A}, b_i \in \bar{B}$ have unit norm, the normal formula for the cosine similarity can be :

$$sim(a_i, b_i) = \frac{a_i \cdot b_i}{|a_i||b_i|} = a_i \cdot b_i \tag{3}$$

Meaning that the cosine similarity between the vectors can be computed using only the dot product between them. In the context of the similarity matrix S, then, we can observe that:

$$S = \begin{bmatrix} a_1 \cdot b_1 & \dots & a_1 \cdot b_n \\ \vdots & \ddots & \vdots \\ a_n \cdot b_1 & \dots & a_n \cdot b_n \end{bmatrix} \tag{4}$$

Meaning that each cell of the matrix $s_ij \in S$ corresponds to the cosine similarity between a_i and b_j. Once obtained this representation, which acts as the prediction of the model, we can observe that due to the fact that only the sentences with the same index are semantically related. For this reason, we can use as labels a diagonal matrix with the same size as S but with the values of the diagonal set to 1, the others set to 0:

$$y = \mathrm{diag}(1, 2, \dots, b_s) \tag{5}$$

Finally, the complete loss is expressed as a double cross-entropy, as first presented in [2]:

$$\mathcal{L}(S, y) = -\frac{1}{2} \left(\frac{1}{b_s} \sum_{i=0}^{b_s} \log \frac{\exp S_i}{\sum_{j=0}^{b_s} \exp S_j} y + \frac{1}{b_s} \sum_{i=0}^{b_s} \log \frac{\exp S_i^T}{\sum_{j=0}^{b_s} \exp S_j^T} y \right) \tag{6}$$

This double cross entropy, then, has the desired outcome of producing almost orthogonal vectors (with cosine similarity close to 0) for non semantically related sentences, while it should produce almost parallel vectors (with cosine similarity close to 1) for semantically related sentences.

With this model, it is possible to produce semantically aware embeddings for sentences. The maximum length of the normative documents, however, does not allow the application of the model to the entire document. For this reason, we developed an approach that is informed by the structure of the document itself, encoded in the Akoma Ntoso XML tree, and which also considers normative references (see Fig. 3). Since our goal is to encode articles and recitals from the preamble, we proceed by first producing a list of inline elements in Akoma Ntoso, meaning those that appear in the middle of text, such as references, dates, etc. With this list, we can populate the leaves of our tree, meaning the elements that have either no children or only inline children. They are also associated with all the textual content that they contain, including text that is inside inline children if they are present. Given a leaf element l of the tree with no references, we can compute its vector representation using the following algorithm:

$$v(l) = M(t(l)) \tag{7}$$

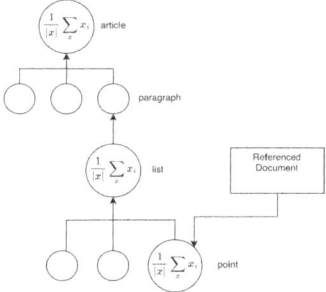

Fig. 3. The strategy used to obtain a vector representation for articles and recitals. Each non-leaf node is represented by a vector obtained from its children, and, if present, the normative references in its text.

where we denote the textual content of l with $t(l)$. For non-leaf nodes, then, we use a recursive approach to reconstruct their vectors from their children:

$$v(e) = \frac{1}{1 + |c(e)|} \left(M(t(e)) + \sum_i v(c_i(e)) \right) \tag{8}$$

where $c(e)$ is a tuple containing all the children of the element e and $c_i(e)$ denotes the nth child of the element e. Our approach is also able to represent information contained in documents that are referenced in the text. In particular, we are able to consider both punctual and non punctual normative references, meaning references that point to a specific portion of a document (e.g., an article, a point, a paragraph, etc.) and those that indicate an entire document, respectively. In order to represent these references, we use two distinct approaches:

$$R(i) = \begin{cases} v(i) & \text{if } i \text{ is a punctual reference} \\ \frac{1}{2} M(title(i)) + v(article_1(i)) & \text{otherwise} \end{cases} \tag{9}$$

where $title(i)$ and $article_1(i)$ represent the title and first article of a document, respectively. This approach uses the vector representation of the element in punctual references, while it represents entire document using its title and first article.

Finally, we can produce the vector representation of a non leaf node containing children and one or more references:

$$v(e) = \frac{1}{2 + |c(e)|} \left(M(t(e)) + \sum_i v(c_i(e)) \frac{1}{r(e)} \sum_j R(r_j(e)) \right) \tag{10}$$

where $r(e)$ is a tuple containing all the references in the text of the node e, while $r_j(e)$ represents the j-th reference. This formula computes the mean between the textual content of each element, its children and a vector representing the references contained in its text, allowing us to obtain vector representations for both recitals and articles, which are aware of the structure of the document and of the references.

The final step in our method is the measurement of the semantic similarity between articles and recitals, which are represented by vectors obtained by the aforementioned procedure, and the SDG targets. Each target is associated with a description, so we can represent it using the model used to represent articles and recitals. The cosine similarity between the articles, recitals and each SDG target are used to obtain a ranking, where each portion of the normative document is associated with a list of SDG targets, from the most similar to the least similar.

5   Results and Validation

In order to evaluate the performance of the model, we opted to use the annotated dataset discussed in Sect. 3, which contains matches between documents the relevant SDG targets. This task is a multi-label classification, in which each document can be assigned one or more SDG targets. Since we do not have a precise threshold that can be used to discriminate between matching and non matching SDG targets for a given ranking, we chose to consider only the top 5 ranking SDGs as matching for any given article or recital. This group of SGDs are called the "predicted matching". While it would be possible to leverage some information about the number of SDG for each document in the gold standard, this would amount to a model that is tuned for the same data used to test it, which is methodologically problematic in our unsupervised setting. Secondly, from the legal point of view, we would be agnostic regarding this parameter for discovering new potential legal knowledge.

In our approach, the semantic similarity with the SDGs is measured on articles and recitals, not entire documents. It is important to underline that while articles constitute the binding part of the normative text, recitals serve as an interpretative guidance and cast light on the overall strategy pursued by the normative instrument. In our case, recitals should be able to provide further context to the scope and the definitions mentioned in the articles. Therefore, their use is a valuable approach as they contain the rationale of a normative act, which can be helpful to classify its role within the SDG framework

For this reason, we chose to compare three different strategies to aggregate the results in order to obtain predictions at the document level:

- **All articles**: we use the union of the predicted matching SDGs for all articles of the document;
- **First four articles**: we use the union of the predicted matching SDGs for the first four articles of the document. This choice is motivated by the intuition that the first four articles of documents generally contain the core scope and context of the regulation which are crucial for the classification.
- **First four articles + recitals**: we use the union of the predicted matching SDGs for the first four articles of the document, as well as the predicted matching SDGs for all the recitals, consistently with observed above with regards to recitals.

With this approach, it is possible to reconstruct, the predicted SDGs for any given document. However, one must consider that this unsupervised approach is very challenging. In particular, our method does not leverage any information about the number of SDG targets that are related to any given document, article or recital. For this reason, the model might produce a higher or a lower number of SDG targets depending on the specific document. Additionally, multiple articles might be predicted as similar to the same SDG target, leading SDGs that are missing from the predictions, especially when the number of ground truth SDGs is high. One other challenging aspect is the fact that, in our dataset, 39 out of 169 targets are not attested. In our evaluation, we chose to consider them despite the fact that they influence the total averages used to compare performance. While it could be possible to remove labels that are not predicted by the model and not annotated at the document level, this would make any comparison between models meaningless, so we opted to keep all the non-attested classes.

In order to evaluate the approach, we present the macro averaged and weighted average precision, recall and F1 score obtained from the 169 SDG targets (Table 1). In addition to the performance metrics obtained from the document-level predictions, we present a random baseline, obtained for each strategy by sampling 5 random SDGs for each article/recital which was used for the evaluation, applied 100 times. We report the mean and standard deviation of the resulting metrics.

Table 1. Precision, recall and F1 score for the four strategies, obtained from Macro and Weighted averages over individual classes. In bold, the best values for each metric. Underlined, the higher metric when comparing each strategy with its baseline. For each baseline we report the means and standard deviations of the metrics over 100 runs.

Strategy	Average	Precision	Recall	F1 Score
All articles	Macro	**0.11**	0.16	0.07
	Weighted	**0.37**	0.22	0.14
Random (All articles)	Macro	0.03 ± 0.0003	0.33 ± 0.008	0.06 ± 0.0004
	Weighted	0.12 ± 0.001	0.41 ± 0.003	0.17 ± 0.001
First four	Macro	0.09	0.09	0.04
	Weighted	0.29	0.12	0.06
Random (First four)	Macro	0.02 ± 0.0006	0.08 ± 0.007	0.03 ± 0.0008
	Weighted	0.09 ± 0.003	0.1 ± 0.003	0.08 ± 0.002
Recitals + first four	Macro	0.09	0.36	**0.10**
	Weighted	0.27	0.44	**0.22**
Random (Recitals + first four)	Macro	0.03 ± 0.0001	0.52 ± 0.008	0.05 ± 0.0002
	Weighted	0.10 ± 0.0008	0.65 ± 0.003	0.16 ± 0.001

While analysing the results of the evaluation, some interesting patterns emerge. In particular, we can see that the difference in terms of macro averaged precision is not substantial when comparing the three models, and that this approach does not produce high precision results. Even if it is a small margin, the best performance in terms of precision is obtained by adopting the "all articles" strategy. However, despite the relatively high number of articles in the document, the performance in terms of recall is quite low, meaning that some of the predicted SDGs might be related to procedural aspects, which are predicted multiple times per document, leading to a low recall value while not impacting the precision. For the first four strategies, the low number of articles seems to penalize the recall values, resulting in a very low overall F1 score. In terms of overall performance, then, the recitals + 4 articles strategy leads to the best overall F1 values, with precision values that are not far from the best ones obtained from the all articles approach, but without the low recall. This strategy is the more promising one and it is the only one to measurably surpass the random baseline F1 scores for both averaging strategies. Incidentally, this finding is also explainable in the light of the legal nature of recitals, which serve as additional context for the binding provisions and, therefore, clarify the scope of the regulation.

Table 2. Top 5,3,1 recall for the manually annotated articles using our model and a random baseline. The random baseline has been executed 100 times and we show the mean and standard deviation for the recalls. In bold, the best results.

Model	Top 5 recall	Top 3 recall	Top 1 recall
Ours	**0.53**	**0.35**	**0.13**
Random Baseline	0.028 ± 0.012	0.017 ± 0.009	0.005 ± 0.006

In an effort to evaluate the fine-grained performance of the model, we annotated 50 articles with their associated SDGs and we proceeded to measure the resulting top 5,3, and 1 recalls (see Table 2), meaning the ratio between the correctly identified SDG targets in the top 5,3,1 ranking predictions and the total number of SDGs associated with the articles. We also report a random baseline, obtained by sampling random SDGs for each of the 50 manually annotated articles, which is applied 100 times and reported in terms of means and standard deviations. These results show that, while going from a fine-grained classification to a document-level one is indeed challenging, our model is able to retrieve the SDGs related to a given article with reasonable performance and that the results are markedly better than a random baseline.

6   Discussion and Final Remarks

The results provide answers to the research questions that are the core of this paper:

- **RQ1**: which parts (Recitals, definition, main body, etc.) of the legislative document are connected with the targets of the SDGs taxonomy? We are now able to precisely detect the classification of the SDGs article-by-article, thus contributing to effective SDGs monitoring and better legislation. We are more successful when using the first articles and recitals. In articles where there is only a normative reference, we should be able to navigate the citation for detecting the text of the destination and include it in the model. Instead, for legislative documents focused on procedural aspects of the European Union (e.g., budget), the mapping is more generic and unspecified (e.g., 1.4, 16.10).
- **RQ2**: what is the evolution of SDGs classification over time? Figs. 5 and 6 allows for a clear understanding of the evolution over time of the EU committments towards certain SDGs

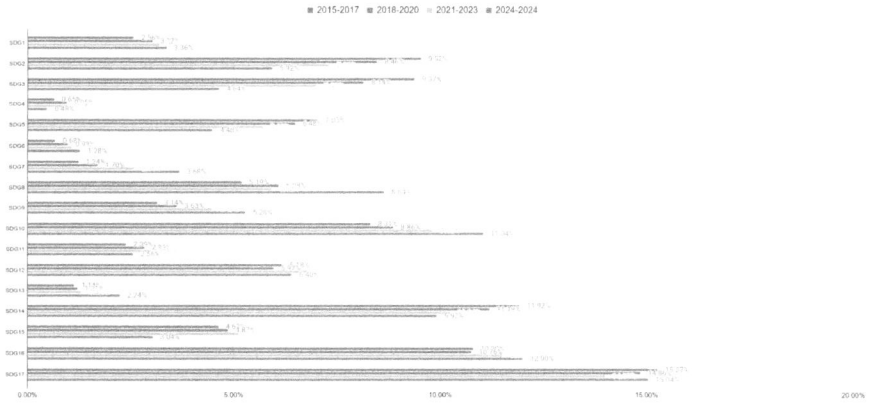

Fig. 4. Percentage distribution of EU legislation across Sustainable Development Goals (SDGs) from 2015 to 2024 - 3-year range

Notable trends include the steady decrease in SDG02 (Zero Hunger) related legislation from about 9.52% in 2018–2020 to 5.92% in 2024. SDG13 (Climate Action) exhibits more modest changes over time, hovering around 2–3% throughout, but with a very recent increase which almost doubles its percentage. Unexpectedly, EU legislation related to SDG03 (Good Health and Well-being) decreases during the 2021–2023 period (4.64%) in comparison to the initial period (9.37%) in the initial period (2015–2017). This decrease in health-related legislation in 2021–2023 seems in contrast to the EU's legislative response to the COVID-19 pandemic.

5-year trends seem to follow a similar distribution with regards to every SDG. Naturally, trends are diluted in a longer period, thus resulting in less evident shifts. However, this analysis allows the comparison between two different Commissions, thus helping legislative drafting and policy monitoring.

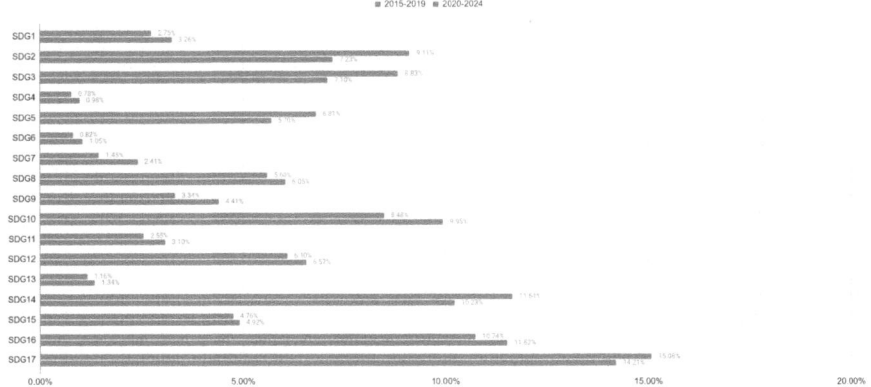

Fig. 5. Percentage distribution of EU legislation across Sustainable Development Goals (SDGs) from 2015 to 2024 - 5-year range

In conclusion, we have used a database of JRC already annotated by human experts with the SDGs classification and an AKN database of legislation for assigning the same classification at the lower granularity (e.g., article vs. document; definition vs. article).

The following findings emerge from the experiments: a) structured documents in AKN-XML are able to handle temporal elements in detecting SDGs; b) documents linked with the main topics of the SDGs work better than documents that describe legal normative procedures of the European or legislative system (e.g., implementation of legislation, modifications, relationship with Member States, derogations, etc.); c) articles describing the scope, definitions, objectives - including Recitals - contribute to the effectiveness of the classifier consistently with their legal function; d) articles that include few sentences and many normative references produce worse results, due to challenges in representing references.

Considering these output the future work will be focused on the following tasks: a) to use EUROVOC for creating a first signal on the good candidates of the SD goals; b) to use definitions and the first five articles for refining the mapping of the targets; c) to navigate the normative references in order to include text from the cited document; d) to navigate the normative references to the updated version, when it is available, allowing us to update the mapping with the evolution of the normative system; e) to map the other articles (from the fifth) using the target only in instances where there are additional SDGs targets as good candidates.

Our work provides better traceability of the SDGs policies in the EU legislation permitting the legislator to detect the articles where the association is weakest. During the legal drafting, our tool could be integrated into the editor to suggest better legal definitions for improving the implementation of the SDGs.

Acknowledgement. This project is conducted with the support of the European Commission funds within ERC HyperModeLex. Grant agreement ID: 101055185.

References

1. Chalkidis, I., Fergadiotis, M., Malakasiotis, P., Aletras, N., Androutsopoulos, I.: LEGAL-BERT: the muppets straight out of law school. In: Cohn, T., He, Y., Liu, Y. (eds.) Findings of the Association for Computational Linguistics: EMNLP 2020, pp. 2898–2904. Association for Computational Linguistics, Online (Nov 2020). https://doi.org/10.18653/v1/2020.findings-emnlp.261, https://aclanthology.org/2020.findings-emnlp.261

2. Chen, Y., Qi, X., Wang, J., Zhang, L.: DisCo-CLIP: a distributed contrastive loss for memory efficient clip training. In: Proceedings of the IEEE/CVF Conference on Computer Vision and Pattern Recognition (CVPR), pp. 22648–22657 (June 2023)

3. Cvejić, A., Grujić, K.G., Cvejić, A., Marković, M., Gostojić, S.: Automatic transformation of plain-text legislation into machine-readable format. In: The 11th International Conference on Information Society, Technology and Management (ICIST 2021) (03 2021)

4. Devlin, J., Chang, M.W., Lee, K., Toutanova, K.: BERT: pre-training of deep bidirectional transformers for language understanding. arXiv preprint arXiv:1810.04805 (2018)

5. Dong, Q., Niu, S.: Legal judgment prediction via relational learning. In: Proceedings of the 44th International ACM SIGIR Conference on Research and Development in Information Retrieval, pp. 983–992. SIGIR '21, Association for Computing Machinery, New York, NY, USA (2021). https://doi.org/10.1145/3404835.3462931

6. European Commission and Joint Research Centre, Borchardt, S., Barbero Vignola, G., Buscaglia, D., Maroni, M., Marelli, L.: Mapping EU policies with the 2030 agenda and SDGs - Fostering policy coherence through text-based SDG mapping. Publications Office of the European Union (2023).https://doi.org/10.2760/110687

7. Flatt, A., Langner, A., Leps, O.: Model-Driven Development of Akoma Ntoso Application Profiles: A Conceptual Framework for Model-Based Generation of XML Subschemas. Springer Nature (2023)

8. Goebel, R., Kano, Y., Kim, M.Y., Rabelo, J., Satoh, K., Yoshioka, M.: Summary of the competition on legal information, extraction/entailment (COLIEE) 2023. In: Proceedings of the Nineteenth International Conference on Artificial Intelligence and Law, pp. 472–480. ICAIL '23, Association for Computing Machinery, New York, NY, USA (2023). https://doi.org/10.1145/3594536.3595176

9. Henderson, P., et al.: Pile of law: learning responsible data filtering from the law and a 256GB open-source legal dataset. Adv. Neural. Inf. Process. Syst. **35**, 29217–29234 (2022)

10. Liu, Y., et al.: RoBerta: a robustly optimized BERT pretraining approach. arXiv preprint arXiv:1907.11692 (2019)

11. Malik, V., et al.: ILDC for CJPE: Indian legal documents corpus for court judgment prediction and explanation. In: Zong, C., Xia, F., Li, W., Navigli, R. (eds.) Proceedings of the 59th Annual Meeting of the Association for Computational Linguistics and the 11th International Joint Conference on Natural Language Processing (Volume 1: Long Papers), pp. 4046–4062. Association for Computational Linguistics, Online (Aug 2021). https://doi.org/10.18653/v1/2021.acl-long.313, https://aclanthology.org/2021.acl-long.313

12. Palmirani, M.: Akoma ntoso for making FAO resolutions accessible. In: Peruginelli, G., Faro, S. (eds.) Knowledge of the Law in the Big Data Age, Conference 'Law via the Internet 2018', Florence, Italy, 11-12 October 2018. Frontiers in Artificial Intelligence and Applications, vol. 317, pp. 159–169. IOS Press (2018). https://doi.org/10.3233/FAIA190018

13. Palmirani, M.: Lexdatafication: Italian legal knowledge modelling in akoma ntoso. In: Rodríguez-Doncel, V., Palmirani, M., Araszkiewicz, M., Casanovas, P., Pagallo, U., Sartor, G. (eds.) AI Approaches to the Complexity of Legal Systems XI-XII - AICOL International Workshops 2018 and 2020: AICOL-XI JURIX 2018, AICOL-XII JURIX 2020, XAILA JURIX 2020, Revised Selected Papers. Lecture Notes in Computer Science, vol. 13048, pp. 31–47. Springer (2020https://doi.org/10.1007/978-3-030-89811-3_3

14. Palmirani, M., Sperberg, R., Vergottini, G., Vitali, F.: Akoma Ntoso Version 1.0 Part 1: XML Vocabulary. OASIS Standard (August 2018). http://docs.oasis-open.org/legaldocml/akn-core/v1.0/akn-core-v1.0-part1-vocabulary.html

15. Palmirani, M., Vitali, F., Bernasconi, A., Gambazzi, L.: Swiss federal publication workflow with akoma ntoso. In: Hoekstra, R. (ed.) Legal Knowledge and Information Systems - JURIX 2014: The Twenty-Seventh Annual Conference, Jagiellonian University, Krakow, Poland, 10-12 December 2014. Frontiers in Artificial Intelligence and Applications, vol. 271, pp. 179–184. IOS Press (2014). https://doi.org/10.3233/978-1-61499-468-8-179

16. Reimers, N., Gurevych, I.: Sentence-BERT: sentence embeddings using siamese BERT-networks. arXiv preprint arXiv:1908.10084 (2019)

17. Sanh, V., Debut, L., Chaumond, J., Wolf, T.: Distilbert, a distilled version of BERT: smaller, faster, cheaper and lighter. arXiv preprint arXiv:1910.01108 (2019)

18. Vaswani, A., et al.: Attention is all you need. Adv. Neural Inf. Process. Syst. **30** (2017)

19. Vitali, F., Palmirani, M., Sperberg, R., Parisse, V.: Akoma Ntoso Version 1.0. Part 2: Specifications. OASIS Standard (August 2018). http://docs.oasis-open.org/legaldocml/akn-core/v1.0/akn-core-v1.0-part2-specs.html

20. Xiao, C., Hu, X., Liu, Z., Tu, C., Sun, M.: Lawformer: a pre-trained language model for Chinese legal long documents. AI Open **2**, 79–84 (2021). https://doi.org/10.1016/j.aiopen.2021.06.003

21. Zheng, L., Guha, N., Anderson, B.R., Henderson, P., Ho, D.E.: When does pre-training help? assessing self-supervised learning for law and the casehold dataset of 53,000+ legal holdings. In: Proceedings of the Eighteenth International Conference on Artificial Intelligence and Law, pp. 159–168. ICAIL '21, Association for Computing Machinery, New York, NY, USA (2021)

Supporting Decision-Making for City Management Through Automated Planning and Execution

Riccardo De Benedictis(✉) ⓘD, Gloria Beraldo ⓘD, Amedeo Cesta ⓘD, and Gabriella Cortellessa ⓘD

Institute of Cognitive Sciences and Technologies (ISTC) - National Research Council of Italy (CNR), via Giandomenico Romagnosi n. 18/A, 00196 Rome, Italy
{riccardo.benedictis,gloria.beraldo,amedeo.cesta,
gabriella.cortellessa}@cnr.it

Abstract. Urban intelligence is an emerging research field that aims at investigating the use of advanced technologies and data analysis techniques to enhance the efficiency, sustainability, and livability of urban areas. One of the components of urban intelligence is decision support which, among the possible implementations, can make use of forms of automated reasoning capable of *planning* the activities that must be carried out on the territory and, at the same time, of *reacting* to its dynamic evolution. Taking inspiration from the dual-process cognitive theories, this paper aims at investigating the integration of automated planning and rule-based systems as a means of supporting decision-making processes in urban management.

Keywords: Urban Intelligence · Planning · Decision Support System

1 Introduction

Cities are complex and dynamic environments that require continuous management to ensure their efficiency, sustainability, and livability. As urban populations grow and become more diverse, the challenges of urban management become increasingly complex [16,19]. In recent years, there has been a growing interest in the use of advanced technologies and data analysis techniques to support decision-making processes in urban management. Urban intelligence, in particular, is an emerging dynamic and evolving field of research that seeks to leverage advanced technologies and data analysis techniques to enhance the efficiency, sustainability, and livability of urban areas [3].

A critical component of the urban intelligence is the support to decisions which enables planners and policymakers to make informed decisions about urban development and management. A Cognitive Decision Support System (CDSS), in particular, is a type of Decision Support System (DSS) that incorporates cognitive theories and models of human decision-making to assist human

A. Artale et al. (Eds.): AIxIA 2024, LNAI 15450, pp. 119–132, 2025.
https://doi.org/10.1007/978-3-031-80607-0_10

decision-makers in complex decision-making tasks [18]. Among the available cognitive theories, the dual processing theory [15] has been widely applied in the development of CDSSs [2,22]. This cognitive theory posits that human cognition operates via two distinct systems or processes, often referred to as System 1 and System 2. More specifically, System 1 refers to fast, automatic, and intuitive thinking that relies on heuristics, mental shortcuts, and previous experience to make decisions or judgments. This system is often associated with our unconscious or intuitive mind and is involved in activities such as perception, pattern recognition, and emotional responses. System 2, on the other hand, refers to slower, deliberate, and analytical thinking that relies on logic, reasoning, and conscious effort to make decisions or judgments. System 2 is often associated with our conscious or rational mind and is involved in activities such as problem-solving, planning, and decision-making.

Taking inspiration from the dual processing theory, this paper presents a cognitive architecture, called COCO (from COmbined deduction and abduCtiOn logic reasoner), that aims at enhancing decision-making in urban management by combining a rule-based system to mimic the behavior of System 1, and a timeline-based planner, extended with semantic reasoning capabilities, to mimic the behavior of System 2. Section 2 provides background information on these two technologies, while Sect. 3 describes the COCO cognitive architecture, which combines a rule-based system and a timeline-based planner. This integration enables the planning of activities over extended time horizons, their execution, dynamic adaptation, and adaptive responses to changes in the urban environment. To demonstrate the effectiveness of this approach, Sect. 4 presents a case study in the city of Matera and provides some results. Finally, Sect. 5 summarizes the key findings and discusses future research directions.

2   Technical Background

This section provides some technical background on the two main components of the proposed approach for urban intelligence: rule-based systems and timeline-based planning. It explains how rule-based systems use a set of rules to make decisions and how they can efficiently react to new information. It also describes how timeline-based planning generates goal-oriented behaviors and is suitable for managing temporal information. Understanding these two components is crucial to understanding how they can be integrated to provide a more robust and flexible approach to urban intelligence.

2.1   Rule-Based Systems

Rule-based systems are a type of Artificial Intelligence (AI) systems that use a set of "if-then" rules to make decisions or draw conclusions [13,14]. These rules typically take the form of logical statements or condition-action pairs, where the condition is a set of input variables and the action is a set of output actions or conclusions. A knowledge base stores these rules along with some facts which are known to be true. The introduction of new facts triggers a reasoning engine which, by applying the rules to the input data or situations, selects the appropriate actions or conclusions.

An example of a rule, for such a system, can be "IF the temperature is above $30\,°C$ AND the humidity is above 70%, THEN activate the sprinkler system in the park". In this example, the rule-based system is programmed to respond to specific environmental conditions (high temperature and humidity) by triggering an action (activating the sprinkler system) to keep lush the vegetation that inhabits the park. By introducing a fact stating that "the temperature is currently $35\,°C$", and a fact stating that "the humidity is currently 75%", the previous rule is activated and the corresponding action is executed. It is worth noticing that when an action is executed, it can generate new facts or modify the existing ones, which can be used in subsequent reasoning and decision-making processes.

Rule-based systems can be particularly valuable in situations where decisions need to be made quickly and reliably. By using a set of pre-defined rules, decision-makers can quickly assess and respond to different situations, without the need for extensive analysis or deliberation. Furthermore, since the knowledge and reasoning process is based on explicitly defined rules, it is easy to understand how a rule-based system arrives at a certain decision or output. This is particularly important in the context of urban intelligence, where decision-makers and stakeholders need to have a clear understanding of how and why certain decisions are made.

2.2 Timeline-Based Planning

Automated planning [12] is another branch of AI that deals with creating computer programs that can generate plans, schedules, and strategies for accomplishing specific goals or tasks. Timeline-based planning [17], also known as constraint-based planning, is a type of automated planning where activities are organized over timelines and scheduled based on their temporal constraints and dependencies. This paper extends the formalization defined in [5] to handle also information not strictly tied to a specific time or time interval.

The basic building block of timeline-based planning, specifically, is the *token* which, intuitively, is used to represent the single unit of information. Through their introduction and their constraining during the planning process, tokens allow to represent the different components of the high-level plans. In its most general form, a token is formally described by an expression like $n\,(x_0, \ldots, x_i)_\chi$. In particular, n is a *predicate* symbol, $x_0, \ldots, x_i$ are its *parameters* (i.e., constants, numeric variables or object variables) and $\chi \in \{f, g\}$ is a constant representing the class of the token (i.e., either a *fact* or a *goal*).

The token's parameters are constituted, in general, by the variables of a *constraint network* $\mathcal{N}$ (refer to [6] for further details) and can be used, among other things, to represent temporal information such as the start or the end of some tasks. The semantics of the χ constant, on the contrary, is borrowed from Constraint Logic Programming (CLP) [1]. Specifically, while the facts are

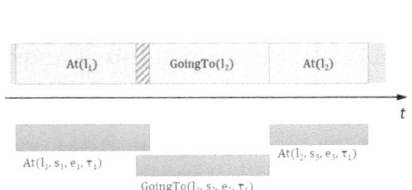

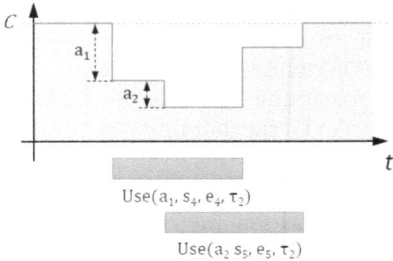

(a) An *inconsistent* state-variable time-line. The first *At* token and the *GoingTo* token are temporally overlapping. The inconsistency can be removed, for example, by introducing a $e_1 \leq s_2$ constraint.

(b) A *consistent* reusable-resource time-line. The overlap of tokens is allowed as long as the simultaneous use of the resource is less than its capacity.

Fig. 1. Different timelines extracted by their associated tokens.

considered inherently true, the goals must be achieved as defined by a set of *rules*. Rules, in particular, are expressions of the form $n(x_0, \ldots, x_k) \leftarrow \mathbf{r}$ where $n(x_0, \ldots, x_k)$ is the *head* of the rule and $\mathbf{r}$ is the *body* of the rule. In particular, $\mathbf{r}$ represents the *requirement* for achieving any goal having the "form" of the head of the rule. Such requirements can be either a token, a *constraint* among tokens (possibly including the $x_0, \ldots, x_k$ variables), a *conjunction* of requirements or a (priced) *disjunction* of requirements. It is worth noting the recursive definition of requirement, which allows the definition of the body of a rule as any logical combination of tokens and constraints. To illustrate, let's consider a rule that outlines the required steps for installing an optical fiber line in a specific road.

$$OpticalFiber\,(r, s, e) \leftarrow \left\{ \begin{matrix} [e - s \geq 20] \wedge \\ Trench\,(r_1 : r, s_1, e_1)_g \wedge \\ [s - e_1 \leq 7] \wedge [e_1 \leq s] \wedge \\ Repair\,(r_2 : r, s_2, e_2)_g \wedge \\ [s_2 - e \leq 8] \wedge [s_2 \geq e] \end{matrix} \right\}$$

According to the previous rule, the installation process takes a minimum of 20 time units. However, prior to commencing the installation, it is essential to excavate a trench along the road. The time between trench excavation and installation should not exceed 7 time units. Lastly, once the optical fiber is installed, the trench must be filled within a maximum of 8 time units to restore the road surface. The Trench and Repair predicates will share similar rules that establish the necessary conditions to accomplish the goals defined in the rule's body.

Similarly to CLP, through the application of the rules it is hence possible to establish and generate relationships among tokens. Compared to CLP, however, timelines introduce an added value: tokens may be equipped with a special object variable τ that identifies the *timeline* affected by the token. Different tokens with the same value for the τ parameter, in particular, affect the same timeline and, depending on the nature of the timeline, might interact with each other. There can be, indeed, different types of timelines. In case of *state-variable* timelines (see Fig. 1a), for example, different tokens on the same state-variable cannot temporally overlap. In case of *reusable-resource* timelines (see Fig. 1b), on the contrary, tokens represent resource usages and can, hence, overlap as long as the concurrent uses remain below the resource's capacity. In this context, timelines can be viewed as a *global constraint* (see, for example, [6]) imposed on the tokens applied to them.

Given the ingredients mentioned above, we can now formally introduce the addressed planning problem. A *timeline-based planning problem*, specifically, is a triple $\mathcal{P} = (\mathbf{O}, \mathcal{R}, \mathbf{r})$, where $\mathbf{O}$ is a set of typed objects, needed for instantiating the initial domains of the constraint network variables and, consequently, the tokens' parameters, $\mathcal{R}$ is a set of rules and $\mathbf{r}$ is the requirement that needs to be satisfied so that the plan achieves the desired objectives. A *solution* is a set of tokens whose parameters assume values so as to guarantee the satisfaction of all the constraints imposed by the problem's requirement, by the application of the rules, as well as by the global constraints imposed by the timelines.

3   Thinking, Fast and Slow, Logically: COCO

In a rule-based system, the inference engine typically applies a set of production rules to a knowledge base in order to *deduce* new information or actions. The rules are usually written in a forward-chaining form, meaning that they are triggered when certain conditions (i.e., antecedents) are met, and then generate new information or actions (i.e., consequents). The search limited to match the rule conditions, enhanced with indexing techniques [8], combined with the almost total absence of backtracking, makes these approaches particularly efficient

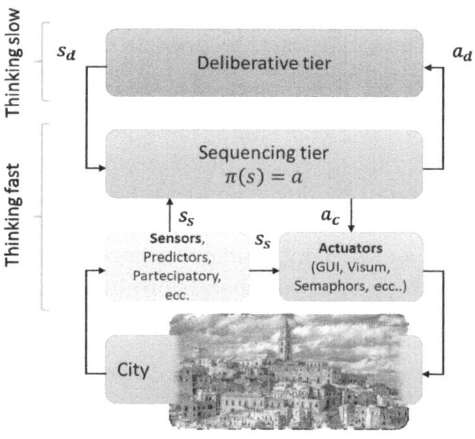

Fig. 2. The COCO three-layer architecture.

in reacting to new information. In timeline-based planning, on the contrary, the system works by searching backwards (*abduction*), from goals, to find a sequence of actions that can achieve that goals. This process involves constructing a plan by recursively applying rules and constraints, searching for valid solutions. When constraints do not propagate, the system backtracks, making the search for a solution more onerous from a complexity point of view. These approache are, nonetheless, specifically designed to handle temporal information and are more suited for generating goal-oriented behaviors that need to be executed within a certain time frame.

The proposed approach, depicted in Fig. 2, aims to exploit the high-reactivity and explainability of the rule-based system, together with the powerful planning capabilities of the timeline-based planner, to enable effective decision-making in dynamic and complex urban environments. Taking inspiration from classical robotics architectures [9], specifically, the COmbined deduction and abduCtiOn logic reasoner (COCO) consists of a *deliberative* tier responsible, through a timeline-based planner, for the generation, the execution and the dynamic adaptation of the plans; a *sequencing* tier which, through the CLIPS[1] rule-based system, executes a sequence of actions according to the current state of the world; and a *sensing* and a *controlling* tier, which respectively interprets data produced by sensors and translates the sequencer's actions into lower level commands for the actuators. The System 1 side is covered by the sequencing tier, which quickly recognizes and responds to familiar patterns and situations, generating abstractions from sensory data and low-level commands for actuators, functioning like automatic, intuitive decision-making. In contrast, the System 2 side is covered by the deliberative tier, which uses semantic and causal reasoning, and logical and arithmetic approaches to generate and adapt high-level plans based on dynamic environmental information.

The COCO state, according to which actions are selected from the sequencer tier, is represented through a set of facts in the rule-based system. Adding, modifying or deleting facts entails the execution of the actions through the activation of the rules. The facts, representing the state, are described by a combination of two distinct sets:

- the s_s set, containing facts generated by the sensing tier through a REST API, characterizes the consequences of the interpretation of sensory data, representing, for example, temperature, humidity, air quality, flows of vehicles on roads, etc.;
- the s_d set, containing facts generated by the deliberative tier, representing the high-level commands produced as a result of the execution of the planned tasks.

Similarly, the actions executed by the sequencer tier can be of two distinct types:

- the a_c actions, towards the controllers, responsible for various tasks, such as directly performing actions (e.g., activating a sprinkler) or indirectly influencing the city (e.g., communicating with municipal technicians or decision-makers);
- the a_d actions, towards the deliberative tier, responsible, for example, for the creation of the planning problems and for the execution and dynamic adaptation of the generated plans.

Notably, the sequencing tier, using the $\pi(s)$ policy, can act on the environment through a_c actions and introspectively on higher-level reasoning through a_d actions. The higher-level tasks (a.k.a. intrinsic motivations [21]) generated

---

[1] https://clipsrules.net.

Table 1. User-defined functions for interacting with the deliberative tier. These functions can be invoked, if necessary, by the sequencing tier.

User-defined function	Description
`new_solver(purpose, files)`	Creates a new solver for the given purpose and starts solving the planning problem contained in the given files.
`start_execution(solver_id)`	Starts the execution of the plan generated by the solver with the given ID.
`delay_task(task_id, delay_time)`	Delays the start of the task with the given ID by the `delay_time` amount of time.
`extend_task(task_id, extend_time)`	Extends the duration of the task with the given ID by the `extend_time` amount of time.
`failure(task_ids)`	Notifies the deliberative tier that the execution of the given set of tasks is failed. The executing plan should be adapted considering that the consequences of the failed tasks will no more be available.
`adapt(solver_id, files)`	Adapts the given plan by introducing new requirements (e.g., new goals).
`delete_solver(solver_id)`	Deletes the given solver and, if present, the corresponding plan.

by the deliberative tier during plan execution are only one factor influencing the sequencing tier's actions. These tasks are not mandatory for the system's autonomy but serve as suggestions for the agent on what to do.

The sequencing tier of the COCO architecture is equipped with several actions that enable it to formulate the planning problem, execute and modify the solutions generated by the planner in a dynamic manner. In particular, the CLIPS system has been enhanced to support user-defined functions, summarized in Table 1, within rule-based system rules. One of these functions is `new_solver`, which creates a new solver from a string indicating the solver's purpose and a set of files comprising the planning model definition and the problem instance. For timeline-based planning, these files contain the rule definitions and the initial problem requirement. Upon invocation, this function generates a new `solver` fact (refer to Table 2 for the facts related to planning that have been considered into the knowledge base) in the knowledge base, which includes the solver's ID, purpose, and state (initially in the `reasoning` state until a solution is found). Notably, the sequencing tier remains active during the planning process, reacting to external inputs and taking into account the planner's reasoning status as necessary.

After the planning process is completed, the `solver` fact is updated to indicate that the planner is now in an `idle` state. At this point, a rule on the sequencing tier, that has a premise with a `solver` fact having the same purpose of the planner and the `idle` state, is used to trigger the execution of the plan through the user-defined function `start_execution`. The presence of this rule

Table 2. Facts asserted and modified during the execution of the plans. The rule-based system reacts to the presence of these facts as to the presence of facts asserted as a consequence of changes in the environment.

Fact	Description
solver(id, purpose, state)	Declares the presence of a solver with a particular ID, purpose, and status. The status can be either reasoning, idle, executing, adapting, finished or failed.
task(solver_id, id, type, pars, vals)	Declares that a task is currently executing. The solver_id and id parameters indicate, respectively, the ID of the solver and the ID of the task. The type parameter indicates the type of the task (i.e., the n predicate symbol of the corresponding token). The pars and vals parameters indicate, respectively, the parameter names of the task and their values (i.e., the $x_0, \ldots, x_i$ names and values of the corresponding token).

enables the option to postpone plan execution until additional conditions arise, if deemed necessary. The planner then modifies the solver fact by putting it in the executing state and starts executing the plan by sending tasks to the sequencing tier in a timely manner. Aside from executing the plan, the sequencing tier can also perform other actions to modify the running plan. For instance, the delay_task and extend_task functions can request the delay of the start or end time of a task, respectively. The failure function can remove an activity from the plan, considering its effects on the execution of future activities. Lastly, the adapt function can introduce new requirements or goals within the current plan. As these adaptations can be quite expensive, effective strategies have been adopted to manage them [4,11].

Reasoning on delays and failures in the sequencing tier results in the modification of the solver fact, which is put in the adapting state. Once the adaptation is complete, the previous state (idle or executing) is restored. In case the planner ends up in an inconsistent state, such as due to excessive delays or too many failures that prevent the achievement of

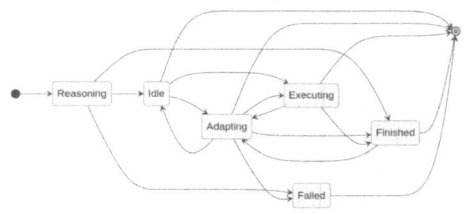

Fig. 3. State-transition diagram illustrating the potential states of the solvers.

the desired goals, the solver fact is updated to indicate a failed state of the planner. Further actions, such as creating a new solver with a new problem, are delegated to the rule-based system. When the execution completes all planned tasks achieving the desired goals, the state of the solver fact becomes finished. It is important to note that the solver fact is a crucial element in the communication and coordination between the planner and the sequencing tier, ensuring effective execution of the plan while managing exceptional cases. Figure 3 illustrates the potential states and transitions of the solvers.

Table 3. Functions called during the execution of plans in the COCO system.

Function	Description
starting(solver_id, id, type, pars, vals)	Queries the sequencing tier to determine if the task with the given id in the plan managed by the solver_id solver, characterized by the type type and with parameters pars taking on values vals, can be initiated. Returns a Boolean value (by default, TRUE) indicating whether the task can start. If not, an optional numerical value may be provided to indicate the estimated delay for starting the activity.
start(solver_id, id, type, pars, vals)	Informs the sequencing tier that the task, identified by the provided parameters, has just begun. By default, this action asserts a corresponding task fact in the knowledge base.
ending(solver_id, id)	Queries the sequencing tier to determine if the task with the given id in the plan managed by the solver_id solver can be terminated. Returns a Boolean value (by default, TRUE) indicating whether the task can finish. If not, an optional numerical value may be provided to indicate the estimated delay for ending the activity.
end(solver_id, id)	Informs the sequencing tier that the task with the given id in the plan managed by the solver_id solver has just finished. By default, this action retracts the corresponding task fact from the knowledge base.

During task execution, effective communication with the sequencing tier is crucial. Task execution in the COCO system requires confirmation from the sequencing tier, which is aware of dynamic environmental updates. Communication is maintained by adding relevant facts to the knowledge base and invoking specific custom functions. These functions are detailed in Table 3. The starting function checks if a task can begin, returning a Boolean value and an optional delay estimate if initiation is not possible. The start function informs the sequencing tier of a task's start, updating the knowledge base. Similarly, the ending function assesses if a task can end, and the end function signals task completion, updating the knowledge base accordingly. These functions ensure clear coordination between the deliberative and sequencing levels within the COCO system.

4   The Case Study of Matera

Matera (a photo of the city is visible within Fig. 2) is a beautiful city in southern Italy known for its ancient town, the "Sassi di Matera", a UNESCO World Heritage Site since 1993. In recent years, Matera has undergone a significant transformation, rebranding itself from a poverty-stricken city in the 1950 s to a modern, thriving hub today, center for innovation and cultural development. The Matera 2019 program, as the European Capital of Culture, included numerous initiatives to promote the city's history, art, and cultural heritage. For the occasion, Matera has been selected to host the "House of Emerging Technologies" project, funded by the Italian Ministry of Economic Development. The project, in particular, has implemented several technological solutions to enhance the city's urban management and improve the quality of life of citizens and visitors. One of these solutions is a data platform that collects information from sensors placed around the city, including data from citizen notifications, which can be used for analysis and decision-making. Additionally, a 3D model of the city, annotated to achieve a semantic 3D representation, provides valuable insights for urban management [20]. The project also employs Dynamic Mode Decomposition to analyze pedestrian and vehicle traffic patterns and predict future states [7]. Path planning algorithms have also been developed to help visitors optimize their visits, finding the optimal route based on user preferences such as shortest paths, minimum slopes, or maximum shade [10].

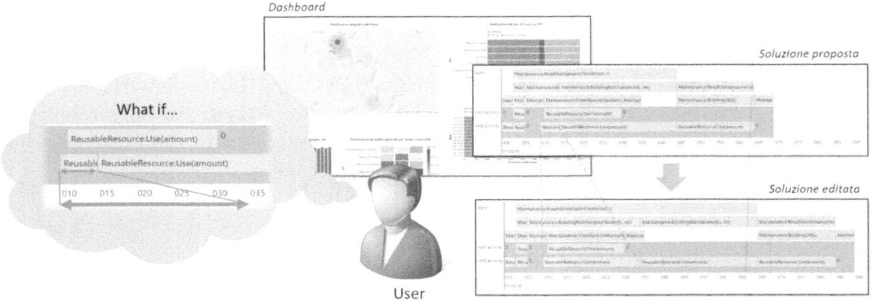

Fig. 4. The COCO web app contains a dashboard for real-time monitoring and for visualizing statistics. Plans can be visualized and edited in order to perform what-if analysis.

The COCO system[2] is one element in this ensemble, aiming to coordinate the operations of the various components, plan necessary activities, and manage part of the information received from sensors. While planning urban interventions, decision-makers and municipal technicians receive real-time suggestions on activities to undertake, and citizens receive pertinent updates on the status of the city (e.g., public events). Both decision-makers and municipal technicians can interact with COCO and, if needed, incrementally adjust the generated solutions by introducing additional constraints, thereby conducting a what-if analysis. For instance, Fig. 4 displays the user-accessible web-based dashboard, presenting information about the city's state and statistics derived from sensors' history. The figure also includes a timeline representation of an executing plan, illustrating the impact of extending a task due to a user-initiated what-if analysis.

---

[2] https://github.com/ratioSolver/COCO.

The rule-based system within COCO maintains a comprehensive dataset related to the city's state. This includes details about the managed sensor types, the specific sensors strategically positioned throughout the city, information about roads (e.g., known condition, length, capacity, slope, etc.), details about buildings (e.g., known condition, energy efficiency, etc.), road traffic and atmospheric simulations, predicted future states (to react to problems before they occur), a registry of users, who have system access, with their associated skills, and so on. Data generated by sensors reaches COCO via a REST API and contributes to the assertion of additional facts, which in turn can trigger the activation of rules and subsequent execution of specific actions. Similarly, the rule-based system has been expanded with user-defined functions to facilitate both direct actions (e.g., activating a sprinkler) and indirect actions (e.g., communicating with municipal technicians or decision-makers). These actions aim to influence the city and may involve suggesting decisions to decision-makers. Suppose, for example, that an air quality sensor sends a pm10 value equal to 55 μg/mc. This information results in adding a (`sensor_data aq0 04042023 55`) fact, in which (`aq0`) is the ID of the air quality sensor, 04042023 is the timestamp of the datum and 55 is the pm10 perceived amount. Since the daily limit threshold, in Italy, is 50 μg/mc, the following rule triggers the sending of a warning message to the person in charge of managing the situation.

```
(defrule pm10
    (sensor_data (id ?s_id) (timestamp ?t) (data ?pm10))
    (sensor (id ?s_id) (location ?lat ?lng) (type_id ?type))
    (sensor_type (id ?type) (name ''air_quality'')) (test (>= ?pm10 50))
    (user (id ?u_id)) (skill (id ?u_id) (name ''air_monitoring'')) =>
    (send_message ?u_id (str-cat "The air quality sensor has perceived a pm10
    value of " ?pm10 " which is above the recomended threshold of 50 Âţg/mc")))
```

Another scenario involves managing participatory data through a web interface where citizens can report issues concerning buildings, roads, and other public amenities. When a certain threshold of reports is reached, the rule-based system activates the deliberative tier by setting a goal for maintaining the reported asset. In modeling the problem, the monitoring of maintenance interventions is entrusted to a

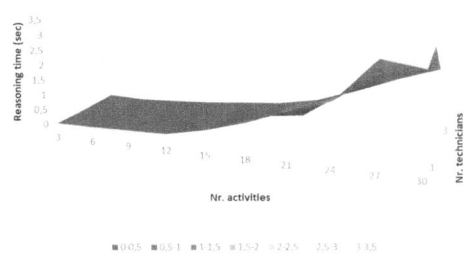

Fig. 5. Planning times based on the number of maintenance goals and the number of municipal technicians.

team of municipal technicians, who are also assigned the task of preparing the documents for the related calls for tenders, aimed at assigning the activities to the companies which, won tenders, will be awarded the contract for the effective implementation of maintenance operations. Each technician has specific skills, limiting their involvement to certain types of maintenance tasks (e.g., road and public green maintenance but not public building maintenance). Additionally, to prevent overloading, no technician can handle more than two activities simultaneously; for instance, in case of three concurrent activities, they can be assigned to two different technicians or scheduled to overlap in a way that respects the limit of two concurrent activities per technician.

The ongoing process of defining rules encompasses both the rules-based system and the deliberative tier. Specifically, the deliberative tier addresses issues related to the maintenance of public goods, urban planning interventions, and the intricacies of procurement procedures, which must navigate the complexities of Italian bureaucracy. On the other hand, rules for the rule-based system primarily consider scenarios where predefined thresholds are exceeded. Employing machine learning techniques, particularly decision tree learning, we leverage data obtained from road simulations to formulate rules for predicting traffic jams on specific roads, based on the monitoring of a selected subset equipped with sensors. To assess the effectiveness of COCO, nonetheless, our focus turned to evaluating the efficiency of the reasoners' resolution processes on a set of benchmark problems of increasing size. This approach allowed us to estimate resolution times as the size of the addressed problems grew. Given that decision-makers might interact with COCO to perform what-if analyses during urban intervention planning, the system's response must be swift. Figure 5 illustrates the resolution times varying with the number of maintainance goals and on the number of municipal technicians in the team. Notably, despite the exponential complexity[3] of the problem, resolution times consistently remain within a few seconds, even with higher numbers of activities. It is worth to note how, the planner has greater freedom in assigning activities, resolution times decrease slightly with more technicians.

5   Conclusions

This paper introduces the COCO system, integrating a rule-based system with automated planners to support decision-making in urban management. Rule-based systems react efficiently to environmental changes, while automated planning provides a more deliberative approach to generating tasks that achieve desired goals. By combining these approaches, urban managers gain a comprehensive tool for managing various aspects of urban life. Pattern-matching techniques enhance the efficiency of rule-based systems in reactive tasks, while the deliberative component, though more computationally intensive, remains feasible for scenario generation, plan adaptation, and what-if analyses.

Defining rules is a critical and often complex process shared by both systems. In future work, we aim to explore machine learning to streamline and, where possible, automate rule definition. Additionally, changes in municipal administrations have delayed tasks like procuring and installing sensors. In the coming

---

[3] The planner must sequence activities while respecting temporal and resource constraints, thus solving an NP-Hard problem in this case.

months, we plan to conduct experiments with real users, including municipal administrators and citizens. We have also begun applying these techniques in the cities of Catania and Milano.

References

1. Apt, K.R., Wallace, M.G.: Constraint Logic Programming Using ECL^{i}PS^e. Cambridge University Press, New York, NY, USA (2007)
2. Arnott, D., Gao, S.: Behavioral economics for decision support systems researchers. Decis. Support Syst. **122**, 113063 (2019). https://doi.org/10.1016/j.dss.2019.05.003
3. Castelli, G., et al.: Urban intelligence: a modular, fully integrated, and evolving model for cities digital twinning. In: 2019 IEEE 16th International Conference on Smart Cities: Improving Quality of Life Using ICT & IoT and AI (HONET-ICT), pp. 033–037 (2019). https://doi.org/10.1109/HONET.2019.8907962
4. De Benedictis, R., Beraldo, G., Cesta, A., Cortellessa, G.: Incremental timeline-based planning for efficient plan execution and adaptation. In: Dovier, A., Montanari, A., Orlandini, A. (eds.) AIxIA 2022 - Advances in Artificial Intelligence, pp. 225–240. Springer International Publishing, Cham (2023)
5. De Benedictis, R., Cesta, A.: Lifted heuristics for timeline-based planning. In: ECAI-2020. 24th European Conference on Artificial Intelligence, pp. 2330–2337. Santiago de Compostela, Spain (2020)
6. Dechter, R.: Constraint Processing. Elsevier Morgan Kaufmann (2003)
7. Diez, M., Serani, A., Campana, E.F., Stern, F.: Data-driven modelling of ship maneuvers in waves via dynamic mode decomposition (2021)
8. Forgy, C.L.: Rete: a fast algorithm for the many pattern/many object pattern match problem. Artif. Intell. **19**(1), 17–37 (1982). https://doi.org/10.1016/0004-3702(82)90020-0
9. Gat, E.: On three-layer architectures. In: Artificial Intelligence and Mobile Robots, pp. 195–210. AAAI Press (1997)
10. Gentile, C., Stecca, G., Mancini, S., Suanno, M.: An application of the orienteering problem with time windows for scheduling visits during social events. In: Joint EURO/ALIO International Conference 2018 on Applied Combinatorial Optimization, Bologna (Italy), June 25 - 27, 2018 (2018)
11. Gerevini, A., Serina, I.: Fast plan adaptation through planning graphs: local and systematic search techniques. In: Chien, S.A., Kambhampati, S., Knoblock, C.A. (eds.) Proceedings of the Fifth International Conference on Artificial Intelligence Planning Systems, Breckenridge, CO, USA, April 14-17, 2000, pp. 112–121. AAAI (2000). http://www.aaai.org/Library/AIPS/2000/aips00-012.php
12. Ghallab, M., Nau, D., Traverso, P.: Automated Planning: Theory and Practice. Morgan Kaufmann Publishers Inc. (2004)
13. Grosan, C., Abraham, A.: Rule-Based Expert Systems, pp. 149–185. Springer Berlin Heidelberg, Berlin, Heidelberg (2011). https://doi.org/10.1007/978-3-642-21004-4_7
14. Hopgood, A.A.: Intelligent Systems for Engineers and Scientists, 3rd Edition (2016)
15. Kahneman, D.: Thinking, Fast and Slow. Farrar, Straus and Giroux, New York (2011)

16. Moreno-Monroy, A.I., Schiavina, M., Veneri, P.: Metropolitan areas in the world. delineation and population trends. J. Urban Economics **125**, 103242 (2021). https://doi.org/10.1016/j.jue.2020.103242, https://www.sciencedirect.com/science/article/pii/S0094119020300139, delineation of Urban Areas

17. Muscettola, N.: HSTS: integrating planning and scheduling. In: Zweben, M. and Fox, M.S. (ed.) Intelligent Scheduling, pp. 169–212. Morgan Kauffmann (1994)

18. Niu, L., Lu, J., Zhang, G.: Cognition-driven decision support for business intelligence: models, techniques, systems and applications / Li Niu, Jie Lu, and Guangquan Zhang. Springer Verlag Berlin (2009)

19. OECD, Commission, E.: Cities in the World (2020). https://doi.org/10.1787/d0efcbda-en, https://www.oecd-ilibrary.org/content/publication/d0efcbda-en

20. Scalas, A., Cabiddu, D., Mortara, M., Spagnuolo, M.: Potential of the geometric layer in urban digital twins. ISPRS Int. J. Geo-Inf. **11**(6), 343 (2022). https://doi.org/10.3390/ijgi11060343, https://www.mdpi.com/2220-9964/11/6/343

21. Schmidhuber, J.: Formal theory of creativity, fun, and intrinsic motivation (1990' 2010). IEEE Trans. Auton. Ment. Dev. **2**(3), 230–247 (2010). https://doi.org/10.1109/TAMD.2010.2056368

22. Tsalatsanis, A., Hozo, I., Kumar, A., Djulbegovic, B.: Dual processing model for medical decision-making: an extension to diagnostic testing. PLoS One **10**(8), e0134800 (2015). https://doi.org/10.1371/journal.pone.0134800

NutriWell: An Explainable Ontology-Based FoodAI Service for Nutrition and Health Management

Berardina De Carolis(✉)🆔, Davide Lofrese(✉), Davide Di Pierro(✉)🆔, and Stefano Ferilli(✉)🆔

Università degli Studi di Bari Aldo Moro, Bari, Italy
{berardina.decarolis,davide.dipierro,stefano.ferilli}@uniba.it,
d.lofrese1@alumni.uniba.it

Abstract. Non-communicable diseases (NCDs) like hypertension, diabetes, osteoporosis, and cancer constitute 80% of the disease burden in European countries, affecting a significant portion of the working-age population. Addressing these numbers requires a strong effort in prevention and management. Nutrition is crucial not only for chronic conditions but also for non-chronic medical needs such as pregnancy, allergies, and intolerances. Artificial Intelligence (AI), especially when integrated with chatbots or social robots, now plays a pivotal role in assisting users with NCD prevention and management, as well as dietary needs. This manuscript introduces *NutriWell*, a framework leveraging AI and the *GraphBRAIN* technology for intelligent knowledge retrieval in nutrition and health management. *NutriWell* informs users about meal suitability based on their nutritional requirements, utilizing explanations that combine feature data and user preferences. Italian websites such as *GialloZafferano* and *AlimentiNUTrizione* provide extensive catalogs of European meals, including ingredients, allergens, and dietary specifics. The contribution of this work is the construction of a personalized diet assistant by utilizing datasets extracted from these websites that, as far as we know, have never been used for these tasks. A key contribution is an API that retrieves graph-based information integrated with an ontology specifying relational constraints. The ontology design, derived from existing frameworks and enhanced to integrate food impacts on disorders, allows for the calculation of meal impact scores tailored to user needs and preferences.

Keywords: Graph Database · Ontology · Health

1 Introduction

Non-communicable diseases (NCDs), also known as chronic diseases, are diseases that are not transmissible from one person to another and include hypertension, diabetes, osteoporosis, and cancer. NCDs are responsible for 80% of the disease

A. Artale et al. (Eds.): AIxIA 2024, LNAI 15450, pp. 133–146, 2025.
https://doi.org/10.1007/978-3-031-80607-0_11

burden in European countries [23] and about one-quarter of the working-age population (23.5%) is affected by at least one chronic disease [22]. Furthermore, multiple chronic conditions (MCCs) often occur at the same time, which is very common in people aged more than 65 years old (65%) and up to 85% in elderly people (aged 85+) [17]. In the next years, these figures are predicted to increase. For example, diabetes diagnoses in Europe have almost tripled over the last two decades, from about 22 million in 2000 to 61 million in 2021, and 2045 expects a further increase of 13% [7]. Genetic and environmental factors contribute to the risk of developing one or more NCDs, but modifiable behavioural risk factors play an essential role. In particular, tobacco use, lack of physical activity, and unhealthy diet increase the risk of NCDs. Indeed, the rise in chronic medical conditions can be linked to diets becoming more and more characterized by high levels of fats and sugars, but lacking in fresh fruits and vegetables [4]. Moreover, about two million deaths each year are attributed to excess salt and sodium intake [8].

Hence, a healthy diet and lifestyle can help in preventing the onset of such diseases. For instance, a diet that is low in fats, refined carbohydrates, and sugar-sweetened beverages, but rich in fruits and vegetables reduces the risk of cardiovascular diseases [24]. In addition, following a healthy diet is useful not only in the prevention of an NCD but also in the treatment and control of an already-developed disease. An example is the DASH (Dietary Approaches to Stop Hypertension) diet which helps reduce blood pressure in hypertensive patients.

Improving eating habits is important for other non-chronic medical conditions as well, such as pregnancy where a high supply of nutrients is necessary, but limiting sugars, salt and saturated fats. Furthermore, people affected with food allergies or intolerances have to be careful in what they eat to avoid the unintentional intake of unsafe food containing allergens that could trigger life-threatening reactions.

To make one's dietary habits better, food and nutrition literacy became very important [18]. Specifically, nutrition literacy is the ability to obtain, understand, and apply nutritional information to make healthy decisions about food consumption. A nutrition-literate person is aware of the food nutrients and how they affect health and, as a consequence, he/she can exercise good judgment in choosing what to eat.

Technologies can help in increasing nutrition literacy and gaining a greater level of nutritional awareness by providing hardware and software tools to support people in managing their nutrition and food intake. For example, digital food diaries can be used to log meals and monitor calories and macronutrients (i.e., carbohydrates, proteins and fats) to keep a balanced diet. Similarly, virtual coaches in the form of chatbots can provide users with personalized diet recommendations based on age, gender and health conditions.

Due to the nature of the problem and the necessity of making people understand what modern AI systems output, explanations for the results need to be provided. We emphasize the personalization factor in this approach since dietary habits, diseases and intolerances make each one of us different.

In this work, we propose a new framework for evaluating how appropriate is a meal for an end-user, taking into account user intolerances, diseases, preferences (e.g. vegetarianism), food ingredients, calories and more. The dataset is constructed by combining information available in some of the most comprehensive food websites, such as *GialloZafferano* and *AlimentiNUTrizione*. The combined dataset has been translated into a graph formalism (specifically Labelled Property Graph [1]) which can be accessed through an API. The graph is empowered with an ontology defining entity and relationship constraints. The ontology also acts as a scheme for the graph and has been designed starting from existing schemes and connecting information about foods with their impact on disorders that is, to the best of our knowledge, an underrepresented way of formalizing schemes in the food domain. The graph and the ontology follow the *GraphBRAIN* technology, next described. This manuscript is structured as follows: Sect. 2 presents existing solutions and comparisons with our framework, Sect. 3 describes data gathering and storage, Sect. 4 describes the *GraphBRAIN* framework and the ontology design process, Sect. 5 describes the overall *NutriWell* framework, Sect. 6 describes the explanatory process and the evaluation, Sect. 7 clarifies possible ethical concerns, and finally Sect. 8 concludes the work and mentions future scenarios.

2   Related Work

The food sector has largely benefited from Artificial Intelligence. The applications are countless [13], but they can be mainly divided into two categories: the control and tracking, from the harvesting to the consumption, and the effects of the aliments on our bodies, more often than not proposing recommendations [21]. One of the first attempts to advertise meals based on the user needs was by Snae et al. [19]. It was based on Korean cuisine and represented a filtering system for diseases. From this earlier stage, we fuzzify the impact by assigning a certain degree of damage (not just a binary choice) and provide explanations by combining ingredients' features.

A more sophisticated recommender system by Toledo et al. [20] has personalization as its main strength and also considers user preferences. One of the main differences with our approach is that we are capable of providing explanations for informing the user about the goodness of a choice. This is due to the use of interpretable graph models (graphs) and symbolic conceptualizations (ontologies).

Regarding the pure ontology designing phase, the attempt to unify food ontologies has been provided by Popovski et al. [14]. However, the unified conceptualization does not include peculiarities details for expressing the impact of the food and ingredients on allergies and/or diseases. In the work, the alignment took into consideration several existing ontologies such as FoodWiki [3], Open Food Facts [16] and others. Nonetheless, these resources cannot be compared with the richness of the Italian websites we are considering here. On the other side, our solution lacks the presence of foreign cuisines.

In the context of food production tracking for sustainability and smart cities, Kamel et al. [12] integrated heterogeneous sources to combine information at different granularity and steps for a holistic production line of food.

In dealing with graphs, Qin et al. [15] constructed a Chinese cuisine knowledge graph with a query answering system retrieving resources gathered from the web. In this work, the ontology is derived from data rather than manually constructed and refined for the task, also because the system was not supposed to be used for a specific use case. Again, the lack of correlation between food and illnesses, or the correlation with the ingredients' features is common.

Without using conceptualization on a graph, as often happened with the LPG model, Bajaj et al. [2] introduced the use of Neo4j for the storage and recommendation of food. This represented a preliminary idea of our work in which the performance can be appreciated and justifies the ongoing research in this field with that representation.

Taking everything into account, many works aimed to recommend personalized food based on diseases/allergies, some of them are not explainable or limited in their interpretation since they do not make use of interpretable data structures or ontologies. The conceptualization of food barely takes into account intolerances and the impact of each ingredient on them. Datasets vary in nationality and there have been attempts to merge them but, as far as we are concerned, nobody took into account two of the most popular Italian websites.

3   Dataset

The first step was to realize a new dataset, that is the result of the combination of existing datasets available in the form of websites. As far as we are concerned, it is the first time *GialloZafferano* and *AlimentiNUTrizione* have been employed for developing an AI-based diet assistant. The main limitation of this dataset is that it is in Italian but it may represent a relevant resource in the field for the community. One of the contributions consists of the collection of these web-based data (through scraping), translation, and dissemination. Diseases, allergies, and intolerances have been manually selected, considering their relation to food, and manually listed by experts who examined the dataset. Afterwards, foods, beverages and ingredients have been provided with an impact on the diseases, which can be positive, neutral, or negative. This assumption holds if the quantities respect the traditional recipe more or less. For instance, an exceeding amount of salt harms every person regardless of his/her physical state.

3.1   Data Gathering

The majority of data on foods comes from the two aforementioned websites. The first one is the most visited recipes website in Italy and contains more than 4,000 recipes. It has been chosen as a data source both for its numerosity and for the presence of nutritional information. Specifically, the nutrients available in *GialloZafferano* are eight: carbohydrates, proteins, fats, sugars, saturated fats, fibers, cholesterol, and sodium. The second website, on the other hand, is curated by the Italian Food and Nutrition Research Center and includes the Food Composition Tables, a collection of composition data for about 900 basic foods. We also included some other sources like *Cookaround* and *leCalorie* to gather a few regional recipes. In summary, *GialloZafferano*, along with other recipe websites, is the data source for nutritional facts of complex recipes (e.g., cheesecake), whereas *AlimentiNUTrizione* is the source for nutritional facts of basic foods (e.g., apple). Fortunately, ingredients in *GialloZafferano* did not need any entity recognition process since no synonyms were used throughout the websites. On the other hand, ingredients in *AlimentiNUTrizione* were manually linked to those available in *GialloZafferano*.

3.2 Data Labelling

After a data cleaning process to remove invalid values and/or redundancies, the labelling step took place. The complete set of the ingredients contained in the recipes has been taken into account to label each ingredient with a category (e.g., fruit, meat, sauce). For this purpose, a set of categories has been defined based on the classes in the HeLiS ontology [5]. In particular, this ontology provides a representation of the food and physical activity domains and has been used in a real-world system for promoting healthy lifestyles in workplaces. Among the food-related concepts included in the ontology, the ingredients are broken down into 137 categories organized in a hierarchical taxonomy. These concepts are represented with a high level of granularity, nonetheless, for this task, a subset of these classes has been considered discarding too specific classes. For instance, the **Red Meat** class has been included, but specific types of red meat have been neglected (e.g., sheep, bovine, goat, and pork red meat). The total classes selected are 35 and the resulting hierarchical structure is shown in Fig. 1.

After defining the categories to use, the ingredients have been manually assigned to the most specific category. For example, **Sliced Beef** has been assigned the **Red Meat** category, instead of the more generic **Meat** category.

Labelling ingredients allows assigning diet and health labels to foods and beverages. More specifically, as in Edamam [6], it has been chosen to supplement foods and beverages with a set of diet and health labels to provide information on nutrient-level and ingredient-level aspects of the foods.

The set of diet and health labels used in this work is based on a subset of the labels provided by Edamam. In particular, 12 labels have been defined (5 diet labels and 7 health labels) and a short description of each is reported in Table 1.

In total, 21 conditions have been chosen, with 12 chronic diseases and health conditions (acne, cancer, diverticulitis, high cholesterol, hypertension, irritable bowel syndrome, migraine, non-alcoholic fatty liver disease, obesity, osteoporosis, pregnancy, type 2 diabetes), 6 food allergies (egg, fish, mollusc, peanut, shellfish, tree nut), and 3 food intolerances (fructose, gluten, lactose).

Following the selection of diseases, a range of values has been defined to express the positive or negative effect of a food, beverage, or ingredient on a

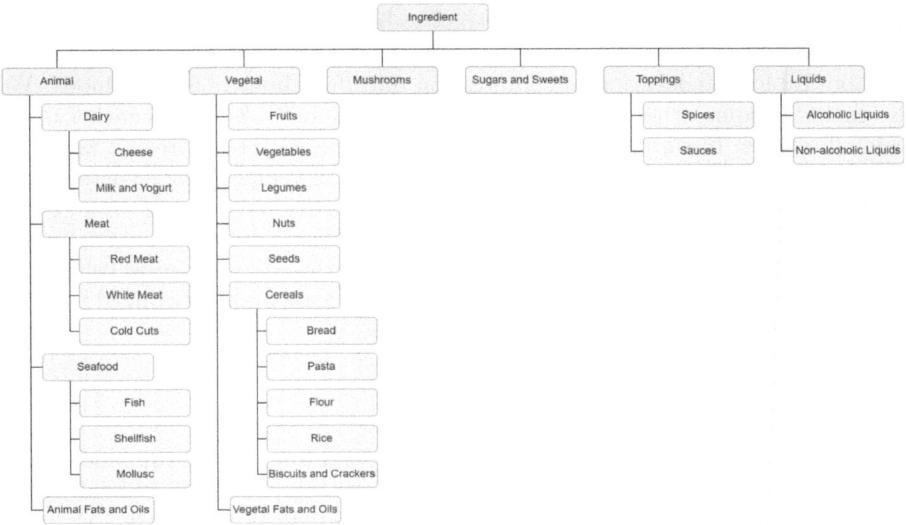

Fig. 1. Ingredients' ontology.

disease, allergy or intolerance. In particular, it has been chosen to assign values in the closed interval $[-1, 1]$ with the following interpretation:

- -1: the food, beverage or ingredient is bad and should be avoided as it worsens or increases the risk of the condition
- 0: the food, beverage or ingredient has a neutral or no impact on the condition (this value is also used when there is no information about the relationship on the disease)
- $+1$: the food, beverage or ingredient has a helpful effect as it improves or prevents the condition

Note that, for generic diseases and medical conditions, values in-between -1 and $+1$ are possible. For instance, a value of -0.5 represents a food, beverage or ingredient that is moderately bad and should be consumed less, but not avoided. The choice of this range has been suggested by experts in the domain, who claimed that a higher level of granularity requires a more fine-grained user knowledge, and hence is not general.

Conversely, for allergies and intolerances, only the three values -1, 0 and $+1$ are possible without in-between values, that is:

- -1: the food, beverage or ingredient cannot be eaten as it contains the allergen
- 0: the food, beverage or ingredient is a little risky and might contain traces of the allergen (this value is also used when there is no information about the relationship on the allergy/intolerance)
- $+1$: the food, beverage, or ingredient is safe to eat as it does not contain the allergen

Table 1. Diet and health labels

Diet	balanced	Balanced ratio of carbohydrates, proteins and fats. Specifically: • % carbohydrates from 45 to 65 • % proteins from 10 to 35 • % fats from 20 to 35
	high-protein	% proteins > 50
	low-carbs	% carbohydrates < 20
	low-fat	% fats < 15
	low-sugar	# grams of sugars for serving < 4
Health	alcohol-free	No alcoholic ingredients
	pork-free	No pork meat ingredients
	red-meat-free	No red meat ingredients
	no-oil-added	No oil added in the food
	pescatarian	No meat ingredients
	vegan	No animal ingredients
	vegetarian	No meat or fish ingredients

First, the ingredient-disease pairs have been manually labelled according to knowledge about the interaction between ingredients and diseases. For instance, the ingredient "Salt" has been assigned the value -1 for hypertension disease as it is one of the ingredients directly linked to high blood pressure and, as such, it should be avoided. For allergies and intolerances, the labelling has been carried out checking, for each ingredient, whether it contains the allergen. For example, the ingredient "Dark chocolate" has been assigned the rating 0 for the egg food allergy, as it might contain the allergen. Next, food-disease pairs have been automatically labelled considering the ingredients in the foods and the previously labelled ingredient-disease pairs. Specifically, the assigned value for a food-disease pair is the average of the ingredient-disease values for each ingredient present in the food. For example, if there is a food containing four ingredients with -1, -1, $+1$ and 0 as ingredient-disease ratings for a specific disease, the food-disease pair will be labelled with -0.25, that is the average of the four ingredient-disease values. This is a safe practical simplification in general, needed to make the process of labelling each recipe feasible. However, this does not apply to allergies where the assigned value for a food-allergy pair is the the minimum of the ingredient-disease values, rather than their average. Consequently, if the food has even one ingredient containing the allergen, the food-allergy pair will be labeled with -1 as it is not safe to eat.

The final dataset is made of 5,239 foods and beverages (4,840 recipes, and 399 basic foods) along with their nutritional facts. In addition, the dataset includes 1,606 ingredients divided into 35 categories. Each food is labelled with a set of diet and health labels chosen among 12 possible labels. Furthermore, the dataset features information on the interaction of foods and ingredients with 21 diseases, allergies and intolerances.

4   GraphBRAIN and Ontology Alignment

For the storage of the dataset, many alternatives are available currently. Due to the relational structure of the data (e.g. connections among foods and ingredients, and ingredients with diseases and allergies), and the need for both competitive performance and interpretability, we opted for a graph-based representation, specifically the Labelled Property Graph [1] supported by Neo4j. While providing efficient query-answering techniques and path interpretability, graph databases lack a general structure and schema, which is a requisite for traditional relational databases [11], making the interpretation of labels blurry when evaluating the different results. Following this need, in *GraphBRAIN* (GB) [9,10] we created a framework to deal with LPG data with a manually-defined upper schema on them. Schemes are the abstraction of nodes and arcs in the graph, representing the following (main) concepts:

- **entity**: set of nodes sharing the same label.
- **relationship**: arc between nodes.
- **attribute**: property of a node (resp. arc) in the LPG.
- **hierarchy**: a label being a specification of another one.

As it can be noticed, schemes are interpreted as ontologies. In the GB setting, data are fully compliant with schemes and no exceptions are allowed. For this purpose, part of the contribution consists in the developing of a new scheme for the food domain collecting structural elements of foods and ingredients, and connecting them with the impact on preferences, allergies and diseases.

A preliminary food conceptualization was already available in GB, but it has been expanded to fulfil the requirements of this work. The main elements of the dataset are these three concepts:

- **Aliment**: a generic aliment, specialized in Food and Beverage.
- **Ingredient**: a generic ingredient, specialized in 35 classes (see Fig. 1).
- **Disease**: a generic disease, specialized in Allergy and Intolerance.

The whole conceptualization (visualized as a graph) is shown in Fig. 2.

GB is available in the form of API to allow end-users to build their graph-based application.

5   NutriWell

NutriWell, the proposed framework, provides intelligent access to nutritional information about foods and beverages (with details on macronutrients, micronutrients and ingredients) but also gives insights on the impact of food on diseases, allergies, and intolerances. This information is accessible using a service designed and developed as a web API following REST architecture principles.

Resources exposed by the API have been identified based on the concepts represented as classes and relationships in the ontology. Specifically, the three

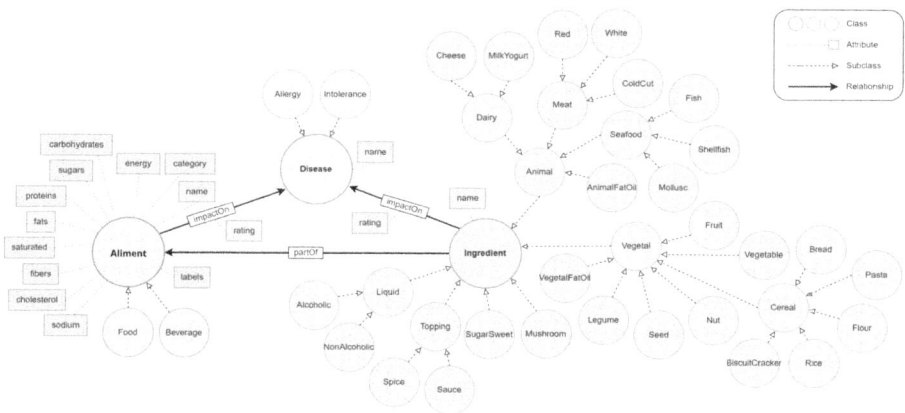

Fig. 2. GB Food Ontology

concepts defined as top-level classes in the ontology, like **Aliment**, **Ingredient** and **Disease**, give rise to two granularities of REST resources: collection resources and singleton resources. The former represents groups of homogeneous items, whereas the latter represents specific items within a collection. For example, the **Aliment** concept results in a collection resource, including all the foods and beverages, and multiple singleton resources, one for each specific food or beverage. The same applies to the **Ingredient** and **Disease** concepts, where a collection groups together the items, which can also be accessed individually.

Relationships among the concepts are represented as nested sub-collection resources. In particular, the *partOf* relationship specifying the ingredients contained in a food is represented as a sub-collection nested within the corresponding singleton food resource. In the opposite direction, the set of foods containing an ingredient is modelled as a sub-collection within the singleton ingredient resource. Similarly, the impact scores of a specific food (ingredient) on diseases are nested within the singleton food (ingredient) resources and, in the opposite direction, the impacts of foods (ingredients) on a specific disease are nested within the singleton disease resource.

Each singleton resource is described with a set of attributes that match the attributes of the respective classes in the ontology. Furthermore, two additional attributes are included in each singleton resource: *id* (the unique numeric identifier of the item) and *type* (the most specific ontology class assigned to the item).

Resources are represented in JSON format and they are accessed via URLs organized into a hierarchy. More specifically, collection resources have URLs based on plural nouns (*/foods, /ingredients, /diseases*), whereas singleton resources are assigned a unique numeric identifier and accessed through their parent collection resource (*/foods/{food-id}, /ingredients/{ingredient-id}, /diseases/{disease-id}*). Instead, nested sub-collection resources are accessed through their parent singleton resource (e.g., */foods/{food-id}/ingredients*, */foods/{food-id}/diseases*).

Operations on resources are defined in terms of standard HTTP methods identifying the type of operation to carry out. *NutriWell* uses five HTTP methods with their standard semantics, namely: GET, POST, PUT, PATCH and DELETE. Hence, the four traditional CRUD operations can be executed on resources. This allows data to change over time by adding new foods, ingredients and diseases.

The API also implements filtering features allowing clients to obtain subsets of large collection resources. In particular, one or more filters can be specified to retrieve a subset of items satisfying some constraints. For instance, the *name* filter parameter can be used to retrieve foods and beverages matching a string according to a similarity measure (namely, the Sørensen-Dice similarity measure).

NutriWell is implemented in Python leveraging *Litestar*, an open-source framework focused on building APIs. The system architecture is outlined in Fig. 3. The server consists of several modules with well-defined responsibilities that cooperate to process requests. In short, a request coming from the client is received from the router and passed to the authorization middleware to check the API key validity. Then, the request reaches the controller that handles it using the service layer which, in turn, accesses the database through the repository layer. Note that the repository does not directly interact with the Neo4j database, but instead, it uses *GraphBRAIN* functionalities through its API.

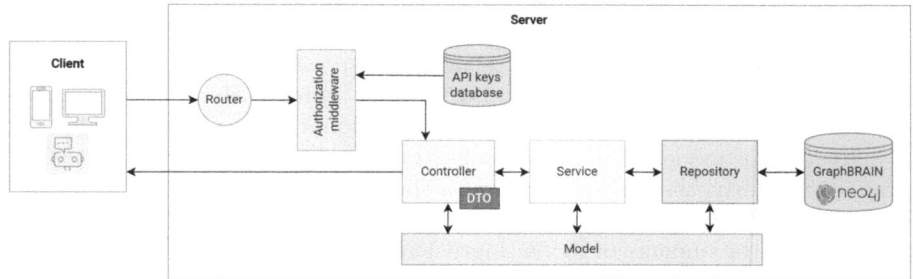

Fig. 3. NutriWell API implementation architecture

The framework is deployed leveraging containerization with two Docker containers (one for the API server, and the other for the Neo4j database) based on custom-built Docker images.

6   Expert Evaluation and Use Case

The evaluation has been conducted with the help of two members of the Department of Science, Food and Nature of the university. They have been chosen of almost the same age and different genders. They were responsible for identifying and pointing out possible misleading values in the labelling phase (Sect. 3.2) and adding further considerations. They were allowed to modify the impact of some aliments on some diseases. Throughout the dataset, the main rationale was that the aliment is the sum of all its ingredients, but this is not always the case. Unfortunately (or luckily) recipes are not standard and this is the first element hindering the accuracy of the solution. For this reason, experts tended to be less permissive when considering some aliments, because it happens that the recipes introduce relationships among ingredients that do not exist when taken individually. The two experts were separated during their evaluation of the labels. At the end of their individual examinations, they exchanged their results and discussed them to reach an agreement. In the end, less than 2% of the impact changed polarity (from 0 to -0.5 or -1). In no case did the polarity change from a positive value to a negative one or vice-versa. One of the evaluators made very few changes from a negative to a neutral impact, but these changes have not been maintained after discussion with the other evaluator. The first evaluator proposed changes in 0.8% of the dataset, while the second in the 1.1%. After the discussion, 1.5% circa was changed. The agreement between the two evaluators after individual analysis was about 40%, which is quite low but not unexpected. The difficulty in the agreement lies in the subjectivity of the evaluation. Factors like quantity, ingredient matching and personal experience come into play. Nonetheless, an agreement was smoothly found and the small percentage of values changed justifies the use of common knowledge to label data.

6.1   Use Case

We present here a stereotypical situation in which an end-user may benefit from the system. Figure 4 reports the interaction with the application querying *Nutri-Well*.

Scenario *Mario is a retired 75-year-old man living in Italy and, despite being widowed and living alone, he leads a quite active life. However, his fondness for sweets has led to health issues in recent years. Indeed, he has been diagnosed with irritable bowel syndrome and high cholesterol. Concerned for his health, he installed on his smartphone a mobile app with diet-tracking capabilities to assist during mealtimes where he can report his health conditions.*

When Mario asks the system to check whether a box of chocolates may fit with its health, he observes that chocolates hurt irritable bowel syndrome (-0.7), but do not affect high cholesterol (0.0). The app also explains to Mario which are the harmful ingredients in chocolates. Thus, he decides to eat only one.

Then, he asks for suggestions on more appropriate meals for his condition. The system looks for meals having at least an impact score equal to 0.5 and presents them to Mario.

7   Ethical Concerns

Although the scraping of *GialloZafferano* and *AlimentiNUTrizione* is not explicitly allowed, we want to remind you that *NutriWell* is not a recipe framework, it uses information about recipes to categorise meals and expose potential risks for users. Under no circumstances could the user get where the information about potential harm comes from, and hence information about recipe authors can never be extracted, since we discard it in the dataset pre-processing.

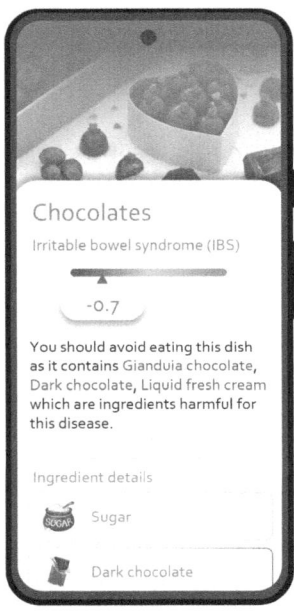

Fig. 4. Example of *NutriWell* response for chocolates

8   Conclusions

In this study, we proposed a novel approach to assist end-users in choosing foods for both preference or health motivations, using and combining structural components of food and ingredients. We provided the assistance in the form of a REST API and contributed to the definition of a new conceptualization for health conditions management. The solution employs the *GraphBRAIN* framework. This work may give rise to several extensions, from the ontological formalization of inter-relationships among ingredients to the definition of exceptions when dealing with aliments' interactions, which is not uncommon. Data labelling may require further analysis in the future but, as far as the two experts were concerned, no relevant criticalities emerged. In addition, a thorough evaluation of the application prototype with end users will be conducted to understand its impact on improving nutrition literacy and awareness.

Disclosure of Interests. The authors have no competing interests to declare that are relevant to the content of this article

References

1. Angles, R.: The property graph database model. In: Alberto Mendelzon Workshop on Foundations of Data Management (2018). https://api.semanticscholar.org/CorpusID:43977243
2. Bajaj, V., Panda, R.B., Dabas, C., Kaur, P.: Graph database for recipe recommendations. In: 2018 7th International Conference on Reliability, Infocom Technologies and Optimization (Trends and Future Directions) (ICRITO), pp. 1–6 (2018). https://doi.org/10.1109/ICRITO.2018.8748827
3. Çelik, D., et al.: FoodWiki: ontology-driven mobile safe food consumption system. Sci. World J. **2015**(1), 475410 (2015)
4. Cena, H., Calder, P.C.: Defining a healthy diet: evidence for the role of contemporary dietary patterns in health and disease. Nutrients **12**(2), 334 (2020)
5. Dragoni, M., Bailoni, T., Maimone, R., Eccher, C.: Helis: an ontology for supporting healthy lifestyles. In: The Semantic Web–ISWC 2018: 17th International Semantic Web Conference, Monterey, CA, USA, October 8–12, 2018, Proceedings, Part II 17, pp. 53–69. Springer (2018)
6. Edamam: Edamam API (2024). https://www.edamam.com/. Accessed 17 Apr 2024
7. Federation, I.D.: IDF Diabetes Atlas (2024). https://diabetesatlas.org/data/en/region/3/eur.html. Accessed 17 Apr 2024
8. Federation, I.D.: IDF Diabetes Atlas (2024). https://www.who.int/news-room/factsheets/detail/noncommunicable-diseases. Accessed 17 Apr 2024]
9. Ferilli, S., Redavid, D.: The GraphBRAIN system for knowledge graph management and advanced fruition. In: Foundations of Intelligent Systems: 25th International Symposium, ISMIS 2020, Graz, Austria, September 23–25, 2020, Proceedings, pp. 308–317. Springer (2020)
10. Ferilli, S., Redavid, D., Di Pierro, D., et al.: LPG-based Ontologies as Schemas for Graph DBs. In: SEBD, pp. 256–267 (2022)
11. Harrington, J.L.: Relational Database Design and Implementation. Morgan Kaufmann (2016)
12. Kamel Boulos, M.N., Yassine, A., Shirmohammadi, S., Namahoot, C.S., Brückner, M.: Towards an "Internet of Food": food ontologies for the internet of things. Future Internet **7**(4), 372–392 (2015)
13. Mavani, N.R., Ali, J.M., Othman, S., Hussain, M., Hashim, H., Rahman, N.A.: Application of artificial intelligence in food industry-a guideline. Food Eng. Rev. **14**(1), 134–175 (2022)
14. Popovski, G., Korousic-Seljak, B., Eftimov, T.: FoodOntoMap: linking food concepts across different food ontologies. In: KEOD, pp. 195–202 (2019)
15. Qin, L., Hao, Z., Zhao, L.: Food safety knowledge graph and question answering system. In: Proceedings of the 2019 7th International Conference on Information Technology: IoT and Smart City, pp. 559–564 (2019)

16. Rakhmawati, N.A., Fatawi, J., Najib, A.C., Firmansyah, A.A.: Linked open data for halal food products. J. King Saud Univ.-Comput. Inf. Sci. **33**(6), 728–739 (2021)
17. Sagan, A., Kowalska-Bobko, I., Bryndová, L., Smatana, M., Chaklosh, I., Gaál, P.: What is being done to respond to the rise of chronic diseases and multi-morbidity in Czechia, Hungary, Poland, and Slovakia? Front. Public Health **10**, 1082164 (2023)
18. Silva, P.: Food and nutrition literacy: exploring the divide between research and practice. Foods **12**(14), 2751 (2023)
19. Snae, C., Bruckner, M.: FOODS: a food-oriented ontology-driven system. In: 2008 2nd ieee International Conference on Digital Ecosystems and Technologies, pp. 168–176. IEEE (2008)
20. Toledo, R.Y., Alzahrani, A.A., Martinez, L.: A food recommender system considering nutritional information and user preferences. IEEE Access **7**, 96695–96711 (2019)
21. Trattner, C., Elsweiler, D.: Food recommender systems: important contributions, challenges and future research directions. arXiv preprint arXiv:1711.02760 (2017)
22. Vlachou, A., et al.: Policy guidelines for effective inclusion and reintegration of people with chronic diseases in the workplace: national and European perspectives. Int. J. Environ. Res. Public Health **15**(3), 493 (2018)
23. World Health Organization: Noncommunicable diseases (2024). https://health.ec.europa.eu/non-communicable-diseases/overview_en Accessed 17 Apr 2024
24. Yu, E., et al.: Diet, lifestyle, biomarkers, genetic factors, and risk of cardiovascular disease in the nurses' health studies. Am. J. Public Health **106**(9), 1616–1623 (2016)

Regular Clocks for Temporal Task Specifications in Reinforcement Learning

Giuseppe De Giacomo[1,2](✉) (iD), Marco Favorito[3] (iD), and Fabio Patrizi[2] (iD)

[1] University of Oxford, Oxford, UK
[2] Sapienza University of Rome, Rome, Italy
degiacomo@diag.uniroma1.it , patrizi@diag.uniroma1.it
[3] Bank of Italy, Rome, Italy
marco.favorito@bancaditalia.it

Abstract. Several recent approaches in reinforcement learning are studying a conceptual architecture where the environment is simultaneously represented at two (or more) levels of abstraction, with the environment providing two traces of data/events/features/fluents, one at a lower-level/finer grain and one at a higher-level/coarser grain. For simplicity, most of this literature assumes that the instants of the two traces match. In this paper, we drop this strong assumption and introduce an explicit mapping between the low-level and the high-level traces that the high-level trace perceives as a clock defined in terms of properties of segments of the low-level one. We investigate the case of regular mappings, where the segments that induce clock ticks are specified by a regular language property or a finite-state machine. We show that if both the clock and the high-level specifications are expressed as finite-state machines, such as reward machines, we can combine the two specifications in polynomial time into a single machine incorporating the clock. We then investigate the case in which both the clock and the high-level task are specified declaratively, e.g., in linear temporal logics on finite traces such as LTL_f and LDL_f, and show that this yields a notable representational advantage wrt a flattened representation where the clock is not explicit.

Keywords: Clock specification · Reinforcement Learning · Temporal Tasks

1 Introduction

Several recent works are focusing on a conceptual architecture where the environment is simultaneously represented at two (or more) levels of abstraction, each providing a different trace (or traces) of data/events/features/fluents: one at a lower-level/finer grain and one at a higher-level/coarser grain [2,3,5,6,15, 16,18,28]. For example, the low-level trace could include environment features directly observed by a reinforcement-learning (RL) agent while the high-level trace could include logical fluents observed by a KR(-based) monitor, such as a temporal specification, and used to reward the RL agent for carrying out some task, according to the fulfilment of the (high-level) specification.

For concreteness, we consider the unclocked setting discussed in [5], depicted in Fig. 1a (the KR monitor was called "restraining bolt" in 1a). As standard in RL, the RL agent interacts with the environment by observing a number of features extracted by a suitable module, e.g., a set of sensors, performing some actions, and possibly obtaining rewards. The observed features produce the low-level trace. Besides, there are additional properties of the environment, called *fluents*, that the RL agent is, in general, unaware of but are observable to an external KR monitor. These correspond to the high-level trace. Fluents can be complex properties which depend on the features but can also be features themselves, possibly inaccessible to the agent due, e.g., to a lack of suitable sensors. The KR monitor requires the agent to fulfil some requirements or carry out an additional task, wrt to that implicitly defined by the standard reward function. This is achieved by defining an additional, possibly non-Markovian reward function, based on the fluents, implemented by the KR monitor. It is important to observe that this setting implicitly makes the assumption that the feature and fluent traces are aligned, i.e., they produce the next observation at the same time, [5,15].

In this paper, we advocate the introduction of a specific component to allow for loosening the synchronicity requirement of the two traces; see Fig. 1b. The clock component generates the time points of the high-level trace for the KR monitor by checking relevant properties of the current prefix of the low-level trace of features. This allows for a better representation of the KR monitor, decoupling the handling of the clock from the high-level specification that uses it. For example, imagine that the high-level property checked by the KR monitor depends only on the data items produced at even time points $(0, 2, 4, \ldots)$. Introducing a clock component allows the KR monitor to offer a reward based only on the time points of interest without needing to keep track of each time point's parity; on the other hand, if the clock module is not present, the KR module must track parity, cluttering the specification of the KR monitor itself.

In this paper, we explore the benefits and the implications of dropping the strong *common-clock* assumption for feature and fluent extractors. We do so by introducing an explicit mapping between the low-level and the high-level traces, which is perceived by the high-level trace as a clock, defined in terms of properties of segments of the low-level trace. We require the mapping to be regular, in the sense of regular languages [13].

We study the case in which the KR monitor consists of a Reward Machine (RM) [15], and the clock consists of a finite state transducer, or automaton, (FSA). We solve reinforcement learning in this setting by showing how to compile the clock aware in a more involved reward machine which although clattered by the handling of the clock and hence less intuitive, can be computed automatically in polynomial time. In this way, we obtain both the representational advantage of decoupling the clock from the KR monitor while still maintaining the effectiveness of the reward machine approach.

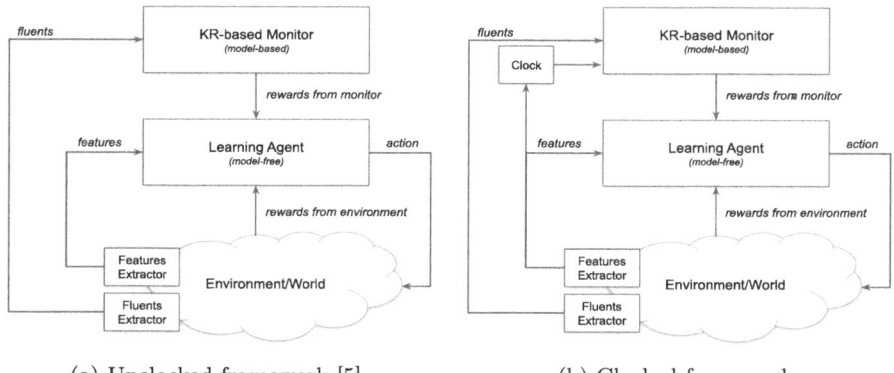

(a) Unclocked framework [5].   (b) Clocked framework.

Fig. 1. The standard agent-environment systems with a KR-based monitor.

We then discuss the case where the clock and KR monitor are specified declaratively using a linear temporal logics on finite traces, in particular, LTL_f or LDL_f [8]. Notice that LDL_f has exactly the expressive power of regular expression (i.e., that of Monodic Second Order Logic on finite traces). Instead LTL_f has the expressive power of star-free regular expressions (i.e., that of First-Order Logic on finite traces). As a result, we can compile LTL_f/LDL_f KR monitor specifications and clock specifications in Reward Machines and FSA specifications, respectively, and adopt the techniques above for doing reinforcement learning. This gives us a procedure that is worst case 2EXPTIME-complete, as in the case of unclocked specifications [2,5]. In fact, the overhead introduced by the clock is minimal.

Finally, a natural question arises: can, at least in principle, clocked specifications in LDL_f and LTL_f be translated into unclocked specifications in LDL_f and LTL_f, respectively? In the case of LDL_f, the answer is obviously positive since LDL_f can capture any regular language and hence also that obtained from compiling the clock into a finite state reward machine. For LTL_f, proving that this is the case is not as simple because it has to show that the specific Cartesian Product construction that we use to compile away the clock specification preserves being star-free. We do show this in the paper.

Note that these expressivity results do not induce an easy (polynomial) way of compiling away the logical specification of the clock into the logical specification of the KR monitor. The specific constructions used for the proof would generate a 2EXPTIME-blowup in the specification. We leave it to future work whether this upper-bound can be improved. In any case, as we show here, the approach does not need this compilation.

2   Preliminaries

LTL$_f$ and LDL$_f$. LTL$_f$ and LDL$_f$ are, respectively, Linear Temporal Logic and Linear Dynamic Logic with finite trace semantics, proposed in [8]. LTL$_f$ shares the same syntax of LTL [22]. It is as expressive as First-Order Logic over finite traces (FOL) or star-free regular expressions, so strictly less expressive than regular expressions, which, in turn, are as expressive as Monadic Second-Order logic over finite traces (MSO). The semantics of such logic formalisms are given in terms of finite traces denoting a finite, possibly empty, sequence $\pi = \pi_0, \ldots, \pi_n$ of elements from the alphabet $2^{\mathcal{P}}$, containing all possible propositional interpretations of the propositional symbols in $\mathcal{P}$. Notice that, differently from [8], we allow the empty trace as in [2,7]. Given a set $\mathcal{P}$ of propositional symbols, LTL$_f$ formulae are built as follows:

$$\varphi ::= tt \mid \phi \mid \neg\varphi \mid \varphi_1 \wedge \varphi_2 \mid \bigcirc\varphi \mid \varphi_1\,\mathcal{U}\,\varphi_2$$

where tt is the tautology (not to be confused with $true = \phi \vee \neg\phi$), ϕ is a propositional formula over $\mathcal{P}$, $\bigcirc$ is the *next* operator, and $\mathcal{U}$ is the until operator. We adopt the usual Boolean abbreviations for disjunction, implication, etc. In addition, we use common abbreviations of temporal operators. For the *weak next* operator $\bullet$, we have $\bullet\varphi \equiv \neg\bigcirc\neg\varphi$ (notice that in the finite trace case $\neg\bigcirc\neg\varphi \neq \bigcirc\varphi$), for the *release* operator $\mathcal{R}$, we have $\varphi_1\,\mathcal{R}\,\varphi_2 \equiv \neg(\neg\varphi_1\,\mathcal{U}\,\neg\varphi_2)$, for *eventually* ($\Diamond$) we have $\Diamond\varphi \equiv true\,\mathcal{U}\,\varphi$, for *always* ($\Box$) we have $\Box\varphi \equiv \neg\Diamond\neg\varphi$. Finally, we have $last \equiv \bullet(false)$.

LDL$_f$ is a temporal logic as natural as LTL$_f$, but with the full expressive power of Monadic Second-Order logic over finite traces. LDL$_f$ is obtained by merging LTL$_f$ with regular expressions (RE$_f$) through the syntax of the well-know logic of programs PDL, *Propositional Dynamic Logic* [10,11], but adopting a semantics based on finite traces. LDL$_f$ is an adaptation of LDL introduced in [27], which, like LTL, is interpreted over infinite traces. We omit the details on the syntax of LDL$_f$ due to lack of space, but one property that we will use is that regular expressions can easily be encoded into a LDL$_f$ formula. The semantics of a LTL$_f$/LDL$_f$ formula is defined over finite traces; its full definition can be found in [2]. Given a finite (possibly empty) trace π, by $\pi, i \models \varphi$ we denote that the LTL$_f$/LDL$_f$ formula φ is satisfied by π at instant $i \in \mathbb{N}$. We write $\pi \models \varphi$, if $\pi, 0 \models \varphi$ and say that π *satisfies* φ. Moreover, from an LTL$_f$/LDL$_f$ formula φ, we can compute a DFA $\mathcal{A}_\varphi$ that accepts all and only the traces that satisfy φ [2,8].

Automata Theory. A deterministic finite-state automaton (DFA) [24] is a 5-tuple $\mathcal{A} = \langle Q, \Sigma, q_0, F, \delta \rangle$ where Q is the (non-empty) finite set of states, Σ is the finite set of input symbols (alphabet), $q_0 \in Q$ is the initial state, $F \subseteq Q$ is the set of accepting states, and $\delta : Q \times \Sigma \to Q$ is the transition function. The extended transition function δ^* of $\mathcal{A}$ is $\delta^*(q, \epsilon) = q$ and $\delta^*(q, wa) = \delta(\delta^*(q, w), a)$. An automaton $\mathcal{A}$ accepts a word w if $\delta^*(q_0, w) \in F$. The language of $\mathcal{A}$, denoted $\mathcal{L}(\mathcal{A})$, is the set of words that $\mathcal{A}$ accepts. A *non-deterministic* finite-state automaton (NFA) is defined in the same way as a DFA, except for δ, which is a relation rather than a function, i.e. $\delta \subseteq Q \times \Sigma \times Q$. A Mealy machine M_e [20] is a 6-tuple $M_e = \langle Q, \Sigma, \Gamma, q_0, \delta, \theta \rangle$ where Q is the finite set of states, Σ is the finite set of input symbols, Γ is the finite set of the output symbols, q_0 is the initial state, $\delta : Q \times \Sigma \to Q$ is the transition function, and $\theta : Q \times \Sigma \to \Gamma$ is the output function that maps transition to output symbols. A Moore machine M_o [21] is like a Mealy machine except that the output function is defined as $\theta : Q \to \Gamma$, i.e., it maps states to output symbols. The output of M_e on word $a_1 \ldots a_n$ is $\theta^*(a_1 \ldots a_n) = \theta(q_0, a_1)\theta(\delta^*(q_0, a_1), a_2) \ldots \theta(\delta^*(q_0, a_1, \ldots, a_{n-1}), a_n)$. An analogous definition exists for M_o. A Mealy/Moore machine M defines a regular *transduction function* $F_M : \Sigma^* \to \Gamma^*$ mapping words over the input alphabet Σ into words over the output alphabet Γ. DFAs and NFAs are known as *acceptors*, while Mealy and Moore machines as *transducers*. From a DFA $\mathcal{A} = \langle Q, \Sigma, q_0, \delta, F \rangle$, we can obtain a Mealy machine $M_{\mathcal{A}} = \langle Q, \Sigma, \Gamma, q_0, \delta, \theta \rangle$, with $\theta(q, a) = accept$ iff $\delta(q', a) \in F$, s.t., for every word $w \in \Sigma^*$, we have that $w \in \mathcal{L}(\mathcal{A})$ iff the last character of $F_{M_{\mathcal{A}}}(w)$ is *accept*. The reverse is possible, too. Likewise, we can transform a Mealy machine into an equivalent Moore machine, and vice versa. See [13, 17].

MDPs and RL. A Markov Decision Process (MDP) $\mathcal{M} = \langle S, A, Tr, R \rangle$ contains a set S of states, a set A of actions, a transition function $Tr : S \times A \to Prob(S)$ that returns for every state s and action a a distribution over the next state, and a reward function $R : S \times A \times S \to \mathbb{R}$ that specifies the reward (a real value) received by the agent when transitioning from state s to state s' by applying action a. A solution to an MDP is a function called a *policy*, assigning an action to each state, possibly depending on past states and actions. The *value* of a policy ρ at state s, denoted $v^\rho(s)$, is the expected sum of (possibly discounted by a factor γ, with $0 \le \gamma \le 1$) rewards when starting at state s and selecting actions based on ρ. Typically, the MDP is assumed to start in an initial state s_0, so policy optimality is evaluated w.r.t. $v^\rho(s_0)$. Every MDP has an *optimal* policy ρ^*. In discounted cumulative settings, there exists an optimal policy that is *Markovian* $\rho : S \to A$, i.e., ρ depends only on the current state, and deterministic [23]. Reinforcement Learning (RL) is the task of learning a possibly optimal policy, from an initial state s_0, on an MDP where only S and A are known, while Tr and R are not—see, e.g., [26]. A *non-Markovian* reward function [1] is defined as $\bar{R} : (S \times A)^* \to \mathbb{R}$, i.e. a real-valued function over finite state-action sequences. Usually, $\bar{R}$ is specified using a pair (φ, r), where φ is a LTL$_f$/LDL$_f$ formula: if the current (partial) trajectory is $\pi = \langle s_0, a_1, \ldots, s_{n-1}, a_n \rangle$, the agent receives at s_n a reward r iff $\pi \models \varphi$ (where $s_i \in 2^\mathcal{P}$) [2]. A *Non-Markov Reward Decision Process (NMRDP)* is like an MDP except that the reward function is non-Markovian.

3   Clocked Framework

Let $\mathcal{M}_{ag} = \langle S, A, Tr_{ag}, R_{ag} \rangle$ be an MDP on which the learning agent acts. Let $f_r : \mathcal{L}^* \to \mathcal{R}$ a *high-level reward function*, with $\mathcal{L} = 2^\mathcal{F}$ the set of possible fluents' configurations, and $\mathcal{R} \subseteq \mathbb{R}$ a finite set of reward values. Additionally, we consider a *clock function* (or simply *clock*) $f_c : \mathcal{L}^* \to \{0, 1\}$, with 0 meaning "low" state and 1 meaning "high" state. We also say that the clock *ticks on trace t* whenever $f_c(t) = 1$. The role of the clock is to exclude particular fluent observations before giving them as input to the high-level reward function. We assume that both f_r and f_c are *regular* functions over histories, therefore they can be represented by a finite-state machine formalism (e.g. Mealy machines or DFA). The diagram in Fig. 1b depicts at a high level the scenario we have in mind: the inner loop (red) of interaction between the learning agent and the environment is similar to the agent-environment loop of an RL scenario, while the outer loop (blue) starts from the *fluents extractor*, which outputs a high-level representation of the world state in the form of a fluent configuration $\ell \in \mathcal{L}$, passes through the clock function evaluation and, if the history so far makes the clock to be in the "high" state, then the fluents observation is fed to the high-level reward function.

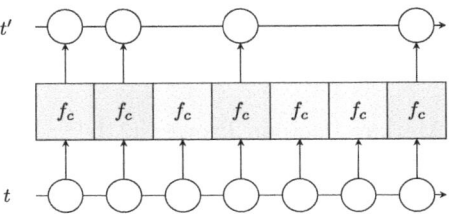

Fig. 2. Intuitive representation of how the clock function f_c projects the low-level trace t into the high-level trace t'.

Figure 2 intuitively explains how the filtering mechanism of the clock function f_c works. Circles represent trace timesteps. The bottom trace t has the finest time granularity. The clock function f_c is evaluated on every trace prefix. Let us introduce some notation for traces: for a trace $t = \ell_0, \ldots, \ell_n$, $\mathsf{length}(t) = n + 1$ (or $|t|$) is a positive integer denoting the length of t, $t[i]$ is the i-th step of t (with $0 \le i < \mathsf{length}(t)$, and $t[i : j]$ be the subtrace $t[i], t[i + 1], \ldots, t[j]$ (with $0 \le i \le j < \mathsf{length}(t)$). If the trace prefix at some time i makes the formula f_c true (i.e. $F(t[0 : i]) = 1$), then the timestep is passed to the evaluation of f_r, and becomes a timestep of the coarser-grained timestep sequence t'. On the other hand, if for some timestep i, the trace prefix up to that timestep does not make f_c to tick, then the configuration at timestep i, i.e. $t[i]$, is ignored at the higher level trace t'.

We now proceed with a complete formalization. To do so, we start with the notion of trace *projection*:

Definition 1 (Trace Projection [9]). *Let $t \in \mathcal{L}^*$ be a trace over the set of fluents configurations $\mathcal{L} = 2^{\mathcal{F}}$, and let f_c be the clock function. The projection of t onto clock function f_c is the trace $t|_{f_c} = \ell'_0, \ell'_1, \ldots, \ell'_n$, where $\ell'_i = t[i]$, if $f_c(t[0 : i]) = 1$, and $\ell'_i = \epsilon$, otherwise.*

Intuitively, the projection is obtained from t after removing the timesteps with index $i = 0, \ldots, n$ for which the prefix of the trace up to position i (included) does not make f_c evaluate to 1. Note that this notion is analogous to that in [9]. However, the crucial difference is that their clock operator only looks at the current instant, while ours can model temporal constraints.

Example 1 Let $t = \langle \{a, b\}, \{b\}, \{c\}, \{a\}, \{b, c\} \rangle$, and for any trace t', let f_c be a clock function such that $f_c(t') = 1$ if $a \in t[\text{length}(t) - 1]$, otherwise 0. Such behaviour can be intuitively explained as "every time a is true, the clock is high". The projected trace $t|_{f_c}$ is then $\{\{a, b\}, \{a\}\}$. The second, third, and fifth timesteps are filtered out because a does not hold.

Example 2 Let $t = \langle \{a\}, \{b\}, \{c\}, \{a\}, \{b\}, \{c\} \rangle$, and let $f_c(t') = 1$ if $\text{length}(t')$ mod $2 = 0$, otherwise 0. Intuitively, the clock is high (resp. low) at each even (resp. odd) time step. The projected trace is $t|_{f_c} = \langle \{a\}, \{c\}, \{b\} \rangle$.

The clock mechanism makes the high-level reward function evaluated only whenever the clock ticks. Given f_c and f_r, the *clocked reward function* $\bar{R}_{cr} : \mathcal{L}^* \to \mathbb{R}$ is as follows:

$$\bar{R}_{cr}(t) = \sum_{i=0}^{|t|-1} \gamma^i f_r(t[0:i+1]|_{f_c}) \cdot f_c(t[0:i+1]) \tag{1}$$

The clocked reward function $\bar{R}_{cr}(t)$ gives rewards at the clock tick only, and the reward function f_r is evaluated only on the trace projected onto the clock f_c. Note also that $\bar{R}_{cr}(t)$ is a non-Markovian reward function since its value depends on the full trace history of fluents configurations t.

In our scenario, we are interested in learning an optimal policy for the MDP $\mathcal{M}_{ag}$, where the reward function to optimize is the expected discounted sum of rewards, both from R_{ag} and $\bar{R}_{cr}$. To do so, as in other works, e.g. [5], we assume that the agent actions in A induce a Markovian transition distribution over the features and fluents configuration: $Tr_{ag}^\ell : S \times \mathcal{L} \times A \to Prob(S \times \mathcal{L})$, and the interaction between the agent and the environment yields a trajectory $\tau = (s_0, \ell_0), a_0, (s_1, \ell_1), a_1, \ldots, (s_n, \ell_n)$. Hence, the value function of a policy ρ takes the form $v^\rho(s_0) = \mathbb{E}_{\tau \sim Tr_{ag}^\ell}[\bar{R}(\tau)]$, where $\bar{R}(\tau) = \sum_{i=0}^n \gamma^i R_{ag}(s_i, a_i) + \bar{R}_{cr}(\ell_0, \ldots, \ell_n)$.

Note that, in general, since the reward function is non-markovian, the optimal policy could be non-Markovian too, i.e. $\bar{\rho} : (S \times \mathcal{L})^* \to A$. We call the NMRDP induced by Tr_{ag}^ℓ and $\bar{R}(\tau)$ as $\mathcal{M}_{ag}^\ell$. We can now state our target problem:

Problem 1. Given the tuple $\langle \mathcal{M}_{ag}^\ell, f_r, f_c \rangle$, where $\mathcal{M}_{ag}^\ell = \langle S \times \mathcal{L}, A, Tr_{ag}^\ell, \bar{R} \rangle$ is a learning agent, $f_r : \mathcal{L}^* \to \mathbb{R}$ is a high-level reward function, and $f_c : \mathcal{L}^* \to \{0, 1\}$ is a clock function, find a policy $\bar{\rho} : (S \times \mathcal{L})^* \to A$ such that $v^{\bar{\rho}}(s_0)$ is maximized.

Observe that this setting is rather general since f_r and f_c are only assumed to be regular functions of histories. Two popular ways of representing regular functions is either via finite-state machines, like transducers, or via declarative languages (e.g. temporal logics). In the next sections, we consider both cases and provide a solution technique to solve our problem.

4   Clocked Reward Machine

In this section, we consider the case where f_r and f_c are specified as finite-state machines. In particular, we consider a *reward transducer* (or *reward machine*) $M_r = \langle Q_r, \mathcal{L}, \mathcal{R}, q_0^r, \delta_r, \theta_r \rangle$ with $\mathcal{R} \subseteq \mathbb{R}$ the output alphabet, i.e. a finite set of reward values, and a *clock transducer* (or *clock machine*) $M_c = \langle Q_c, \mathcal{L}, \{0, 1\}, q_0^c, \delta_c, \theta_c \rangle$. In particular, for a trace $t = \ell_0, \dots, \ell_n$, we define $f_{M_r}(t) = \theta_r(\delta_r^*(q_0^r, \ell_0, \dots, \ell_{n-1}), \ell_n)$ as the reward function of M_r, i.e. $f_{M_r}(t)$ is the last outputted reward by M_r on input t, while $f_{M_c}(t) = \theta_c(\delta^*(q_0, \ell_0, \dots, \ell_{n-1}), \ell_n)$ as the clock function of M_c. The reward transducer is a well-known concept in reinforcement learning for high-level task specifications, e.g. see [4,14,15].

We show how, given M_c and M_r, we can compute a new Mealy machine $M_{cr} = \langle Q_{cr}, \mathcal{L}, \mathcal{R} \cup \{0\}, q_0^{cr}, \delta_{cr}, \theta_{cr} \rangle$, that we call the *clocked reward machine*, such that the function it represents is precisely $\bar{R}_{cr}$ when $f_r = f_{M_r}$ and $f_c = f_{M_c}$. Such machine M_{cr} is defined as follows:

- $Q_{cr} = Q_c \times Q_r$;
- $q^{cr} = (q_0^c, q_0^r)$;
- $\delta_{cr}((q_c, q_r), \ell) = \begin{cases} (\delta_c(q_c, \ell), q_r) & \text{if } \theta_c(q_c, \ell) = 0 \\ (\delta_c(q_c, \ell), \delta_r(q_r, \ell)) & \text{if } \theta_c(q_c, \ell) = 1 \end{cases}$;

- $\theta_{cr}((q_c, q_r), \ell) = \begin{cases} 0 & \text{if } \theta_c(q_c, \ell) = 0 \\ \theta_r(q_r, \ell) & \text{if } \theta_c(q_c, \ell) = 1 \end{cases}$

Intuitively, the clocked reward machine is like the classical synchronous product between two transducers, except that the state component coming from the reward machine q_r is progressed only if the clock component q^c, after reading the symbol ℓ, is such that the clock output is 1. The *clocked reward function* corresponding to M_{cr} is $\bar{R}_{M_{cr}}(t) = \sum_{i=0}^n \gamma^i \theta_{cr}(\delta^*(q_0^{cr}, t[0 : i - 1]), t[i])$.
The correctness follows by construction:

Theorem 1. *Let M_r and M_c be a reward machine and a clock machine, respectively, and let f_r and f_c their reward and clock functions. Let the clocked reward machine M_{cr}. Moreover, let $\bar{R}_{cr}(t)$ be a clocked reward function with $f_r = f_{M_r}$ and $f_c = f_{M_c}$. We have that, for all traces t, $\bar{R}_{M_{cr}}(t) = \bar{R}_{cr}(t)$*

Proof. We prove the claim by induction on the length of the trace $t = \ell_1, \dots, \ell_n$. If $t = \epsilon$, then $\bar{R}_{M_{cr}}(t) = \bar{R}_{cr}(t) = 0$. Now assume the claim holds for $t_{n-1} = \ell_1, \dots, \ell_{n-1}$, and let $t_n = t_{n-1}\ell_n$, Let $q_{n-1}^{cr} = \delta_{cr}^*(t_{n-1})$ be the last state of the run over trace t_{n-1}. On one hand, we have $\bar{R}_{M_{cr}}(t_n) = \bar{R}_{M_{cr}}(t_{n-1}) + \gamma^n \theta_{cr}(q_{n-1}^{cr}, \ell_n)$, by definition of $\bar{R}_{M_{cr}}$, while on the other hand we have $\bar{R}_{cr}(t_n) = \bar{R}_{cr}(t_{n-1}) + \gamma^n f_{M_r}(t_n|_{f_{M_c}}) \cdot f_{M_c}(t_n)$, by definition of $\bar{R}_{cr}$ (Eq. 1) and by assumption. Since $\bar{R}_{M_{cr}}(t_{n-1}) = \bar{R}_{cr}(t_{n-1})$ by inductive hypothesis, it remains to prove that $\theta_{cr}(q_{n-1}^{cr}, \ell_n) = f_{M_r}(t_n|_{f_{M_c}}) \cdot f_{M_c}(t_n)$. We have two cases: either $\theta_c(q_{n-1}^c, \ell_n) = 0$, or $\theta_c(q_{n-1}^c, \ell_n) = 1$. In the former case, by construction of θ_{cr}, we have $\theta_{cr}(q_{n-1}^{cr}, \ell_n) = f_{M_c}(t_n) = 0$. Hence, the claim holds. In

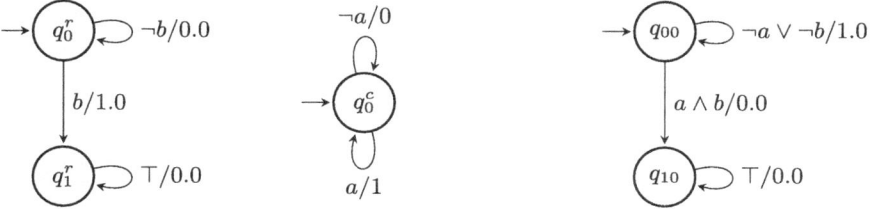

Fig. 3. M_r, M_c, and M_{cr} of Example 3.

the latter case, on one hand we have $\theta_{cr}(q^{cr}_{n-1}, \ell_n) = \theta_r(q^r_{n-1}, \ell_n)$, by definition of θ_{cr}, and on the other hand $f_{M_r}(t_n) = \theta_r(q^r_{n-1}, \ell_n)$. Hence, both terms are equal.

Example 3. Let M_r be the reward machine for the goal "reach b" (Fig. 3, left), and let $\mathcal{A}_c$ be the clock machine that ticks whenever a is true (Fig. 3, middle). The clock product M_{cr} is shown in Fig. 3, right. Note that the transition of the M_r-component of the state is made only if the clock is high, i.e. when the symbol a holds in the current timestep.

Based on the clocked reward machine construction, we now provide a solution to Problem 1 in case f_r and f_c are specified as Mealy machines M_r and M_c, respectively. Starting from $\mathcal{M}^\ell_{ag}$ and M_{cr}, we construct the MDP $\mathcal{M}' = \langle S', A', Tr', R' \rangle$, defined as follows:

- $S' = S \times \mathcal{L} \times Q_{cr}$;
- $A' = A$
- $Tr'((s, \ell, q), a, (s', \ell', q')) = \begin{cases} Tr(s, a, s') & \text{if } q' = \delta(q, \ell') \\ 0 & \text{otherwise.} \end{cases}$
- $R'((s, \ell, q), a, (s', \ell', q')) = R_{ag}(s, a, s') + \theta_{cr}(q, \ell')$

By construction, and by Theorem 1, it holds that the MDP $\mathcal{M}'$ is equivalent to the NMRDP $\mathcal{M}^\ell_{ag}$, in the sense of [1], and therefore optimal policies ρ' for $\mathcal{M}'$ can be transformed in optimal policies for $\mathcal{M}^\ell_{ag}$:

Theorem 2. *An optimal policy for the NMRDP $\mathcal{M}^\ell_{ag}$ with $f_r = f_{M_r}$ and $f_c = f_{M_c}$, can be learned by learning corresponding optimal policies for the MDP $\mathcal{M}'$.*

In other words, one can solve Problem 1 by first finding an optimal (memoryless) policy ρ' for $\mathcal{M}'$, and then by defining an equivalent policy on $\mathcal{M}^\ell_{ag}$, as follows: let $\tau = (s_0, \ell_0), a_1, (s_1, \ell_1), \ldots, (s_{n-1}, \ell_{n-1}, a_n)$ be the current trajectory of the process leading to state (s_n, ℓ_n). Let q_n denote the current state of Mealy machine M_{cr}, given input $t = \ell_0, \ldots, \ell_n$. Then, we define $\bar{\rho}(\tau) := \rho'(s_n, \ell_n, q_n)$.

In fact, by using a technique analogous to [5], one can show that we can restrict the policies of interest by dropping the fluents configurations $\mathcal{L}$ from the agent features. Hence, the resulting state space of the new MDP $\mathcal{M}''$ would be $S \times Q_{cr}$, with the state component Q_{cr} being progressed correctly by the environment.

Theorem 3. *An optimal policy for the NMRDP $\mathcal{M}_{ag}^{\ell}$ with $f_r = f_{M_r}$ and $f_c = f_{M_c}$ can be learned by learning corresponding optimal policies for the MDP $\mathcal{M}''$.*

Proof sketch. By Theorem 2, there exist an optimal policy ρ' such that $\bar{\rho}$ computed from ρ is also optimal for $\mathcal{M}_{ag}^{\ell}$. There exists a corresponding optimal policy for $\mathcal{M}''$, $\rho'' : S \times Q_{cr} \to A$, which differs from ρ' by dropping the $\mathcal{L}$ component of the state; optimality of ρ'' wrt $\mathcal{M}''$ can be shown by marginalizing the transition function distribution T'' over ℓ' (see proof of Theorem 6 in [5]).

As a consequence of Theorem 3, one can solve the learning problem of Problem 1 by learning an optimal policy for $\mathcal{M}''$.

5   Declarative Clock Specifications

In this section, we study a variant of Problem 1 where the reward and clock functions are specified *declaratively* using a formal regular language, e.g. LTL$_f$ and LDL$_f$. The main advantages of doing so are *(i)* the use of a high-level, human-understandable language, *(ii)* succinctness with respect to the finite-state machine formalism (in the best case, a doubly-exponential gain), and *(iii)* better modularity and composability of specifications. Note that any logic formalism with finite trace-based semantics that is not more expressive than regular expressions can be used in our framework (e.g. Pure-Past LTL [7]). At a high level, the solution method in the declarative setting works by transforming both the reward and clock specifications into a reward machine and a clock machine; then, we rely on the solution introduced in Sect. 4.

More formally, we have a *reward specification* (φ_r, r), where φ_r is the LTL$_f$/LDL$_f$ formula that has to be satisfied in order to give the reward signal r to the agent (as in [2,4,5]), plus a *clock specification* φ_c, another LTL$_f$/LDL$_f$ formula which specifies the clock function. Their respective reward function f_{φ_r} and the clock function f_{φ_c} are defined as follows:

$$f_{\varphi_r}(t) = \begin{cases} r & \text{if } t \models \varphi_r \\ 0 & \text{otherwise.} \end{cases} \qquad f_{\varphi_c} = \begin{cases} 1 & \text{if } t \models \varphi_c \\ 0 & \text{otherwise.} \end{cases}$$

Intuitively, the reward function $f_{\varphi_r}(t)$ returns r whenever $t \models \varphi_r$, otherwise it gives no reward signal. Similarly, the clock function $f_{\varphi_c}(t)$ is 1 iff $t \models \varphi_c$. A *clocked reward specification* is the triple $(\varphi_r, \varphi_c, r)$, and the derived clocked reward function $\bar{R}_{\varphi_r, \varphi_c}$ is defined by starting from $\bar{R}_{cr}$ and by setting $f_r = f_{\varphi_r}$ and $f_c = f_{\varphi_c}$.

Example 4. Continuing Example 3, let the reward specification be (φ_r, r), where $\varphi_r = \Diamond b$ and $r = 1$, and $\varphi_c = \Diamond(a \wedge last)$. We have that $f_{\varphi_r} = f_{M_r}$ and $f_{\varphi_c} = f_{M_c}$.

In order to solve this declarative variant of Problem 1, we resort to a reduction to the solution shown in Sect. 4. To do so, we proceed in steps. First, from the reward specification (φ_r, r), we compute the DFA equivalent to φ_r, $\mathcal{A}_{\varphi_r} = \langle Q, \mathcal{L}, q_0, F, \delta \rangle$. Then, we define the Moore machine $M' = \langle Q, \mathcal{L}, \{0, r\}, q_0, \delta, \theta \rangle$

where $\theta(q) = r$ if $q \in F$, otherwise $\theta(q) = 0$. From M', we can compute its equivalent Mealy reward machine M_{φ_r}. An analogous transformation can be made for the clock specification, i.e. from φ_c to the clock machine M_{φ_c}. Finally, we can resort to the solution presented in Sect. 4 to solve our problem.

Theorem 4. *Let $\langle \mathcal{M}_{ag}^\ell, f_{\varphi_r}, f_{\varphi_c} \rangle$ be an instance of Problem 1 in which f_{φ_r} and f_{φ_c} are specified by a LTL$_f$/LDL$_f$ reward specification (φ_r, r) and φ_c, respectively. Then, optimal policies for $\langle M_{ag}^\ell, f_{M_{\varphi_r}}, f_{M_{\varphi_c}} \rangle$ are also optimal policies for $\langle \mathcal{M}_{ag}^\ell, f_{\varphi_r}, f_{\varphi_c} \rangle$.*

Proof. By construction and by Theorem 1.

6   Unclocked-Equivalent Specifications

Given a LTL$_f$/LDL$_f$ clocked reward specification $(\varphi_r, \varphi_c, r)$ we ask ourselves whether there exist an *unclocked-equivalent reward specification* (φ_{cr}, r) such that for all traces t, $\bar{R}_{\varphi_{cr}}(t) = \bar{R}_{cr}(t)$, where $\bar{R}_\varphi(t) = \sum_{i=0:t[0:i] \models \varphi}^n \gamma^i r$. We answer positively, and we explain a way to compute φ_{cr}, given a clocked specification $(\varphi_r, \varphi_c, r)$. The following theorem shows how, by construction:

Theorem 5. *Given a clocked reward specification $(\varphi_r, \varphi_c, r)$, there exist a LDL$_f$ reward specification (φ_{cr}, r) such that $\bar{R}_{\varphi_r, \varphi_c} = \bar{R}_{cr}$.*

Proof. First, we compute the DFAs $\mathcal{A}_r$ and $\mathcal{A}_c$, which are the DFAs equivalent to φ_r and φ_c, respectively. Then, we consider their equivalent Mealy machines $M_{\mathcal{A}_r}$ and $M_{\mathcal{A}_c}$, as explained in the Preliminaries, from which we can compute M_{cr} using the clocked product (see Sect. 4, with the only difference that the output alphabet is not a set of rewards f_r but instead $\{accept\}$). Since M_c behaves as an acceptor, we can compute its equivalent DFA $\mathcal{A}_{cr}$. Then, we can compute an equivalent regular expression for $\mathcal{A}_{cr}$ in exponential time, and thus get a regular expression that is at most exponentially-larger than the DFA [13]. Finally, we can convert the regular expression to an LDL$_f$ formula φ_{cr} with constant blow-up [8]. By construction, $t \models \varphi$ iff M_{cr} with input t would have outputted $accept$ in place of r, iff the clock condition was satisfied (Theorem 1).

In fact, if φ_r and φ_c are both LTL$_f$ formulas, then the language recognized by the *clocked* DFA *product* $\mathcal{A}_{cr}$ (i.e. the acceptor version of M_{cr}) is a star-free language, and so it can be defined by some LTL$_f$ formula [8].

Theorem 6. *If $(\varphi_r, \varphi_c, r)$ is a LTL$_f$ clocked specification, then there exist an unclocked-equivalent LTL$_f$ reward specification (φ_{cr}, r).*

Proof. The crux of the proof is to show that the clocked product $\mathcal{A}_{cr}$ is a counter-free automaton [19], and therefore $\mathcal{L}(\mathcal{A}_{cr})$ is a star-free language [25]. The claim follows since the class of star-free regular languages is equivalent to the class of LTL$_f$-definable languages [8], and by the equivalence of $\mathcal{A}_{cr}$ with the clocked semantics for $(\varphi_r, \varphi_c, r)$ as per Theorem 1. First, observe that both $\mathcal{A}_r$ and $\mathcal{A}_c$ are

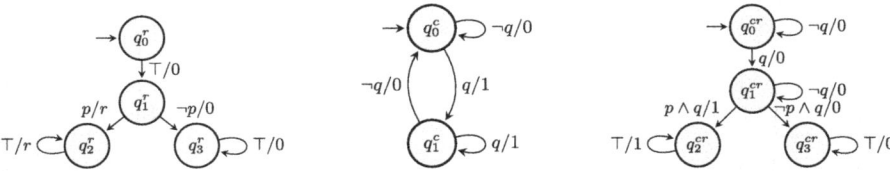

Fig. 4. Machines for Example 5, from left to right: reward machine for $(\mathsf{O}p, r)$, clock machine for φ_c, and reward machine for the unlocked-equivalent specification (φ_{cr}, r)

counter-free automata, since they are semantically equivalent to LTL_f formulas φ_r and φ_c, respectively. Assume by contradiction that $\mathcal{A}_{cr}$ has a *permutation*, i.e. for some set $P = \{q_1, \ldots, q_m\}$, $m \geq 2$, of states of $\mathcal{A}_{cr}$, there is a run $q_1 \ldots q_m$ such that $\delta'(q_i, \ell_i) = q_{i+1}$, for $1 \leq i \leq m - 1$, and $\delta'(q_m, \ell_m) = q_1$. Now, consider the same set of states but only considering the state components coming from $\mathcal{A}_c$, i.e. $\{q_1^c, \ldots, q_m^c\}$. Note that there cannot be self-loops in this path, i.e. $q_i^c \neq q_j^c$ for all $i \neq j$. By construction of clocked product, and in particular by definition of δ', it is easy to see that P is also a permutation for $\mathcal{A}_c$. Since for a DFA being permutation-free is equivalent to being counter-free [19], we have that $\mathcal{A}_c$ does have a counter, and therefore we get a contradiction.

Differently from Theorem 5, Theorem 6 only tells us that an unclocked-equivalent LTL_f exists, but not how to compute it. Now we give a possible automata-based approach for the LTL_f case. Given a clocked LTL_f specification, compute $\mathcal{A}_{cr}$, which can be doubly-exponentially larger. Then, reverse all transitions to get an NFA $\mathcal{A}^R$ that accepts the reverse of the language of $\mathcal{A}_{cr}$, then determinize this NFA to get an equivalent DFA $\mathcal{A}'^R$. Note that $\mathcal{A}'^R$ may be exponentially larger than $\mathcal{A}^R$. Now, apply Theorem 11 of [7] to transform this DFA into an equivalent PLTL_f formula ψ. Finally, form the swap ψ^{sw} for the reverse language of ψ. Then, ψ^{sw} is the LTL_f formula equivalent to the PLTL_f formula φ.

Such translations for LDL_f (resp. LTL_f) are very impractical, as we incur in three (resp. four) exponential blowups in the size of the original clocked specification. It would be interesting to devise direct translations from clocked $\text{LTL}_f/\text{LDL}_f$ specifications into classical $\text{LTL}_f/\text{LDL}_f$ formulas, but we leave this as future work.

Example 5. In this example, we give an idea about how an unclocked-equivalent formula can be more verbose and counterintuitive than a clocked specification. Consider $(\varphi_r, \varphi_c, r)$, with $\varphi_r = \mathsf{O}p$ and $\varphi_c = \Diamond(q \wedge last)$. The clock formula intuitively means "evaluate the goal formula only when q is true in the current timestep". The equivalent machines for these specifications are shown in Fig. 4. Intuitively, the clocked specification transitions to the next state only when q holds. However, the second time this happens, p must hold to satisfy the specification. It can be shown that the formula $\varphi_{cr} = \neg q\,\mathcal{U}(q \wedge \mathsf{O}(\neg q\,\mathcal{U}(p \wedge q)))$ is unclocked-equivalent to the clocked reward specification. The formula includes an $\mathcal{U}$ operator and a nested O and $\mathcal{U}$ operator.

7   Conclusion

In this paper, we investigated the separation of a clock specification from the temporal specification itself, allowing the time granularity of the temporal specification to be coarser than the actual time. Our work can be extended to consider multi-clocked specifications, which are needed for certain applications. One nice example is reported in [12] where temporal specifications for space missions are formalized in a variant of LTL$_f$ at different time-granularities, called *types*, to represents conditions with different frequencies like second, hours, days, etc. In this context, our work may give the basis for developing sophisticated multi-clocked specifications where clocks are specified in LTL$_f$/LDL$_f$.

Acknowledgements. This work has been partially supported by the ERC-ADG WhiteMech (No. 834228), the PRIN project RIPER (No. 20203FFYLK), the PNRR MUR project FAIR (No. PE0000013), and the Sapienza project MARLeN (Multi-layer Abstraction for Reinforcement Learning with Non-Markovian Rewards).

References

1. Bacchus, F., Boutilier, C., Grove, A.J.: Rewarding behaviors. In: AAAI/IAAI, vol. 2, pp. 1160–1167. AAAI Press / The MIT Press (1996)
2. Brafman, R.I., De Giacomo, G., Patrizi, F.: LTLf/LDLf non-Markovian rewards. In: AAAI, pp. 1771–1778. AAAI Press (2018)
3. De Giacomo, G., Favorito, M., Iocchi, L., Patrizi, F.: Imitation learning over heterogeneous agents with restraining bolts. In: ICAPS, pp. 517–521. AAAI Press (2020)
4. De Giacomo, G., Favorito, M., Iocchi, L., Patrizi, F., Ronca, A.: Temporal logic monitoring rewards via transducers. In: KR, pp. 860–870 (2020)
5. De Giacomo, G., Iocchi, L., Favorito, M., Patrizi, F.: Foundations for restraining bolts: reinforcement learning with LTLf/LDLf restraining specifications. In: ICAPS, pp. 128–136. AAAI Press (2019)
6. De Giacomo, G., Iocchi, L., Favorito, M., Patrizi, F.: Restraining bolts for reinforcement learning agents. In: AAAI, pp. 13659–13662. AAAI Press (2020)
7. De Giacomo, G., Stasio, A.D., Fuggitti, F., Rubin, S.: Pure-past linear temporal and dynamic logic on finite traces. In: IJCAI, pp. 4959–4965. ijcai.org (2020)
8. De Giacomo, G., Vardi, M.Y.: Linear temporal logic and linear dynamic logic on finite traces. In: IJCAI, pp. 854–860. IJCAI/AAAI (2013)
9. Eisner, C., Fisman, D., Havlicek, J., McIsaac, A., Van Campenhout, D.: The definition of a temporal clock operator. In: Baeten, J.C.M., Lenstra, J.K., Parrow, J., Woeginger, G.J. (eds.) ICALP 2003. LNCS, vol. 2719, pp. 857–870. Springer, Heidelberg (2003). https://doi.org/10.1007/3-540-45061-0_67
10. Fischer, M.J., Ladner, R.E.: Propositional dynamic logic of regular programs. J. Comput. Syst. Sci. **18**, 194–211 (1979)
11. Harel, D.: Dynamic logic. In: Gabbay, D.M., Guenthner, F. (eds.) Handbook of Philosophical Logic, vol. 4, pp. 497–604. Springer, Dordrecht (1984). https://doi.org/10.1007/978-94-017-0456-4_2

12. Hariharan, G., Kempa, B., Wongpiromsarn, T., Jones, P.H., Rozier, K.Y.: MLTL multi-type (MLTLM): a logic for reasoning about signals of different types. In: Isac, O., Ivanov, R., Katz, G., Narodytska, N., Nenzi, L. (eds.) NSV/FoMLAS@CAV. LNCS, vol. 13466, pp. 187–204. Springer, Cham (2022). https://doi.org/10.1007/978-3-031-21222-2_11

13. Hopcroft, J.E., Ullman, J.D.: Introduction to Automata Theory, Languages and Computation. Addison-Wesley, London (1979)

14. Icarte, R.T., Klassen, T.Q., Valenzano, R.A., McIlraith, S.A.: Using reward machines for high-level task specification and decomposition in reinforcement learning. In: ICML. Proceedings of Machine Learning Research, vol. 80, pp. 2112–2121. PMLR (2018)

15. Icarte, R.T., Klassen, T.Q., Valenzano, R.A., McIlraith, S.A.: Reward machines: exploiting reward function structure in reinforcement learning. J. Artif. Intell. Res. **73**, 173–208 (2022). https://doi.org/10.1613/JAIR.1.12440

16. Li, X., Vasile, C.I., Belta, C.: Reinforcement learning with temporal logic rewards. In: IROS, pp. 3834–3839. IEEE (2017)

17. Linz, P., Rodger, S.H.: An Introduction to Formal Languages and Automata. Jones & Bartlett Learning, Boston (2022)

18. Littman, M.L., Topcu, U., Fu, J., Jr., C.L.I., Wen, M., MacGlashan, J.: Environment-independent task specifications via GLTL. CoRR **abs/1704.04341** (2017)

19. McNaughton, R., Papert, S.A.: Counter-Free Automata (MIT Research Monograph No. 65). The MIT Press, Cambridge (1971)

20. Mealy, G.H.: A method for synthesizing sequential circuits. Bell Syst. Tech. J. **34**(5), 1045–1079 (1955)

21. Moore, E.F.: Gedanken-experiments on sequential machines. In: Automata Studies.(AM-34), Volume 34, pp. 129–154. Princeton University Press (2016)

22. Pnueli, A.: The temporal logic of programs. In: FOCS, pp. 46–57. IEEE Computer Society (1977)

23. Puterman, M.L.: Markov Decision Processes: Discrete Stochastic Dynamic Programming. Wiley Series in Probability and Statistics, Wiley (1994)

24. Rabin, M.O., Scott, D.S.: Finite automata and their decision problems. IBM J. Res. Dev. **3**(2), 114–125 (1959)

25. Schützenberger, M.P.: On finite monoids having only trivial subgroups. Inf. Control **8**(2), 190–194 (1965)

26. Sutton, R.S., Barto, A.G.: Reinforcement learning - an introduction. MIT Press, Adaptive computation and machine learning (1998)

27. Vardi, M.Y.: The rise and fall of linear time logic. In: GandALF (2011). http://www.cs.rice.edu/~vardi/papers/gandalf11-myv.pdf

28. Xu, Z., Topcu, U.: Transfer of temporal logic formulas in reinforcement learning. In: IJCAI, pp. 4010–4018. ijcai.org (2019)

A Real-Time Support with Haptic Feedback for Safer Driving Using Monocular Camera

Giorgio De Magistris[1] , Lorenzo Guercio[1], Francesco Starna[1],
Samuele Russo[2] , Natalia Kryvinska[3], and Christian Napoli[1](✉)

[1] Department of Computer, Control, and Management Engineering,
Sapienza University of Rome, via Ariosto 25, 00185 Rome, Italy
{demagistris,cnapoli}@diag.uniroma1.it
[2] Department of Psychology, Sapienza University of Rome, via Dei Marsi 78,
Roma 00185, Italy
samuele.russo@uniroma1.it
[3] Faculty of Management, Comenius University in Bratislava, Bratislava, Slovakia
Natalia.Kryvinska@uniba.sk

Abstract. Each year, car accidents impact billions of people, resulting in numerous casualties. Consequently, road safety remains a top priority for nations worldwide. This project aims to enhance driver safety through a feedback system that relies solely on a monocular camera mounted atop the vehicle. The proposed system is a real-time application designed to warn drivers of imminent road hazards, which are classified by their level of risk. Our method employs various computer vision techniques and incorporates a simple 2D-3D correspondence to estimate the longitudinal and lateral distances of objects ahead of the vehicle, under certain simplifying assumptions. The system conducts a comprehensive danger analysis by evaluating potential hazards within the vehicle's path. Depending on the danger level, warnings are delivered to the driver with varying degrees of invasiveness, using haptic feedback The proposed method was tested on the KITTI dataset, yielding positive results.

Keywords: Haptic Feedback · Computer Vision · Deep Learning

1 Introduction

In recent years, Artificial Intelligence for autonomous driving systems has become more and more important and is having a huge impact in our life. The most recent driving systems have been equipped with driver assistance functions such as Lane Keeping Assistant (LKA) [2,6,18,29], Adaptive Cruise Control (ACC) [30] and Brake Assist System (BAS) [17], in order to increase safety in driving. All of these assistant functions rely on Computer Vision algorithms, in particular on object detection and distance estimation [7]. Those techniques may

A. Artale et al. (Eds.): AIxIA 2024, LNAI 15450, pp. 161–174, 2025.
https://doi.org/10.1007/978-3-031-80607-0_13

rely on different kinds of sensors, such as a LiDAR scanner [24,38], monocular [9] or stereo [23] cameras, and GPS [21]. The LiDAR scanner creates a 3D map of the surrounding environment and it is more accurate than 2D information, but it can be very expensive. GPS alone is not adequate for real time assistance. Camera images, instead, provide enough data to build a driver assistance function, and it is also a cheap sensor that can be easily installed in every vehicle. In this paper we focus on developing a haptic feedback function that is complementary with the Emergency Brake Assistant (EBA), to ensure safe driving and avoid potential risks before the latter is activated. At each frame we first take the image coming from a monocular camera, placed above the vehicle roof. Then we detect and classify the objects in the scene using YOLOv4, that is a one-stage object detector. We manipulate the camera calibration matrix in order to recover longitudinal and lateral distances from the vehicle to the objects detected. After that, we apply an object tracking algorithm on the objects in order to track their motion. Then, for each object detected, we evaluate the potential danger based on different specific criteria. Finally, we warn the driver with a haptic feedback that is proportional to the level of danger. In particular, the higher the value the more intrusive the feedback, until we reach the maximum danger, where the EBA function will break the vehicle to avoid a hazard. We evaluate our method on the KITTI raw dataset, using mean average precision (mAP) for object detection, and root mean square error (RMSE) for distance estimation.

2   Related Works

Recent advancements in haptic feedback systems have improved driving safety by providing non-visual, non-auditory alerts. These systems use tactile or kinesthetic feedback via the steering wheel, seat, or pedals to communicate critical information like lane departures, proximity warnings, and collision risks. Haptic feedback keeps drivers visually focused on the road while delivering essential cues, proving more effective than visual or auditory alerts in some high-load situations. As noted in [11], haptic systems are classified as either assistance systems, which provide continuous feedback for tasks like navigation or parking, or warning systems, which alert drivers to immediate dangers like collisions. These systems reduce driver response times and enhance spatial awareness, making them essential in modern Advanced Driver Assistance Systems (ADAS). Studies show that combining haptic feedback with other sensory modalities further enhances performance and reaction times in complex environments.

2.1   Object Detectors

State-of-the-art object detectors are mainly divided into two-stage and one-stage detectors. Two-stage detectors (i) use a Region Proposal Network (RPN) to identify regions of interest, and (ii) classify objects and refine bounding boxes. These methods, such as R-CNN [13] and Faster R-CNN [35], are accurate but slower [4,5]. In contrast, one-stage detectors treat detection as a regression problem, predicting bounding boxes and class probabilities in a single step, making them faster but generally less accurate [36]. Notable one-stage detectors include SSD [8,27] and YOLO [33]. For real-time systems, achieving over 10 FPS is crucial, as the human visual system perceives individual images below this threshold and motion above it [31]. Given its speed and performance, YOLOv4 [3] was chosen for our system.

For further details, refer to the survey by [19], which covers various object detection methods.

2.2   Distance Estimation

Current distance estimation in autonomous driving often relies on LiDAR, which, like radar, calculates distance via time of flight. However, LiDAR is expensive. In our work, we focus on monocular cameras, a cost-effective alternative. Stereo cameras usually estimate depth through triangulation, but monocular cameras can estimate 3D distances using techniques like inverse perspective mapping (IPM) and 2D-3D correspondences under simplifying assumptions. This monocular approach, while less complex than stereo setups, provides adequate distance estimation for most road scenarios. Stereo cameras require more complex hardware and calibration to maintain alignment, adding to setup and maintenance complexity. Monocular systems avoid these challenges.

Many recent works use IPM to compute longitudinal distances. For example, [20] combines IPM and YOLO for object detection and distance estimation. Similarly, [32] uses IPM, camera matrices, and lane detection to compute Euclidean distances, while [1] employs IPM and HSV colormap to define the region of interest and retrieve distances. However, IPM depends on the road's vanishing point, which can fail in curves.

Machine learning offers another approach to distance estimation. DisNet [15] uses YOLO to train a neural network for supervised distance estimation, providing a dataset with 2D bounding boxes and distances. [22] developed FisheyeDistanceNet, which estimates depth from fisheye images. While effective, machine learning methods require extensive training and data.

Our approach is faster and simpler. By manipulating the camera matrix and using 3D-2D correspondences from the Pinhole camera model, we efficiently estimate longitudinal and lateral distances.

3   Pipeline

In this section we present our work. Each step of the pipeline (illustrated in Fig. 1) is designed to be executed frame by frame in real time during the driving.

3.1   Object Detection

To evaluate potential dangers, we first need to detect all objects in the scene. Our approach focuses on the one-stage detector YOLOv4, the fourth improved

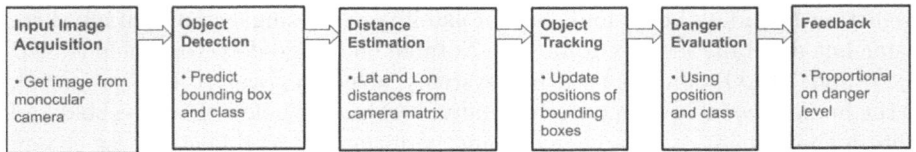

Fig. 1. The complete pipeline of the proposed method.

version of YOLO, chosen based on its balance between inference time and average precision. A modern one-stage object detector generally consists of three key components. First, the backbone, which serves as a feature extractor, is typically pre-trained on large datasets such as ImageNet [10]. Second, the neck is responsible for analyzing and refining features from different stages of the backbone. Finally, the head is tasked with generating bounding boxes and making class predictions.

In the specific case of YOLOv4, the backbone used is CSPDarknet53, an efficient architecture designed for feature extraction. The neck integrates Spatial Pyramid Pooling (SPP) and PANet, which aggregate and process features across multiple scales to enhance detection accuracy. The head is derived from YOLOv3, responsible for generating precise bounding boxes and classifying objects within them. This combination allows YOLOv4 to provide a strong balance of accuracy and speed, making it ideal for real-time object detection.

Backbone. The Cross Stage Partial Network (CSPNet) [37] was introduced to reduce the computation of heavy neural networks, which is fundamental to develop real-time applications on small devices. YOLOv4 applied CSPNet to Darknet53, which is a convolutional neural network using residual connections introduced in YOLOv3 [34].

Neck. As an additional block placed after the backbone YOLOv4 implements Spatial Pyramid Pooling (SPP) [16], which is a more robust method to image deformations (crop/warp) for both object detection and classification. To complete the section, the Path Aggregation Network (PANet) [26] is added to enhance the entire feature hierarchy, in order to let useful information in each feature level propagate directly to the following proposal subnetworks.

Head. YOLO divides the image into an S × S grid and for each grid cell predicts B bounding boxes, each one consisting of 5 predictions: x, y, w, h and *confidence*. Each grid cell also predicts C conditional class probabilities: *Prob (Class|Object)*. YOLOv3's main idea is totally based on the original work, even if it predicts boxes across three different scales, using a similar concept to Feature Pyramid Networks [25]. For this reason, the predictions for the third scale benefit from all the prior computation as well as fine grained features from early on in the network. The 2D bounding box predictions are sufficient to estimate the distances from the vehicle to all the objects in the scene, since we need to know only the lower side of the box, which represents the contact point of the object with the road.

3.2   Distance Estimation

Before going into details, we have to state two simplifying assumptions: (a1) the road on which the vehicle and all the objects in the scene lie, must be a planar surface, (a2) the camera installed on the vehicle must be stationary. These simplifications allowed us to develop an efficient, easy and fast computational method for distance estimation.

Camera Matrix. *Multiple View Geometry in Computer Vision* [14] describes how the pinhole camera model maps world points to image points. Using homogeneous coordinates we can write:

$$P = K[R \mid t] = \begin{bmatrix} f_x & s & x_0 \\ 0 & f_y & y_0 \\ 0 & 0 & 1 \end{bmatrix} \begin{bmatrix} R_{11} & R_{12} & R_{13} & t_1 \\ R_{21} & R_{22} & R_{23} & t_2 \\ R_{31} & R_{32} & R_{33} & t_3 \end{bmatrix}$$

where: K is the 3×3 camera calibration matrix containing the intrinsic parameters, describing the focal length, the optical center, and the skew coefficient, and R and t are the extrinsic parameters, namely rotation and translation of a rigid transformation from 3D world coordinate system to the 3D camera's coordinate system.

In order to obtain the camera matrix, it is necessary to perform a camera calibration process that can be done in different ways and it is implemented in computer vision libraries like OpenCV. The camera matrix P defines how a world point X is mapped to an image point x:

$$\begin{pmatrix} x \\ y \\ 1 \end{pmatrix} = P \begin{pmatrix} X \\ Y \\ Z \\ 1 \end{pmatrix} \quad (1)$$

3.3   2D-3D Correspondence

We start by defining the camera frame RF_c, which we will use from now on for every transformation, it is a right-hand coordinate system with the y axis pointing down (x axis points to the left and the z axis points out of the screen). Given the camera matrix P, the height of the camera from the road to the vehicle roof h, and the longitudinal distance from the camera to the front bumper of the car b, we can now manipulate the camera in order to obtain a one-to-one correspondence that maps image points x to world points on the road X. We first translate the camera by multiplication with a transformation matrix T:

$$P_t = PT = P \begin{bmatrix} 1 & 0 & 0 & 0 \\ 0 & 1 & 0 & h \\ 0 & 0 & 1 & b \end{bmatrix}$$

where $b = camera2bumper$ and $h = camera\ height$

As we can see in Image 2, we have translated the camera matrix on the road (height = 0) and towards the front side of the vehicle, through sequence of homogeneous transformations, so that the distances are computed directly from the central point of the bumper. At this point the assumptions come handy. Thanks to (a1) we simply eliminate from the camera matrix P_t the Y column, meaning that all the points projected to the real world have height equal to zero. This is beneficial for computing the inverse projective mapping of (1), from world point to image point:

$$\begin{pmatrix} X \\ Z \\ 1 \end{pmatrix} = P_{t,y=0}^{-1} \begin{pmatrix} x \\ y \\ 1 \end{pmatrix} \quad (2)$$

Thanks to (a2) we are able to define this mapping in every camera frame, ignoring all the disturbances due to road irregularities and vehicle movements. With this mapping it is easy to estimate longitudinal and lateral distances. Given a generic 2D bounding box ($x1$, $x2$, $x3$, $x4$), coming from the object detection step, we take the two contact points of the object with the road in image coordinates, and we apply the inverse mapping (2), which gives us the left end and right end sides in world coordinates. At this point we take the midpoint between the two (t_{long}, t_{lat}, 1), which corresponds to longitudinal and lateral planar distances from the vehicle bumper to that object.

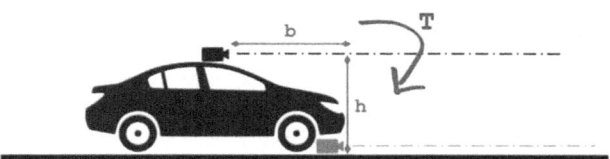

Fig. 2. Visualization of the T matrix transformation

3.4   Object Tracking

With the purpose of obtaining more specific information about the objects in the scene, we implemented an Euclidean object tracking system. It works by storing a dictionary of objects' longitudinal and lateral distances, with their IDs as keys. For each object detected in a generic frame, the tracker is updated, taking as input the vector (t_{long}, t_{lat}) of that object. The tracker compares the vector with the stored dictionary, using Euclidean difference, and if the new vector is sufficiently "close" to something, the dictionary entry of the corresponding point is updated with the new distances, otherwise it is marked as a new ID. The tracker works really well with objects detected within a certain lateral distance range, beyond which we are no more interested in tracking. Once we have the IDs of the objects in the scene, we can compute a few more properties such as the relative longitudinal and lateral velocities (v_{long}, v_{lat}) of the objects with respect to the vehicle, which are important in the danger evaluation phase for making predictions of potential collisions.

3.5 Danger Evaluation

The evaluation of potential danger situations, in order to provide a danger haptic feedback (DHF) complementary to the EBA function, is the core of our project. We apply different criteria according to the following lateral distance subdivisions (distances are considered laterally in both directions):1) **danger zone**: from 0 to 2 m. These are all the objects detected right in front of the vehicle, considering a total span of 4 m; 2) **attention zone**: from 2 to 5 m. These are all the objects detected just close to the vehicle; 3) **safe zone**: from 5 to 10 m. Further objects.

The zone limits have been chosen according to some considerations: 1) the danger zone corresponds to the maximum lane width (3.75 m) approximated to the next integer, 2) the attention zone comprises the next lane and an eventual sidewalk, 3) the safe zone extends till the predictions of the object recognition system give reliable results laterally (10 m). Distances are taken in modulus and computed starting from the midpoint of the front bumper of the vehicle, positive to the right.

Table 1. Table of vulnerability coefficient for evaluating dangerousness for different classes.

	Car	Van	Truck	Tram	Misc	Pedestrian	Cyclist
Vulnerability	1.0	1.0	0.8	0.9	1.0	1.5	1.5

Table 2. Different level of haptic feedbacks depending on the dangerousness value

Dangerousness D	$7 \leq D < 8$	$8 \leq D < 9$	$9 \leq D < 10$	≥ 10
Haptic Feedback	1-level	2-level	3-level	Break (EBA)

We assigned to each zone a support coefficient and to each object class a vulnerability coefficient. Such coefficients are: 1 for the *Danger Zone*, 0.8 for the *Attention Zone* and 0.5 for the *Safe Zone*. The support coefficients add a reduction contribution to dangerousness, according to the zone where the object is detected. The further the zone, the less dangerous the situation. The vulnerability coefficients take into consideration the class of the detected object. Colliding a cyclist or a pedestrian, for example, is more dangerous than colliding a truck, because it may cause a serious damage to the integrity and security of people with a higher probability.

Evaluation. For each detected object, we evaluate the dangerousness of a potential accident in the following manner:

$$D = $$
$$remap(V_{cr} * \alpha_v * \beta_z)$$

where D is the evaluated dangerousnees, V_{cr} is the criterion value, α_v is the vulnerability class coefficient, β_z is the zone coefficient, and the *remap* function remaps the value to the range 0, 10. Essentially the output value of the chosen criteria is smoothed by the two coefficients and finally remapped to a valuable range. The criterion are: stopping (longitudinal) distance, Euclidean distance, intersection distance.

In this way we restrict the value of the multiplication from 0 to 10 applying different criteria according to the zone on which the object is laying. In every zone, we make use of the longitudinal velocity of the vehicle v_e, which can be retrieved by sensors, such as Active Sensor Bearing (ASB), GPS or Inertial Measurement Unit (IMU).

Danger Zone . When considering an object detected in front of the vehicle, the danger comes from the possible collision due to insufficient *stopping distance* t_{stop}. In fact, in each frame, we take into consideration the closest (longitudinally) objects detected in the scene, taking their longitudinal distance. The smaller $t_{stop} - t_{long}$, the higher the probabilities to collide, if the object in front of the vehicle unexpectedly stops. We compute the stopping distance as the sum of the perception-reaction distance and the braking distance as:

$$v_e * t_{reaction} + v_e^2/(2 * \mu * g)$$

where $t_{reaction}$ is the reaction time, μ is the friction coefficient and g is the gravity of the earth. Reasonable values for $t_{reaction}$ and μ are respectively 1 s and 0.8, but these can vary according to the age of the vehicle driver and to what kind of vehicle he is driving.

Attention Zone. In the nearby zone, the danger comes from the possibility of some objects to unexpectedly cross the danger zone and appear in front of the vehicle. In this case we increase or decrease the danger according to the following rules:

- If some object is going towards the danger zone and if the predicted lateral shift of that object intersects the predicted longitudinal shift of the vehicle (the directions of the object and the vehicle intersect), and it happens in less than 3 s, the danger increase inversely proportional to the intersection time. We call this criteria *intersection distance.*

– Otherwise, we consider only the *Euclidean distance*, from the vehicle to the objects laying on the attention zone.

Safe Zone. Objects detected at a lateral distance higher than 5 m are not dangerous at all. In order to preserve the previous criteria and provide continuity to danger evaluation, especially in the case of objects crossing from the safe to the attention zone, we use as a criterion the *Euclidean distance*, from the vehicle to the objects laying on the safe zone. Image 3 shows some examples of danger evaluation, in different scenarios.

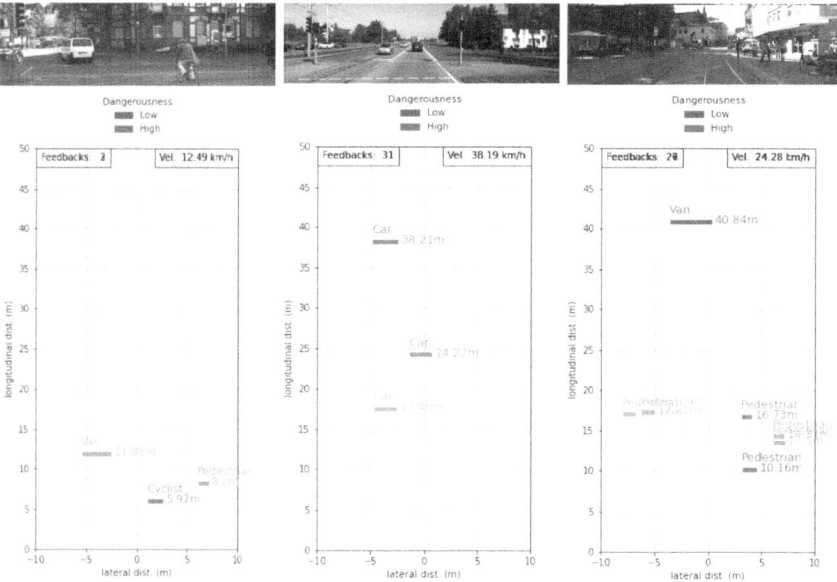

Fig. 3. Examples of Danger Evaluation

3.6   Haptic Feedback

The value of dangerousness computed in the last step is used to give feedback to the driver. Different kinds of actuators for our feedback system are possible, e.g. vibration system installed on the steering wheel, smart band on the wrist, etc. Every system is capable of generating a vibration on a intensity scale from 1 to 3. The values of dangerousness may be relevant and worthy of attention when greater than 7. According to that value, we can map our haptic feedback system together with the EBA as shown in Table 2.

4   Experiments

In this section we report the experiments and the results that we obtained, also mentioning the data used and the hardware we used.

4.1   Dataset

We tested our work on the KITTI [dataset] [12], which provides an annotated dataset for 2D and 3D object detection, and also a raw dataset for testing purposes. We used the object data for training and validating the object detection model, while the raw data was used for testing the object detection, the distance estimation and the object tracking, since the IMU information is provided only for the least. We focused on the scenarios 0005, 0015, and 0091 of the raw data, which respectively represent urban, highway and limited traffic zone scenarios.

4.2   Performances

We developed and tested our project on a Tesla T4 GPU with 12 GB of memory. With this architecture our pipeline runs at 15 FPS.

Object Detection. We trained the YOLOv4 model on KITTI 2D object data, consisting of 7481 images randomly divided into 80% train, 10% validation and 10% test. The network has been initialized with pre-trained weights on ImageNet. Training has been done using stochastic gradient descent with warm

Table 3. Performances on two different scenarios. The 0005 is calculated considering distances from a front cyclist. The 0015 is calculated considering distances from a front car. Empty values are reported when measures were not available or not enough to compute the relative metric.

Scenario	Long. Distance	Long. RMSE	Lateral. Distance	Lateral RMSE
0005	<10 m	0.908	<2 m	0.228
	10 m-30 m	1.931	2 m-5 m	0.306
	30 m-50 m	-	5 m-10 m	-
	Total	1.492	Total	0.262
0015	<10 m	-	<2 m	0.151
	10 m-30 m	2.425	2 m-5 m	-
	30 m-50 m	3.785	5 m-10 m	-
	Total	3.025	Total	0.151

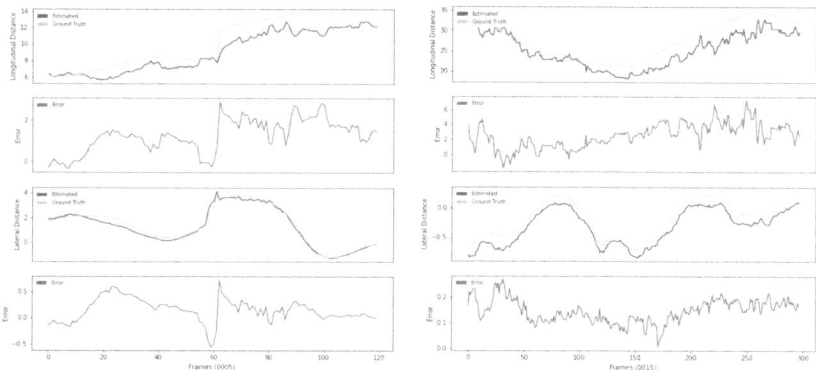

Fig. 4. distance performances in two different scenarios

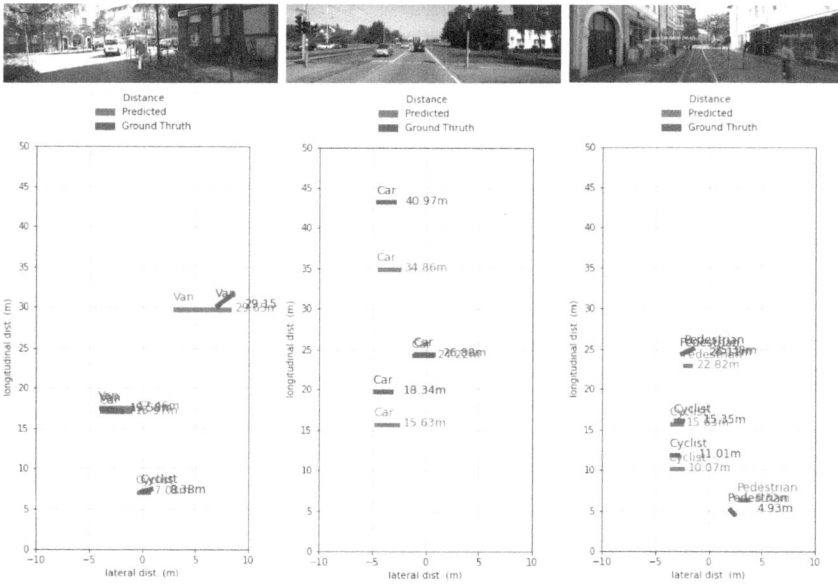

Fig. 5. Detection and distance estimation plots

restart (SGDR) [28] optimizer, with momentum 0.9, learning rate 10^{-3}, and decay $5*10^{-4}$, with batch size 64, for a total of 7500 iterations (about 60 epochs). We evaluated the object detection on a small amount of data (about 750 images), because unfortunately the test set is not annotated. We obtained a mean Average Precision (mAP) of 92.8%.

Distance Estimation. We evaluated the distances with the RMSE metric, distinguishing between short/long and longitudinal/lateral distances. Longitudinal distances are evaluated within 50 m, while lateral distances within the zone dimensions. Table 3 shows the results of the RMSE metric over two different KITTI videos, while in Image 4 the error plots can be seen. Image 5 shows some qualitative results of detection and distance estimation.

5   Conclusions

The proposed method has proved considerably effective in the conditions established at the beginning of the paper and the budget necessary for its implementation is very low. However, some aspects must be considered before applying the method in a real scenario: for example the method totally rely on object detection: if there are errors in this step of the pipeline, there is no other type of check is performed. Moreover the object detector works up to more or less 50 m: it would be better if the detection reached about 100 m (in order to be more effective in highways for example). The proposed method may not work properly in case of adverse visibility conditions or at night, due to the worse performances of the object detection. Moreover, due to the initial assumptions, we have a considerable margin of error when the machine "goes up and down" due to the bumps.

References

1. Adamshuk, R., et al.: On the applicability of inverse perspective mapping for the forward distance estimation based on the hsv colormap. In: 2017 IEEE International Conference on Industrial Technology (ICIT), pp. 1036–1041 (2017). https://doi.org/10.1109/ICIT.2017.7915504
2. Alfarano, A., De Magistris, G., Mongelli, L., Russo, S., Starczewski, J., Napoli, C.: A novel convmixer transformer based architecture for violent behavior detection. Lecture Notes in Computer Science (including subseries Lecture Notes in Artificial Intelligence and Lecture Notes in Bioinformatics) **14126 LNAI**, 3–16 (2023). https://doi.org/10.1007/978-3-031-42508-0_1
3. Bochkovskiy, A., Wang, C.Y., Liao, H.Y.M.: Yolov4: Optimal speed and accuracy of object detection (2020)
4. Bonanno, F., Capizzi, G., Coco, S., Napoli, C., Laudani, A., Sciuto, G.L.: Optimal thicknesses determination in a multilayer structure to improve the spp efficiency for photovoltaic devices by an hybrid fem - cascade neural network based approach. In: 2014 International Symposium on Power Electronics, Electrical Drives, Automation and Motion, SPEEDAM 2014, pp. 355 – 362 (2014). https://doi.org/10.1109/SPEEDAM.2014.6872103
5. Bonanno, F., Capizzi, G., Sciuto, G.L., Napoli, C., Pappalardo, G., Tramontana, E.: A cascade neural network architecture investigating surface plasmon polaritons propagation for thin metals in openmp. Lecture Notes in Computer Science (including subseries Lecture Notes in Artificial Intelligence and Lecture Notes in Bioinformatics) **8467 LNAI**(PART 1), 22 – 33 (2014). https://doi.org/10.1007/978-3-319-07173-2_3

6. Brandizzi, N., Russo, S., Brociek, R., Wajda, A.: First studies to apply the theory of mind theory to green and smart mobility by using gaussian area clustering. In: CEUR Workshop Proceedings. vol. 3118, pp. 71 – 76 (2021)
7. Brociek, R., Magistris, G.D., Cardia, F., Coppa, F., Russo, S.: Contagion prevention of covid-19 by means of touch detection for retail stores. In: CEUR Workshop Proceedings, vol. 3092, pp. 89 – 94 (2021)
8. Capizzi, G., Bonanno, F., Napoli, C.: A wavelet based prediction of wind and solar energy for long-term simulation of integrated generation systems. In: SPEEDAM 2010 - International Symposium on Power Electronics, Electrical Drives, Automation and Motion, pp. 586 – 592 (2010). https://doi.org/10.1109/SPEEDAM.2010.5542259
9. Chen, X., Kundu, K., Zhang, Z., Ma, H., Fidler, S., Urtasun, R.: Monocular 3d object detection for autonomous driving. In: 2016 IEEE Conference on Computer Vision and Patter Recognition (CVPR), pp. 2147–2156 (2016). https://doi.org/10.1109/CVPR.2016.236
10. Deng, J., Dong, W., Socher, R., Li, L.J., Li, K., Fei-Fei, L.: Imagenet: A large-scale hierarchical image database. In: 2009 IEEE Conference on Computer Vision and Pattern Recognition, pp. 248–255 (2009)
11. Gaffary, Y., Lécuyer, A.: The use of haptic and tactile information in the car to improve driving safety: A review of current technologies. Front. ICT 5, 5 (2018)
12. Geiger, A., Lenz, P., Stiller, C., Urtasun, R.: Vision meets robotics: The kitti dataset. Int. J. Robot. Res. (IJRR) (2013). http://www.cvlibs.net/datasets/kitti/index.php
13. Girshick, R., Donahue, J., Darrell, T., Malik, J.: Rich feature hierarchies for accurate object detection and semantic segmentation (2014)
14. Hartley, R., Zisserman, A.: Multiple View Geometry in Computer Vision. Cambridge University Press, 2 edn. (2004). https://doi.org/10.1017/CBO9780511811685
15. Haseeb, M.A., Guan, J., Ristic-Durrant, D., Gräser, A.: Disnet: A novel method for distance estimation from monocular camera (2018)
16. He, K., Zhang, X., Ren, S., Sun, J.: Spatial pyramid pooling in deep convolutional networks for visual recognition. LNCS, pp. 346–361 (2014). https://doi.org/10.1007/978-3-319-10578-9_23
17. Hirose, T., Taniguchi, T., Hatano, T., Takahashi, K., Tanaka, N.: A study on the effect of brake assist systems (bas). SAE Int. J. Passenger Cars - Mech. Syst. 1(1), 729–735 (apr 2008). https://doi.org/10.4271/2008-01-0824
18. Ishida, S., Gayko, J.: Development, evaluation and introduction of a lane keeping assistance system. In: IEEE Intelligent Vehicles Symposium, 2004. pp. 943–944 (2004). https://doi.org/10.1109/IVS.2004.1336512
19. Jiao, L.: A survey of deep learning-based object detection. IEEE Access 7, 128837–128868 (2019). https://doi.org/10.1109/access.2019.2939201
20. Kim, Y., Kum, D.: Deep learning based vehicle position and orientation estimation via inverse perspective mapping image. In: 2019 IEEE Intelligent Vehicles Symposium (IV), pp. 317–323 (2019). https://doi.org/10.1109/IVS.2019.8814050
21. Kumar, S., Moore, K.B.: The evolution of global positioning system (gps) technology. J. Sci. Educ. Technol. 11(1), 59–80 (2002). https://doi.org/10.1023/A:1013999415003
22. Kumar, V.R., et al.: Fisheyedistancenet: Self-supervised scale-aware distance estimation using monocular fisheye camera for autonomous driving. In: 2020 IEEE International Conference on Robotics and Automation (ICRA), pp. 574–581 (2020)

23. Li, P., Chen, X., Shen, S.: Stereo r-cnn based 3d object detection for autonomous driving (2019)
24. Li, Y., Ibanez-Guzman, J.: Lidar for autonomous driving: the principles, challenges, and trends for automotive lidar and perception systems. IEEE Signal Process. Mag. **37**(4), 50–61 (2020). https://doi.org/10.1109/MSP.2020.2973615
25. Lin, T.Y., Dollár, P., Girshick, R., He, K., Hariharan, B., Belongie, S.: Feature pyramid networks for object detection (2017)
26. Liu, S., Qi, L., Qin, H., Shi, J., Jia, J.: Path aggregation network for instance segmentation (2018)
27. Liu, W., et al.: Ssd: Single shot multibox detector. LNCS, pp. 21–37 (2016). https://doi.org/10.1007/978-3-319-46448-0_2
28. Loshchilov, I., Hutter, F.: Sgdr: Stochastic gradient descent with warm restarts (2017)
29. Mammeri, A., Lu, G., Boukerche, A.: Design of lane keeping assist system for autonomous vehicles. In: 2015 7th International Conference on New Technologies, Mobility and Security (NTMS), pp. 1–5 (2015). https://doi.org/10.1109/NTMS. 2015.7266483
30. Marsden, G., McDonald, M., Brackstone, M.: Towards an understanding of adaptive cruise control. Transport. Res. Part C: Emerg. Technol. **9**(1), 33–51 (2001). https://doi.org/10.1016/S0968-090X(00)00022-X, https://www. sciencedirect.com/science/article/pii/S0968090X0000022X
31. Połap, D., Woźniak, M., Napoli, C., Tramontana, E.: Real-time cloud-based game management system via cuckoo search algorithm. Int. J. Electron. Telecommun. **61**(4), 333–338 (2015). https://doi.org/10.1515/eletel-2015-0043
32. Qiao, D., Zulkernine, F.: Vision-based vehicle detection and distance estimation. In: 2020 IEEE Symposium Series on Computational Intelligence (SSCI), pp. 2836–2842 (2020). https://doi.org/10.1109/SSCI47803.2020.9308364
33. Redmon, J., Divvala, S., Girshick, R., Farhadi, A.: You only look once: Unified, real-time object detection (2016)
34. Redmon, J., Farhadi, A.: Yolov3: An incremental improvement (2018)
35. Ren, S., He, K., Girshick, R., Sun, J.: Faster r-cnn: Towards real-time object detection with region proposal networks (2016)
36. Soviany, P., Ionescu, R.T.: Optimizing the trade-off between single-stage and two-stage object detectors using image difficulty prediction (2018)
37. Wang, C.Y., Liao, H.Y.M., Yeh, I.H., Wu, Y.H., Chen, P.Y., Hsieh, J.W.: Cspnet: A new backbone that can enhance learning capability of cnn (2019)
38. Wang, Y., Chao, W., Garg, D., Hariharan, B., Campbell, M., Weinberger, K.Q.: Pseudo-lidar from visual depth estimation: Bridging the gap in 3d object detection for autonomous driving. CoRR **abs/1812.07179** (2018). http://arxiv.org/abs/1812.07179

Relating Explanations with the Inductive Biases of Deep Graph Networks

Michele Fontanesi$^{(\boxtimes)}$ (iD), Alessio Micheli$^{(\boxtimes)}$ (iD), and Marco Podda$^{(\boxtimes)}$ (iD)

Department of Computer Science, University of Pisa, Largo B. Pontecorvo 3,
56127 Pisa, Italy
`michele.fontanesi@phd.unipi.it, micheli@di.unipi.it, marco.podda@unipi.it`

Abstract. Deep Graph Networks (DGNs), i.e. neural networks able to process graphs directly, feature an iterative message passing (MP) step that implements the node embeddings computation. However, the inductive and architectural biases of different DGNs in relation to the type and number of MP iterations are yet to be unveiled. Here, we investigate this important topic using eXplainable Artificial Intelligence (XAI) techniques for graphs. Specifically, we use the XAI metric of plausibility to detect explanatory patterns and to relate this information to the biases exploited by the underlying DGN to correctly learn graph classification tasks. We use this method to gather evidence on the rich diversity of DGN biases in relation to the type and number of iterations of MP when applied to XAI benchmarks. In addition, we show that when the MP conditions are fixed, the learned explanatory pattern may change based on the norm of the learned weights, signifying that the training procedure, in particular cases, influences the generalization dynamics.

Keywords: Deep Graph Networks · Explainable Artificial Intelligence · Inductive Bias

1 Introduction

The increasing use of graph structures to model complex relational phenomena coupled with the latest peak of interest in Machine Learning have made neural networks able to handle graph data directly, a.k.a. Deep Graph Networks (DGNs) [2], the *de facto* technology to tackle classification and regression tasks on graphs. Since their introduction [11,17], different types of DGNs have been developed, most commonly based on the message passing (MP) paradigm [6]. Loosely speaking, MP is a generic three-step iterative procedure whose objective is to update node embeddings based on the graph topology, which each DGN implements internally in different flavors.

While DGNs have been repeatedly shown to generalize to unseen graphs, the inductive biases [13], i.e., the set of assumptions implicitly made by the model that make this generalization possible, are still not completely characterized, since they are encoded into a large set of learned parameters. Nevertheless,

A. Artale et al. (Eds.): AIxIA 2024, LNAI 15450, pp. 175–187, 2025.
https://doi.org/10.1007/978-3-031-80607-0_14

knowing which inductive bias DGNs exploit is paramount to understanding and interpreting their decisions, enhancing their trustworthiness [15] and as a consequence, their widespread adoption in safety-critical applications.

In this work, we contribute to this topic by applying eXplainable Artificial Intelligence (XAI) techniques for graphs [1,7,8,20] to analyze the behavior of DGNs in synthetic graph classification tasks, deriving insights about the rich landscape of the inductive biases that they implicitly exploit. By using the Class Activation Mapping (CAM) [16,21] explainer, we first notice that different DGNs (characterized by different MP variants) achieve almost perfect generalization despite showing two different explanatory patterns (i.e., importance scores) at the node level. This suggests that there are different learning "routes", all valid, that a DGN can take to achieve the ultimate goal of generalization. We then use the XAI metric of plausibility [9] to detect which explanatory pattern the DGN has picked up, and show how it relates to the specific MP implementation. More precisely, we show experimentally that the explanatory patterns align with known properties of certain MP variants, and we show that by varying the MP configuration the model shifts from one explanatory pattern to the other.

Our results shed light on how the different inductive biases that DGNs use are leveraged to learn graph classification tasks. Moreover, they suggest that all kinds of inductive biases are equally important and play a prominent role in the end goal of generalization.

2   Background

In this section, we provide the notions to understand the proposed analysis.

2.1   Preliminary Notions on Graphs

A graph $G = (V_G, E_G)$ [3] is defined as a tuple consisting of a set of vertices $V_G = \{v_1, ..., v_n\}$ and a set of edges $E_G \subseteq (V_G \times V_G) = \{(u, v) \mid u, v \in V\}$. The graph connectivity is usually formalized as an *adjacency matrix* $\mathbf{A} \in \mathbb{R}^{n \times n}$ with $\mathbf{A}_{u,v} = \mathbb{1}[(u, v) \in E_G]$. The neighborhood of a node v is the set $\mathcal{N}_v = \{u \in V \mid (u, v) \in E_G\}$ of nodes connected to v by an edge. Graph nodes are associated with feature vectors $\mathbf{x}_v \in \mathbb{R}^d$ for some $d \in \mathbb{N}$, and we use the notation $\mathbf{X} \in \mathbb{R}^{n \times d}$ to indicate the matrix of node features stacked row-wise. Therefore, for the purposes of this work, we encode a graph with the tuple $(\mathbf{A}, \mathbf{X})$. Two graphs G and G' are said to be (structurally) isomorphic if there exists a bijection $\phi : V_G \to V_{G'}$ such that $\forall u, v \in V_G, (u, v) \in E_G \iff (\phi(u), \phi(v)) \in E_{G'}$.

2.2   Deep Graph Networks

In this work, we focus on graph classification tasks consisting of learning an unknown function f that maps graphs $G \in \mathcal{G}$ to class labels $y_G \in \mathcal{C}$, where $\mathcal{G}$ and $\mathcal{C}$ indicate a set of graphs and the discrete set of possible labels, respectively. In this setting, a DGN implements a parameterized function f_Θ which assigns a predicted label $\hat{y}_G$ to input graphs. During training, the parameters Θ are adjusted such that f_Θ well approximates f. In this work, we specify a DGN as the following function composition:

$$f_\Theta = f_{\theta_1}^{\text{trans}} \circ f_{\theta_2}^{\text{pool}} \circ f_{\theta_3}^{\text{out}}, \tag{1}$$

where

- $f_{\theta_1}^{\text{trans}}$ implements an isomorphic transduction of the input graph which maps the node features $\mathbf{x}_v$ to node embeddings $\mathbf{h}_v^L \in \mathbb{R}^{d'}$, $d' \in \mathbb{N}$, by applying MP for $L \geq 1$ iterations.
- $f_{\theta_2}^{\text{pool}}$ is a pooling operator that sums up the embeddings into a single graph representation vector

$$\sum_{v \in V_G} \mathbf{h}_v^L \in \mathbb{R}^{d'}.$$

- $f_{\theta_3}^{\text{out}}$ is a downstream classifier (in this work, it is a logistic regression model) that outputs a $|\mathcal{C}|$-dimensional vector of class probabilities based on the graph representation:

$$\hat{\mathbf{y}}_G = \text{softmax}\left(\theta^{\text{out}} \sum_{v \in V_G} \mathbf{h}_v^L\right).$$

The output of a DGN is the most likely class according to the output vector:

$$\hat{y}_G = \arg\max \hat{\mathbf{y}}_G.$$

2.3   Message Passing Variants

Usually, DGNs realize $f_{\theta_1}^{\text{trans}}$ with some form of MP. Generally speaking, MP is a blueprint defined at the node level as follows:

$$\mathbf{h}_v^{l+1} = \text{Upd}\left(\mathbf{h}_v^l, \text{Agg}(\{\text{Msg}(\mathbf{h}_v^l, \mathbf{h}_u^l) \mid u \in \mathcal{N}_v\})\right), \tag{2}$$

where the Msg function computes a message between every node and its neighbors; Agg combines all the messages received by each node from its neighborhood in a permutation-invariant fashion; and Upd updates every node embedding by combining the current node embedding and the aggregated messages. Each DGN implements its own version of MP; broadly speaking, MP implementations can be categorized as convolutional or recursive. Convolutional DGNs [2] implement $f_{\theta_1}^{\text{trans}}$ by stacking $L \geq 1$ MP layers, creating deep, end-to-end trainable architectures that progressively expand the receptive field of the node embeddings [11]. Instead, recursive DGNs implement $f_{\theta_1}^{\text{trans}}$ as a recursive contractive dynamical system. This process is executed until convergence, with each iteration corresponding to a single MP computation. This study focuses on three convolutional DGNs and one recursive DGN architecture, as described in the following. Notice that l indexes the layer for convolutional MP, while for recursive MP, it indexes the iterations.

Graph Isomorphism Network. (GIN) [19] convolutional layers implement MP as follows (with $1 \leq l \leq L$, where L is a hyper-parameter):

$$\mathbf{h}_v^0 = \mathbf{x}_v, \tag{3}$$

$$\mathbf{h}_v^l = \text{MLP}_{\boldsymbol{\Theta}^{l-1}} \left((1 + \epsilon^{l-1}) \mathbf{h}_v^{l-1} + \sum_{u \in \mathcal{N}_v} \mathbf{h}_u^{l-1} \right), \tag{4}$$

where ϵ is a learnable or fixed parameter, Msg returns the neighboring embedding, Agg is the sum function, and Upd is a sum function followed by a multilayer perceptron (MLP) parameterized with layer-dependent weights $\boldsymbol{\Theta}$.

GraphConv. (GC) [14] convolutional layers implement MP as follows (with $1 \leq l \leq L$, where L is a hyper-parameter):

$$\mathbf{h}_v^0 = \mathbf{x}_v, \tag{5}$$

$$\mathbf{h}_v^l = \text{ReLU} \left(\boldsymbol{\Theta}_1^{l-1} \mathbf{h}_v^{l-1} + \boldsymbol{\Theta}_2^{l-1} \sum_{u \in \mathcal{N}_v} \mathbf{h}_u^{l-1} \right), \tag{6}$$

where Msg returns the neighboring embedding, Agg is the sum function, and Upd is a sum function followed by a ReLU nonlinearity. Notice that the current node embedding and the aggregated neighborhood embedding are weighted with layer-dependent parameters $\boldsymbol{\Theta}_1$ and $\boldsymbol{\Theta}_2$.

The **Principal Neighbourhood Aggregation** (PNA) [4] convolutional layer implements MP as follows (with $1 \leq l \leq L$, where L is a hyper-parameter):

$$\mathbf{h}_v^0 = \mathbf{x}_v, \tag{7}$$

$$\mathbf{h}_v^l = \text{MLP}_{\boldsymbol{\Theta}_1^{l-1}} \left(\mathbf{h}_v^{l-1}, \bigoplus_{u \in \mathcal{N}_v} \text{MLP}_{\boldsymbol{\Theta}_2^{l-1}} (\mathbf{h}_v^{l-1}, \mathbf{h}_u^{l-1}) \right) \tag{8}$$

with

$$\bigoplus = \begin{bmatrix} 1 \\ S(\mathbf{D}, \alpha = 1) \\ S(\mathbf{D}, \alpha = -1) \end{bmatrix} \otimes \begin{bmatrix} mean \\ std \\ min \\ max \end{bmatrix} \tag{9}$$

where Msg and Upd are MLPs with layer-dependent parameters $\boldsymbol{\Theta}_1$ and $\boldsymbol{\Theta}_2$. Similarly, the function $\bigoplus$ realizes Agg, with $S(\mathbf{D}, \alpha)$ being a degree-based scaler, 1 being an identity scaler, $\otimes$ being a tensor product and *mean, std, min, max* being the mean, standard deviation, minimum and maximum functions to aggregate neighborhood messages, respectively.

Lastly, **Graph Echo State Networks** (GESN) [5] provides the following efficient recursive message passing variant based on Reservoir Computing:

$$\mathbf{h}_v^0 = \mathbf{0}, \tag{10}$$

$$\mathbf{h}_v^l = \tanh\left(\bar{\boldsymbol{\Theta}}\,\mathbf{x}_v + \boldsymbol{\Theta}\sum_{j\in\mathcal{N}_v}\mathbf{h}_j^{l-1}\right) \tag{11}$$

where $\bar{\boldsymbol{\Theta}}$ is a weight matrix introducing residual connections, and $\boldsymbol{\Theta}$ is the recursive weight matrix shared across all L iterations. The efficiency and further specific bias of this architecture come from the fact that both weight matrices are untrained but carefully initialized, creating a contractive/Markovian dynamical system that provides meaningful node embeddings to solve a task at convergence. Specifically, the recursive matrix $\boldsymbol{\Theta}$ must be initialized such that for every input $\mathbf{x}_v$ and every initial state of the system, as the number of iterations grows to infinity each node embedding reaches a stable fixed point. This is known as the Graph Embedding Stability property for which one sufficient and one necessary condition have been identified. The sufficient condition requires $\|\boldsymbol{\Theta}\|\|\mathbf{A}\| < 1$ while the necessary condition requires $\rho(\boldsymbol{\Theta}) < 1/\alpha$, where ρ indicates the spectral radius and α is the graph spectral radius [12]. The matrix $\bar{\boldsymbol{\Theta}}$, instead, is randomly initialized sapling values from the interval $[-\omega, \omega]$. It should be noted that both ρ and ω constitute hyperparameters of the architecture. However, L is not a hyperparameter as it is for the convolutional variants. In GESN, L is a stopping criterion in the form of the maximum number of allowed iterations, and therefore MP operations, for the dynamical system to reach the required convergence and provide meaningful node embeddings. As a consequence, L is usually large as the convergence of the system is a prerequisite to solving tasks with GESN.

2.4   The CAM Attribution Method

The class activation mapping (CAM) technique is a local post-hoc XAI method that assigns an *importance score* to each node in a graph. Specifically, given a graph G and a DGN f_Θ, the CAM method computes importance scores for each node by exploiting the following equivalence in the $f_{\theta_3}^{\mathrm{out}}$ module:

$$logit_{(y)} = \theta_{(y)}^{\mathrm{out}}\sum_{v\in V_G}\mathbf{h}_v^L = \sum_{v\in V_G}\theta_{(y)}^{\mathrm{out}}\mathbf{h}_v^L. \tag{12}$$

where $logit_{(y)}$ identifies the score associated to class y by its readout unit, $\theta_{(y)}^{\mathrm{out}}$ is the weight vector of the readout unit associated with class y, and $\mathbf{h}_v^L$ are the node embeddings computed by the model at the last layer L. In particular, CAM exploits the observation that the final logits of a DGN, usually computed as a linear transformation of the graph embedding $\sum_{v\in V}\mathbf{h}_v^L$, can be seen as the sum of a weighted contribution of each node $\theta_{(y)}^{\mathrm{out}}\mathbf{h}_v^L$ to the logit.

Ultimately, the CAM method returns a vector $\hat{\mathbf{t}}_G \in \mathbb{R}^n$ where the i-th position stores the contribution (i.e., the importance score) of the i-th node to the overall graph prediction. Among the many explainers for DGN architectures available in the literature (see e.g., [18,20]), CAM was chosen since it does not require the specification of hyperparameters, making it a suitable choice to compare different MP-based DGNs on equal terms.

3   Method

We develop our methodology on multiple XAI graph classification datasets of the form $\mathcal{D} = \{(G, y_G, \mathcal{T}) \mid G \in \mathcal{G}, y \in \mathcal{C}\}$ where graphs G are associated to target classes y as well as to sets of *ground truth explanations* $\mathcal{T} = \{\mathbf{t}_G^p \in \{0,1\}^n \mid p \in \mathcal{P}\}$ collecting a diverse *ground truth* (GT) for a given explanatory pattern p in the set of explanatory patterns $\mathcal{P}$. Specifically, the ground truth explanation is a binary vector encoding the relevance (1) or irrelevance (0) of each node to the graph prediction, while the explanatory pattern refers to the properties of the substructure identified by the relevant nodes within the graph. Our objective is to detect which explanatory pattern p is learned by different MP configurations – number of layers for the convolutional variants. Moreover, at fixed MP conditions, we also analyze the effect of training on the learned policy by studying the 2-norms of the weights of the convolutional MP layers.

3.1   Explanatory Pattern Detection

The identification of the explanatory pattern proceeds as follows:

1. First, the dataset $\mathcal{D}$ is partitioned into a training set $\mathcal{D}_{\text{train}}$ and a hold out test set $\mathcal{D}_{\text{test}}$. The training set is used to train and select the DGNs f_Θ, while the test set $\mathcal{D}_{\text{test}}$ is used for model assessment.
2. Once f_Θ has been learned and its generalization is assessed, graphs in $\mathcal{D}_{\text{test}}$ are processed by the CAM explainer, generating a set of explanations $\{\hat{\mathbf{t}}_G = \text{CAM}(G, f_\Theta) \mid G \in \mathcal{D}_{\text{test}}\}$;
3. Finally, given an explanatory pattern p, we compute its plausibility $\bar{Pl}s_p$, which consists of the sample-wise Area Under the Receiver Operating Characteristic curve (AUROC) between the explanations provided by CAM $\hat{\mathbf{t}}_G$ with the corresponding ground truth explanations $\mathbf{t}_G^p$:

$$\bar{Pl}s_p = \frac{1}{|\mathcal{D}_{\text{test}}|} \sum_{G \in \mathcal{D}_{\text{test}}} \text{AUROC}(\hat{\mathbf{t}}_G, \mathbf{t}_G^p), \tag{13}$$

We compute $\bar{Pl}s_p$ for each explanatory pattern $p \in \mathcal{P}$, and we determine the detected explanatory pattern as the one that maximizes $\bar{Pl}s_p$. The choice of plausibility to establish the explanatory pattern is due to the fact that its computation does not require the definition of a threshold to transform explanations into binary versions, which is mandatory for metrics like accuracy.

3.2   Analysis Procedure to Detect the Training Effect

Given a set of DGN models, characterized by the same MP type and iteration number we compute the norms of all the learned weights as an indicator
of their differences due to the convergence of the training procedure to different local minima. Then, we relate the average plausibility values of all models
$\bar{Pls}_p$, $\forall p \in \mathcal{P}$, to their corresponding total norm values to understand the relationship between a learned policy and the models' characteristics determined by
the training process at fixed MP conditions.

4   Experiments

4.1   Datasets and Prediction Policies

We tested our approach on three different synthetic binary classification graph
datasets originally associated with a single explanatory pattern based on the
detection of diverse motifs in the graphs [9,10]. In particular, the BA2Motif
dataset consists of 960 graphs with 25 nodes on average and assigns class 1 to
Barabási-Albert (BA) graphs linked to a house motif and class 0 to BA graphs
linked to a 5-node cycle motif; the BA2grid dataset consists of 2000 graphs with
22 nodes on average and assigns class 1 to BA graphs linked to a 3×3 grid motif
and class 0 to plain BA graphs; the GridHouse dataset consists of 2000 graphs
with 24 nodes on average and assigns class 1 to BA graphs linked to a 3×3 grid
and a house motif, class 0 to BA graphs linked to either the grid or the house.
However, each of these datasets admits a second explanatory pattern based on
the degree of each node. Specifically, perfect classifiers can be constructed using
only the average degree of the input graphs.

Table 1. Minimum and maximum average degrees by target class for each dataset.

	Class 0		Class 1	
	min	max	min	max
BA2grid	1.87	1.93	2.20	2.4
BA2Motif	2	2	2.08	2.08
GridHouse	2.06	2.3	2.34	2.5

In Table 1, we show that the maximum average degree characterizing class 0
graphs is always lower than the minimum average degree characterizing class 1
graphs for each dataset. Therefore, a DGN that learned this threshold would be
able to separate the two classes. Moreover, we also constructed the set of associated ground truth explanations for the degree explanatory pattern, exploiting
the characteristic that the minimum average degree for class 1 graphs is always
above 2. Specifically, the associated ground truth vector marks nodes with a

degree $\geq$ 3 as relevant (since they move the average towards class 1) and all other nodes as irrelevant. Thus, in our experiments, $\mathcal{P} = \{Degree, Motif\}$. Figure 1 shows the different explanatory patterns that can be picked up by the different DGNs during training.

4.2 Model Selection

The models used in this study have similar hyper-parameters, allowing for the comparison between different MP variants. In particular, all convolutional models comprise a varying number of layers (up to a maximum of 5) followed by a sum pooling operation to generate the graph embedding and a single layer MLP to map graph embeddings into class probabilities. The only exception to the shared model scheme is GESN, as recursive architectures do not map MP iterations to different layers. Consequently, for this MP variant, we only tested a one-layer configuration while keeping the number of iterations large enough (up to a maximum of 50) for the node embeddings to reach a stable fixed point useful for classification purposes. The model selection procedure adheres to the following scheme:

1. We split each dataset into training (80%) and test (20%) sets stratifying the splits following the class distributions.
2. We perform a 5-fold cross-validation technique over the training set, testing multiple hyperparameter configurations. In particular, for convolutional MP-

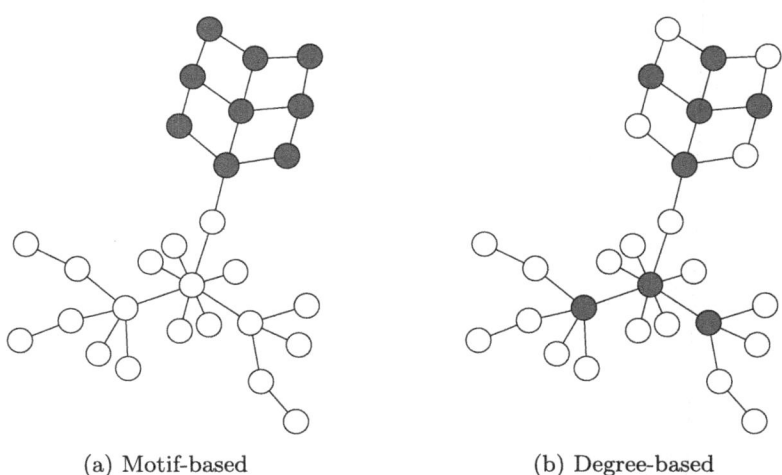

(a) Motif-based   (b) Degree-based

Fig. 1. We show the two possible explanatory patterns associated with the data employed in this study, using the BA2Grid dataset as an example. In both cases, the graph is assigned class 1 if the graph contains the pattern (i.e., the subset of nodes in blue). For the motif-based explanatory pattern (a), this subset identifies a 3×3 grid motif. For the degree-based explanatory pattern (b), the subset includes all nodes with degree $\geq$ 3.

DGNs, we used a grid search approach testing multiple values of the learning rate, weight decay, number of units inside each layer, and number of layers. As this latter hyperparameter is a key target of the analysis we kept its grid-search range fixed across all convolutional MP variants (from 1 up to a maximum of 5 layers). Other hyperparameter ranges instead have been tuned to increase the number of models achieving high enough performances to be kept as subjects of the analysis. Concerning, GESN, instead, the number of layers has been kept fixed to 1 but we tested different values for the ρ hyperparameter, the σ input scaler, the size of the untrained reservoir and the l2 regularization coefficient of the trained readout. It is important to stress that we kept the range of studied ρ values in the range between 0 and 1 to satisfy the Graph Embedding Stability property and keep GESN in a contractive regime.

3. For the analysis purpose, we collected all models whose hyperparameter configurations exceed an average Accuracy value across all folds of 90%.

Once we identified all suitable models we applied, to all of them, the procedures to identify the learned explanatory pattern as well as the procedure to gather information concerning the influence of training in the learned policy through the computation of the norm of the weights.

5   Results

In Table 2, we show the average $\bar{Pls}_{Degree}$ and the $\bar{Pls}_{Motif}$ values across the selected hyperparameters configurations for each MP variant while grouping results based on the number of MP iterations. From the table, it is possible to see that both explanatory patterns have been picked up by the different DGNs examined. This highlights that both patterns are useful and allow generalization, despite their very different nature. In general, we observe that the preferred explanatory pattern changes across MP variants as well as across different layers (for convolutional MPs).

Delving into the results, two interesting phenomena can be observed. First, on some convolutional MP variants, the explanatory pattern changes as the number of MP layers increases. Specifically, GIN and GC with a low number of MP layers (1-2) pick up the degree explanatory pattern; however, they switch to the motif pattern at higher iterations. This result agrees with the expected inductive bias of these models, which are able to capture low-order structures such as degree at the lowest layers, and tend to capture more complex substructures such as motifs with a large number of layers. Interestingly enough, while GIN with two layers picks up the motif explanatory pattern, GC still prefers to pick up the degree explanatory pattern with the same number of layers. This indicates that even if the two MP variants have similar shifts from low-order to high-order explanatory patterns, their learning behavior, dictated by their respective inductive biases, is slightly different.

Second, there are MP variants whose explanatory pattern does not change when varying the iteration number. Specifically, PNA constantly picks up the

Table 2. Average values across the selected hyperparameter configurations of $\bar{Pls}_{Degree}$ and $\bar{Pls}_{Motif}$, here indicated with Motif and Degree tags, respectively, while grouped by the number of MP iterations (1-5). As GESN features one layer, only a single value is reported. Higher values across MP types, iterations, and prediction policies are shown in **bold**.

		BA2grid					BA2Motif					GridHouse				
	Iterations	1	2	3	4	5	1	2	3	4	5	1	2	3	4	5
GIN	Motif	0.79	**0.95**	**0.99**	**1.00**	**0.99**	0.78	**0.83**	**0.92**	**0.95**	**0.96**	0.76	**0.90**	**0.98**	**0.99**	**0.99**
	Degree	**1.00**	0.84	0.83	0.77	0.75	**1.00**	0.74	0.80	0.69	0.61	**1.00**	0.83	0.85	0.80	0.79
GC	Motif	0.79	0.85	**0.98**	**1.00**	**1.00**	0.78	0.83	**0.92**	**0.95**	0.95	0.76	0.85	**0.96**	**0.99**	**0.99**
	Degree	**1.00**	**0.99**	0.87	0.78	0.76	**1.00**	**0.96**	0.81	0.70	0.67	**1.00**	**0.96**	0.87	0.82	0.80
PNA	Motif	0.79	0.83	0.84	0.84	0.84	0.77	0.78	0.77	0.78	0.77	0.76	0.76	0.75	0.75	0.75
	Degree	**1.00**	**1.00**	**1.00**	**1.00**	**1.00**	**1.00**	0.99	0.98	0.96	0.97	**1.00**	**1.00**	**1.00**	**1.00**	**1.00**
GESN	Motif	0.80					0.78					0.70				
	Degree	**1.00**					**1.00**					**0.99**				

degree explanatory pattern regardless of the number of MP layers; a behavior that we associate with the model's direct and easy access to the degree information via the scaler $S(\mathbf{D}, \alpha)$. Similarly, GESN, which is based on recursive MP, picks up the degree explanatory pattern, independently by the explored hyperparameter configuration space. In the latter case, this behavior is in agreement with the nature of recursive MP, since GESN matrices initialization imposes a contractive/Markovian dynamics on the model, which leads the model to favor localized information such as the degree. Overall, these results show that we can trace back to the inductive biases exploited by the DGNs by detecting which explanatory patterns they have picked up in relation to their architecture.

Figure 2 summarizes the analysis of the influence of training on the learned explanatory patterns. The figure displays how the plausibility of the two explanatory patterns picked up by a 2-layered GIN model varies as the 2-norm of the weights increases. Intuitively, smaller norms indicate that the learning dynamics are more similar to a 1-layered variant (i.e., one that is only capable of detecting low-order structures such as the degree) than larger norms. As can be seen, when the 2-norm is smaller, the degree explanatory pattern has the highest plausibility, while the setting slowly reverses and the motif explanatory pattern has higher plausibility as the norm increases. This plot shows that in certain MP configurations, the training dynamics (i.e., the local minima to which the training procedure has converged, which itself is related to the norm of the weights) play a role in determining which inductive bias is exploited by the DGN to generalize. Contrast this finding with Fig. 3, where a 1-layered GIN variant is depicted. In this case, the training dynamics are not influential, as the weights norm does not determine a shift of explanatory pattern. In general, we observe that when the inductive bias favors the degree explanatory pattern (i.e., 1-layered convolutional variants or recursive variants with strong Markovianity), the training procedure has little to no influence in determining the generalization dynamics.

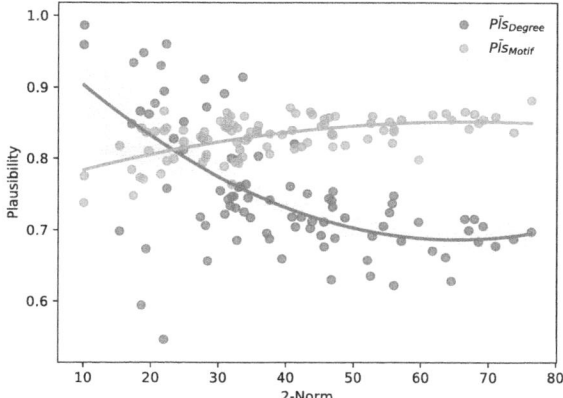

Fig. 2. Plausibility trends of the degree-based pattern and the motif-based pattern with respect to the 2-norm of the learned weights for a soft biased MP variant (2-layers GIN) on the BA2Motif dataset. A single model generates two points as its explanations are scored against both available policies.

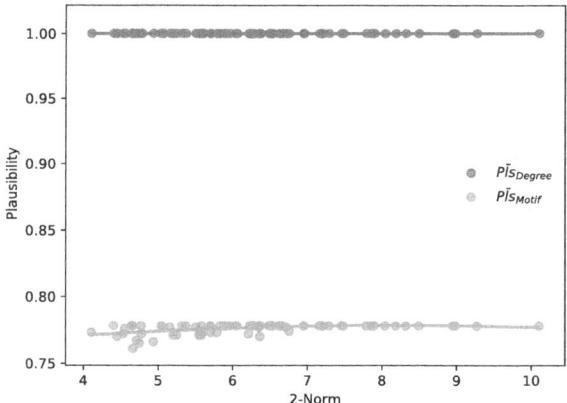

Fig. 3. Plausibility trends of the degree-based pattern and the motif-based pattern with respect to the 2-norm of the learned weights for a hard biased MP variant (1-layer GIN) on the BA2Motif dataset. A single model generates two points as its explanations are scored against both available policies.

6   Conclusions

In this work, we studied the inductive biases of DGNs under the lens of XAI. Starting from the fact that DGNs achieve generalization according to different mechanisms that are relatable to their inductive biases, we have shown that we can use tools from the XAI literature to unveil these mechanisms, drawing a connection between the downstream explanatory pattern (which itself relates to how the graph prediction is formed) and the upstream inductive bias of the MP implementation.

Our experiments highlighted that even in controlled environments like synthetic benchmarks, we can (i) witness the emergence of different explanatory patterns and (ii) gain insights into the inductive bias of diverse MP variants by identifying which pattern has been learned by each variant. Our analysis revealed several differences across the studied MP variants. First, there are convolutional variants that align to different explanatory patterns depending on the number of MP layers (specifically, GC and GIN). Second, for certain intermediate MP configurations (e.g., GIN with 2 layers), the 2-norm of the convolutional weights (which depends on the training procedure) impacts the generalization dynamics more than the MP specifics. Lastly, PNA (convolutional) and GESN (recursive) consistently align to the degree explanatory pattern, indicating that PNA's particular MP formulation and GESN's contractive dynamics characterize their inductive bias.

We believe our results are relevant since they present novel insights concerning the relationships between different DGNs, their MP implementation, and the inductive bias they embody. The undisclosed rich diversity of inductive biases grants Machine Learning practitioners multiple opportunities to solve their tasks and reach generalization capabilities by leveraging possibly diverse patterns. As a consequence of the inductive biases' effects on explanatory patterns, we encourage Machine Learning practitioners to test multiple message-passing variants to solve a given problem and use XAI techniques to check which explanatory patterns grant good generalization and to which inductive biases they can be related.

In subsequent works, our intention is to perform this analysis on a larger scale, considering different (possibly real-world) datasets, further architectures, and other XAI methods.

Acknowledgments. Research partly funded by PNRR - M4C2 - Investimento 1.3, Partenariato Esteso PE00000013 -"FAIR - Future Artificial Intelligence Research" - Spoke 1 "Human-centered AI", funded by the European Commission under the NextGeneration EU programme.

Disclosure of Interests. The authors have no competing interests to declare that are relevant to the content of this article.

References

1. Arrieta, A.B., et al.: Explainable artificial intelligence (xai): Concepts, taxonomies, opportunities and challenges toward responsible AI. Inform. Fusion **58** (2020)
2. Bacciu, D., Errica, F., Micheli, A., Podda, M.: A gentle introduction to deep learning for graphs. Neural Netw. **129** (2020). https://doi.org/10.1016/j.neunet.2020.06.006
3. Bondy, J.A., Murty, U.S.R.: Graph Theory with Applications. Elsevier, New York (1976)

4. Corso, G., Cavalleri, L., Beaini, D., Liò, P., Veličković, P.: Principal neighbourhood aggregation for graph nets. Advances in Neural Information Processing Systems **33** (2020)
5. Gallicchio, C., Micheli, A.: Graph echo state networks. In: The 2010 International Joint Conference on Neural Networks (IJCNN) (2010). https://doi.org/10.1109/IJCNN.2010.5596796
6. Gilmer, J., Schoenholz, S.S., Riley, P.F., Vinyals, O., Dahl, G.E.: Neural message passing for quantum chemistry. In: Precup, D., Teh, Y.W. (eds.) Proceedings of the 34th International Conference on Machine Learning. Proceedings of Machine Learning Research, vol. 70. PMLR (2017)
7. Gunning, D., Aha, D.: DARPA's explainable artificial intelligence (XAI) program. AI magazine **40**(2) (2019)
8. Kakkad, J., Jannu, J., Sharma, K., Aggarwal, C., Medya, S.: A survey on explainability of graph neural networks. arXiv:2306.01958 (2023)
9. Longa, A., Azzolin, S., Santin, G., Cencetti, G., et al., P.L.: Explaining the explainers in graph neural networks: a comparative study. arXiv:2210.15304 (2022)
10. Luo, D., Cheng, W., Xu, D., Yu, W., et al., B.Z.: Parameterized explainer for graph neural network. In: Advances in Neural Information Processing Systems. vol. 33. Curran Associates, Inc. (2020)
11. Micheli, A.: Neural network for graphs: A contextual constructive approach. IEEE Trans. Neural Netw.**20**(3) (2009). https://doi.org/10.1109/TNN.2008.2010350
12. Micheli, A., Tortorella, D.: Addressing heterophily in node classification with graph echo state networks. Neurocomputing **550** (2023). https://doi.org/10.1016/j.neucom.2023.126506
13. Mitchell, T.M.: Machine Learning. McGraw-Hill, New York (1997)
14. Morris, C., Ritzert, M., Fey, M., Hamilton, W.L., et al., J.E.L.: Weisfeiler and leman go neural: Higher-order graph neural networks. Proc. AAAI Conf. Artif. Intell. **33**(01) (2019). https://doi.org/10.1609/aaai.v33i01.33014602
15. Oneto, L., Navarin, N., Biggio, B., Errica, F., et al., A.M.: Towards learning trustworthily, automatically, and with guarantees on graphs: An overview. Neurocomputing **493** (2022). https://doi.org/10.1016/j.neucom.2022.04.072
16. Pope, P.E., Kolouri, S., Rostami, M., Martin, C.E., Hoffmann, H.: Explainability methods for graph convolutional neural networks. In: IEEE/CVF Conference on Computer Vision and Pattern Recognition (CVPR) (2019). https://doi.org/10.1109/CVPR.2019.01103
17. Scarselli, F., Gori, M., Tsoi, A.C., Hagenbuchner, M., Monfardini, G.: The graph neural network model. IEEE Trans. Neural Netw. **20**(1) (2009). https://doi.org/10.1109/TNN.2008.2005605
18. Wu, Z., Pan, S., Chen, F., Long, G., et al., C.Z.: A comprehensive survey on graph neural networks. IEEE Trans. Neural Netw. Learn. Syst. **32**(1) (2021). https://doi.org/10.1109/TNNLS.2020.2978386
19. Xu, K., Hu, W., Leskovec, J., Jegelka, S.: How powerful are graph neural networks? arXiv preprint arXiv:1810.00826 (2018)
20. Yuan, H., Yu, H., Gui, S., Ji, S.: Explainability in graph neural networks: a taxonomic survey. IEEE Trans. Pattern Anal. Mach. Intell. **45**(05) (2023). https://doi.org/10.1109/TPAMI.2022.3204236d
21. Zhou, B., Khosla, A., Lapedriza, A., Oliva, A., Torralba, A.: Learning deep features for discriminative localization. In: Proceedings of the IEEE Conference on Computer Vision and Pattern Recognition, pp. 2921–2929 (2016)

Integrating Temporal Planning and Knowledge Representation to Generate Personalized Touristic Itineraries

Silvia Gola[1(✉)], Donatella Capaldi[2], Alessandra Chivirì[3], Mohamed Ali Jaziri[3], Laura Leopardi[2], Saverio Giulio Malatesta[2], Irene Muci[3], Andrea Orlandini[1], Alessandro Umbrico[1], and Alberto Bucciero[3]

[1] CNR - Institute of Cognitive Sciences and Technologies, Rome, Italy
silvia.gola@istc.cnr
[2] Sapienza University - DIGILAB, Rome, Italy
[3] CNR - Institute of Heritage Science, Rome, Italy

Abstract. The *HERitage sMart social mEdia aSsistant* project offers innovative services enabling contextualized and multi-perspective, cross-cultural explorations of the rich and various cultural heritage of a territory. The project proposes the integration of Artificial Intelligence technologies to contextualize and personalize cultural paths according to users' interests and implicit/explicit relationships among tangible and intangible cultural entities. This work describes the designed AI-based architecture, the integration of Ontology-based Knowledge Representation and Reasoning, and Automated Planning to achieve the needed levels of contextualization and customization.

Keywords: Cultural Heritage · Knowledge Representation and Reasoning · Automated Planning · Customization

1 Introduction

The tourism industry is undergoing a profound transformation driven by the diffusion of smart technologies. Smart applications have emerged as powerful tools capable of enhancing the travel experience by offering personalized and dynamic touristic itineraries. This evolution is particularly significant in cultural heritage, where the richness and diversity of historical, artistic, and cultural assets offer many opportunities for tailored visitor experiences [8,13,16]. The diffusion of apps on smartphones offers enriched narrative experiences, allowing visitors to engage with cultural heritage in innovative ways. Through interactive content, users can gain deeper insights into historical contexts and cultural stories, fostering a more meaningful connection with the explored locations.

This paper presents the main features of a smart application developed as part of a research initiative promoted by Regione Lazio. The *HERitage sMart*

A. Artale et al. (Eds.): AIxIA 2024, LNAI 15450, pp. 188–199, 2025.
https://doi.org/10.1007/978-3-031-80607-0_15

social mEdia aSsistant (HerMeS) project, a joint effort of the National Research Council of Italy and La Sapienza University, aims to offer tools and innovative services to promote Lazio's Cultural Heritage through advanced AI and ICT methodologies and technologies. HerMeS' mission is, therefore, to enhance the fruition of cultural heritage through AI-generated touristic itineraries, tailored to users' needs and interests. The main outcome is an AI-enhanced smartphone application allowing different actors (i.e., tourists, citizens, economic operators, and public administration) to share experiences, feedback, and services.

The HerMeS app combines the socialization of the cultural experience with the development of AI technologies. This AI system takes into account users' interests (for instance, Nature, Archaeology, Eno-gastronomy, etc.) and needs (for example, visiting time, area of interest, special needs, etc.) to create a personalized tourist itinerary that maximizes the visitor's experience. Such a technology also offers useful information for defining targeted intervention strategies to the Public Administration and economic operators, which can lead to the development of solutions for territorial growth.

The touristic itinerary generation problem was examined from different perspectives and investigated through diverse AI techniques [3]. The most common solutions pursue a search and route generation approach (e.g., [14]) or recommendation techniques (e.g., [9,17]) or machine learning (e.g., [4]) to maximize users' satisfaction of visiting a given destination. User preferences are usually considered limited to preferred points of interest and whole journey duration ([10]) or selecting a list of locations based on several criteria such as mandatory visits, tour duration, and endpoints of the tour. Similar to our approach, several works leverage AI-based solutions like, e.g., [1] to adapt touristic itineraries to users' preferences. Works generally formulate users' preferences and features of points of interest as mathematical problems solved through optimization algorithms capable of considering multiple (possibly conflicting) constraints and objectives (e.g., [11]). However, our work seems to pursue an original approach by leveraging an ontology-based knowledge base and contextual temporal planning to support thematic reasoning and personalized generation of cultural paths (i.e., users' itineraries). Furthermore, HerMeS adopted an interdisciplinary approach leveraging the partners' experience in pushing the innovation of knowledge, conservation, and fruition of Cultural Heritage.

The long-term objective of our work is to pave the way toward innovative applications that can transform cultural tourism, promote sustainable practices, and enrich individual experiences. In this regard, our research aims to contribute to the ongoing integration of technology and cultural heritage, highlighting the benefits and challenges of adopting smart solutions.

2   A Recommendation System for Cultural Itineraries

HerMeS provides a range of AI-based functionalities to enhance the enjoyment and exploration of Cultural Heritage, assisting stakeholders, especially tourists, in connecting their heterogeneous needs and interests. This is done through

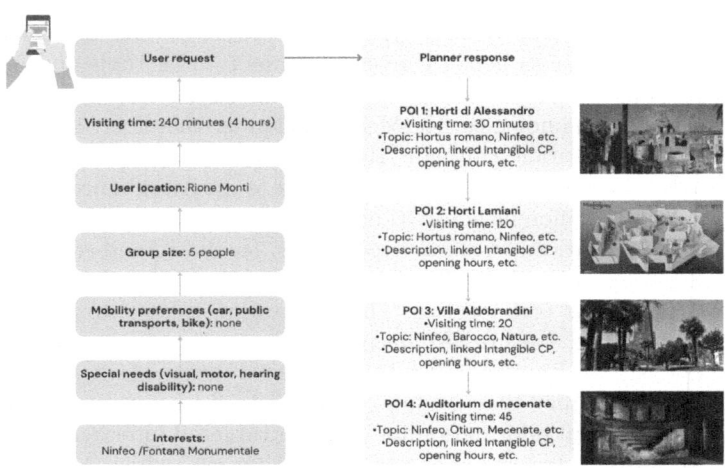

Fig. 1. Sample of HerMeS app flow

a bottom-up participatory model and advanced IT technologies, including AI algorithms, that analyze several variables (e.g., user preferences, historical data, and current trends) to generate personalized itineraries enriched with valuable touristic information. The app recommends touristic itineraries, tailored to users' interests, that combine cultural sites (tangible cultural objects) with ephemeral experiences (intangible cultural objects) to promote off-road, unconventional, and hidden aspects of Lazio's cultural heritage.

To this end, an ICT infrastructure has been defined [5] to develop an app and a central database that serves the client apps installed on smartphones and provides access to its intelligent functionalities. The central database collects knowledge from different and highly heterogeneous sources, while a recommendation system selects a set of *cultural items* and proposes personalized itineraries based on user preferences. To support the recommendation system, a Knowledge Base (KB), based on ArCO [6], was designed to characterize a wide set of information concerning cultural heritage, such as geographical location, mobility information, type of cultural object (tangible vs. intangible), cultural object thematic descriptions, cultural object data properties (visiting time, inclusive accessibility, visiting hours, visiting price, etc.), relationships between cultural objects (a semantic relationship describing a close correlation between cultural objects), and correlations with cultural topics.

2.1   Extending the ArCO Ontology

HerMeS relies on the ArCO ontology framework, a network of 13 ontologies describing the domain of cultural heritage[1] [6, 7]. The key advantage of the ArCO

---

[1] http://wit.istc.cnr.it/arco.

ontology is its modularity, which supports flexible integration and usage within HerMeS. ArCO defines general concepts and properties that are suitable for interpreting pieces of knowledge and integrating existing thesauri e.g., PICO 4.1[2] However, while ArCO focuses on the representation of Cultural Objects, with a traditionally descriptive approach, what we wanted to achieve with HerMeS was the representation of Cultural Places - territorial structures with cultural significance, characterized by a stratification of tangible and intangible cultural objects. For this reason, HerMeS extends ArCO concepts to support a structured (and layered) description of a territory identifying parts (areas) that are relevant from a heritage perspective.

Among the main extensions to ArCO are: the introduction of new classes (Territorial Unit, Topographic Context, Monumental Unit, Monumental Complex, Cultural Property Description, etc.); the refinement of existing classes (Cultural Property Residual, Intangible Cultural Property, Topic); the introduction of new data properties (Visiting Time, Inclusive Accessibility, etc.), and; the integration of the PROV-O ontology[3] [15] to track the POI's provenance. The resulting formalism supports compositional descriptions of tangible and intangible cultural objects and contextual correlations with topics. The introduced taxonomy of topics supports a thematic indexing of cultural objects. We can thus easily retrieve cultural entities from general topics to more specific ones during the reasoning phase. Such a structure is crucial to flexibly personalize touristic itineraries according to users' interests, specified in terms of preferred topics (e.g., Fig. 2).

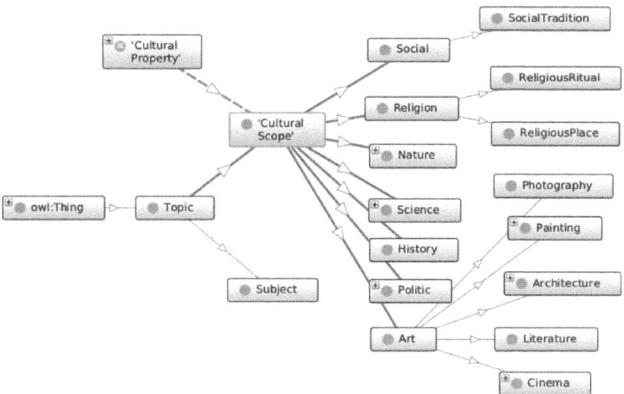

Fig. 2. Excerpt of the HerMeS taxonomy of topics.

HerMeS combines the semantic representation of cultural entities with automated planning to tailor user-specific itineraries. It requires synergetic reasoning on thematic cultural objects and related technical data of the visit like visit

[2] https://www.vocabularyserver.com/pico/it/index.php.
[3] https://www.w3.org/TR/prov-o.

duration, previous visits, expected number of visitors, and potential congestion. The implemented decision-making process addresses a numeric planning problem aiming to optimize user experience by balancing the number of cultural entities visited with the temporal constraints of the visit.

2.2 Dataset Collection for HerMeS

A key element of the HerMeS project is to generate touristic itineraries that contain tangible cultural heritage (physical cultural places) and intangibles (festivities, traditions, proverbs, legends, etc.). With the collaboration of DigiLab Sapienza and ISPC teams, we managed to create a dataset of the tangible and intangible cultural heritage of two districts in the historical center of Rome (the Rioni Monti and Esquilino), which we used to populate our ontological framework. We obtained a knowledge graph of 100 cultural places: 76 tangibles (including 35 from Rione Esquilino and 41 from Rione Monti) and 24 intangibles. Figure 3 aggregates the modeled POIs by considering their geographic distribution over the territory. The intensity level characterizes the expected visit duration of the POIs (aggregated by geographic areas).

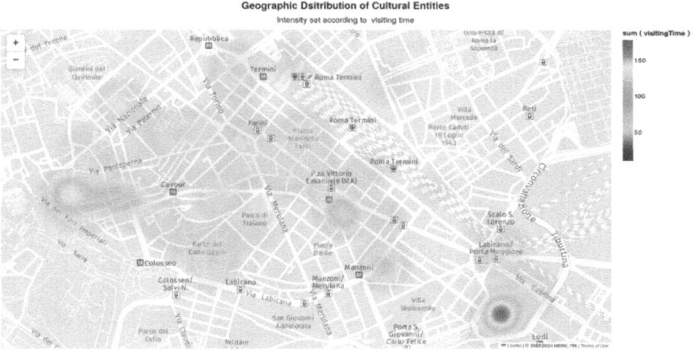

Fig. 3. Distribution of POIs considered for the Rione Monti and Esquilino in Rome.

3   AI-Based Cultural Heritage Exploration

The implemented HerMeS services are the result of a pipeline of AI-based modules that retrieve and contextualize cultural heritage knowledge according to the requests and related preferences specified by the users. Figure 4 shows the functional flow implementing the personalization of users' itineraries. First, the user sends a trip request using the HerMeS app. A request encapsulates the user's interests (i.e., a list of preferred topics), and visit preferences (i.e., geographic area, duration of the visit, accessibility, and mobility requirements).

Each request is intercepted by HerMeS REST API and forwarded to the back end AI-based reasoning components. The semantic-based recommendation component retrieves information about the cultural objects that match the specified interests and preferences. It relies on HerMeS ontology to extract a contextualized view of cultural entities given by the thematic correlations with intangibles and compositional relationships with other tangibles.

The extracted set of tangibles is used to build and refine a travel dataset containing information about the expected travel distance between any pair of tangibles according to different mobility preferences (e.g., bus, metro, foot). Such a dataset is incrementally populated and refined by integrating third-party APIs (e.g., Distance Matrix API from Google) that provide reliable and updated mobility data. The travel-time dataset and the outcome of the semantic-based recommender system are input to the component that automatically generates the planning problem specification. The temporal planning component then synthesizes a *cultural path* by explicitly reasoning about temporal requirements (i.e., the total time available for the visit and the visiting time of each tangible) and the travel time of alternative sequences of visited tangibles. The resulting optimized (and personalized) cultural path is sent back to the user issuing the (synchronous) trip request as the response. The HerMeS app then interacts with the user by showing the planned tangibles and contextual associated information (i.e., correlated tangibles and intangibles).

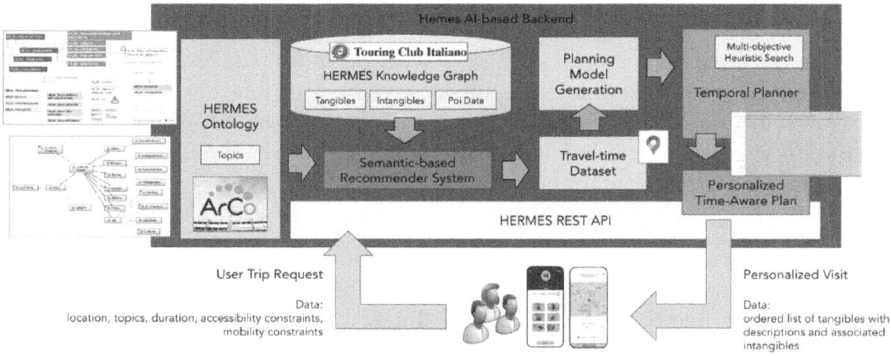

Fig. 4. The structure of the AI-based pipeline implemented by HerMeS back-end.

4   Personalizing Explorations Through Planning

Integrated decision-making skills allow HerMeS to reason about temporal requirements and users' interests and synthesize consistent cultural paths. The developed temporal planner evaluates alternative sequences of cultural entities by considering the expected duration of the entire visit, the expected visit time of each cultural entity, and the expected travel time between pairs of entities. The optimal sequence is selected, encapsulated into a list of aggregated POIs, and returned to the user. This section introduces the temporal planning formalism used and then delves into the details of the algorithm developed to handle the *Visit Planning Problem*.

4.1   Reasoning on Time and Causality

The planning module of HerMeS relies on the timeline-based planning formalism introduced in [12]. Briefly, a timeline-based specification describes valid behaviors of domain features to be controlled over time. Given a description (i.e., a model), a timeline-based planning process synthesizes a set of flexible behaviors, i.e., timelines. The timelines describe how the modeled domain features should evolve to correctly realize the desired behaviors (i.e., the flexible sequences of states and actions each domain feature should respectively assume or perform).

More formally, a state variable is a tuple $SV = \langle V, T, D \rangle$ describing the set of valid behaviors of a domain feature:

- V is a set of values $v_i \in V$ representing states or actions the feature can assume or perform over time;
- $T : V \to 2^V$ is a state transition function describing possible successors on a timeline and thus valid transitions for each value $v \in V$;
- $D : V \to \mathbf{T} \times \mathbf{T}$ is a duration function specifying expected duration bounds, expressed in some temporal domain $\mathbf{T}$ (typically $\mathbf{N}^+$), for each value $v_i \in V$.

Temporal flexibility is crucial to deal with temporal uncertainty and robust execution of plans. A flexible timeline for a state variable sv_i is a sequence of (flexible) temporal intervals called tokens. Together these tokens describe an envelope of valid temporal behaviors of a domain feature. If $SV_i = \langle V, T, D \rangle$ is a state variable, a token x_j for the variable has the form $x_j = \langle v_k, [e_j, e'_j], [d_j, d'_j] \rangle$ where $v_k \in V$ is the value assumed by the token x_j, $[e_j, e'_j]$ is the end-time interval of x_j (with $e < e'$) and $[d_j, d'_j]$ is the minimum and maximum duration of x_j. The planned duration of a token should be consistent with the duration bounds of the associated value v_k. A timeline is a continuous sequence of tokens describing the behavior of a domain feature from a temporal origin to (at least) a desired planning horizon H. The start-time interval of a token is not explicitly represented since it coincides with the end-time interval of the previous token in the timeline i.e., the first token of a timeline starts the temporal origin $[0, 0]$. A timeline FTL_i for a state variable $SV_i = \langle V, T, D \rangle$ is a continuous and finite sequence of tokens of the form

$$x_1 = \left(v_1, [e_1, e_1^i], [d_1, d_1'] \right), \ ..., \ x_m = \left(v_m, [e_m, e_m^i], [d_m, d_m'] \right)$$

where $v_1, .., v_m \in V$ and for all J=1, ..., m-1, $v_{j+1} \in T(v_j)$. Denoting with start (x_j) the computed start time interval of a token x_j then, for all j = 1, ..., m-1, $[e_j, e'_j] = $ start (x_{j+1}).

State variables specify valid behaviors of domain features (i.e., local consistency). Complex behaviors however require the coordination of the behaviors of different state variables. Additional constraints are therefore necessary to coordinate simultaneous behaviors of state variables (i.e., enforce global consistency). *Synchronization rules* specify such constraints, necessary to synthesize valid plans (i.e., complex behaviors of state variable achieving desired goals). A synchronization rule has the form

$$a_0[SV_0 = v_0] \rightarrow a_1[SV_1 = v_1], ..., a_n[SV_n = v_n].\mathcal{C}$$

where every $a_i[SV_i = v_i]$ is a token variable denoting a temporal interval in which a state variable SV_i assumes the value v_i. The left-hand part of the synchronization rule $(a_0[SV_0 = v_0])$ is called the trigger. The set $\mathcal{C}$ specifies temporal relations between token variables. Synchronization rules with the same trigger are treated as disjunctions and represent alternative constraints that should hold between different sets of token variables.

The HerMeS planner has been developed as extension of the open-source framework PLATINUm [18,19]. It integrates a novel search heuristics and solving procedure to generate cultural paths recursively. The next sections delve into the details of the modeled planning problem and the developed solving procedure.

4.2   Preference-Aware Visit Planning

The *Visit Planning Problem* consists of deciding the sequence of cultural entities that best fit users' interests and constraints among known tangible cultural properties. Planning choices are made among tangible cultural properties only. Correlated intangibles and tangibles are aggregated dynamically into the final POI structures sent back to the app.

Following the pipeline depicted in Fig. 4, the temporal planning component receives dynamically generated problem specification as input and synthesizes an optimal temporal plan representing a personalized visit. The problem consists of building a timeline describing the personalized visit for a user. Planning decisions concern the incremental definition of the cultural path of a user (i.e., the user's timeline). Each incremental step selects the next tangible to insert into the visit according to the visit time of the next tangible and the travel time from the previous tangible in the timeline. The total duration of the planned visit should not exceed the input duration specified by the user. To achieve this, the developed heuristic search minimizes the visit's *coverage*. Figure 5 shows a conceptual view of the planning choices made during the iterative synthesis of a user timeline.

Planning choices concern the decision of the next tangible to add to the user timeline (*where to go next?*). Such choices are modeled through synchronization rules modeling alternative ways of instantiating a *Visit* token on the user timeline. It is worth underscoring that the number of such synchronization rules dynamically varies depending on the number of tangibles inferred by the knowledge-reasoning components. Therefore each visit choice has a branching

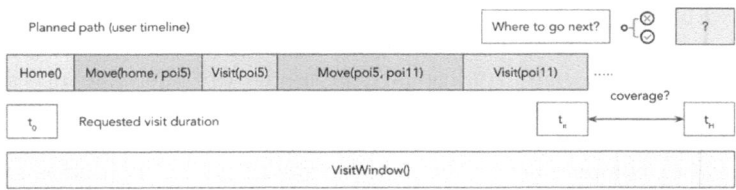

Fig. 5. Planning choices for deciding the cultural visit (i.e., user timeline).

factor equal to the number of tangibles that are considered relevant to user interests (i.e., user-selected topics). This modeling choice leads to a high branching factor of the search space. However, it is necessary to give the planner full flexibility in the synthesis of user cultural paths. A specifically designed heuristic supports these choices by evaluating alternative tangibles for visits (i.e., alternative tangibles that can be added to the timelines in the next iterations), and minimizing the differences between the requested time of the visit (i.e., the time horizon, t_H, of the planning problem) and the expected total time of the planned visit π. Interestingly, heuristic evaluation would consider alternative travel times between consecutive tangibles based on user preferences about mobility.

Algorithm 1 Domain independent iterative refinement of timelines.

1: **function** SOLVE($\mathcal{P}$, $\mathcal{S}$, $\mathcal{H}$)
2:     $\pi \leftarrow InitialPlan\,(\mathcal{P})$, $F_{pc} \leftarrow \emptyset$
3:     **while** $\neg IsSolution\,(\pi)$ **do**
4:         $\Phi^* = \{\phi_1^*, ..., \phi_m^*\} \leftarrow DetectFlaws\,(\pi, \mathcal{H})$
5:         **for** $\phi_i^* \in \Phi^*$ **do**   ▷ Compute flaw solutions
6:             $N_{\phi_i^*} = \{n_1, ..., n_t\} \leftarrow HandleFlaw\,(\phi_i^*, \pi)$
7:             **if** $N_{\phi_i^*} = \emptyset$ **then**   ▷ Unsolvable flaws
8:                 $Backtrack(\pi, Dequeue(F_{pc}))$
9:             **for** $n_j \in N_{\phi_i^*}$ **do**   ▷ Branching for each solution
10:                $F_{pc} \leftarrow Enqueue\,(n_j, \mathcal{S})$
11:        **if** $\neg IsEmpty\,(F_{pc})$ **then**   ▷ Iterative refinement
12:            $\pi \leftarrow Refine\,(\pi, Dequeue\,(F_{pc}))$
13:        **else**
14:            **return** $Failure$ ▷ No plan to explore and no solution found
15:    **return** π

More specifically, the solving procedure of a timeline-based planner iteratively refines a set of partially instantiated timelines. A dedicated data structure (the fringe) collects all the alternative partial plans that constitute the search space. At each iteration, the planner extracts the most promising partial plan from the fringe and analyzes the consistency of the timelines and the *goal conditions*. If the planner finds some flaws (i.e., conditions affecting the completeness and consistency of the timelines) the current plan is not a solution, and some operations should be made to solve the flaws and refine the plan. Each possible refinement (i.e., solution to a flaw) determines an alternative partial plan that is collected into the fringe. Algorithm 1 summarizes this general procedure implemented by PLATINUm [18,19].

Depending on the characteristics of the domains, the solving procedure could be extended through dedicated heuristics. Heuristics are generally necessary to make better choices while expanding the search space and refining timelines. Such choices affect the quality of plans and the solving efficiency by analyzing qualities of partial plans to explore (i.e., possible solutions collected in the fringe) and discriminating among detected flaws of a refined plan.

In the *Visit Planning Problem*, a challenge concerns a missing *goal condition* suitable to identify a solution plan. The intrinsic recursive nature of the planning choices sketched in Fig. 5 requires to "keep open" the possibility of adding a new step (i.e., tangible) to the visit. The planner cannot know how many tangibles a user can visit within the specified visit window. The total number depends on the duration of each visit and its schedule (i.e., the planned sequences of the tangibles) which determines different travel times. Therefore, the planning process should add tangibles to the visit incrementally until the partial plan meets a minimum quality condition (i.e., the *goal condition*). In this case, we set the *quality threshold* on coverage to 80% (i.e., at least 80% of the temporal window should be filled by the visit). Consequently, plans with no flaws but with the coverage below a certain threshold are discarded allowing the search to continue towards better solutions. Furthermore, we developed a new heuristic comparing partial plans based on their coverage. To synthesize reliable visits we encapsulated an evaluation criterion to polarize choices toward plans with less tangibles. Namely, we polarized planning choices towards plans that covered the visiting window with fewer steps.

Figure 6 depicts statistical data obtained within a solving instance. The *Fringe Size* clearly shows the recursive nature of the planning problem. The number of partial plans populating the fringe increases constantly which contrasts the typical behavior of seeing the fringe decreasing when planning choices move

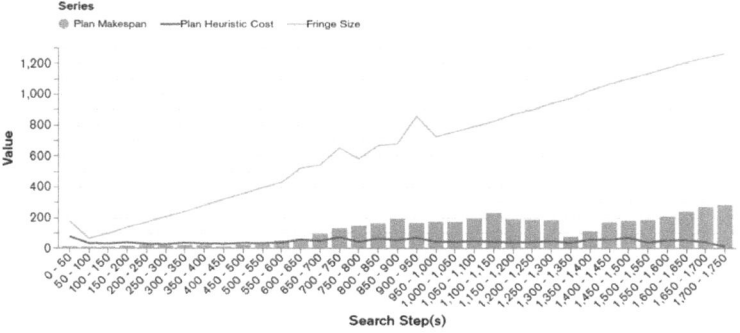

Fig. 6. Planning choices within the synthesis of a visit timeline.

close to a solution. Despite this challenge, the planner addressed trip requests from users effectively and efficiently. A total number of 258 requests were issued during testing. The average response time of the planner was in the order of minutes (20 s at the lowest, 196 s at the highest) which was considered feasible for the application.

5   Conclusions

The HerMeS project allowed us to demonstrate the potential of a system that combines knowledge reasoning and planning in the context of cultural heritage. The knowledge graph enables us to represent complex data in a structured manner. Each point of interest (POI) is tagged with a series of properties and connected to other POIs in a network of semantic relations, allowing for inferential reasoning. However, the digitization and tagging of cultural heritage datasets with tourism-related metadata remain open issues. In this initial phase of HerMeS, which represents a proof of concept, we opted for manual data collection to showcase the potential of this tool with high-quality data. However, this approach is not scalable if we decide to expand the geographical area of reference. Automating data collection and tagging is, therefore, a future research direction.

This proof of concept shows that the HerMeS system is highly flexible and can be integrated with other frameworks. HerMeS's planning algorithm has shown effective decisions concerning cultural paths. A central aspect was the effective reasoning on the time necessary for visiting tangibles and the expected traveling times between consecutive visits. The designed heuristic concretely evaluates alternative paths selecting the ones that achieve high quality. In this regard, planning technology supports flexible reasoning that can easily be tailored to different scenarios by integrating and evaluating different quality metrics of plans. Namely, the decision-making component could be extended to adapt planning choices to environmental contexts, and online knowledge about simultaneous visits planned on the territory. This latter aspect, combined with the capability of gathering real-time data from the environment (e.g., traffic, visiting queues, etc.) would strongly improve the *awareness* of planning choices.

Closing the loop between the planning process and the world state as in classical deliberative architectures [2] would strongly enhance the adaptability of planned paths and the experience of single users by better distributing the "cultural traffic". Future works would also focus on incorporating real-time data from other users' planned visits in the same area to better shape visits. The app is currently in its early stage of development. Usability tests to evaluate the effectiveness of the user interface will be conducted next.

Acknowledgments. The authors were partially supported by Regione Lazio and Lazio Innova within the HerMeS project (POR FESR LAZIO 2014-2020 Cod. A0375E0110).

References

1. Abbasi-Moud, Z., Vahdat-Nejad, H., Sadri, J.: Tourism recommendation system based on semantic clustering and sentiment analysis. Expert Syst. Appl. **167** (2021)
2. Alami, R., Chatila, R., Fleury, S., Ghallab, M., Ingrand, F.: An architecture for autonomy. International Journal of Robotics Research, Special Issue on Integrated Architectures for Robot Control and Programming **17**(4), 315–337 (1998)
3. Aliano Filho, A., Morabito, R.: An effective approach for bi-objective multi-period touristic itinerary planning. Expert Syst. Appl. **240** (2024)
4. Beraldi, P., De Maio, A., Olivito, F., Potrino, G., Straface, I., Violi, A.: A decision support system for trip tourism recommendation. Int. J. Transp. Develcp. Integr. **5** (2021)
5. Bucciero, A., et al.: Hermes: Heritage smart social media assistant. In: Extended Reality. Springer Nature Switzerland (2023)
6. Carriero, V.A., et al.: Arco: The Italian cultural heritage knowledge graph. In: Ghidini, C., et al. (eds.) The Semantic Web - ISWC 2019, pp. 36–52. Springer International Publishing, Cham (2019)
7. Carriero, V.A., Gangemi, A., Mancinelli, M.L., Nuzzolese, A.G., Presutti, V., Veninata, C.: Pattern-based design applied to cultural heritage knowledge graphs. Semantic Web **12**(313–357), 2 (2021)
8. Ceccarelli, S., et al.: Evaluating visitors' experience in museum: comparing artificial intelligence and multi-partitioned analysis. Digital Appl. Archaeol. Cult. Eerit. **33**, e00340 (2024)
9. Cesta, A., et al.: Personalizing technology-enhanced learning for cultural visits. In: Adjunct Publication of the 28th ACM Conference on User Modeling, Adaptation and Personalization. UMAP '20 Adjunct, Association for Computing Machinery (2020)
10. Chia-Ling, H., Wei-Lin, C., Chia-Ho, O.: Constructing a personalized travel itinerary recommender system with the internet of things. Wireless Networks (2023)
11. Choi, K.C., et al.: Genetic algorithm for tourism route planning considering time constrains. Int. J. Eng. Trends Technol. **70**(3) (2022)
12. Cialdea Mayer, M., Orlandini, A., Umbrico, A.: Planning and execution with flexible timelines: a formal account. Acta Informatica **53**(6–8), 649–680 (2016)
13. Daga, E., et al.: Integrating citizen experiences in cultural heritage archives: Requirements, state of the art, and challenges. J. Comput. Cult. Herit. **15**(1) (2022)
14. Expósito, A., Mancini, S., Brito, J., Moreno, J.A.: A fuzzy grasp for the tourist trip design with clustered pois. Expert Syst. Appl. **127** (2019)
15. Lebo, T., et al.: Prov-o: The prov ontology. W3C Recomm. **30** (2013)
16. Silvestri, S., Tricomi, G., Bassolillo, S.R., De Benedictis, R., Ciampi, M.: An urban intelligence architecture for heterogeneous data and application integration, deployment and orchestration. Sensors **24**(7) (2024)
17. Tenemaza, M., Luján-Mora, S., De Antonio, A., Ramírez, J.: Improving itinerary recommendations for tourists through metaheuristic algorithms: An optimization proposal. IEEE Access **8** (2020)
18. Umbrico, A., Cesta, A., Cialdea Mayer, M., Orlandini, A.: Integrating resource management and timeline-based planning. In: The 28th International Conference on Automated Planning and Scheduling (ICAPS) (2018)
19. Umbrico, A., Cesta, A., Cialdea Mayer, M., Orlandini, A.: Platinum: A new framework for planning and acting. In: AI*IA 2017 Advances in Artificial Intelligence, pp. 498–512 (2017)

ASR Systems Under Acoustic Challenges: A Multilingual Study

Sergei Katkov$^{(\boxtimes)}$ ⓘ, Antonio Liotta ⓘ, and Alessandro Vietti ⓘ

Free University of Bozen-Bolzano, Bolzano 39100, Italy
sergei.katkov@student.unibz.it

Abstract. The performance of automatic speech recognition (ASR) systems in acoustically challenging environments is crucial for the effectiveness of various voice-controlled applications. This study presents an extensive experimental evaluation of the robustness of different ASR models against a range of acoustic disturbances, including white noise, reverberation, time stretch, and pitch shift. By comparing the performance of these models in English, Italian, and German, this research provides a cross-linguistic perspective. The findings reveal a significant decline in performance across all models when subjected to these audio distortions, highlighting the varying degrees of resilience across different languages. By incorporating multiple languages, this study offers valuable insights into the unique challenges and potential opportunities for enhancing ASR technologies, addressing both well-researched and less-explored linguistic domains. Our comparative study highlights that although ASRs are reaching near-human accuracy in ideal acoustic conditions, ASR performance under the whole range of distortions is still well below human performance

Keyword: Automatic Speech Recognition

1 Introduction

Recent advancements in automatic speech recognition (ASR) have introduced models like Whisper [28], Conformer [13], and QuartzNet [19]. These developments have significantly enhanced ASR efficiency and speed, which is essential for a wide range of applications.

However, the accuracy of ASR models, especially under acoustically challenging conditions, remains crucial. Prior studies [5,14,21] have highlighted the importance of improving ASR systems' resilience to noise and other acoustic distortions. Improving ASR robustness to noise is a direct approach to enhancing performance, particularly under conditions with significant noise.

This research evaluates the robustness of ASR models, including the Whisper family, QuartzNet, Conformer, and Fast Conformer, under various audio transformations - such as white noise, reverberation, time stretching, and pitch

© The Author(s), under exclusive license to Springer Nature Switzerland AG 2025
A. Artale et al. (Eds.): AIxIA 2024, LNAI 15450, pp. 200–213, 2025.
https://doi.org/10.1007/978-3-031-80607-0_16

shifting - chosen to replicate common auditory challenges encountered in real-life and online communication scenarios. These transformations are selected to mimic common auditory challenges encountered in real life and online communication.

Our study seeks to contribute to the ASR field by systematically investigating various ASR models under diverse acoustic conditions and across multiple languages. The findings are intended to inform future developments in speech recognition technology, optimizing its application in varied real-world scenarios and expanding its utility across different linguistic domains.

2   Related Work

Advances in automatic speech recognition (ASR) technology, especially with models like Whisper [28], Conformer [13], and QuartzNet [19], have been significant.

The native multilingual capabilities of models like Whisper [28], compared to fine-tuning methods [16], represent different strategies for adapting ASR technologies across languages and conditions, enhancing their generalizability and utility.

While the Whisper model shows resilience in basic noise environments [22, 28], its performance under extensive acoustic variations remains less explored. Conformer's integration into denoising pipelines [7, 20] showcases improvements in recognition amidst noise. Developing noisy datasets [6] and noise augmentation techniques [1] has been essential, though their applicability to Whisper and QuartzNet requires more exploration.

In [18], it is shown that ASR models degrade significantly at high noise levels in Italian, even when human listeners can transcribe accurately. In [17], Whisper models struggle with audio transformations and chunk length variations, particularly for German. However, the study lacks a multilingual comparison, highlighting the need for broader cross-linguistic analysis.

Research on noise removal [21, 32] and speech dereverberation [30, 31] offers solutions to mitigate auditory distortions, which are common challenges in ASR applications. These studies lay a foundation for enhancing ASR robustness to noise and reverberation.

QuartzNet, when fine-tuned with noise augmentations, shows improvements in handling noisy samples while maintaining performance on clean data [3], demonstrating the potential of targeted noise augmentation.

Pitch manipulation research aims to reduce performance gaps between male and female voices [9], a critical area for ensuring ASR systems handle cross-speaker variation effectively.

In summary, ASR has progressed significantly with models like Whisper, Conformer, and QuartzNet, but further exploration is needed in noise handling, unconventional transformations, and multilingual support. These areas offer promising paths for enhancing ASR robustness and versatility.

Our research evaluates the robustness of Whisper, QuartzNet, Conformer, and Fast Conformer models under diverse acoustic disturbances in English, Italian, and German languages.

3   Methodology

This study assesses Whisper, QuartzNet, Conformer, and Fast Conformer ASR models' robustness to audio disturbances, focusing on English, Italian, and German languages. We conduct transformations to mimic challenges encountered in online communications and real-world environments, evaluating their performance and identifying areas for enhancement.

3.1   Models

The Whisper, QuartzNet, Conformer, and Fast Conformer models were selected for their architectural characteristics and their different approaches to handling multilingual data and noise.

Whisper Models. We utilized the Whisper base, medium, and large-v3 models [28], leveraging their multilingual capabilities by specifying the target language (English, German, or Italian) during inference. These models are designed to support multiple languages, allowing for optional language selection at inference.

QuartzNet 15x5. QuartzNet [19] 15x5, featuring a deep 79-layer architecture and 18.9 million parameters, was initially pretrained on English datasets such as LibriSpeech [24], Fisher Corpus [4], Switchboard-1 [10], WSJ-0, and WSJ-1 [25]. It was subsequently fine-tuned for various languages using the Common Voice [2] dataset.

Conformer CTC Large. The Conformer CTC Large model, which uses around 120 million parameters, employs the Connectionist Temporal Classification (CTC) loss function [12]. It was trained on datasets such as Common Voice [2], Multilingual LibriSpeech [27], and VoxPopuli [33], and utilizes a SentencePiece tokenizer [11].

Conformer-Transducer Large. This model utilizes the Recurrent Neural Network Transducer (RNNT) loss and decoder [34] for automatic speech recognition. It was trained on the same datasets as the Conformer CTC Large.

FastConformer Hybrid Transducer-CTC Large. The FastConformer [29] Hybrid Transducer-CTC model combines the strengths of both CTC and Transducer models. It was trained on the same speech data as the Conformer models. The architecture of this model is optimized with 8x depthwise-separable convolutional downsampling.

Table 1 provides a summary of the model architectures and parameter counts for each ASR model evaluated in this study.

Table 1. Model architectures and parameter counts

Model	Architecture	Parameters (millions)
Whisper Base	Transformer	74
Whisper Medium	Transformer	769
Whisper Large-v3	Transformer	1550
QuartzNet 15x5	CNN	18.9
Conformer-CTC Large	Conformer	120
Conformer-Transducer Large	Conformer	120
FastConformer Hybrid	Conformer	114

3.2 Dataset

To evaluate the efficiency of the ASR models in environments augmented with audio disturbances, we utilized the test subsets of the Common Voice 13.0 dataset [2] for English, Italian, and German. The dataset consists of approximately 13,000 utterances per language, providing a balanced representation of various accents and speech contexts encountered in real-world scenarios.

3.3 Evaluation Metrics

To assess the performance of speech recognition systems in our study, we employ the Word Error Rate (WER) metric. The WER is calculated as follows:

$$\text{WER} = \frac{S + D + I}{N}, \tag{1}$$

where S, D, and I denote the numbers of substitutions, deletions, and insertions needed to match the system's transcription to the reference text. N represents the total count of words in the reference text.

This measure serves as an indicator of transcription accuracy, with lower WER values reflecting better performance. Typically, a WER below 0.1 is considered excellent, 0.1–0.2 is acceptable but may indicate potential issues, and above 0.2 denotes significant transcription errors, making the ASR output difficult to understand.

For text normalization, punctuation and other non-alphanumeric symbols were removed, and all text was converted to lowercase.

3.4 Audio Transformations

To evaluate the performance of ASR models under realistic acoustic conditions, specific audio transformations were applied. These transformations were chosen to replicate common auditory challenges.

The white noise transformation adds uniform noise across various frequencies, simulating background noise found in crowded places, urban settings, and telecommunications or online communications due to signal interference or compression artifacts. Time stretch transformation changes the duration of an audio signal without altering its pitch, mimicking scenarios where speech speed varies, such as in spontaneous conversations. Pitch shift transformation changes the pitch of an audio signal, representing different speaker fundamental frequency, singing voices, and speech patterns of individuals with certain medical conditions, testing the model's adaptability to varying vocal pitches. Reverberation adds echo effects to simulate environments like large halls, reflective rooms, and phone calls, testing the model's ability to handle echoes.

The transformations are defined as follows, inspired by real-world auditory conditions to evaluate model robustness:

- **White Noise:** A uniform noise signal added across various frequencies to simulate background noise in urban settings or online communications, expressed as

$$n(t) = \alpha \cdot \text{rand}(t), \tag{2}$$

where α represents the amplitude.
- **Time Stretch:** Modifies the duration of an audio signal without altering its pitch, representing variations in speech speed in conversations, described by

$$y(t) = x(a \cdot t), \tag{3}$$

where a is the stretch factor.
- **Pitch Shift:** Alters the pitch using Fourier Transform techniques, reflecting different vocal pitches, given by

$$y(t) = F^{-1}\{F\{x(t)\} \cdot e^{j2\pi\Delta f t}\}, \tag{4}$$

with Δf indicating the frequency shift.
- **Reverberation:** Simulates echo effects as in large rooms or phone calls, represented as

$$y(t) = x(t) + \alpha \cdot x(t - \Delta t), \tag{5}$$

where α is the decay rate and Δt is the delay time.

4   Results

We analyzed Whisper, QuartzNet, and Conformer models under acoustic disturbances like white noise, time stretch, pitch shift and reverberation to explore their robustness in the English, Italian and German context.

The results in Table 2 show that the Whisper Large model and Conformer variants consistently outperform other models, while QuartzNet's lower accuracy reflects its simpler architecture. The Whisper Base model, despite being the smallest in the advanced Whisper series, has the highest WER, highlighting its limitations in achieving optimal accuracy as a compact transformer model. This result underscores the trade-off between model complexity and performance,

Table 2. WER for ASR Models in Noise-Free Scenario

Model/Language	English	Italian	German
Whisper Base	0.26	0.37	0.30
Whisper Medium	0.13	0.10	0.09
Whisper Large-v3	0.11	0.06	0.06
QuartzNet	0.22	0.17	0.14
Conformer-CTC Large	0.10	0.07	0.07
Conformer-Transducer Large	0.08	0.05	0.06
FastConformer-Hybrid CTC/Transducer	0.10	0.06	0.05

particularly in noise-free environments. Across different languages, this tendency persists. While the Whisper Base model excels in English, the more advanced Whisper Large-v3 model performs better in Italian and German. The superior performance of QuartzNet and Conformer models can be attributed to the use of the Common Voice dataset for tuning non-English languages, enabling these models to better adapt to the distribution in the test set.

4.1   English Language Experiments

We performed a set of experiments on all previously listed models for the English language.

The almost linear degradation in quality is evident for nearly all models, as shown in Fig. 1. The Whisper Base model appears to be the least robust, with

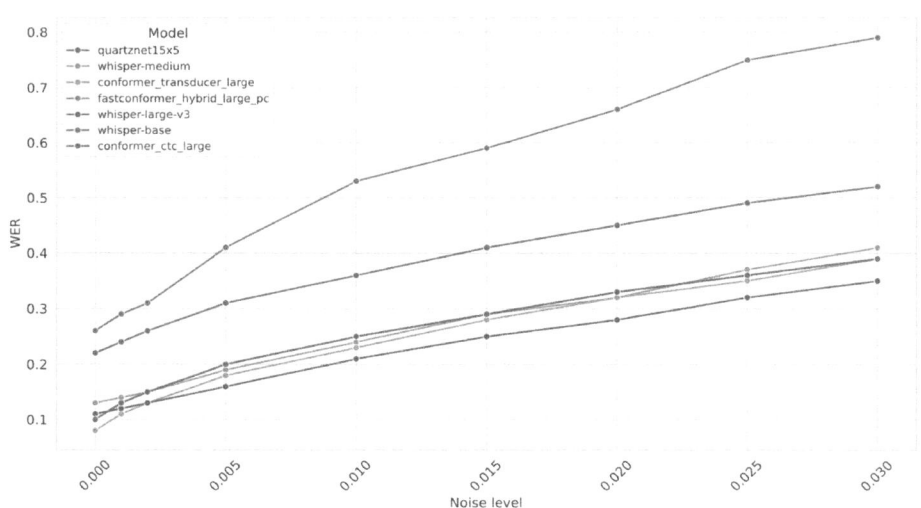

Fig. 1. WER comparison for different models under white noise for English language

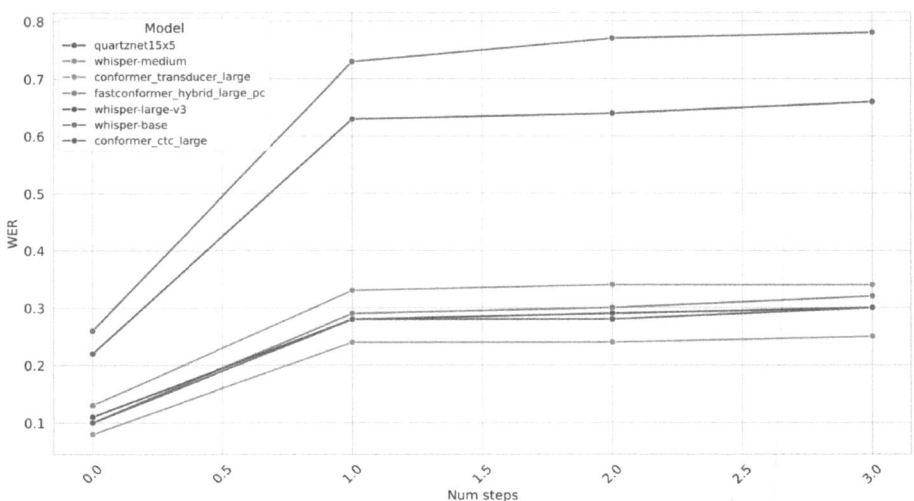

Fig. 2. WER comparison for different models under pitch shift for English language

its WER increasing more rapidly than that of other models. Among the other models, QuartzNet demonstrates poorer performance compared to the rest. At a noise level of 0.03, all models experience a marked reduction in quality, highlighting a clear deviation from the human ability to comprehend and interpret audio content in similar conditions [26].

Although pitch changes do not greatly affect human comprehension of audio, these modifications result in a noticeable and fairly consistent decline in ASR model performance across all tested levels. Of the models evaluated, the Conformer Transducer Large shows the greatest resilience to pitch alterations, as indicated in Fig. 2. It is important to note that the specific level of pitch variation has minimal impact on the model. It seems that merely shifting the signal out of the training set distribution is sufficient to significantly degrade performance.

At altered time stretch levels, there is a universal decline in performance across all models, as shown in Fig. 3. The x-axis value of 1.0 represents no transformation, with values to the left indicating slowed down audio and values to the right indicating sped up audio. However, the Whisper models, particularly the smaller variants, experience a more pronounced performance drop and are prone to generating repetitive phrases in their outputs. This phenomenon, known as "hallucination" is widely observed in sequence generation models and affects both ASR [8] and broader language generation [15], leading to significantly inflated WER. Notably, even at stretch rates of 0.9 or 1.1, where humans find the audio completely intelligible [23], there is still a noticeable decline in recognition accuracy for these models. Interestingly, the Conformer Transducer Large per-

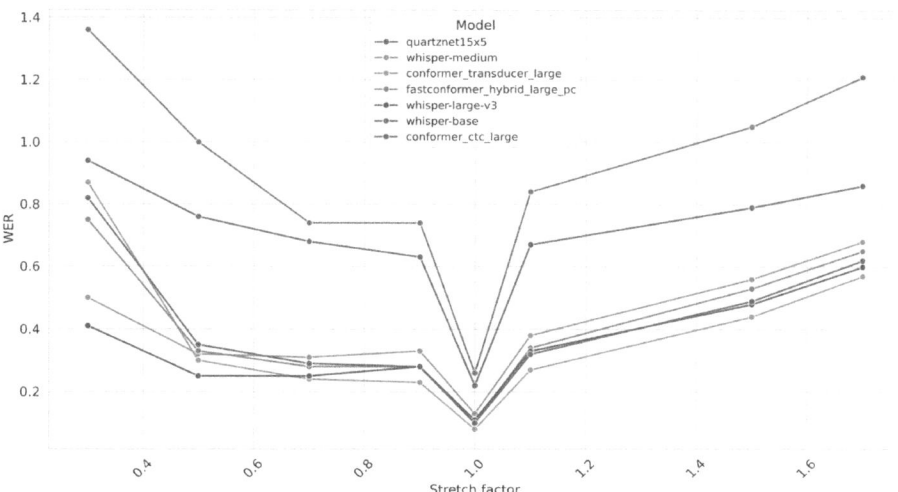

Fig. 3. WER comparison for different models under time stretch for English language

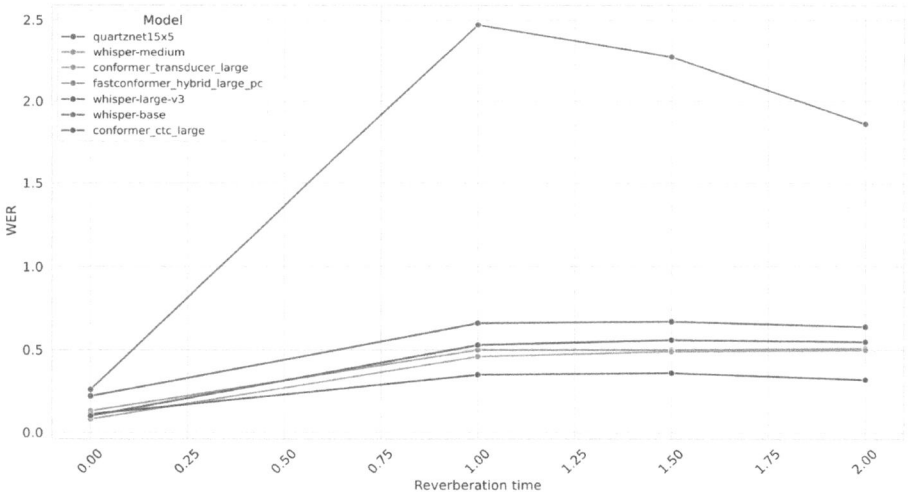

Fig. 4. WER comparison for different models under reverberation for English language

forms better with sped-up audio, while Whisper Large-v3 handles slowed-down audio more effectively.

Figure 4 illustrates the superior performance the Whisper Large-v3 model, in handling reverberated audio. In contrast, the Whisper Base model struggles significantly with these transformations. Notably, across all tested reverberation times, we observe a nearly uniform degradation in model performance, indicating

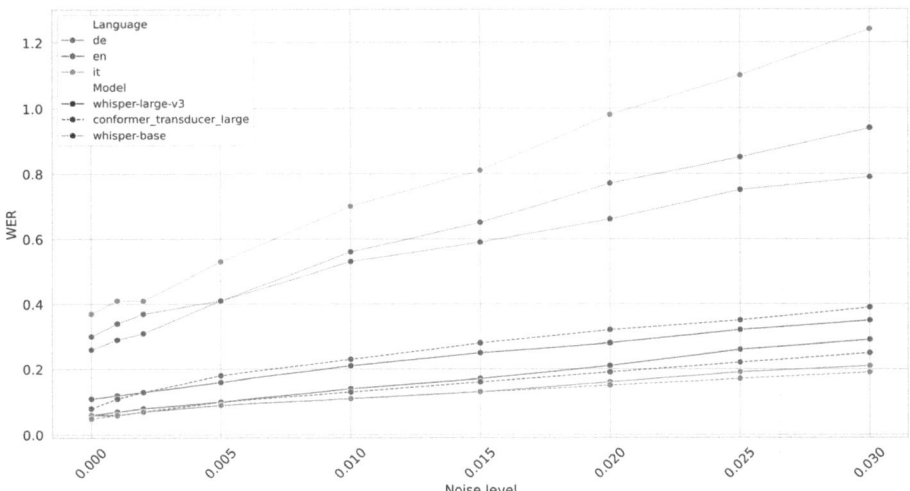

Fig. 5. WER comparison for different models and languages under white noise

that these ASR systems are sensitive to the presence of reverberation rather than its intensity.

4.2 Multilingual Experiments

Experiments were conducted for English, Italian, and German languages. To maintain concise and clear visual representations, we present the results only for the Whisper Large-v3, Whisper Base, and Conformer Transducer Large models. For each language, a distinct color is used, and for each model, a unique line style is applied. Specifically, the Whisper Large-v3 model is represented with a solid line, the Conformer Transducer Large with dashed lines, and the Whisper Base with dotted lines.

The Conformer model demonstrates superior robustness in Italian and German, while the Whisper Large-v3 model performs better in English. As shown in Fig. 5, both the models achieve commendable results, with their performance in Italian and German surpassing that in English. This may be attributed to the phonetic properties of these languages. The Whisper Base model, however, exhibits significantly lower quality in Italian compared to other languages. Conversely, for English, the Whisper Base model shows relatively good performance, whereas the Whisper Large-v3 and Conformer models have higher WER.

The same tendency persists for pitch shift transformations. As shown in Fig. 6, the Whisper Large-v3 model performs almost equally well for both German and Italian languages. The Conformer model, however, demonstrates slightly better performance in the Italian language.

For time stretch transformations, the Whisper Large-v3 and Conformer models perform at a similar quality overall. However, the Conformer model performs

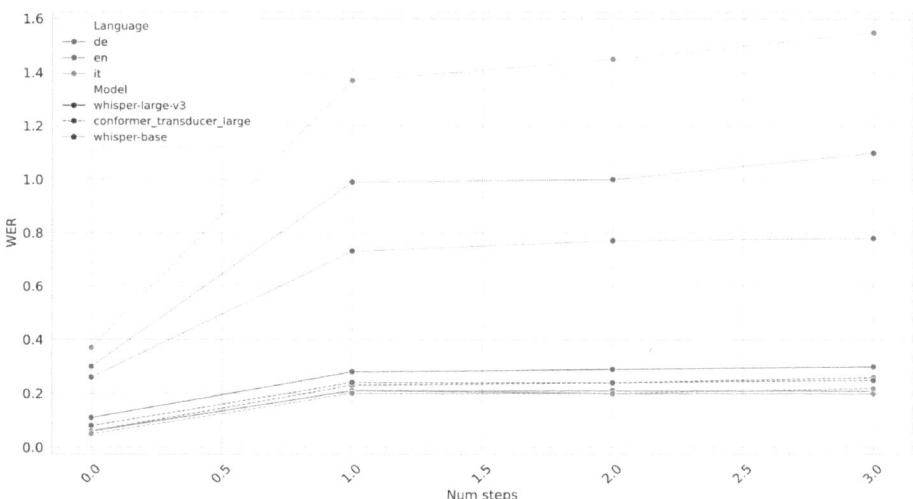

Fig. 6. WER comparison for different models and languages under pitch shift

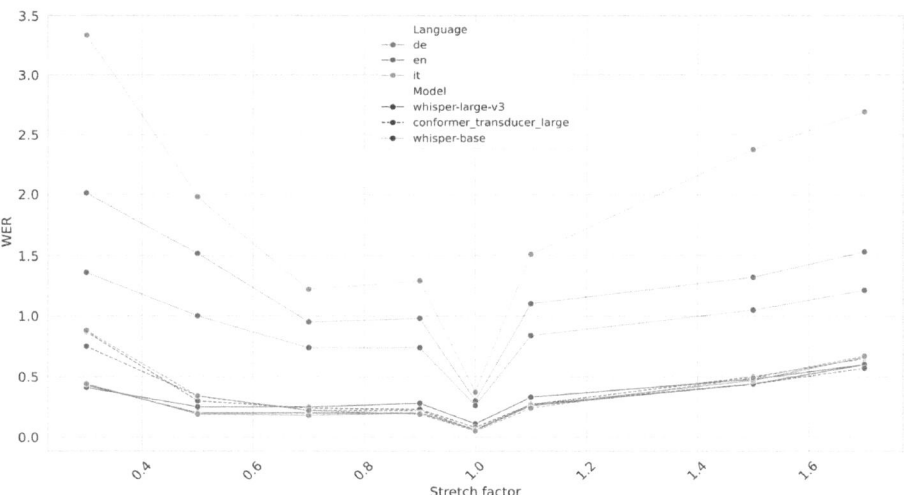

Fig. 7. WER comparison for different models and languages under time stretch

better for stretch factors greater than 1.0, while the Whisper Large-v3 model performs better for stretch factors less than 1.0, as shown in Fig. 7.

It can be observed that the Whisper Large-v3 model is the most robust to reverberation across all languages. Although the WER remains relatively high, it is significantly lower compared to other models, as illustrated in Fig. 4.

The performance differences across languages can be attributed to linguistic features. Italian and German have more consistent phoneme-to-grapheme map-

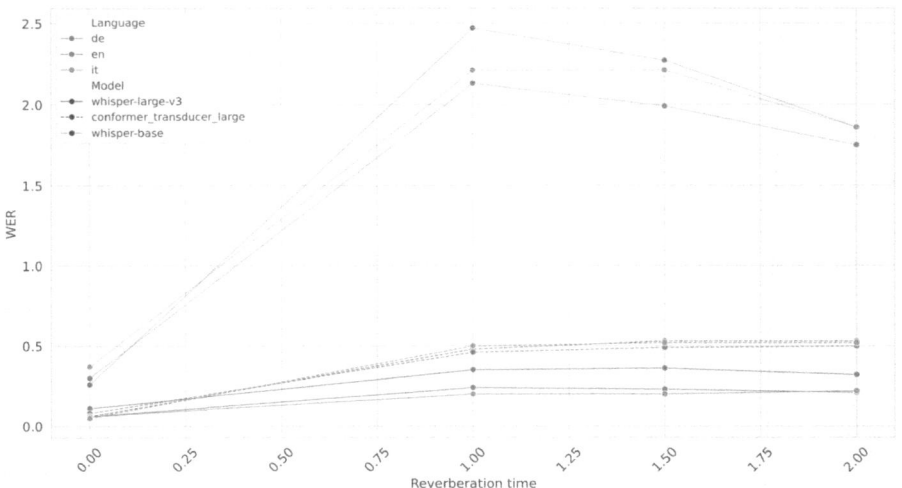

Fig. 8. WER comparison for different models under reverberation

pings than English, possibly explaining the better model performance. Additionally, German compound words and Italian vowel-rich phonetics pose unique challenges. Future work could explore these nuances further to optimize ASR model training and fine-tuning for specific languages.

Overall, the Whisper Large-v3 model is more robust to transformations such as reverberation and time stretch with a stretch factor less than 1.0 (slowing down). In contrast, the Conformer model performs better under conditions such as white noise. This robustness can be attributed to the specific fine-tuning processes applied to these models.

5 Conclusion

This study evaluates Whisper, QuartzNet, and Conformer ASR models against acoustic disturbances (white noise, reverberation, time stretch, pitch shift) across English, Italian, and German. The findings highlight each model's unique response to these challenges, with larger models like Whisper Large-v3 and Conformer generally performing better, though they still struggle with certain transformations. Whisper Base, with its limited parameters, exhibits significant robustness issues and a tendency to hallucinate.

Interestingly, despite more training data for English, Italian and German often show better ASR performance, suggesting language-specific factors in ASR accuracy. Whisper's multilingual capability is notable, but it sometimes underperforms compared to specialized Conformer models, indicating a trade-off between versatility and accuracy.

Different audio transformations uniquely affect ASR model performance. For example, reverberation shows a uniform degradation across models, suggesting a need for specialized training to handle such transformations better.

While ASR achieves near-human accuracy under ideal conditions, its performance under distortions is still below human levels. Noises that humans can easily compensate for result in high WER for ASR systems. For instance, white noise often produces high WER despite humans understanding the speech relatively well. Similarly, time stretch transformations might not significantly hinder human comprehension but can drastically increase WER for ASR models.

Future research should explore advanced noise augmentation techniques, understand linguistic nuances contributing to performance differences, and ensure balanced language representation in training data. Additionally, the acoustic transformations used in this study could provide insights for improving ASR systems for pathological speech, which often exhibits irregular pitch, breathiness, and other distortions. Addressing these aspects will make ASR systems more inclusive and capable of serving users with a wide range of speech characteristics. Furthermore, investigating the impact of mixed noise scenarios - where multiple types of acoustic disturbances, such as background noise and reverberation, occur simultaneously - can offer a more comprehensive understanding of ASR robustness in complex real-world environments, guiding the development of more resilient systems.

It is also essential to investigate the discrepancies between human and machine intelligibility of distorted speech, aiming to develop ASR systems that align more closely with human auditory perception. These steps will help develop ASR technologies that are robust, reliable, and effective across diverse linguistic contexts.

Acknowledgement. This research was conducted as part of the RATTLE (Voice Recogniser based on Artificial Intelligence) project, kindly funded by the Fondazione Pfizer.

References

1. Adolfi, F., Bowers, J.S., Poeppel, D.: Successes and critical failures of neural networks in capturing human-like speech recognition. Neural Netw. **162**(C), 199–211 (may 2023). https://doi.org/10.1016/j.neunet.2023.02.032
2. Ardila, R., et al.: Common voice: A massively-multilingual speech corpus. In: International Conference on Language Resources and Evaluation (2019). https://api.semanticscholar.org/CorpusID:209376338
3. Balam, J., Huang, J., Lavrukhin, V., Deng, S., Majumdar, S., Ginsburg, B.: Improving noise robustness of an end-to-end neural model for automatic speech recognition (2020)
4. Cieri, C., Miller, D., Walker, K.: The fisher corpus: A resource for the next generations of speech-to-text (01 2004)
5. Cui, T., Xiao, J., Li, L., Jiang, X., Liu, Q.: An approach to improve robustness of nlp systems against asr errors. ArXiv **abs/2103.13610** (2021). https://api.semanticscholar.org/CorpusID:232352551

6. Duarte, J.C., Colcher, S.: Building a noisy audio dataset to evaluate machine learning approaches for automatic speech recognition systems. ArXiv **abs/2110.01425** (2018). https://api.semanticscholar.org/CorpusID:238259030

7. Eickhoff, P., Möller, M., Pekarek-Rosin, T., Twiefel, J., Wermter, S.: Bring the noise: Introducing noise robustness to pretrained automatic speech recognition. In: International Conference on Artificial Neural Networks (2023). https://api.semanticscholar.org/CorpusID:261559431

8. Frieske, R., Shi, B.E.: Hallucinations in neural automatic speech recognition: Identifying errors and hallucinatory models (2024)

9. Fucci, D., Gaido, M., Negri, M., Cettolo, M., Bentivogli, L.: No pitch left behind: Addressing gender unbalance in automatic speech recognition through pitch manipulation. 2023 IEEE Automatic Speech Recognition and Understanding Workshop (ASRU), pp. 1–8 (2023). https://api.semanticscholar.org/CorpusID:263830339

10. Godfrey, J., Holliman, E., McDaniel, J.: Switchboard: telephone speech corpus for research and development. In: [Proceedings] ICASSP-92: 1992 IEEE International Conference on Acoustics, Speech, and Signal Processing. vol. 1, pp. 517–520 vol.1 (1992). https://doi.org/10.1109/ICASSP.1992.225858

11. Google: Sentencepiece. https://github.com/google/sentencepiece

12. Graves, A., Fernández, S., Gomez, F., Schmidhuber, J.: Connectionist temporal classification: Labelling unsegmented sequence data with recurrent neural 'networks. vol. 2006, pp. 369–376 (01 2006). https://doi.org/10.1145/1143844.1143891

13. Gulati, A., et al.: Conformer: Convolution-augmented Transformer for Speech Recognition (2020)

14. Higuchi, Y., Tawara, N., Ogawa, A., Iwata, T., Kobayashi, T., Ogawa, T.: Noise-robust attention learning for end-to-end speech recognition. In: 2020 28th European Signal Processing Conference (EUSIPCO).,pp. 311–315 (2021). https://doi.org/10.23919/Eusipco47968.2020.9287488

15. Holtzman, A., Buys, J., Forbes, M., Choi, Y.: The curious case of neural text degeneration. CoRR **abs/1904.09751** (2019). http://arxiv.org/abs/1904.09751

16. Huang, J., et al.: Cross-language transfer learning, continuous learning, and domain adaptation for end-to-end automatic speech recognition (2020)

17. Katkov, S., Liotta, A., Vietti, A.: Benchmarking whisper under diverse audio transformations and real-time constraints. In: Proceedings of the 26th International Conference on Speech and Computer (SPECOM) (2024)

18. Katkov, S., Liotta, A., Vietti, A.: Evaluating the robustness of ASR systems in adverse acoustic conditions. In: Proceedings of the Fifth International Conference on Intelligent Data Science Technologies and Applications (IDSTA) (2024)

19. Kriman, S., et al.: Quartznet: Deep automatic speech recognition with 1d time-channel separable convolutions. In: ICASSP 2020 - 2020 IEEE International Conference on Acoustics, Speech and Signal Processing (ICASSP), pp. 6124–6128 (2020). https://doi.org/10.1109/ICASSP40776.2020.9053889

20. Lee, G.W., Kim, H.K.: Two-step joint optimization with auxiliary loss function for noise-robust speech recognition. Sensors (Basel, Switzerland) **22** (2022). https://api.semanticscholar.org/CorpusID:250942334

21. Li, J., Deng, L., Gong, Y., Häb-Umbach, R.: An overview of noise-robust automatic speech recognition. IEEE/ACM Transactions on Audio, Speech, and Language Processing **22**, 745–777 (2014), https://api.semanticscholar.org/CorpusID:14557362

22. Mauch, M., Ewert, S.: The audio degradation toolbox and its application to robustness evaluation. In: International Society for Music Information Retrieval Conference (2013). https://api.semanticscholar.org/CorpusID:11675708

23. Müller, J.A., Wendt, D., Kollmeier, B., Debener, S., Brand, T.: Effect of speech rate on neural tracking of speech. Front. Psychol. **10** (2019). https://doi.org/10.3389/fpsyg.2019.00449, https://www.frontiersin.org/journals/psychology/articles/10.3389/fpsyg.2019.00449

24. Panayotov, V., Chen, G., Povey, D., Khudanpur, S.: Librispeech: An asr corpus based on public domain audio books. In: 2015 IEEE International Conference on Acoustics, Speech and Signal Processing (ICASSP), pp. 5206–5210 (2015). https://doi.org/10.1109/ICASSP.2015.7178964

25. Paul, D.B., Baker, J.M.: The design for the wall street journal-based csr corpus. In: Proceedings of the Workshop on Speech and Natural Language. p. 357–362. HLT '91, Association for Computational Linguistics, USA (1992). https://doi.org/10.3115/1075527.1075614

26. Payton, K.L., Uchanski, R.M., Braida, L.D.: Intelligibility of conversational and clear speech in noise and reverberation for listeners with normal and impaired hearing. J. Acoust. Society America **95**(3), 1581–1592 (03 1994). https://doi.org/10.1121/1.408545

27. Pratap, V., Xu, Q., Sriram, A., Synnaeve, G., Collobert, R.: Mls: A large-scale multilingual dataset for speech research. In: Interspeech 2020. ISCA (Oct 2020). https://doi.org/10.21437/interspeech.2020-2826

28. Radford, A., Kim, J.W., Xu, T., Brockman, G., McLeavey, C., Sutskever, I.: Robust speech recognition via large-scale weak supervision (2022)

29. Rekesh, D., et al.: Fast conformer with linearly scalable attention for efficient speech recognition (2023)

30. Saito, K., et al.: Unsupervised vocal dereverberation with diffusion-based generative models (2022)

31. Schwartz, B., Gannot, S., Habets, E.: Online speech dereverberation using kalman filter and em algorithm. IEEE/ACM Trans. Audio, Speech, Lang. Process. **23**, 394–406 (2015). https://api.semanticscholar.org/CorpusID:2413399

32. Shrawankar, U., Thakare, V.: Noise estimation and noise removal techniques for speech recognition in adverse environment. In: Shi, Z., Vadera, S., Aamodt, A., Leake, D. (eds.) Intelligent Information Processing V, pp. 336–342. Springer Berlin Heidelberg, Berlin, Heidelberg (2010). https://doi.org/10.1007/978-3-642-16327-2_40

33. Wang, C., et al.: Voxpopuli: A large-scale multilingual speech corpus for representation learning, semi-supervised learning and interpretation. CoRR **abs/2101.00390** (2021). https://arxiv.org/abs/2101.00390

34. Zhang, Q., Lu, H., Sak, H., Tripathi, A., McDermott, E., Koo, S., Kumar, S.: Transformer transducer: A streamable speech recognition model with transformer encoders and rnn-t loss. In: ICASSP 2020 - 2020 IEEE International Conference on Acoustics, Speech and Signal Processing (ICASSP), pp. 7829–7833 (2020). https://doi.org/10.1109/ICASSP40776.2020.9053896

Automating Resume Analysis: Knowledge Graphs via Prompt Engineering

Giorgio Lazzarinetti[1,2](✉) ⓘ, Sara Manzoni[1] ⓘ, and Italo Zoppis[1] ⓘ

[1] Universitá degli Studi Milano-Bicocca, Milano, Italy
{giorgio.lazzarinetti,sara.manzoni,italo.zoppis}@unimib.it
[2] BID Company S.r.l., Milano, Italy
https://www.bidcompany.it/

Abstract. The rapid digitization of recruitment processes and the growing complexity of resume data have posed significant challenges in managing and extracting information from such sources. Traditional methods necessitate innovative approaches that can adapt and scale effectively. This paper introduces a methodology employing Large Language Models (LLMs) facilitated by advanced prompt engineering techniques, to construct Knowledge Graphs (KGs) directly from resumes. Our approach bypasses the extensive customization typically required for domain-specific tasks, leveraging the intrinsic capabilities of LLMs to interpret and organize complex data. We evaluate our methodology, focusing particularly on Named Entity Recognition (NER) as a measure of effectiveness. The results demonstrate superior performance of our system against baseline models. Additionally, we explore the practical applicability of our system through a novel self-consistency metric, which further attests to the method's ability to accurately capture and reproduce essential resume information in KG format. This study not only underscores the potential of LLMs in automated information extraction but also opens up new avenues for research and application in the HR technology domain and beyond.

Keywords: Knowledge Graph · Resume Analysis · Deep Learning · Large Language Model · Prompt Engineering · Text to Graph

1 Overview

Online recruitment platforms such as LinkedIn have revolutionized job advertising, offering significant time efficiencies for employers and job seekers alike. However, the increasing volume of data on these platforms complicates the effective analysis of each resume, a challenge that has attracted considerable research interest [1]. Resumes, which are primarily text-based and lack a uniform format, contain diverse information types, creating structural uncertainties.

Traditionally, resume review was a manual task where HR professionals extracted information and matched skills against job descriptions to identify suitable candidates [2]. To overcome the limitations of manual processes, automated techniques like keyword retrieval and Document Object Model (DOM)

A. Artale et al. (Eds.): AIxIA 2024, LNAI 15450, pp. 214–227, 2025.
https://doi.org/10.1007/978-3-031-80607-0_17

tree-based methods have been developed [1]. While keyword retrieval is straight-forward, it often lacks accuracy due to textual noise [2–4]. DOM tree approaches, on the other hand, face scalability challenges because they depend on manual input and are template-specific [5].

Recent advances in Natural Language Processing (NLP) have introduced machine learning-based methods, predominantly using Named Entity Recognition (NER) and pattern matching, to extract and structure resume information [6–8]. Despite their efficiency in handling large volumes of data, these methods struggle with complex, time-sensitive information and scaling to new, unseen entities in a dynamic job market [9].

To address these issues, the use of Knowledge Graphs (KGs) has gained traction in resume parsing and skill matching, providing a more expressive framework than traditional tables for organizing and analyzing information [10,11]. However, constructing KGs from unstructured texts remains a challenging task, often tackled using various Deep Learning (DL) methods [12], such as Large Language Models (LLMs) pre-trained on extensive corpora and fine-tuned on real data [13–15]. However, only recently, the increasing size of these models has enabled LLMs to perform complex, practical tasks effectively even without fine-tuning, benefiting significantly from advancements in prompt engineering - a burgeoning field aimed at optimizing prompt design to enhance LLMs performance across different applications and research initiatives [16].

Despite the proliferation of tools and applications for managing resume data, there has been limited research focused on assessing the effectiveness of prompt-based techniques for constructing KGs from text, particularly resumes. In this study, we investigate whether modern LLMs can successfully build KGs from resumes in a way similar to a professional human analyst. The main goal of this research is to explore the feasibility and effectiveness of prompt engineering in automating the resume parsing process. For this reason we propose a prompt-based methodology to create KGs from resumes using a pre-trained LLM, aiming to provide both theoretical insights into specific prompting techniques and a comprehensive evaluation of the proposed method.

The paper is structured as follows: Sect. 2 introduces LLMs and prompt engineering techniques; Sect. 3 outlines our approach to convert texts to KGs, the ontology for resume parsing and the evaluation schema; Sect. 4 discusses the datasets used and experimental results; Sect. 5 offers final thoughts.

2   Background

2.1   Large Language Models

LLMs are advanced artificial intelligence systems that utilize DL techniques to understand, interpret, and generate human language. They are pre-trained on expansive corpora and have demonstrated remarkable capabilities across a diverse array of NLP tasks [17]. A fundamental component underpinning the success of most LLMs is their reliance on the Transformer architecture [18], which is distinguished by its incorporation of encoder and decoder modules, both of which are enhanced through the self-attention mechanism. Predicated on their architectural framework, LLMs can be systematically classified into one of three distinct categories: (i) encoder-only models like BERT [13] and RoBERTa [14], which are adept at understanding word relationships and are used in tasks such as text classification and NER; (ii) encoder-decoder models such as T5 [15], which excels in context-based sentence generation tasks like summarization, translation, and question answering; and (iii) decoder-only models, including GPT-4 [19], which focus on generating text from minimal prompts without additional modifications [20]. Decoder-only models excel in free-form text generation, creative writing, and dialog systems where the generation of coherent and contextually relevant responses is crucial. The flexibility of these models is particularly advantageous in scenarios requiring adaptive responses or generating content based on sparse inputs.

2.2   Prompt Engineering

Prompt engineering is an area of inquiry that concentrates on the formulation and refinement of prompts to enhance the performance of LLMs across a myriad of applications and research domains [16]. Within this framework, a prompt is conceptualized as a sequence of natural language inputs tailored to a specific task, such as sentiment classification, and is composed of distinct elements: (i) *instruction*, i.e., a concise directive that guides the model in executing a particular task; (ii) *context*, which furnishes the relevant backdrop for the input text or supplies few-shot examples; and (iii) *input text*, denoting the textual content subject to the model's processing. This discipline endeavors to augment the efficacy of LLMs in executing an array of complex tasks, encompassing question answering, sentiment analysis, and the elucidation of common sense reasoning.

Several primary techniques have been identified, each contributing distinctively to the functionality of LLMs. Among these, Zero-shot Learning (ZsL), Few-shot Learning (FsL), and Chain-of-Thought (CoT) are particularly prevalent. ZsL allows models to execute tasks based solely on prompt instructions, showcasing their ability to generalize across various tasks [21]. FsL enhances this by incorporating a limited number of task examples within the prompt, enabling LLMs to leverage pattern recognition to understand and perform tasks [20]. CoT, in contrast, prompts the model to articulate intermediate steps or reasoning processes before producing a final answer, facilitating deeper engagement with complex reasoning tasks by encouraging the model to "think aloud" [22]. Additionally, as prompt engineering is an active area of research, several innovative techniques have emerged. Notable among these are Retrieval Augmented Generation [23], Tree-of-Thought Prompting [24], and Graph-of-Thought Prompting [25], each offering sophisticated methods to enhance the effectiveness and applicability of LLMs in diverse computational tasks.

3 Prompt-Based Solution

3.1 Text to Knowledge Graph Pipeline

To design our framework we begin with an analysis of the prevailing methods in the literature for constructing KGs from textual data [12]. The development of a KG involves multiple phases, each tailored to overcome specific obstacles encountered during the conversion of unstructured text into a structured form of knowledge representation.

1. **Entity Recognition and Classification**: detects and classifies entities within the text, such as people, places, and organizations, which are essential for constructing nodes in the KG.
2. **Relationship Extraction**: determines the relationships between entities, which form the edges of the KG, crucial for mapping the connections within the graph.
3. **Entity Disambiguation and Linking**: addresses the challenge of distinguishing between entities with similar names and correctly linking them to existing entries in a knowledge base, ensuring accurate entity representation.
4. **Knowledge Integration**: entities and relationships are integrated into an existing KG or used to create a new one. It involves resolving inconsistencies and integrating new knowledge using technologies like RDF and SPARQL.
5. **Knowledge Refinement and Enrichment**: the KG is continuously refined and updated with new information, corrections, and enhancements to improve its accuracy and quality.

3.2 Resume Data Schema

The outlined stages present a generalized framework for transforming textual data into a KG, emphasizing the need for adaptation to specific business domains for accurate representation. In the context of our research, we focus on candidate resumes, necessitating a tailored approach to precisely identify domain-specific concepts. Various ontologies for modeling resumes and job offers have been suggested [26–28]. Referencing them, we seek to define the key entities, attributes, and relationships that should be extracted from resumes to accurately and flexibly represent real-world scenarios. Our schema, detailed in Table 1, provides a comprehensive view of an individuals professional and academic achievements. We have specified attributes for each entity to reflect essential and commonly encountered data. In the proposed schema, we identify seven principal entities which focus on distinct yet interconnected aspects of a professional profile:

- **Person**: acts as the central node, linking all other entities, with attributes including name, contact details, and demographics.
- **Education**: details academic qualifications and training, with attributes like institution name, degree, field of study, and graduation dates.
- **Professional Experience**: outlines employment history, including employer names, job titles, employment dates, and responsibilities.

- **Skill**: covers specific competencies, both technical and soft, with attributes such as skill name, proficiency level, and years of experience.
- **Certification**: documents certifications and licenses, with attributes including certification name, issuing organization, and validity.
- **Achievement**: highlights significant accomplishments, including awards or recognitions, with relevant details such as the award name, issuing body, and date.
- **Publication**: represents scholarly work, with attributes including title, description, publication date, and outlet.

Table 1. KG's schema for individuals derived from resume data, detailing seven primary entities along with their respective attributes and relationships.

Entities	Attributes	Relationships
Person	Name, Contact Information, (email, phone number), Location, LinkedIn Profile	HasEducation, HasExperience, HasSkill, HasCertification, HasAchievement, HasPublication
Education	Degree, Field of Study, Educational Institution, Start Date, End Date	ObtainedBy (inverse of HasEducation), RelatedToField
Professional Experience	Job Title, Company Name, Industry, Start Date, End Date, Responsibilities, Achievements	UndertakenBy (inverse of HasExperience), InIndustry, UsesSkill
Skill	Skill Name, Proficiency Level, Years of Experience	UsedInJob (inverse of UsesSkill)
Certification	Certification Name, Issuing Organization, Issue Date, Expiry Date	ObtainedBy (inverse of HasCertification), RelatedToSkill
Achievement	Achievement Title, Description, Date,	AchievedBy (inverse of HasAchievement), RelatedToSkill, RelatedToExperience
Publications	Title, Description, Date, Journal, Conference	PublishedBy (inverse of HasPublication), RelatedToSkill, RelatedToExperience

3.3   CoT Prompt for Resume to Knowledge Graph

Analyzing the general pipeline for converting text into a graph detailed in Sect. 3.1 reveals a highly sequential process that incorporates logical reasoning at various stages to enhance the outcome. CoT prompting, as used with language models for complex problem-solving or reasoning tasks, exemplifies this approach. It involves guiding the model through intermediate steps or reasoning paths towards a conclusion, similar to human problem-solving strategies. This method is particularly useful where direct answers require information synthesis, logical reasoning, or nuanced context understanding, leveraging the model's capability to generate relevant text sequences from structured prompts.

Consequently, we crafted a specialized CoT prompt that integrates the standard procedures for text-to-graph conversion, with tailored modifications to align with HR-specific requirements. The structure of the prompt is outlined in Algorithm 1. The prompt sets out clear instructions for the LLM on handling entities (nodes), their identifiers, and the treatment of numerical data and dates. We recommend using simple, textual identifiers, particularly for the *Person* entity, to keep the node identification straightforward and interpretable. Numerical data and dates are treated as attributes, not nodes, to minimize complexity.

Algorithm 1: Resume2KnowledgeGraph Prompt Main Structure

You are an algorithm designed for extracting information in structured formats from resumes to build a knowledge graph. In order to do it consider the following statements.

Preliminary Considerations

- **Nodes**: Nodes represent entities and concepts. Ensure you use basic or elementary types for node labels. For example, when you identify an entity representing a person, always label it as "person".
- **Nodes ID**: Never utilize integers as node IDs. Node IDs should be names or human-readable identifiers found in the text.
- **Numerical Data and Dates**: Numerical data, like age or other related information, should be incorporated as attributes or properties of the respective nodes. Always attach them as attributes or properties of nodes. Properties must be in a key-value format.

To build the knowledge graph then follow the steps and the instructions described in Algorithm *Resume2KnowledgeGraph Steps*.

Additional Considerations

- Incorporate nodes for Languages with attributes for proficiency and usage context, linked to Person entities, to capture linguistic capabilities.
- Add nodes for Volunteer Experience similar to Professional Experience, including attributes like Role, Organization, and Date, to capture non-work-related skills and achievements.
- Consider temporal relationships between experiences to infer career progression paths and potential skill development over time.

The extraction methodology is further detailed in Algorithm 2, customized per our schema in Table 1. It includes specific examples and focal points to guide the model in aligning with the predefined schema and includes steps for

---

Algorithm 2: Resume2KnowledgeGraph Steps Prompt

Step 1: Entity Recognition and Classification

– Action: Scan the resume text to identify and classify entities according to predefined categories: Person, Education, Professional Experience, Skill, Certification, Achievement, and Publications.
– Customization: Pay special attention to keywords and phrases that signify the beginning and end of sections (e.g., "Education", "Experience", "Skills"), and use formatting cues like bullet points and headings to distinguish between different entities and their attributes.

Step 2: Relationship Extraction

– Action: Analyze the context around identified entities to extract relationships between them. This involves understanding how different entities like Education and Person or Professional Experience and Skill are connected.
– Customization: Focus on verbs and prepositions that indicate relationships, such as "earned" for Education and "worked on" for Professional Experience, to map the defined relationships accurately (e.g., HasEducation, UsesSkill).

Step 3: Entity Disambiguation and Linking

– Action: Resolve ambiguities among entities (e.g., differentiating between Java the programming language and Java the island) and link entities to unique identifiers where possible (e.g., using LinkedIn profiles for disambiguation).
– Customization: For the HR domain, prioritize disambiguation of educational institutions, company names, and certification bodies by cross-referencing known databases or lists to ensure accuracy in entity identification.

Step 4: Knowledge Integration

– Integrate the extracted entities and relationships into a cohesive knowledge graph structure, ensuring that each entity is represented as a node with its attributes and that the relationships between entities are accurately depicted as edges.
– Customization: Ensure that nodes for Person entities serve as central hubs, linking to various aspects of their professional profile (Education, Experience, Skills, etc.) to reflect the comprehensive nature of a resume.

Step 5: Knowledge Refinement and Enrichment

– Action: Refine the knowledge graph by checking for consistency, removing duplicates, and filling in missing information. Enrich the graph by adding inferred relationships or attributes (e.g., inferring skill proficiency levels from years of experience or job responsibilities).
– Customization: Consider adding nodes for Industries to connect Professional Experience and Skills, enhancing the graph's utility for HR purposes by facilitating industry-specific analysis and talent mapping.

---

information validation through cross-referencing and directives on managing the *Person* entity as a central link to other relevant entities.

Additionally, the main prompt incorporates guidance for handling contextual information not covered in the schema, such as language skills or volunteer activities, and advises on assessing temporal relationships to deduce career paths and skills. These additional guidelines aim to ensure the model captures both structured and contextual dimensions of resume data, thus enhancing the utility and accuracy of HR analytics.

3.4 Proposed Evaluation Approach

Evaluating the quality of a KG presents significant challenges, particularly when approached as an unsupervised task. Typically, the evaluation targets individual sub-tasks within the KG construction pipeline such as NER, Triple Extraction (TE) or Entity Linking. In our unified framework, where the output comprises entities, attributes and relations forming the complete KG, it is not feasible to evaluate each sub-task individually. Notably, while TE generally poses challenges in converting texts to KGs, it is somewhat simplified in our context since each entity directly connects to the main entity *Person*, easing the identification process.

To assess the effectiveness of our approach in constructing KGs from resumes, we focus on measuring the NER capability of our solution, given its critical role, using standard classification metrics: Precision, Recall, F1-score and Accuracy. These metrics are computed on a publicly available dataset from Kaggle [29] that includes resume texts alongside identified entities. We benchmark these results against two state-of-the-art methods: a RoBERTa-based model and a spaCy-based model. Finetuning for RoBERTa is performed on the *roberta-base* model [30] with token classification head for NER. All parameters are fine-tuned with Adam [31] optimizer at a learning rate of $E \times 10^{-4}$. Weight decay of 0.01 is applied to all parameters except biases and normalization parameters, which were exempt to stabilize training. Training is conducted over 10 epochs, employing gradient clipping with a max norm of 1.0 to prevent gradient explosion. For the spaCy model, we adopt the *en-core-web-sm* model [32] adding the NER component and training for 20 epochs with a dropout rate of 0.3. Default stochastic gradient descent optimizer is adopted, with its built-in decay mechanism, L2 regularization and gradient clipping strategy [33]. To fine-tune the baseline models we apply a 70–30 ratio split of the dataset.

Additionally, to assess the quality of KGs built from resumes we developed a novel self-consistency metric. Typically, to evaluate correctness, completeness, and consistency of the extracted information used to construct the KG, a ground truth is necessary. However creating a scalable ground truth in real-world scenarios is impracticable. For this reason, we have opted to introduce a self-consistency metric to measure the quality of the KGs generated. This metric involves reverting the generated KG back into a textual resume format using GPT-4 (with a simple yet effective ZsL approach), then quantitatively comparing the regenerated resume to the original one. For this comparison, we use a pre-trained sentence transformer [34] to compute the cosine similarity between embeddings of the original and regenerated texts of the resume. To interpret these similarity scores, we create a dataset comprising triplets of resumes: a reference resume, a second resume deemed similar by human evaluators, and a third one deemed different. We calculate average cosine similarities for both similar and different resume sets. The effectiveness of our method is gauged by comparing these similarity scores, aiming for our results to approach the upper similarity bounds established by the comparable resumes. Although this task involves a translation model, we have chosen not to use standard translation model evaluation metrics (e.g., BLEU, ROUGE, or METEOR), since transforming the KG into a resume is not done in a supervised manner, as is typical for translation models. Consequently, because the ultimate goal is not to produce a resume that closely mirrors the original one but rather one that includes all essential information from the original resume, we use this self-consistency metric that correctly quantifies the fidelity of the information retained in the KG.

4   Experimental Results

4.1   Datasets Description

As mentioned in Paragraph 3.4, to test our methodologies we used three datasets.

The *NER Dataset*, is a dataset publicly available on Kaggle [29] that contains resumes and tagged entities for NER. It is composed of 220 resumes and a total of 3556 entities divided in the following 10 types: Name, Email Address, Location, College Name, Degree, Graduation Year, Companies Worked at, Designation, Skills, Years of Experience. Each of these maps to the set of entities or attributes designed in Table 1. This dataset is used to evaluate the performance of the LLM in extracting entities after steps 1 to 3 of Algorithm 2 have been performed.

The *Resumes Dataset*, used to directly measure the information extraction and KG construction capabilities of the algorithms together, is composed of 188 resumes in PDF format. These are resumes from professionals of different sectors (e.g., IT, Banking, Finance, Fashion, Food, Industry) and with different seniority level (e.g., junior, mid and senior). These resumes have been synthetically generated starting from real-world data collected from LinkedIn.

Finally, the *Triplets Dataset*, is composed of 50 triplets of resumes. We randomly extract 50 resumes from the Resumes Dataset, and for each of these reference resumes we manually build a similar resume so that it contains all the information of the reference one expressed in a different way. Finally, we add a third resume to the triplet, by getting one from the same sector and possibly similar professional experience, but with different information. As an example, Table 2 shows the similar sentence and the different sentence built as part of the triplet with respect to a reference sentence. This dataset is used as ground truth to benchmark the performance of the LLM in building the KG from the resume, based on its ability to build the resume back from the constructed KG.

Table 2. Example of reference sentence, similar sentence and different sentence from the Triplet Dataset used to evaluate the approach in a qualitative way.

Reference Sentence	Computer Science engineer with one year of experience in DevOps. Competent in using various automation tools and able to work in environments with agile methodologies. Motivated to constantly improve technical skills and to bring innovation within projects.
Similar Sentence	Passionate Computer engineer with a year's experience in DevOps, skilled in employing diverse automation tools and adept at operating within agile methodologies. Eager to continuously enhance technical abilities and introduce new techniques and tools in projects.
Different Sentence	DevOps engineer with 6 years of experience in building and managing scalable and reliable infrastructures. Expert in using CI/CD tools to optimize development and deployment operations. Skilled in team collaboration and solving complex problems.

4.2 Named Entity Recognition

As described, the effectiveness of NER directly influences the accuracy and integrity of the resultant KG. To assess the quality of NER in our study, we employed classical NER performance metrics: Precision, Recall, F1-Score, and Accuracy. These metrics provide a comprehensive view of our model's capability to correctly identify and classify entities within resumes. They are presented in Table 3, which shows a comparative analysis between the baseline models - a fine-tuned RoBERTa model and a fine-tuned spaCy model - and our proposed CoT prompt-based methodology applied on the GPT-4 model.

Table 3. Results of the NER task in terms of Precision, Recall, F1-score and Accuracy, that show how the CoT prompt-based model outperforms the baseline models.

Model	Precision	Recall	F1-score	Accuracy
spaCy	0,86	0,85	0,86	0,86
RoBERTa	0,91	0,89	0,90	0,89
GPT-4	0,94	0,90	0,92	0,92

Results are computed on the 30% of test data (73 resumes with a total of 1175 entities). Here, our methodology demonstrates superior performance across all metrics. These metrics signify not only an enhancement in identifying correct entities but also in reducing false positives and negatives, crucial for building reliable KG. To visualize the GPT-4 model's capability to extract entities based on our CoT prompt, Fig. 1 shows an example of extracted KG from a resume.

4.3 Self Consistency Metric

As mentioned, to evaluate the quality of the KGs generated, we compute a self-consistency metric by serving the KGs generated from the original resume

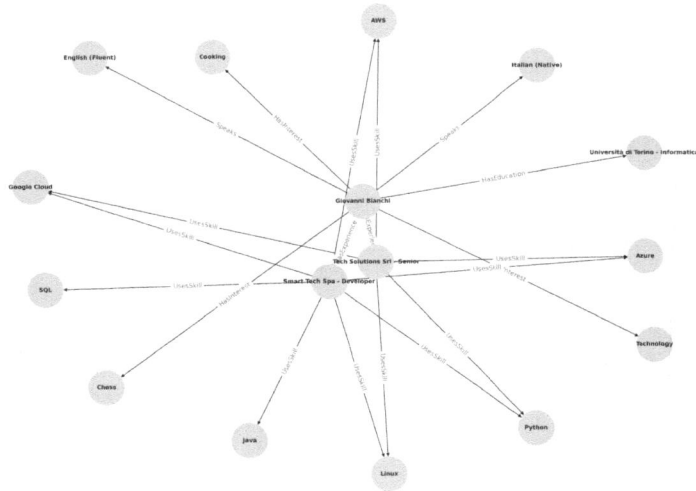

Fig. 1. Example of a generated KG with Person as central entity connected to information about Education, Professional Experience, Languages, Interests and Skills.

texts as input to GPT-4 to regenerate, with a ZsL prompt-based approach, the resume texts and subsequently measuring the cosine similarity between these texts (properly embedded with a pre-trained sentence transformer) to assess fidelity and accuracy. The effectiveness of our KG-based reconstruction is quantified by comparing the cosine similarity scores of the regenerated resumes against those of two control groups: a set of similar and a set of different resumes. These control groups, composed of 50 resumes serve to establish benchmark similarity ranges for evaluation. The results of these comparisons are summarized in Table 4, which shows that the average cosine similarity score between the original resumes and their KG-based reconstructions (Test Group) is 0.876. This closely approaches the 0.942 average for manually identified similar resumes (Positive Control Group), indicating that the KG effectively captures and reproduces key resume information. Only a few reconstructions fall below the threshold set as the maximum similarity score of the Negative Control Group (0.698), with the

Table 4. Comparison of cosine similarity scores on the Triplets Dataset (with a support of 50 resumes) and on test instances (with a support of 220 resumes).

Control Group	Min Sim	Avg Sim	Max Sim	Support
Positive	0,823	0,942	0,977	50
Negative	0,182	0,46	0,698	50
Test	0,655	0,876	0,932	220

lowest of the Test Group being 0.655. Moreover, the average similarity with the Negative Control Group at 0.46 is significantly lower with respect to the lowest of the Test Group, clearly differentiating between relevant and non-relevant content in the KG reconstructions, as depicted in Fig. 2. These results highlight the precision of the information captured by our KG-based method in replicating resume content, demonstrating performance nearly equivalent to human-judged similar texts and significantly surpassing the threshold for non-similar texts.

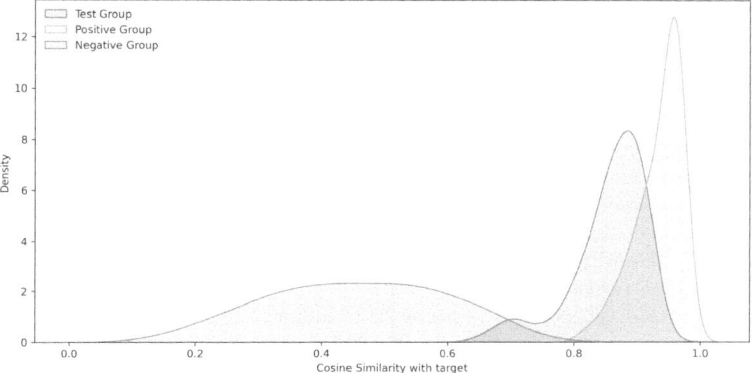

Fig. 2. Distribution of the cosine similarity of each control group with respect to target.

5 Conclusion and Future Works

In this paper, we investigated whether modern LLMs can successfully build KGs from resumes akin to professional human analyst. We designed a CoT prompt-based methodology that leverages advanced LLMs to convert texts into KGs that encapsulate professional profiles. The primary objective of our research was to explore the feasibility and effectiveness of prompt engineering in automating the resume parsing process and subsequently creating detailed KGs. We focused on NER to benchmark the effectiveness of our system against traditional models, showing that our approach achieved superior performance compared to state-of-the-art models without extensive fine-tuning. We also propose a self-consistent approach to measure the ability of our method in generating KG from resumes. The obtained results suggests that our method can accurately capture and reproduce critical information from resumes.

While our results are promising, several avenues remain open for future exploration, such as testing different LLMs or prompting strategies, ethical considerations, the integration with real-time systems and cross-domain adaptability.

References

1. Chen, J., Zhang, C., Niu, Z.: A two-step resume information extraction algorithm. Math. Probl. Eng. **2018**(1), 1–8 (2018)
2. Jagwani, V., Meghani, S., Pai, K., Dhage, S.: Resume Evaluation through Latent Dirichlet Allocation and Natural Language Processing for Effective Candidate Selection. arXiv preprint arXiv:2307.15752 (2023)
3. Maheshwari, S., Sainani, A., Reddy, P.K.: An approach to extract special skills to improve the performance of resume selection. In: Kikuchi, S., Sachdeva, S., Bhalla, S. (eds.) Databases in Networked Information Systems, pp. 256–273. Springer Berlin Heidelberg, Berlin, Heidelberg (2010). https://doi.org/10.1007/978-3-642-12038-1_17
4. Kopparapu, S.K.: Automatic extraction of usable information from unstructured resumes to aid search. In: 1st IEEE International Conference on Progress in Informatics and Computing (PIC '10), vol. 1, pp. 99–103. IEEE, China (2010)
5. Ji, X., Zeng, J., Zhang, S., Wu, C.: Tag tree template for Web information and schema extraction. Expert Syst. Appl. **37**(12), 8492–8498 (2010)
6. Rasal, P., Balwaik, Y.: Resume parser analysis using machine learning and natural language processing. Int. Res. J. Modern. Eng. Technol. Sci. **5**(3), (2023)
7. Bhaliya, N., Gandhi, J., Singh, D.K.: NLP based Extraction of Relevant Resume using Machine Learning. IJITEE (2020)
8. Bhor, S., Gupta, V., Nair, V., Shinde, H., Kulkarni, M.: Resume parser using NLP Techniques. www.ijres.org **9**(6), 01–06 (2021)
9. de Groot, M., Schutte, J., Graus, D.: Job posting-enriched knowledge graph for skills-based matching. In: RECSYS in HR 2022, Co-located with the 16th ACM Conference on Recommender Systems, US (2022)
10. Goyal, N., Kalra, J.S., Sharma, C., Mutharaju, R., Sachdeva, N., Kumaraguru, P.: JobXMLC: extreme multi-label classification of job skills with graph neural networks. In: Vlachos, A., Augenstein, I. (eds.) Findings of the Association for Computational Linguistics: EACL 2023, pp. 2181–2191. Association for Computational Linguistics, Dubrovnik, Croatia (2023)
11. Wang, Y., Allouache, Y., Joubert, C.: Analysing CV corpus for finding suitable candidates using knowledge graph and BERT. In: 13th International Conference on Advances in Databases. Knowledge, and Data Applications (DBKDA 2021), pp. 256–273. Valencia, Spain (2021)
12. Zhong, L., Wu, J., Li, Q., Peng, H., Wu, X.: A comprehensive survey on automatic knowledge graph construction. ACM Comput. Surv. **56**, (2023). https://doi.org/10.1145/3618295
13. Devlin, J., Chang, M.-W., Lee, K., Toutanova, K.: BERT: Pre-training of deep bidirectional transformers for language understanding. In: Proceedings of the 2019 Conference of the North American Chapter of the Association for Computational Linguistics: Human Language Technologies, Volume 1 (Long and Short Papers), pp. 4171–4186. Association for Computational Linguistics, Minneapolis, Minnesota (2019)
14. Liu, Y., et al.: RoBERTa: a robustly optimized bert pretraining approach. In: Proceedings of the 23rd Conference on Empirical Methods in Natural Language Processing (EMNLP 2019), pp. 4248–4258. Association for Computational Linguistics, Hong Kong, China (2019)
15. Raffel, C., et al.: Exploring the limits of transfer learning with a unified text-to-text transformer. J. Mach. Learn. Res. **21**(1), 5485–5551 (2020)

16. Amatriain, X.: Prompt Design and Engineering: Introduction and Advanced Methods.arXiv preprint, arXiv:2401.14423 (2024)
17. Yang, J., et al.: Harnessing the power of llms in practice: a survey on ChatGPT and beyond. ACM Trans. Knowl. Discov. Data **18**(6), Article 160, 32 pages (2024)
18. Vaswani, A., et al.: Attention is all you need. In: Proceedings of the 31st Conference on Neural Information Processing Systems (NIPS 2017), Long Beach, CA, USA (2017)
19. OpenAI: GPT-4 Technical Report. arXiv preprint. arXiv:2303.08774 (2023)
20. Brown, T., et al.: Language models are few-shot learners. Adv. Neural. Inf. Process. Syst. **33**, 1877–1901 (2020)
21. Wei, J., et al.: Finetuned language models are zero-shot learners. In: International Conference on Learning Representations (ICLR 2022), pp. 1–2. (2022)
22. Wei, J., et al.: Chain-of-thought prompting elicits reasoning in large language models. In: 36th Conference on Neural Information Processing Systems (NeurIPS 2022), pp. 1882–1893. (2022)
23. Lewis, P., et al.: Retrieval-augmented generation for knowledge-intensive NLP tasks. In: Proceedings of the 34th Conference on Neural Information Processing Systems (NeurIPS 2020), pp. 9459–9474. Vancouver, Canada (2020)
24. Yao, S., et al.: Tree of thoughts: deliberate problem solving with large language models. In: Advances in Neural Information Processing Systems 36 (NeurIPS 2023), NeurIPS (2023)
25. Besta, M., et al.: Graph of thoughts: solving elaborate problems with large language models. In: 30th International Conference on Neural Information Processing Systems (NeurIPS 2023), pp. 15682–15690. ETH Zurich, Zurich, Switzerland (2023)
26. Zaouga, W., Ben Arfa Rabai, L.: Modeling and evaluating a human resource management ontology. In: Computer Science On-line Conference, pp. 1–2. (2019)
27. Ahmed, N., Khan, S., Latif, K.: Job description ontology. In: 2016 International Conference on Frontiers of Information Technology (FIT), pp. 217–222. Islamabad, Pakistan (2016)
28. Javed, Z., Qazi, H., Khoja, S.A.: An ontology-based knowledge management model for e-recruitment utilizing MOOCs data. In: 2019 8th International Conference on Information and Communication Technologies (ICICT), pp. 124–128. Karachi, Pakistan (2019)
29. Kaggle - Resume Entities for NER. https://www.kaggle.com/datasets/dataturks/resume-entities-for-ner/data. Accessed 09 June 2024
30. Hugging Face - FacebookAI - RoBERTa Base Model. https://huggingface.co/FacebookAI/roberta-base. Accessed 26 Aug 2024
31. Kingma, D., Ba, J.: Adam: a method for stochastic optimization. In: proceeding of the 3rd International Conference on Learning Representations (ICLR) , San Diego, USA (2015)
32. Hugging Face - spaCy - en-core-web-sm Model. https://huggingface.co/spacy/en_core_web_sm. Accessed 26 Aug 2024
33. SpaCy - Initialize Method. https://spacy.io/api/language#initialize. Accessed 26 Aug 2024
34. Hugging Face - Sentence Transformers. https://huggingface.co/sentence-transformers. Accessed 09 June 2024

Combined Text-Visual Attention Models for Robot Task Learning and Execution

Giuseppe Rauso$^{(\boxtimes)}$, Riccardo Caccavale$^{(\boxtimes)}$, and Alberto Finzi$^{(\boxtimes)}$

University of Naples Federico II, Naples, Italy
{giuseppe.rauso,riccardo.caccavale,alberto.finzi}@unina.it

Abstract. In this work, we explore the interplay between text and visual attention mechanisms in a robot reinforcement learning setting, where robotic tasks are conveyed through natural language instructions. Specifically, we propose a novel approach aimed at enhancing robot task learning and execution by leveraging an integrated multimodal attention model that associates task-relevant environmental features with related words in the natural language mission text. We illustrate the overall framework architecture along with the learning process, emphasizing the interaction between textual and visual feature-based attention mechanisms. The method is trained in MiniGrid environments using the Proximal Policy Optimization algorithm, and its performance is evaluated by comparing the proposed architecture with a baseline that lacks attentional mechanisms. Experimental results demonstrate the efficacy of the approach also highlighting its potential in behavior transparency.

Keywords: Language Conditioned Reinforcement Learning ·
Multi-modal Attention · Behavior Transparency · Robot Task Learning

1 Introduction

This work presents a novel approach for enhancing robot task learning and execution through the integration of combined text and visual attention models. The concept of attention, extensively studied in cognitive neuroscience, underpins various cognitive models introduced to explain different behaviors, ranging from active perception to cognitive control, with visual attention being the most examined form. Attention models and mechanisms have been also widely adopted and utilized in the field of artificial intelligence, with particular success in machine learning. This is primarily due to the ability to improve performance and accelerate training in many cases, also making the development of models more efficient. In particular, attention mechanisms in transformers have revolutionized the field of natural language processing (NLP) by enabling models to weigh the relevance of different words in sentences contextually, thus capturing long-range dependencies and interrelated patterns in texts.

In this work, we investigate the interaction between text and visual attention models in a reinforcement learning setting, where robotic agents are instructed

© The Author(s), under exclusive license to Springer Nature Switzerland AG 2025
A. Artale et al. (Eds.): AIxIA 2024, LNAI 15450, pp. 228–240, 2025.
https://doi.org/10.1007/978-3-031-80607-0_18

to accomplish tasks specified by natural language sentences. We address this issue within a language conditioned reinforcement learning setting, where joint representations of observation and textual representations are typically used to enhance policy generalization and transferability to novel/unseen environments [1,19–21] or to enhance learning from human demonstration [8]. In this context, we assume textually specified mission goals and train the robotic agent to generate and exploit a combined multimodal attention model, where task-relevant words in the mission description are mapped into related salient visual features detected by the agent. This is achieved in a reinforcement learning setting by training the agent to generate and exploit word-related attention maps, which are suitably combined to coherently relate textual description with visual features and effectively orient the agent behavior. Such attention mechanisms are intended to support the agent's ability to focus solely on objects that correspond to the words present in the given mission, thereby enhancing the effectiveness of task learning and execution. Moreover, the alignment between salient visual features and task-relevant words aims to support the transparency of the agent's attentional behavior during task execution. We address these issues by proposing an integrated framework endowed with combined attention mechanisms, which is trained to accomplish simple tasks in MiniGrid environments using the Proximal Policy Optimization algorithm. We illustrate and discuss the overall architecture along with the learning process, emphasizing the interaction between textual and visual attention models. The approach is evaluated by comparing the proposed system with a baseline framework that lacks attentional mechanisms.The evaluation also includes assessing the quality of word-feature associations in the generated attention maps. The experimental results demonstrate the advantage of our approach in terms of efficacy and transparency.

2   Related Work

Over the years, various models of attentional mechanisms have been proposed in the context of machine learning, primarily inspired by studies derived from neuroscience [13]. Indeed, models of this type have been used in various contexts, including image and video classification and captioning [15,23], translation [5,26], and even in combination with text for question answering [3,4]. Attention mechanisms have also been used in the context of reinforcement learning, as in [25], where the *Deep Attention Recurrent Q-Network* (DARQN) is proposed, adding a soft attention and a hard attention to the *Recurrent Deep Q-Network* (RDQN) [12], or in [18], where a soft attention mechanism is used to highlight the task-relevant features of the frames in combination with the *Deep Q-Network* (DQN) [16]. In this cases, the saliency maps are learned exclusively through rewards and highlight the most important visual features in a given frame that the agent needs to focus on. In [10], a multi-attention mechanism is proposed, which is used in parallel on different segments of sensory inputs for navigation in a grid environment. This approach allows the model to focus on smaller parts of the input, achieving greater sample efficiency during learning. In the literature, we also find applications of the *self-attention* mechanism in a reinforcement learning context, such as [14], where the Markovian property underlying reinforcement learning is leveraged to achieve spatio-temporal attention, or in [27], where self-attention is used to calculate the relationships between observed entities. Other works, however, have studied the application of attention mechanisms that leverage different sources, thus making it no longer a "self" attention. This is the case in [17], where the query vectors are produced from the output of an LSTM layer, while the key and value vectors are produced from the encoding of the visual observation. However, in our work, we aim to study the interactions between natural language and what the agent observes in the environment. In the field of *language conditioned reinforcement learning*, several works have explored this possibility to define goals or instructions, such as in [1,2,20,21], also leveraging gated attention mechanisms [11], and combining images and text in the calculation of attention [19]. Indeed, the idea of directly comparing the representation of text with what the agent perceives to achieve *multimodal attention*, as seen in [19], aligns closely with the concept underlying this work. However, their goals are fundamentally different; they focus on conceptual reinforcement learning where, besides maximizing reward, the objective is to extract concepts from entities in the environment based on textual scene descriptions. In our case, the text provided to the agent represents the goal, and the aim is to demonstrate how words in the task are mapped to what the agent observes in the environment. This involves creating attention maps and weights for each word, thereby enhancing both the agent's performance and the interpretability of the relationships between the text and observations developed during training using only the reward as a feedback.

3   Proposed Approach

We assume a robot task learning problem, where goals are provided in natural language. In this setting, we propose an approach based on multimodal attention mechanisms that leverages both the observed features and the words of the sentence representing the task. Our goal here is twofold: beyond enhancing the learning and execution process, our aim is to simultaneously ground the words to the associated observed features (related to objects and their characteristics, such as colors) through per-word attentional maps and weights. As a side effect, the proposed method allows for an additional level of transparency in the agent's behavior, as text attention and feature attention values are trained to be aligned and related to the task under execution. The proposed architecture is end-to-end, and both the execution of tasks and the learning of attentional maps, crucial for achieving better performance, occur solely through the reward obtained in the environment. We operate within a reinforcement learning context and employ the *Proximal Policy Optimization* (PPO) [22] algorithm for training. In the following we detail the proposed method.

3.1   Minigrid Environment

We demonstrate our approach in environments defined in *BabyAI* [8], a platform based on *MiniGrid* [9] that features grid-based simulated scenarios and tasks (see Fig. 1) formulated using a subset of a synthetic language called *Baby language*. This language is a small subset of English but is combinatorially rich; indeed, although intentionally kept simple, it contains 2.48×10^{19} possible instructions. These instructions include tasks such as reaching, picking up, opening doors, and placing objects next to others, as well as combinations like the "and" of two tasks or a sequence (before/after). In this work, we use only instructions of the type "go to <Descr>" and "pick up <Descr>," where <Descr> describes the object with an article, color (including none), and type of object. Therefore, possible sentences in the environments used for this study include phrases like "go to the red key", "pick up a box", "go to the ball".

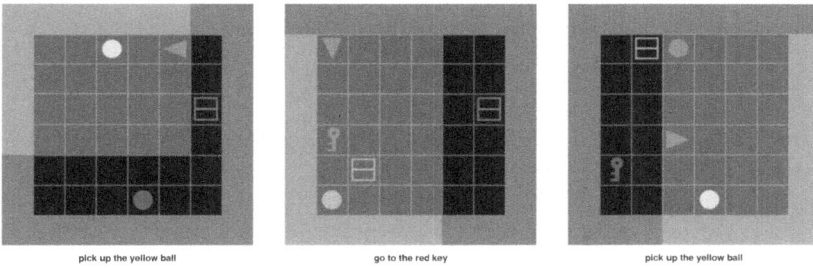

Fig. 1. Examples of MiniGrid environments used for this work, featuring "go to" and "pick up" tasks.

3.2   Background

We frame our approach in the context of a reinforcement learning problem, where the agent interacts with the environment to maximize cumulative reward. Formally, at each time step t, the agent is in some state $s_t \in S$ and chooses the next action $a_t \in A$ based on a policy π that can be deterministic, defined as $\pi : S \rightarrow A$, or stochastic, thereby determining a probability $\pi(a_t|s_t)$. The agent receives a reward r_{t+1} according to a reward function $R : S \times A \rightarrow \mathbb{R}$. Then, with a probability $p(s_{t+1}|s_t, a_t)$ it moves to the next state s_{t+1}. In particular, the environments are created based on the MiniGrid environments and associated with goal-augmented *Partially Observable Markov Decision Processes* (POMDPs), formally described by the tuple $(S, A, \Omega, p, R, G, O, \gamma)$, where Ω is the observation space, O the probabilistic observation model, G the goal space and γ the discount factor. The reward function thus becomes a goal-conditioned reward function $R : S \times A \times G \rightarrow \mathbb{R}$. We use PPO to solve the problem, which is an on-policy policy gradient algorithm that maximizes the following objective:

$$L^{CLIP}(\theta) = \hat{\mathbb{E}}_t[\min(r_t(\theta)\hat{A}_t, \text{clip}(r_t(\theta), 1 - \epsilon, 1 + \epsilon)\hat{A}_t)] \tag{1}$$

where ϵ is a hyperparameter, $\hat{A}_t$ is an estimator of the advantage function at timestep t, measuring the value of the selected action compared to the expected value of the state, $r_t(\theta) = \frac{\pi_\theta(a_t|s_t)}{\pi_{\theta_{old}}(a_t|s_t)}$ is the ratio between the new and old policies π parametrized by θ and θ_{old} respectively. This objective penalizes overly abrupt changes in the policy, aiming to keep the ratio $r_t(\theta)$ from deviating too much from 1. We rely on the original version of the approach [22] where the overall objective function is formulated as follows:

$$L_t^{\text{PPO}}(\theta) = \hat{\mathbb{E}}_t[L_t^{\text{CLIP}}(\theta) - c_1 L_t^{\text{VF}}(\theta) + c_2 S[\pi_\theta](s_t)] \tag{2}$$

with c_1, c_2, c_3 coefficients, S an entropy bonus, and $L_t^{\text{VF}} = (V_\theta(s_t) - V_t^{\text{targ}})^2$.

3.3   System Architecture and Learning Framework

The system we propose takes as input the features observed in the agent's field of view along with the mission defined in natural language and generates the associated policy exploiting world-related attention maps. The learning framework is detailed as follows (see Fig. 2). Let $O \in \mathbb{R}^{f_h \times f_w \times 3}$ and $g \in \mathbb{R}^m$ be, respectively, the portion of the grid observed by the agent (field of view) with height and width f_h and f_w, and m the maximum length (in words) of the task specification. We define $\tilde{O} = Conv(O)$ as the encoding of the observation through a convolutional network, and $\tilde{g} = Embedding(g)$ as the embedding of the task tokens. Let $\tilde{O}_{\text{flatten}}$ denote the flattening of the feature maps outputted by the convolutional network, transitioning from shape (K_{out}, f_h, f_w) to $(f_h \cdot f_w, K_{out})$, where K_{out} is number of filters used in the last convolutional layer. Drawing inspiration from the *scaled dot-product attention* mechanism with query, key, and value proposed in [26], we obtain the attention matrix

$$A = \text{softmax}\left(\frac{QK^T}{\sqrt{d_k}}\right) \tag{3}$$

where Q and K are, respectively, the projection of the embedding of the task (or mission) $\tilde{g}$ and the encoding of the observation $\tilde{O}_{\text{flatten}}$ onto a space of dimension d_k. By reshaping the rows of this matrix back to a shape of (f_h, f_w), we obtain m attention maps, one for each word. Each of these maps highlights the cells related to the corresponding word in the portion of the grid observed by the agent (see Fig. 3). However, we consider the attention maps as row vectors of A for the subsequent formalizations. To amplify or reduce the signal in relevant positions in the observed feature map based on the mission words, instead of directly multiplying A by a matrix of values (as in [26]), we propose the alternative method detailed below. We aim to derive attention weights for individual words based on what the agent is observing. Specifically, we want to determine which words are more "salient" for the portion of the grid that the agent is observing.

To this end, we compute the *Shannon entropy* [24] on the rows of the matrix A, which represent categorical distributions:

$$\forall i = 1, \ldots, m, \qquad H(A_i) = -\sum_{j=1}^{f_h \cdot f_w} A_{ij} \cdot \log A_{ij} \tag{4}$$

To obtain the attention weights for individual words, we apply the softmax to the negated entropy vector:

$$w = \text{softmax}\left(\begin{bmatrix} -H(A_1) \\ \vdots \\ -H(A_m) \end{bmatrix}\right) \tag{5}$$

Finally, to obtain the attention map, we calculate the weighted sum of the m rows of the matrix A, where the weights are the entropies obtained for each row:

$$M = \sum_{i=1}^{m} w_i \cdot A_i \tag{6}$$

This map M is applied to each feature map to highlight only the cells that represent some element in the mission text:

$$\forall i = 1, \ldots, f_h \cdot f_w, \qquad F_i = \tilde{O}_{\text{flatten}}^i \cdot M_i \tag{7}$$

Thus, by assessing the word-cell relevance, we effectively exploit a multimodal attention mechanism. The filtered feature maps are then fed into an LSTM recurrent layer, enabling the agent to operate in a partially observable environment. The output of this layer is concatenated with the output of a GRU recurrent layer that processes the mission text.

4   Empirical Evaluation

The proposed framework is assessed considering both the system performance and the quality of the word-feature grounding in the generated attention maps. We assess the effectiveness of the multimodal attention system by comparing its performance during both training and testing phases with a baseline system lacking attention mechanisms. Specifically, the baseline is created by removing the Attention Module (see the dotted box in Fig. 2) and directly passing the convolutional network encoding $\tilde{O}_{\text{flatten}}$ to the LSTM recurrent network, while concatenating the output with the text encoding from the GRU recurrent network which receives the word embeddings $\tilde{g}$.

4.1   Training

To train the agents we employed an environment defined by a single 8×8 room without walls (except for the perimeter ones) containing 4 randomly chosen and

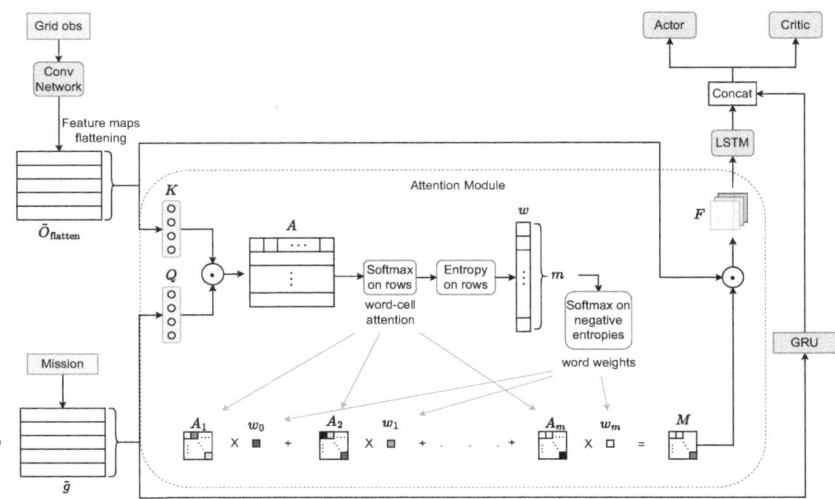

Fig. 2. System architecture. The components of the attention module are enclosed within the turquoise dotted box. The attention maps $A_1, \ldots, A_m$ are displayed as matrix form for clarity, but they are row vectors of matrix A as detailed in Sect. 3.3.

colored objects. For each task, one object is to be reached or picked up, while the other 3 are distractors. We use the observation encoding proposed with the MiniGrid environments, namely a 7×7 grid with 3 channels, representing the agent's field of view, where each cell of the grid is encoded as a tuple *(object id, object color, object state)*. The reward function follows the framework's default environment settings, providing a reward ranging from 0 to 1 only at the end of the episode based on the steps taken to complete the task; in case of failure, the reward is 0. We use the 'done' action to prompt the agent to recognize when it has successfully completed an episode-ending action, such as reaching a specific object (in the case of 'go to') or picking up an object (in the case of 'pick up'). However, the agent can still pick up objects without issuing a 'done' action, for example, to clear obstacles from its path. The agents were trained for 15 million steps in the described environment. The evolution of the average reward can be observed in Fig. 4, where the model without attention converges to a lower value and exhibits significant instability compared to the model with attention.

4.2 Testing

After training, we can evaluate the performance of the proposed framework and the accuracy of the trained attentional mechanisms in word-feature grounding.

Performance. The performance of the proposed framework is compared to a setup without attention. The evaluation is conducted across various environments with different dimensions and numbers of objects to assess the models'

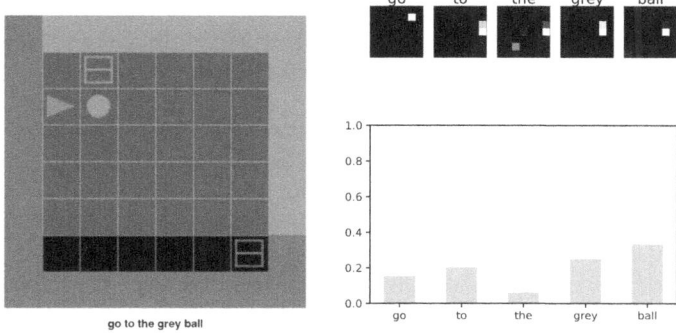

Fig. 3. Snapshot of the grid scenario (left) with the associated per-word attention maps (Top right) and the word weights w (Bottom right). The per-word maps are agent-centric with the agent positioned in the middle of the right side, facing left, with the positions of objects relative to the agent mirrored along the vertical axis. In this case, the agent must complete task described by the phrase "go to the grey ball". (Color figure online)

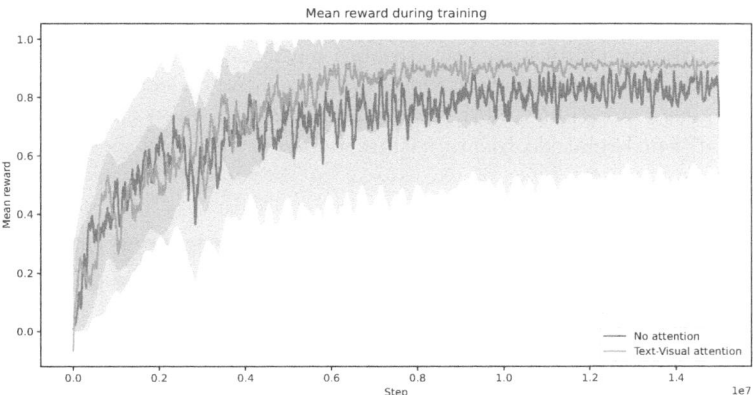

Fig. 4. Evolution of the reward for the model with attention and the one without attention during training.

robustness in larger settings. These environments present greater challenges, as agents operate with a more limited field of view and encounter additional distractors. Figure 6 shows the average reward and success rate over 100 episodes, averaged across 5 different seeds for both agents. The collected results demonstrate the robustness of the agent equipped with the multimodal attention mechanisms compared to the agent without attention. Indeed, the former experiences a significantly smaller decline in performance as the number of distractors increases. In the most challenging scenarios, it maintains a mean reward between 0.8 and 0.85 and around a 90% success rate. In contrast, the model without attention experiences a more significant performance drop, showing that the proposed attentional approach not only enhances performance, but also improves generalization and robustness to environmental changes.

Accuracy Evaluation. To evaluate the quality of the generated attention maps, we aim to measure how well the system places higher values in the maps at the positions of the visible objects referred by the words in the mission specification. As illustrated in Sect. 3.3, each word ω in the mission text is associated with an attention map A^ω. For each word ω, we can also identify n_ω related objects in the agent's field of view (e.g., the words "red" is associated with n_{red} visible objects). We refer to $A^\omega_{x_i,y_i}$ as the value of the A^ω attention map at the coordinates (x_i, y_i), representing the actual position of the i-th visible object. Given a set of objects in the agent field of view, the accuracy of the attention map A^ω can be defined as follows:

$$ \text{acc}_\omega = \frac{\sum_i^{n_\omega} \text{p}_i^\omega}{n_\omega} \quad \text{with} \quad \text{p}_i^\omega = \begin{cases} 1 & \text{if } A^\omega_{x_i,y_i} \geq \alpha \frac{1}{n_\omega} \\ 0 & \text{otherwise} \end{cases} \tag{8} $$

where $\frac{\alpha}{n_\omega}$ is a threshold to determine whether the object is correctly detected (hit) or not (miss). Here, $\alpha \in [0, 1]$ is a parameter representing a percentage of $\frac{1}{n_\omega}$. This fraction calibrates the threshold with respect to the total weight of the map divided by the number of visible word-related objects, representing the value an object's position would have in an attention map that assigns equal weights to all word-related objects within the agent's field of view.

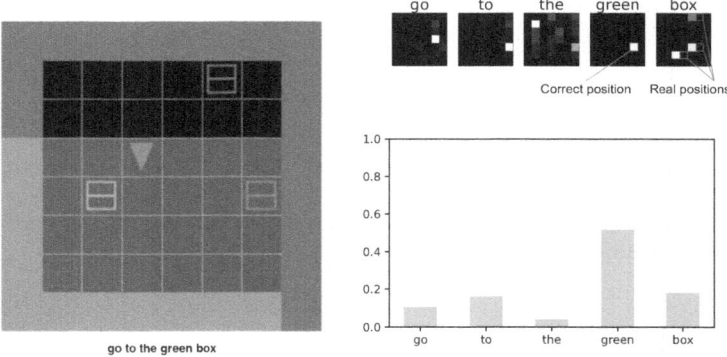

Fig. 5. During the execution of "go to the green box" the agent highlights salient task-related values aligning text salience (bottom right) and attention maps (top right). Here, the green box is correctly related and emphasized, while the box position shifted forward by one. (Color figure online)

The accuracy measure introduced above assesses the system's ability to correlate words with the precise target positions. To relax this notion, we introduce variations of this accuracy measure accounting for hits near the target. In this regard, we introduce the accuracy measure in the neighborhood of the object's position $acc_{\omega,ng}$ that evaluates whether in the attention map there is at least one cell that exceeds the threshold in the proximity of the object position. This is defined as follows.

$$acc_{\omega,ng} = \frac{\sum_i^{n_\omega} p_{i,ng}^\omega}{n_\omega} \quad \text{with} \quad p_{i,ng}^\omega = \begin{cases} 1 & \text{if } \exists(k,z) \in ng(x_i,y_i) : A_{k,z}^\omega \geq \alpha\frac{1}{n_\omega} \\ 0 & \text{otherwise} \end{cases}$$

$$(9)$$

where $ng(x_i, y_i)$ is the set of coordinate pairs of positions surrounding the real position of the object, meaning the positions at distance 1 in each direction. However, during the experiments, we noticed biased directions for displacements in the object proximity, i.e., shifted one step forward from the actual position in the agent's visual field of view (see Fig. 5). To account for these small biases we introduce a more focused accuracy assessment in the target's neighborhood where the hits are shifted in some direction. In particular, we focus on hits with a forward shift as the bias:

$$acc_{\omega,bs} = \frac{\sum_i^{n_\omega} p_{i,bs}^\omega}{n_\omega} \quad \text{with} \quad p_{i,bs}^\omega = \begin{cases} 1 & \text{if } A_{x_i,\overline{y_i}}^\omega \geq \alpha\frac{1}{n_\omega} \\ 0 & \text{otherwise} \end{cases} \quad (10)$$

where $\overline{y}$ is the shifted coordinate. Then, we can measure the accuracy $acc_{\omega,cmb}$ of the combined hit of the actual and shifted positions of the target objects:

$$acc_{\omega,cmb} = \frac{\sum_i^{n_\omega} p_{i,cmb}^\omega}{n_\omega} \quad \text{with} \quad p_{i,cmb}^\omega = \begin{cases} p_i^\omega \vee p_{i,bs}^\omega & \text{if } y_i > 0 \\ p_i^\omega & \text{otherwise} \end{cases} \quad (11)$$

Accuracy Results. To assess the system performance we focus on words related to the objects and colors using the accuracy measures introduced above. During testing, we evaluate the maps only when at least one object of the type/color mentioned in the mission sentence is in the agent's field of view. For the accuracy measures we set $\alpha = 0.5$, averaging the results over the number of evaluation step for each episode (i.e., a task mission). We further average the collected values over 100 episodes and across executions with 5 different seeds. The results are provided in Fig. 7 for the object-related maps and in Fig. 8 for the color-related maps. For these cases, we illustrate the accuracy values as the the grid dimension and the number of objects increase. The accuracy in the neighborhood $acc_{\omega,ng}$ (green line in Fig. 7 and 8), as expected, is higher than the others, ranging from over 90% to around 80%. However, the combined accuracy $acc_{\omega,cmb}$ (red line in Fig. 7) remains close, with a slight degradation as the number of objects -and distractors- increases. Therefore, the agent remains capable of correlating colors and objects with their associated positions in the attention maps, despite a fixed bias that occasionally shifts objects and colors forward. We can also observe that this shift is more evident for the object-related maps (see Fig. 7), where the accuracy of the actual position acc_ω (dotted blue line) is lower than the shifted accuracy $acc_{\omega,bs}$ (dotted orange line). On the other hand, higher acc_ω values can be

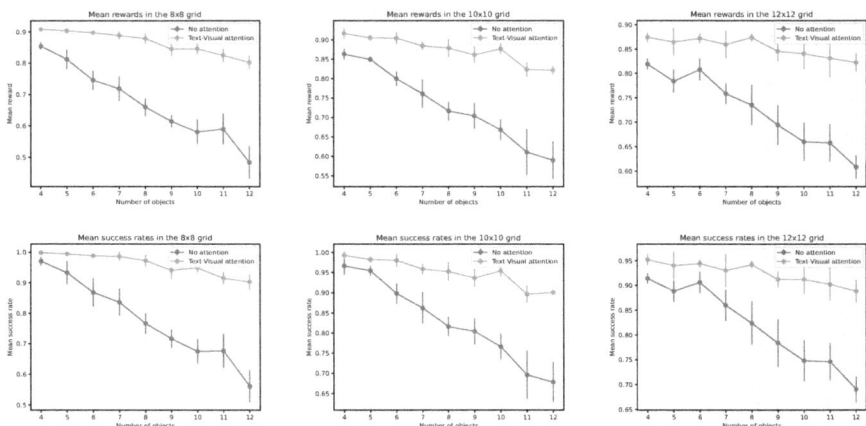

Fig. 6. Average reward (first row) and success rate (second row) with standard deviations in the test phase over 100 episodes, averaged over 5 seeds for both the model with attention and the model without attention varying with the number of objects and grid size.

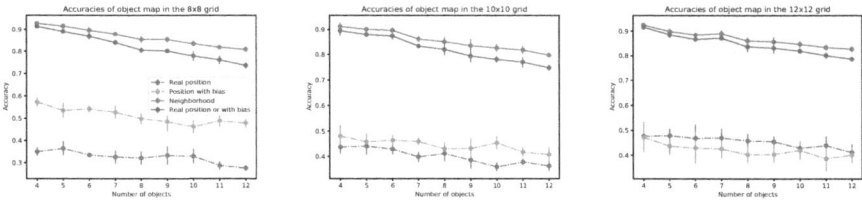

Fig. 7. Mean and standard deviation of the accuracies for the object attention maps described in Sect. 4.2, averaged over 100 episodes and then averaged across 5 seeds, varying with the number of objects and grid size.

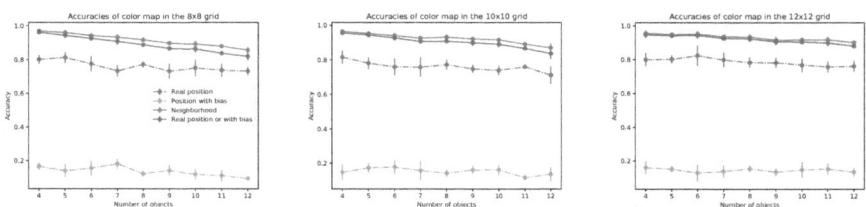

Fig. 8. Mean and standard deviation of the accuracies for the color attention maps described in Sect. 4.2, averaged over 100 episodes and then averaged across 5 seeds, varying with the number of objects and grid size.

observed for the color-related attention maps (see Fig. 8). Here the values range between 80% and 70%, with a relatively stable performance as the number of objects increases. Overall, the accuracy evaluation shows the system's capability to correlate objects, colors, and values in the word-related attentional maps.

This ability is maintained even in increasingly complex scenarios not accounted for during training. The generated attention maps can then establish a coherent alignment between saliency in the linguistic and feature domains, providing insights about the agent's attentional focus during task execution.

5 Conclusions

We presented a novel approach to task learning, with agents instructed in natural language, that leverages multimodal attention mechanisms aligning mission words and observations relevance. Specifically, in the proposed method the agent is trained to generate per-word attention maps, thereby grounding the task words along with their relevance in the environmental observations. We show that the generated attention maps not only enhance learning and execution performance, but also provide an additional level of transparency in the agents attentional behavior, in that key words from input sentences guide the agent during task execution, enabling focused interactions with specific features and locations within the environment grid. The empirical results demonstrate the advantage of the approach in terms of average reward and success rate compared to the architecture without the proposed mechanisms. Moreover, the study on word-feature association shows the system ability to ground relevant words in the environment with high accuracy. In future work, we aim to investigate the robustness of the proposed attentional mechanisms in more complex scenarios and with more structured tasks. We plan to explore the feasibility of incremental learning, starting with simpler tasks to establish the grounding of words in the environment, as proposed in this study. Subsequently, we will leverage this capability to learn more complex tasks, in these settings, we intend to explore the integration of executive attentional mechanisms [6] suitable for flexible task orchestration [7].

Acknowledgments. This work was partially supported by the projects: EU Horizon INVERSE (grant 101136067) and euROBIN (grant 101070596), Melody (PRIN PNRR prot. P2022XALNS), SPACE IT UP (PE15 ASI/MUR).

References

1. Akakzia, A., Colas, C., Oudeyer, P.Y., Chetouani, M., Sigaud, O.: Grounding language to autonomously-acquired skills via goal generation. arXiv:2204.04308 (2021)
2. Anderson, P., et al.: Vision-and-language navigation: Interpreting visually-grounded navigation instructions in real environments. arXiv:1711.07280 (2018)
3. Andreas, J., Rohrbach, M., Darrell, T., Klein, D.: Learning to compose neural networks for question answering. arXiv:1601.01705 (2016)
4. Andreas, J., Rohrbach, M., Darrell, T., Klein, D.: Neural module networks. arXiv:1511.02799 (2017)
5. Bahdanau, D., Cho, K., Bengio, Y.: Neural machine translation by jointly learning to align and translate. arXiv:1409.0473 (2016)

6. Caccavale, R., Finzi, A.: Learning attentional regulations for structured tasks execution in robotic cognitive control. Auton. Robot. **43**, 2229–2243 (2019)
7. Caccavale, R., Finzi, A.: A robotic cognitive control framework for collaborative task execution and learning. Top. Cogn. Sci. **14**(2), 327–343 (2022)
8. Chevalier-Boisvert, M., et al.: Babyai: A platform to study the sample efficiency of grounded language learning. arXiv:1810.08272 (2019)
9. Chevalier-Boisvert, M., et al.: Minigrid & miniworld: Modular i& customizable reinforcement learning environments for goal-oriented tasks. arXiv:2306.13831 (2023)
10. Choi, J., Lee, B.J., Zhang, B.T.: Multi-focus attention network for efficient deep reinforcement learning. ArXiv **abs/1712.04603** (2017). https://api.semanticscholar.org/CorpusID:3824441
11. Colas, C., et al.: Language as a cognitive tool to imagine goals in curiosity-driven exploration. arXiv:2002.09253 (2020)
12. Hausknecht, M., Stone, P.: Deep recurrent q-learning for partially observable mdps. arXiv:1507.06527 (2017)
13. Lindsay, G.W.: Attention in psychology, neuroscience, and machine learning. Front. Comput. Neurosci. **14** (2020). https://doi.org/10.3389/fncom.2020.00029, https://www.frontiersin.org/articles/10.3389/fncom.2020.00029
14. Manchin, A., Abbasnejad, E., van den Hengel, A.: Reinforcement learning with attention that works: A self-supervised approach. arXiv:1904.03367 (2019)
15. Mnih, V., Heess, N., Graves, A., Kavukcuoglu, K.: Recurrent models of visual attention. arXiv:1406.6247 (2014)
16. Mnih, V., et al.: Human-level control through deep reinforcement learning. Nature **518**, 529–533 (2015). https://api.semanticscholar.org/CorpusID:205242740
17. Mott, A., Zoran, D., Chrzanowski, M., Wierstra, D., Rezende, D.J.: Towards interpretable reinforcement learning using attention augmented agents. arXiv:1906.02500 (2019)
18. Mousavi, S., Schukat, M., Howley, E., Borji, A., Mozayani, N.: Learning to predict where to look in interactive environments using deep recurrent q-learning. arXiv:1612.05753 (2017)
19. Peng, S., et al.: Conceptual reinforcement learning for language-conditioned tasks. arXiv:2303.05069 (2023)
20. Röder, F., Eppe, M.: Language-conditioned reinforcement learning to solve misunderstandings with action corrections. arXiv:2211.10168 (2022)
21. Röder, F., Eppe, M., Wermter, S.: Grounding hindsight instructions in multi-goal reinforcement learning for robotics. arXiv:2204.04308 (2022)
22. Schulman, J., Wolski, F., Dhariwal, P., Radford, A., Klimov, O.: Proximal policy optimization algorithms. arXiv:1707.06347 (2017)
23. Shan, M., Atanasov, N.: A spatiotemporal model with visual attention for video classification. arXiv:1707.02069 (2017)
24. Shannon, C.E.: A mathematical theory of communication. Bell Syst. Tech. J. **27**(3), 379–423 (1948). https://doi.org/10.1002/j.1538-7305.1948.tb01338.x
25. Sorokin, I., Seleznev, A., Pavlov, M., Fedorov, A., Ignateva, A.: Deep attention recurrent q-network. arXiv:1512.01693 (2015)
26. Vaswani, A., et al.: Attention is all you need. arXiv:1706.03762 (2023)
27. Zambaldi, V.F., et al.: Deep reinforcement learning with relational inductive biases. In: International Conference on Learning Representations (2018). https://api.semanticscholar.org/CorpusID:59233950

ICE: An Evaluation Metric to Assess Symbolic Knowledge Quality

Federico Sabbatini[1]([⊠]) and Roberta Calegari[2]([⊠])

[1] University of Urbino, Urbino, Italy
f.sabbatini1@campus.uniurb.it
[2] University of Bologna, Bologna, Italy
roberta.calegari@unibo.it

Abstract. The automated assessment of symbolic knowledge, derived, for instance, from extraction procedures, facilitates the autotuning of machine learning algorithms, obviating inherent biases in subjective human evaluations. Despite advancements, comprehensive metrics for evaluating knowledge quality are missing in the literature. To address this gap, our study introduces ICE, a novel evaluation metric designed to measure the quality of symbolic knowledge. This metric computes a score by considering three quality sub-indices, namely, predictive performance, human readability and completeness, and it can be tailored to suit the specific requirements of the case at hand by adjusting the weights assigned to each sub-index. We present here the mathematical formulation of the ICE score, and show its effectiveness through comparative analyses with existing quality scores applied to real-world tasks.

Keywords: Explainable artificial intelligence · Symbolic knowledge extraction · AutoML

1 Introduction

In the current landscape of artificial intelligence (AI), symbolic knowledge extraction (SKE) has gained widespread utilisation to address the interpretability challenges associated with sub-symbolic AI, characterised by efficacy in predictions, but often relying on complex models which pose challenges in terms of interpretability and explainability [14,33]. SKE methodologies involve knowledge extraction from "black-box" models [15,18], aiming to construct surrogate symbolic representations. These techniques play a crucial role in enhancing the interpretability and explainability of machine learning (ML) models, enabling human understanding and trust in decision-making processes.

The literature on SKE techniques emphasises the absence of universally optimum solutions [3,6,7,26,28,34,36,37]. This inherent variability necessitates the systematic exploration of multiple SKE techniques to select the optimum approach for a given case. The extracted knowledge quality is linked to factors such as data distribution, pre-processing strategies, and feature selection techniques.

A. Artale et al. (Eds.): AIxIA 2024, LNAI 15450, pp. 241–256, 2025.
https://doi.org/10.1007/978-3-031-80607-0_19

Consequently, a rigorous evaluation of the knowledge is imperative to compare the efficacy of diverse techniques within the specific context of interest. Assessing the quality of knowledge derived through SKE involves several indices, including accuracy, completeness, and readability [10,20,39]. However, manual evaluation of these indices is time-consuming and subject to subjective biases. Automation of this evaluation process aligns with an automated machine learning (AutoML) perspective [13], offering efficiency and objectivity in the selection of suitable SKE techniques.

While recent efforts have introduced metrics for automated evaluation, these metrics remain limited in scope, lacking the comprehensive coverage of necessary evaluation criteria and the integration of user feedback and customisation. Accordingly, in this paper we propose the Index for Complete quality Evaluation (ICE) as a scoring metric designed to comprehensively evaluate knowledge quality. ICE aims to advance the state of the art by facilitating the automated evaluation and comparison of symbolic knowledge, providing a complete, objective and quantitative assessment of the outputs from SKE procedures.

2   Related Works and Background Notions

SKE techniques currently find application in addressing a diverse exhibition of real-world challenges, particularly in critical domains where interpretability and human comprehension are imperative [2,11]. These methods typically yield knowledge outputs represented symbolically, facilitating interpretable predictions. The literature encompasses numerous SKE techniques, necessitating the execution of various experiments to identify optimum approaches. The comparison of different outcomes – i.e., the knowledge extracted – is essential in this selection process to select the best approach.

Existing literature widely recognises that knowledge quality can be assessed based on predictive performance, human readability, and completeness [1,7,12, 19,35,40]. The results of these evaluations depend on both the chosen SKE algorithm and the user-defined parameters controlling the algorithm's behaviour. Consequently, comparisons can be conducted not only between distinct extraction procedures, but also between instances of the same extractor with varying parametrisations. For knowledge to be deemed of high quality, it must concurrently exhibit superior predictive performance, human readability, and completeness. Predictive performance concerns the knowledge's ability to provide accurate outputs. Readability quantifies the human effort required to comprehend the rationale behind the predictions. Completeness measures the proportion of predictions that the knowledge can provide in response to user queries. The conventional approach to knowledge comparisons typically involves a manual examination of individual quality indices. However, such a method is susceptible to human subjectivity (and possible biases) and lacks the capability for automated assessments. Moreover, the comparison of a set of knowledge is straightforward when there exists a candidate knowledge that maximises all three indices, rendering it the optimum knowledge within the set. Regrettably, real-world applications often present a fidelity/readability trade-off, wherein a comparison is made between knowledge exhibiting high predictive performance but limited readability and knowledge characterised by enhanced human readability but diminished predictive performance [17]. In such scenarios, selecting the best knowledge necessitates a thorough consideration of all three quality indices, free from human bias or material errors. Nonetheless, it remains crucial to offer human users the ability to assign appropriate weights to different quality indices, enabling adaptation of the comparison to the sensitivity and objectives of the given task. This is particularly relevant in situations where the emphasis may vary, such as instances where predictive performance is prioritised over readability, as opposed to scenarios where readability is an imperative consideration.

To the best of our knowledge, to date, only two metrics have been established for the explicit purpose of evaluating the knowledge quality: FIRE [24] and Q_s [27]. FIRE, while overlooking knowledge completeness in its quality assessment, allows for the incorporation of a user-defined parameter to adjust the importance of knowledge readability and predictive performance, respectively. The metric is as a multiplicative scoring function, considering predictive performance and human readability as "losses", i.e., predictive loss as predictive error and readability loss as knowledge size. Consequently, smaller FIRE scores are indicative of higher knowledge quality, given that losses are essentially multiplied. Similarly, Q_s is grounded in the multiplication of index losses. Noteworthy distinctions from FIRE lie in the inclusion of knowledge completeness loss and the exclusion of user-defined capabilities to adjust relative loss weights. No other metrics evaluating symbolic knowledge quality have been proposed in the literature. Consequently, a comprehensive metric is lacking—one that incorporates predictive performance, human readability, and completeness indices while allowing for the customisation of their relative importance in overall score calculation.

Such a metric would serve as a foundational element for enabling an unbiased, standardised, and concise evaluation of symbolic knowledge quality. It would be also crucial for AutoML procedures, as it facilitates the automatic selection of high-quality symbolic knowledge representations, leading to more precise and efficient ML-based systems. Without such an evaluation metric, AutoML algorithms may inadvertently choose suboptimum symbolic knowledge representations, resulting in subpar model performance and resource wastage.

In this study we introduce ICE as a comprehensive scoring function addressing the current literature gap for knowledge quality assessment. The ICE score enhances the efficacy of previously introduced metrics (FIRE and Q_s) by incorporating all three indices from the literature to evaluate symbolic knowledge (predictive performance, readability, and completeness). As a result it provides a quantitative assessment of knowledge quality, also empowering users to customise weight parameters, assigning varying importance to the three indices based on the task and user requirements. Consequently, different symbolic knowledge instances can be easily compared using the ICE metric.

Quality Indices. The evaluation of knowledge quality commonly relies on three primary indices: predictive performance, human-readability extent, and completeness [10,39]. Each index lacks a unique definition since it often depends on the task at hand. Predictive performance evaluation mirrors approaches applicable to black-box models or other predictors. The assessment may involve comparing the ground truth of a data set or the outputs of an opaque model emulated by the symbolic knowledge. Task-dependent evaluations prevail, with accuracy and F_1 scores being standard for classification tasks, while mean absolute/squared error (MAE/MSE) and the R^2 score are commonplace for regression tasks. Readability is often associated with knowledge size [8]. For instance, an SKE algorithm generating a list of n rules may be deemed more human-readable than another procedure presenting a list or tree with $2n$ rules or leaves. While readability information can extend to the complexity of individual knowledge items, quantitative and formal assessments of this complexity are currently unavailable. For example, comparing a tree leaf's readability describing an M-of-N logic rule to a decision table entry associated with a fuzzy rule lacks established techniques [24]. Consequently, knowledge size is generally considered sufficient to express readability due to its straightforward interpretation. Completeness is estimated as the percentage of the input feature space covered by the knowledge, representing the subspace where predictions can be made. In instances where this measurement proves impractical, such as data sets with a multitude of input features, completeness estimation can be achieved by querying the knowledge with a set of instances and calculating the percentage of provided responses.

3   The ICE Score

The ICE (Index for Complete quality Evaluation) score provides an evaluation encompassing predictive performance, human readability and completeness of the analysed knowledge. To achieve this goal the first two indices are squashed in the $(0, 1)$ open interval with a generalised sigmoid function (parametrised by the user) and then they are multiplied together and by the completeness index. The user-defined parameters used inside the generalised sigmoid functions enable the ICE score to assign a customised relative relevance to predictive performance and human readability. No parameters are required for the completeness importance since this latter is assumed equal to 1 by default to avoid an unnecessary complex score formulation. The completeness does not need to be normalised in the specified interval, because it is naturally expressed as a percentage, and thus it always lies within the $[0, 1]$ closed interval.

ICE is a multiplicative metric assuming that good quality knowledge is associated with high values of all the three underlying indices and, conversely, bad quality is associated with small values of at least one index. Therefore, the ICE score can assume values in the $[0, 1)$ half-open interval. Ideally, good knowledge should have ICE score as close as possible to 1. The ICE score is defined as the following continuous and differentiable function:

$$ICE : (\mathbb{R}_{\leq 1} \times \mathbb{R}_{>0} \times [0,1] \times \mathbb{R}_{>0} \times \mathbb{R}_{>0}) \mapsto [0,1), \tag{1}$$

$$ICE(p,\ r,\ c,\ \varphi,\ \rho) \quad = \quad P(p,\ \varphi) \cdot R(r,\ \rho) \cdot c, \tag{2}$$

where p, r and c are the raw knowledge predictive performance, size and completeness measurements, respectively, φ is the relative importance assigned to the raw predictive performance, and ρ is the one assigned to the knowledge size. $P(\cdot)$ and $R(\cdot)$ are the continuous and differentiable functions expressing the knowledge *accuracy* and *readability*, respectively, defined as follows:

$$P : (\mathbb{R}_{\leq 1} \times \mathbb{R}_{>0}) \mapsto (0,1), \tag{3}$$

$$P(p,\varphi) = \left(1 + e^{5(\varphi(1-p)-1)}\right)^{-1}, \tag{4}$$

$$R : (\mathbb{R}_{>0} \times \mathbb{R}_{>0}) \mapsto (0,1), \tag{5}$$

$$R(r,\rho) = \left(1 + e^{0.3\rho r - 5}\right)^{-1}. \tag{6}$$

The accuracy function $P(p,\varphi)$ used for the ICE calculation is an ad-hoc function representing the knowledge raw predictive performance p squashed in $(0,1)$ and weighted with respect to the user-defined importance parameter φ. Analogously, the readability function $R(r,\rho)$ squashes in the same interval the raw human-readability extent (i.e., the knowledge size) r and weights it according to the user-defined importance parameter ρ. Since the completeness importance is always considered equal to 1 in the ICE score calculation, users can act on the φ and ρ parameters to decide the relative importance of knowledge predictive performance and size with respect to each other and the completeness by selecting values smaller or larger than 1. If both φ and ρ are equal to 1, then the ICE score equally weights the three indices. The ICE score trend for different values of its parameters is reported in Fig. 1.

We point out that the fixed values used to parametrise the exponentials within the $P(\cdot)$ and $R(\cdot)$ functions have been carefully tuned to obtain "well-behaved" sigmoid functions suitable to be customised by users only by providing a single additional importance parameter. In this context, a well-behaved sigmoid *(i)* tends to 1 when representing desirable knowledge properties (e.g., high predictive performance or human readability), *(ii)* tends to 0 when denoting poor knowledge quality, and *(iii)* exhibits a growth rate tunable via a single user-defined parameter, representing the importance of the sigmoid function in the overall ICE score calculation. The fixed values of Eqs. (4) and (6) (e.g. 0.3, 5) were chosen after a thorough study of the aforementioned properties and utilizing optimisation tools that provide sigmoid curve fitting.

In the following, we analyse the ICE function domain, the properties of the accuracy and readability functions and those resulting in the ICE score.

3.1   ICE Function Domain

The ICE scoring function is defined in the domain reported in Eq. (1), given the following assumptions: (i) knowledge raw predictive performance (p) assessed

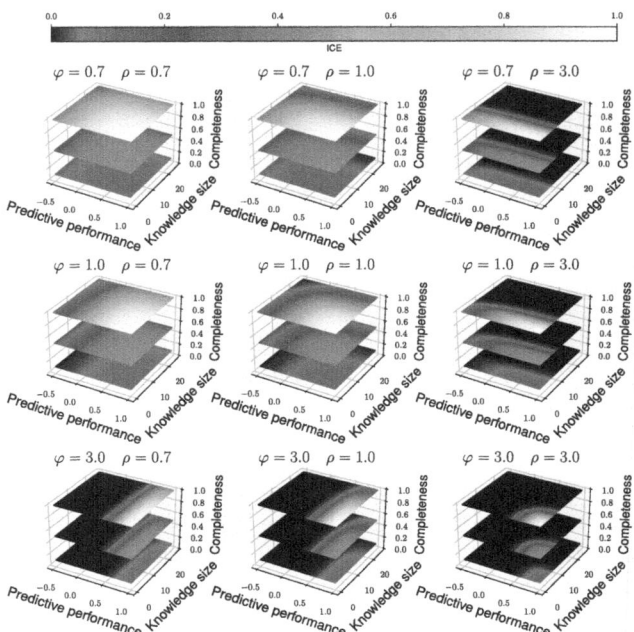

Fig. 1. ICE score for different values of knowledge predictive performance p (x-axis), size r (y-axis) and completeness c (z-axis), predictive performance importance φ (rows) and size importance ρ (columns). Different colours represent different ICE score values (top colourbar). (Color figure online)

via task-dependent scores equal to 1 in the best case, may have no lower-bound in the worst case; (ii) knowledge size (r) an integer number greater or equal to 1 (knowledge contains at least one item). To enhance score flexibility the corresponding considered range has been extended to all positive real numbers; (iii) knowledge coverage (c) expressed as a percentage and mapped in the $[0, 1]$ interval; (iv) predictive performance importance (φ) a positive real number by design; (v) knowledge size importance (ρ) a positive real number by design.

3.2   ICE Accuracy Function

ICE adopts the $P(\cdot)$ accuracy function shown in Eqs. (3) and (4) and depicted in the left panel of Fig. 2 to apply the user-defined weight φ to the raw predictive performance p measured for the knowledge. The left part of Fig. 3 reports the accuracy for different fixed values of the φ weight and the function's first and second partial derivatives with respect to p. The function is bounded in $(0, 1)$

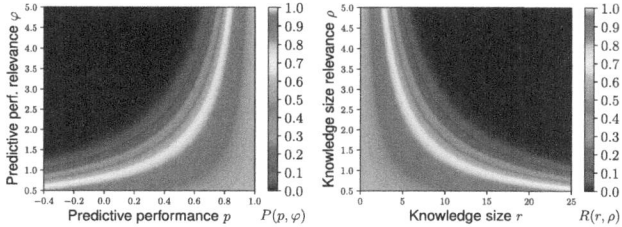

Fig. 2. ICE accuracy and readability function trends in their domains. Functions' input parameters are reported in the axes, the corresponding value is represented by the colour (small values are associated with dark colours).

for any possible value of p and φ. Indeed, from Eq. (4):

$$\lim_{p \to -\infty} P(p, \varphi) = 0, \quad \forall \varphi > 0, \tag{7}$$

$$\lim_{p \to 1} P(p, \varphi) = 1, \quad \forall \varphi > 0, \tag{8}$$

$$\lim_{\varphi \to \infty} P(p, \varphi) = 0, \quad \forall p < 1, \tag{9}$$

$$\lim_{\varphi \to 0} P(p, \varphi) = 1, \quad \forall p < 1. \tag{10}$$

The accuracy function is monotonically increasing with respect to p and decreasing with respect to φ, indeed:

$$0 \;<\; \frac{\partial P}{\partial p} \;=\; \frac{5\,\varphi\,e^{5(\varphi(1-p)-1)}}{\left(1 + e^{5(\varphi(1-p)-1)}\right)^2}, \tag{11}$$

$$0 \;>\; \frac{\partial P}{\partial \varphi} \;=\; -\frac{5\,(1-p)\,e^{5(\varphi(1-p)-1)}}{\left(1 + e^{5(\varphi(1-p)-1)}\right)^2}, \tag{12}$$

$$p_1 \;<\; p_2 \iff P(p_1, \varphi) < P(p_2, \varphi), \tag{13}$$

$$\varphi_1 \;<\; \varphi_2 \iff P(p, \varphi_1) > P(p, \varphi_2). \tag{14}$$

Equations from (11) to (14) hold $\forall p, p_1, p_2 \in \mathbb{R}_{\leq 1}$, $\forall \varphi, \varphi_1, \varphi_2 \in \mathbb{R}_{>0}$, with the only exception of Eq. (12) strictly requiring $p < 1$.

Another interesting property of the accuracy function is the flex point observed for a fixed value of φ. The flex point analysis gives an insight about the relationship between p and φ within the accuracy function. Equating to 0 the second partial derivative of $P(\cdot)$ with respect to p we obtain:

$$\frac{\partial^2 P}{\partial p^2} = 25\,\varphi^2\,\frac{e^{5(\varphi(1-p)-1)} - e^{10(\varphi(1-p)-1)}}{\left(1 + e^{5(\varphi(1-p)-1)}\right)^3} = 0, \qquad p = 1 - \frac{1}{\varphi}. \tag{15}$$

It is possible to obtain the same result through the second partial derivative for φ. Anyway, given the flex point properties of generic sigmoid functions ranging in $(0, 1)$, $P(p, \varphi) = 0.5 \; \forall p, \varphi \mid p = 1 - \frac{1}{\varphi}$.

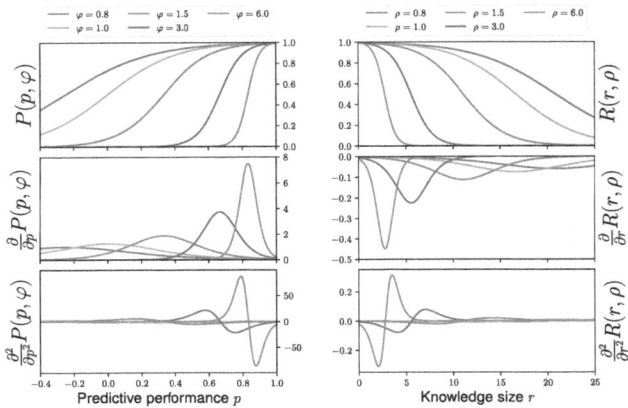

Fig. 3. ICE accuracy and readability functions with respect to predictive performance p, knowledge size r, φ and ρ (top panels). First and second partial derivatives (middle and bottom panels, respectively) for p and r.

3.3   ICE Readability Function

ICE adopts the $R(\cdot)$ readability function reported in Equations (5) and (6) to apply the user-defined weight ρ to the measured knowledge size r. The function is shown in the right panels of Figs. 3 and 2. In Fig. 3 the readability score obtained for a set of ρ weight values is reported. Similarly to the accuracy, also the readability function is bounded in $(0, 1)$ for any possible value of its parameters, as ensured by Equation (6), indeed:

$$\lim_{r \to \infty} R(r, \rho) = 0, \quad \forall \rho > 0, \tag{16}$$

$$\lim_{r \to 0} R(r, \rho) = 1, \quad \forall \rho > 0, \tag{17}$$

$$\lim_{\rho \to \infty} R(r, \rho) = 0, \quad \forall r > 0, \tag{18}$$

$$\lim_{\rho \to 0} R(r, \rho) = 1, \quad \forall r > 0. \tag{19}$$

The readability function is monotonically decreasing with respect to r and ρ:

$$0 \; > \; \frac{\partial R}{\partial r} \; = \; -\frac{0.3 \, \rho \, e^{0.3\rho r - 5}}{\left(1 + e^{0.3\rho r - 5}\right)^2}, \tag{20}$$

$$0 \; > \; \frac{\partial R}{\partial \rho} \; = \; -\frac{0.3 \, r \, e^{0.3\rho r - 5}}{\left(1 + e^{0.3\rho r - 5}\right)^2}, \tag{21}$$

$$r_1 \; < \; r_2 \; \Longleftrightarrow \; R(r_1, \rho) > R(r_2, \rho), \tag{22}$$

$$\rho_1 \; < \; \rho_2 \; \Longleftrightarrow \; R(r, \rho_1) > R(r, \rho_2). \tag{23}$$

Equations from (20) to (23) hold $\forall r, r_1, r_2, \rho, \rho_1, \rho_2 \in \mathbb{R}_{>0}$.

Also in this case it is interesting to study the flex point observed for a fixed value of ρ. By equating to 0 the second partial derivative of $R(\cdot)$ with respect to r we obtain that $R(r, \rho) = 0.5 \; \forall r, \rho \mid r = \frac{5}{0.3\rho}$.

3.4 ICE Function Properties

The overall ICE score is calculated by multiplying the accuracy function, the readability function and the completeness measurement. Given the properties of the two functions and the fact that completeness may be considered as a multiplicative constant, several properties may be demonstrated for the ICE score. Information on the ICE function range may be derived:

$$0 \le ICE(p, r, c, \varphi, \rho) < 1, \; \forall \; p, \; r, \; c, \; \varphi, \; \rho. \tag{24}$$

From Eqs. (7) to (10) and (16) to (19) the ICE asymptotic behaviour may be inferred. In particular, the ICE score tends to 0 if the knowledge predictive performance tends to $-\infty$, or if at least one amongst knowledge size, predictive performance importance or size importance tends to ∞. Formally,

$$\lim_{P(p,\varphi) \to 0} ICE(p, r, c, \varphi, \rho) = 0, \quad \forall r, \; \rho, \; c, \tag{25}$$

$$\lim_{R(r,\rho) \to 0} ICE(p, r, c, \varphi, \rho) = 0, \quad \forall p, \; \varphi, \; c. \tag{26}$$

Furthermore, it is trivial to demonstrate that

$$ICE(p, r, c, \varphi, \rho) = 0 \quad \Longleftrightarrow \quad c = 0. \tag{27}$$

The ICE score tends to 1 if *(i)* the knowledge predictive performance also tends to 1 or the corresponding user-defined relevance tends to 0 and, at the same time, *(ii)* the knowledge size or its importance tends to 0, and *(iii)* the knowledge completeness is equal to 1. Formally,

$$ICE(p, r, c, \varphi, \rho) \simeq 1 \quad \Longleftrightarrow \quad P(p, \varphi) \simeq 1, \; R(r, \rho) \simeq 1, \; c = 1. \tag{28}$$

ICE score values near 0 and 1 descend from the elementary properties of multiplication. Indeed *at least one* amongst accuracy, readability or completeness terms near 0 is sufficient to drag the ICE score towards 0. Conversely, *all of them* need to be near 1 to enable an ICE score close to 1. Monotonicity of the ICE function may be trivially deduced for individual projections of the involved variables, except when $c = 0$ (in this case the ICE score is always 0).

3.5 Flexibility of the ICE Score

ICE has been designed to satisfy flexibility requirements for the fidelity/readability trade-off, that may not be sufficiently handled by the existing Q_s and FIRE scores, despite their dedicated customisation parameters. For instance, let us consider the comparison of a knowledge described by 4 rules covering the whole input space having accuracy score = 0.95 and another exhaustive knowledge with only one rule having accuracy = 0.75. Both alternatives are equivalent if considering completeness, whereas the former maximises the predictive performance and the latter maximises the human-readability extent. Depending on the specific application (e.g., if human readability is more or less important than the predictive performance), end-users may prefer one knowledge or the other. A flexible metric to evaluate knowledge quality should allow users to tune the importance of the underlying quality indices to reflect this necessity. However, the knowledge with 4 rules is the best according to the Q_s score, without any provision for human intervention to alter the rating based on fidelity/readability trade-off preferences. Furthermore, it is trivial to demonstrate analytically that with the FIRE metric it is not possible to find a value for the trade-off parameter such that the single-ruled knowledge is considered better than the other. Conversely, the ICE importance parameters for the predictive performance and readability may be set equal to 0.5 and 2, respectively, to privilege the knowledge with fewer rules, or equal to 2 and 0.5, respectively, to privilege the one with highest predictive performance. ICE is thus more flexible than FIRE, which is not capable of satisfying all possible users' needs.

4   Experiments

The effectiveness of the ICE scoring function in evaluating symbolic knowledge quality has been assessed through the comparison of the outputs provided by different SKE algorithms based on clustering, trees and/or hypercubes [21, 29, 31]: ExACT [22], CREAM [23], ITER [12], GRIDEX [32] and CART [4]. We relied on the ML models and SKE techniques implemented within the scikit-learn and PSYKE[1] Python libraries [5,16,25,30]. The ICE score is thus applied to give a quantitative assessment of the outputs provided by this pool of extractors. Other analogous metrics (i.e., the FIRE and Q_s scores) have also been applied to the same outputs as benchmarks.

Experiments are carried out on the Wine [9] and Wisconsin breast cancer (WBC) [38] classification data sets. SKE algorithms have been applied to unbounded decision trees (DTs) previously trained on them. For each combination of data set and extraction technique, the corresponding output symbolic knowledge has been evaluated based on its raw predictive performance via the F_1 score, its size and its completeness. Given that ITER and GRIDEX provide knowledge in the form of a logic rule list, the knowledge size corresponds to the number of rules. ExACT, CREAM and CART, conversely, provide tree-structured symbolic knowledge and therefore the size corresponds to the number of leaf nodes. Completeness has been calculated as the percentage of the input feature space volume covered by the extracted rules with respect to the whole volume. Tree-based knowledge has always completeness = 1.

---

[1] https://github.com/psykei/psyke-python.

Since the Q_s and FIRE metrics require knowledge quality indices to be expressed as losses, we calculated the predictive loss as $1 - F_1$, the readability loss as the knowledge size and the completeness loss as $2 - completeness$, as suggested in [27]. We recall here that completeness ranges in [0, 1] and therefore a loss calculated as $1 - completeness$ is not suitable for multiplicative quality evaluations, as the case of Q_s, since exhaustive completeness (i.e., a loss equal to 0) would zero the score regardless of the predictive and readability loss values.

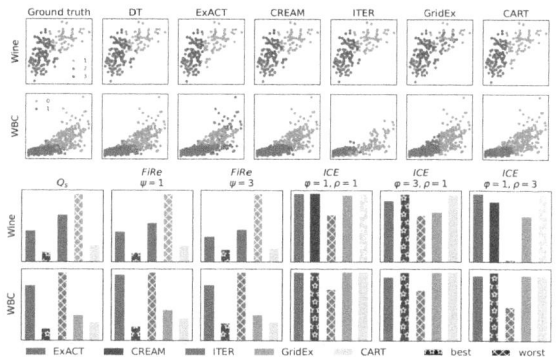

Fig. 4. Experiment results.

Table 1. Experimental results (EX = ExACT, CR = CREAM, G = GRIDEX).

Data set	Wine					WBC				
Quality metric	EX	CR	ITER	G	CART	EX	CR	ITER	G	CART
F_1 score	0.80	**0.95**	0.92	*0.73*	0.89	*0.82*	**0.94**	0.89	0.92	**0.94**
Knowledge size	**3**	4	9	5	**3**	3	**2**	5	3	3
Completeness	**1.00**	**1.00**	*0.75*	**1.00**	**1.00**	**1.00**	**1.00**	*0.76*	**1.00**	**1.00**
Q_s	0.608	**0.203**	0.926	*1.340*	0.338	0.536	**0.118**	0.672	0.246	0.178
FIRE, $\psi = 1$	0.643	**0.217**	0.829	*1.452*	0.357	0.566	**0.122**	*0.590*	0.260	0.188
FIRE, $\psi = 3$	0.214	**0.109**	0.276	*0.581*	0.119	0.189	**0.061**	*0.236*	0.087	0.063
ICE, $\varphi = 1, \rho = 1$	0.966	0.970	*0.678*	0.946	**0.972**	0.968	**0.979**	*0.733*	0.974	0.975
ICE, $\varphi = 3, \rho = 1$	0.862	**0.964**	*0.669*	0.706	0.949	0.896	**0.972**	*0.717*	0.962	0.968
ICE, $\varphi = 1, \rho = 3$	0.892	0.795	*0.032*	0.607	**0.898**	0.894	**0.952**	*0.470*	0.900	0.901

Q_s does not require user-defined parameters, so it is applied to the loss measurements without customisations. For the fidelity-readability trade-off parameter (ψ) required by the FIRE score, we selected $\psi = 1$ and $\psi = 3$ to test the metric under different conditions (equal importance for predictive and readability losses and higher importance for the predictive loss since high values of ψ tend to neglect the impact of the readability loss). Finally, for the ICE score we tested three different cases: $\varphi = 1$ and $\rho = 1$; $\varphi = 3$ and $\rho = 1$; $\varphi = 1$ and $\rho = 3$. Results of the experiments are reported in Fig. 4, i.e., a comparison of the data sets' ground truth with the predictions of DTs and SKE algorithms in the top panels and the corresponding knowledge quality evaluations in the bottom ones. Star- and cross-hatched bars highlight the best and worst score values, respectively. We recall that differently from ICE, knowledge evaluated via the Q_s and FIRE metrics has good quality if associated with *small* scores. Table 1 reports for each case study the quality indices for all the adopted SKE extractors and the corresponding Q_s, FIRE and ICE scores calculated upon these indices. Corresponding index losses are not reported since they can be trivially obtained as described above. For each index and metric, the best(worst) values are highlighted in bold(italic) font.

Case Studies. In the Wine Data Set case study there is no candidate knowledge having all the best quality indices at the same time: CREAM has the best F_1 score and complete coverage, but it provides one rule more than CART and ExACT. These two alternatives have comparable completeness but smaller F_1 scores, especially ExACT. However, this evaluation is somehow limiting because there may be situations where higher readability (fewer rules) is preferred over accuracy. It is worth noticing that in these scores readability (as per literature) only considers the size of the knowledge, but it could include more advanced evaluations based on its human interpretability. The FIRE and Q_s scores are unanimous in declaring the symbolic knowledge extracted via CREAM the one having the best quality. ICE accepts human customisation and assigns the highest quality to CART when setting $\varphi < \rho$ (knowledge readability has a predominant role with respect to predictive performance). Conversely, when $\varphi > \rho$ the best SKE algorithm is CREAM since its output knowledge has the highest predictive performance, which in this case is the prevalent term in the ICE calculation. Finally, with $\varphi = \rho$ both terms are equally weighted, resulting in a very slight difference in the evaluation of CART and CREAM.

For the WBC data set there is an SKE technique minimising knowledge size and maximising its completeness and F_1 score at the same time. Thus, CREAM is considered the best technique according to all quality metrics. ITER is clearly the algorithm providing the worst knowledge, given that its individual quality indices are all suboptimum. Of particular interest in this case study is the comparison between ExACT and GRIDEX. They produce knowledge having the same completeness and size, however, GRIDEX has a higher F_1 score. This latter is obviously considered better than ExACT according to all quality metrics, however, the difference is slight if the quality is evaluated through ICE with $\varphi \leq \rho$, since it assigns more relevance to the knowledge size than to the predictive performance. On the contrary, the difference in quality is far more evident when assessed via ICE with $\varphi > \rho$, assigning larger weights to the F_1 score impact.

5   Conclusions

ICE is a new metric evaluating the quality of symbolic knowledge according to a set of relevant indices, such as predictive performance, human-readability extent, and completeness. It proves to be effective in carrying out automated assessments and comparisons, also enabling human tuning of the weights to be assigned to individual quality indices. For this reason, ICE results are more flexible than existing alternatives. We believe that complete scoring functions for symbolic knowledge as ICE may be effective in developing algorithmic solutions for automated tuning of parameters required by SKE procedures, therefore avoiding time-consuming manual selection performed by humans, possibly leading to suboptimum results. Future works will be devoted to a deeper investigation of interpretability including readability information about the individual knowledge items. Furthermore, we plan to study a more sound approach to avoid subjectivity in the ICE score's weight adjustment, currently still lacking unambiguity.

Acknowledgments. This work has been supported by PNRR – M4C2 – Investimento 1.3, Partenariato Esteso PE00000013 – "FAIR—Future Artificial Intelligence Research" – Spoke 8 "Pervasive AI", funded by the European Commission under the NextGenerationEU programme and by the European Unions Horizon Europe AEQUITAS research and innovation programme under grant number 101070363.

References

1. Augasta, M.G., Kathirvalavakumar, T.: Reverse engineering the neural networks for rule extraction in classification problems. Neural Process. Lett. **35**(2), 131–150 (2012). https://doi.org/10.1007/s11063-011-9207-8
2. Baesens, B., Setiono, R., Mues, C., Vanthienen, J.: Using neural network rule extraction and decision tables for credit-risk evaluation. Manage. Sci. **49**(3), 312–329 (2003). https://doi.org/10.1287/mnsc.49.3.312.12739
3. Barakat, N., Diederich, J.: Eclectic rule-extraction from support vector machines. Int. J. Comput. Inf. Eng. **2**(5), 1672–1675 (2008). https://doi.org/10.5281/zenodo.1055511
4. Breiman, L., Friedman, J., Stone, C.J., Olshen, R.A.: Classification and Regression Trees. CRC Press (1984)
5. Calegari, R., Sabbatini, F.: The PSyKE technology for trustworthy artificial intelligence. In: Dovier, A., Montanari, A., Orlandini, A. (eds.) AIxIA 2022. LNCS, vol. 13796, pp. 3–16. Springer, Cham (2023). https://doi.org/10.1007/978-3-031-27181-6_1
6. Castillo, L.A., González Muñoz, A., Pérez, R.: Including a simplicity criterion in the selection of the best rule in a genetic fuzzy learning algorithm. Fuzzy Sets Syst. **120**(2), 309–321 (2001). https://doi.org/10.1016/S0165-0114(99)00095-0

7. Craven, M.W., Shavlik, J.W.: Extracting tree-structured representations of trained networks. In: Touretzky, D.S., Mozer, M.C., Hasselmo, M.E. (eds.) Advances in Neural Information Processing Systems 8. Proceedings of the 1995 Conference, pp. 24–30. The MIT Press (1996). http://papers.nips.cc/paper/1152-extracting-tree-structured-representations-of-trained-networks.pdf

8. Czarnowski, I., Caballero, A.M., Howlett, R.J., Jain, L.C.: Intelligent Decision Technologies 2016: Proceedings of the 8th KES International Conference on Intelligent Decision Technologies (KES-IDT 2016)–Part I, vol. 56. Springer, Cham (2016). https://doi.org/10.1007/978-3-319-39627-9

9. Forina, M., Leardi, R., Armanino, C., Lanteri, S., Conti, P., Princi, P.: Parvus: an extendable package of programs for data exploration, classification and correlation. J. Chemom. **4**(2), 191–193 (1988)

10. d'Avila Garcez, A.S., Broda, K., Gabbay, D.M.: Symbolic knowledge extraction from trained neural networks: a sound approach. Artif. Intell. **125**(1–2), 155–207 (2001)

11. Hofmann, A., Schmitz, C., Sick, B.: Rule extraction from neural networks for intrusion detection in computer networks. In: 2003 IEEE International Conference on Systems, Man and Cybernetics, vol. 2, pp. 1259–1265. IEEE (2003). https://doi.org/10.1109/ICSMC.2003.1244584

12. Huysmans, J., Baesens, B., Vanthienen, J.: ITER: an algorithm for predictive regression rule extraction. In: Tjoa, A.M., Trujillo, J. (eds.) DaWaK 2006. LNCS, vol. 4081, pp. 270–279. Springer, Heidelberg (2006). https://doi.org/10.1007/11823728_26

13. Karmaker, S.K., Hassan, M.M., Smith, M.J., Xu, L., Zhai, C., Veeramachaneni, K.: Automl to date and beyond: challenges and opportunities. ACM Comput. Surv. (CSUR) **54**(8), 1–36 (2021)

14. Kenny, E.M., Ford, C., Quinn, M., Keane, M.T.: Explaining black-box classifiers using post-hoc explanations-by-example: the effect of explanations and error-rates in XAI user studies. Artif. Intell. **294**, 103459 (2021). https://doi.org/10.1016/j.artint.2021.103459

15. Lipton, Z.C.: The mythos of model interpretability. Queue **16**(3), 31–57 (2018). https://doi.org/10.1145/3236386.3241340

16. Pedregosa, F., et al.: Scikit-learn: machine learning in Python. J. Mach. Learn. Res. (JMLR) **12**, 2825–2830 (2011). https://doi.org/10.5555/1953048.2078195

17. Puiutta, E., Veith, E.M.S.P.: Explainable reinforcement learning: a survey. In: Holzinger, A., Kieseberg, P., Tjoa, A.M., Weippl, E. (eds.) CD-MAKE 2020. LNCS, vol. 12279, pp. 77–95. Springer, Cham (2020). https://doi.org/10.1007/978-3-030-57321-8_5

18. Rocha, A., Papa, J.P., Meira, L.A.A.: How far do we get using machine learning black-boxes? Int. J. Pattern Recognit. Artif. Intell. **26**(02), 1261001–(1–23) (2012). https://doi.org/10.1142/S0218001412610010

19. Saad, E.W., Wunsch, D.C., II.: Neural network explanation using inversion. Neural Netw. **20**(1), 78–93 (2007). https://doi.org/10.1016/j.neunet.2006.07.005

20. Sabbatini, F., Calegari, R.: Achieving complete coverage with hypercube-based symbolic knowledge-extraction techniques. In: Nowaczyk, S., et al. (eds.) ECAI 2023, Part I. CCIS, vol. 1947, pp. 179–197. Springer, Cham (2023). https://doi.org/10.1007/978-3-031-50396-2_10

21. Sabbatini, F., Calegari, R.: Bottom-up and top-down workflows for hypercube- and clustering-based knowledge extractors. In: Calvaresi, D., et al. (eds.) Explainable and Transparent AI and Multi-Agent Systems. LNCS, vol. 14127, pp. 116–129. Springer, Cham (2023). https://doi.org/10.1007/978-3-031-40878-6_7

22. Sabbatini, F., Calegari, R.: ExACT explainable clustering: unravelling the intricacies of cluster formation. In: Baker, C.K., Gómez Álvarez, L., Heyninck, J., Meyer, T., Peñaloza, R., Vesic, S. (eds.) Joint Proceedings of the 2nd Workshop on Knowledge Diversity and the 2nd Workshop on Cognitive Aspects of Knowledge Representation co-located with 20th International Conference on Principles of Knowledge Representation and Reasoning (KR 2023), Rhodes, Greece, September 3–4, 2023. CEUR Workshop Proceedings, vol. 3548. CEUR-WS.org (2023). https://ceur-ws.org/Vol-3548/paper3.pdf

23. Sabbatini, F., Calegari, R.: Explainable clustering with CREAM. In: Marquis, P., Tran, C.S., Kern-Isberner, G. (eds.) 20th International Conference on Principles of Knowledge Representation and Reasoning (KR 2023), September 2–8 , Rhodes, Greece, pp. 593–603. IJCAI Organization (2023). https://doi.org/10.24963/kr.2023/58

24. Sabbatini, F., Calegari, R.: Symbolic knowledge-extraction evaluation metrics: the FiRe score. In: Gal, K., Nowé, A., Nalepa, G.J., Fairstein, R., Rădulescu, R. (eds.) Proceedings of the 26th European Conference on Artificial Intelligence, ECAI 2023, Kraków, Poland. September 30 – October 4, 2023 (2023). https://doi.org/10.3233/FAIA230496, https://ebooks.iospress.nl/doi/10.3233/FAIA230496

25. Sabbatini, F., Calegari, R.: Unlocking insights and trust: the value of explainable clustering algorithms for cognitive agents. In: Falcone, R., Castelfranchi, C., Sapienza, A., Cantucci, F. (eds.) Proceedings of the 24th Workshop "From Objects to Agents", Roma, Italy, November 6–8, 2023. CEUR Workshop Proceedings, vol. 3579, pp. 232–245. CEUR-WS.org (2023). https://ceur-ws.org/Vol-3579/paper18.pdf

26. Sabbatini, F., Calegari, R.: Unveiling opaque predictors via explainable clustering: the CReEPy algorithm. In: Boella, G., et al. (eds.) Proceedings of the 2nd Workshop on Bias, Ethical AI, Explainability and the role of Logic and Logic Programming co-located with the 22nd International Conference of the Italian Association for Artificial Intelligence (AI*IA 2023), Rome, Italy, November 6, 2023. CEUR Workshop Proceedings, vol. 3615, pp. 1–14. CEUR-WS.org (2023), https://ceur-ws.org/Vol-3615/paper1.pdf

27. Sabbatini, F., Calegari, R.: On the evaluation of the symbolic knowledge extracted from black boxes. AI Ethics 4(1), 65–74 (2024). https://doi.org/10.1007/s43681-023-00406-1

28. Sabbatini, F., Calegari, R.: Untying black boxes with clustering-based symbolic knowledge extraction. Intelligenza Artificiale 18(1), 21–34 (2024). https://doi.org/10.3233/IA-240026

29. Sabbatini, F., Ciatto, G., Calegari, R., Omicini, A.: Hypercube-based methods for symbolic knowledge extraction: towards a unified model. In: Ferrando, A., Mascardi, V. (eds.) WOA 2022 – 23rd Workshop "From Objects to Agents", CEUR Workshop Proceedings, vol. 3261, pp. 48–60. Sun SITE Central Europe, RWTH Aachen University (2022). http://ceur-ws.org/Vol-3261/paper4.pdf

30. Sabbatini, F., Ciatto, G., Calegari, R., Omicini, A.: Symbolic knowledge extraction from opaque ML predictors in PSyKE: platform design & experiments. Intelligenza Artificiale 16(1), 27–48 (2022). https://doi.org/10.3233/IA-210120

31. Sabbatini, F., Ciatto, G., Calegari, R., Omicini, A.: Towards a unified model for symbolic knowledge extraction with hypercube-based methods. Intelligenza Artificiale 17(1), 63–75 (2023). https://doi.org/10.3233/IA-230001

32. Sabbatini, F., Ciatto, G., Omicini, A.: GridEx: an algorithm for knowledge extraction from black-box regressors. In: Calvaresi, D., Najjar, A., Winikoff, M., Främling, K. (eds.) EXTRAAMAS 2021. LNCS (LNAI), vol. 12688, pp. 18–38. Springer, Cham (2021). https://doi.org/10.1007/978-3-030-82017-6_2

33. Sabbatini, F., Grimani, C., Calegari, R.: Bridging machine learning and diagnostics of the ESA LISA space mission with equation discovery via explainable artificial intelligence. Adv. Space Res. **74**(1), 505–517 (2024). https://doi.org/10.1016/j.asr.2024.04.041, https://www.sciencedirect.com/science/article/pii/S0273117724003880

34. Saito, K., Nakano, R.: Extracting regression rules from neural networks. Neural Netw. **15**(10), 1279–1288 (2002). https://doi.org/10.1016/S0893-6080(02)00089-8

35. Schmitz, G.P.J., Aldrich, C., Gouws, F.S.: ANN-DT: an algorithm for extraction of decision trees from artificial neural networks. IEEE Trans. Neural Networks **10**(6), 1392–1401 (1999). https://doi.org/10.1109/72.809084

36. Setiono, R., Liu, H.: NeuroLinear: from neural networks to oblique decision rules. Neurocomputing **17**(1), 1–24 (1997). https://doi.org/10.1016/S0925-2312(97)00038-6

37. Setiono, R., Thong, J.Y.L.: An approach to generate rules from neural networks for regression problems. Eur. J. Oper. Res. **155**(1), 239–250 (2004). https://doi.org/10.1016/S0377-2217(02)00792-0

38. Street, W.N., Wolberg, W.H., Mangasarian, O.L.: Nuclear feature extraction for breast tumor diagnosis. In: Acharya, R.S., Goldgof, D.B. (eds.) Biomedical Image Processing and Biomedical Visualization. vol. 1905, pp. 861 – 870. International Society for Optics and Photonics, SPIE (1993). https://doi.org/10.1117/12.148698

39. Tran, S.N., d'Avila Garcez, A.S.: Knowledge extraction from deep belief networks for images. In: IJCAI-2013 Workshop on Neural-Symbolic Learning and Reasoning (2013)

40. Zhou, Z., Jiang, Y., Chen, S.: Extracting symbolic rules from trained neural network ensembles. AI Commun. **16**(1), 3–15 (2003). http://content.iospress.com/articles/ai-communications/aic272

Hierarchical Knowledge Extraction from Opaque Machine Learning Predictors

Federico Sabbatini[1(✉)] and Roberta Calegari[2]

[1] University of Urbino, Urbino, Italy
f.sabbatini1@campus.uniurb.it
[2] University of Bologna, Bologna, Italy
roberta.calegari@unibo.it

Abstract. Adopting opaque machine learning predictors, which achieve very high predictive performance, often necessitates incorporating symbolic knowledge-extraction techniques. These techniques aim to explain the opaque predictions, thus making them applicable in high-stakes scenarios. The development of symbolic knowledge-extraction procedures is evolving alongside the dynamic machine learning landscape. However, there are recurring drawbacks that tend to be overlooked or addressed in a suboptimum way. Common examples include the non-exhaustiveness of the global explanations generated for a black-box predictor or the unwanted discretisation introduced in the prediction of continuous variables. To tackle these challenges, in this work, we introduce the HEx algorithm, its formalisation and its properties. This algorithm aims to obtain a symbolic, hierarchical representation of the knowledge acquired by opaque machine learning classifiers and regressors, always ensuring knowledge exhaustiveness and avoiding any output discretisation. Experiments demonstrating the superior capabilities of HEx compared to state-of-the-art competitors in terms of predictive performance, completeness, and human readability are presented.

Keywords: Explainable artificial intelligence · Symbolic knowledge extraction · PSyKE

1 Introduction

Inherently interpretable models, where humans can understand the reasoning behind the outputs, may not be sufficiently complex to accurately capture the nuances of the domain, resulting in suboptimum predictive capabilities. Conversely, there are machine learning (ML) predictors with a high degree of complexity that enables them to achieve superior predictive performance. However, these models lack interpretability, especially concerning internal decision-making processes and input feature exploitation. This leads to an impossibility for human users to trace and thus understand the exact workflow leading to a given outcome starting from an input query [8]. Despite the unfortunate proof of an inverse proportionality relationship between human interpretability and predictive performance [10,30], there is a growing demand for interpretable and explainable predictions. This demand has resulted in the rejection of opaque models in critical decision systems, despite their capability to provide highly accurate predictions [17,18]. The criticality of a system is determined by the extent to which important aspects of human lives are affected by the predictive system. For example, critical domains include finance, security, and medicine. In such contexts, transparent models are preferred over opaque ones, even if they may have limitations in predictive performance.

To keep the advantages coming along with complexity and opaqueness, different strategies have been proposed by the explainable artificial intelligence community [5,22]. One consists of performing symbolic knowledge extraction (SKE; [26]) to provide human-interpretable surrogates of the opaque ML predictors. These surrogate models are interpretable for humans and preserve as much as possible the predictive capabilities of the original, opaque predictor.

SKE techniques recently proposed in the literature are mostly designed to be applied upon specific sorts of ML models, typically artificial neural networks [11,15,24,43]. The adoption of model-agnostic extractors seems to have lost momentum, despite the increasing diversity of available ML models. When SKE techniques are tailored specifically to narrow clusters of opaque predictors, it can result in a fossilisation of the decision-making system. For instance, a system leveraging a fuzzy neural network may be empowered with the SKE algorithm proposed in [43] to achieve human interpretability. As a result, minimum changes in the model architecture (e.g., another kind of neural network or switching to a random forest) would result in the compelling modification of the SKE technique, which is only suitable for fuzzy neural networks. Conversely, model-agnostic extractors are not strictly bound to specific subsets of ML predictors. Therefore, they enable the avoidance of these unwanted dependencies.

Accordingly, we introduce here the HEx algorithm, a novel task- and model-agnostic SKE procedure to explain opaque ML predictors accepting continuous input features. HEx provides a symbolic human-interpretable model whose predictions are drawn according to a tree-based hypercubic partitioning of the input feature space [38,40]. Our experiments show that opaque models of any kind can be explained via HEx with higher predictive performance, completeness and human-readability extent than state-of-the-art knowledge-extraction techniques.

The manuscript is organised as follows. Related works are described in Sect. 2. The design and implementation of the novel HEx algorithm for hierarchical symbolic knowledge extraction are reported in Sect. 3. Experiments assessing the effectiveness and usability of HEx compared to state-of-the-art competitors are detailed in Sect. 4. Conclusions are finally drawn in Sect. 5.

2 Related Works

When facing opaqueness deriving from sophisticated algebraic calculations constituting the core of sub-symbolic predictors, SKE procedures provide human interpretability through a symbolic approximation of the original, opaque predictor behaviour [28,42]. The literature offers a wide range of different alternatives, even though these are mostly constrained in their actual applicability. The most appropriate SKE technique to adopt in a specific scenario should be identified in the light of the candidates' peculiarities, constraints and overall achieved quality. Beyond mandatory requirements, also the kind of knowledge outputted by SKE methods should be taken into consideration. In particular, shape and expressiveness of the knowledge are relevant aspects to analyse. Knowledge shapes typically adopted are lists and trees of rules. The expressiveness of knowledge items ranges from propositional *if-then* rules to more sophisticated M-of-N, fuzzy and oblique rules.

Requirements of SKE Techniques. The three main requirements constraining the applicability scope of SKE techniques are detailed in the following.

The degree of inspection inside the internal structure of the opaque model during the knowledge extraction is defined *translucency*. There are three distinct classes of SKE algorithms based on translucency, namely, decompositional, pedagogical and eclectic [2]. Decompositional SKE procedures analyse the model's internal parameters, for instance, support vectors in a support vector machine or connection weights in neural networks. Pedagogical extractors only consider the input/output response of the opaque predictor to generate symbolic knowledge. Eclectic procedures combine elements of both categories. It is worth emphasising that decompositional techniques are bounded to individual classes of black boxes, e.g., only tree ensembles, or fuzzy neural networks, or any kind of feed-forward neural networks for the most general procedures. Conversely, pedagogical models are model-agnostic and thus present fewer applicability constraints.

SKE techniques may be applicable only in some domains, depending if they are compatible only with opaque classifiers, only with regressors, or with both categories. The majority of extractors are limited to classification tasks [13, 16,46,48], with some exceptions for regression tasks [23,43,45]. A very narrow subset of extractors results to be task-agnostic [7,27,35,37,44].

Depending on the specific peculiarities of SKE algorithms, these may be compatible with different subsets of input features. More in detail, feature kinds typically accepted are binary and/or discrete and/or real-valued. It is worth highlighting that it is possible to adopt conversion routines to map features into the desired domain (e.g., one-hot encoding, discretisation and binarisation methods). These processing phases should be performed before training the opaque predictor and performing SKE.

Evolution of Translucency over Time. A review of recent literature about SKE shows an increasing propensity to design novel decompositional techniques. For instance, during the last two years the following knowledge extractors were proposed: 2 pedagogical algorithms for regression tasks [25,31] and 1 for classification tasks [12]; 1 decompositional extractor for decision tree ensembles [29], 1 for support vector machines [3] and 6 for neural networks. More in detail, these latter are explicitly designed for convolutional neural networks [24], fuzzy neural networks [11,43] or networks with exactly four layers [15]. The remaining 2 are more general and assume no constraints on the network structure [4,20]. All these decompositional extractors are only applicable to classification tasks except the one proposed in [43].

An analogous trend may be observed in 2021 (10 decompositional and 3 pedagogical algorithms). As a result, it can be noticed that recent SKE procedures are mostly decompositional and focused on opaque classifiers. Given the undeniable general applicability of pedagogical techniques, we argue that the research community could benefit from the proposal of novel algorithms overcoming the hindrances of existing ones.

State-of-the-Art Pedagogical SKE Techniques. We conclude this section by briefly reviewing state-of-the-art pedagogical extraction algorithms inspiring HEx and adopted as benchmarks in our experiments.

The ITER SKE algorithm can be adopted to explain opaque regressors accepting continuous input features [23]. It is based on a bottom-up iterative strategy leading to the construction of a set of hypercubes within the input feature space. Cubes are disjoint and possibly non-exhaustive. Predictions are made based on the output values associated with the cubes enclosing the queries. Cubes' output values are calculated during the knowledge extraction and they are constant values, therefore a discretisation of the predicted outputs is introduced.

Other SKE techniques applicable to explain opaque regressors via disjoint hypercubes are GRIDEX and GRIDREX [31,41] also accepting only continuous input features. They induce a recursive, top-down partitioning of the input feature space. As in the case of ITER, explainability is obtained through a human-interpretable hypercubic partitioning. However, GRIDEX and GRIDREX perform an input feature analysis to prune the least relevant features from the output knowledge. Only GRIDREX avoids prediction discretisation by adopting linear combinations of the input variables instead of constant values as cube outputs.

The CART algorithm may be exploited to induce a decision tree explaining the outcomes of opaque classifiers or regressors, without constraints on the input feature kind. The output of CART is a binary tree where leaves are associated with constant predictions and internal nodes are constraints on the input variables [7]. Complete paths from the tree root to each leaf correspond to the explanations for the opaque outcomes.

3   Hierarchical Knowledge Extraction

HEx (Hierarchical EXtractor) is a pedagogical SKE technique applicable to opaque predictors operating on continuous attributes. Its algorithm merges the advantages of existing SKE techniques to achieve better predictive performance and conciseness than its competitors. More in detail, it exploits the hierarchical nature of tree-based systems and the human interpretability of hypercubes. Similarly to CART, it can explain opaque classifiers as well as regressors and the hypercubes it identifies can be associated with constant values, as in ITER, or with linear combinations of the input variables, as in GRIDREx.

Given the domain of input features accepted by HEx, the hypercubes it identifies are described in terms of interval-inclusion constraints over continuous input attributes. Hypercubes are not disjoint, since smaller cubes may be enclosed within a bigger one. Nonetheless, predictions based on HEx hypercubes are not ambiguous, because cubes are ordered. Inner cubes have the highest priority than outer ones when predicting a query. Therefore, if a query is enclosed within more than a cube, only the innermost is considered.

The hierarchical, hypercubic partitioning provided by HEx is always exhaustive since the last identified cube is used as *default* cube. All queries not covered by other cubes are thus enclosed by it.

HEx requires a predictor and a training set to be provided by users. The training set may be the same as the one previously used to train the opaque model. During the knowledge extraction phase, HEx supports classification by finding the most frequently predicted class label inside each hypercube and by using it as an interpretable prediction for all queries falling inside that cube. Similarly, in regression tasks where constant outputs are used, the average of all opaque predictions within each cube is used. Otherwise, when expressing outputs as linear combinations of the input variables, a linear fit within each cube is performed to correlate the training inputs with the opaque predictions provided by the ML model.

The human-interpretable knowledge provided by HEx is generated by converting each hypercube identified during the extraction phase into an *if-then* rule having as precondition a formal description of the hypercube boundaries and as postcondition the associated prediction. The conversion is performed methodically from the innermost cubes to the default one.

Algorithmically, HEx partitions the input feature space according to a top-down strategy, preserving information about parent cubes and corresponding child cubes through a tree structure. It differs from existing hypercube-based extractors since its decisions are grounded on the notion of *gain* between cubes. More in detail, when splitting a parent cube, the gain from replacing the ancestor cube with its child sub-cubes is computed, and only descendants showing a favourable gain are retained. The gain is always calculated between a cube and its children/descendants.

To give an abstract evaluation of the quality of symbolic knowledge generated by HEx, we refer to the 3 most used proxies for knowledge quality: predictive performance, readability and completeness [14,19,32,33,47]. HEx completeness is ensured by design. Its predictive performance may be measured through the same scoring metric adopted for the underlying ML model, by comparing the HEx predictions to the data set ground truth or the opaque predictions. Finally, the human-readability extent is typically assessed based on the symbolic knowledge size, e.g., the number of items it contains. In the case of HEx, readability is bounded to the quantity of identified hypercubes, by considering that readability decreases if the number of cubes increases. Thanks to the knowledge-extraction strategy it employs, HEx can generate more concise knowledge pieces (i.e., with fewer items) than other state-of-the-art competitors.

The overall predictive performance and readability exhibited by the knowledge extracted with HEx depends on the user-defined hyper-parameters provided as inputs, clearly impacting the steps executed during the algorithm. These parameters and the HEx algorithm are detailed in the following subsections, respectively. It is important to notice that the user-defined parameters of HEx can be automatically tuned via the existing PEDRO procedure without any modification [31].

HEx Hyper-Parameters. The HEx knowledge extractor requires 4 input parameters to be tuned by users: the maximum depth of its recursions (δ), the minimum quantity of samples to consider within each hypercube (m), the error threshold deemed acceptable during the extraction (θ), and the strategy to adopt at each recursion to partition the input feature space ($S_1, \ldots, S_\delta$).

δ is the upper-bound for the number of recursive splits to perform. It is defined as an integer number greater or equal to 1, formally: $\delta \in \mathbb{N} \setminus \{0\}$. For $\delta = 1$ only a single partitioning step is performed. This parameter is an upper-bound since the algorithm may pre-emptively terminate if all hypercubes found during recursion $i, i < \delta$ have a predictive error below θ. δ is strictly bounded with the overall human-interpretability extent of the knowledge outputted by HEx, since growing δ values generally lead to larger quantities of identified hypercubes and therefore to larger knowledge pieces.

m is the lower-bound for the number of training instances to consider when creating a hypercubic partition. It is defined as an integer number greater or equal to 1, formally: $m \in \mathbb{N} \setminus \{0\}$. After the cube creation, if it contains less than m training instances, the training data set is augmented by generating random samples inside the cube, up to the user-defined value. Large values of m are employed to obtain more robust results in presence of outliers.

θ is the user-defined error threshold adopted to discern between hypercubic regions that need to be refined during successive recursive iterations of HEx and regions to be considered final, i.e., those having predictive error below the threshold. The definition of θ depends on the task at hand. When executing classification, θ is a threshold on the cubes' classification accuracy. It is thus defined as a real number in the [0, 1] interval. On the other hand, when performing regression, it represents a threshold on the mean absolute error of hypercubes. Therefore, $\theta \in \mathbb{R}^+$.

θ represents a sensitivity parameter controlling the overall predictive performance of the knowledge provided by HEx. Small values of θ indicate a priority for maximising predictive performance, potentially sacrificing human readability. This occurs because HEx recursions may not be terminated prematurely before reaching δ. This parameter is also used to check if adjacent hypercubes may be merged and if there is a gain in splitting a parent cube into child sub-cubes, as detailed in Sect. 3.

$S_1, \ldots, S_\delta$ are the splitting strategies to adopt during recursive iterations $1, \ldots, \delta$. Two different strategies are supported by HEX, namely, fixed or adaptive. Fixed strategies are parametrised with an integer value, k, identifying the number of partitions that are created along *every* input variable. In this case, a parent cube is split into k^d child sub-cubes, by assuming d input features. Nonetheless, the actual number of produced cubes may be decreased after the HEX merging phase. Differently, adaptive strategies are parametrised with a monotone increasing function f defined as $f : [0, 1] \rightarrow \mathbb{N} \setminus \{0\}$ and generating $f(r)$ partitions along input dimensions having relevance equal to r. This allows for conducting a sensitivity analysis on the impact of individual input features on predictions and subsequently performing a finer slicing on the most important ones. For the least important features, it is possible to select a coarser partitioning as well as to avoid any slicing. In this case, input dimensions that are never sliced are considered irrelevant to the predictions, and therefore, they are not included in the generated symbolic knowledge. In other words, these features are not useful to explain the predictions of the underlying opaque model.

We highlight here that the feature relevance may be assessed through any procedure external to HEX, for instance via the f_classif and f_regression functions of the sklearn.feature_selection Python library. Other adequate methods may be found in the literature [1,49,50]. The only requirement of HEX is that the feature importance ranking should be normalised in the [0, 1] interval. The most relevant feature is thus associated with a value of 1.

HEX Algorithm. The HEX algorithm applied to explain a predictor P trained on a data set D is summarised in Algorithm 1. We point out here that G represents a grid object, concisely enclosing both concepts of maximum depth and splitting strategies. In other words, G encapsulates the δ and $S_1, \ldots, S_\delta$ user-defined parameters.

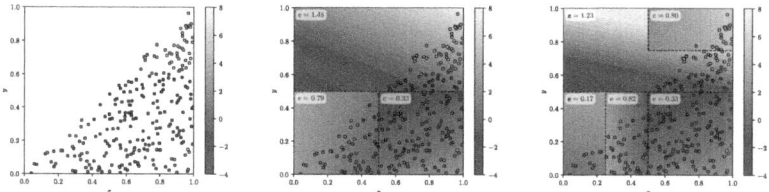

Fig. 1. Example of HEX instances applied to an artificial regression data set.

The HEX algorithm starts by identifying the *surrounding hypercube*, i.e., the minimal cube enclosing all the training instances. The root of the tree induced by HEX is therefore initialised with the surrounding cube, with no parent and

Algorithm 1. HEx pseudocode

```
 1: function HEX(P, D, G, θ, m)
 2:     H₀ ← the minimal hypercube including all the samples of D
 3:     root ← NEWNODE(H₀, ∅, P, D, θ)
 4:     SPLIT(1, root, P, D, G, θ, m)
 5:     Π ← post-ordered depth-first search from root
 6:     Π ← {node.cube | node ∈ Π ∧ node.gain}
 7:     if D \ ⋃_{H∈Π} H ≠ ∅ then Π ← Π ∪ {H₀}
 8:     return Π
 9: function NEWNODE(H, parent, P, D, θ)
10:     node ← new Node()
11:     node.cube ← H        node.parent ← parent        node.children ← ∅
12:     node.gain ← GAIN(node, P, D, θ)
13:     return node
14: function GAIN(node, P, D, θ)
15:     parent ← node.parent                                          ▷ Outer cube
16:     while !parent.gain do
17:         parent ← parent.parent
18:     if task is classification ∧ output of node.cube ≠ output of parent.cube then return true
19:     else if task is regression then
20:         e_o ← PREDICTIVEERROR(parent.cube \ node.cube, P, D)       ▷ Outer cube error
21:         e_i ← PREDICTIVEERROR(node.cube, P, D)                     ▷ Inner cube error
22:         if e_o − e_i > 0.6 θ then return true
23:     else return false
24: function PREDICTIVEERROR(H, P, D)
25:     return the average predictive error of {P(x) | x ∈ H ∩ D}
26: function SPLIT(i, node, P, D, G, θ, m)
27:     if i > depth of G ∨ PREDICTIVEERROR(node.cube) ≤ θ then return
28:     Π ← all the partitions of node.cube according to the i-th level of grid G
29:     D ← D ∪ ⋃_{H∈Π} GENERATESAMPLESIN(node.cube, D, m)
30:     Π ← MERGE(Π, P, D, θ)
31:     node.children ← ⋃_{H∈Π} NEWNODE(H, node, P, D, θ)
32:     for all n ∈ node.children do
33:         SPLIT(i + 1, n, P, D, G, θ, m)                            ▷ Recursion
34: function MERGE(Π, P, D, θ)
35:     C ← ADJACENTCUBES(Π)
36:     while (|C| > 0) do
37:         (H₁*, H₂*) ← arg min_{(H₁,H₂)∈C} { PREDICTIVEERROR(H₁ ∪ H₂, P, D) }
38:         H ← H₁* ∪ H₂*
39:         if PREDICTIVEERROR(H, P, D) ≤ θ then
40:             Π ← Π \ {H₁*, H₂*} ∪ {H}
41:             C ← ADJACENTCUBES(Π)
42:         else return Π
43:     return Π
44: function GENERATESAMPLESIN(H, D, m)
45:     c ←| H ∩ D |
46:     if c < m then return { (m − c) random points in H }
47:     else return ∅
48: function ADJACENTCUBES(Π)
49:     return ⋃_{H∈Π} { (H, H') | (H' ∈ Π \ {H}) ∧ (H and H' are adjacent) }
```

no children. Then, the following steps are recursively executed for the tree root and any child node successively created (the *current node*, in the following): (i) the cube associated with the current node is split according to the strategy chosen by the user, as described by the grid G; (ii) the data set D is augmented to have at least m instances inside each created sub-cube. New samples are randomly generated and the predictor P is employed as an oracle to predict the corresponding outputs; (iii) the sub-cubes are merged, if possible. The merging phase consists of iteratively trying to unify pairs of adjacent cubes until there are eligible pairs. Two cubes are merged only if the resulting cube has a predictive error below the user-defined θ threshold; (iv) the resulting cubes are encapsulated within tree nodes, having the current node as parent; (v) the gain of new nodes is calculated. This measure is a Boolean value indicating whether preserving a child node improves predictive performance or not. It is calculated relative to the nearest ancestor with a positive gain. In other words, ancestors with negative gain are disregarded as they will not contribute to the resulting symbolic knowledge. The gain is defined differently based on the performed ML task. For classification, a child node has positive gain if its cube is associated with a class label that is different from that of the closest ancestor (i.e., the child cube identifies a region where a different prediction is dominant). For regression tasks, a child node has positive gain if the predictive error of its cube (e_i) is smaller than that of the closest ancestor (e_o). More in detail, this inequality should hold: $e_o - e_i > 0.6\ \theta$; (vi) the workflow is repeated for each one of these child nodes if their cubes have predictive error above the θ threshold, until the maximum user-defined depth.

After the tree induction, all nodes are linearised according to a post-ordered depth-first search starting from the root. However, the root is not included in the ordered list at this stage. All nodes having negative gain are discarded; the cubes associated with the remaining nodes are translated into ordered symbolic rules composing the output human-interpretable knowledge. As a last step, HEx checks if the knowledge covers the whole input feature space. If not, the surrounding cube is also translated into a rule and queued to the knowledge. The final rule of knowledge is always generalised to a default rule.

Figure 1 exemplifies the execution of HEx applied to a synthetic regression data set with two continuous input features (x and y, see left panel). An instance of HEx with $\theta = 0.5$ and $\delta = 1$ is depicted in the middle panel of Fig. 1. A fixed splitting strategy performing 2 splits for each input dimension has been adopted. As a result, 4 hypercubes are identified, one containing no training samples (top-left), one with a predictive error $e < \theta$ ($e = 0.33$; bottom-right) and two with an error above θ. In this case, the cube with no samples is merged with an adjacent cube (top-right) without losses in the predictive performance. The resulting cubes are finally translated into knowledge with as many *if-then* rules.

An instance of HEx with $\delta = 2$ and the same other parameters as described above is shown in the right panel of Fig. 1. The second recursion of HEx starts after the merging of the two top cubes. In this scenario, the bottom-right cube is no further partitioned, provided its error is below θ. The bottom-left cube is split into four sub-cubes, vertically merged pairwise. One of these merged sub-cubes is marked with positive gain (the leftmost, $e = 0.17$), the other with negative gain. As a result, in the final knowledge there is a rule corresponding to the inner region ($0.00 < x < 0.25, 0.00 < y < 0.50$) followed by a rule derived for the closest parent region having positive gain ($0.00 < x < 0.50, 0.00 < y < 0.50$). Analogously,

Listing 1. Example of knowledge extracted with HEx for the Iris data set.

```
iris is Setosa if petal length <= 1.93
iris is Virginica if petal length > 4.73
iris is Versicolor otherwise
```

Listing 2. Example of knowledge extracted with HEx for the Adult data set.

```
income is > 50K if education-num is > 13
income is <= 50K otherwise
```

the top merged cube is split into four sub-cubes and only one is marked with positive gain (the top-right one, with $e = 0.80$). All the others are marked with negative gain and neglected when generating the output knowledge. The overall knowledge of the HEx instance with $\delta = 2$ has five rules corresponding to as many hierarchical hypercubes, with a weighted average predictive performance of 0.61, in contrast to the 3 rules and the average error of 0.73 exhibited by the HEx instance with $\delta = 1$. This constitutes an example of the fidelity/readability trade-off typically observed for knowledge-extraction techniques, where an enhancement in predictive performance is often counterbalanced with a worsening in the knowledge human interpretability [10,30]. Examples of classification rules extracted with HEx are reported in Listings 1 and 2 for the Iris [21] and Adult Income [6] data sets, respectively. The corresponding decision boundaries are shown in Fig. 2a and 2b, respectively.

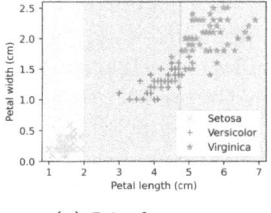 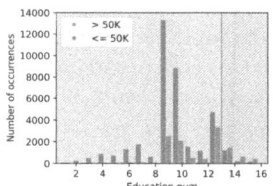

(a) Iris data set.   (b) Adult Income data set.

Fig. 2. Decision boundaries identified by HEx.

4   Experiments

The effectiveness of HEx has been assessed through experiments involving classification and regression tasks. It has been compared to state-of-the-art SKE techniques available in the PSyKE framework [9,34,39] applied to different black boxes. Knowledge quality has been evaluated on human readability (i.e., knowledge size), input space coverage and F_1 or R^2 scores. The Q_s score [36] is also shown as a concise quality assessment encompassing the aforementioned indices (low scores are associated with good quality). Results reported here are averaged over 10 runs. Given the standard deviations close to 0, we only report averages.

Our classification case study is based on the Adult Income data set [6]. It comprises 14 input attributes and 48 842 instances representing information about adult persons, whereas the output feature is a binary label expressing if an individual is likely to receive an income below or above 50 000 dollars. Three different black-box classifiers have been trained on the Adult Income data set, namely, a gradient boosting (GB) predictor, a random forest (RF) and a decision tree (DT). A train/test splitting with a 1:1 ratio has been performed. The training set has been employed for hyper-parameter tuning via 3-fold cross-validation.

Six knowledge extractors were successively applied to each one of these black boxes, namely, ITER, GRIDEX, HEX and three instances of CART. Knowledge size, coverage and F_1 scores with respect to the data set ground truth are reported and compared in Table 1, with best values highlighted in bold.

It can be noticed that HEX provides knowledge pieces with only two rules (one for the positive class and one for the negative) with an F_1 score of 0.66, slightly lower with respect to the highest score of 0.68 observed for CART. However, this CART instance produces 4 rules, thus denoting a stark worsening in the human-readability extent. The comparison between ITER and HEX is favourable for the latter, achieving the highest F_1 score, readability and completeness simultaneously. Also, the comparison with GRIDEX privileges HEX, since they have the same coverage and F_1 scores, however HEX outputs more concise knowledge bases. In general, by observing the Q_s scores computed for the HEX knowledge pieces, our proposed algorithm results capable of providing the highest quality knowledge.

Table 1. Results for the Adult Income data set.

		CART max depth = 1	CART max depth = 2	CART max leaves = 3	ITER	GRIDEX	HEX
GB	F_1	0.65	**0.68**	0.67	0.66	0.66	0.66
	Rules	**2.00**	4.00	3.00	8.20	3.00	**2.00**
	Coverage	1.00	1.00	1.00	0.86	1.00	1.00
	Q_s	0.70	1.28	1.00	3.19	1.02	**0.68**
RF	F_1	0.60	**0.67**	**0.67**	0.65	0.66	0.66
	Rules	**2.00**	4.00	3.00	7.90	3.00	**2.00**
	Coverage	1.00	1.00	1.00	0.83	1.00	1.00
	Q_s	0.80	1.31	1.00	3.24	1.02	**0.68**
DT	F_1	0.60	**0.67**	**0.67**	0.63	0.66	0.66
	Rules	**2.00**	4.00	3.00	8.40	3.00	**2.00**
	Coverage	1.00	1.00	1.00	0.79	1.00	1.00
	Q_s	0.80	1.31	1.00	3.81	1.02	**0.68**

Table 2. Results for the StairwAI data sets.

Data set	DT R^2	CART R^2	Rules	Q_s	GRIDEX R^2	Rules	Q_s	GRIDREX R^2	Rules	Q_s	HEX R^2	Rules	Q_s
#1	1.00	0.93	4	0.299	0.64	2	0.713	**1.00**	**2**	**0.009**	**1.00**	**2**	**0.009**
#2	0.92	0.89	4	0.458	0.69	2	0.627	**0.90**	**2**	**0.199**	**0.90**	**2**	**0.199**
#3	1.00	0.70	4	1.200	0.34	2	1.316	**0.99**	**2**	**0.024**	**0.99**	**2**	**0.024**
#4	1.00	0.88	4	0.488	−1.44	2	4.879	**0.99**	**2**	**0.013**	**0.99**	**2**	**0.013**
#5	1.00	0.93	4	0.285	0.63	2	0.738	**1.00**	2	0.008	**1.00**	**1**	**0.005**
#6	0.99	**0.09**	4	3.648	−1.11	2	4.222	-0.19	2	**2.381**	-0.19	**2**	**2.381**

Our regression case study employs six data sets from real use cases taken from the StairwAI EU Project and composed of up to 5 continuous input features. A different DT with maximum depth equal to 50 and an unbounded number of leaves has been trained for each data set. The pool of SKE algorithms adopted for the data sets is composed of CART, GRIDEX, GRIDREX and HEX. ITER proved incapable of providing comparable results, and therefore it is not considered in this case study.

Several combinations of hyper-parameters have been tested for the extractors. We report in Table 2 the assessments conducted for the underlying black boxes and for the instances of knowledge extractors providing the best results for each black box. The coverage of SKE techniques is not shown, since it is equal to 1.00 for all of them. It is clear how GRIDREX and HEX, being able to describe the outputs of regression rules as linear functions, outperform CART and GRIDEX, only providing constant outputs. HEX provides results very similar to those obtained with GRIDREX, nonetheless for one data set it can achieve the same predictive performance of GRIDREX with a single regression rule, resulting in higher knowledge quality. This can be verified by comparing the Q_s score of HEX (0.005) with that of GRIDREX (0.008).

5 Conclusions

In this work, we introduce HEX to perform SKE from any kind of opaque ML model designed for classification or regression tasks with continuous input attributes. HEX demonstrates superior compared to existing alternative techniques in terms of predictive accuracy, completeness and human-interpretability extent.

The HEX algorithm ensures a total input feature space coverage thanks to its tree-based knowledge extraction. Human readability is achieved via a hierarchical input space partitioning aimed at identifying only relevant predictive rules to be included in a concise output knowledge. Finally, HEX offers sensitive enhancements in the predictive performance when applied to regression tasks given its non-constant predictions based on linear combinations of the input variables.

HEx can be tuned by users via a set of hyper-parameters, that may also be handled automatically with the existing PEDRO procedure, designed for similar SKE algorithms. This ensures that HEx provides high-quality knowledge with minimum user effort.

Our future research will focus on developing more sophisticated and effective regression rules, to overcome the limitations of constant values and linear combinations. Furthermore, we plan to extend the identification of decision boundaries from perpendicular to oblique with respect to the data set axes.

Acknowledgments. This work has been supported by PNRR – M4C2 – Investimento 1.3, Partenariato Esteso PE00000013 – "FAIR—Future Artificial Intelligence Research" – Spoke 8 "Pervasive AI", funded by the European Commission under the NextGenerationEU programme and by the European Union's Horizon Europe AEQUITAS research and innovation programme under grant number 101070363.

References

1. Altmann, A., Toloşi, L., Sander, O., Lengauer, T.: Permutation importance: a corrected feature importance measure. Bioinformatics **26**(10), 1340–1347 (2010)
2. Andrews, R., Diederich, J., Tickle, A.B.: Survey and critique of techniques for extracting rules from trained artificial neural networks. Knowl.-Based Syst. **8**(6), 373–389 (1995). https://doi.org/10.1016/0950-7051(96)81920-4
3. Barbado, A., Corcho, Ó., Benjamins, R.: Rule extraction in unsupervised anomaly detection for model explainability: application to oneclass SVM. Expert Syst. Appl. **189**, 116100 (2022). https://doi.org/10.1016/j.eswa.2021.116100
4. Barbiero, P., Ciravegna, G., Giannini, F., Liò, P., Gori, M., Melacci, S.: Entropy-based logic explanations of neural networks. In: Thirty-Sixth AAAI Conference on Artificial Intelligence, AAAI 2022, Thirty-Fourth Conference on Innovative Applications of Artificial Intelligence, IAAI 2022, The Twelveth Symposium on Educational Advances in Artificial Intelligence, EAAI 2022 Virtual Event, February 22 - March 1, 2022, pp. 6046–6054. AAAI Press (2022). https://ojs.aaai.org/index.php/AAAI/article/view/20551
5. Barredo Arrieta, A., et al.: Explainable explainable artificial intelligence (XAI): Concepts, taxonomies, opportunities and challenges toward responsible AI. Inf. Fusion **58**(December 2019), 82–115 (2020). https://doi.org/10.1016/j.inffus.2019.12.012
6. Becker, B., Kohavi, R.: Adult. UCI Machine Learning Repository (1996). https://doi.org/10.24432/C5XW20
7. Breiman, L., Friedman, J., Stone, C.J., Olshen, R.A.: Classification and Regression Trees. CRC Press (1984)
8. Burrell, J.: How the machine 'thinks': Understanding opacity in machine learning algorithms. Big Data Soc. **3**(1) (2016). https://doi.org/10.1177/2053951715622512
9. Calegari, R., Sabbatini, F.: The PSyKE technology for trustworthy artificial intelligence **13796**, 3–16 (2023). https://doi.org/10.1007/978-3-031-27181-6_1, xXI International Conference of the Italian Association for Artificial Intelligence, AIxIA 2022, Udine, Italy, November 28 - December 2, 2022, Proceedings

10. Calvaresi, D., et al.: EXPECTATION: personalized explainable artificial intelligence for decentralized agents with heterogeneous knowledge. In: Calvaresi, D., Najjar, A., Winikoff, M., Främling, K. (eds.) Explainable and Transparent AI and Multi-Agent Systems. Third International Workshop, EXTRAAMAS 2021, Virtual Event, May 3–7, 2021, Revised Selected Papers, LNCS, vol. 12688, pp. 331–343. Springer Nature, Basel, Switzerland (2021). https://doi.org/10.1007/978-3-030-82017-6_20

11. de Campos Souza, P.V., Lughofer, E.: EFNN-NullUni: an evolving fuzzy neural network based on null-uninorm. Fuzzy Sets Syst. **449**, 1–31 (2022). https://doi.org/10.1016/j.fss.2022.01.010

12. Ciravegna, G., Barbiero, P., Giannini, F., Gori, M., Liò, P., Maggini, M., Melacci, S.: Logic explained networks. Artif. Intell. **314**, 103822 (2023). https://doi.org/10.1016/j.artint.2022.103822

13. Dattachaudhuri, A., Biswas, S.K., Chakraborty, M., Sarkar, S.: A transparent rule-based expert system using neural network. Soft. Comput. **25**(12), 7731–7744 (2021). https://doi.org/10.1007/s00500-020-05547-7

14. Demner-Fushman, D., Rogers, W.J., Aronson, A.R.: MetaMap lite: an evaluation of a new java implementation of MetaMap. J. Am. Med. Inform. Assoc. **24**(4), 841–844 (2017)

15. Diao, H., Lu, Y., Deng, A., Zou, L., Li, X., Pedrycz, W.: Convolutional rule inference network based on belief rule-based system using an evidential reasoning approach. Knowl. Based Syst. **237**, 107713 (2022). https://doi.org/10.1016/j.knosys.2021.107713

16. Espinosa Zarlenga, M., Shams, Z., Jamnik, M.: Efficient decompositional rule extraction for deep neural networks. CoRR **abs/2111.12628** (2021). https://arxiv.org/abs/2111.12628

17. European Commission: AI Act – Proposal for a regulation of the European parliament and the council laying down harmonised rules on artificial intelligence (Artificial Intelligence Act) and amending certain union legislative acts (2021). https://eur-lex.europa.eu/legal-content/EN/TXT/?uri=CELEX:52021PC0206

18. European Commission, Directorate-General for Communications Networks, C., Technology: Ethics guidelines for trustworthy AI. Publications Office (2019). https://doi.org/10.2759/346720

19. Fan, J., Kalyanpur, A., Gondek, D.C., Ferrucci, D.A.: Automatic knowledge extraction from documents. IBM J. Res. Dev. **56**(3.4), 5–1 (2012)

20. Ferreira, J., de Sousa Ribeiro, M., Gonçalves, R., Leite, J.: Looking inside the black-box: Logic-based explanations for neural networks. In: Kern-Isberner, G., Lakemeyer, G., Meyer, T. (eds.) Proceedings of the 19th International Conference on Principles of Knowledge Representation and Reasoning, KR 2022, Haifa, Israel. July 31 - August 5, 2022 (2022). https://proceedings.kr.org/2022/45/

21. Fisher, R.A.: The use of multiple measurements in taxonomic problems. Ann. Eugen. **7**(2), 179–188 (1936). https://doi.org/10.1111/j.1469-1809.1936.tb02137.x, https://onlinelibrary.wiley.com/doi/abs/10.1111/j.1469-1809.1936.tb02137.x

22. Guidotti, R., Monreale, A., Ruggieri, S., Turini, F., Giannotti, F., Pedreschi, D.: A survey of methods for explaining black box models. ACM Comput. Surv. **51**(5), 1–42 (2018). https://doi.org/10.1145/3236009

23. Huysmans, J., Baesens, B., Vanthienen, J.: ITER: An algorithm for predictive regression rule extraction. In: Data Warehousing and Knowledge Discovery (DaWaK 2006), pp. 270–279. Springer (2006) https://doi.org/10.1007/11823728_26

24. Irfan, M., Zheng, J., Iqbal, M., Masood, Z., Arif, M.H.: Knowledge extraction and retention based continual learning by using convolutional autoencoder-based learning classifier system. Inf. Sci. **591**, 287–305 (2022) https://doi.org/10.1016/j.ins.2022.01.043

25. Johansson, U., Sönströd, C., Löfström, T., Boström, H.: Rule extraction with guarantees from regression models. Pattern Recognit. **126**, 108554 (2022). https://doi.org/10.1016/j.patcog.2022.108554

26. Kenny, E.M., Ford, C., Quinn, M., Keane, M.T.: Explaining black-box classifiers using post-hoc explanations-by-example: the effect of explanations and error-rates in XAI user studies. Artif. Intell. **294**, 103459 (2021). https://doi.org/10.1016/j.artint.2021.103459

27. Konig, R., Johansson, U., Niklasson, L.: G-REX: a versatile framework for evolutionary data mining. In: 2008 IEEE International Conference on Data Mining Workshops (ICDM 2008 Workshops), pp. 971–974 (2008).https://doi.org/10.1109/ICDMW.2008.117

28. Lipton, Z.C.: The mythos of model interpretability. Queue **16**(3), 31–57 (2018). https://doi.org/10.1145/3236386.3241340

29. Obregon, J., Jung, J.: RuleCOSI+: rule extraction for interpreting classification tree ensembles. Inf. Fusion **89**, 355–381 (2023). https://doi.org/10.1016/j.inffus.2022.08.021

30. Rudin, C.: Stop explaining black box machine learning models for high stakes decisions and use interpretable models instead. Nat. Mach. Intell. **1**(5), 206–215 (2019). https://doi.org/10.1038/s42256-019-0048-x

31. Sabbatini, F., Calegari, R.: Symbolic knowledge extraction from opaque machine learning predictors: GridREx & PEDRO. In: Kern-Isberner, G., Lakemeyer, G., Meyer, T. (eds.) Proceedings of the 19th International Conference on Principles of Knowledge Representation and Reasoning, KR 2022, Haifa, Israel. July 31 - August 5, 2022 (2022).https://doi.org/10.24963/kr.2022/57, https://proceedings.kr.org/2022/57/

32. Sabbatini, F., Calegari, R.: Achieving complete coverage with hypercube-based symbolic knowledge-extraction techniques. In: Nowaczyk, S., Biecek, P., Chung, N.C., Vallati, M., Skruch, P., Jaworek-Korjakowska, J., Parkinson, S., Nikitas, A., Atzmüller, M., Kliegr, T., et al. (eds.) Artificial Intelligence. ECAI 2023 International Workshops – XAI³, TACTIFUL, XI-ML, SEDAMI, RAAIT, AI4S, HYDRA, AI4AI, Kraków, Poland, September 30 – October 4, 2023, Proceedings, Part I. Communications in Computer and Information Science, vol. 1947, pp. 179–197. Springer (2023https://doi.org/10.1007/978-3-031-50396-2_10

33. Sabbatini, F., Calegari, R.: Symbolic knowledge-extraction evaluation metrics: The FiRe score. In: Gal, K., Nowé, A., Nalepa, G.J., Fairstein, R., Rădulescu, R. (eds.) Proceedings of the 26th European Conference on Artificial Intelligence, ECAI 2023, Kraków, Poland. September 30 – October 4, 2023 (2023). https://doi.org/10.3233/FAIA230496, https://ebooks.iospress.nl/doi/10.3233/FAIA230496

34. Sabbatini, F., Calegari, R.: Unlocking insights and trust: the value of explainable clustering algorithms for cognitive agents. In: Falcone, R., Castelfranchi, C., Sapienza, A., Cantucci, F. (eds.) Proceedings of the 24th Workshop "From Objects to Agents", Roma, Italy, November 6–8, 2023. CEUR Workshop Proceedings, vol. 3579, pp. 232–245. CEUR-WS.org (2023). https://ceur-ws.org/Vol-3579/paper18.pdf

35. Sabbatini, F., Calegari, R.: Unveiling opaque predictors via explainable clustering: The CReEPy algorithm. In: Boella, G., et al. (eds.) Proceedings of the 2nd Workshop on Bias, Ethical AI, Explainability and the role of Logic and Logic Programming co-located with the 22nd International Conference of the Italian Association for Artificial Intelligence (AI*IA 2023), Rome, Italy, November 6, 2023. CEUR Workshop Proceedings, vol. 3615, pp. 1–14. CEUR-WS.org (2023). https://ceur-ws.org/Vol-3615/paper1.pdf
36. Sabbatini, F., Calegari, R.: On the evaluation of the symbolic knowledge extracted from black boxes. AI Ethics **4**(1), 65–74 (2024). https://doi.org/10.1007/s43681-023-00406-1
37. Sabbatini, F., Calegari, R.: Untying black boxes with clustering-based symbolic knowledge extraction. Intelligenza Artificiale **18**(1), 21–34 (2024). https://doi.org/10.3233/IA-240026
38. Sabbatini, F., Ciatto, G., Calegari, R., Omicini, A.: Hypercube-based methods for symbolic knowledge extraction: towards a unified model. In: Ferrando, A., Mascardi, V. (eds.) WOA 2022 – 23rd Workshop "From Objects to Agents", CEUR Workshop Proceedings, vol. 3261, pp. 48–60. Sun SITE Central Europe, RWTH Aachen University (2022). http://ceur-ws.org/Vol-3261/paper4.pdf
39. Sabbatini, F., Ciatto, G., Calegari, R., Omicini, A.: Symbolic knowledge extraction from opaque ML predictors in PSyKE: Platform design & experiments. Intelligenza Artificiale **16**(1), 27–48 (2022). https://doi.org/10.3233/IA-210120
40. Sabbatini, F., Ciatto, G., Calegari, R., Omicini, A.: Towards a unified model for symbolic knowledge extraction with hypercube-based methods. Intelligenza Artificiale **17**(1), 63–75 (2023). https://doi.org/10.3233/IA-230001
41. Sabbatini, F., Ciatto, G., Omicini, A.: GridEx: an algorithm for knowledge extraction from black-box regressors. In: Calvaresi, D., Najjar, A., Winikoff, M., Främling, K. (eds.) Explainable and Transparent AI and Multi-Agent Systems. Third International Workshop, EXTRAAMAS 2021, Virtual Event, May 3–7, 2021, Revised Selected Papers, LNCS, vol. 12688, pp. 18–38. Springer Nature, Basel, Switzerland (2021). https://doi.org/10.1007/978-3-030-82017-6_2
42. Sabbatini, F., Grimani, C., Calegari, R.: Bridging machine learning and diagnostics of the ESA LISA space mission with equation discovery via explainable artificial intelligence. Adv. Space Res. **74**(1), 505–517 (2024). https://doi.org/10.1016/j.asr.2024.04.041, https://www.sciencedirect.com/science/article/pii/S0273117724003880
43. Salimi-Badr, A., Ebadzadeh, M.M.: A novel learning algorithm based on computing the rules' desired outputs of a TSK fuzzy neural network with non-separable fuzzy rules. Neurocomputing **470**, 139–153 (2022). https://doi.org/10.1016/j.neucom.2021.10.103
44. Schmitz, G.P.J., Aldrich, C., Gouws, F.S.: ANN-DT: an algorithm for extraction of decision trees from artificial neural networks. IEEE Trans. Neural Netw. **10**(6), 1392–1401 (1999). https://doi.org/10.1109/72.809084
45. Setiono, R., Leow, W.K., Zurada, J.M.: Extraction of rules from artificial neural networks for nonlinear regression. IEEE Trans. Neural Netw. **13**(3), 564–577 (2002). https://doi.org/10.1109/TNN.2002.1000125
46. Setiono, R., Liu, H.: NeuroLinear: from neural networks to oblique decision rules. Neurocomputing **17**(1), 1–24 (1997). https://doi.org/10.1016/S0925-2312(97)00038-6
47. Smith, C.A., Hetzel, S., Dalrymple, P., Keselman, A.: Beyond readability: investigating coherence of clinical text for consumers. J. Med. Internet Res. **13**(4), e1842 (2011)

48. Towell, G.G., Shavlik, J.W.: Extracting refined rules from knowledge-based neural networks. Mach. Learn. **13**(1), 71–101 (1993). https://doi.org/10.1007/BF00993103
49. Zhuang, J., Dvornek, N.C., Li, X., Yang, J., Duncan, J.: Decision explanation and feature importance for invertible networks. In: 2019 IEEE/CVF International Conference on Computer Vision Workshop (ICCVW), pp. 4235–4239. IEEE (2019)
50. Zien, A., Krämer, N., Sonnenburg, S., Rätsch, G.: The feature importance ranking measure. In: Joint European Conference on Machine Learning and Knowledge Discovery in Databases (ECML PKDD 2009), pp. 694–709. Springer (2009) https://doi.org/10.1007/978-3-642-04174-7_45

On Different Symbolic Music Representations for Algorithmic Composition Approaches Based on Neural Sequence Models

Felix Schön$^{(\boxtimes)}$ iD and Hans Tompits$^{(\boxtimes)}$ iD

Institute of Logic and Computation E192-03, Technische Universität Wien,
Favoritenstraåe 9-11, 1040 Vienna, Austria
{schoen,tompits}@kr.tuwien.ac.at

Abstract. Among the different approaches for automated music composition, those based on neural sequence models like the transformer show particular promise. A critical aspect for such approaches is how given music data sets are represented, or *tokenised*, for serving as suitable inputs for such models, as the choice of representation influences the quality of the produced output. In this paper, we introduce seven novel tokenisation techniques for converting MIDI data into numeric sequences. We compare characteristics of our tokenisers based on sets of musical data translated using our approaches. Our results show that some of our techniques greatly outperform the approaches found in the literature with respect to different metrics such as sequence length, information density, or memory requirements. Moreover, to evaluate the influence of our tokenisation approaches on the quality of the output of a model, we trained an ensemble of transformer models on the sets of tokenised musical data and performed a user study to assess the quality of the generated music pieces. The result of the study shows that the quality of pieces produced using our most promising techniques is equal to or outperforms state-of-the-art approaches.

Keywords: Algorithmic Composition · Symbolic Music Generation · Transformer Neural Networks

1 Introduction

The term *algorithmic composition* (AC) refers to the technique of creating music by means of a formal set of rules or algorithms. While many different automated AC methods have been realised [1,3,4,9,21], the arguably most successful systems developed in recent years are those based on the *transformer neural network architecture* [27], like the MusicTransformer [16] and MuseNet [23].

As the transformer is a *neural sequence model*, AC methods based on such an architecture treat music as a *language*, where a given digital representation of a musical score is translated into discrete elements, called *tokens*, which are then processed by the network model. These sequence-based methods constitute *symbolic music generation* techniques where pieces of music are represented using sequences of symbols from a specific vocabulary representing, e.g., notes, rests, or time signature changes.

Now, the particular representation of the discrete tokens critically influences the network's ability to learn the underlying structure of the input [13]. Furthermore, representation lengths and vocabulary sizes significantly influence memory and computing resource requirements, an often limiting factor for real-world applications.

While research on transformer-based AC methods have for the most part focused on tuning the machine-learning algorithms [6–8,17], the question of the influence of the token representation has received much less attention. Indeed, notable exceptions in this regard include the works by Huang and Yang [17], who introduced REMI, a representation that explicitly models note durations, CP, due to Hsiao et al. [15], which is based on REMI, and Note Tuple [14].

In this paper, we introduce a suite of different symbolic music representation specifications, also referred to as *tokenisation approaches*. In particular, our main focus lies on reducing the average input sequence length while retaining the same output quality as with representations using longer sequences. More specifically, we present seven tokenisations, classified into so-called MIDI-*like approaches* and *note-like approaches*, respectively. In the former category, representations are based on the way the MIDIprotocol [20] represents musical data, whilst tokenisations in the latter category are inspired by the way traditional sheet music is written. For some of our note-like approaches, we make use of a greater vocabulary size. As a result, individual tokens can provide more information than their regular counterparts, e.g., both the pitch of a note and its duration.

Our note-like representations use a similar approach as REMI [15], where note durations are modeled explicitly. However, in contrast to REMI, we do not require these durations to be defined on a per-note basis but rather make use of a *running duration*, allowing for note durations to apply to all successive notes until superseded by the next duration. In the CP [15] method, the model architecture is modified to produce "super tokens" which combine several different REMI tokens. In contrast, our so-called *large-vocabulary representations* similarly represent multiple note attributes using a single token, but can be used without modifying the architecture of a model, making them compatible with more general models and requiring no additional computational effort.

In order to assess the different tokenisations introduced in this paper, we compare them with respect to certain parameters, like sequence length, information density, and memory requirements, applied on a combination of three training sets. Moreover, in order to evaluate the quality of pieces generated with our representations, we trained an ensemble of transformer models on the used data set and compared their output in a user study. The results show that some of our representations significantly reduce the average number of tokens needed to represent a musical sequence—in some cases as much as 40% compared to commonly used approaches such as REMI—without compromising on the output quality.

2   Background

We first provide some basic terminology from music theory (for more information on this subject, cf., e.g., the works of Benward and Saker [2] or Laitz [18]).

In musical scores, *notes* correspond to a tone of a specific pitch. The higher the note is situated on the score, the higher is the corresponding pitch. In general, 88 different notes are used, ranging from A0 (the lowest note) to C8. Notes have a *value*, which is a property that refers to the duration of the tone it represents. This duration is relative with regard to the *bar* it is contained in. A bar is a grouping of notes with a specific overall duration. Commonly, a bar can fit up to four consecutive quarter notes or any combination of (simultaneous) notes that take the same amount of time to play. Using *time signatures*, the capacity of a bar can be specified, usually in terms of how many consecutively played quarter notes it can fit. *Rests* mark pauses in the composition, and, in a similar fashion to notes, the length of these pauses is determined by their value. This, in combination with note values, allows for the construction of *rhythm*.

Relevant for our purposes is also the MIDIfile format [20], which is an industry standard for connecting electronic music and audio devices. MIDIfiles can be used to store musical performance data using sequential blocks of binary data. These blocks can constitute *events*, which consist of a *time-delta* definition, stating how many *ticks* (units of time) passed between the last and the current event, and a *message*, containing musical performance data. Commonly, MIDIuses 24 ticks for the duration of a quarter note.

Important for us are only the so-called "note on" and "note off" messages, indicating the start and end of a note, respectively. These can be used to model, e.g., the pressing and releasing of a piano key. Here, the message contains information about its exact type, the note's pitch, and its *velocity* value. The latter indicates how "loud" or with how much expression a note is played. For the sake of clarity, we represent MIDImessages using a textual representation, e.g., (note on A4) for the message indicating the start of A4.

As neural sequence models can only accept numerical input sequences, musical input compositions need to be translated into such a format before they can be used to train the models. This process is referred to as *tokenisation*. Formally, we are interested in transforming a sequence $S_{source} = (x_1, \ldots, x_n)$, where $x_i \in V_{target}$, for $1 \le i \le n$, into a sequence $S_{target} = (y_1, \ldots, y_m)$, where $y_i \in V_{target}$, for $1 \le i \le m$. Here, n and m give the lengths of the sequences, respectively, while $V_{target} = \{x_1, \ldots, x_s\}$ and $V_{target} = \{y_1, \ldots, y_t\}$ are vocabularies of size s and t, respectively.

For our purposes, V_{target} is the set of all MIDImessages, i.e., $V_{target} = V_{midi}$, where $V_{midi} := \{\ldots, (\text{note on A4}), (\text{note off A4}), \ldots\}$, while V_{target} contains the tokens used by the specific tokenisation approaches discussed in Sect. 3.

The resulting sequence S_{target} can then be used during the *training* process, where the model is tasked to learn the underlying probability distribution of the corpus of input sequences. In the *inference* step, the model is then used to generate new sequences. This is done by repeatedly tasking it to predict y_i based on $(y_0, \ldots, y_{i-1})$, where $y_1, \ldots, y_{i-1}$ are the predictions made in previous steps. Finally, the resulting output sequence $(y_1, \ldots, y_m)$ can be translated back into a sequence $(x_1, \ldots, x_n)$, where $x_i \in V_{\text{target}}$, for $1 \leq i \leq n$. Using this approach, neural sequence models can be utilised to compose new musical pieces.

3   Representations

We now introduce our tokenisation approaches for musical sequences. From an abstract point of view, a *tokenisation*, or *representation*, is a function mapping a sequence of elements from the MIDIvocabulary V_{midi} to a sequence of elements of the vocabulary of the tokeniser, which in our setting are sequences of natural numbers.

Our tokenisers can be categorised using the following three characteristics: (i) *temporal representation* (MIDI-like or note-like), (ii) *pitch representation* (absolute, relative, or circle-of-fifths), and (iii) *vocabulary size* (regular or large-vocabulary).

In what follows, we use the following notation: For any set X, $[X]^*$ denotes the set of all finite sequences of elements from X. Then, a *tokenisation* is a function $f : [V_{\text{midi}}]^* \to [V_f]^*$, where the codomain $[V_f]^*$ of f is a set of sequences of natural numbers and the set V_f is referred to as the *target vocabulary* of f.

Based on specific choices of the target vocabulary, we introduce the following tokenisations:

(i) the *relative MIDI-like representation*, $\mathcal{T}_{\text{midi}}^{\text{rel}}$, with target vocabulary $V_{\text{midi}}^{\text{rel}}$ $:= \{x \in \mathbb{N} | 0 \leq x \leq 392\}$);

(ii) the *circle-of-fifths* (CoF) *MIDI-like representation*, $\mathcal{T}_{\text{midi}}^{\text{cof}}$, with target vocabulary $V_{\text{midi}}^{\text{cof}} := \{x \in \mathbb{N} | 0 \leq x \leq 84\}$);

(iii) the *regular note-like representation*, $\mathcal{T}_{\text{note}}^{\text{reg}}$, with target vocabulary $V_{\text{note}}^{\text{reg}} :=$ $\{x \in \mathbb{N} | 0 \leq x \leq 132\}$);

(iv) the *large-vocabulary note-like representation*, $\mathcal{T}_{\text{note}}^{\text{lvoc}}$, with target vocabulary $V_{\text{note}}^{\text{lvoc}} := \{x \in \mathbb{N} | 0 \leq x \leq 1450\}$);

(v) the *relative note-like representation*, $\mathcal{T}_{\text{note}}^{\text{rel}}$, with target vocabulary $V_{\text{note}}^{\text{rel}} :=$ $\{x \in \mathbb{N} | 0 \leq x \leq 219\}$);

(vi) the *circle-of-fifths note-like representation*, $\mathcal{T}_{\text{note}}^{\text{cof}}$, with target vocabulary $V_{\text{note}}^{\text{cof}} := \{x \in \mathbb{N} | 0 \leq x \leq 73\}$); and

(vii) the *large-vocabulary circle-of-fifths note-like representation*, $\mathcal{T}_{\text{note}}^{\text{lcof}}$, with target vocabulary $V_{\text{note}}^{\text{lcof}} := \{x \in \mathbb{N} | 0 \leq x \leq 3307\}$).

For the sake of clarity, we represent the target vocabularies of our tokenisations using a textual representation rather than their numerical value, e.g., "(note on A4)" stands for "77". Furthermore, the shorthand "(note on _)" refers to all possible variations of a message, e.g., (note on A0) through (note on C8). In Table 1 we give a comparison of textual and numerical representations of tokens for a selection of different representations.

Table 1. Textual and numerical representations of the basic tokens used by our tokenisers

Textual Representation	Numerical Representation
Common to all Tokenisers	
(pad), (start), (stop)	0, 1, 2
Relative MIDI-like Tokeniser $\mathcal{T}_{\mathrm{midi}}^{\mathrm{rel}}$	
(wait 1) – (wait 24)	$4 - 27$
(note on -87) – (note on +87)	$28 - 202$
(note off -87) – (note off +87)	$203 - 376$
Regular Note-like Tokeniser $\mathcal{T}_{\mathrm{note}}^{\mathrm{reg}}$	
(wait)	4
(value definition 1) – (value definition 24)	$5 - 28$
(note play A0) – (note play C8)	$29 - 116$
Large-Vocabulary Note-like Tokeniser $\mathcal{T}_{\mathrm{note}}^{\mathrm{lvoc}}$	
(wait 1) – (wait 24)	$4 - 27$
(note value 2 play A0) – (note value 2 play C8)	$28 - 115$
⋮	⋮
(note value 96 play A0) – (note value 96 play C8)	$1348 - 1435$
Circle-of-Fifths Note-like Tokeniser $\mathcal{T}_{\mathrm{note}}^{\mathrm{cof}}$	
(wait)	4
(value definition 1) – (value definition 24)	$5 - 28$
(octave shift -8) – (octave shift +8)	$29 - 45$
(note play cof -5) – (note play cof +6)	$46 - 57$

Common to all our representations are the (start) and (stop) tokens which mark the beginning and end of a composition, respectively, a (pad) token that does not represent any musical element and is only used to pad sequences to a specific length, and 15 (time signature _) tokens used to define the time signature of a bar, determining how much capacity it has. We support time signatures ranging from $\frac{2}{16}$ up to $\frac{16}{16}$. Here, each (time signature _) token represents exactly one of the supported time signatures. We do not make use of *velocity* tokens for our representations but argue that including them would be straightforward, e.g., by using a set of (velocity _) tokens.

Rather than discuss the individual representations, we will illustrate the differences between the three characteristics mentioned above. This way, the representations are defined implicitly. We refer to Table 1 for more details on the basic token types.

The source code for our tokenisation approaches, the code used to train the models, the weights of the trained models, the generated samples, and the raw survey results can be found at

https://github.com/FelixSchoen/AIxIA-2024.

Temporal Representation. The MIDI-*like temporal representation*, as its name suggests, is based on the way the MIDIprotocol [20] represents musical data.

For our tokenisers, we make use of 88 (`note on _`) tokens to represent the start of a note, and 88 accompanying (`note off _`) tokens to mark the end of it. Furthermore, we make use of 24 (`wait _`) tokens, which correspond to the passing of the respective amount of *ticks*. Using this resolution, we can represent note values as small as thirty-second triplets—which have a duration of 2 ticks— using our representation.

Figure 1 depicts a visual representation of the MIDI-like temporal representation. Here, the beginnings and ends of notes have to be modeled explicitly.

Our *note-like representations* are inspired by the way traditional sheet music works. Instead of using a combination of (`note on _`) and (`note off _`) tokens to represent a single note, we use a (`value definition _`) token to define the length of the successive note, indicated by a (`note play _`) token, e.g., a (`value definition 24`) followed by a (`note play _`) token constitutes a quarter note. This greatly reduces the risk of invalid tokens, e.g., a (`note off _`) for a note that has not been previously opened.

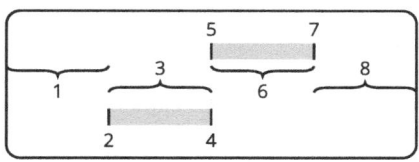 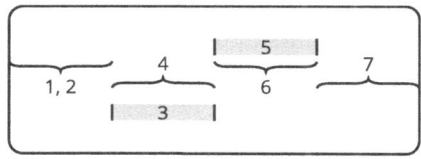

Fig. 1. A graph of the MIDI-like representation for one bar. (1: (`wait 6`), 2: (`note on A4`), 3: (`wait 6`), 4: (`note off A4`), 5: (`note on C5`), 6: (`wait 6`), 7: (`note off C5`), 8: (`wait 6`))

Fig. 2. A graph of the note-like representation for one bar. (1: (`value definition 6`), 2: (`wait`), 3: (`note play A4`), 4: (`wait`), 5: (`note play C5`), 6: (`wait`), 7: (`wait`))

A novel feature of our note-like temporal representation is the notion of a *running value*. Instead of having to define a value for each note, the current value applies to all subsequent tokens until it is replaced. This approach can greatly reduce the number of tokens in a sequence, reducing the computational costs associated with training neural sequence models.

In order to represent rests, we make use of a singular (`wait`) token, which marks an advancement in time in the current sequence. This token also accepts a value definition, or—in the case of a running value—makes use of the current active value.

We allow for consecutive (`value definition _`) tokens. In this case, the total amount of ticks is summed up and applied to the succeeding tokens. This way, notes or rests that last longer than the maximum amount supported by (`value definition _`) tokens can be defined.

Figure 2 depicts a visual representation of a note-like representation. In contrast to the MIDI-like approach, only the start of a note has to be modeled explicitly, its duration is given by previous value definitions.

Pitch Representation. We consider three different pitch representation types: *absolute, relative,* and *circle-of-fifths* type.

With the absolute approach, pitches are defined using only their key number on the piano, e.g., 49 for an A4.

With the relative approach, a pitch is defined by the distance to its predecessor. This is modeled using 175 (`note on _`) and the same amount of (`note off _`) tokens, indicating the distance of the current pitch to the previous one within the interval $[-87, +87]$. As the first note in a sequence has no predecessor, we define its representation as the distance from the international standard pitch A4 to it.

With the circle-of-fifths approach, distances between pitches are given by their distance on the *circle of fifths*, which is a categorisation of pitch classes. Any two adjacent classes on this circle, e.g., C and G, or A and E, are exactly 7 semi-tones apart, an interval commonly used in music. We use 12 (`note on _`) and the same amount of (`note off _`) tokens to represent the distance between two pitches on the circle of fifths and 17 (`octave shift _`) messages to be able to model shifts in octaves between two pitches of -8 to $+8$.

Vocabulary Size. In contrast to the regular vocabulary size, with the *large-vocabulary approach*, we replace the use of individual pairs of (`value definition _`) and (`note play _`) tokens by a single (`value _ play _`) token, specifying both value and pitch of a note. This approach requires a large amount of unique tokens in order to model all possible combinations. It works analogously for other pitch representation types, e.g., note value and relative distances can be combined into a single token.

Note that this approach only works for note-like temporal representations as here note values are modeled explicitly.

4   Experiments and Evaluation

To compare between our different tokenisers, we conducted an analysis of the sets of tokenised sequences produced using our approaches. These sets were obtained by tokenising the MIDI files from the dataset discussed in Sect. 4.1 below. To evaluate the differences in quality between neural sequence models trained using different tokenisation approaches, we conducted a survey on the output of an ensemble of transformer models trained on the same sets of tokenised sequences.

Note that for the sake of comparison, we include in our analysis both the regular MIDI-like tokeniser as found throughout literature [16,22,23] and a REMI-like tokeniser similar to the one used by the state-of-the-art Museformer [28] that does not make use of a running value but is otherwise identical to our regular note-like tokeniser.

4.1   Experimental Settings

Model Parameters. We use the original transformer architecture as introduced by Vaswani et al. [27] for our evaluation since we want to isolate the evaluation of our tokenisation processes and make it as replicable as possible. We used as hyperparameters a model dimensionality of 256, 1024 neurons per feed-forward layer, 4 attention heads, 4 encoder layers, and a dropout rate of 0.15 with a length limit of 1024 for all tokenisers. We utilise the AdamW optimiser [19] with beta values of 0.9, 0.98, an epsilon value of 1×10^{-9}, and a weight decay value of 0.1. For the learning rate we adapted the original transformer learning rate with 8000 warm-up steps and a multiplicative factor of 2, training for up to 64 epochs with a batch size of 2 over 8 accumulation steps, resulting in a practical batch size of 16. The training was conducted on the CLIP cluster[1] using four NVIDIA Quadro RTX 6000 cards per node.

Dataset. In order to test our tokenisation approaches on a wide variety of musical pieces, we used a combination of three different datasets, namely the *piano-midi.de*, the *ADL Piano MIDI* [10], and the *ASAP* [11] dataset. We utilised our music library S-Coda [25, 26] to preprocess and tokenise the MIDI files. Each piece was first checked for eligibility based on metrics such as number of tracks and empty bars and then split into chunks of 8 consecutive bars. We used a *stride* of 4 bars, i.e., every fourth bar in a piece of the dataset marks the beginning of an 8-bar chunk used for training.

4.2   Analysis of the Sets of Tokenised Sequences

Table 2 shows the numerical results of several analysis approaches of the sets of tokenised musical sequences. As their name suggests, the large-vocabulary approaches exhibit significantly higher vocabulary sizes than their regular counterparts. Note that although larger vocabulary sizes require more computational resources during the embedding step, for transformer models, the main bottleneck stems from the overall length of sequences. The large-vocabulary approaches perform exceptionally well in this regard. They are able to outperform all other approaches in this aspect, improving upon the regular note-like representation by almost 25%, over 40% for the regular MIDI-like representation, and over 50% compared to the REMI-like representation. Both the regular note-like and relative note-like approaches outperform the conventionally used MIDI-like representation techniques and could serve as a good alternative to their large-vocabulary counterparts if smaller vocabulary sizes or the inclusion of information such as, e.g., velocity values is desired.

Interesting to note are the values for the standard deviation. The non-large-dictionary approaches making use of a circle-of-fifths representation exhibit especially high values here, suggesting that the range of sequence lengths is quite high. This has a particularly severe impact, as in a batch, all sequences are

---

[1] https://clip.science.

Table 2. Results of the analysis on the different sets of tokenised sequences

Tokeniser	Vocab. Size	Avg. Seq. Len.	Std. Dev. Seq. Len.	Entropy	Gini Coeff.	Final Loss	Memory Req.	Survey Wins
Regular MIDI-like Tokeniser	219	317.68	148.98	6.60	0.63	0.84	7.52 GB	60%
Relative MIDI-like Tokeniser	393	317.68	148.98	6.2	0.80	0.75	6.60 GB	37%
CoF MIDI-like Tokeniser	85	460.90	224.92	4.85	0.72	0.68	6.25 GB	40%
Regular Note-like Tokeniser	133	252.83	109.93	5.05	0.75	0.99	2.35 GB	57%
REMI-like Tokeniser	133	385.77	169.36	4.6	0.81	0.65	8.09 GB	56%
Large Vocabulary Note-like Tokeniser	1451	190.12	84.17	7.30	0.86	1.29	1.95 GB	61%
Relative Note-like Tokeniser	220	252.84	109.93	4.96	0.84	0.88	3.75 GB	53%
CoF Note-like Tokeniser	74	329.58	147.55	4.35	0.77	0.84	12.41 GB	37%
Large Voc. CoF Note-like Tokeniser	3308	190.12	84.17	7.27	0.90	1.2	2.21 GB	48%

padded to the highest sequence length among them, drastically increasing memory requirements.

We compared our approaches also with respect to *entropy*, which is used to measure the information content of a random variable, where a higher entropy indicates a more random distribution and thus a larger amount of information per observation [24]. It is calculated using the formula

$$H(X) := - \sum_{x \in \mathcal{X}} P(x) log_2 P(x),$$

where X is a random variable with domain $\mathcal{X}$ and $P(x)$ is the probability of X having value $x \in \mathcal{X}$. Lower values of entropy indicate a higher predictability of next words while higher values imply larger vocabulary sizes and greater information gain per word.

Both large-vocabulary approaches exhibit significantly higher entropy values than their regular-vocabulary counterparts. This is in accordance with the decreased sequence lengths as each word carries a larger amount of information for these approaches. On the other hand, the regular circle-of-fifths approaches carry the least amount of information per word.

Another parameter we considered is the *Gini coefficient* [5,12], which can be used to measure statistical inequality in the distribution of values across a set of classes. It is given by

$$G = \frac{1}{2n^2 \overline{x}} \sum_{i=1}^{n} \sum_{j=1}^{n} |x_i - x_j|,$$

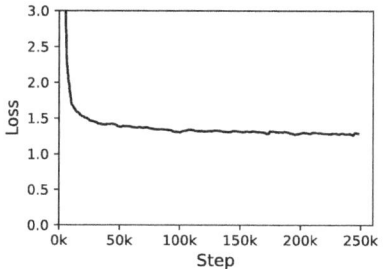 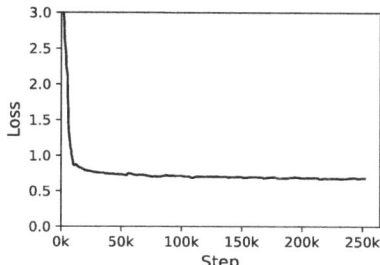

(a) Learning curve of the model trained using the large vocabulary note-like tokenisation approach.

(b) Learning curve of the model trained using the circle-of-fifths MIDI-like tokenisation approach.

Fig. 3. Learning rates of two models trained on the same dataset using two different tokenisation approaches

where n is the number of classes, x_i is the number of values that belong to class i, and $\bar{x}$ is the average of values per class. Alternatively, if $x_i \leq x_{i+1}$ holds, we can calculate the Gini coefficient as follows:

$$G = \frac{1}{n} \sum_{i=1}^{n} (2i - n - 1)x_i \cdot \left(\sum_{i=1}^{n} x_i \right)^{-1}.$$

The Gini coefficient provides a measure of how equally observations are distributed over a number of classes. $G = 0$ indicates a perfectly equivalent distribution while $G = 1$ indicates a maximally imbalanced distribution, e.g., all samples belonging to a single class.

The Gini coefficient is relatively high for all our representation approaches, suggesting that a few single tokens are heavily prioritised over others. We argue that this most likely stems from the repeated usage of the (wait) token which is essential for the construction of rhythm and temporal resolution. Although in practice this did not pose problems, future variations of our representations could try to tackle this shortcoming. We note that, for the calculation of the Gini coefficient and the entropy value, we only considered tokens of the vocabulary that were used in the dataset in order not to dilute the results due to a large number of unused tokens.

We trained an ensemble of nine transformer models on the dataset, for each of the representation techniques, respectively. For the sake of reproducibility, we report the final loss values achieved for each of the models after the last epoch. Note that due to the differences in vocabulary size between the approaches, the loss values are not directly comparable. This is reflected in Fig. 3, showing learning curves for two of the models. Although the learning curve in Fig. 3b seems to outperform the one in Fig. 3a, in practice the former model exhibits significantly higher output quality compared to the latter.

Lastly, we include the highest reported memory usage during the training of the models using the respective representation (cf. Sect. 4.1 for the exact hyperparameters used). In contrast to the loss values, these values are directly comparable and provide important insights. Here, our large-vocabulary approaches perform exceptionally well, reducing the memory requirements by approximately 70% compared to the regular MIDI-like- and REMI-like representation. Despite the large difference in average sequence length, the memory requirement of the regular note-like representation is comparable to our large-vocabulary approaches. We argue that this is due to the overhead induced by the significantly larger vocabulary size. Increasing the number of layers would likely result in the regular note-like approach consuming drastically more memory as the space requirements are dependant on the square of the sequence lengths.

4.3   Evaluation of the Quality of the Generated Music

In order to evaluate qualitative differences between pieces generated by the models trained on the different sets of tokenised sequences, we performed a survey involving 11 participants. For each of the nine models, we generated 64 compositions. Here, the models were only primed with the (start) token and tasked to predict new tokens until the (stop) token or a length of 1024 is reached. Note that we did not remove any failure samples in this process as this could potentially skew the results of the survey.

The participants were provided with eight pairs of two compositions, randomly sampled from the output of one of the trained models. Note that the origin in a pair of samples was mutually exclusive. We then asked the participants to select which of the pieces they believed to be more musically sophisticated, interesting, or less computer-generated. Table 2 shows the percentage of match-ups won for each of the tokenisers. As the pieces were randomly drawn for each instance of the survey, we allowed for multiple submissions. We asked the participants to mark their entries as repeats in this case. In total, we received 17 submissions comparing 272 compositions generated by our models.

The survey shows that with 60.6% of 33 match-ups won, our large-vocabulary note-like tokeniser performed best. This is an encouraging result as it suggests that the quality of pieces produced using this technique is on par or better compared to pieces produced using more traditional approaches, even though the sequence length is greatly reduced.

All of the regular MIDI-like tokenisers, the regular note-like tokeniser, and the REMI-like tokeniser showed good promise as well, winning 60% of 30, 57.1% of 28, and 56.3% of 32 match-ups, respectively. Contrary to our assumptions, the relative and circle-of-fifths approaches did not perform as well, often exhibiting frantic jumps between notes and disharmonic melodies.

Figure 4 depicts score representations for two samples generated by two of our models. More specifically, Fig. 4a shows a piece generated by our large-vocabulary note-like model which exhibits typical rhythmic and melodic struc-

(a) Score representation of a piece generated using the large vocabulary note-like tokenisation approach.

(b) Score representation of a piece generated using the circle-of-fifths MIDI-like tokenisation approach.

Fig. 4. Score representation of two pieces generated by models trained on the same dataset using two different tokenisation approaches

ture. On the other hand, in Fig. 4b, a piece generated by the circle-of-fifths MIDI-like model is given. Here, erratic jumps in pitch and inconsistent rhythm can be observed.

5 Conclusion

In this paper, we introduced seven novel tokenisation techniques for symbolic music generation. These techniques can be categorised into two main categories: (i) MIDI-like tokenisers and (ii) note-like tokenisers. Our large-vocabulary note-like tokeniser shows particular promise. It makes use of a note-like temporal representation style while using a large vocabulary of tokens to indicate pitch and value of a note using a single token. This way, we are able to reduce the average length of a sequence needed to represent a musical composition by more than 40% compared to the most commonly used and the REMI-like approach.

Our user study shows that the output quality of models trained using our large-vocabulary note-like tokeniser is not negatively impacted by the reduction of sequence lengths.

Concerning future work, we plan on adapting our tokenisers to a multi-track setting, potentially supporting a variety of instruments. Here, the large-vocabulary approaches could be extended by additional sets of tokens representing a specific instrument or track. Furthermore, for the note-like approaches, an idea analogous to the running value could be implemented, specifying the current instrument for all subsequent messages until replaced.

References

1. Bell, C.: Algorithmic music composition using dynamic Markov chains and genetic algorithms. J. Comput. Sci. Coll. **27**(2), 99–107 (2011)
2. Benward, B., Saker, M.: Music in Theory and Practice:, vol. 1. USA, eighth edn, McGraw-Hill, New York, NY (2009)
3. Biles, J.A.: Autonomous GenJam: Eliminating the fitness bottleneck by eliminating fitness. In: Poon, J., Maher, M.L. (eds.) Proceedings of the GECCO 2001 Workshop on Non-routine Design with Evolutionary Systems (2001)
4. Boenn, G., Brain, M., De Vos, M., Fitch, J.P.: Automatic music composition using answer set programming. Theory Pract. Logic Program. **11**(2–3), 397–427 (2011). https://doi.org/10.1017/S1471068410000530
5. Breiman, L., Friedman, J., Olshen, R., Stone, C.J.: Classification and Regression Trees. Chapman and Hall, New York (1984)
6. Child, R., Gray, S., Radford, A., Sutskever, I.: Generating long sequences with sparse transformers. CoRR **abs/1904.10509** (2019)
7. Dai, Z., Yang, Z., Yang, Y., Carbonell, J., Le, Q., Salakhutdinov, R.: Transformer-XL: Attentive language models beyond a fixed-length context. In: Korhonen, A., Traum, D.R., Màrquez, L. (eds.) Proceedings of the 57th Annual Meeting of the Association for Computational Linguistics (ACL 2019), pp. 2978–2988. University of Chicago Press (2019)
8. Donahue, C., Mao, H.H., Li, Y.E., Cottrell, G.W., McAuley, J.: Lakhnes: Improving multi-instrumental music generation with cross-domain pre-training. In: Flexer, A., Peeters, G., Urbano, J., Volk, A. (eds.) Proceedings of the 20th International Society for Music Information Retrieval Conference (ISMIR 2019), pp. 685–692 (2019)
9. Eigenfeldt, A., Pasquier, P.: Realtime generation of harmonic progressions using constrained Markov selection. In: Ventura, D., Pease, A., y Pérez, R.P., Ritchie, G., Veale, T. (eds.) Proceedings of the 1st International Conference on Computational Creativity (ICCC 2010), pp. 16–25. computationalcreativity.net (2010)
10. Ferreira, L.N., Lelis, L.H.S., Whitehead, J.: Computer-generated music for tabletop role-playing games. In: Lelis, L., Thue, D. (eds.) Proceedings of the 16th AAAI Conference on Artificial Intelligence and Interactive Digital Entertainment (AIIDE 2020), pp. 59–65. AAAI Press (2020)
11. Foscarin, F., McLeod, A., Rigaux, P., Jacquemard, F., Sakai, M.: ASAP: A dataset of aligned scores and performances for piano transcription. In: Cumming, J., Lee, J.H., McFee, B., Schedl, M., Devaney, J., McKay, C., Zangerle, E., de Reuse, T. (eds.) Proceedings of the 21th International Society for Music Information Retrieval Conference (ISMIR 2020), pp. 534–541 (2020)
12. Gini, C.: On the measure of concentration with special reference to income and statistics. Colorado Coll. Public., General Series **208**, 73–79 (1936)
13. Goodfellow, I.J., Bengio, Y., Courville, A.C.: Deep Learning. MIT Press, Adaptive computation and machine learning (2016)

14. Hawthorne, C., Huang, C.A., Eck, D.I.D.: Transformer-NADE for piano performances. In: Elliott, L., Dieleman, S., Fiebrink, R., Roberts, A., Engel, J., White, T. (eds.) Proceedings of the NeurIPS Workshop on Machine Learning for Creativity and Design (2018)

15. Hsiao, W., Liu, J., Yeh, Y., Yang, Y.: Compound Word Transformer: Learning to compose full-song music over dynamic directed hypergraphs. In: Guerzhoy, M., Torrey, L. (eds.) Proceedings of the 11th Symposium on Educational Advances in Artificial Intelligence (EAAI 2021), pp. 178–186. AAAI Press (2021). https://doi.org/10.1609/AAAI.V35I1.16091

16. Huang, C.A., et al.: Music Transformer: Generating music with long-term structure. In: Levine, S., Livescu, K., Mohamed, S. (eds.) Proceedings of the 7th International Conference on Learning Representations (ICLR 2019). OpenReview.net (2019)

17. Huang, Y., Yang, Y.: Pop music transformer: beat-based modeling and generation of expressive pop piano compositions. In: Chen, C.W., Cucchiara, R., Hua, X., Qi, G., Ricci, E., Zhang, Z., Zimmermann, R. (eds.) Proceedings of the 28th International Conference on Multimedia (ACM 2020), pp. 1180–1188. ACM (2020)

18. Laitz, S.G.: The Complete Musician: An Integrated Approach to Tonal Theory, Analysis, and Listening, 3rd edn. Oxford University Press, Oxford, England (2012)

19. Loshchilov, I., Hutter, F.: Decoupled weight decay regularization. In: Levine, S., Livescu, K., Mohamed, S. (eds.) Proceedings of the 7th International Conference on Learning Representations (ICLR 2019). OpenReview.net (2019)

20. MIDI Manufacturers Association: The Complete MIDI 1.0 Detailed Specification. https://midi.org/ (1996)

21. Opolka, S., Obermeier, P., Schaub, T.: Automatic genre-dependent composition using answer set programming. In: Schiphorst, T., Pasquier, P. (eds.) Proceedings of the 21st International Symposium on Electronic Art (ISEA 2015), pp. 627–632. ISEA International, Brighton, UK (2015)

22. Payne, C.: Clara: A neural net music generator. https://christinemcleavey.com/clara-a-neural-net-music-generator. Accessed 04 June 2024

23. Payne, C.: MuseNet. https://openai.com/research/musenet (2019). Accessed 20 June 2023

24. Russell, S., Norvig, P.: Artificial Intelligence: A Modern Approach. Pearson, 4th edn. (2020)

25. Schön, F.: PAUL-2: A Transformer-Based Algorithmic Composer of Two-Track Piano Pieces. Diploma Thesis, Technische Universität Wien, Institute of Logic and Computation, E192-03 (2023)

26. Schön, F., Tompits, H.: PAUL-2: An upgraded Transformer-based redesign of the algorithmic composer PAUL. In: Basili, R., Lembo, D., Limongelli, C., Orlandini, A. (eds.) Proceedings of the 22nd International Conference of the Italian Association for Artificial Intelligence (AIxIA 2023). Lecture Notes in Computer Science, vol. 14318, pp. 278–291. Springer (2023). https://doi.org/10.1007/978-3-031-47546-7

27. Vaswani, A., et al.: Attention is all you need. In: Guyon, I., von Luxburg, U., Bengio, S., Wallach, H.M., Fergus, R., Vishwanathan, S.V.N., Garnett, R. (eds.) Proceedings of the 30th Annual Conference on Neural Information Processing Systems (NIPS 2017), pp. 5998–6008 (2017)

28. Yu, B., et al.: Museformer: Transformer with fine- and coarse-grained attention for music generation. In: Koyejo, S., Mohamed, S., Agarwal, A., Belgrave, D., Cho, K., Oh, A. (eds.) Proceedings of the 36th Annual Conference on Neural Information Processing Systems (NeurIPS 2022) (2022)

DR-Minerva: A Multimodal Language Model Based on Minerva for Diagnostic Information Retrieval

Irene Siragusa[1,2] [ID], Salvatore Contino[1(✉)] [ID], and Roberto Pirrone[1] [ID]

[1] Department of Engineering, University of Palermo, 90128 Palermo, Sicily, Italy
{salvatore.contino01,roberto.pirrone}@unipa.it
[2] Department of Computer Science, IT University of Copenhagen,
2300 København S, Denmark
irene.siragusa02@unipa.it

Abstract. This paper illustrates the development of Minerva Diagnostic Retriever (DR-Minerva), a Visual Language Model specialized in the medical domain. Prompted using a textual input with the patient's information along with a CT or MR scan, the model provides information about the body part and the scanning modality of the given image. The model relies on the Flamingo architecture, which is well known for its good in-context and few-shot learning capabilities, and it encodes textual data using Minerva, a novel Large Language Model trained on English and Italian data. Model performances are improved via fine-tuning the aforementioned model, and using external knowledge by means of a Retrieval Augmented Generation approach. At inference time, the model is injected with the retrieved examples in form of in-context learning. The authors developed a rearranged version of the MedPix® multi-modal medical dataset, that was used for both the development and the test of the model as long as for retrieval. A detailed description of the system is reported along with the experimental results that are discussed in thoroughly. Dataset and models used are available on GitHub (https://github.com/CHILab1/MedPix-2.0.).

Keywords: Multimodal Language Model · Retrieval Augmented Generation · Information Retrieval · Minerva · Flamingo · MedPix

1 Introduction

The spread of Artificial Intelligence (AI) in the medical domain has been revolutionary, beginning to transform the way in which diagnosis, treatment, and monitoring of patients are carried out. In particular, in recent years, the development of AI-based technologies for decision making support for physicians, gained a relevant interest in the scientific community, through the use of increasingly complex and precise Deep Neural Networks (DNNs) capable of analysing the whole variety of data available from clinical departments [5]. Today, the development of increasingly precise support systems is the natural development for computer applications within this domain, which must, however, not only develop

A. Artale et al. (Eds.): AIxIA 2024, LNAI 15450, pp. 288–300, 2025.
https://doi.org/10.1007/978-3-031-80607-0_22

predictive capabilities, but also an ever-increasing level of trustworthiness for physician and patient safety. To achieve these goals, DNNs need to be trained on an ever-increasing amount of data to improve their generalization capability. Unfortunately, the shortage of data is the biggest obstacle that does not allow rapid progress towards this goal to date. Currently, the models developed by the scientific community are based on public domain datasets, which are of poor quality because they are collected episodically without an established protocol for adding new data to the set. Often, such datasets are assembled for a scientific challenge, and their metadata only reflect the purpose of the scientific question behind the competition. The data needed to build reliable AI-enabled Medical Decision Support Systems (MDSS) must be collected directly from clinical sources, and their metadata must be standardized, especially for Vision Language Models (VLM) or on a Multimodal architecture of various kinds (Large Multimodal Model, LMM). It is precisely these models that are perfectly suited to the role required for physician support, thanks to their ability to integrate and process textual and visual information, providing rapid and objective support by analysing the features extracted from the data provided.

We present a new implementation of a VLM, based on Flamingo [2] and Minerva LLM, called Minerva Diagnostic Retriever (DR-Minerva), which have been trained through fine-tuning for the classification and prediction of two main features of biomedical data, i.e. the *modality* that contains the information inherent to the type of source of the biomedical image (e.g. CT, MRI) and the *location* that instead refers to the anatomical region that has been examined. The proposed neural architecture aims to perform few-shot predictions by identifying both modality and location, and if required returns the join of both predictions given a medical image and a short text with the information of the patient. Few-shot prediction is done via a Retrieval Augmented Generation (RAG) approach [15], leveraging on the peculiar textual information provided and the re-arranged version of the MedPix® [1] was used.

The paper is arranged as follows: Sect. 2 illustrates the relevant contributions within LMM in the medical domain. The architecture of the developed systems is reported in Sect. 3 along with the dataset used, while the experimental setups and results are reported and discussed in Sect. 4. Future works and concluding remarks are drawn in Sect. 5 and 6 respectively.

2   Related Works

Since development of transformed-based Language Models (LM) [28] like BERT [6], considerable improvements were done in building LMs till to Large Language Models (LLM). Those systems reach competitive performances with State Of The Art (SOTA) BERT-based models in most of the traditional Natural Language Processing (NLP) tasks [10], but they are intrinsically full of issues. Recent LLMs are very large, averaging from 70B to 175B as for Llama models [20,27] and GPT-3.5 [4], and a full fine-tuning of these models is actually impracticable due to the high computational cost and resources required. Moreover, there is no open information about the training procedure or the data involved of both models. Despite those issues, the interest of the scientific community is looking towards Large Multimodal Model (LMM), which leverage both textual, visual or audio data. Since Medical Imaging is intrinsically a multimodal domain, and it deeply focuses on analyzing both images and the related reports [8], Visual Language Models are the most used within these applications.

Most of the medical VLM rely on SOTA models, such as CLIP [24], LLaVA [19], and OpenFlamingo [3], an open-source version of Flamingo [2] and via a fine-tuning procedure, they succeed in developing their corresponding medical versions, BiomedCLIP [29], LLaVa-Med [16], and Med-Flamingo [21]. These models share a common pipeline, where images and text are encoded separately with their respectively visual and textual models, and then merged together to generate the textual output.

CLIP is trained to learn a multi-modal embedding space by jointly training both an image encoder and a text encoder to maximize the cosine similarity of the paired image and text embeddings while minimizing the cosine similarity of the incorrect pairings [24].

Both LLaVA and Flamingo rely on the pre-trained CLIP visual encoder to extract the visual features from a given image. LLaVA projects the obtained visual features to the word embedding space via a linear layer to pass them to the LM [19]. Analogously in Flamingo, visual tokens are extracted from the visual features through a "Perceiver Resampler" and then are incorporated with the textual encoding via a cross-attention layer, which is interleaved between the frozen pre-trained LM layers [2].

BiomedCLIP [29], LLaVa-Med [16], and Med-Flamingo, follow the training strategies of the models they are based on, and they are fine-tuned on data sets containing pairs of medical images and their caption, such as MTB [21], PMC-OA [17] and then are evaluated with the medical dataset for Visual Question Answering (VQA) like VQA-RAD [14], PathVQA [9] and SLAKE [18]. Both VQA-RAD and SLAKE collect radiologic images, while PathVQA contains pathology images, and the models are expected to reply to the given question based on the information derived from the proposed image.

3   System Description

In the following sub-sections a detailed description of the proposed system is given along with the design choices, and the overview of the dataset is provided along with the metrics used for the evaluation phase.

3.1   RAG-Based Flamingo

The overall DR-Minerva architecture is shown in Fig. 1. The system relies on both the Flamingo architecture [2] and Minerva [23], a novel LLM trained from scratch on English and Italian data as part of the activities in the PNRR FAIR

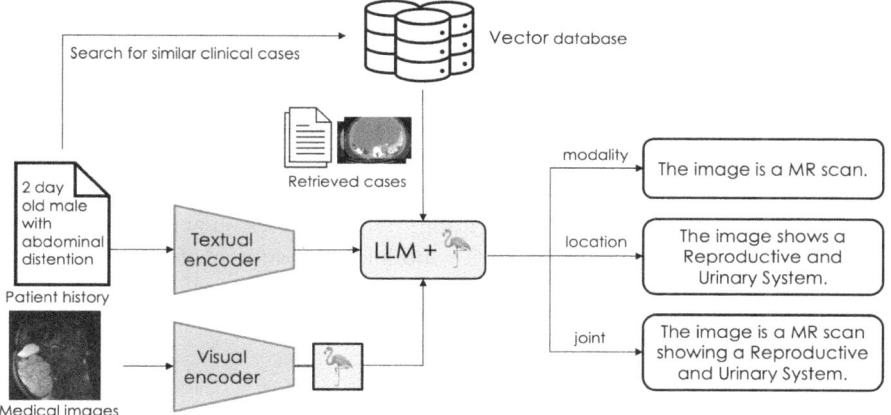

Fig. 1. Overview of DR-Minerva architecture

Transversal Project 2: "Vision, Language and Multimodal Challenges"[1]. The project is an effort made by almost twenty Italian Universities, and the authors are involved in the research for developing LMMs tailored for specific domains. We chose Minerva since it is a completely open-source model, since training set, architecture and weights are freely available, and its training set is half in English and half Italian, making it suitable for further experiments with the developed architecture and Italian data.

We used Open Flamingo [3], the open-source version of Flamingo, in the 3B parameters version[2]. As it is well known, the Flamingo architecture exhibits good in-context learning capabilities that make it suitable to adapt in diverse domains [2]. We maintained the CLIP ViT-L/14 [24] as the visual encoder, and we adopted Minerva-3B[3] as language encoder. The overall model is queried using the prompt reported in Table 1 to instruct the model on how to behave and generate the desired output.

We developed a suitable RAG component for our system [15] so, at inference time, the model is provided with an enriched prompt that can improve its performance. Since the AI models are required to be as precise as possible, in particular in medical domain, we query DR-Minerva with both the target medical image and a template built from some personal information of the patient (e.g. age and sex) followed by the history of the patient in order to prevent empty textual samples. Then the closest clinical cases are retrieved w.r.t. the patient's history, and they are attached to the prompt as few-shot learning examples.

---

[1] https://fondazione-fair.it/en/transversal-projects/tp2-vision-language-and-multimodal-challenges/.

[2] https://huggingface.co/openflamingo/OpenFlamingo-3B-vitl-mpt1b.

[3] https://huggingface.co/sapienzanlp/Minerva-3B-base-v1.0.

The RAG module picks (up to) the four closest clinical cases to the query, and it is build via the LangChain framework[4] that in turn uses a FAISS [7] vector database where data are stored using Linq-Embed-Mistral [13]. This is recognized as the best model in Massive Text Embedding Benchmark (MTEB) [22] for Information Retrieval[5].

To effectively evaluate RAG performance, we run the evaluation experiments with and without adding the retrieved examples, at inference time. It is worth noticing that in the no-RAG configuration, two examples showing two different scanning modalities are provided to the model to guide it at generation phase. During the developing process, some experiments were done querying the model providing just the instruction, i.e. in zero-shot configuration, as it is reported in Sect. 4.

Table 1. The structure of the prompt is reported as well as the template of the corresponding expected answers

Type	Prompt	Response
Modality	"Given the following medical images and the patient history, provide information about the scanning modality."	The image is a MR scan.
Location	"Given the following medical images and the patient history, provide information about the body part shown in the image."	The image shows a head.
Join	"Given the following medical images and the patient history, provide information about the scanning modality and the body part shown in the image."	The image is a MR scan showing a head.

3.2 The Dataset

To develop DR-Minerva, we used a re-arranged version of the MedPix® dataset [26][6]. MedPix® [1] is a multimodal semi-structured dataset of clinical cases released by the National Institutes of Health (NIH). For each case, a clinical report of the patient is reported along with some generic information about the disease, and some medical images with additive information related to both the scanning modality and the body part.

MedPix® dataset is freely available but the textual information is not provided in a suitable format for training AI system. The re-arranged version we used, collects all the information and structure them in two JSON files, namely the case-topic and the description file. The former collects the clinical cases, identified by their *uid* code, all the patient information, such as age, sex and her/his history, the diagnostic finding and the suggested treatment (case information), and general information about the disease from an academic point of view (topic information). The latter collects the caption of the medical images: for each image the *uid* code is reported, along with the scanning modality, the caption of the image and the body part shown. The aforementioned information

[4] https://www.langchain.com/.
[5] as in https://huggingface.co/spaces/mteb/leaderboard in June 2024.
[6] https://github.com/CHILab1/MedPix-2.0.

are reported as key-value pair following the JSON format: values are textual strings that can be a single word, as for the scanning modality, or a paragraph as for the differential diagnosis in the case information.

Given the data in a more accessible format, it was possible to select the relevant pieces of information and consequently create the classification tasks. We decided to focus on three evaluation setting, namely *modality*, *location* and *join*. The scanning modality evaluation consist in determining if a given image is a Computed Tomography (CT) or a Magnetic Resonance (MR) scan, while the location requires to individuate the body part shown, and the join setting asks for information about both modality and location. A single location is assigned to each image and refers to the macro-area shown[7] and are Thorax, Head, Abdomen, Reproductive and Urinary System and Spine and Muscles. The original dataset considers also General and Nervous System labels, but, since samples belonging to these categories were few compared to the others, images belonging to these location were re-assigned by a specialist to the aforementioned five. There is also worth mentioning that each image is associated to one location and one scanning modality, while a clinical case can contain multiple images, obtained with different scanning modality and showing different body part.

Thus, for each clinical case, we considered the history of the patient, his/her sex and age, and we created a sample document that, within the annotated images with modality and location labels, constitute the multimodal dataset for DR-Minerva. A sample of the dataset is reported in the figure below (Fig. 2).

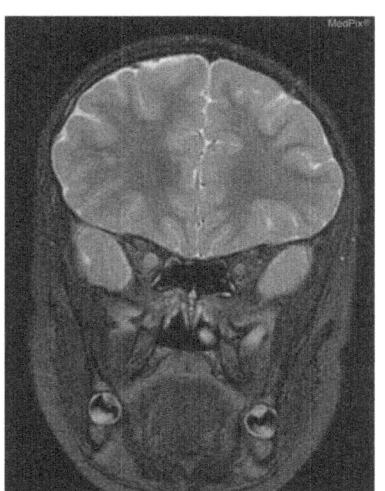

Example of some of the structured information from MedPix 2.0

UID: *MPX1463*
CT: *MPX1463_synpic17575*
MRI: *MPX1463_synpic17576, MPX1463_synpic17577*
Age: *6 y.o.*
Sex: *female*
History: *A 6 YO female presented to the emergency department with a 3 day history of right eye pain and severe decreasing visual acuity.*
Disease: *Optic Neuritis*
Modality: *MR*
Location: *Head*

RAG document

6 y.o. female patient suffering from a Optic Neuritis (imaging and clinical findings combined to verify diagnosis) .
A 6 YO female presented to the emergency department with a 3 day history of right eye pain and severe decreasing visual acuity.

Inference query

6 y.o. female patient. A 6 YO female presented to the emergency department with a 3 day history of right eye pain and severe decreasing visual acuity.

Fig. 2. A simple representation of a multimodal sample of the dataset. The actual structure of the RAG documents and the inference query, derived from the JSON file of the dataset are reported

---

[7] a more detailed location information is provided but not considered.

A semi-automatic 80%-10%-10% split was built from the documents keeping images from the same clinical case in the same split and assuring a balance for modality and location labels, as it is shown in Table 2. Maintaining the balance, we further split the training set in train-1 and train-2. Demographics and history of the patient and the clinical diagnosis from train-1, following ad hoc designed template, are saved as documents (e.g. .txt file) and used to build the vector database and used as retriever corpus at inference time; train-2 samples are used for Flamingo fine-tuning, while both training splits are used for Minerva fine-tuning. At inference time, the model is queried to provide information about the *modality* the image is captured, the body part *location* shown and both characteristics (*join*). At inference time, depending on the evaluation setting, the designed prompt reported in Table 1 is used, along with the retrieved documents and the corresponding images, from train-1 split, the inference image and the textual input, constructed with a template reporting sex, age and history of the patient, as in Fig. 1.

To the best of our knowledge, there is no available dataset and related classification tasks, that covers such a variety of information regarding scanning modality and body part. The majority of dataset focuses on a scanning modality or body part, like chest [12] or brain [11], thus making impossible to develop more complex tasks where diverse scanning modality and body part are jointly taking into account and that shares also homogeneous textual information that can be used for train Multimodal Models.

Table 2. Below an overview of the used dataset is provided. We refer to Reproductive and Urinary System as RaUS and to Spine and Muscles as SaM (inside the brackets the number of images is reported)

Train	Dev	Test
• Images (1653)	• Images (197)	• Images (200)
∗ TAC (878)	∗ TAC (84)	∗ TAC (100)
∗ MRI (775)	∗ MRI (113)	∗ MRI (100)
• Location	• Location	• Location
∗ Thorax (263)	∗ Thorax (30)	∗ Thorax (41)
∗ Head (742)	∗ Head (66)	∗ Head (76)
∗ Abdomen (264)	∗ Abdomen (23)	∗ Abdomen (32)
∗ RaUS (127)	∗ RaUS (20)	∗ RaUS (11)
∗ SaM (257)	∗ SaM (58)	∗ SaM (40)

4 Experiments

4.1 Experimental Set-up

The whole architecture was developed on server with 96 Intel(R) Xeon(R) Gold 6442Y CPUs and 2 48 GB NVIDIA RTX 6000 Ada Generation.

We instruction-tuned Minerva for 20 epochs on a single GPU taking approximately 4 h: we follow Alpaca-LoRA[8] setting and trained the model with all the training set. Starting from the multimodal split, we created the training sample by adding to the instruction in Table 1, the patient demographics and history. We further added the Flamingo's special tokens `<image>` and `<|endofchunk|>` generating a training set of 4959 samples, three times larger than the original since samples where created for the three query, namely modality, location and join.

Due to computational restrictions, we fine-tuned Flamingo, with the fine-tuned version of Minerva, per 10 epochs over the CPU with batch size of 1, following the train hyperparameters of Open Flamingo[9]. The whole process last approximately 3 days.

As for inference, runs where no RAG context was considered took 20 min on average on a single GPU, while the ones with RAG, approximately one hour and half and samples with a bigger RAG context that didn't fit the GPU, where manually queried in CPU.

4.2   Metrics

The created evaluation tasks can be considered as multi-class classification tasks, which performances can be evaluated with classical classification metrics such as accuracy, precision, recall and F1 score, after an output standardization phase. Since the predicted labels came out from a generative model, it is necessary to check if the generated output matches with or contains one of the possible labels: if an exact match is found, a valid predicted label can be associated with the generated text, otherwise an error label is assigned. This assignment is necessary for metrics calculation and it provides the information that the model generates something unmeaning, like a label spelled incorrectly, not generated at all or invalid, that is the case where a plausible label is generated, but does not meet the task constrains. E.g. at inference time for modality evaluation, if the model labels a image as a PET, it would be considered as an error since the task considers only CT and MR as possible scanning modalities. For precision, recall and F1 score, macro average is considered.

4.3   Results

In the subsections below are reported the obtained experimental results over the test set and a relative discussion for each evaluation setting. As for the evaluation with the fine-tuned version of Flamingo, we report the evaluation after 5 epochs (flamingo-ft-5) and after 10 epochs (flamingo-ft-10). Regardless the evaluation setting, at least a one-shot example should be provided to the model to generate a meaningful answer. Experiments with only prompt and query, not only are unsatisfactory, but also lack of consistency since the model start generating

---

[8] https://github.com/tloen/alpaca-lora.
[9] https://github.com/mlfoundations/open_flamingo.

unmeaning output and it is not following the provided instruction. In general, 5 epochs of fine-tuning Flamingo are enough for reaching satisfactory results and further training can decrease its performances.

Table 3. Experimental results for test set in modality evaluation setting. The starred line represent the inference in a zero-shot evaluation mode

LLM model	Flamingo version	RAG	Accuracy	Precision	Recall	F1 score
Minerva-3B *	flamingo-base *	*	0.17 *	0.174 *	0.113 *	0.137*
Minerva-3B	flamingo-base		0.36	0.369	0.24	0.278
Minerva-3B	flamingo-base	x	0.305	0.419	0.203	0.194
Minerva-3B ft	flamingo-base		0.405	0.463	0.27	0.341
Minerva-3B ft	flamingo-base	x	0.425	0.322	0.283	0.264
Minerva-3B ft	flamingo-ft-5		0.865	0.894	0.865	0.862
Minerva-3B ft	flamingo-ft-5	x	0.88	0.593	0.587	0.59
Minerva-3B ft	**flamingo-ft-10**		**0.935**	**0.94**	**0.935**	**0.935**
Minerva-3B ft	flamingo-ft-10	x	0.82	0.583	0.547	0.551

Modality Evaluation Setting In Table 3 are collected the experimental results over the test set for modality evaluation setting. In this evaluation setting, no significant improvement is provided by the RAG module, while performances highly benefit from Flamingo fine-tuning and the model fine-tuned over 10 epochs without RAG, reaches the best performances for every considered metric, reaching at least 0.93 for accuracy, precision, recall and F1 score. Overall these performances are not surprising, since this evaluation setting is the easiest one and can be considered as a binary classification task as it is structured: generally speaking, CT and MR are not the only possibilities as for scanning modality, but in the used dataset those are the only two option considered.

In order to verify the effectiveness of using the visual encoder of Flamingo, a comparison with state-of-the-art approaches was conducted. In fact, in the task modality the results obtained with Flamingo are higher than those reported at the state of the art in the paper by Raffy et al. [25] The latter in the diagnostic modality classification obtained an average Recall value of 92.4% (92.5% for CT and of 92.3% for MRI) lower than the performance achieved by our model.

Location Evaluation Setting. In Table 4 are collected the experimental results over the test set for location evaluation setting. Given the starting accuracy of 0.03 of the base model with RAG, the best results are obtained with Flamingo fine-tuned over 5 epochs, reaching an accuracy of 0.72 while precision, recall and F1 are stable around 0.51. Differently from the modality evaluation setting, this is a harder task for the model that, despite enhancing its performances via the usage of RAG, cannot reach highly satisfactory results, compared to the ones in Table 3, but surprisingly high compared to the starting point.

In this case further fine-tuning of Flamingo for 10 epochs, is not beneficial for the model, by contrast we aim that the textual information provided along with the image for location classification, improves and guide the general-purpose visual encoder that do not use any segmentation techniques to analyze the provided images for sub-sequentially classification.

Table 4. Experimental results for test set in location evaluation setting. The starred line represent the inference in a zero-shot evaluation mode

LLM model	Flamingo version	RAG	Accuracy	Precision	Recall	F1 score
Minerva-3B*	flamingo-base*	*	0.0*	0.0*	0.0*	0.0*
Minerva-3B	flamingo-base		0.0	0.0	0.0	0.0
Minerva-3B	flamingo-base	x	0.03	0.292	0.022	0.041
Minerva-3B ft	flamingo-base		0.0	0.0	0.0	0.0
Minerva-3B ft	flamingo-base	x	0.035	0.146	0.015	0.028
Minerva-3B ft	flamingo-ft-5		0.285	0.245	0.242	0.142
Minerva-3B ft	**flamingo-ft-5**	**x**	**0.72**	**0.524**	**0.507**	**0.512**
Minerva-3B ft	flamingo-ft-10		0.39	0.365	0.272	0.225
Minerva-3B ft	flamingo-ft-10	x	0.625	0.479	0.464	0.457

Join Evaluation Setting. In Table 5 are collected the experimental results over the test set for join evaluation setting, that is considered yet for the combined prediction task yet for the separate evaluations of both modality and location. Here can be clearly be notice how the combined prediction of modality and location and location alone can be difficult for the model, and how can be substantially improved with the RAG module, as for ACC-J that grows from 6.50% to 25.50% and as for ACC-L from 7.50% to 55.00% without any fine-tuning. As expected, fine-tuning Flamingo leads to the best performances that, as for the join evaluation setting, that reaches an accuracy of only 0.65: this result, shows that there is a substantial room for improvement in this evaluation setting and it confirms that, the multi-label classification task for determining the location of a given images, i.e. the location evaluation, is really challenging for the model despite five macro body part are considered.

5 Future Works

The final objective of our work is to build an AI system that can effectively help physicians during the diagnostic process, not only providing a detailed explanation of the proposed clinical image, but also adding some general information, about the found lesion or the disease. We are currently working on a second version of the model that, in a purely generative setting, provides a free-text clinical report, leveraging a re-defined RAG. The idea is to retrieve not only clinical reports, but also general information about the diseases, coming from

Table 5. Experimental results for test set in join evaluation setting, EM stands for exact match and ACC stands for accuracy, PREC for precision and REC for recall. ACC-M, ACC-L and ACC-J refers to the accuracy with the **M**odality, **L**ocation and **J**oin evaluation setting respectively. The starred line represent the inference in a zero-shot evaluation mode

LLM model	Flamingo version	RAG	ACC-M	ACC-L	ACC-J	PREC-M	PREC-L	PREC-J	REC-M	REC-L	REC-J	F1-M	F1-L	F1-J
Minerva-3B*	flamingo-base*	*	0.25*	0.0*	0.0*	0.194*	0.0*	0.0*	0.167*	0.0*	0.0*	0.179*	0.0*	0.0*
Minerva-3B	flamingo-base		0.2	0.075	0.065	0.129	0.0255	0.0121	0.133	0.061	0.0303	0.131	0.036	0.0173
Minerva-3B	flamingo-base	x	0.45	0.55	0.255	0.168	0.517	0.173	0.3	0.396	0.19	0.215	0.426	0.163
Minerva-3B-ft	flamingo-base		0.5	0.265	0.19	0.412	0.201	0.0631	0.333	0.176	0.183	0.298	0.127	0.0769
Minerva-3B-ft	flamingo-base	x	0.51	0.625	0.3	0.417	0.46	0.277	0.34	0.437	0.2	0.284	0.42	0.166
Minerva-3B-ft	**flamingo-ft-5**		0.925	0.425	0.37	0.935	0.621	**0.462**	0.925	0.365	0.304	0.925	0.338	0.235
Minerva-3B-ft	**flamingo-ft-5**	x	0.89	**0.72**	**0.65**	0.597	**0.622**	0.434	0.593	**0.632**	**0.389**	0.595	**0.613**	**0.382**
Minerva-3B-ft	**flamingo-ft-10**		**0.93**	0.55	0.5	**0.936**	0.512	0.401	**0.93**	0.382	0.366	**0.93**	0.362	0.302
Minerva-3B-ft	flamingo-ft-10	x	0.845	0.675	0.565	0.588	0.511	0.37	0.563	0.504	0.37	0.564	0.488	0.34

the same dataset or built from high-quality sources as textbooks, and arranged in a graph database, thus resembling a medical Knowledge Base that can be better navigated to reach the relevant documents for report generation. To develop this model, we will use Leonardo supercomputer[10] via a ISCRA-C application.

Another objective relies on the choice of the LLM used: Minerva is trained from scratch from English and Italian data, and our purpose is to develop and analyze an Italian version of DR-Minerva via a translation procedure of the dataset used, i.e. and Italian version of MedPix 2.0.

6 Conclusions

We presented DR-Minerva, a Multimodal Language Model for medical domain based on Minerva LLM that employs a RAG based approach to enhance its classification capabilities for classifying a medical image considering the scanning modality, the body part shown or both. Our experiments reveal that the join proposed task for determine both modality and location is challenging for the model and there is room for improvement with the given task setting and for further generation-related tasks in free-text modality.

Aknowledgment. We would like to thank the Sapienza NLP group for developing Minerva LLM. This work is supported by the cup project B73C22000810001, project code ECS_00000022 "SAMOTHRACE" (Sicilian MicronanoTech Research And Innovation Center).

Disclosure of Interests. The authors declares that they have no relevant or material financial interests that relate to the research described in this paper.

---

[10] https://leonardo-supercomputer.cineca.eu/it/home-it/.

References

1. Medpix. https://medpix.nlm.nih.gov/home
2. Alayrac, J.B., et al.: Flamingo: a visual language model for few-shot learning (2022)
3. Awadalla, A., et al.: Openflamingo: an open-source framework for training large autoregressive vision-language models. arXiv preprint arXiv:2308.01390 (2023)
4. Brown, T.: Language models are few-shot learners. Adv. Neural. Inf. Process. Syst. **33**, 1877–1901 (2020)
5. Davenport, T., Kalakota, R.: The potential for artificial intelligence in healthcare. Fut. Healthc. J. **6**(2), 94–98 (2019). https://doi.org/10.7861/futurehosp.6-2-94
6. Devlin, J., Chang, M.W., Lee, K., Toutanova, K.: Bert: pre-training of deep bidirectional transformers for language understanding. arXiv preprint arXiv:1810.04805 (2018)
7. Douze, M., et al.: The Faiss library (2024). https://arxiv.org/abs/2401.08281
8. Hartsock, I., Rasool, G.: Vision-language models for medical report generation and visual question answering: a review. arXiv preprint arXiv:2403.02469 (2024)
9. He, X., Zhang, Y., Mou, L., Xing, E., Xie, P.: Pathvqa: 30000+ questions for medical visual question answering. arXiv preprint arXiv:2003.10286 (2020)
10. Hromei, C.D., Croce, D., Basile, V., Basili, R.: Extremita at evalita 2023: multitask sustainable scaling to large language models at its extreme. In: Proceedings of the Eighth Evaluation Campaign of Natural Language Processing and Speech Tools for Italian. Final Workshop (EVALITA 2023), Parma, Italy. CEUR.org (2023)
11. Jack Jr, C.R., et al.: The Alzheimer's disease neuroimaging initiative (ADNI): MRI methods. J. Magn. Reson. Imaging Off. J. Int. Soc. Magn. Reson. Med. **27**(4), 685–691 (2008)
12. Johnson, A.E., et al.: Mimic-CXR, a de-identified publicly available database of chest radiographs with free-text reports. Sci. Data **6**(1), 317 (2019)
13. Junseong, K., et al.: Linq-embed-mistral:elevating text retrieval with improved gpt data through task-specific control and quality refinement. Linq AI Res. Blog (2024). https://getlinq.com/blog/linq-embed-mistral/
14. Lau, J.J., Gayen, S., Ben Abacha, A., Demner-Fushman, D.: A dataset of clinically generated visual questions and answers about radiology images. Sci. Data **5**(1), 1–10 (2018)
15. Lewis, P., et al.: Retrieval-augmented generation for knowledge-intensive NLP tasks. Adv. Neural. Inf. Process. Syst. **33**, 9459–9474 (2020)
16. Li, C., et al.: Llava-med: training a large language-and-vision assistant for biomedicine in one day. In: Advances in Neural Information Processing Systems, vol. 36 (2024)
17. Lin, W., et al.: PMC-clip: contrastive language-image pre-training using biomedical documents. In: Greenspan, H., et al. (eds.) MICCAI 2023. LNCS, vol. 14227, pp. 525–536. Springer, Cham (2023). https://doi.org/10.1007/978-3-031-43993-3_51
18. Liu, B., Zhan, L.M., Xu, L., Ma, L., Yang, Y., Wu, X.M.: Slake: a semantically-labeled knowledge-enhanced dataset for medical visual question answering. In: 2021 IEEE 18th International Symposium on Biomedical Imaging (ISBI), pp. 1650–1654. IEEE (2021)
19. Liu, H., Li, C., Wu, Q., Lee, Y.J.: Visual instruction tuning. In: Advances in Neural Information Processing Systems, vol. 36 (2024)
20. Llama Team, A..M.: The llama 3 herd of models (2024). https://arxiv.org/abs/2407.21783

21. Moor, M., et al.: Med-flamingo: a multimodal medical few-shot learner. In: Machine Learning for Health (ML4H), pp. 353–367. PMLR (2023)
22. Muennighoff, N., Tazi, N., Magne, L., Reimers, N.: MTEB: massive text embedding benchmark. arXiv preprint arXiv:2210.07316 (2022).https://doi.org/10.48550/ARXIV.2210.07316, https://arxiv.org/abs/2210.07316
23. Orlando, R., Moroni, L., Huguet Cabot, P.L., Conia, S., Barba, E., Navigli, R.: Minerva technical report (2024). https://nlp.uniroma1.it/minerva/
24. Radford, A., et al.: Learning transferable visual models from natural language supervision (2021)
25. Raffy, P., Pambrun, J.F., Kumar, A., Dubois, D., Patti, J.W., Cairns, R.A., Young, R.: Deep learning body region classification of MRI and CT examinations. J. Digit. Imaging **36**(4), 1291–1301 (2023). https://doi.org/10.1007/s10278-022-00767-9
26. Siragusa, I., Contino, S., Ciura, M.L., Alicata, R., Pirrone, R.: Medpix 2.0: a comprehensive multimodal biomedical dataset for advanced AI applications. In: Proceedings of the 3rd Italian Conference on Big Data and Data Science, ITADATA2024 (to appear). Pisa, Italy (2024). https://arxiv.org/abs/2407.02994
27. Touvron, H., et al.: Llama 2: open foundation and fine-tuned chat models (2023)
28. Vaswani, A., et al.: Attention is all you need. In: Advances in Neural Information Processing Systems, vol. 30 (2017)
29. Zhang, S., et al.: Biomedclip: a multimodal biomedical foundation model pretrained from fifteen million scientific image-text pairs. arXiv preprint arXiv:2303.00915 (2023)

REPAIR Platform: Robot-AidEd PersonAlIzed Rehabilitation

Christian Tamantini⬤, Alessandro Umbrico(✉)⬤, and Andrea Orlandini⬤

Institute of Cognitive Sciences and Technologies, National Research Council of Italy, 00196 Rome, Italy

Abstract. Physical rehabilitation is essential for restoring functionality and improving the quality of life for individuals affected by neurological or musculoskeletal conditions. Rehabilitation robots emerged as key-enabling technology to deliver intensive treatments and objectively quantify patients' motor performance. In the context of Healthcare 5.0, personalization of the treatment is paramount to improve the effectiveness of the interventions. Personalization can be implemented reactively, by providing real-time physical assistance and feedback, and deliberatively, by planning sessions based on therapeutic goals. Inspired by Kahneman's dual-system theory, this paper proposes a cognitive architecture for a robot-aided rehabilitation platform capable of delivering personalized treatment through deliberative and reactive techniques. The proposed cognitive architecture is described and validated through experimental sessions. Six healthy participants were enrolled in the experiments, simulating a robot-aided rehabilitation session with a TIAGo service robot serving as the physical interface to deliver the planned session. The results highlight that the plans generated according to different clinical objectives elicited distinct physiological responses from the participants, demonstrating the effectiveness of the personalized approach.

Keywords: Robot-aided rehabilitation · Physical rehabilitation · Automated Planning · Task Planning

1 Introduction

Physical rehabilitation is a crucial component in the recovery process for individuals affected by different disabilities, ranging from neurological conditions to musculoskeletal injuries, aiming to restore lost functionality and improve the quality of life and independence. In 2019, over 2.4 billion people worldwide were living with health conditions that could benefit from rehabilitation, highlighting the immense need for physical treatments [1]. Conventional physical therapy involves a complex interaction between a physiotherapist and the patient, including physically manipulating the patient's body and developing an empathetic relationship [2]. Physiotherapists assess the patient's condition and create tailored rehabilitation exercise plans to push forward motor recovery and promote active participation [3].

A. Artale et al. (Eds.): AIxIA 2024, LNAI 15450, pp. 301–314, 2025.
https://doi.org/10.1007/978-3-031-80607-0_23

In this scenario, rehabilitation robots have started to play an increasingly important role thanks to their capabilities to i) deliver highly intensive and repetitive treatments, ii) implement different care paradigms, iii) integrate feedback systems to gamify exercise and iv) objectively quantify patients' motor performance [4]. Among the opportunities that robotics provides in physical rehabilitation, personalization is one of the features that stands out the most as it enables the delivery of engaging treatments that promote active participation and improve motor recovery [5]. Personalization of robot-aided rehabilitation could be implemented at multiple levels: reactive and deliberative ones. The former generates reactive actions to support the execution of the individual task in real-time according to the patient's needs and state by providing tunable physical assistance or contextualized feedback [6]. The other acts at a higher level to recommend rehabilitation plans consistent with the motor recovery of the individual user [7]. In other words, robot-aided rehabilitation systems can be designed drawing inspiration from Kahneman's dual-system theory [8]. This allows for slow, deliberate planning of each rehabilitation session based on therapeutic goals and fast, real-time feedback and corrections during the execution of individual exercises. This dual approach ensures that each session is optimally tailored to the patient's progress and needs, enhancing the overall effectiveness of the rehabilitation program.

In this context, we propose a cognitive architecture for a robot-aided rehabilitation platform designed to personalize treatment by combining the two reasoning perspectives: deliberately, by generating a physiotherapy exercise plan suitable for the clinical goals of each session, by monitoring task execution and providing contextual feedback in real-time. This work introduces the main functional components of the architecture. A preliminary validation involving six healthy participants in a simulated robot-aided rehabilitation session with the TIAGo robot, demonstrating the feasibility of the approach.

The rest of the paper is structured as follows. Section 2 presents the scientific literature investigating the development of cognitive architectures to provide physical therapy. Section 3 introduces the proposed approach to personalize the rehabilitation treatment, its experimental implementation, and validation with healthy participants. Section 4 shows and discusses the results obtained in the experimental validation. Lastly, Sect. 5 summarises the main contributions and results and outlines future developments.

2   Related Works

Cognitively sophisticated architectures have been proposed in the literature in the healthcare context to provide robotic systems for rehabilitation with more complex comprehension and adaptation capabilities than traditional robot-mediated rehabilitation systems.

In [9,10], a control architecture for a social robot in rehabilitation is proposed, which handles both physical and cognitive interactions. Monitoring systems analyze users' movements, facial expressions, and spoken sentences to manage different behaviors following the "Stimulus-Response" approach [11]. The robot shifts roles from Demonstrator, the robot explains the motor task, to Observer, it monitors the patient's movements, and to Helper, it physically assists in task execution. This responsive platform effectively engages participants by integrating multimodal monitoring and natural language communication skills. However, it does not customize the treatment plan based on the patient's condition.

Automatic planning techniques have recently begun to contaminate robotic rehabilitation systems as they allow the generation of plans that consider the patient's condition at admission and generate an appropriate schedule of exercises to achieve certain goals within a session [12]. In particular, automatic planning methodologies were used to administer clinical scales, such as the Comprehensive Geriatric Assessment and the Quality of Upper Extremity Skills Test [13]. Both clinical scales require the patient to replicate a series of poses. Once the patient reaches the required pose, the robotic system, which includes the NAO robot and a Kinect camera for upper limb kinematics monitoring, calculates the deviation of the achieved pose from the desired one and automatically compiles the assessment sheet. A similar architecture has been applied to provide physical training to children with neurological disorders such as Cerebral Palsy or Obstetric brachial plexus palsy [14,15]. This autonomous system plans rehabilitation sessions for children by offering two games: Mirror and Simon [16]. In these games, children mimic upper limb poses demonstrated by the robot. The system employs an automated planning process to generate pose sequences, thereby ensuring the inclusion of various poses within each session, and dynamically adjusting error thresholds for personalized treatment. The poorer the performance, the higher the tolerance. Although this architecture demonstrates its capabilities in generating more engaging and tailored sessions and leading to a notable motor recovery, this planning system has the only objective of planning a session of a certain duration structured as a sequence of warm-up, training, and cool-down phases. Recent research has concentrated on automated planning methodologies for rehabilitation sessions. These methodologies involve the design of choreographies to challenge participants in specific aspects, such as energy expenditure or balance [17]. This system uses the patient's motor condition to generate step sequences targeting the specific clinical objectives. However, this platform lacks a monitoring system to assess the impact of the generated plans on users.

Despite the development of sophisticated robotic rehabilitation systems, existing methodologies frequently fail to i) personalize treatment plans according to the specific circumstances of individual patients; ii) adapt exercise sequences in real-time, and; iii) comprehensively monitor and evaluate the impact of rehabilitation plans on users' progress. Therefore, there is a critical need for a control architecture in robotic rehabilitation that personalizes treatment based on patient-specific conditions and therapist-set clinical objectives. This system should integrate real-time monitoring and feedback to adapt the treatment plan, enhancing the effectiveness of interventions through tailored and responsive care.

3 Materials and Methods

3.1 Proposed Approach

We introduce the REPAIR platform capable of integrating deliberative planning and fast motion classification to support personalized assistance in physical rehabilitation. The architecture is organized according to the Dual Process theory and combines (slow) deliberative and (fast) reactive reasoning capabilities [7,18]. The deliberative layer is in charge of deciding the proper exercise set to administer to the patient and adapting planned and interacting behaviors according to clinicians' feedback and observed state and performance. The reactive layer is in charge of controlling robot actions as well as evaluating the execution of planned activities through the monitoring of patient's movements and physiological state. Figure 1 shows the organization of the functional components and the resulting control flow. It is worth noticing that REPAIR pursues a human-in-the-loop methodology [19] where feedback from clinicians is crucial to tailor reasoning and acting capabilities to specific clinical needs and objectives.

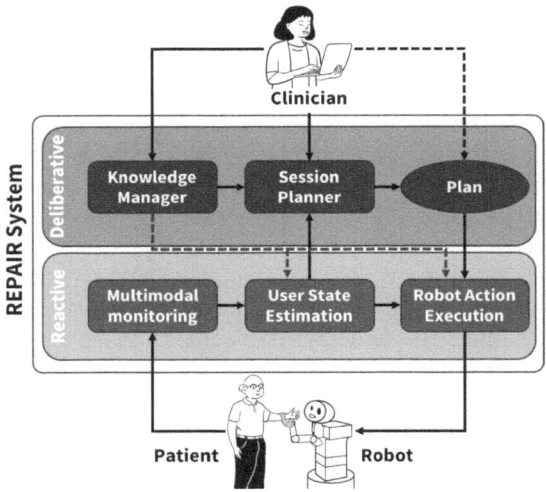

Fig. 1. Architecture of the proposed robot-aided rehabilitation platform

The overall process begins with the clinician administering a set of clinical scales providing a clear overview of the patient's condition. In this regard, the clinician has the crucial role of endowing the system with the health-related knowledge necessary to make decisions that comply with the clinical practice. Namely, the clinician initializes a *Knowledge Base* encapsulated in the *Knowledge Manager* by providing domain-specific knowledge suitable to contextualize planning decisions according to different clinical objectives. For example, the clinician's input is crucial to model and characterize the effects of physical exercises on health-related conditions/features of patients [17].

Given the specific pathological condition and the patient's level of disability, the clinician specifies a clinical goal to reach in the current session and possibly additional constraints or preferences, e.g. the maximum session duration. Such a goal is fed into the automated planning module, also named *Session Planner*, that leverages the information stored in the *Knowledge Manager*, i.e. the list of exercises that can be used to generate the session along with their characteristics, to compute a proper *Plan*. Automated planning methodologies can be exploited inside the *Session Planner* to solve the planning problem of finding a personalized *Plan* for the patient under examination. In this context, a *Plan* is represented by a list of physical exercises (*stimuli*) that ensures the achievement of the specific clinical goal set by the clinician. Furthermore, the clinician can access the plan generated by the autonomous rehabilitation agent and modify it as appropriate, including the addition, removal, or modification of exercises, to ensure accurate supervision of the session (see dashed line in Fig. 1).

The execution of the rehabilitation session is managed at a low level by the reactive layer. It includes a module for user *Multimodal Monitoring* that collects raw information from several perspectives, ranging from kinematics to physiological measurements, useful to estimate user state. Indeed, the *User State Estimation* module takes as input the data collected from a set of sensors and estimates the complex state of the patient [20]. The user state represents, in an abstract symbolic manner, the quality of the movement performed by the user as well as information regarding the physical or cognitive spheres during the execution of a task. Such an estimation has a twofold effect: it triggers the *Robot Action Execution* in the reactive layer, such as the returning of verbal feedback or providing physical assistance, and it returns the information to the *Session Planner* to check whether re-planning is needed.

Lastly, it is worth noting that the *Knowledge Manager* is interconnected with both the estimation and action modules. This allows it to adapt the reactive modules according to its internal knowledge. The focus of the estimation process may change depending on the context, as well as the action module can generate different behaviors based on the robot's capabilities. For instance, a humanoid robot can physically mirror the tasks, a robot with an anthropomorphic arm can physically support task execution, and a digital system can provide vocal feedback.

3.2   Experimental Evaluation

To validate the proposed methodology, we implemented the approach described in Sect. 3.1 on a robotic platform to conduct robot-aided rehabilitation sessions. Moreover, a monitoring system was employed to track the user's state throughout the sessions. The following sections provide a detailed account of the materials used in the experimental setup and explain the implementation of each functional block of the architecture to achieve the desired behaviors.

Experimental Setup The service robot TIAGo (PAL Robotics S.L., Spain) was used as the physical robotic system. TIAGo features an anthropomorphic arm with 7°C of freedom (DoFs), a liftable torso, and a mobile base on wheels. Additionally, the robot is equipped with a microphone and speakers to manage audio input and output. Its head, which also has pan and tilt degrees of freedom, mounts an Asus Xtion RGB-D camera capable of providing RGB and depth images with a resolution of 640×480 at a frame rate of 30 Hz. Moreover, the participants were asked to wear a GARMIN Vivosmart 4 wristband to collect their Heart Rate (HR) [21]. Figure 2 shows the experimental setup used to evaluate the proposed methodology. All the software components run under the robot operating system (ROS Melodic).

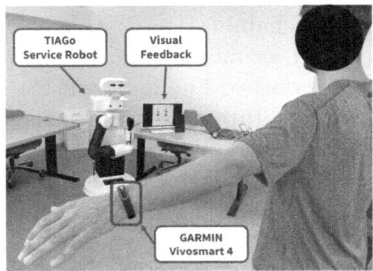

Fig. 2. Experimental setup used to evaluate the proposed methodology

Knowledge Manager. The *Knowledge Manager* is the central data repository for patient profiles and exercise information. It maintains comprehensive profiles for each patient, including their clinical history, current condition, and progress. Additionally, it houses a detailed list of potential rehabilitation exercises, each described in terms of intensity levels. In the system tested in this paper, 23 exercises were extracted from the"PhysioTherapy eXercises" database [22], see Table 1. The selection of these exercises was based on their capacity to elicit a range of intensities, thereby engaging all major muscle groups. This repository is of critical importance for the *Session Planner* module, which accesses the *Knowledge Manager* to generate personalized and effective session plans.

Session Planner. The *Session Planner* is the high-level reasoning component that decides the sequence of physical stimuli suited for a rehabilitation session. The component relies on timeline-based planning [23,24] and integrates search strategies capable of reasoning on the numeric effects of physical stimuli [17]. Specifically, we have extended the open-source planning framework PLATINUm[1] [25] with a heuristic search suitable to evaluate the clinical qualities of partial plans. Algorithm 1 briefly describes the structure of the search procedure. The

---

[1] https://github.com/pstlab/PLATINUm.git.

Table 1. List of the exercises implemented in the Knowledge Base

ID	Exercise	Intensity	ID	Exercise	Intensity
A1	Arm circles	1	A13	Frontal lunges	3
A2	Side stretches	1	A14	Squat	3
A3	Side leg raises	1	A15	Military press	3
A4	Scarecrow arms rotation	1	A16	Side lunges	3
A5	Forward bend stretch	1	A17	Butt kicks	3
A6	Cross-body arm stretch	1	A18	Boxing	4
A7	Standing quad stretch	1	A19	High knees	4
A8	Bicep curl	1	A20	Jumping jacks	4
A9	Arm lateral raise	2	A21	High kick	4
A10	Arm front raise	2	A22	Jump squats	5
A11	Cross-body toe touches	3	A23	Running in place	5
A12	Body crunches	3			

planner receives as input the clinical objective encapsulated into a heuristic function $\mathcal{H}_\pi$ and the number of exercises to be administrated $\mathcal{N}$.

Algorithm 1. Heuristic search procedure of the Session Planner.

Input: $\mathcal{H}_\pi, \mathcal{N}$
Output: $\pi = (FTL, R)$
1: $\Pi' \leftarrow \emptyset$
2: $\pi \leftarrow$ initialize $(\mathcal{SV}, \mathcal{S})$
3: **while** ¬meetsRequirements $(\pi, \mathcal{N})$ **do**
4:     $\Pi' = \{\pi'_1, \pi'_2, ..., \pi'_m\} \leftarrow$ refine (π)
5:     $\pi \leftarrow$ select $(\Pi', \mathcal{H}_\pi)$
6: **end while**
7: **return** π

The termination condition represents a novel aspect of the implemented search procedure. Unlike "classical" planning problems requiring to achieve a certain state or decompose a certain task, the objective here is to synthesize a plan π which considers a sufficient number of stimuli. Plan refinement thus should always consider the possibility of recursively making additional planning decisions (i.e., subgoals) until plan requirements are met (rows 3–5). In the considered problem, the requirement conditions concern the number of stimuli $\mathcal{N}$ specified by the clinician. Alternatively, the clinician can specify the minimum duration of the session instead of the minimum number of exercises.

The planner should search for plans π that achieve a certain (clinical) objective within the specified requirements. In the current work, we consider two extremal clinical objectives: (i) LOW intensity $\mathcal{H}_\pi^{LOW}$; (ii) $HIGH$ intensity $\mathcal{H}_\pi^{HIGH}$. Equation 1 intuitively describes the objective function $f_i(\Pi)$ of the planning problem.

It leverages data about exercise intensity in Table 1 to evaluate the cumulative intensity of the subset of selected exercises in a given plan π.

$$f_i(\pi) = \sum_{a_i \in \pi} \text{intensity}(a_i) \tag{1}$$

Two search strategies $\mathcal{H}_\pi^{LOW}$, $\mathcal{H}_\pi^{HIGH}$ have been developed to evaluate sequences of physical exercises $a_i \in \pi$ of a plan π that respectively minimize and maximize the cumulative intensity $f_i(\pi)$. Although we have considered the two simple objective functions mentioned above, the developed approach can support a wider set of more detailed/complex objectives provided by a therapist [17]. It is then worth underlining that our system can be extended to support many different clinical requirements and applications. It is worth noticing that the system has been designed with the explicit intention of assisting healthcare professionals, and not to supplant their role. This ensures that the expertise and judgment of therapists remain at the core of patient care.

Multimodal Monitoring. In this experiment, the multimodal monitoring system collects data related to two dimensions: movement and cardiac activity. The TIAGo robot's built-in camera tracks the user's kinematics during the task execution. Specifically, once a frame is captured by the RGB camera, the Mediapipe pose algorithm is employed to retrieve the user's anatomical landmarks [26]. The three-dimensional joint coordinates in the real world, expressed in the user's origin frame, which is situated between the hips, are collected at a frequency of 30 Hz. In particular, the coordinates of the shoulders, elbows, wrists, hips, knees, and ankles were considered, as the objective was to monitor total body motions. Furthermore, the user's heart rate is collected throughout the session from the wrist-worn device at a frequency of 1 Hz.

User State Estimation. The user state estimation module is responsible for recognising, classifying and counting the user's movements. This software module identifies which of the known activities the user is performing and tracks the duration of each action.

To train the action classification algorithm, data were collected from four healthy participants (26.2 ± 4.1 mean age, 4 males). For each of the 23 exercises, data were gathered over 20 s at a sampling rate of 30 Hz, resulting in 600 observation per exercise. Additionally, a further class was included (A0), representing the resting condition, with data collected under identical conditions. Each observation comprised the three-dimensional coordinates of anatomical landmarks of the upper and lower limbs, monitored over 30 frames (equivalent to one second). The supervised model employed in this study to perform action recognition was a Support Vector Machine (SVM) with a radial basis function kernel. The choice of the SVM classifier was driven by its effectiveness in handling high-dimensional data, robustness to overfitting, and its suitability to perform real-time inferences during robot-aided rehabilitation sessions [27].

Robot Action Execution. The robotic tasks considered in this scenario are: i) displaying the currently administrated exercise, and; ii) providing visual and vocal feedback on the task execution. The monitor of the robotic system provides visual feedback, displaying the physical motion to be performed. Additionally, the robot may deliver verbal feedback to guide the user through the exercises. This dual feedback mechanism ensures clear communication and helps maintain user engagement and correct execution of the rehabilitation tasks. The feedback phase allows for the real-time correction and reinforcement of the user's movements. The administration of visual and verbal feedback facilitates the user's comprehension of and ability to modify their task execution, thereby ensuring continuous engagement and immediate guidance [10].

Experimental Protocol. In this experiment, 6 healthy right-handed participants (30.8 ± 5.3 mean age, 5 males and 1 female) were enrolled. They provided written consent to participate in the study. To test the capability of the system to deliver different rehabilitation sessions, each participant was asked to perform two sessions, specifically planned with the objectives of *LOW* and *HIGH* intensities and the same requirement in terms of duration, i.e. the session is required to be composed of 10 exercises.

Performance Indicators. The offline performance of the implemented action classification model was initially evaluated. Since data from four participants were recorded, a leave-one-subject-out (LOSO) cross-validation approach was employed. This method entails training the model on data from three participants and testing it on the data from the remaining one. This process is repeated for each enrolled participant, thereby ensuring a robust evaluation of the model's performance. Given that the dataset was balanced, accuracy was selected as the metric to assess the classification performance. Moreover, the time needed to train (T_{train}^{SVM}) the model as well as the time to perform inference ($T_{predict}^{SVM}$) were computed.

To quantify the efficacy of the *Session Planner* in generating tailored plans and the impact of the session on the enrolled subjects, the following performance indicators were computed:

- Cumulative Plan Intensity (ΣPI): This indicator quantifies the overall intensity of all exercises incorporated into a rehabilitation session. The indicator is calculated by summing the individual intensities of each exercise and reflects the planner's ability to generate plans with different intensities according to specific input intensity requirements.
- Session Duration (T_{tot}): total time taken to complete a rehabilitation session is defined as the entire period from the beginning to the end of the session, including any intervals or breaks, and is expressed in minutes. The monitoring of T_{tot} enables the assessment of whether plans generated at different intensity levels require different amounts of time.

– Normalized Hear Rate (HR_n): the user's HR mean response, calculated as

$$HR_n = mean\left(\frac{HR - HR_{base}}{HR_{base}}\right) \qquad (2)$$

where HR is the actual heart rate during the session and HR_{base} is the baseline heart rate at the beginning of the session. The value of HR_n provides information on the physiological impact of the planned session on the user.

The Mann-Whitney test was employed to ascertain whether there were any statistically significant differences between the computed metrics when *LOW* and *HIGH* intensity plans were administered to the participants. Furthermore, Pearson's linear correlation test was used to compute the relationship between the ΣPI and HR_n. The significance level was set for both statistical tests at a p-value of 0.05.

4   Results and Discussion

Figure 3A reports the normalized confusion matrix obtained by appending all the predictions inferred on the testing subjects during the LOSO validation. The mean accuracy was found to be 81.80 ± 4.11%. These results demonstrate the model's capacity to maintain accuracy across diverse individuals, which is a crucial attribute for models that handle user characteristic variability while ensuring consistent performance levels. The training time for the SVM model was $T_{train}^{SVM} = 597.25 \pm 50.16$ s, and the inference time per observation was $T_{predict}^{SVM} = 0.07 \pm 0.03$ s. These results suggest that while the SVM model requires a reasonable training period, its quick inference time per observation makes it suitable for applications requiring rapid decision-making and real-time processing of data.

Figure 3B illustrates the frequency of occurrence of the various exercises in the planes generated at *LOW* and *HIGH* intensities. The two conditions are represented by different colours: green and red for *LOW* and *HIGH*, respectively. The graph illustrates how the rehabilitation plans are adapted according to the required intensity level, employing a combination of exercises to optimize the effectiveness of the session. The *LOW*-intensity plans comprise a more diverse range of exercises, distributed throughout the session in a more balanced manner. In contrast, the *HIGH*-intensity plans focus on a smaller set of exercises, including squats, frontal lunges, and high knees, which are selected by the planner with greater frequency. This distinction reflects the adaptation of the plans to enhance the efficacy of the workout, with a greater emphasis on variety and balance in the low-intensity plans and a more concentrated approach to high-impact exercises in the high-intensity plans.

Figure 4 shows the performance indicators computed during the experiments carried out in the validation of the proposed planning system. As expected, ΣPI values reflect the clear statistically significant difference between the LOW and HIGH conditions (p-value< $1 \cdot 10^{-2}$). The HIGH condition requires a greater

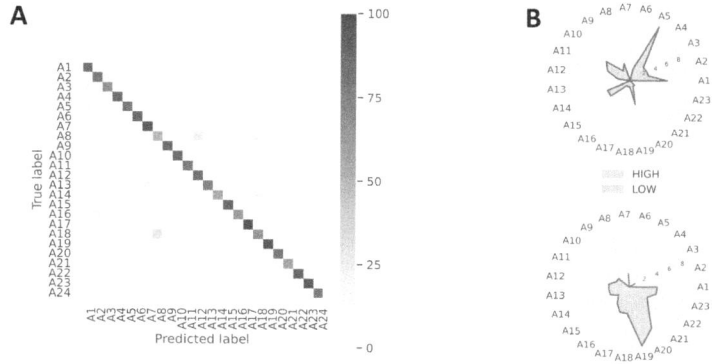

Fig. 3. A. Normalized confusion matrix of the trained SVM model for action classification. B. Occurrences of the exercises in the plans for *LOW* and *HIGH* intensity

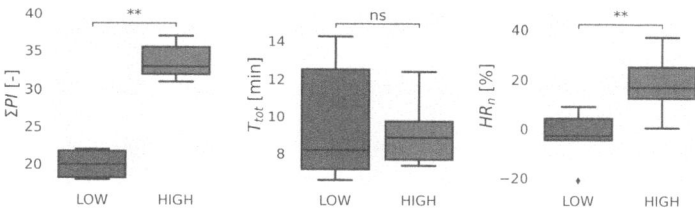

Fig. 4. Performance indicators computed during the experimental validation, categorized by the LOW and HIGH experimental conditions. *ns* indicates no statistically significant difference, and ∗∗ denotes a significant difference (p-value < 0.01)

ΣPI, consistent with generating more intense sessions and therefore tailoring the session according to the specific clinical goal.

Although the average session duration is slightly longer in the HIGH condition, there is some overlap between the two groups and the distributions are not statistically different (p-value= 0.7). This suggests that HIGH sessions, while more intense, do not always take significantly longer than LOW sessions. Variations in sessions duration may be influenced by several factors, such as individual responses to tasks and variability in exercise performance.

The HR_n metric demonstrates a statistically significant difference between the LOW and HIGH conditions (p-value$< 1 \cdot 10^{-2}$). The mean HR_n values in the HIGH condition are significantly higher, suggesting that the more intense the plan is, the higher the physiological response. This aligns with the expectation that more intensive sessions (HIGH) cause a greater increase in heart rate compared to less intensive sessions (LOW). Negative HR_n values in some LOW sessions indicate minimal or negative physiological response, i.e. a lower HR

with respect to the baseline condition, likely due to the relatively low intensity of the exercises. Such a result is also stressed by Pearson's linear correlation between ΣPI and HR_n demonstrating a statistically significant strong linear relationship $\rho = 0.68$ (p-value= 0.01).

5 Conclusions

This work presents a cognitive architecture for a robot-aided rehabilitation platform designed to provide personalized treatment by integrating deliberate exercise planning and real-time reactive feedback. The proposed system was validated with six healthy participants using the TIAGo robot to simulate rehabilitation sessions. Despite the relatively modest cohort size of enrolled subjects, the findings indicate that the planner can effectively produce different sessions according to the input intensity level. Different exercises were selected and the ΣPI reflects the intensity. Moreover, the multimodal monitoring system revealed that *HIGH* intensity sessions significantly impacted the participants' HR, reflecting a greater physiological response. Indeed, a statistically significant strong linear correlation was found between the HR_n and ΣPI. The results demonstrate that the planned sessions elicited disparate effects on the body's response.

The preliminary findings demonstrate the platform's capacity to adapt exercise intensity and impact patient response, thereby generating personalized rehabilitation sessions. The long-term objective is to circumvent repetitive exercises and target specific body areas for varied and efficacious rehabilitation. The system can be expanded to support a greater number of therapeutic programs and integrate additional sensors to endow the REPAIR platform with the capability to estimate psychophysiological processes and enhance the *Session Planner* with comprehensive user state estimates for more sophisticated rehabilitation plans. Moreover, from a clinical point of view, extensive experiments will be carried out enrolling the pathological population to assess the applicability of such a system in real clinical practice.

Acknowledgments. This work was supported by the Italian Ministry of Research, under the complementary actions to the NRRP "Fit4MedRob - Fit for Medical Robotics" Grant PNC0000007, (CUP: B53C22006990001).

Disclosure of Interests. The authors have no competing interests to declare that are relevant to the content of this article.

References

1. Cieza, A., et al.: Global estimates of the need for rehabilitation based on the global burden of disease study 2019: a systematic analysis for the global burden of disease study 2019. Lancet **396**(10267), 2006–2017 (2020)
2. Kleiner, M.J., Kinsella, E.A., Miciak, M., Teachman, G., McCabe, E., Walton, D.M.: An integrative review of the qualities of a good physiotherapist. Physiotherapy Theory Pract. **39**(1), 89–116 (2023)

3. Naylor, J., Killingback, C., Green, A.: What are the views of musculoskeletal physiotherapists and patients on person-centred practice? A systematic review of qualitative studies. Disabil. Rehabil. **45**(6), 950–961 (2023)

4. Duret, C., Grosmaire, A.G., Krebs, H.I.: Robot-assisted therapy in upper extremity hemiparesis: overview of an evidence-based approach. Front. Neurol. **10**, 438977 (2019)

5. Rodgers, H., et al.: Robot assisted training for the upper limb after stroke (RATULS): a multicentre randomised controlled trial. Lancet **394**(10192), 51–62 (2019)

6. Tamantini, C., et al.: Tailoring upper-limb robot-aided orthopedic rehabilitation on patients' psychophysiological state. IEEE Trans. Neural Syst. Rehabl. Eng. (2023)

7. Umbrico, A., De Benedictis, R., Fracasso, F., Cesta, A., Orlandini, A., Cortellessa, G.: A mind-inspired architecture for adaptive HRI. Int. J. Soc. Robot. **15**(3), 371–391 (2023)

8. Bonnefon, J.-F., Rahwan, I.: Machine thinking, fast and slow. Trends Cogn. Sci. **24**(12), 1019–1027 (2020)

9. Cristofori, L., et al.: HeAL9000: an intelligent rehabilitation robot. In: CEUR Workshop Proceedings, vol. 3060, pp. 29–41 (2021)

10. Tamantini, C., et al.: Integrating physical and cognitive interaction capabilities in a robot-aided rehabilitation platform. IEEE Syst. J. (2023)

11. Johnson, M.J., Mohan, M., Mendonca, R.: Therapist-patient interactions in task-oriented stroke therapy can guide robot-patient interactions. Int. J. Soc. Rob. **14**(6), 1527–1546 (2022)

12. Fuentetaja, R., García-Olaya, A., García, J., González, J.C., Fernández, F.: An automated planning model for HRI: use cases on social assistive robotics. Sensors **20**(22), 6520 (2020)

13. Martín, A., Pulido, J.C., González, J.C., García-Olaya, Á., Suárez, C., et al.: A framework for user adaptation and profiling for social robotics in rehabilitation. Sensors **20**(17), 4792 (2020)

14. González, J.C., Pulido, J.C., Fernández, F.: A three-layer planning architecture for the autonomous control of rehabilitation therapies based on social robots. Cogn. Syst. Res. **43**, 232–249 (2017)

15. Pulido, J.C., et al.: A socially assistive robotic platform for upper-limb rehabilitation: a longitudinal study with pediatric patients. IEEE Rob. Autom. Mag. **26**(2), 24–39 (2019)

16. Turp, M., González, J.C., Pulido, J.C., Fernández, F.: Developing a robot-guided interactive Simon game for physical and cognitive training. Int. J. Humanoid Rob. **16**(01), 1950003 (2019)

17. Umbrico, A., et al.: Combining clinical and spatial constraints into temporal planning to personalize physical rehabilitation. In: Proceedings of the International Conference on Automated Planning and Scheduling, vol. 33 (2023)

18. Grady Booch, et al.: Thinking fast and slow in AI. In: Proceedings of the AAAI Conference on Artificial Intelligence, vol. 35, no.17 (2021)

19. Sorrentino, A., et al.: Personalizing care through robotic assistance and clinical supervision. Front. Rob. AI **9** (2022)

20. Tamantini, C., et al.: A data-driven fuzzy logic method for psychophysiological assessment: an application to exoskeleton-assisted walking. IEEE Trans. Med. Rob. Bionics (2024)

21. Schyvens, A.-M., et al.: Accuracy of Fitbit charge 4, Garmin Vivosmart 4, and WHOOP versus polysomnography: systematic review. JMIR Mhealth Uhealth **12**(1), e52192 (2024)

22. Glinsky, J., Harvey, L., Sherrington, C., Katalinic, O.: www.physiotherapyexercises.com–new exercises and features to help physiotherapists prescribe home exercise programs. Physiotherapy **101**, e1381 (2015)

23. Muscettola, N.: HSTS: integrating planning and scheduling. In Zweben, M., Fox, M.S. (eds.) Intelligent Scheduling. Morgan Kauffmann (1994)

24. Cialdea Mayer, M., Orlandini, A., Umbrico, A.: Planning and execution with flexible timelines: a formal account. Acta Inf. **53**(6), 649–680 (2016)

25. Umbrico, A., Cesta, A., Cialdea Mayer, M., Orlandini, A.: PLATINUm: a new framework for planning and acting. In: Esposito, F., Basili, R., Ferilli, S., Lisi, F. (eds.) AI*IA 2017 Advances in Artificial Intelligence, pp. 498–512. Springer, Cham (2017)

26. Dill, S., et al.: Accuracy evaluation of 3D pose estimation with mediapipe pose for physical exercises. In: Current Directions in Biomedical Engineering, volume 9, pp. 563–566. De Gruyter (2023)

27. Nguyen, T.-T., Pham, D.-T., Hai, V., Le, T.-L.: A robust and efficient method for skeleton-based human action recognition and its application for cross-dataset evaluation. IET Comput. Vis. **16**(8), 709–726 (2022)

Integrating Classical Planners with GPT-Based Planning Policies

Massimiliano Tummolo(✉), Nicholas Rossetti, Alfonso Emilio Gerevini(✉),
Matteo Olivato, Luca Putelli, and Ivan Serina

Dipartimento di Ingegneria dell'Informazione, Università degli Studi di Brescia,
Via Branze 38, Brescia, Italy
{massimiliano.tummolo,alfonso.gerevini}@unibs.it

Abstract. Recent works on Large Language Models (LLMs) have demonstrated their effectiveness in learning general policies in automated planning. In particular, a system called PLANGPT has achieved impressive performance in terms of coverage in various domains. However, it may produce invalid plans that either satisfy only some goal fluents of the corresponding planning problem or violate the planned actions' preconditions. To overcome this limitation, we propose a novel neuro-symbolic approach that combines PLANGPT with a planner capable of repairing (or completing) the plan generated by PLANGPT, thereby leveraging model-based reasoning. When PLANGPT generates a candidate plan for a specific planning problem, we validate it using a symbolic validator. If the generated plan is invalid, we execute the repair procedure of the planner LPG to obtain a valid solution plan from it. In this paper, we empirically evaluate the effectiveness of our approach and demonstrate its performances across various planning domains. Our results show significant improvements in the performance of both PLANGPT and LPG, highlighting the effectiveness of combining learning methods with traditional planning techniques.

1 Introduction

Attention-based architectures such as Transformers [33], BERT [4], and GPT [17] have driven recent advancements in Natural Language Processing (NLP). These models have achieved impressive results in machine translation and summarisation and have shown promise in understanding factual knowledge and common sense [7,12,16,24]. However, their reasoning abilities, especially for planning tasks, remain limited [1,30,32]. Current prompting methods and fine-tuning Large Language Models (LLMs) struggle to generate valid plans for automated planning problems [1,14,15,32].

More promising results were obtained by PLANGPT [20,21], a novel GPT-based model specifically trained to generate plans for classical planning domains.

M. Tummolo was enrolled in the National Doctorate on AI conducted by Sapienza, University of Rome with the University of Brescia.

A. Artale et al. (Eds.): AIxIA 2024, LNAI 15450, pp. 315–329, 2025.
https://doi.org/10.1007/978-3-031-80607-0_24

However, a limitation of this system is that it cannot correct invalid plans at generation time (plans with unsatisfied preconditions or unachieved goals), returning in these cases an incorrect solution for the planning problem.

As other machine learning models [2,3,8], PLANGPT is able to learn a general policy which can be used to solve many planning problems. However, they can be also used in combination with a planner: in the work of [29] general policies are exploited as heuristics by planners; in the work in [31] instead a LLM-generated plans are subsequently corrected by a planner. Following these works, in this paper we combine PLANGPT with the LPG planner [6] to address invalid or incomplete plans that may arise during generation. By integrating learning and model-based techniques, our aim is to improve the reliability and accuracy of plan generation by LLMs.

2 Related Work

Recent works have studied and analysed the capabilities of LLMs in planning and reasoning in the last few years. In [1,30], the authors showed how pre-trained GPT models (GPT-3.5 and GPT-4) can be used to generate plans starting from the problem description without a customised training. Unfortunately, their results highlight that pre-trained LLMs often fail to generate correct plans, even with a neural validator that checks the executability of the actions.

In [14,15], the authors fine-tuned a Code-T5 model [34] with solved problems in several planning domains obtaining a new model, Plansformer. This model showed interesting results, producing more valid plans than the prompting approach in various domains limited in the number of objects. These approaches use an LLM to generate a plan given the initial state, the goal, and the domain description as input, similar to the context of general policies. The main difference from our approach is that we train GPT from scratch with a custom dataset of planning instances.

In another line of work, researchers have exploited different deep-learning architectures to learn general policies. Instead of generating the sequence of actions, these systems compute a heuristic for all the states reachable by applicable actions, starting from the current state and the goal. For instance, in [27,28], authors proposed a Graph Neural Network (GNN) to address the problems in various benchmark domains. Following this work, the authors tried to integrate the learnt general policies with a greedy first search, obtaining a learned domain-specific planner called Muninn [29]. A similar work was presented in [2,3,8] where the authors use GNNs with other graph representations, ranking of the search state and machine learning methods to compute different heuristics.

These approaches produce a numeric heuristic that evaluates the current state and guides the search, and must be continually called upon by the planner. Instead, in our approach, the model directly generates the sequence of actions. For example, in [31], a pre-trained LLM generates a candidate plan that is given as the initial seed to a plan repair system. However, a crucial difference to our work is that the generated plan is provided as input to the planner without any modification.

Instead of using pre-trained LLMs, an initial experiment to train a Language Model from scratch, in the automated planning context, is available in [23]. Moreover, recently we proposed PLANGPT [20,21], a general policy based on the GPT architecture trained from scratch on a dataset of planning instances. PLANGPT obtains SoTA performances in generating valid plans in various benchmark domains. However, PLANGPT can generate invalid or incomplete plans that violate an action or do not satisfy the goal. In this paper, to address this limitation, we integrate PLANGPT with a plan repair planner, LPG, to correct invalid plans using different candidate plan initialisations.

3 Background: Classical Planning, GPT and PLANGPT

3.1 Classical Planning

Following the formalisation presented in [20] to represent deterministic, fully observable planning problems, a classical planning problem is a pair $P = (D, I)$ where D is a planning domain and I is a problem instance. More specifically, D contains a set of predicate symbols p and a set of action schemas with preconditions and effects given by atoms $p(x_1, ..., x_k)$, where each x_i is an argument of the schema; I is a tuple $I = (O, Init, Goal)$, where O is a (finite) set of objects names c_i, and $Init$ and $Goal$ are sets of ground atoms $p(c_1, ..., c_k)$ representing the initial state and the goal of the problem. A classical planning problem $P = (D, I)$ encodes a state model $S(P) = (S, s_0, S_G, Act, A, f)$ where each state $s \in S$ is a set of ground atoms from P, s_0 is the set of fluents of the initial state $Init$, S_G is the set of goal states $s \in S$ such that $Goal \subseteq s$, Act is the set of ground actions in P, $A(s)$ is the set of ground actions whose preconditions are true in s, and f is the transition function so that $f(a, s)$, for $a \in A(s)$, represents the state resulting from applying action a to state s. An action sequence $a_0, ..., a_n$ is applicable in P if $a_i \in A(s_i)$ and $s_{i+1} = f(a_i, s_i)$, for $i = 0, ..., n$, and it is a solution plan if $s_{n+1} \in S_G$. The plan cost is assumed to be its length; therefore, a plan is optimal if no shorter plan exists.

A plan validator [10] is a reasoning tool that, given a domain, a problem instance, and a plan, validates whether the plan solves the problem. The validator checks the applicability of each plan action a_i by verifying the truth of its preconditions in the current state s_i ($a_i \in A(s_i)$), and progresses s_i to s_{i+1} ($s_{i+1} = f(a_i, s_i)$). If an action violates the preconditions ($a_i \notin A(s_i)$), then the validator terminates returning an invalid plan. Otherwise the validator verifies whether the last state of the plan reaches the problem goal ($s_{i+1} \in S_G$); in that case, it returns the generated plan as a solution plan, or the invalid plan.

Generalised planning studies the representation and computation of general policies to solve multiple problems in the same planning domain [11,25,26]. A general policy can be defined as a function $\pi(Init, Goal, a_0, ..., a_{i-1})$ that provides the next action in Act to apply given the initial state $Init$, the goal $Goal$ of the problem instance and the list of i actions previously obtained by π auto-regressively. A policy π solves a set of classical planning instances for the same domain D if each of these instances $I = (O, Init, Goal)$ is solved by the sequence of actions $A_\pi = (a_0, ..., a_i)$ obtained by applying auto-regressively π, i.e. $a_0 = (Init, Goal)$, $a_1 = (Init, Goal, a_0)$, $a_2 = (Init, Goal, a_0, a_1)$ ..., $a_i = (Init, Goal, a_{i-1})$.

3.2   Generative Pretrained Transformer (GPT)

In this section, we briefly introduce the architecture of GPT, the neural component of PLANGPT and how it works. A GPT model [17,18] is the decoder stack of the Transformer architecture [33] developed to generate sequences of elements for NLP tasks. We selected the smallest GPT-2 version because it is the latest open-source version of GPT and, requires less training data and fewer computational resources for training than bigger versions. This model completes the sentence given as input, known as prompt, with the most likely next words. The completion process continues step-by-step, appending the generated word to the input and outputting the most likely next word. In our example, given the input "Rome is the capital", GPT predicts the following words "of" and "Italy". The main component of GPT-2 is the attention mechanism. This neural component tries to correlate each couple of tokens in the prompt to extract the various relationships between the sentence, obtaining a meaningful semantic of the prompt to generate the most valuable token. This generation process requires a preliminary tokenization step using a tokenizer, in this case, WordPiece [4], mapping the words in the prompt into individual words or word fragments called *tokens*.

More formally, this strategy is the standard strategy of GPT called **greedy decoding**. At each step, the model takes the prompt as input and outputs the token with the highest probability from the vocabulary (adding it to the prompt). This generation has the issue of producing less varied outputs, as it always selects the most probable token greedily without exploring other tokens. Another method called **top-p sampling** addresses these limitations. In top-p sampling, instead of always selecting the token with the highest probability, the model creates a reduced set of tokens at each step and then randomly samples the next one from the probability distribution over this reduced set. At each step, the strategy cumulatively sums the probabilities of the tokens in descending order until the sum exceeds a threshold p. This token selection ensures that only the most likely tokens, which account for a probability mass of at least p, are considered for sampling.

3.3   PLANGPT

In our previous work, PLANGPT [20], we trained from scratch the architecture of GPT-2 on a customised planning dataset, following the idea that LLMs could understand the grammar and solve a planning problem as shown by [5]. In the context of general policies, after training, PLANGPT can solve complex planning problems similar to those from the International Planning Competition (IPC), achieving state-of-the-art performance across various classical planning domains using the top-p sampling generation.

PLANGPT receives in input a set of fluents representing the initial state and the goal of a planning and has to compute a plan to solve a problem. In order to do that, it has to predict sequentially all the actions of a plan as if they were words. Mapping fluents and action into words is done through the tokenization. During tokenization, we split each fluent (and each action) into its components, the fluent (or action) name, and its associated objects. For example, for fluent (*At Truck1 Loc1*) we have three tokens: *At*, *Truck1* and *Loc1*; for action (*Drive Truck1 Loc1 Loc3*), four tokens: *Drive*, *Truck1*, *Loc1* and *Loc3*. After training, given as input the fluents of the initial state and the goal of a problem, PLANGPT generates the solution plan by generating the next token (the action name or the object name) in an auto-regressive mode with different generation strategies.

At the end of the generation, the validator unites the tokens into actions. Finally, the validator checks the validity of the plan. However, a current limitation of our approach is that if an action fails due to a violation of a precondition or the plan does not satisfy the goal, the plan is considered invalid by the validator, and PLANGPT cannot correct it.

3.4   Local Search for Planning Graphs

The standard method for solving classical planning problems is the use of a planner. A planner is a system that addresses planning problems without leveraging particular domain properties or biases, but using only the domain definition and search methods. Given as input the domain description D and the problem I, a planner will produce a plan to solve the problem I. In literature, numerous planners such as LAMA [19], Fast-Downward [9] and LPG [6] exploit different kinds of heuristics and search to solve automated planning problems. In this work, we consider using the Local search for Planning Graphs (LPG) [6] as it offers the possibility of plan repair and completion.

The basic search scheme of LPG was inspired by Walksat [13], an efficient procedure to solve SAT problems. The search space of LPG consists of *action graphs*, particular sub-graphs of the planning graph representing partial plans. The search steps are graph modifications, transforming an action graph into another one. LPG exploits a compact representation of the planning graph to define the search neighbourhood and to evaluate its elements building relaxed planning graphs. This is achieved by an anytime process that produces a sequence of plans, each of which improves the quality of the previous ones.

In addition to generating a plan from scratch, LPG offers a plan repair solution: starting from an invalid or incomplete plan LPG solves the problem by leveraging the knowledge in that plan and correcting it.

4   PLANGPT Seed as Input of LPG

The main contribution of this work is integrating the LPG planner in the generation phase of PLANGPT. Given that PLANGPT has the potential to generate invalid plans, we use the LPG repair plan option to correct these invalid plans.

Starting from an already generated plan, instead of an empty seed as usual, LPG can compute an action graph from the current invalid plan that corrects inconsistencies and improves the quality of the final solution, reducing the search time required and exploiting the knowledge in the generated plan.

The proposed architecture includes a neural system, PLANGPT, which produces a plan (valid or not), a symbolic validator that can check its validity, and LPG that can repair it. We refer to this combined system as R-PLANGPT.

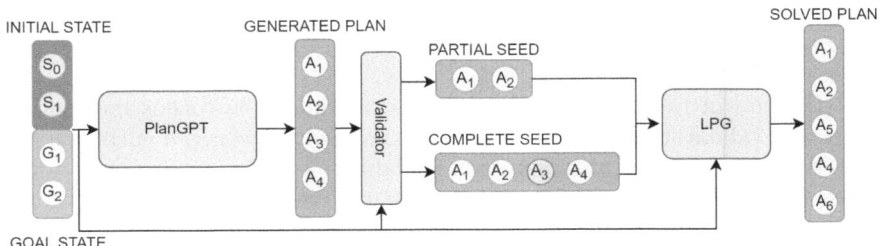

Fig. 1. Example of input/output for a planning problem with two fluents in the initial state (S_0 and S_1) and two fluents (G_0 and G_1) forming the goal. PLANGPT generates the plan A_1, ..., A_4. The validator verifies the correctness of the candidate plan and, if it finds it invalid, generates the partial and complete seeds. Then LPG generates a valid plan using the seed with the repair option

Following Fig. 1, the generation process of the system starts from the component PLANGPT, which takes the initial state and goals as input and generates a candidate plan. In this example, given the fluents S_0 and S_1 and the goal fluents G_1 and G_2, PLANGPT generates a plan composed of 4 actions: A_1, A_2, A_3, A_4. Then, the symbolic validator checks the actions' validity and the satisfaction of the goal. In the example, the validator analyses the actions A_1, A_2, A_3, A_4, discovering that the action A_3 is invalid.

We implement two strategies to create the LPG candidate seed: the **partial seed**, where the validator discards some actions from the original generated plan, or the **complete seed**, where LPG takes as input the whole generated plan.

In the partial seed, if the plan has an action that violates a precondition, the validator prunes all the actions from the violation, obtaining the candidate plan. Instead, suppose the plan has no preconditions' violations. In that case, the validator produces the candidate plan by selecting all the actions up to the last one that satisfies the problem's last solved goal. Furthermore, the validator checks the presence of loops in the candidate plan computed, i.e. sequences of actions that repetitively reach the same state without progressing towards the goals, and removes them. The idea is to provide LPG with a correct initial candidate plan to complete that satisfies various goal fluents and does not provide any violated preconditions or loops. In Fig. 1, for the partial seed, since action

A_3 is invalid, the validator prunes actions A_3, A_4 and produces the candidate plan A_1, A_2.

In the complete seed, instead, the candidate plan for LPG consists of the plan from PLANGPT without any modifications. This approach enabled LPG to take advantage of the knowledge of the plan generated after a precondition violation and, therefore, to provide details on the subsequent phases of the plan. By correcting the violation of the preconditions, if any, it is possible that the remaining plan is valid and helps LPG in its search. In Fig. 1, for the complete seed, the candidate plan is A_1, A_2, A_3, A_4.

Finally, LPG searches for a solution starting from the input candidate plan and gives the final plan solution as output. In Fig. 1, LPG takes as input the complete seed and produces the new plan A_1, A_2, A_5, A_4, A_6 substituting action A_3 with action A_5 and adding action A_6 to obtain a valid solution to the problem. In our experimental evaluation, we also considered an empty candidate plan as input to LPG.

5   Experimental Results

Starting from the available trained PLANGPT [20], we extended its generation process with the integration of a validator and the LPG planner in the eight benchmark domains used in [20]: BLOCKSWORLD, DEPOTS, DRIVERLOG, FLOOR-TILE, LOGISTICS, SATELLITE, VISITALL and ZENOTRAVEL.

For each domain, we used more than 6000 testing problems (Tset). The planning problems in Tset are similar to those used in the International Planning Competition (IPC) and are created using the available PDDL generators [22]. The choice to use this dataset is to compare a larger number of problems since the test set of IPC contains only between 30 and 100 problems for each domain. The PLANGPT models are run on an NVIDIA A100 GPU with 40 GB. Regarding the planners, for each problem, we generate solution plans on an Intel (R) Xeon (R) Gold 6140M CPU @ 2.30GHz with a standard time limit of 300s.

To evaluate our experiments, we use classical planning metrics such as the coverage, the plan length and the *IPCScore-Quality* (IPCQ) and *IPCScore-Agile* (IPCA) as defined in the last International Planning Competition (IPC 2023):

- **Coverage**: the percentage of valid plans over the total number of generated plans.
- **Plan Length**: the score of a problem is the number of actions of a solution plan. The score of a model is the mean of its score for the problems solved by all the models.
- **IPCScore-Quality**: The score of a problem is the ratio C^*/C where C is the cost of the plan discovered by the model and C^* is the cost of a reference plan (the cheapest plan obtained by all models for that problem). The score of an unsolved problem is 0. The score of a model is the sum of its scores for all problems.

– **IPCScore-Agile**: The score of a problem on a solved task is 1 if the task was solved within 1 second and 0 if not solved within the resource limits. If the problem is solved in T seconds ($1 \leq T \leq 300$) then its score is $1 - log(T)/log(300)$. The score of a model is the sum of its scores for all problems.

In the following, we evaluate PLANGPT and LPG in terms of coverage and plan length compared on Tset considering different execution time thresholds. Next, we evaluate R-PLANGPT, combining the repair process of LPG using partial, and complete seed on the invalid plans generated by PLANGPT in terms of coverage, plan length, and execution time to find the best solution compared to LPG with an empty seed. Finally, we compare the performances of R-PLANGPT with LAMA, FD, PLANGPT and LPG in the IPC benchmark problems for our domains in terms of coverage, IPCQ and IPCA.

5.1   PLANGPT Vs LPG

This section compares PLANGPT (using top p sampling) and LPG (initialised with an empty seed) over the Tset on coverage and plan length, evaluating different execution times. PLANGPT generates a single solution, while LPG produces multiple solutions in an interval of 5 minutes of incremental quality. Considering that PLANGPT was trained on suboptimal planning instances solved by LPG, this comparison demonstrates the model's capabilities relative to its teacher, highlighting instances where it can surpass the performances of LPG. Table 1 shows the coverage of PLANGPT and LPG considering different execution time thresholds: 10 seconds, 20 seconds, 1 minute and 5 minutes. Both systems obtain high coverage in under 10 seconds of execution with almost perfect scores on BLOCKSWORLD, SATELLITE, VISITALL and ZENOTRAVEL. Instead, DEPOTS and DRIVERLOG obtain lower levels of coverage due to the high number of states to evaluate in the search, while FLOORTILE's performances are affected by the numerous dead-ends of the domain. After 20 seconds, we can observe that even DEPOTS and DRIVERLOG obtain high coverages, while FLOORTILE obtains high coverages only after 1 minute for both systems. Finally, considering the time threshold of 5 minutes, LPG obtains higher coverages than PLANGPT having a difference up to 5% (0% in BLOCKSWORLD, 5% in DEPOTS, 2% in DRIVER-LOG and SATELLITE, and 0.1% in VISITALL and ZENOTRAVEL). We can observe a notable difference in the LOGISTICS domain where LPG obtains a higher coverage than PLANGPT (98% vs 77%). This domain is very complex for PLANGPT since it belongs to the C3-fragment of the first-order logic. Lastly, we observe that PLANGPT obtains higher coverage than LPG (99% vs 93%) in FLOORTILE, because the LPG search is affected by the numerous dead-ends present in this domain.

Table 2 shows the results of the plan length of PLANGPT and LPG of the problems solved by both systems considering the time ranges of 10 seconds, 20 seconds, 1 minute and 5 minutes. In general, we observe that, in less than 10 seconds, PLANGPT obtains plans of shorter length; after 1 minute, the two systems are comparable in different domains. Given more time, LPG obtains a

Table 1. Percentage coverage of PLANGPT and of LPG over Tset. For each time frame we highlight in bold the best results.

domain	< 10 s		< 20 s		< 1 m		< 5 m	
	LPG	PLANGPT	LPG	PLANGPT	LPG	PLANGPT	LPG	PLANGPT
BLOCKSWORLD	**99.3**	**99.3**	99.9	**100.0**	**100.0**	**100.0**	**100.0**	**100.0**
DEPOTS	**77.6**	76.0	**99.4**	94.5	**99.8**	94.8	**99.9**	94.9
DRIVERLOG	**61.1**	61.0	**98.1**	96.3	**99.8**	97.8	**99.9**	97.9
FLOORTILE	40.8	**41.2**	58.0	**62.6**	93.2	**99.3**	93.5	**99.6**
LOGISTICS	**98.0**	77.2	**99.9**	77.3	**99.9**	77.3	**99.9**	77.3
SATELLITE	**100.0**	98.1	**100.0**	98.1	**100.0**	98.1	**100.0**	98.1
VISITALL	**99.8**	99.8	**100.0**	99.9	**100.0**	99.9	**100.0**	99.9
ZENOTRAVEL	**100.0**	99.9	**100.0**	99.9	**100.0**	99.9	**100.0**	99.9

Table 2. Plan length of PLANGPT and of LPG over Tset for the problem solved by both systems. For each time frame we highlight in bold the best results

domain	< 10 s		< 20 s		< 1 m		< 5 m	
	LPG	PLANGPT	LPG	PLANGPT	LPG	PLANGPT	LPG	PLANGPT
BLOCKSWORLD	40.4	**38.0**	39.4	**38.2**	38.3	**38.2**	**37.5**	38.2
DEPOTS	35.0	**33.9**	38.8	**37.6**	37.9	**37.7**	**36.8**	37.7
DRIVERLOG	69.5	**67.5**	85.9	**84.7**	**80.2**	85.6	**73.4**	85.7
FLOORTILE	51.5	**43.8**	76.5	**55.8**	70.4	**58.8**	61.9	**59.0**
LOGISTICS	**19.3**	21.7	**19.1**	21.7	**18.8**	21.7	**18.5**	21.7
SATELLITE	**29.8**	29.9	**29.8**	29.9	**29.7**	29.9	**29.7**	29.9
VISITALL	**41.7**	44.8	**40.9**	44.9	**39.9**	44.9	**38.9**	44.9
ZENOTRAVEL	41.3	**40.3**	**39.8**	40.3	**38.3**	40.3	**36.3**	40.3

better quality in all domains, except for FLOORTILE, where PLANGPT obtains the best plan length. Given that PLANGPT generates a single plan and stops the generation, we expect that LPG obtains shorter plans in the long run because it continues to produce solutions of incremental quality. In BLOCKSWORLD and DEPOTS, within 1 minute, PLANGPT obtains shorter plans of an action. After 1 minute, LPG produces plans of similar length. In DRIVERLOG, we can observe that LPG obtains better plans after 1 minute with a more significant number of actions (5 after 1 minute and 12 after 5 minutes). Overall, in the domain of LOGISTICS, there is always a difference of 3 actions between the systems. In VISITALL, this difference is around 3 to 5 actions in favour of LPG. In ZENOTRAVEL, first PLANGPT has a higher quality, but then LPG obtains lesser and lesser actions up to a difference of 4 actions. In SATELLITE, the two systems obtain the same plan length. Finally, we can observe that in FLOORTILE, PLANGPT generates plans having better quality for each timeframe: a difference of 8 actions

before 10 seconds, 11 before 1 minutes, since PLANGPT has already generated
all the plans, and 3 after 2 minutes when LPG completes its search. This surprising result in the FLOORTILE domain implies that learning a policy from valid
plans can be helpful when the search uses a negative-effect relaxation in the
heuristics leading to explore numerous undetected dead-ends.

5.2 PLANGPT as Initial Seed of LPG

Table 3. Percentage coverage (cov), plan length (length), CPU time of problem
unsolved by PLANGPT and corrected by the complete system R-PLANGPT, using
the partial and complete seed strategies. In the first columns we show also the results
obtained by LPG without seed on the same set of problems

| | LPG | | | R-PLANGPT | | | | | |
| | Empty | | | Partial | | | Complete | | |
domain	cov	length	time	cov	length	time	cov	length	time
DEPOTS	**100.0**	55.2	128.9	**100.0**	56.4	**84.9**	97.8	**54.8**	105.9
DRIVERLOG	99.9	**127.6**	169.6	**100.0**	128.8	**101.1**	87.4	128.2	126.6
LOGISTICS	99.5	52.6	104.5	99.8	**51.8**	**86.9**	97.3	51.9	89.9
SATELLITE	**100.0**	40.5	**14.8**	**100.0**	40.6	18.7	**100.0**	40.8	18.2

In Table 3, we show the integration of PLANGPT and LPG, R-PLANGPT,
using different initialisation strategies (partial and complete plan seed) given to
the planner LPG to solve the unsolved problem of PLANGPT and comparing
against LPG with an empty seed. We show the coverage, plan length, and the
average execution time used by LPG to obtain the best solution for each seed. We
analyse DEPOTS (356), DRIVERLOG (158), LOGISTICS (1504) and SATELLITE (123)
since these domains have at least 100 invalid plans generated by PLANGPT.
The execution time of the generation of PLANGPT and the validation (in the
partial and complete seed) is added to the LPG computation time to show a
fair comparison to the empty seed, which does not require PLANGPT. On the
other side, the LPG search time limit is 5 minutes.

From Table 3, concerning coverage, the quality of the empty and partial
seeds is comparable, solving most of the problems unsolved by PLANGPT. However, we have a drop in performances with the complete seed. More specifically,
we observe that using the partial seed in DRIVERLOG and LOGISTICS slightly
enhances the coverage of LPG. On the contrary, in SATELLITE, using a seed is
not helpful to LPG. However, using the complete seed, we observe a drop of
the coverage in SATELLITE (-2.2%), DEPOTS (-12.5%) and LOGISTICS (-2.2%).
LPG struggles to correct very long plans (also with cycles) or plans with multiple
violations and, therefore, the useful actions that can be extracted from the plan
are insufficient to compensate for this problems. Although individually LPG and
PLANGPT cannot compute a valid solution for 20 problems in FLOORTILE, when
combined using the partial seed, R-PLANGPT solves these problems, obtaining

valid plans exploiting the knowledge of PLANGPT and refining the plan with the LPG search.

Concerning the plan length, the quality of the plans for the 3 seeds is comparable overall, with a mean difference of a single action. For DEPOTS and SATELLITE, the best seed is the complete seed. In the case of DRIVERLOG, LPG without PLANGPT obtains the best length. While for LOGISTICS, the best seed is the partial seed.

Regarding the time to generate a solution, using the partial or complete seeds allows a notable reduction in the heuristic search of LPG to obtain the best solution. We observe that the time between the plan generated by LPG from scratch compared to the candidate plans of partial seed decreases with a delta from $44s$ in DEPOTS, $68s$ in DRIVERLOG, $18s$ in LOGISTICS. Also in the complete seed, we note a decrease in the execution time, but it is less remarkable than the partial seed, because LPG must correct and remove loops in the candidate plan: $23s$ in DEPOTS, $43s$ in DRIVERLOG and $15s$ in LOGISTICS. The only exception is in SATELLITE, where having a seed for LPG does not lower the time for the heuristic search, but neither increases it. This result shows how introducing a plan seed (which contains helpful information on the plan) helps the planner to carry out a more targeted heuristic search, reducing its execution time.

Therefore, from our results, the partial seed is a better strategy for the combined system R-PLANGPT because the cutting strategy can obtain a helpful prefix seed, which the planner can use to start from. The integration of PLANGPT and LPG produces plans of comparable plan length with a significant decrease in the generation of the solution.

5.3   Comparison with SoTA Planners on IPC

In Table 4, we compare the different state-of-the-art classical planners with LPG, PLANGPT, and the combined system R-PLANGPT with the partial seed strategy using a time limit of 5 minutes. It is important to note that the system R-PLANGPT uses different configurations for each domain, so it is a domain dependent approach, and the classical planners considered are domain independent. We used the IPCQuality and IPCAgile metrics. We evaluated the system using the IPC competition problems. Each domain contains 20 planning instances except for BLOCKSWORLD with 35 instances, DEPOTS, 22 and LOGISTICS, 30.

Regarding coverage, FD and LAMA solve all the problems except for DEPOTS (77% and 95%) and FLOORTILE (10%). The last instances of DEPOTS are complex because they have many objects. Although FLOORTILE is complex because it contains multiple dead-ends that are not detected by delete-relaxation heuristics. PLANGPT managed to solve with high coverage in almost all the domains (90% in DEPOTS and 95% in DRIVERLOG and VISITALL) with the exceptions of LOGISTICS (53%) and SATELLITE (70%), providing various invalid plans. In SATELLITE, PLANGPT struggles when a precondition is bound to an object selected by a previous action which is far away from the current one. For instance, in LOGISTICS, PLANGPT struggles to correlate the positions of the truck and the object simultaneously. In contrast, in SATELLITE, PLANGPT struggles to select an instrument with the correct mode to take an image. The best-performing systems proved to be LPG and R-PLANGPT, which solved all the provided planning problems.

Table 4. Comparison of IPCQ and IPCA metrics between classical planners (FD, LAMA and LPG), PLANGPT and R-PLANGPT with the partial seed using the IPC test set

domain	FD		LAMA		LPG		PLANGPT		R-PLANGPT	
	IPCQ	IPCA	IPCQ	IPCA	IPCQ	IPCA	IPCQ	IPCA	IPCQ	IPCA
BLOCKSWORLD	27.61	**35.00**	33.93	34.88	**35.00**	**35.00**	34.73	34.20	34.73	34.20
DEPOTS	15.15	14.65	19.45	20.22	18.59	**21.85**	17.42	14.27	**21.40**	17.17
DRIVERLOG	18.79	**19.06**	19.73	18.96	18.59	18.79	17.08	15.95	17.46	16.32
FLOORTILE	2.00	1.46	2.00	1.44	17.36	**15.99**	**19.64**	10.39	**19.64**	10.39
LOGISTICS	26.41	**30.00**	26.55	**30.00**	24.99	29.90	14.02	13.05	**27.12**	22.53
SATELLITE	18.51	**20.00**	18.64	**20.00**	19.74	**20.00**	11.94	11.61	19.68	17.12
VISITALL	19.07	15.46	**19.60**	12.38	19.46	**19.86**	16.53	16.41	17.46	16.48
ZENOTRAVEL	18.85	**20.00**	19.82	**20.00**	19.22	19.38	15.71	16.01	17.51	17.50
TOTAL	146.39	155.63	159.72	157.88	172.95	**180.77**	147.07	131.89	**175.00**	151.62

Regarding the IPCQ metric, we observe that R-PLANGPT reaches the highest score in DEPOTS (21.40), FLOORTILE (19.64), and LOGISTICS (27.12). In the case of FLOORTILE, the results are provided by the solution plans generated by PLANGPT. In the case of DEPOTS and LOGISTICS, instead, the integration with the plan-repair procedure of LPG produces the shortest plans. LAMA reaches the best quality in DRIVERLOG (19.73), VISITALL (19.60), and ZENO-TRAVEL (19.82), while LPG obtains the shortest plan in BLOCKSWORLD (35.00) and SATELLITE (19.74). Finally, PLANGPT obtains the best quality in FLOOR-TILE and comparable performances in the other domains.

Regarding the IPCA metric, we observe that all the planners are faster than PLANGPT and, therefore, than R-PLANGPT. PLANGPT is generally slower to compute a solution because it generates only a single solution with higher quality. In SATELLITE, all the planners compute the plans in less than 1 second. In BLOCKSWORLD FD and LPG take less time to compute one solution compared to the other systems. The same behaviour happens in LOGISTICS and ZENOTRAVEL with FD and LAMA. FD is the faster planner in DRIVERLOG (19.06), while LPG obtains the best results in DEPOTS (21.85), FLOORTILE (15.99) and VISITALL (19.86).

In conclusion, considering the IPC test set, we evaluated the ability of learned general policies derived from LLM, combined with a plan-repair planner, to provide enhanced results in various domains and show comparable performances with SoTA planners. More in-depth, the FLOORTILE domain is particularly appealing because planners based on delete-relaxation heuristics struggle to acquire a solution, while R-PLANGPT obtains perfect coverage.

6   Conclusions

In this work, we investigated the possibility of integrating a neural solution based on the GPT architecture, PLANGPT, with a symbolic one, LPG. Firstly, we analysed the comparison between LPG and PLANGPT, where PLANGPT showed comparable performance to LPG in some domains in a limited time window and better coverage and quality in the case of FLOORTILE. Then, we proposed our combined system, R-PLANGPT. We showed that PLANGPT can give information, as a seed, for LPG and guide the heuristic search to a solution in less time than LPG alone. In fact, R-PLANGPT corrects the majority of the test problems using the partial or complete seed obtained from the invalid plans generated from PLANGPT. Finally, we evaluated R-PLANGPT in the context of the IPC competition against state-of-the-art classical planners with comparable performances. Current and future work includes training PLANGPT on other challenging domains for planners, integrating the domain knowledge in the training phase, and overcoming the current limits due to the maximum number of objects in the vocabulary and the length of the context window.

Acknowledgements. This work was been supported by EU H2020 project AIPlan4EU (GA 101016442), EU ICT-48 2020 project TAILOR (GA 952215), MUR PRIN project RIPER (No. 20203FFYLK), Climate Change AI project (No. IG-2023-174), Regione Lombardia through the initiatives "Il Piano Lombardia - Interventi per la ripresa economica" and "Programma degli interventi per la ripresa economica: sviluppo di nuovi accordi di collaborazione con le università per la ricerca, l'innovazione e il trasferimento tecnologico" - DGR n. XI/4445/2021 and by SERICS (PE00000014) under the MUR National Recovery and Resilience Plan funded by the European Union - NextGenerationEU.

References

1. Arora, D., Kambhampati, S.: Learning and leveraging verifiers to improve planning capabilities of pre-trained language models. arXiv preprint arXiv:2305.17077 (2023)
2. Chen, D., Thiébaux, S., Trevizan, F.: Learning domain-independent heuristics for grounded and lifted planning. In: Proceedings of 38th AAAI Conference on Artificial Intelligence (2024). http://felipe.trevizan.org/papers/chen24:goose.pdf
3. Chen, D., Trevizan, F., Thiébaux, S.: Return to tradition: learning reliable heuristics with classical machine learning. In: Proceedings of 34th International Conference on Automated Planning and Scheduling (ICAPS) (2024). http://felipe.trevizan.org/papers/chen24:wlkernel.pdf
4. Devlin, J., Chang, M., Lee, K., Toutanova, K.: BERT: pre-training of deep bidirectional transformers for language understanding. In: NAACL-HLT, pp. 4171–4186. Association for Computational Linguistics (2019)
5. Geib, C.W., Steedman, M.: On natural language processing and plan recognition. In: IJCAI, pp. 1612–1617 (2007)
6. Gerevini, A., Saetti, A., Serina, I.: Planning through stochastic local search and temporal action graphs in LPG. J. Artif. Intell. Res. **20**, 239–290 (2003). https://doi.org/10.1613/jair.1183

7. Geva, M., Khashabi, D., Segal, E., Khot, T., Roth, D., Berant, J.: Did Aristotle use a laptop? A question answering benchmark with implicit reasoning strategies. Trans. Assoc. Comput. Linguistics **9**, 346–361 (2021)

8. Hao, M., Trevizan, F., Thiébaux, S., Ferber, P., Hoffmann, J.: Guiding GBFS through learned pairwise rankings. In: Proceedings of 33rd International Joint Conference on AI (IJCAI) (2024). http://felipe.trevizan.org/papers/hao24:ranking.pdf

9. Helmert, M.: The fast downward planning system. J. Artif. Intell. Res. **26**, 191–246 (2006)

10. Howey, R., Long, D., Fox, M.: VAL: automatic plan validation, continuous effects and mixed initiative planning using PDDL. In: ICTAI, pp. 294–301. IEEE Computer Society (2004)

11. Hu, Y., De Giacomo, G.: Generalized planning: synthesizing plans that work for multiple environments. In: IJCAI, pp. 918–923. IJCAI.org (2011)

12. Jiang, Z., Xu, F.F., Araki, J., Neubig, G.: How can we know what language models know. Trans. Assoc. Comput. Linguistics **8**, 423–438 (2020)

13. Kautz, H., Selman, B.: Pushing the envelope: planning, propositional logic, and stochastic search. In: Proceedings of the National Conference on Artificial Intelligence, vol. 2 (1999)

14. Pallagani, V., et al.: Plansformer: generating symbolic plans using transformers. arXiv preprint arXiv:2212.08681 (2022)

15. Pallagani, V., et al.: Plansformer tool: demonstrating generation of symbolic plans using transformers. In: IJCAI, pp. 7158–7162. IJCAI.org (2023)

16. Petroni, F., et al.: Language models as knowledge bases? In: EMNLP/IJCNLP, pp. 2463–2473. Association for Computational Linguistics (2019)

17. Radford, A., Narasimhan, K.: Improving language understanding by generative pre-training (2018). https://api.semanticscholar.org/CorpusID:49313245

18. Radford, A., Wu, J., Child, R., Luan, D., Amodei, D., Sutskever, I.: Language models are unsupervised multitask learners (2019). https://api.semanticscholar.org/CorpusID:160025533

19. Richter, S., Westphal, M.: The LAMA planner: guiding cost-based anytime planning with landmarks. J. Artif. Intell. Res. **39**, 127–177 (2010)

20. Rossetti, N., et al.: Learning general policies for planning through GPT models. In: 34th International Conference on Automated Planning and Scheduling (2024)

21. Rossetti, N., Tummolo, M., Gerevini, A.E., Putelli, L., Serina, I., Olivato, M.: Enhancing GPT-based planning policies by model-based plan validation. In: Proceedings of the 18th International Conference on Neural-Symbolic Learning and Reasoning (2024)

22. Seipp, J., Torralba, A., Hoffmann, J.: PDDL generators (2022). https://github.com/AI-Planning/pddl-generators

23. Serina, L., Chiari, M., Gerevini, A.E., Putelli, L., Serina, I.: A preliminary study on BERT applied to automated planning. In: Proceedings of the 10th Italian workshop on Planning and Scheduling (IPS 2022), RCRA Incontri E Confronti (RiCeRcA 2022), and the workshop on Strategies, Prediction, Interaction, and Reasoning in Italy (SPIRIT 2022) co-located with 21st International Conference of the Italian Association for Artificial Intelligence (AI*IA 2022), November 28 – December 2, 2022, University of Udine, Udine, Italy. CEUR Workshop Proceedings, vol. 3345. CEUR-WS.org (2022)

24. Serina, L., Putelli, L., Gerevini, A.E., Serina, I.: Synonyms, antonyms and factual knowledge in BERT heads. Future Internet **15**(7), 230 (2023). https://doi.org/10.3390/fi15070230

25. Srivastava, S., Immerman, N., Zilberstein, S.: Learning generalized plans using abstract counting. In: AAAI, pp. 991–997. AAAI Press (2008)
26. Srivastava, S., Immerman, N., Zilberstein, S.: A new representation and associated algorithms for generalized planning. Artif. Intell. **175**(2), 615–647 (2011)
27. Ståhlberg, S., Bonet, B., Geffner, H.: Learning general optimal policies with graph neural networks: expressive power, transparency, and limits. In: ICAPS, pp. 629–637. AAAI Press (2022)
28. Ståhlberg, S., Bonet, B., Geffner, H.: Learning generalized policies without supervision using GNNs. In: KR, pp. 474–483. IJCAI Org. (2022)
29. Stahlberg, S., Bonet, B., Geffner, H.: Muninn (2023). https://ipc2023-learning.github.io/abstracts/muninn.pdf
30. Valmeekam, K., Hernandez, A.O., Sreedharan, S., Kambhampati, S.: Large language models still can't plan, a benchmark for LLMs on planning and reasoning about change. arXiv preprint arXiv:2206.10498 (2022)
31. Valmeekam, K., Marquez, M., Sreedharan, S., Kambhampati, S.: On the planning abilities of large language models - a critical investigation. In: NeurIPS (2023)
32. Valmeekam, K., Sreedharan, S., Marquez, M., Hernandez, A.O., Kambhampati, S.: On the planning abilities of large language models, a critical investigation with a proposed benchmark. arXiv preprint arXiv:2302.06706 (2023)
33. Vaswani, A., et al.: Attention is all you need. In: NIPS, pp. 5998–6008. Curran Associates Inc. (2017)
34. Wang, Y., Wang, W., Joty, S.R., Hoi, S.C.H.: CodeT5: identifier-aware unified pre-trained encoder-decoder models for code understanding and generation. In: EMNLP, pp. 8696–8708. Association for Computational Linguistics (2021)

Probabilistic Traces in Declarative Process Mining

Michela Vespa[1]([✉])(iD), Elena Bellodi[1]([✉])(iD), Federico Chesani[2]([✉])(iD),
Daniela Loreti[2]([✉])(iD), Paola Mello[2]([✉])(iD), Evelina Lamma[1]([✉])(iD),
Anna Ciampolini[2]([✉])(iD), Marco Gavanelli[1]([✉])(iD), and Riccardo Zese[3]([✉])(iD)

[1] Dipartimento di Ingegneria, Universitá di Ferrara, Via Saragat 1, Ferrara, Italy
{Michela.Vespa,Elena.Bellodi,Evelina.Lamma,Marco.Gavanelli}@unife.it
[2] Dipartimento di Informatica - Scienza e Ingegneria, Viale Risorgimento 2,
Bologna, Italy
{Federico.Chesani,Daniela.Loreti,Paola.Mello,Anna.Ciampolini}@unibo.it
[3] Dipartimento di Scienze Chimiche, Farmaceutiche ed Agrarie - Universitá di
Ferrara, Via Borsari 46, Ferrara, Italy
Riccardo.Zese@unife.it

Abstract. When dealing with real-world processes, it is essential to consider their inherent uncertainty to more accurately represent their nature. In this work, we consider cases in which some information in the log might be unreliable. We propose a novel semantics for probabilistic process traces, based on the Distribution Semantics from Probabilistic Logic Programming, which allows one to annotate event executions of an observed trace with a probability representing the uncertainty of the event as the degree of our belief in that event happening. Then, we propose a novel definition of probabilistic compliance of a probabilistic process trace w.r.t. a declarative process specification, and how to compute it using a probabilistic abduction proof-procedure. Experimental results on a real-world healthcare protocol are presented to evaluate the feasibility of the proposed semantics on conformance checking.

Keywords: Process Mining · Probabilistic compliance · Declarative language · Distribution Semantics

1   Introduction

In the Business Process Mining (BPM) community [24], the integration of probability into various aspects of process modeling is a growing research topic, reflecting an interest in enhancing process analysis under conditions of uncertainty in real-world domains. Uncertainty can be found at various levels, such as process constraints, events, event attributes, or traces.

For instance, in declarative process mining, [2] introduced the notion of probabilistic process constraints, by associating probabilities to DECLARE constraints with a frequency-based approach. A probabilistic constraint is satisfied over the log if the number of traces satisfying the constraint over the log cardinality achieves the mathematical relation established by the relational operator and the probability assigned. A constraint c_1 with assigned probability $(0.6, \geq)$ is

A. Artale et al. (Eds.): AIxIA 2024, LNAI 15450, pp. 330–345, 2025.
https://doi.org/10.1007/978-3-031-80607-0_25

satisfied if the number of traces complaint with c_1 is at least $\geq 60\%$ of the total traces. They propose how to discover such constraints and how to carry out monitoring and conformance checking.

In procedural process mining, [6,14,15] handle probabilities at the level of traces or events in a trace. In [6], traces are supposed generated by a stochastic process model, which outputs a variety of possible sequences, each associated with a certain probability. Then, probabilistic trace alignment - i.e. the comparison between the model traces and the observed trace - is done by identifying the k model traces nearest to a particular observed log trace. [15] defines probability distributions over all possible realizations of an uncertain trace, where uncertainty may come from partial timestamps, indeterminate events, and activity labels. Uncertainty is divided into two types: strong uncertainty, where the probability distributions of events are unknown, and weak uncertainty, where events follow known probability distributions. The conformance score is calculated as the cost of the optimal alignment between the trace and a Petri net model. [14] consider the analysis of a specific class of event logs, those containing uncertain events, i.e. recordings of executions of specific activities in a process which are enclosed with an indication of uncertainty in the event attributes. Specifically, attributes of an event are not recorded as a precise value but as a range or a set of alternatives, and they perform conformance checking by assessing upper and lower bounds on the conformance score for possible values of the attributes in an uncertain trace.

Differently from previous work, we propose a novel semantics to handle uncertainty at the level of *events* in a trace in a *declarative* process mining setting. In fact, some information in a process trace could be unreliable and a domain expert might be allowed to indicate a *degree of belief* on that information. Such degree is expressed by an *epistemic probability* value [20] which may be associated to an event execution. To better explain the idea, we provide an example based on a real medical protocol about elective colorectal surgery [23]. In the ERAS® (Enhanced Recovery After Surgery) guidelines, the administration of preoperative antibiotics is crucial for reducing infection risks. However, there might be cases where this administration is not logged correctly due to human error or system issues. For instance, if a surgeon recalls ordering antibiotics for a patient before surgery but later finds no documentation of this in the medical records, she might estimate, based on routine practice, interactions with the nursing staff, and protocol recommendations, that there was a 95% probability the antibiotics were administered as needed. This estimation is not based on quantitative data but rather on the surgeon's *confidence/belief* in her standard procedures.

From a formal point of view, we introduce the concept of Probabilistic Event and Probabilistic Trace starting from Probabilistic Logic Programming (PLP) and the Distribution Semantics [22]. In a PLP program, logic formulas are annotated with probabilities, defining a probability distribution over normal logic programs called worlds. These probabilities represent the likelihood of the formulas appearing in a normal logic program. Likewise, the probability of an event is treated as the probability that such event will appear (or not) in a world, similarly to how scenarios (or realizations) are treated in [15]. However, we consider uncertainty related to the event as a whole, without considering event attributes. According to our semantics, all worlds including one such event "inherit" its probability, while those not including the event take into account the complement to 1 of its probability. We also tackle the problem of probabilistic conformance checking of a probabilistic trace with DECLARE constraints: the conformance score is defined as the sum of the probabilities of the worlds where the trace is compliant.

This work makes the following contributions: we define a semantics for probabilistic events and traces in the setting of declarative process specifications, introduce a new concept of compliance, and show their application to the ERAS® protocol. Then, we exploit previous results, in particular (i) the mapping provided to DECLARE in terms of the SCIFF modeling language [13] and (ii) the extension of the Distribution Semantics to Abductive Logic Programming (ALP) in the SCIFF framework [3], in order to implement our proposed semantics and compute a compliance probability.

Experiments show that the approach is able to manage a large number of DECLARE constraints and probabilistic events.

The paper is organized as follows: Sect. 2 introduces background on declarative languages and the distribution semantics, Sect. 3 presents the proposed semantics, Sect. 4 describes how we perform probabilistic compliance. Section 5 describes experimental results and Sect. 6 concludes the paper.

2   Background

2.1   Process Traces and DECLARE

In the BPM context, the starting point is observing a process execution through the activities that constitute the process. Each execution, or *process instance*, is referred to as a *trace*, with each activity execution known as an *activity instance*. Activities are identified by names and typically marked with a temporal timestamp, establishing an order within the same trace. Traces are often represented as sequences of activity names, ordered by their timestamps. However, depending on the context, timestamps can be omitted, as is the case in our approach.

Formally, we assume a finite alphabet of symbols Σ representing the activity names. A trace and a log then are defined as follows:

Definition 1. (Trace t and Log $\mathcal{L}$) Given a finite set Σ of symbols (i.e., activity names), a trace t is a finite, ordered sequence of symbols over Σ, i.e. $t \in \Sigma^*$, where the latter is the infinite set of all the possible finite sentences over Σ. A log $\mathcal{L}$ is a finite set of traces.

In a log of the process, each trace t represents a different process instance. Different process instances may have the same trace, although referring to different executions. It might make sense to count the number of appearances of a specific trace. Formally:

Definition 2 ($\mathcal{L}(\cdot)$ function). With an abuse of notation, $\mathcal{L}(\cdot)$ will be used to indicate also a function that counts the occurrences of a trace t in the log $\mathcal{L}$.

Example 1. Let us suppose that a process is made of activities a, b, c, and d. $\Sigma = \{a, b, c, d\}$. An example of a log might be: $\mathcal{L} = \{t_1 = \langle a, b, c \rangle, t_2 = \langle a, b, a, d \rangle, t_3 = \langle a, a, d \rangle, t_4 = \langle a, b, c \rangle\}$.
  It holds that: $\mathcal{L}(t_1) = \mathcal{L}(t_4) = 2, \mathcal{L}(t_2) = 1, \mathcal{L}(t_3) = 1$.

The DECLARE modeling language, introduced by [16], counters the inflexibility of procedural models by focusing on defining key process properties rather than specific execution steps. It models processes through *constraints*, rules governing the activities within a trace with qualitative temporal relations among the activities. For instance, the constraint response(a, b) mandates that each instance of activity a be eventually followed by b, focusing on what must happen *after* a in a forward-looking way. DECLARE offers a variety of constraint patterns, such as response(x, y), init(x), requiring every process to start with activity x, and precedence(x, y), ensuring that an activity x has occurred *before* an activity y, in a backward-looking way. DECLARE also provides a graphical representation for these patterns (see Fig. 1) and is based on two different logic formal semantics.

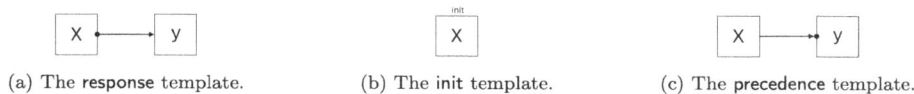

(a) The response template.   (b) The init template.   (c) The precedence template.

Fig. 1. Examples of the DECLARE graphical notation: x and y are placeholders that should be substituted with proper activity names

In the original formulation in [16] the semantics was given using the *LTL* temporal logic; subsequent works have shown the feasibility of adopting the *LTL$_f$* logic [12]: for a recent recap see [7]. A second formal semantics has been proposed in [13], where the SCIFF language and ALP [1] has been exploited. Both the semantics exploit the idea that each DECLARE template can be mapped onto one or more logic formulas φ, and that logical entailment can be used to define the notion of *compliance/violation* of a trace t w.r.t. a constraint formula φ. We provide an intuitive definition of compliance/violation, where the meaning of the entailment symbol $\models$ should be referred to the chosen semantics (*LTL$_f$* or ALP).

Definition 3 (Compliance/violation of a trace versus a constraint). A trace t is *compliant* with a DECLARE constraint if, named φ the corresponding logic formula modelling that constraint, it holds: $t \models \varphi$.
  A trace t *violates* a DECLARE constraint if it does not entail the corresponding formula φ, i.e. if $t \not\models \varphi$.

Definition 4 (Declarative Process Specification, from [7]). A *declarative process specification* is a tuple DS=(REP, Σ, C) where:

- REP is a finite non-empty set of *templates*, where each *template* is a predicate $c(x_1, \ldots, x_m) \in$ REP on variables $x_1, \ldots, x_m$ (with $m \in \mathbb{N}$ the arity of c);
- Σ is a finite non-empty set of *activity names*;
- C is a finite set of *constraints*, obtained by instantiating templates from REP to Σ; we will compactly denote such constraints with $c(a_1, \ldots, a_m)$, $a_1, \ldots, a_m \in \Sigma$.

Usually the constraints $c(a_1, \ldots, a_m)$ in a DS are considered as being in *logical conjunction*. The notion of compliance can be then lifted from a trace vs. a constraint towards a trace vs. a DS as follows:

Definition 5 (Compliance of a trace versus a Declarative Process Specification). A trace is compliant with a DS if it entails the conjunction of the formulas φ_i corresponding to the $c_i \in C$:

$$t \models \varphi_1 \wedge \ldots \wedge \varphi_m$$

where m is the cardinality of C.

Example 2. Let us consider the log introduced in Example 1, and the following DS (REP and Σ are omitted for the sake of simplicity):

$$C = \{ \quad c_1 = \mathsf{response(a,b)}$$
$$c_2 = \mathsf{init(a)} \quad \}$$

Even without considering the corresponding formal semantics, we can notice that t_1 and t_4 are compliant with c_1; t_2 is not compliant with c_1 because the second occurrence of activity a is not followed by an occurrence of activity b; t_3 is not compliant with c_1 because two occurrences of a are not followed by an occurrence of b; $t_1, \ldots, t_4$ are all compliant with c_2.

2.2   Distribution Semantics and Probabilistic Logic Programming

Probabilistic Logic Programming (PLP) has recently garnered increasing attention due to its capability to incorporate probability into logic programming, thereby handling uncertain information more effectively. Among the various PLP approaches, the one based on the distribution semantics [22] has become particularly popular, in fact it serves as the foundation for numerous other languages, including Probabilistic Logic Programs [8], Probabilistic Horn Abduction (PHA) [18], Independent Choice Logic (ICL) [17], pD [10], Logic Programs with Annotated Disjunctions (LPADs) [26], ProbLog [9] and CP-logic [25]. Such semantics is particularly appealing for its intuitiveness and because efficient inference algorithms were proposed.

A program in one of these languages defines a probability distribution over normal logic programs called *worlds*. We consider here the case of the distribution semantics for programs that do not contain function symbols (i.e., they have a finite set of worlds) for the sake of simplicity; for the treatment of function symbols see [21]. A survey of the distribution semantics in PLP can be found in [4]. In the following, the distribution semantics will be described with reference to LPADs.

Formally, a LPAD consists of a finite set of "annotated disjunctive clauses", where the head is a disjunction in which each atom is annotated with a probability. If the body holds true, only one of the atoms in the head will be true with the associated probability. An annotated disjunctive clause R_i is of the form

$$h_{i1} : p_{i1}; \ldots; h_{in_i} : p_{in_i} :- b_{i1}, \ldots, b_{im_i},$$

where $h_{i1}, \ldots, h_{in_i}$ are logical atoms and $\{p_{i1}, \ldots, p_{in_i}\}$ are real numbers in the interval $[0, 1]$ such that $\sum_{k=1}^{n_i} p_{ik} \leq 1$; $b_{i1}, \ldots, b_{im_i}$ is indicated with $body(R_i)$. If $\sum_{k=1}^{n_i} p_{ik} < 1$, the head implicitly contains an extra atom $null$ that does not appear in the body of any clause and whose annotation is $1 - \sum_{k=1}^{n_i} p_{ik}$. We denote by $ground(T)$ the grounding of an LPAD T.

An *atomic choice* [17] is a triple (R_i, θ_j, k) where $R_i \in T$, θ_j is a substitution that grounds R_i and $k \in \{1, \ldots, n_i\}$ identifies one of the head atoms. (R_i, θ_j, k) means that, for the ground clause $R_i\theta_j$, the head h_{ik} was chosen. A set of atomic choices κ is *consistent* if only one head is selected from the same ground clause; we assume independence between the different choices. A *composite choice* κ is a consistent set of atomic choices [17]. The *probability* $P(\kappa)$ *of a composite choice* κ is the product of the probabilities of the independent atomic choices, i.e. $P(\kappa) = \prod_{(R_i, \theta_j, k) \in \kappa} p_{ik}$.

A *selection* σ is a composite choice that, for each clause $R_i\theta_j$ in $ground(T)$, contains an atomic choice (R_i, θ_j, k). Let us indicate with S_T the set of all selections. A selection σ identifies a normal logic program w_σ defined as $w_\sigma = \{(h_{ik} \leftarrow body(R_i))\theta_j | (R_i, \theta_j, k) \in \sigma\}$. w_σ is called a (possible) *world* of T. Since selections are composite choices, we can assign a probability to worlds: $P(w_\sigma) = P(\sigma) = \prod_{(R_i, \theta_j, k) \in \sigma} p_{ik}$.

We denote the set of all worlds of T by W_T. $P(W_T)$ is a probability distribution over worlds, i.e., $\sum_{w \in W_T} P(w) = 1$. A composite choice κ identifies a set of worlds $w_\kappa = \{w_\sigma | \sigma \in S_T, \sigma \supseteq \kappa\}$. Similarly we can define the set of possible worlds associated to a set of composite choices K: $W_K = \bigcup_{\kappa \in K} w_\kappa$.

Example 3. Consider the following LPAD T encoding the effect of flu and hay fever on the sneezing symptom.

(R_1) $strong\_sneezing(X) : 0.3; moderate\_sneezing(X) : 0.5 : - flu(X)$.
(R_2) $strong\_sneezing(X) : 0.2; moderate\_sneezing(X) : 0.6 : - hay\_fever(X)$.
(R_3) $flu(bob)$.
(R_4) $hay\_fever(bob)$.

If somebody has the flu or hay fever, there is the possibility that he experiences sneezing symptoms with different intensity: if she has the flu, then she might show strong sneezing with probability 0.3, or moderate sneezing with probability 0.5; similarly for the second clause. She might not experience any symptom with probability 0.2 in both cases. We know for sure that Bob has both the flu and hay fever. T has $3 \cdot 3 = 9$ worlds, as each probabilistic clause has one grounding $\theta_1 = \{X/bob\}$. Worlds are shown in Table 1.

Table 1. Worlds for Example 3. The probabilities of the worlds sum up to 1

World id	World	$P(w)$
w_1	strong_sneezing(bob):-flu(bob). strong_sneezing(bob):-hay_fever(bob). flu(bob). hay_fever(bob).	$0.3 \times 0.2 = 0.06$
w_2	strong_sneezing(bob):-flu(bob). moderate_sneezing(bob):-hay_fever(bob). flu(bob). hay_fever(bob).	$0.3 \times 0.6 = 0.18$
w_3	strong_sneezing(bob):-flu(bob). flu(bob). hay_fever(bob).	$0.3 \times 0.2 = 0.06$
w_4	moderate_sneezing(bob):-flu(bob). strong_sneezing(bob):-hay_fever(bob). flu(bob). hay_fever(bob).	$0.5 \times 0.2 = 0.1$
w_5	moderate_sneezing(bob):-flu(bob). moderate_sneezing(bob):-hay_fever(bob). flu(bob). hay_fever(bob).	$0.5 \times 0.6 = 0.3$
w_6	moderate_sneezing(bob):-flu(bob). flu(bob). hay_fever(bob).	$0.5 \times 0.2 = 0.1$
w_7	strong_sneezing(bob):-hay_fever(bob). flu(bob). hay_fever(bob).	$0.2 \times 0.2 = 0.04$
w_8	moderate_sneezing(bob):-hay_fever(bob). flu(bob). hay_fever(bob).	$0.2 \times 0.6 = 0.12$
w_9	flu(bob). hay_fever(bob).	$0.2 \times 0.2 = 0.04$

Given a goal G, its probability $P(G)$ can be defined by marginalizing the joint probability of the goal and the worlds:

$$P(G) = \sum_{w \in W_T} P(G, w) = \sum_{w \in W_T} P(G|w)P(w) = \sum_{w \in W_T : w \models G} P(w) \qquad (1)$$

The probability of a goal G given a world w is $P(G|w) = 1$ if $w \models G$ and 0 otherwise. $P(w) = P(w_\sigma) = P(\sigma)$, i.e. is the product of the annotations p_{ik} of the atoms selected in σ. Therefore, the probability of a goal G can be computed by summing the probability of the worlds where the goal is true. In practice, given a goal to solve, it is unfeasible to enumerate all the worlds where G is entailed. Inference algorithms, instead, find *explanations* for a goal: a composite choice κ is an *explanation* for G if G is entailed by every world of w_κ. In particular, algorithms find a covering set of explanations w.r.t. G, where a set of composite choices K is *covering* with respect to G if every program $w_\sigma \in W_T$ in which G is entailed is in w_K.

3   Probabilistic Process Traces Under the Distribution Semantics

In this Section, we propose a new semantics for handling uncertainty at the level of event executions, that is highly inspired by the Distribution Semantics introduced in Sect. 2.2.

The motivation behind this proposal relies in the fact that in certain domains it might not be possible to completely observe the evolution of a process instance; as a consequence, there is no certainty of the happening of some events in the observed trace. However, due to the domain's characteristics, it may be the case that some events happened with a certain probability. Such probability can be interpreted as an *epistemic probability*, i.e. as the degree of our belief in that event, as done in [19,20].

Example 4. In a hospital department the log of the patients' events is usually updated by healthcare professionals. They might forget to log one or more events. A probabilistic trace would take in consideration the fact that, even if not logged, some events might have happened with a probability p. The trace:

$$t = \langle 0.7 : \mathsf{check\_fever}, \mathsf{drug\_prescription}, \mathsf{check\_fever}, 0.95 : \mathsf{check\_fever}, \mathsf{dim\ ssion} \rangle$$

describes the situation where the healthcare professional logged only the second event (drug_prescription), the third event (check_fever), and the fifth event (dimission). Two events of type check_fever were not logged, however it is probable that they happened anyway due to the patient's disease and treatment. In these cases we have a degree of belief 0.7 and 0.95 respectively in the occurrence of those events, i.e. we *believe* that those events happened with that probability.

We propose to deal with this scenario by applying the Distribution Semantics as follows.

Definition 6 (Probabilistic Event). A *Probabilistic Event* is a couple:

$$Prob : \mathsf{EventDescription}$$

where EventDescription is a symbol describing an event (EventDescription $\in \Sigma$), while $Prob \in [0,1]$ is the epistemic probability that the event happened. A probability value of 1 means the event happened, and we will refer to it as "certain"; for ease of reading such probability will be omitted.

For the sake of simplicity, we will adopt the notation $Prob : \mathsf{E}_i$ indicating that the generic event E appearing in the i-th position in the trace has a degree of belief $Prob$.

Definition 7 (Probabilistic Trace). A *Probabilistic Trace* is a trace where at least one event is probabilistic.

Recalling the Distribution Semantics, for each probabilistic event we can make an *atomic choice*, which determines whether a probabilistic event appears or not in the trace.

Definition 8 (Atomic choice and Composite choice). An *Atomic Choice* is a pair (E_i, k) where E_i is a probabilistic event E appearing in the i-th position in a probabilistic trace and $k \in \{0,1\}$. k indicates whether E_i is chosen to be included in a world with probability p_i (k=1), or not with probability $1 - p_i$ (k=0). We assume independence between the different atomic choices.

A *Composite Choice* $\kappa(t)$ is a consistent set of atomic choices over probabilistic events in t, i.e., $(E_i, k) \in \kappa(t), (E_i, m) \in \kappa(t) \Rightarrow k = m$ (only one decision for each probabilistic event). The *probability* $P(\kappa)$ *of a composite choice* κ is $P(\kappa) = \prod_{(E_i,1) \in \kappa} p_i \prod_{(E_i,0) \in \kappa} (1 - p_i)$, where p_i is the probability associated with E_i.

Note that here we do not need the substitution θ as in the definition of atomic choice in Subsect. 2.2, since, according to Def. 1, the events are ground.

Definition 9. (Selection over a trace t) A *Selection* $\sigma(t)$ over a probabilistic trace t is a composite choice containing an atomic choice (E_i, k) for each probabilistic event in the trace t.

A selection $\sigma(t)$ identifies a world w_σ in this way: $w_\sigma = \{E_i | (E_i, 1) \in \sigma\}$.

Let us indicate with $S(t)$ the set of all selections and with $W(t)$ the set of all worlds.

Example 5 (continued from previous). Given the trace t:

$t = \langle 0.7 : \text{check\_fever}_1, \text{drug\_prescription}_2, \text{check\_fever}_3, 0.95 : \text{check\_fever}_4, \text{dimission}_5 \rangle$

where we explicitly add a pedix for each event due to the multiple appearance of the check_fever activity, the set $S(t)$ of possible selections $\sigma(t)$ is:

$$\sigma_1(t) = \{(\text{check\_fever}_1, 1), (\text{check\_fever}_4, 1)\}$$
$$\sigma_2(t) = \{(\text{check\_fever}_1, 1), (\text{check\_fever}_4, 0)\}$$
$$\sigma_3(t) = \{(\text{check\_fever}_1, 0), (\text{check\_fever}_4, 1)\}$$
$$\sigma_4(t) = \{(\text{check\_fever}_1, 0), (\text{check\_fever}_4, 0)\}$$

The set $W(t)$ of possible worlds $w(t)$ is:

$w_{\sigma 1}(t) = \langle \text{check\_fever}_1, \text{drug\_prescription}_2, \text{check\_fever}_3, \text{check\_fever}_4, \text{dimission}_5 \rangle$
$w_{\sigma 2}(t) = \langle \text{check\_fever}_1, \text{drug\_prescription}_2, \text{check\_fever}_3, \text{dimission}_5 \rangle$
$w_{\sigma 3}(t) = \langle \text{drug\_prescription}_2, \text{check\_fever}_3, \text{check\_fever}_4, \text{dimission}_5 \rangle$
$w_{\sigma 4}(t) = \langle \text{drug\_prescription}_2, \text{check\_fever}_3, \text{dimission}_5 \rangle$

Note that certain (non probabilistic) events always appear in the generated worlds.

Definition 10 (Probability of a Selection). The probability of a selection $\sigma(t)$ is defined as:

$$P(\sigma(t)) = \prod_{(E_i,1) \in \sigma(t)} p_i \prod_{(E_i,0) \in \sigma(t)} (1 - p_i)$$

The probability of a selection corresponds to the probability of a world w_σ, i.e. $P(w_\sigma(t)) = P(\sigma(t))$.

The probability of a world is obtained by multiplying the probabilities associated to each alternative (presence or absence of an event) as these are considered independent of each other. This gives a probability distribution $P(w(t))$ over the worlds, i.e. $\sum_{w(t) \in W(t)} P(w(t)) = 1$.

Example 6 (continued from previous).
The trace t has four worlds, corresponding to the selections listed in Example 5, and their probabilities are:

$$
\begin{aligned}
P(\sigma_1(t)) &= P(w_{\sigma 1}(t)) = 0.7 * 0.95 & = 0.665 \\
P(\sigma_2(t)) &= P(w_{\sigma 2}(t)) = 0.7 * (1 - 0.95) & = 0.035 \\
P(\sigma_3(t)) &= P(w_{\sigma 3}(t)) = (1 - 0.7) * 0.95 & = 0.285 \\
P(\sigma_4(t)) &= P(w_{\sigma 4}(t)) = (1 - 0.7) * (1 - 0.95) & = 0.015
\end{aligned}
$$

Note that 0.665+0.035+0.285+0.015=1.

Example 5 allows us to highlight some characteristics of the semantics proposed in this paper. First of all, thanks to the notion of *world*, we started from a probabilistic trace, and ended up with a set of regular (non-probabilistic) traces, that correspond to the worlds $w_{\sigma i}(t)$.

4   Probabilistic Compliance

In this Section we will define the notion of *compliance* of a probabilistic trace w.r.t. a Declarative Process Specification. Given a model M and a notion of compliance of a trace t w.r.t. M, we can extend this notion to a probabilistic trace by considering the compliance of each world $w_\sigma(t)$ generated by a trace, and by summing up the probabilities of the worlds compliant with M.

Definition 11 (Compliance of a probabilistic trace). Given a model M, a probabilistic trace t, and a set $S(t)$ of all the selections $\sigma_i(t)$, we define the compliance Comp(M,t) of a probabilistic trace t w.r.t. M as the sum of the probabilities of the worlds $w_{\sigma i}(t)$ for which the compliance function returns true.

$$
Comp(M,t) = \sum_{w(t) \in W(t)} \begin{cases} P(w(t)) & \text{if } w(t) \text{ is compliant with } M, \\ 0 & \text{otherwise.} \end{cases}
$$

Example 7 (continued from previous). Suppose we have a model M that prescribes that before any drug_prescription, a check_fever must be executed. Only worlds $w_{\sigma 1}(t)$ and $w_{\sigma 2}(t)$ are compliant with the prescribed model. Hence:

$$
Comp(M,t) = P(w_{\sigma 1}(t)) + P(w_{\sigma 2}(t)) = 0.665 + 0.035 = 0.7
$$

We will say that t is compliant w.r.t. model M with a probability of 0.7.

Definition 12 (Compliance of a log with probabilistic traces). Given a model M and a log $\mathcal{L}$ with probabilistic traces t_i, we define the compliance of a log with probabilistic traces as the weighted sum of the compliance of t_i, where where $\mathcal{L}(t_i)$ counts the occurrences of trace ti in the log L (see Def. 2).

$$Comp(M, \mathcal{L}) = \sum_{t_i \in \mathcal{L}} \frac{\mathcal{L}(t_i)}{|\mathcal{L}|} * Comp(M, t_i)$$

We might observe that, w.r.t. Def. 5, we move forward from a crisp boolean concept towards a *degree* of compliance: this is an expected consequence of introducing probabilities in the traces' events. The proposed semantics accommodates for both probabilistic and non-probabilistic traces: the latter are treated as traces with only certain events as usual in Process Mining, and the derived worlds w_{σ_i} will always contain them.

5   Implementation and Evaluation

In this Section we describe how we compute the compliance of a probabilistic trace w.r.t a Declarative Process Specification, by means of the framework implemented in [5]. This framework enables reasoning on ALP programs that incorporate "integrity constraints" (ICs) á la IFF [11], extended with the possibility of annotating them with a probability. The programs, known as IFF^{Prob} programs, define a probability distribution over IFF programs based on the distribution semantics. IFF^{Prob} is based on the $\mathcal{S}CIFF$ proof-procedure [1]. In [5], the IFF sub-language is extended with a CHR constraint that represents the current explanation with its probability in the current derivation branch. Here, *expl* is a set of pairs (C_i, k), where C_i represents a (possibly) probabilistic integrity constraint and the Boolean value k determines whether C_i is included in *expl*.

To perform the experiments, firstly we described, in the CLIMB language [13], a DECLARE process model for elective colorectal surgery based on the ERAS® (Enhanced Recovery After Surgery) Society guidelines for perioperative care [23]. The model comprises 21 constraints regarding crucial perioperative events, from patient admission to post-surgery recovery. CLIMB (Computational Logic for the Verification and Modeling of Business constraints) is a rule-based language which employs forward rules to bind event occurrences with *expected* courses of interaction. An event execution status is denoted as happened (H), expected (E), or forbidden (though forbidden activities are not considered here). For example, the fact that an atomic activity a has happened at time T can be denoted by $H(\text{exec}(a), T)$, while $E(\text{exec}(a), T)$ states that a is expected to occur at time T. Being the body of integrity constraints universally quantified with scope the entire rule, every time a group of event occurrences makes its body true, then the rule triggers, generating the expectations contained in the head. An excerpt of our model is:

$$\text{true} \rightarrow E(\text{exec}(\text{program\_admission}), 0). \hspace{3cm} (ic_1)$$

$$H(\text{exec}(\text{program\_admission}), T_1) \rightarrow E(\text{exec}(\text{counseling}), T_2) \wedge T_2 > T_1. \hspace{0.5cm} (ic_2)$$

Integrity constraint ic_1 specifies that the process must always start with the event *program admission* of the patient, occurring at time 0 (init template). ic_2 represents the response constraint, indicating that whenever a *program admission* happens, the pre-operative *counseling* (patient education) must eventually follow at a time T2 later than T1.

Secondly, we made one or more events probabilistic in a process trace by relying on the same syntax used for the constraints. Every event is represented as a happened (H) event in the head of a rule with body *true*, so that the head is always enacted. This is enabled by the $\mathcal{S}$CIFF-lite extension [13], where the head of the IC may include happened events. To assign a probability p to uncertain events, we place p :: before the rule. An example of an execution trace composed of both certain and probabilistic events is the following:

$$true \longrightarrow H(event(program\_admission), 0).$$
$$0.75::true \longrightarrow H(event(counseling), 5).$$
$$0.95::true \longrightarrow H(event(fasting), 80).$$

We created a process trace using 21 events, each one corresponding to a different activity provided by the protocol. Of these, we decided to keep the main three as certain given their meaning: program_admission, start_surgery, and end_surgery, while all the remaining events were kept as certain or were assigned a probability value of 0.5, representing the degree of belief associated with each event's occurrence (see in the following for more details). For our purposes, there is no difference in associating 0.5 or any other probability value.

We ran two scalability tests to evaluate how the execution time for computing the probability of compliance of a probabilistic trace w.r.t a DS scales, (a) by increasing the number of probabilistic events (PEs) in the trace, given a fixed number of ICs, or (b) by increasing the number of ICs in the model, given a fixed number of probabilistic events.

Tests were executed on a Linux machine equipped with an Intel® Xeon® E5-2630v3 processor, at 2.40 GHz, 20 GB of RAM and a maximum execution time of 8 h for each job. In test (a), the number of probabilistic events in the trace was increased from 1 to 18 at steps of 1, while the number of ICs was increased in multiples of 3, from 1 to 12. Starting from 13 ICs, constraints were added at steps of 1 up to 21 ICs, in order to identify the configurations leading to timeout. Here, the "larger" configuration (in terms of number of ICs + number of PEs) reaching timeout was 13 ICs and 18 PEs. Results are shown in Fig. 2a. In test (b) the number of PEs was increased in multiples of 3, from 1 up to 9, then at steps of 1 from 10 to 18. The number of ICs was increased from 1 to 21 at steps of 1. The larger configuration that led to timeout was the one with 10 PEs and 21 ICs. Figure 2b illustrates the results.

In both cases the framework is able to manage a remarkable number of PEs and constraints in the model at the same time, even if it shows an exponential trend in execution times as the number of constraints or of probabilistic events increases. In particular, it is able to compute the compliance probability within about one minute with, for instance, 4 PEs and 15 ICs, or 9 PEs and 12 ICs,

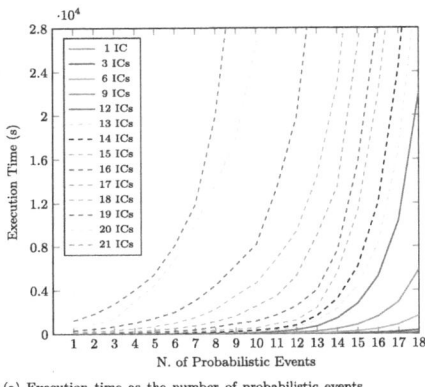
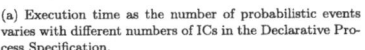
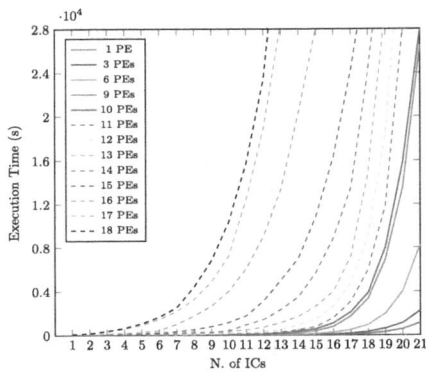

(a) Execution time as the number of probabilistic events varies with different numbers of ICs in the Declarative Process Specification.

(b) Execution time as the number of ICs varies with different numbers of probabilistic events (PEs).

Fig. 2. Execution time for computing the compliance of a probabilistic trace against a Declarative Process Specification, with varying probabilistic events (a) and ICs (b). Dashed curves indicate that the T.O. was reached

Table 2. N. of explanations corresponding to each experiment of test (a). "T.O." indicates that the execution timed out

#IC	Number of Probabilistic Events																	
	1	2	3	4	5	6	7	8	9	10	11	12	13	14	15	16	17	18
1	2	4	8	16	32	64	128	256	512	1024	2048	4096	8192	16384	32768	65536	131072	262144
3	1	2	4	8	16	32	64	128	256	512	1024	2048	4096	8192	16384	32768	65536	131072
6	1	2	4	8	8	8	8	16	32	64	128	256	512	1024	2048	4096	8192	16384
9	1	1	1	1	1	1	1	2	4	8	16	32	64	128	256	512	1024	2048
12	1	1	1	1	1	1	1	1	1	1	2	4	8	16	32	64	128	256
13	1	1	1	1	1	1	1	1	1	1	1	2	4	8	16	32	64	T.O.
14	1	1	1	1	1	1	1	1	1	1	1	1	2	4	8	16	32	T.O.
15	1	1	1	1	1	1	1	1	1	1	1	1	2	4	8	16	T.O.	T.O.
16	1	1	1	1	1	1	1	1	1	1	1	1	1	2	4	T.O.	T.O.	T.O.
17	1	1	1	1	1	1	1	1	1	1	1	1	1	1	2	T.O.	T.O.	T.O.
18	1	1	1	1	1	1	1	1	1	1	1	1	1	1	T.O.	T.O.	T.O.	T.O.
19	1	1	1	1	1	1	1	1	1	1	1	1	T.O.	T.O.	T.O.	T.O.	T.O.	T.O.
20	1	1	1	1	1	1	1	1	1	1	T.O.	T.O.	T.O.	T.O.	T.O.	T.O.	T.O.	T.O.
21	1	1	1	1	1	1	1	1	1	T.O.	T.O.	T.O.	T.O.	T.O.	T.O.	T.O.	T.O.	T.O.

11 PEs and 9 ICs, 13 PEs and 6 ICs (plus the 3 main certain events in all cases). We also computed, for case (a), the number of explanations generated (see Table 2), which initially grows exponentially with few ICs and increasing number of probabilistic events, and then becomes constrained as more ICs need to be fulfilled. The exponential number of explanations results from each probabilistic event having two atomic choices, present or absent, in a world.

6 Conclusions and Future Work

In this paper, we introduced a new semantics for handling uncertainty at the level of events in declarative process traces. A probabilistic trace is able to incorporate probabilistic events where the probability represents the degree of belief in such events. The semantics is inspired by the Distribution Semantics from Probabilistic Logic Programming. We then propose to compute the compliance probability of a probabilistic trace against a DECLARE process model. The computation of the compliance relies on an existing algorithm. Tests show that, even if the execution time increases exponentially with additional probabilistic events and constraints, the approach used is able to manage combinations of a large number of model constraints and probabilistic events. Future research will focus on expanding experimental validation, extending the new semantics to manage uncertainty at the level of traces or the log itself, defining the compliance of probabilistic trace(s) w.r.t *probabilistic* DECLARE models, and studying the profiles of energy consumption when computing the probability of compliance.

Acknowledgments.

Research funded by the Italian Ministerial grant PRIN 2022 "Probabilistic Declarative Process Mining (PRODE)", n. 20224C9HXA - CUP F53D23004240006, funded by European Union - Next Generation EU. Research partly funded by the Italian Ministry of University and Research through PNRR - M4C2 - Investimento 1.3 (Decreto Direttoriale MUR n. 341 del 15/03/2022), Partenariato Esteso PE00000013 -"FAIR - Future Artificial Intelligence Research" - Spoke 8 "Pervasive AI" - CUP J33C22002830006, funded by the European Union under the NextGeneration EU programme". This work was realized by Daniela Loreti with a research contract co-financed by the European Union (PON Ricerca e Innovazione 2014-2020 art. 24, comma 3, lett. a), della Legge 30/12/2010, n. 240 e s.m.i. e del D.M. 10/08/2021 n. 1062).

References

1. Alberti, M., Chesani, F., Gavanelli, M., Lamma, E., Mello, P., Torroni, P.: Verifiable agent interaction in abductive logic programming: the SCIFF framework. ACM Trans. Comput. Log. **9**(4), 29:1–29:43 (2008). https://doi.org/10.1145/1380572.1380578
2. Alman, A., Maggi, F.M., Montali, M., Peñaloza, R.: Probabilistic declarative process mining. Inf. Syst. **109**, 102033 (2022). https://doi.org/10.1016/J.IS.2022.102033
3. Azzolini, D., Bellodi, E., Ferilli, S., Riguzzi, F., Zese, R.: Abduction with probabilistic logic programming under the distribution semantics. Int. J. Approx. Reason. **142**, 41–63 (2022). https://doi.org/10.1016/J.IJAR.2021.11.003
4. Bellodi, E.: The distribution semantics in probabilistic logic programming and probabilistic description logics: a survey. Intelligenza Artificiale **17**(1), 143–156 (2023). https://doi.org/10.3233/IA-221072

5. Bellodi, E., Gavanelli, M., Zese, R., Lamma, E., Riguzzi, F.: Nonground abductive logic programming with probabilistic integrity constraints. Theory Pract. Logic Program. **21**(5), 557–574 (2021). https://doi.org/10.1017/S1471068421000417
6. Bergami, G., Maggi, F.M., Montali, M., Peñaloza, R.: Probabilistic trace alignment. In: 2021 3rd International Conference on Process Mining (ICPM), pp. 9–16 (2021). https://doi.org/10.1109/ICPM53251.2021.9576856
7. Ciccio, C.D., Montali, M.: Declarative process specifications: reasoning, discovery, monitoring. In: van der Aalst, W.M.P., Carmona, J. (eds.) Process Mining Handbook, LNBIP, vol. 448, pp. 108–152. Springer (2022). https://doi.org/10.1007/978-3-031-08848-3_4
8. Dantsin, E.: Probabilistic logic programs and their semantics. In: Russian Conference on Logic Programming. LNCS, vol. 592, pp. 152–164. Springer (1991)
9. De Raedt, L., Kimmig, A., Toivonen, H.: ProbLog: A probabilistic prolog and its application in link discovery. In: Veloso, M.M. (ed.) 20th International Joint Conference on Artificial Intelligence (IJCAI 2007), vol. 7, pp. 2462–2467. AAAI Press (2007)
10. Fuhr, N.: Probabilistic datalog: implementing logical information retrieval for advanced applications. J. Am. Soc. Inf. Sci. **51**, 95–110 (2000)
11. Fung, T.H., Kowalski, R.A.: The IFF proof procedure for abductive logic programming. J. Log. Program. **33**(2), 151–165 (1997). https://doi.org/10.1016/S0743-1066(97)00026-5
12. Giacomo, G.D., Vardi, M.Y.: Linear temporal logic and linear dynamic logic on finite traces. In: Rossi, F. (ed.) IJCAI 2013, Proceedings of the 23rd International Joint Conference on Artificial Intelligence, Beijing, China, August 3-9, 2013, pp. 854–860. IJCAI/AAAI (2013). http://www.aaai.org/ocs/index.php/IJCAI/IJCAI13/paper/view/6997
13. Montali, M.: Specification and verification of declarative open interaction models - a logic-based approach, LNBIP, vol. 56. Springer (2010). https://doi.org/10.1007/978-3-642-14538-4
14. Pegoraro, M., van der Aalst, W.M.: Mining uncertain event data in process mining. In: 2019 International Conference on Process Mining (ICPM), pp. 89–96 (2019). https://doi.org/10.1109/ICPM.2019.00023
15. Pegoraro, M., Bakullari, B., Uysal, M.S., van der Aalst, W.M.P.: Probability estimation of uncertain process trace realizations. In: Munoz-Gama, J., Lu, X. (eds.) Process Mining Workshops, pp. 21–33. Springer, Cham (2022)
16. Pesic, M.: Constraint-based workflow management systems : shifting control to users, PhD thesis, (research tu/e / graduation tu/e), proefschrift, Industrial Engineering and Innovation Sciences (2008). https://doi.org/10.6100/IR638413
17. Poole, D.: The independent choice Logic for modelling multiple agents under uncertainty. Artif. Intell. **94**, 7–56 (1997)
18. Poole, D.: Logic programming, abduction and probability - a top-down anytime algorithm for estimating prior and posterior probabilities. Nat. Gener. Comput. **11**(3), 377–400 (1993)
19. Riguzzi, F., Bellodi, E., Lamma, E., Zese, R.: Epistemic and statistical probabilistic ontologies. In: Bobillo, F., et al. (eds.) Proceedings of the 8th International Workshop on Uncertain Reasoning for the Semantic Web (URSW2012), Boston, USA, 11 November 2012, pp. 3–14, No. 900 in CEUR Workshop Proceedings, Sun SITE Central Europe, Aachen, Germany (2012)
20. Riguzzi, F., Bellodi, E., Lamma, E., Zese, R.: Reasoning with probabilistic ontologies. In: Yang, Q., Wooldridge, M.J. (eds.) Proceedings of the Twenty-Fourth International Joint Conference on Artificial Intelligence, IJCAI 2015, Buenos Aires,

Argentina, July 25-31, 2015, pp. 4310–4316. AAAI Press (2015). http://ijcai.org/Abstract/15/613

21. Riguzzi, F., Swift, T.: Welldefinedness and efficient inference for probabilistic logic programming under the distribution semantics. Theory Pract. Logic Program. **13**(2), 279–302 (2013). https://doi.org/10.1017/S1471068411000664

22. Sato, T.: A statistical learning method for logic programs with distribution semantics. In: Sterling, L. (ed.) Logic Programming, Proceedings of the Twelfth International Conference on Logic Programming, Tokyo, Japan, June 13-16, 1995, pp. 715–729. MIT Press (1995)

23. Gustafsson, U.O., et al.: Guidelines for perioperative care in elective colorectal surgery: enhanced recovery after surgery (eras®) society recommendations: 2018. World J. Surg. **43**(3), 659–695 (2019). https://doi.org/10.1007/s00268-018-4844-y

24. Van der, Aalst, et al.: Process mining manifesto. In: Daniel, F., Barkaoui, K., Dustdar, S. (eds.) Business Process Management Workshops - BPM 2011 International Workshops, Clermont-Ferrand, France, August 29, 2011, Revised Selected Papers, Part I. LNBIP, vol. 99, pp. 169–194. Springer (2011). https://doi.org/10.1007/978-3-642-28108-2_19

25. Vennekens, J., Denecker, M., Bruynooghe, M.: CP-logic: a language of causal probabilistic events and its relation to logic programming. Theory Pract. Logic Program. **9**(3), 245–308 (2009). https://doi.org/10.1017/S1471068409003767

26. Vennekens, J., Verbaeten, S., Bruynooghe, M.: Logic programs with annotated disjunctions. In: Demoen, B., Lifschitz, V. (eds.) 20th International Conference on Logic Programming (ICLP 2004). LNCS, vol. 3131, pp. 431–445. Springer (2004). https://doi.org/10.1007/978-3-540-27775-0_30

Author Index

A. Artale et al. (Eds.): AIxIA 2024, LNAI 15450, pp. 347–348, 2025.
https://doi.org/10.1007/978-3-031-80607-0

The manufacturer's authorised representative in the EU is Springer
Nature Customer Service Centre GmbH, Europaplatz 3, 69115 Heidelberg,
Germany. If you have any concerns regarding our products, please
contact ProductSafety@springernature.com

Printed and bound by CPI Group (UK) Ltd, Croydon, CR0 4YY
27/04/2026
02097586-0010